Taking Sides: Clashing Views
on Moral Issues, 14/e,
Expanded

Owen M. Smith and Anne Collins Smith

http://create.mheducation.com

ISBN-10: 1259345785   ISBN-13: 9781259345784

Contents

Preface

This text contains essays arranged in pro and con pairs that address controversial issues in morality and moral philosophy. Each of the issues is expressed in terms of a single question in order to draw the lines of debate more clearly.

Some of the questions included in this volume have been in the mainstream of moral philosophy for hundreds or even thousands of years and are central to the discipline. These include abstract questions about relativism and the relationship between morality and religion. Other questions relate to specific topics of contemporary concern, such as cloning, abortion, affirmative action, and the relinquishment of technology.

The authors of the selections presented here take a strong stand on a given issue and provide the best defenses of their own positions. The selections were chosen for their usefulness in defending a position and for their accessibility to students. The authors include philosophers, scientists, and social critics from a wide variety of backgrounds. Each presents us with a well-defined and closely argued answer on an issue—even if we ultimately cannot accept the answer as our own.

Each issue is accompanied by an introduction, which sets the stage for the debate, and concludes with a question about middle ground, which explores the possibility of agreement. Learning outcomes, questions for critical thinking and reflection, suggestions for further reading, and Internet resources may also be found in each issue, along with biographical information about the contributors on each side of the debate.

Taking Sides: Clashing Views on Moral Issues is a tool to encourage critical thought on important moral issues. Readers are charged with the task of developing a critical and informed view of these issues, and should not feel confined to the views expressed in the selections. Some readers may see important points on both sides of an issue and construct for themselves a new and creative approach, which may incorporate the best of both sides or provide an entirely new vantage point for understanding.

Owen M. Smith
Stephen F. Austin State University

Anne Collins Smith
Stephen F. Austin State University

Editors of This Volume

OWEN M. SMITH, an Associate Professor of Philosophy and Classical Studies at Stephen F. Austin State University, earned a PhD in Philosophy from the joint program in Classics and Philosophy at the University of Texas at Austin. His primary areas of specialization are applied ethics, philosophy of religion, and natural theology in late antiquity. His research and teaching interests include gnosticism and the application of mythological and philosophical principles to popular culture.

ANNE COLLINS SMITH, an Associate Professor of Philosophy and Classical Studies at Stephen F. Austin State University, earned a PhD in Philosophy from the joint program in Classics and Philosophy at the University of Texas at Austin. Her primary areas of specialization are medieval metaphysics, natural theology, and applied ethics. Her current research and teaching interests include the use of popular culture to exemplify philosophical problems.

The editors have also written and translated graphic novels for children and young adults.

Acknowledgments We owe a debt of thanks to Stephen Satris, the original and longtime editor of *Taking Sides: Clashing Views on Moral Issues;* without his pioneering efforts, we would have had neither the opportunity nor the honor of continuing his work.

To our parents with gratitude for their heritage and to our son with hope for the future.

Academic Advisory Board Members

Judith Wagner DeCew
Clark University

L.M. Ed monds
Arizona State University

Christian Fossa-Andersen
DeVry University

Amber E. George
SUNY Cortland

Andreas Kiryakakis
College of St. Benedict

Elizabeth Langevin
University of Phoenix

Robert Micallef
Madonna University

Robert L. Muhlnickel
Monroe Community College

Ronald Novy
University of Central Arkansas

Andreas W. Reif
Manchester Community College

William Rodriguez
Bethune Cookman University

Karen Scialabba
Marist College

Matt Zwolinski
University of San Diego

Introduction

Making decisions about what is right and wrong, what should and shouldn't be done, is an activity that we do thousands of times every day. In fact, many of these decisions are so clear-cut, so straightforward that we are scarcely, if at all, aware that we are making them. Rarely do we seriously entertain the notion of running red lights, driving onto the sidewalk and scattering pedestrians, or even ramming the cars of drivers who annoy us. True, the legal consequences of such actions provide a deterrent to indulging in these fantasies, but legal issues are not the only reasons we exercise self-discipline and self-control. While running red lights might get us to our destinations faster, it is only *fair* that everyone take their turn. Driving onto the sidewalks might enable us to get around traffic jams, but people could get hurt that way, and it's just not *worth* hurting people to save a little time. Ramming other cars might make us feel better, but the other drivers are people too, and they deserve our *respect* even when they annoy us.

In fact, only when these types of decisions are not clear-cut do we actually have to sit down and reflect on the various options that we are facing, what factors favor each option, and what factors oppose each option, in order to figure out how to act. Even then, making a decision about how to act is not like making a simple factual determination, like how many bones there are in the typical human foot. Facts are important in making these types of decisions, but they are only incidental to the process. Rather, the central part of the decision-making process involves general ideas about the sorts of actions that are right and the sorts of actions that are wrong. These ideas, known as moral principles, are then applied in specific situations by specific people. Moreover, different people may arrive at different conclusions about how to act, even if they were placed in exactly the same situation. In fact, unlike in strictly factual disputes that have only one correct answer, it is possible to respect the decision made by another person, even though you would have made a different decision.

Identifying the reasons for disputes about the proper way to act can be difficult. Sometimes there is a difference of opinion about what the facts are. Sometimes there may be agreement about what the facts are, but a difference about what they mean or how to interpret them. More fundamentally, there may be a difference in fundamental moral principles, about the very sorts of actions that are right and wrong. Often, a dispute arises not just from one type of difference, but from many different types of reasons. Simply identifying the reason or reasons behind the dispute may not be enough to resolve the dispute. It might be the case that some disputes about how to act can never be resolved.

Judgments about the proper way to act in a specific situation are called moral judgments. Morality is a philosophical discipline that addresses how moral judgments are made in specific situations. The investigation into the principles used in making moral judgments is known as ethics. Various philosophers have proposed ethical theories about the meaning of basic moral terms such as good and bad, right and wrong. These theories often have consequences about whether disputes about moral judgments can ever be resolved. Often, people who proceed from different ethical theories end up making different moral judgments. Oddly enough, it is not uncommon for people who proceed from different ethical theories to arrive at the same moral judgment, although they provide different justifications or rationales for their judgment. People who proceed from the same ethical theories may also arrive at different moral judgments, most often because they emphasize different moral principles in making their judgments.

So, what are you to do when faced with a difficult decision about how to act, a decision that is not clear-cut or straightforward? Since the issue is not strictly a factual issue, you will have to arrive at your own decision by careful thought. Try as best you can to imagine yourself holding each position; in this way you can identify the assumptions each position makes, work carefully through the steps justifying each position, identify the advantages and disadvantages of each position, and determine how important these advantages and disadvantages are. Moreover, you should maintain an open mind toward all the positions. Strive to assume the position of an impartial judge, who can accurately state each position and can fairly assess its strengths and weaknesses. In order to accomplish these tasks, a degree of introspection is necessary. Be aware of your own initial thoughts and feelings on the issue and be sure to identify any assumptions or preconceived ideas you may possess; these assumptions and ideas will need to be tested before making a final judgment. If you have a strong prior attachment to one position, guard against unfairly favoring this position as you consider the issue. Finally, once each position has been clearly understood and carefully considered, make a choice. Morality is a practical discipline, and judgment cannot be postponed indefinitely. However, when the time for informed judgment arrives, remember that while you must make a choice, you need not choose either of the positions presented to you. There may be another way of approaching the issue, a way of establishing common ground among the incompatible positions which allows you to escape the conflict and incorporate the best parts of each position.

The process of making moral judgments is modelled for you in each of the issues discussed in this text. A practical question is posed, and two opposed positions are presented for your careful consideration. Read through each author's arguments, reasons, and examples, and decide which have merit. The questions and issues that are raised here require careful analysis and evaluation, and you may be unsatisfied with the positions expressed in the selections. View these shortcomings as an opportunity to modify and correct these positions until they are as strong and persuasive as then can be. Then reason through the issue yourself and come to your own conclusion about the moral course of action.

Decisions about how to act not only say a lot about the sort of person you are, but also can actually determine the sort of person you come to be. This process, moreover, is never over. People who are dissatisfied with themselves can become a different sort of person by consistently making different decisions about how to act; so too those who are satisfied with the sort of person they are can start down the road of becoming dissatisfied with themselves by making different decisions. In this way, morality and moral decision making have consequences beyond any given issue. There is no final exam in morality. After all, we make decisions about what is right and wrong, what should and shouldn't be done, thousands of times every day.

"It is our choices . . . that show what we truly are, far more than our abilities."

J. K. Rowling, *Harry Potter and the Chamber of Secrets*

Owen M. Smith
Anne Collins Smith

Unit 1

UNIT

Fundamental Issues in Morality

*E*ven before confronting particular moral issues, we often encounter diverging views about morality itself. Some people assert that there is no such thing as objective morality, and thus moral conflicts cannot be resolved. Such people commonly hold the view that moral judgments are simply the expression of individual or cultural views, which vary from time to time and place to place. Other people assert that morality is the product of divine revelation, and thus without religion, there is no morality. These and other ideas are discussed in this unit.

Selected, Edited, and with Issue Framing Material by:
Owen M. Smith, *Stephen F. Austin State University*
and
Anne Collins Smith, *Stephen F. Austin State University*

ISSUE

Is Moral Relativism Correct?

YES: **Torbjörn Tännsjö**, from "Moral Relativism," *Philosophical Studies* (2007)

NO: **Louis P. Pojman**, from "The Case Against Moral Relativism," in *The Moral Life: An Introductory Reader in Ethics and Literature* (Oxford University Press, 2007)

Learning Outcomes

After reading this issue, you will be able to:

- Explain the distinction between cultural moral relativism and individual moral relativism.
- Explain the central concept and basic justification of ontological relativism.
- Explain the central concept and basic justification of moral realism.
- Formulate your own position on whether morality is relative and identify evidence supporting your position.
- Identify the main objections to your position and formulate responses to these objections.

ISSUE SUMMARY

YES: Torbjörn Tännsjö distinguishes among several types of relativism and argues in favor of one of them, which he calls "ontological relativism." According to this view, two people may disagree radically on a moral question, and yet both may be right, because each of them inhabits a different socially-constructed moral universe.

NO: Louis Pojman carefully distinguishes what he calls the diversity thesis—that moral rules differ from society to society—from ethical relativism. The diversity thesis is a straightforward description of what are acknowledged differences in the moral beliefs and practices of various human groups. But he argues that moral relativism does not follow from this diversity.

Moral realism is the view that there are objective moral standards that can be applied to all actions, no matter who performs them or in what circumstances they are performed. One important aspect of moral realism is the ability to make a definitive judgment about the morality of an action: it is either morally right or morally wrong, much like a claim about reality is either factually correct or factually incorrect.

When people are discussing conflicting moral judgments, the assertion that "morality is relative" almost inevitably comes up. Such statements are often attempts to cut the discussion short, since they undermine any objective basis for establishing which moral judgments might be correct or incorrect. Moreover, the statement "morality is relative" is frustratingly vague and incomplete. To understand what is meant by that assertion, we need to answer the question "What factor or factors is morality relative to?"

Sometimes "morality is relative" means that moral judgments are relative to various aspects of a specific situation. Something as simple as washing a car might be morally permissible under normal circumstances, but morally wrong during a drought. In other cases, "morality is relative" means that moral judgments are relative to a person's interpretation of a situation, so that people who interpret the same situation differently will make different moral judgments about the right thing to do. For example, someone who believes that washing a car will make it rain might consider it morally necessary to wash a car during a drought, while those who do not share that belief would consider the same action morally wrong. Moreover, it is entirely possible that the people making different moral judgments hold the same moral values and the difference in their moral judgments arise only from the differences in their situations or from the differences in their interpretations of the same situation, not from a genuine conflict between their values. Both the car-washer (who believes that washing the car will make it rain) as well as the non-washer (who believes that washing the car will simply waste water) value responsibility to the community and respect for the environment; they merely disagree about the best way to fulfill their shared values. Because we make moral judgments in specific contexts, these kinds of relativity are inherent in all moral reasoning. Thus, the assertion that "morality is relative" does not usually refer to these kinds of relativity.

Instead, the assertion that "morality is relative" usually means that moral judgments are relative to moral values. Such relativists hold the view that there are no objective moral standards that apply in every circumstance or situation. Instead, there are many sets of different moral standards, all of which are equally correct. There are two distinct forms of this type of relativism: cultural moral relativism, which asserts that the morality of an action is determined by the culture in which the action is performed, and individual ethical relativism, which asserts that the morality of an action is determined by the opinion of the person performing the action.

While many people initially find this approach to morality attractive, most people who have thought and written about this issue reject moral relativism. As a result, the supporters of moral relativism are in the minority. Among those, however, who think moral relativism is correct, Torbjörn Tännsjö's work—excerpted here—stands out. After briefly mentioning the view that people should be tolerant of the moral problem-solving principles of other cultures, Tännsjö distinguishes between semantic relativism and ontological relativism.

Semantic relativism corresponds fairly closely to cultural moral relativism. According to semantic relativism, people make moral judgments based solely on the moral framework established within their culture. Therefore, when a person asserts that an action is morally right or morally wrong, he or she is really asserting that the action is morally permissible or morally impermissible within his or her culture. Accordingly, specific moral judgments may be both correct and incorrect, that is, they may be correct according to the principles of one culture and incorrect according to the principles of another culture. Tännsjö explicitly rejects this form of relativism.

Rather, Tännsjö argues in favor of a kind of relativism that he calls ontological relativism. Ontological relativism is akin to individual moral relativism. According to this view, each of us inhabits a separate moral universe, which we construct from the moral framework of the societies in which we live. Each person, therefore, makes moral judgments from the perspective of his or her own moral universe. Ontological relativism differs from semantic relativism, according to Tännsjö, because in ontological relativism moral judgments cannot be both correct and incorrect, they must be either correct or incorrect. They are correct if they correspond to the principles I have established in my moral universe; they are incorrect if they do not corrrepond to the principles I have established in my universe. People who make moral judgments that conflict with my moral judgments are not just different, they are wrong. It is true that people who inhabit different moral universes can make different moral judgments, but within the moral universe of each person, there is only one correct set of moral principles, and hence only one moral judgment can be correct in that universe.

In contrast, Louis Pojman argues that commonly held forms of relativism such as cultural moral relativism and individual moral relativism are incorrect. After examining the underlying principles of these positions, he offers a detailed critique of them by dissecting the premises that appear to support them. Pojman also undermines these positions by using a type of argument known as *reductio ad absurdum*. In this type of argument, he points out the absurd consequences of following the underlying principles of these forms of relativism to their logical conclusion. Finally, he asserts that what appear to be differences in moral principles between cultures may simply be differences in the way that moral principles are applied depending on particular elements or interpretations of given situations, which leaves open the possibility that different cultures can share common moral principles.

YES

Torbjörn Tännsjö

Moral Relativism

Introduction

Moral relativism comes in many varieties. One is a substantial moral doctrine, according to which we ought to respect other cultures, and allow them to solve moral problems as they see fit. I will say nothing about this kind of moral relativism in the present context.

Other kinds of relativism are metaethical doctrines. According to these doctrines, there are more than one way correctly to answer a moral question. At least this is how I am going to use the term 'relativism' in the present context. This means that I do not count expressivism and emotivism and prescriptivism as relativist doctrines. According to expressivism, emotivism, or prescriptivism, there is no moral truth. According to these doctrines, there exist no moral facts. I prefer to classify these doctrines as nihilist. Relativism is the doctrine that there exists more than one truth about some moral cases. . . .

In the present context I will focus on metaethical forms of moral relativism and set nihilism to one side. Moral (metaethical) relativism, in turn, comes in at least three forms.

One kind of moral (metaethical) relativism is semantic (or 'indexical') moral relativism, according to which, when we pass moral judgements, we make an implicit reference to some system of morality (our own). According to this kind of moral relativism, when I say that a certain action is right, my statement is elliptic. What I am really saying is that, according to some (adequate) moral framework or system S, to which I adhere, for example the one prevailing in my culture, this action is permitted.[1] I will reject this kind of relativism.

According to another kind of (metaethical) moral relativism, which we may call epistemic, it is possible that, when one person (belonging to one culture) makes a certain moral judgement, such as that this action is right, and another person (belong[ing] to another culture) makes the judgement that the very same action is wrong, they may have just as good reasons for their respective judgements; it is even possible that, were they fully informed about all the facts, equally imaginative, and so forth, they would still hold on to their respective (conflicting) judgements. They are each fully justified in their belief in conflicting judgements.[2] I will comment on this form of moral relativism in passing.

Finally, however, there is a third kind of (metaethical) moral relativism we could call ontological, according

to which, when two persons pass conflicting moral verdicts on a certain action, they may both be right. Neither of them make judgements with any implicit reference to any system of norms. They both use their moral vocabulary in an absolute sense. An objectivist non-natural moral analysis (in the style of G.E. Moore or Henry Sidgwick) of what they say gives a correct representation of what they are doing. And yet, for all that, they pass conflicting judgements. The explanation why they can both, in an absolute sense, be 'right' in their judgements, is that they inhabit different moral (socially constructed) universes. So while it is true in the first person's moral universe that a certain action is right, it is true in the second person's moral universe that the very same action is wrong. I intend to explain and defend this version of ontological moral relativism.

Moral Universes

How Are We to Think of Moral Universes?

A moral universe consists of a system of common sense morality. We may compare common sense morality to grammar. And we should remember that it is possible to distinguish between descriptive and regulative grammar. In descriptive grammar we observe how language is actually used. We formulate hypotheses, and we try to find general answers to questions about language use. But we may also discuss a language from a regulative point of view. We may try to answer questions such as: is it correct to use certain words in a certain order? We may want to articulate general principles also in regulative grammar. However, these principles are not descriptive of the language in question. Rather, they answer the question: what makes a certain way of using language a proper or correct one? They provide reasons for answers to this question.

In regulative grammar we take for granted that there are facts of the matter. There are right and wrong ways of using language. These are facts. These facts do not exist independently of us, of course. We may think of them as social constructions, i.e. as constituted by us. If we were to speak differently, then different facts would obtain. And yet, for all that, these facts are in a sense objective. We may be ignorant about them. By sound argument we may be set straight with respect to them. . . .

It is worth observing that there are two different kinds of answers to the question what 'makes' a certain use of language a proper or correct one. One (regulative) kind of answer does indeed stipulate a reason for a judgement about the case: it is wrong to put the words in a certain order because, in the language in question, the noun phrase must precede the verb phrase. This is the kind of reason stated in a principle or rule of regulative grammar. However, the same question, i.e. the question what 'makes' a certain use of language a proper or correct one, can also be understood as an ontological question about what constitutes right and wrong in a language. And then the answer must be along the following lines: the correctness of a certain way of using the words is constituted by the fact that this is how the words are actually used in the linguistic community in question. But this is not the end of the matter. It is also crucial how experts on grammar assess this way of using words. If they condone this way of using the words, this contributes to this way's being a proper one. And, of course, one reason why the experts condone a certain way of using the words is that this is how the words are being used. But it is also true, to some extent, at least, that the fact that this way of using the words is condoned by the experts contributes to the explanation of why the words are used this way.

In a similar vein we may think of (conventional common sense) morality (in a society). Conventional common sense morality is learnt by children in a manner similar to how they learn their mother tongue. They learn that it is right or wrong to perform certain actions. Why is it right or wrong to perform a certain action? Once again there exist two ways of understanding and answering the question. A certain rule can be given, providing a reason to perform, or not perform, the action in question. Or, the question may be understood as an ontological question as to what constitutes right and wrong action. Once again, the answer to the latter (ontological) question has something to do with both how people actually behave, but also with how moral experts, or even people in general, tend to judge this kind of behaviour. These facts, in turn, may have, and certainly must have, some kind of natural explanation, for example one in terms of evolutionary biology.

Socially constituted moral norms seem to come to us in the form of a moral universe. This means that we think of them, ideally, at any rate, as complete. We demand of the norms making up our moral universe that, in principle, they answer all moral questions (even though the answers may be hard to come by for us) in an unambiguous way. And the set of answers to these questions is the moral universe (a set of moral facts). . . .

In general, if we want to find out about what constitutes right and wrong action in a certain society, we should focus more on how people justify their actions than on what they do. A crucial feature of morality is that we can use the morality a person explicitly adheres to when we want to criticise his or her actions, once they are at variance with this morality. But, at the same time, if everybody tend to perform a certain action, condemned

by common sense morality, this may mean that, at the end of the day, this action is actually condoned by common sense morality. Common sense morality is in much way a malleable and changing entity. . . .

How are we to distinguish moral (socially constituted) facts from other kinds of (socially constituted) facts, such as facts concerning etiquette, the existing legal situation, and so forth?

I suppose one distinguishing fact is that moral facts are more basic. Moral considerations seem to override other kinds of consideration. In fact, only moral considerations provide us with, in Kant's sense, categorical norms. Even if, linguistically speaking, it is proper to put a comment in one way and improper to put it in another way, this does not mean that one ought to put it in the proper way. In a similar vein, even if a certain action is legally prescribed, economically advantageous, and so forth, this does not as such mean that we ought to perform it. This fact may be hidden, to some extent, by the fact that we may believe that we have a moral obligation to obey the law. Some may even believe that we have a moral obligation to use language properly. However, without such obligations taken for granted, law and regulative grammar lack categorical normative force.

Moreover, to be accepted as a 'morality' a normative outlook must not be too idiosyncratic, i.e., it has to [be] shared to some extent, it has to be supported by a kind of common sense.

It is a moot question to what extent, within an existing common sense morality, we can really find principles explaining all actual cases of right- and wrongdoing. This problem has a clear parallel within grammar. However, even if, in the final analysis, experts must take up a rather 'particularistic' view, and concede that they find no deterministic principles capable of explaining all cases of right- or wrong-doing (or proper or improper grammar), we all tend to believe that, in many cases, there are correct answers to these questions. Even if we cannot tell for certain why this is so, we know that it is wrong to perform certain actions (or we know that certain grammatical constructions are ill formed). . . .

It would perhaps be far-fetched to claim that, just as there are different languages, there are completely different moralities (in different societies).[3] However, I think it safe to claim at least that, just as there are somewhat different dialects or even idiolects existing within a linguistic community, there are somewhat different moralities existing in different societies.

Here is a possible example. In most (all) actual societies (with their corresponding moral universes) women are in many respects treated worse than men. However, while in some societies such unequal treatment can be defended on the ground that, by treating women worse than men, all get what they deserve, such a defence is not possible in another society (with another and different moral universe, where the value of women and men is constituted as equal).

Or, should we adopt some constraint to do with the content of a moral universe and claim that the former universe is not moral? This is something we do when we pass moral judgements, of course. If we feel that men and women are of equal worth we may hesitate to speak of the view that men are more valuable than women as a 'moral' one. We will speak of it as immoral. However, when pursuing metaethics, it might be a good idea not to include any requirement that a socially constituted system of norms should have any content in particular in order to count as a 'moral' universe. The crucial thing is that the norms composing it have an overriding nature and are not too idiosyncratic.

All this means that while, from the perspective of one existing common sense morality (society), an action may be right, it may yet, for all that, be wrong, when judged from the perspective of another existing common sense morality. . . .

Back to Semantic Relativism?

But does not all this mean that we are back to a semantic relativism of a naturalistic, indexical kind? Is the claim made above not just that, when a person in one society asserts that a certain action is right, what this person is saying is that, from the perspective of the set of moral rules operative in his or her society, this action is right?

No, this is not the proper way of understanding the claim. Note that we have distinguished between descriptive and regulative grammar; in a similar vein we ought to distinguish between descriptive and normative ethics. So, when a person asserts that a certain action is right, this assertion is indeed normative. The assertion is that the action in question is right, period. The analysis of the assertion is non-naturalist. No implicit reference to the system of norms is made; an objective claim, with reference to socially constituted moral facts, is being made. We may say that this assertion is true in the moral universe in question if and only if the action in question is right. The explanation of why it is right, simpliciter can be given, however, with reference to (the content of, not the existence of) principles in this system of morality – to the extent that moral principles can be formulated within this system of morality. The claim as such makes no reference to the existence of these principles. It is normative and categorical and objective and allows of non-naturalistic analysis.

What are we to say about a situation where two persons from different cultures make conflicting judgements about a certain action?

Well, in order for this scenario to be possible, at least one of the systems must have a general scope. If both systems restrict their judgements to actions within their respective societies, no conflict will emerge. However, while this policy of live and let live is comparatively common in a linguistic context (especially between different languages but also, to some extent, between different dialects), this kind of moral relativism (with such a restricted scope) is rare. We tend to judge, from the point of view of our own morality, the manners of others. This is rendered possible by the fact that two different moral universes may share (a part of) the one and only existing actual empirical universe. If a certain concrete action is part of both moral universes, it may be right in one of the universes while wrong in the other universe. And, as I have stressed above, if we conceive of ourselves as inhabiting a moral universe, there will be a drive towards completeness. We want answers to all moral questions, also those arising in alien cultures.

Suppose the two persons are actually making conflicting moral judgements about the very same action. Let us suppose, for example, that while one person asserts that a certain action, such as the circumcision performed on a young woman in the society to which this person belongs ought to take place, another person, belonging to another society, asserts that this very same action ought not to take place, how are we to understand their conflict?

This is indeed a conflict. So we should avoid interpreting the judgements as elliptical, with an implicit reference to each person's own system of norms (somehow corrected). They are both to be taken as issuing categorical judgements about the very same action. And these judgements are indeed, we may assume, true in each moral universe. And they are 'objective' in the sense that they may be true, irrespective of whether anyone knows about this. But does not this mean that they cannot be contradictory?

I believe we should say that these people do not, strictly speaking, contradict each other. And this is due to the fact that their respective judgements differ in meaning. In saying so, we assume a moderate amount if externalism about meaning, of course. Each person, in each universe, refers to a simple property, but the properties differ between universes. One judgement is true in virtue of facts obtaining in one universe; the other is true in virtue of facts obtaining in the other universe. People inhabiting different moral universes may agree, of course, that it is true (in their universe) that a certain action is right, if and only if this action is right, but this, seemingly identical truth condition, has different meaning in different moral universes. We cannot analyse this meaning in any natural terms. In each universe, the notion of obligation is simple and not definable in any non-moral terms. However, even if the truth-conditions of each judgement are in a way inscrutable, they differ. And this means that these persons do not contradict each other after all. The reason is that they have constituted to themselves different moral universes. They need not themselves be aware of this, of course. Each may think that there is one true morality (theirs).[4] . . .

What has now been said seems to imply that we face a kind of semantic relativism after all. And in a way we do.

However, this is a new and subtler form of semantic relativism (as compared to the traditional variety described in the opening paragraph) since, taking norms to be categorical, it is compatible with the fact that the judgements in question are in conflict.

How are we to conceive of this conflict? Well, even if the judgements are logically compatible, they, and not only those who issue them, are in conflict in a practical sense. This practical conflict is rendered possible by the fact that these normative judgements have not only truth-conditions, but satisfaction conditions as well. The claim that the woman in question ought to be circumcised is satisfied if, and only if, the women is actually circumcised. And note that this satisfaction-condition is the same in all moral universes (since it is not cast in moral terms).

The normative claims that the circumcision ought to take place, and that it ought not to take place are, therefore, even if logically consistent (because issued from different moral universes using the word 'ought' in different ways), still incompatible. There is no way to satisfy both these claims.

This practical inconsistency explains why persons belonging to different moral universes, making moral judgements that are, from a strict logical point of view, consistent, may feel a need to sort out their conflicts. Even if they need not feel any intellectual drive to do so, they may well, for practical reasons, find it urgent to reach an agreement. . . .

Moral Explanation

Furthermore, while it is hard to see how we could offer moral explanations, if semantic relativism of the naturalistic, indexical, variety were true, this is something we can do on the (objectivist) version of relativism here defended. If 'This is wrong' means that, according to a certain (adequate,) framework or system of norms S, this is not permitted, then there seems to be no way of explaining what it is that makes the action in question wrong. There may be a causal explanation why the action has come to be prohibited, but there is no possibility of finding any moral explanation of its wrongness. However, on the version of relativism here defended, we may easily find a moral explanation of why the action in question is wrong, provided the moral universe is rich enough to provide such an explanation. We may say, for example, that it is wrong since it means that an innocent person is harmed (provided it is wrong to harm innocent persons in the universe in question). But this fact cannot explain why, according to S, it is not permitted. The (social) fact that it is not permitted by S, if it can be explained at all, must be explained in terms that seem to be morally irrelevant. The explanation might be, for example, that the action in question is condemned in the system because the system condemning these kinds of actions have had a certain function, explaining why it has been selected, and so forth. Such an explanation is interesting from a sociological point of view but irrelevant from a moral point of view. . . .

Logical Relations between Moral Judgements

According to the kind of moral absolutism here defined, there are indeed moral judgements, capable of being true or false. It is true that the meaning of words such as 'right' and 'wrong' tend to vary between different moral universes, but within each moral universe there exist true and false moral judgements. This means that we can conceive of logical relations in terms of truth. A moral argument is valid if, and only if, necessarily, . . . the premises of the argument are true, then the conclusion of the argument is true as well. To obtain the right moral implications we need to clarify the normative terminology, of course. But this can easily be done, for example in the following manner. A particular action is right if and only if it is not wrong. And an action is obligatory if and only if it is wrong not to perform it. Since rightness, wrongness and obligatoriness are, even if socially constituted, yet objective and genuine properties of particular actions we need only standard first-order predicate logic to get our deontic logic off the ground. . . .

When we take our moral judgements to be true or false, we may conceive of moral inconsistencies in the 'ordinary' way. Two inconsistent norms cannot both be true. And we will thus, in our pursuit for truth, have an incentive to get rid also of moral inconsistencies. When we think of moral facts as constitutive of a moral 'universe', it becomes imperative that all moral truth can be combined into one single and true (consistent) conjunction describing this universe. And our well-known epistemic goal of believing a proposition if it is true, and of not believing it if it is false, applies to our moral beliefs just as well as to other aspects of our belief system. . . .

Moral Relativism and Moral Realism

It should be noted that if moral ontological relativism, of the kind here described, is true, then epistemic moral relativism is trivially true. It is obvious that, if conflicting moral judgements, made by people living in different moral universes, may be true, then each advocate of each one of the conflicting views may have equally good reasons to support his or her favoured position. But what should a 'transcendental' moral realist of Moore's or Sidgwick's brand say about the view just outlined?

It is true that most philosophers who have advocated some kind of social constructivist view of ethics have been 'nihilists', in the sense that they have denied that there are any moral facts, existing independent of our thinking and acting.[5] Social constructivism has been resorted to by them as a kind of ersatz realism. However, this does not mean that social constructivism is inconsistent with strong moral realism. Indeed, I think it would be foolhardy of a 'transcendental' moral realist, who believes that there are objective moral reasons and facts existing independently of us to deny that different (conventional) moral universes of the kind here described exist as well. Moral realists should be prepared to accept that, when some people pass moral verdicts on actions, they express their views from the perspective of the conventional morality into which they have been socialised. So normative ontological relativism is made true by the existence of this kind of socially constituted or constructed conventional morality. However, a moral realist, who believes that there exist moral facts independently of our conceptualisation or actions, should be expected to want to add to this picture that, once the existing different moral universes have been described, there is a way of transcending them all. One more question remains to be asked and answered: which one, if any among competing moral claims, is the uniquely correct one? They must be supposed to ask for reasons that are not only categorical and objective but also such that they are in no way of our making.

When the moral realist of Moore's or Sidgwick's variety poses this question, using the standard moral terminology in the way he or she does, it is quite possible that the question cannot be answered with reference to any principles designed to rationalise any actual conventional morality. And, more importantly, the answer to the question, if such an answer exists, cannot be taken to be constituted by us. On the contrary, it is assumed that the answer is 'out there', to be found, in the same way that answers to questions posed by physicists are thought to be 'out there' to be found.

Suppose the moral realist is right about this. Let us suppose that the moral realist is right in insisting that, when different conventional moralities have been identified, there is one more question to be asked and to be answered: which one (if any one) of two competing moral claims is the correct one?[6] What does this mean?

Well, it is obvious that the moral realist is here using the moral vocabulary in a slightly different sense from the senses used in the two competing conventional moral universes. But it is no coincidence that all the parties to this controversy translate the relevant words into 'right' and 'wrong' in their own terminology. For even if these terms, when they occur in different moral universes, take on a somewhat different meaning, they all share an important function. They are all categorical and they do all guide choices. . . .

What does all this mean for how we should understand the moral conversation between a moral realist and a person who has never contemplated this 'further' question about absolute rightness, merely passing moral judgements from his or her conventional moral universe?

The obvious answer is that we should understand this difference of opinion in a way similar to how we understood the conflict between people belonging to different (conventional) moral universes. The moral realist and the person issuing moral judgements from the perspective of a particular conventional moral universe pass moral judgements that are logically consistent (because they have different truth-conditions); however, these judgements are, since they are categorical and normative, and therefore without implicit reference to any moral universe, truly conflicting. In many cases these persons will find that there is no way of satisfying the moral demands put forward by the other party. So there will be a drive somehow to solve the conflict.

Conclusion

Global ontological relativism is a self-defeating position, or so I would be prepared to argue. However, the existence of many different conventional moral systems or moral 'universes' prepares the way for a more restricted kind of moral ontological relativism. I have argued that such moral ontological relativism is true. Here Nelson Goodman's daring metaphor of 'world-making' is indeed appropriate.

It is noteworthy that even a moral realist who believes that there exists one uniquely true morality 'out there', to be found by us, may concede that moral ontological relativism of the kind here described is true. The moral realist need not reject relativism, but only add a realistic element to the picture.

Notes

1. This version of relativism is famously defended (in several places) by David Wong and Gilbert Harman. It should be noted that Harman doesn't put forward his theory as a claim about what we actually mean by a word like 'right'; rather, if we want to understand the use of 'right' in moral context as contributing to claims that have truth-values, then this is how we should understand these uses.
2. I know of no philosopher who has actually defended this (indeed quite defensible) position.
3. Some moral relativists may be prepared to make this claim, but I find it exaggerated; in general, relativists tend to exaggerate the degree to which different moral communities hold on to different basic moral positions. It seems to me that much apparent moral disagreement can be explained away as depending on different empirical beliefs.
4. This is true of semantic, indexical kinds of relativism as well, of course. Neither Harman nor Wong need to insist that it is obvious to speakers referring to different frameworks or systems, that this is what they are actually doing.
5. For example, this seems to me to be a correct diagnosis of John McDowell. See for example his 'Non-Cognitivism and Rule-Following', in Steven H. Holtzman and Christopher M. Leich

(eds.), *Wittgenstein: to Follow a Rule*, London: Routledge & Kegan Paul, 1981.

6. Note that even if the moral realist is right about this, there may be no way of finding out the answer to this question. If this is not possible, a kind of strong moral epistemic relativism seems to emerge. On this version of epistemic relativism a unique moral truth exits, so two conflicting moral opinions cannot both be right. And yet, for all that, two people may have equally and perfectly good reasons to believe in their favoured solution to the moral problem.

TORBJÖRN TÄNNSJÖ has been the Kristian Claëson Professor of Practical Philosophy at Stockholm University since 2002; he is also Director at the Stockholm University Stockholm Centre for Health Care Ethics, a cooperation between Stockholm University (SU), Karolinska Instistute (KI), and the Royal Institute of Technology (KTH). He is also an Affiliated Professor of Medical Ethics at Karolinska Institute. He has written and edited a number of important books in the field of ethics and has published over a hundred articles.

Louis P. Pojman

 **NO**

The Case Against Moral Relativism

"Who's to Judge What's Right or Wrong?"

> Like many people, I have always been instinctively a moral relativist. As far back as I can remember . . . it has always seemed to be obvious that the dictates of morality arise from some sort of convention or understanding among people, that different people arrive at different understandings, and that there are no basic moral demands that apply to everyone. This seemed so obvious to me I assumed it was everyone's instinctive view, or at least everyone who gave the matter any thought in this day and age.
>
> —Gilbert Harman[1]

> Ethical relativism is the doctrine that the moral rightness and wrongness of actions vary from society to society and that there are not absolute universal moral standards on all men at all times. Accordingly, it holds that whether or not it is right for an individual to act in a certain way depends on or is relative to the society to which he belongs.
>
> —John Ladd[2]

Gilbert Harman's intuitions about the self-evidence of ethical relativism contrast strikingly with Plato's or Kant's equal certainty about the truth of objectivism, the doctrine that universally valid or true ethical principles exist. . . . "Two things fill the soul with ever new and increasing wonder and reverence the oftener and more fervently reflection ponders on it: the starry heavens above and the moral law within," wrote Kant. On the basis of polls taken in my ethics and introduction to philosophy classes in recent years, Harman's views may signal a shift in contemporary society's moral understanding. The polls show a two-to-one ratio in favor of moral relativism over moral absolutism, with fewer than five percent of the respondents recognizing that a third position between these two polar opposites might exist. Of course, I'm not suggesting that all of these students had a clear understanding of what relativism entails, for many who said they were relativists also contended in the same polls that abortion except to save the mother's life is always wrong, that capital punishment is always wrong, or that suicide is never morally permissible. . . .

1. An Analysis of Relativism

Let us examine the theses contained in John Ladd's succinct statement on ethical (conventional) relativism that appears at the beginning of this essay. If we analyze it, we derive the following argument:

1. Moral rightness and wrongness of actions vary from society to society, so there are no universal moral standards held by all societies.
2. Whether or not it is right for individuals to act in a certain way depends on (or is relative to) the society to which they belong.
3. Therefore, there are no absolute or objective moral standards that apply to all people everywhere.

1. The first thesis, which may be called the *diversity thesis*, is simply a description that acknowledges the fact that moral rules differ from society to society. The Spartans of ancient Greece and the Dobu of New Guinea believe that stealing is morally right, but we believe it is wrong. The Roman father had the power of life and death . . . over his children, whereas we condemn parents for abusing their children. A tribe in East Africa once threw deformed infants to the hippopotamuses, and in ancient Greece and Rome infants were regularly exposed, while we abhor infanticide. Ruth Benedict describes a tribe in Melanesia that views cooperation and kindness as vices, whereas we see them as virtues. While in ancient Greece, Rome, China and Korea parricide was condemned as "the most execrable of crimes," among Northern Indians aged persons, persons who were no longer capable of walking, were left alone to starve. Among the California Gallinomero, when fathers became feeble, a burden to their sons, "the poor old wretch is not infrequently thrown down on his back and securely held while a stick is placed across his throat, and two of them seat themselves on the ends of it until he ceases to breathe."[3] Sexual practices vary over time and place. Some cultures permit homosexual behavior, while others condemn it. Some cultures practice polygamy, while others view it as immoral. Some cultures condone while others condemn premarital sex. Some cultures accept cannibalism, while the very idea revolts us. Some West African tribes perform clitoridectomies on girls, whereas we deplore such practices. Cultural relativism is

From *The Moral Life: An Introductory Reader in Ethics and Literature*, by Louis P. Pojman and Lewis Vaughn, eds., 2007, pp. 166–180, 190 (excerpts). Copyright © 2007 by Oxford University Press, Inc. Reprinted by permission.

well documented, and "custom is the king o'er all." There may or may not be moral principles that are held in common by every society, but if there are any, they seem to be few at best. Certainly it would be very difficult to derive any single "true" morality by observing various societies' moral standards.

2. The second thesis, the *dependency thesis,* asserts that individual acts are right or wrong depending on the nature of the society from which they emanate. Morality does not occur in a vacuum, and what is considered morally right or wrong must be seen in a context that depends on the goals, wants, beliefs, history, and environment of the society in question. As William G. Sumner says,

> We learn the morals as unconsciously as we learn to walk and hear and breathe, and [we] never know any reason why the [morals] are what they are. The justification of them is that when we wake to consciousness of life we find them facts which already hold us in the bonds of tradition, custom, and habit.[4]

Trying to see things from an independent, noncultural point of view would be like taking out our eyes in order to examine their contours and qualities. There is no "innocent eye." We are simply culturally determined beings.

We could, of course, distinguish between a weak and a strong thesis of dependency, for the nonrelativist can accept a certain degree of relativity in the way moral principles are *applied* in various cultures, depending on beliefs, history, and environment. For example, Jewish men express reverence for God by covering their heads when entering places of worship, whereas Christian men uncover their heads when entering places of worship. Westerners shake hands upon greeting each other, whereas Hindus place their hands together and point them toward the person to be greeted. Both sides adhere to principles of reverence and respect but apply them differently. But the ethical relativist must maintain a stronger thesis, one that insists that the moral principles themselves are products of the cultures and may vary from society to society." The ethical relativist contends that even beyond environmental factors and differences in beliefs, a fundamental disagreement exists among societies. . . .

In a sense we all live in radically different worlds. But the relativist wants to go further and maintain that there is something conventional about *any* morality, so that every morality really depends on a level of social acceptance. Not only do various societies adhere to different moral systems, but the very same society could (and often does) change its moral views over place and time. For example, the majority of people in the southern United States now view slavery as immoral, whereas one hundred and forty years ago they did not. Our society's views on divorce, sexuality, abortion, and assisted suicide have changed somewhat as well—and they are still changing.

3. The conclusion that there are no absolute or objective moral standards binding on all people follows from the first two propositions. Combining cultural relativism (*the diversity thesis*) with *the dependency thesis* yields ethical relativism in its classic form. If there are different moral principles from culture to culture and if all morality is rooted in culture, then it follows that there are no universal moral principles that are valid (or true) for all cultures and peoples at all times.

2. Subjectivism

Some people think that this conclusion is still too tame, and they maintain that morality is dependent not on the society but rather on the individual. As my students sometimes maintain, "Morality is in the eye of the beholder." They treat morality like taste or aesthetic judgments—person relative. This form of moral subjectivism has the sorry consequence that it makes morality a very useless concept, for, on its premises, little or no interpersonal criticism or judgment is logically possible. Suppose that you are repulsed by observing John torturing a child. You cannot condemn him if one of his principles is "torture little children for the fun of it." The only basis for judging him wrong might be that he was a hypocrite who condemned others for torturing. But suppose that another of his principles is that hypocrisy is morally permissible (for him); thus we cannot condemn him for condemning others for doing what he does.

On the basis of subjectivism Adolf Hitler and the serial murderer Ted Bundy could be considered as moral as Gandhi, so long as each lived by his own standards, whatever those might be. . . .

Notions of good and bad, or right and wrong, cease to have interpersonal evaluative meaning. We might be revulsed by the views of Ted Bundy, but that is just a matter of taste. A student might not like it when her teacher gives her an F on a test paper, while he gives another student an A for a similar paper, but there is no way to criticize him for injustice, because justice is not one of his chosen principles.

Absurd consequences follow from subjectivism. If it is correct, then morality reduces to aesthetic tastes about which there can be neither argument nor interpersonal judgment. Although many students say they espouse subjectivism, there is evidence that it conflicts with other of their moral views. They typically condemn Hitler as an evil man for his genocidal policies. A contradiction seems to exist between subjectivism and the very concept of morality, which it is supposed to characterize, for morality has to do with *proper* resolution of interpersonal conflict and the amelioration of the human predicament. . . . Whatever else it does, morality has a minimal aim of preventing a Hobbesian state of nature . . . , wherein life is "solitary, poor, nasty, brutish, and short. But if so, subjectivism is no help at all, for it rests neither on social agreement of principle (as the conventionalist maintains) nor on an objectively independent set of norms that bind all people for the common good. If there were only one person on earth, there would be no occasion for morality, because there wouldn't be any interpersonal conflicts to resolve or others whose suffering he or she would have a duty to ameliorate. Subjectivism implicitly assumes something of this solipsism, an atomism in which isolated individuals make up separate universes.

Subjectivism treats individuals like billiard balls on a societal pool table where they meet only in radical collisions, each aimed at his or her own goal and striving to do in the others before they themselves are done in. This atomistic view of personality is belied by the facts that we develop in families and mutually dependent communities in which we share a common language, common institutions, and similar rituals and habits, and that we often feel one another's joys and sorrows. As the poet John Donne wrote, "No man is an island, entire of itself; every man is a piece of the continent."

Radical individualistic ethical relativism is incoherent. If so, it follows that the only plausible view of ethical relativism must be one that grounds morality in the group or culture. This form is called *conventionalism.*

3. Conventionalism

Conventional ethical relativism, the view that there are no objective moral principles but that all valid moral principles are justified (or are made true) by virtue of their cultural acceptance, recognizes the social nature of morality. That is precisely its power and virtue. It does not seem subject to the same absurd consequences which plague subjectivism. Recognizing the importance of our social environment in generating customs and beliefs, many people suppose that ethical relativism is the correct meta-ethical theory. Furthermore, they are drawn to it for its liberal philosophical stance. It seems to be an enlightened response to the sin of ethnocentricity, and it seems to entail or strongly imply an attitude of tolerance toward other cultures. Anthropologist Ruth Benedict says, that in recognizing ethical relativity, "We shall arrive at a more realistic social faith, accepting as grounds of hope and as new bases for tolerance the coexisting and equally valid patterns of life which mankind has created for itself from the raw materials of existence."[5] The most famous of those holding this position is the anthropologist Melville Herskovits, who argues even more explicitly than Benedict that ethical relativism entails intercultural tolerance.

1. If morality is relative to its culture, then there is no independent basis for criticizing the morality of any other culture but one's own.
2. If there is no independent way of criticizing any other culture, we ought to be tolerant of the moralities of other cultures.
3. Morality is relative to its culture. Therefore,
4. We ought to be tolerant of the moralities of other cultures.[6]

Tolerance is certainly a virtue, but is this a good argument for it? I think not. If morality simply is relative to

each culture, then if the culture in question does not have a principle of tolerance, its members have no obligation to be tolerant. Herskovits seems to be treating the *principle of tolerance* as the one exception to his relativism. He seems to be treating it as an absolute moral principle. But from a relativistic point of view there is no more reason to be tolerant than to be intolerant and neither stance is objectively morally better than the other.

Not only do relativists fail to offer a basis for criticizing those who are intolerant, but they cannot rationally criticize anyone who espouses what they might regard as a heinous principle. If, as seems to be the case, valid criticism supposes an objective or impartial standard, relativists cannot morally criticize anyone outside their own culture. Adolf Hitler's genocidal actions, so long as they are culturally accepted, are as morally legitimate as Mother Teresa's works of mercy. If Conventional Relativism is accepted, racism, genocide of unpopular minorities, oppression of the poor, slavery, and even the advocacy of war for its own sake are as equally moral as their opposites. And if a subculture decided that starting a nuclear war was somehow morally acceptable, we could not morally criticize these people. Any actual morality, whatever its content, is as valid as every other, and more valid than ideal moralities—since the latter aren't adhered to by any culture.

There are other disturbing consequences of ethical relativism. It seems to entail that reformers are always (morally) wrong since they go against the tide of cultural standards. William Wilberforce was wrong in the eighteenth century to oppose slavery; the British were immoral in opposing suttee in India (the burning of widows, which is now illegal in India). The early Christians were wrong in refusing to serve in the Roman army or to bow down to Caesar, since the majority in the Roman Empire believed that these two acts were moral duties. In fact, Jesus himself was immoral in breaking the law of His day by healing on the Sabbath day and by advocating the principles of the Sermon on the Mount, since it is clear that few in His time (or in ours) accepted them.

Yet we normally feel just the opposite, that the reformer is a courageous innovator who is right, who has the truth, against the mindless majority. Sometimes the individual must stand alone with the truth, risking social censure and persecution. . . . Yet if relativism is correct, the opposite is necessarily the case. Truth is with the crowd and error with the individual. . . .

There is an even more basic problem with the notion that morality is dependent on cultural acceptance for its validity. The problem is that the notion of a *culture* or *society* is notoriously difficult to define. This is especially so in a pluralistic society like our own where the notion seems to be vague with unclear boundary lines. One person may belong to several societies (subcultures) with different value emphases and arrangements of principles. A person may belong to the nation as a single society with certain values of patriotism, honor, courage, laws (including some which are controversial but have majority acceptance, such as the current law on abortion). But he or she may also belong to a church which opposes some of the laws of the State. He may also be an integral member of a socially mixed community where different principles hold sway, and he may belong to clubs and a family where still other rules are adhered to. Relativism would seem to tell us that where he is a member of societies with conflicting moralities he must be judged both wrong and not-wrong whatever he does. For example, if Mary is a U.S. citizen and a member of the Roman Catholic Church, she is wrong (qua Catholic) if she chooses to have an abortion and not-wrong (qua citizen of the U.S.A.) if she acts against the teaching of the Church on abortion. As a member of a racist university fraternity, KKK, John has no obligation to treat his fellow Black student as an equal, but as a member of the university community itself (where the principle of equal rights is accepted) he does have the obligation; but as a member of the surrounding community (which may reject the principle of equal rights) he again has no such obligation; but then again as a member of the nation at large (which accepts the principle) he is obligated to treat his fellow with respect. What is the morally right thing for John to do? The question no longer makes much sense in this moral Babel. It has lost its action-guiding function.

Perhaps the relativist would adhere to a principle which says that in such cases the individual may choose which group to belong to as primary. If Mary chooses to have an abortion, she is choosing to belong to the general society relative to that principle. And John must likewise choose among groups. The trouble with this option is that it seems to lead back to counter-intuitive results. If Murder Mike of Murder, Incorporated, feels like killing Bank President Ortcutt and wants to feel good about it, he identifies with the Murder, Incorporated society rather than the general public morality. Does this justify the killing? In fact, couldn't one justify anything simply by forming a small subculture that approved of it? Ted Bundy would be morally pure in raping and killing innocents simply by virtue of forming a little coterie. How large must the group be in order to be a legitimate subculture or society? Does it need ten or fifteen people? How about just three? Come to think about it, why can't my burglary partner and I found our own society with a morality of its own? Of course, if my partner dies, I could still claim that I was acting from an originally social set of norms. But why can't I dispense with the interpersonal agreements altogether and invent my own morality—since morality, on this view, is only an invention anyway? Conventionalist relativism seems to reduce to subjectivism. And subjectivism leads, as we have seen, to moral solipsism, to the demise of morality altogether. . . .

. . . I don't think you can stop the move from conventionalism to subjectivism. The essential force of the validity of the chosen moral principle is that it is dependent on choice. The conventionalist holds that it is the choice of the group, but why should I accept the group's silly choice, when my own is better (for me)? Why should anyone give such august authority to a culture of society? If this is all morality comes to, why not reject it altogether—even though one might want to adhere to its directives when others are looking in order to escape sanctions?

4. A Critique of Ethical Relativism

However, while we may fear the demise of morality, as we have known it, this in itself may not be a good reason for rejecting relativism. That is, for judging it false. Alas, truth may not always be edifying. But the consequences of this position are sufficiently alarming to prompt us to look carefully for some weakness in the relativist's argument. So let us examine the premises and conclusion listed at the beginning of this essay as the three theses of relativism.

1. *The Diversity Thesis.* What is considered morally right and wrong varies from society to society, so that there are no moral principles accepted by all societies.
2. *The Dependency Thesis.* All moral principles derive their validity from cultural acceptance.
3. *Ethical Relativism.* Therefore, there are no universally valid moral principles, objective standards which apply to all people everywhere and at all times.

Does any one of these seem problematic? Let us consider the first thesis, the diversity thesis, which we have also called cultural relativism. Perhaps there is not as much diversity as anthropologists like Sumner and Benedict suppose. One can also see great similarities between the moral codes of various cultures. E. O. Wilson has identified over a score of common features,[7] and before him Clyde Kluckhohn has noted much significant common ground between cultures.

> Every culture has a concept of murder, distinguishing this from execution, killing in war, and other "justifiable homicides." The notions of incest and other regulations upon sexual behavior, the prohibitions upon untruth under defined circumstances, of restitution and reciprocity, of mutual obligations between parents and children—these and many other moral concepts are altogether universal.[8]

Colin Turnbull's description of the sadistic, semidisplaced, disintegrating Ik in Northern Uganda supports the view that a people without principles of kindness, loyalty, and cooperation will degenerate into a Hobbesian state of nature.[9] But he has also produced evidence that underneath the surface of this dying society, there is a deeper moral code from a time when the tribe flourished, which occasionally surfaces and shows its nobler face.

On the other hand, there is enormous cultural diversity and many societies have radically different moral codes. Cultural relativism seems to be a fact, but, even if it is, it does not by itself establish the truth of ethical relativism. Cultural diversity in itself is neutral between theories. For the objectivist could concede complete cultural relativism, but still defend a form of universalism; for he or she could argue that some cultures simply lack correct moral principles.

On the other hand, a denial of complete cultural relativism (i.e., an admission of some universal principles) does not disprove ethical relativism. For even if we did find one or more universal principles, this would not prove that they had any objective status. We could still *imagine* a culture that was an exception to the rule and be unable to criticize it. So the first premise doesn't by itself imply ethical relativism and its denial doesn't disprove ethical relativism.

We turn to the crucial second thesis, the dependency thesis. Morality does not occur in a vacuum, but rather what is considered morally right or wrong must be seen in a context, depending on the goals, wants, beliefs, history, and environment of the society in question. We distinguished a weak and a strong thesis of dependency. The weak thesis says that the application of principles depends on the particular cultural predicament, whereas the strong thesis affirms that the principles themselves depend on that predicament. The nonrelativist can accept a certain relativity in the way moral principles are *applied* in various cultures, depending on beliefs, history, and environment. For example, a raw environment with scarce natural resources may justify the Eskimos' brand of euthanasia to the objectivist, who in another environment would consistently reject that practice. The members of a tribe in the Sudan throw their deformed children into the river because of their belief that such infants *belong* to the hippopotamus, the god of the river. We believe that they have a false belief about this, but the point is that the same principles of respect for property and respect for human life are operative in these contrary practices. They differ with us only in belief, not in substantive moral principle. This is an illustration of how nonmoral beliefs (e.g., deformed children belong to the hippopotamus) when applied to common moral principles (e.g., give to each his due) generate different actions in different cultures. In our own culture the difference in the nonmoral belief about the status of a fetus generates opposite moral prescriptions. The major difference between pro-choicers and pro-lifers is not whether we should kill persons but whether fetuses are really persons. It is a debate about the facts of the matter, not the principle of killing innocent persons.

So the fact that moral principles are weakly dependent doesn't show that ethical relativism is valid. In spite of this weak dependency on nonmoral factors, there could still be a set of general moral norms applicable to all cultures and even recognized in most, which are disregarded at a culture's own expense.

What the relativist needs is a strong thesis of dependency, that somehow all principles are essentially cultural inventions. But why should we choose to view morality this way? Is there anything to recommend the strong thesis over the weak thesis of dependency? The relativist may argue that in fact we don't have an obvious impartial standard from which to judge. "Who's to say which culture is right and which is wrong?" But this seems to be dubious. We can reason and perform thought experiments in order to make a case for one system over another. We may not be able to know with certainty that our moral beliefs are closer to the truth than those of another culture or those of others within our own culture, but we may be *justified* in believing that they are. If we can be closer to the truth regarding factual or scientific matters, why can't we be closer to the truth on moral matters? Why can't a culture be simply confused or wrong about its moral perceptions? Why can't we say that the society like the Ik which sees nothing wrong with enjoying watching its own children fall into fires is less moral in that regard than the culture that cherishes children and grants them protection and equal rights? To take such a stand is not to commit the fallacy of ethnocentricism, for we are seeking to derive principles through critical reason, not simply uncritical acceptance of one's own mores.

Many relativists embrace relativism as a default position. Objectivism makes no sense to them. I think this is Ladd and Harman's position, as the latter's quotation at the beginning of this article seems to indicate. Objectivism has insuperable problems, so the answer must be relativism. . . .

In conclusion I have argued (1) that cultural relativism (the fact that there are cultural differences regarding moral principles) does not entail ethical relativism (the thesis that there are no objectively valid universal moral principles) [and] (2) that the dependency thesis (that morality derives its legitimacy from individual cultural acceptance) is mistaken. . . .

So "Who's to judge what's right or wrong?" We are. We are to do so on the basis of the best reasoning we can bring forth, and with sympathy and understanding.[10]

Notes

1. Gilbert Harman, "Is There a Single True Morality?" in *Morality, Reason and Truth,* eds. David Copp and David Zimmerman (Rowman & Allenheld, 1984).
2. John Ladd, *Ethical Relativism* (Wadsworth, 1973).
3. Reported by the anthropologist Powers, *Tribes of California,* p. 178. Quoted in E. Westermarck, *Origin and Development of Moral Ideals* (London, 1906), p. 386. This work is a mine of examples of cultural diversity.
4. W. G. Sumner, *Folkways* (Ginn & Co., 1906), p. 76.
5. Ruth Benedict, *Patterns of Culture* (New American Library, 1934), p, 257.

6. Melville Herskovits, *Cultural Relativism* (Random House, 1972).
7. E. O. Wilson, *On Human Nature* (Bantam Books, 1979), pp. 22–23.
8. Clyde Kluckhohn, "Ethical Relativity: Sic et Non," *Journal of Philosophy,* LII (1955).
9. Colin Turnbull, *The Mountain People* (New York: Simon & Schuster, 1972).
10. Bruce Russell, Morton Winston, Edward Sherline, and an anonymous reviewer made important criticisms on earlier versions of this article, issuing in this revision.

Louis P. Pojman (1935–2005) was a prolific American philosopher who published (as editor or author) over 30 books and wrote more than 100 articles. His writing extends widely and embraces many areas of philosophy, but Pojman is best remembered as a writer on ethical, social, and political issues. He was particularly concerned to make ideas clear to nonphilosophers.

EXPLORING THE ISSUE

Is Moral Relativism Correct?

Critical Thinking and Reflection

1. How can disagreements about right and wrong between people within the same culture be solved: (a) within a framework of moral relativism and (b) within framework of moral realism?
2. How can disagreements about right and wrong between people from different cultures be resolved: (a) within a framework of moral relativism and (b) within a framework of moral realism?
3. Both Pojman and Tännsjö criticize cultural moral relativism (also known as semantic relativism). How are these criticisms similar? How are they different? Are these criticisms consistent with one another?
4. Find an example of an action that is considered morally right in one culture and morally wrong in another culture. How might the different moral judgments be explained without cultural moral relativism? Do you find these explanations persuasive?
5. As a result of the rapid development of communication technology, such as the Internet, differences among societies are decreasing and a more uniform international culture is developing. If this process continues, then a single society might be influencing the construction of each person's individual reality, thereby introducing a uniformity among these realities. In this case, could this uniformity result in the development of a universal, and hence quasi-objective, moral standard by which to judge actions?

Is There Common Ground?

It seems unlikely that an author who defends ethical relativism would also be sympathetic to moral realism. The objective moral standards described by Tännsjö within the framework of ontological relativism are objective only from the perspective of a specific person's socially constructed reality. There need be no objective moral standards beyond these individual realities that apply to the socially constructed realities of every single person. However, Tännsjö wraps up his article by saying that his position is entirely consistent with the possibility that objective moral standards do exist, although it would be a challenge for a person to "break out" of his/her own reality in order to discover such a universal moral standard.

While Pojman's objectivist system allows no room for moral relativism, he nonetheless allows for what he calls "a certain relativity" in the application of moral principles to form judgments. He can thus provide a sympathetic account of how societies that appear to have radically different ethical views may in fact share common norms with other cultures. Rather than stating that these cultures are simply mistaken about objective moral standards, Pojman asserts that they may hold different beliefs that account for the different ways in which these common norms are expressed.

Create Central

www.mhhe.com/createcentral

Additional Resources

Maria Baghramian, *Relativism* (Routledge, 2004)

Michael C. Brannigan, *Ethics Across Cultures* (McGraw-Hill, 2005)

Neil Levy, *Moral Relativism: A Short Introduction* (One-World Publications, 2002)

Paul K. Moser and Thomas L. Carson, eds., *Moral Relativism: A Reader* (Oxford University Press, 2000)

Internet References . . .

Ethics Updates: Introduction to Moral Theory

http://ethics.sandiego.edu/theories/Intro/index.asp

Internet Encyclopedia of Philosophy: Moral Philosophy

www.iep.utm.edu/moral-re/

Online Guide to Ethics and Moral Philosophy: Ethical Relativism

http://caae.phil.cmu.edu/cavalier/80130/part2/sect6.html

Selected, Edited, and with Issue Framing Material by:
Owen M. Smith, *Stephen F. Austin State University*
and
Anne Collins Smith, *Stephen F. Austin State University*

ISSUE

Does Morality Need Religion?

YES: **C. Stephen Layman,** from "Ethics and the Kingdom of God.," in *The Shape of the Good: Christian Reflections on the Foundations of Ethics* (University of Notre Dame Press, 1991)

NO: **John Arthur,** from "Religion, Morality, and Conscience," in *Morality and Moral Controversies* (Prentice Hall, 1996)

Learning Outcomes
After reading this issue, you will be able to: • Describe the reasons people give for choosing to behave morally.   • Discuss each author's position on the relationship between religion and morality.   • Formulate your own position on whether morality needs religion and identify evidence supporting your position.   • Identify the main objections to your position and formulate responses to these objections.

ISSUE SUMMARY

YES: Philosopher C. Stephen Layman argues that morality makes the most sense from a theistic perspective and that a purely secular perspective is insufficient. The secular perspective, Layman asserts, does not adequately deal with secret violations, and it does not allow for the possibility of fulfillment of people's deepest needs in an afterlife.

NO: Philosopher John Arthur counters that morality is logically independent of religion, although there are historical connections. Religion, he believes, is not necessary for moral guidance or moral answers; morality is social.

There is a widespread feeling that morality and religion are connected. One view is that religion provides a ground for morality, so without religion there is no morality. Thus, a falling away from religion implies a falling away from morality.

Such thoughts have troubled many people. The Russian novelist Dostoyevsky (1821–1881) wrote, "If there is no God, then everything is permitted." Many Americans today also believe that religious faith is important. They often maintain that even if doctrines and dogmas cannot be known for certain, religion nevertheless leads to morality and good behavior. President Dwight D. Eisenhower is reputed to have said that everyone should have a religious faith but that it did not matter what that faith was. And many daily newspapers throughout the country advise their readers to attend the church or synagogue of their choice. Apparently, the main reason why people think it is important to subscribe to a religion is that only in this way will one be able to attain morality. If there is no God, then everything is permitted and there is moral chaos. Moral chaos can be played out

in societies and, on a smaller scale, within the minds of individuals. Thus, if you do not believe in God, then you will confront moral chaos; you will be liable to permit (and permit yourself to do) anything, and you will have no moral bearings at all.

Such a view seems to face several problems, however. For example, what are we to say of the morally good atheist or of the morally good but completely nonreligious person? A true follower of the view that morality derives from religion might reply that we are simply begging the question if we believe that such people *could* be morally good. Such people might do things that are morally right and thus might *seem* good, the reply would go, but they would not be acting for the right reason (obedience to God). Such people would not have the same anchor or root for their seemingly moral attitudes that religious persons do.

Another problem for the view that links morality with religion comes from the following considerations: If you hold this view, what do you say of devoutly religious people who belong to religious traditions and who support moralities that are different from your own? If morality is indeed derived from religion, if different people are thus led to follow different moralities, and if the original religions are not themselves subject to judgment, then it is understandable how different people arrive at different moral views. But the views will still be different and perhaps even incompatible. If so, the statement that morality derives from religion must mean that one can derive *a* morality from *a* religion (and not that one derives morality itself from religion). The problem is that by allowing this variation among religions and moralities back into the picture, we seem to allow moral chaos back in, too.

The view that what God commands is good, what God prohibits is evil, and without divine commands and prohibitions nothing is either good or bad in itself is called the *divine command theory,* or the *divine imperative view.* This view resists the recognition of any source of good or evil that is not tied to criteria or standards of God's own creation. Such a recognition is thought to go against the idea of God's omnipotence. A moral law that applied to God but was not of God's own creation would seem to limit God in a way in which he cannot be limited. But, on the other hand, this line of thought (that no moral law outside of God's own making should apply to him) seems contrary to the orthodox Christian view that God is good. For if good means something in accordance with God's will, then when we say that God is good, we are only saying that he acts in accordance with his own will—and this just does not seem to be enough.

In the following selections, C. Stephen Layman argues that a religious perspective makes better sense of moral commitment than a secular perspective. Indeed, in his view, it is not even clear that a secular individual who followed the dictates of morality would be rational. John Arthur asserts that morality does not need a religious foundation at all and that morality is social.

YES

C. Stephen Layman

Ethics and the Kingdom of God

Why build a theory of ethics on the assumption that there is a God? Why not simply endorse a view of ethics along . . . secular lines . . . ? I shall respond to these questions in [two] stages. First, I contrast the secular and religious perspectives on morality. Second, I explain why I think the moral life makes more sense from the point of view of theism [belief in God] than from that of atheism. . . .

⁕

As I conceive it, the modern secular perspective on morality involves at least two elements. First, there is no afterlife; each individual human life ends at death. It follows that the only goods available to an individual are those he or she can obtain this side of death.[1]

Second, on the secular view, moral value is an *emergent* phenomenon. That is, moral value is "a feature of certain effects though it is not a feature of their causes" (as wetness is a feature of H_2O, but not of hydrogen or oxygen).[2] Thus, the typical contemporary secular view has it that moral value emerges only with the arrival of very complex nervous systems (viz., human brains), late in the evolutionary process. There is no Mind "behind the scenes" on the secular view, no intelligent Creator concerned with the affairs of human existence. As one advocate of the secular view puts it, "Ethics, though not consciously created [either by humans or by God], is a product of social life which has the function of promoting values common to the members of society."[3]

By way of contrast, the religious point of view (in my use of the phrase) includes a belief in God and in life after death. God is defined as an eternal being who is almighty and perfectly morally good. Thus, from the religious point of view, morality is not an emergent phenomenon, for God's goodness has always been in existence, and is not the product of nonmoral causes. Moreover, from the religious point of view, there are goods available after death. Specifically, there awaits the satisfaction of improved relations with God and with redeemed creatures.

It is important to note that, from the religious perspective, *the existence of God and life after death* are not independent hypotheses. If God exists, then at least two lines of reasoning lend support to the idea that death is not final. While I cannot here scrutinize these lines of reasoning, I believe it will be useful to sketch them.[4] (1) It has often been noted that we humans seem unable to find complete fulfillment in the present life. Even those having abundant material possessions and living in the happiest of circumstances find themselves, upon reflection, profoundly unsatisfied. . . . [I]f this earthly life is the whole story, it appears that our deepest longings will remain unfulfilled. But if God is good, He surely will not leave our deepest longings unfulfilled provided He is able to fulfill them—at least to the extent that we are willing to accept His gracious aid. So, since our innermost yearnings are not satisfied in this life, it is likely that they will be satisfied after death.

(2) Human history has been one long story of injustice, of the oppression of the poor and weak by the rich and powerful. The lives of relatively good people are often miserable, while the wicked prosper. Now, if God exists, He is able to correct such injustices, though He does not correct all of them in the present life. But if God is also good, He will not leave such injustices forever unrectified. It thus appears that He will rectify matters at some point after death. This will involve benefits for some in the afterlife—it may involve penalties for others. (However, the . . . possibility of post-mortem punishment does not necessarily imply the possibility of hell as *standardly conceived*.)

We might sum up the main difference between the secular and religious views by saying that the only goods available from a secular perspective are *earthly* goods. Earthly goods include such things as physical health, friendship, pleasure, self-esteem, knowledge, enjoyable activities, an adequate standard of living, etc. The religious or theistic perspective recognizes these earthly goods *as good,* but it insists that there are non-earthly or *transcendent* goods. These are goods available only if God exists and there is life after death for humans. Transcendent goods include harmonious relations with God prior to death as well as the joys of the afterlife—right relations with both God and redeemed creatures.

⁕

[One secular] defense of the virtues amounts to showing that society cannot function well unless individuals have moral virtue. If we ask, "Why should we as individuals care about society?", the answer will presumably be along the following lines: "Individuals cannot flourish apart from a well-functioning society, *so morality pays for the individual.*"

This defense of morality raises two questions we must now consider. First, is it misguided to defend morality by an appeal to self-interest? Many people feel that morality and self-interest are fundamentally at odds: "If you perform an act because you see that it is in your interest to do so, then you aren't doing the right thing *just because it's right*. A successful defense of morality must be a defense of duty for duty's sake. Thus, the appeal to self-interest is completely misguided." Second, *does* morality really pay for the individual? More particularly, does morality always pay in terms of earthly goods? Let us take these questions up in turn.

(1) Do we desert the moral point of view if we defend morality on the grounds that it pays? Consider an analogy with etiquette. Why should one bother with etiquette? Should one do the well-mannered thing simply for its own sake? Do we keep our elbows off the table or refrain from belching just because these things are "proper"?

To answer this question we must distinguish between the *justification of an institution* and *the justification of a particular act within that institution*. (By 'institution' I refer to any system of activities specified by rules.) This distinction can be illustrated in the case of the game (institution) of baseball. If we ask a player why he performs a particular act during a game, he will probably give an answer such as, "To put my opponent out" or "To get a home run." These answers obviously would not be relevant if the question were, "Why play baseball at all?" Relevant answers to this second question would name some advantage for the individual player, e.g., "Baseball is fun" or "It's good exercise." Thus, a justification of the institution of baseball (e.g., "It's good exercise") is quite different from a justification of a particular act within the institution (e.g., "To get a home run").

Now let's apply this distinction to our question about etiquette. If our question concerns the justification of a particular act within the institution of etiquette, then the answer may reasonably be, in effect, "This is what's proper. This is what the rules of etiquette prescribe." . . .

But plainly there are deeper questions we can ask about etiquette. Who hasn't wondered, at times, what the point of the institution of etiquette is? Why do we have these quirky rules, some of which seem to make little sense? When these more fundamental questions concerning the entire institution of etiquette are being asked, it makes no sense to urge etiquette for etiquette's sake. What is needed is a description of the human *ends* the institution fulfills—ends which play a justificatory role similar to fun or good exercise in the case of baseball. And it is not difficult to identify some of these ends. For example, the rules of etiquette seem designed, in part, to facilitate social interaction; things just go more smoothly if there are agreed upon ways of greeting, eating, conversing, etc.

If anyone asks, "Why should I as an individual bother about etiquette?", an initial reply might be: "Because if you frequently violate the rules of etiquette, people will shun you." If anyone wonders why he should care about being shunned, we will presumably reply that good social relations are essential to human flourishing, and hence that a person is jeopardizing his own best interests if he places no value at all on etiquette. Thus, in the end, a defense of the institution of etiquette seems to involve the claim that the institution of etiquette *pays* for those who participate in it; it would not be illuminating to answer the question, "Why bother about etiquette?" by saying that etiquette is to be valued for its own sake.

Now, just as we distinguish between justifying the institution of etiquette (or baseball) and justifying a particular act within the institution, so we must distinguish between justifying the institution of morality and justifying a particular act within the institution. When choosing a particular course of action we may simply want to know what's right. But a more ultimate question also cries out for an answer: "What is the point of the institution of morality, anyway? Why should one bother with it?" It is natural to respond by saying that society cannot function well without morality, and individuals cannot flourish apart from a well-functioning society. In short, defending the institution of morality involves claiming that morality pays for the individual in the long run. It seems obscurantist to preach duty for duty's sake, once the more fundamental question about the point of the institution of morality has been raised.

But if morality is defended on the grounds that it pays, doesn't this distort moral motivation? Won't it mean that we no longer do things because they are right, but rather because they are in our self-interest? No. We must bear in mind our distinction between the reasons that justify a particular act within an institution and the reasons that justify the institution itself. A baseball player performs a given act in order to get on base or put an opponent out; he does not calculate whether this particular swing of the bat (or throw of the ball) is fun or good exercise. A well-mannered person is not constantly calculating whether a given act will improve her relations with others, she simply does "the proper thing." Similarly, even if we defend morality on the grounds that it pays, it does not follow that the motive for each moral act becomes, "It will pay" for we are not constantly thinking of the philosophical issues concerning the justification of the entire system of morality; for the most part we simply do things because they are right, honest, fair, loving, etc. Nevertheless, our willingness to plunge wholeheartedly into "the moral game" is apt to be vitiated should it become clear to us that the game does not pay.

At this point it appears that the institution of morality is justified only if it pays for the individuals who participate in it. For if being moral does not pay for individuals, it is difficult to see why they should bother with it. The appeal to duty for duty's sake is irrelevant when we are asking for a justification of the institution of morality itself.

(2) But we must now ask, "Does morality in fact pay?" There are at least four reasons for supposing that morality

does not pay from a *secular* perspective. (a) One problem for the secular view arises from the fact that the moral point of view involves a concern for *all* human beings—or at least for all humans affected by one's actions. Thus, within Christian theology, the parable of the good Samaritan is well known for its expansion of the category of "my neighbor." But human societies seem able to get along well without extending full moral concern to all outsiders; this is the essence of tribal morality. Thus, explorers in the 1700s found that the Sioux Indians followed a strict code in dealing with each other, but regarded themselves as free to steal horses from the Crow. Later on, American whites repeatedly broke treaties with the American Indians in a way that would not have been possible had the Indians been regarded as equals. It is no exaggeration to say that throughout much of human history tribal morality has been the morality humans lived by.

And so, while one must agree . . . that the virtues are necessary for the existence of society, it is not clear that this amounts to anything more than a defense of tribal morality. . . . From a purely secular point of view, it is unclear why the scope of moral concern must extend beyond one's society—or, more precisely, why one's concern must extend to groups of people outside of one's society *who are powerless and stand in the way of things one's society wants.* Why should the members of a modern industrial state extend full moral consideration to a tiny Amazonian tribe? . . .

(b) A second problem for secular views concerns the possibility of secret violations of moral rules. What becomes of conscientiousness when one can break the rules in secret, without anyone knowing? After all, if I can break the rules in secret, I will not cause any social disharmony. Of course, there can be no breaking of the rules in secret if there is a God of the Christian type, who knows every human thought as well as every human act. But there are cases in which it is extraordinarily unlikely that any *humans* will discover one's rule breaking. Hence, from a secular perspective, there are cases in which secret violations of morality are possible.

Consider the following case. Suppose A has borrowed some money from B, but A discovers that B has made a mistake in his records. Because of the mistake, B believes that A has already paid the money back. B even goes out of his way to thank A for prompt payment on the loan. Let us further suppose that B is quite wealthy, and hence not in need of the money. Is it in A's interest to pay the money back? Not paying the money back would be morally wrong; but would it be irrational, from a secular point of view? Not necessarily. Granted, it might be irrational in some cases, e.g., if A would have intense guilt feelings should he fail to repay the loan. But suppose A will not feel guilty because he really needs the money (and knows that B does not need it), and because he understands that secret violations belong to a special and rare category of action. Then, from a secular point of view, it is doubtful that paying the loan would be in A's interest.

The point is not that theists never cheat or lie. Unfortunately they do. The point is rather that secret violations of morality arguably pay off from a secular point of view. And so, once again, it seems that there is a "game" that pays off better (in terms of earthly goods) than the relatively idealistic morality endorsed by the great ethicists, viz., one allowing secret "violations."

(c) Even supposing that morality pays for some people, does it pay for *everyone* on the secular view? Can't there be well-functioning societies in which some of the members are "moral freeloaders"? In fact, don't all actual societies have members who maintain an appearance of decency, but are in fact highly manipulative of others? How would one show, on secular grounds, that it is in the interest of these persons to be moral? Furthermore, according to psychiatrists, some people are highly amoral, virtually without feelings of guilt or shame. Yet in numerous cases these amoral types appear to be happy. These "successful egoists" are often intelligent, charming, and able to evade legal penalties for their unconventional behavior.[5] How could one show, on secular grounds, that it is in the interests of such successful egoists to be moral? They seem to find their amoral lives amply rewarding.

(d) Another problem from the secular perspective stems from the fact that in some cases morality demands that one risk death. Since death cuts one off from all earthly goods, what sense does it make to be moral (in a given case) if the risk of death is high?

This point must be stated with care. In many cases it makes sense, from a secular point of view, to risk one's life. For example, it makes sense if the risk is small and the earthly good to be gained is great; after all, one risks one's life driving to work. Or again, risking one's life makes sense from a secular point of view if failing to do so will probably lead to profound and enduring earthly unhappiness. Thus, a woman might take an enormous risk to save her child from an attacker. She might believe that she would be "unable to live with herself" afterward if she stood by and let the attacker kill or maim her child. Similarly, a man might be willing to die for his country, because he could not bear the dishonor resulting from a failure to act courageously.

But failing to risk one's life does not always lead to profound and enduring earthly unhappiness. Many soldiers play it safe in battle when risk taking is essential for victory; they may judge that victory is not worth the personal risks. And many subjects of ruthless tyrants entirely avoid the risks involved in resistance and reform. Though it may be unpleasant for such persons to find themselves regarded as cowards, this unpleasantness does not necessarily lead to profound and enduring earthly unhappiness. It seems strained to claim that what is commonly regarded as moral courage always pays in terms of earthly goods.

At this point it appears that the institution of morality cannot be justified from a secular point of view. For, as we have seen, the institution of morality is justified only if it pays (in the long run) for the individuals who participate in it. But if by "morality" we mean the relatively idealistic code urged on us by the great moralists, it appears that the institution of morality does not pay, according to the secular point of view. This is not to say that no moral code could pay off in terms of earthly goods; a tribal morality of some sort might pay for most people, especially if it were to include conventions which skirt the problems inherent in my "secret violation" and "risk of death" cases. But such a morality would be a far cry from the morality most of us actually endorse.

Defenders of secular morality may claim that these difficulties evaporate if we look at morality from an evolutionary point of view. The survival of the species depends on the sacrifice of individuals in some cases, and the end of morality is the survival of the species. Hence, it is not surprising that being highly moral will not always pay off for individuals.

This answer is confused for two reasons. First, even if morality does have survival value for the species, we have seen that this does not by itself justify the individual's involvement in the institution of morality. In fact, it does not justify such involvement if what is best for the species is not what is best for the individual member of the species. And I have been arguing that, from a secular point of view, the interests of the species and the individual diverge.

Second, while evolution might explain why humans *feel* obligated to make sacrifices, it is wholly unable to account for genuine moral obligation. If we did not feel obligated to make sacrifices for others, it might be that the species would have died out long ago. So, moral *feelings* may have survival value. However, *feeling obligated* is not the same thing as *being obligated*. . . . Thus, to show that moral feelings have survival value is not to show that there are any actual moral obligations at all. . . . The point is, the evolutionary picture does not require the existence of real obligations; it demands only the existence of moral feelings or beliefs. Moral feelings or beliefs would motivate action even if there were in actuality no moral obligations. For example, the belief that human life is sacred may very well have survival value even if human life is not sacred. Moral obligation, as opposed to moral feeling, is thus an unnecessary postulate from the standpoint of evolution.

At this point defenders of the secular view typically make one of two moves: (i) They claim that even if morality does not pay, there remain moral truths which we must live up to; or (ii) they may claim that morality pays in subtle ways which we have so far overlooked. Let us take these claims up in turn.

(i) It may be claimed that moral obligation is just a fact of life, woven into the structure of reality. Morality may not always pay, but certain moral standards remain true, e.g., "Lying is wrong" or "Human life is sacred." These are not made true by evolution or God, but are necessary truths, independent of concrete existence, like "1 + 1 = 2" or "There are no triangular circles."

There are at least three difficulties with this suggestion. First, assuming that there are such necessary truths about morality, why should we care about them or pay them any attention? We may grant that an act is correct from the moral point of view and yet wonder whether we have good reason to participate in the institution of morality. So, even if we grant that various statements of the form "One ought to do X" are necessarily true, this does not show that the institution of morality pays off. It just says that morality is a "game" whose rules are necessary truths. . . . To defend the institution of morality simply on the grounds that certain moral statements are necessarily true is to urge duty for duty's sake. And . . . this is not an acceptable defense of the institution of morality.

Second, the idea that some moral truths are necessary comports poorly with the usual secular account. As Mavrodes points out, necessary moral truths seem to be what Plato had in mind when he spoke about the Form of the Good. And Plato's view, though not contradicted by modern science, receives no support from it either. Plato's Form of the Good is not an emergent phenomenon, but is rather woven into the very structure of reality, independently of physical processes such as evolution. So, Plato's view is incompatible with the typically modern secular view that moral value is an emergent phenomenon, coming into existence with the arrival of the human nervous system. For this reason, Plato's views have "often been taken to be congenial . . . to a religious understanding of the world."[6]

Third, it is very doubtful that there are any necessary truths of the form "One ought to do X." We have seen that the institution of morality stands unjustified if participation in it does not pay (in the long run) for individuals. And why should we suppose that there are *any* necessary moral truths if the institution of morality is unjustified? . . . [S]tatements of the form "One ought to do X" are not *necessary* truths, though they may be true *if* certain conditions are met. . . . Hence, if there are any necessary moral truths, they appear to be conditional (if then) in form: If certain conditions exist, one ought to do X. Among the conditions, as we have seen, is the condition that doing X pays for the individual in the long run. So, it is very doubtful that there are any necessary moral truths of the form "One ought to do X."[7] The upshot is that morality is partly grounded in those features of reality which guarantee that morality pays; and the secular view lacks the metaphysical resources for making such a guarantee. . . .

(ii) But some have claimed that, if we look closely at human psychology, we can see that morality does pay *in terms of earthly goods*. For example, Plato suggested that only a highly moral person could have harmony between the various elements of his soul (such as reason and desire). Others have claimed that being highly moral is the only means to inner satisfaction. We humans are just so constituted that violations of morality never leave us with a net gain. Sure, we may gain earthly goods of one sort or another by lying, stealing, etc., but these are always outweighed by inner discord or a sense of dissatisfaction with ourselves.

There are several problems with this. First, some may doubt that moral virtue is the best route to inner peace. After all, one may experience profound inner discord when one has done what is right. It can be especially upsetting to stand up for what is right when doing so is unpopular; indeed, many people avoid "making waves" precisely because it upsets their inner peace. . . .

Second, how good is the evidence that inner peace *always* outweighs the benefits achievable through unethical action? Perhaps guilt feelings and inner discord are a reasonable price to pay for certain earthly goods. If a cowardly act enables me to stay alive, or a dishonest act makes me wealthy, I may judge that my gains are worth the accompanying guilt feelings. A quiet conscience is not everything.

Third, if inner discord or a sense of dissatisfaction stems from a feeling of having done wrong, why not reassess my standards? Therapists are familiar with the phenomenon of false guilt. For example, a married woman may feel guilty for having sex with her spouse. The cure will involve enabling the patient to view sex as a legitimate means of expressing affection. The point is that just because I feel a certain type of act is wrong, it does not follow that the only route to inner peace is to avoid the action. I also have the option of revising my standards, which may enable me to pursue self-interested goals in a less inhibited fashion. Why drag along any unnecessary moral baggage? How could it be shown, on secular grounds, that it is in my interest to maintain the more idealistic standards endorsed by the great moralists? Certainly, some people have much less idealistic standards than others, and yet seem no less happy.

By way of contrast with the secular view, it is not difficult to see how morality might pay if there is a God of the Christian type. First, God loves all humans and wants all included in his kingdom. So, a tribal morality would violate his demands, and to violate his demands is to strain one's most important personal relationship. Second, there are no secret violations of morality if God exists. Since God is omniscient, willful wrongdoing of any sort will estrange the wrongdoer from God. Third, while earthly society may be able to function pretty well even though there exists a small number of "moral freeloaders," the freeloaders themselves are certainly not attaining harmonious relations with God. Accordingly, their ultimate fulfillment is in jeopardy. Fourth, death is the end of earthly life, but it is not the end of conscious existence, according to Christianity. Therefore, death does not end one's opportunity for personal fulfillment; indeed, if God is perfectly good and omnipotent, we can only assume that the afterlife will result in the fulfillment of our deepest needs—unless we willfully reject God's efforts to supply those needs.

So, it seems to me that the moral life makes more sense from a theistic perspective than from a secular perspective. Of course, I do not claim that I have proved the existence of God, and a full discussion of this metaphysical issue would take us too far from matters at hand.[8] But if I have shown that the moral life makes more sense from a theistic perspective than from a secular one, then I have provided an important piece of evidence in favor of the rationality of belief in God. Moreover, I believe that I have turned back one objection to the Christian teleological view, namely, the allegation that theism is unnecessary metaphysical baggage.

Notes

1. It can be argued that, even from a secular perspective, some benefits and harms are available after death. For example, vindicating the reputation of a deceased person may be seen as benefiting that person. See, for example, Thomas Nagel, *Mortal Questions* (London: Cambridge University Press, 1979), pp. 1–10. But even if we grant that these are goods for the deceased, it is obvious that, from the secular point of view, such post-mortem goods cannot be consciously enjoyed by the deceased. They are not available in the sense that he will never take pleasure in them.

2. George Mavrodes, "Religion and the Queerness of Morality," in *Rationality, Religious Belief, and Moral Commitment,* ed. Robert Audi and William J. Wainwright (Ithaca, N.Y.: Cornell University Press, 1986), p. 223.

3. Peter Singer, *Practical Ethics* (London: Cambridge University Press, 1970), p. 209.

4. For an excellent discussion of arguments for immortality, see William J. Wainwright, *Philosophy of Religion* (Belmont, Calif.: Wadsworth, 1988), pp. 99–111.

5. My source for these claims about "happy psychopaths" is Singer, *Practical Ethics*, pp. 214–216. Singer in turn is drawing from Hervey Cleckley, *The Mask of Sanity,* (*An Attempt to Clarify Some Issues About the So-Called Psychopathic Personality*), 5th ed. (St. Louis, Mo.: E. S. Cleckley, 1988).

6. Mavrodes, "Religion and the Queerness of Morality," p. 224. I am borrowing from Mavrodes throughout this paragraph.

7. Those acquainted with modal logic may have a question here. By a principle of modal logic, if p is a necessary truth and p necessarily implies q, then q is a necessary truth. So, if it is necessarily true that "certain conditions are met" and necessarily true that "If they are met, one ought to X," then, "One ought to do X" is a necessary truth. But I assume it is not *necessarily true* that "certain conditions are met." In my judgment it would be most implausible to suppose, e.g., that "Morality pays for humans" is a necessary truth.

8. Two fine discussions of moral arguments for theism are Robert Merrihew Adams, "Moral Arguments for Theistic Belief," in *Rationality and Religious Belief*, ed. C. F. Delaney (Notre Dame, Ind.: University of Notre Dame Press, 1979), pp. 116–140, and J. L. Mackie, *The Miracle of Theism* (Oxford: Oxford University Press, 1982), pp. 102–118.

C. Stephen Layman is a Professor of Philosophy at Seattle Pacific University. He has published in logic, metaphysics, and the philosophy of religion. His books include *The Shape of the Good* (University of Notre Dame Press, 1991), *The Power of Logic*, 3rd ed. (McGraw-Hill, 2005), and *Letters to a Doubting Thomas: A Case for the Existence of God* (Oxford University Press, 2007).

John Arthur  **NO**

Religion, Morality, and Conscience

My first and prime concern in this paper is to explore the connections, if any, between morality and religion. I will argue that in fact religion is not necessary for morality. Yet despite the lack of any logical or other necessary connection, I will claim, there remain important respects in which the two are related. In the concluding section I will discuss the notion of moral conscience, and then look briefly at the various respects in which morality is "social" and the implications of that idea for moral education. First, however, I want to say something about the subjects: just what are we referring to when we speak of morality and of religion?

Morality and Religion

A useful way to approach the first question—the nature of morality—is to ask what it would mean for a society to exist without a social moral code. How would such people think and behave? What would that society look like? First, it seems clear that such people would never feel guilt or resentment. For example, the notions that I ought to remember my parents' anniversary, that he has a moral responsibility to help care for his children after the divorce, that she has a right to equal pay for equal work, and that discrimination on the basis of race is unfair would be absent in such a society. Notions of duty, rights, and obligations would not be present, except perhaps in the legal sense; concepts of justice and fairness would also be foreign to these people. In short, people would have no tendency to evaluate or criticize the behavior of others, nor to feel remorse about their own behavior. Children would not be taught to be ashamed when they steal or hurt others, nor would they be allowed to complain when others treat them badly. (People might, however, feel regret at a decision that didn't turn out as they had hoped; but that would only be because their expectations were frustrated, not because they feel guilty.)

Such a society lacks a moral code. What, then, of religion? Is it possible that a people lacking a morality would nonetheless have religious beliefs? It seems clear that it is possible. Suppose every day these same people file into their place of worship to pay homage to God (they may believe in many gods or in one all-powerful creator of heaven and earth). Often they can be heard praying to God for help in dealing with their problems and thanking Him for their good fortune. Frequently they give sac-

rifices to God, sometimes in the form of money spent to build beautiful temples and churches, other times by performing actions they believe God would approve such as helping those in need. These practices might also be institutionalized, in the sense that certain people are assigned important leadership roles. Specific texts might also be taken as authoritative, indicating the ways God has acted in history and His role in their lives or the lives of their ancestors.

To have a moral code, then, is to tend to evaluate (perhaps without even expressing it) the behavior of others and to feel guilt at certain actions when we perform them. Religion, on the other hand, involves beliefs in supernatural power(s) that created and perhaps also control nature, the tendency to worship and pray to those supernatural forces or beings, and the presence of organizational structures and authoritative texts. The practices of morality and religion are thus importantly different. One involves our attitudes toward various forms of behavior (lying and killing, for example), typically expressed using the notions of rules, rights, and obligations. The other, religion, typically involves prayer, worship, beliefs about the supernatural, institutional forms and authoritative texts.

We come, then, to the central question: What is the connection, if any, between a society's moral code and its religious practices and beliefs? Many people have felt that morality is in some way dependent on religion or religious truths. But what sort of "dependence" might there be? In what follows I distinguish various ways in which one might claim that religion is necessary for morality, arguing against those who claim morality depends in some way on religion. I will also suggest, however, some other important ways in which the two are related, concluding with a brief discussion of conscience and moral education.

Religious Motivation and Guidance

One possible role that religion might play in morality relates to motives people have. Religion, it is often said, is necessary so that people will DO right. Typically, the argument begins with the important point that doing what is right often has costs: refusing to shoplift or cheat can mean people go without some good or fail a test; returning a billfold means they don't get the contents. Religion is therefore said to be necessary in that it provides motivation to do the right thing. God rewards those who follow

His commands by providing for them a place in heaven or by insuring that they prosper and are happy on earth. He also punishes those who violate the moral law. Others emphasize less self-interested ways in which religious motives may encourage people to act rightly. Since God is the creator of the universe and has ordained that His plan should be followed, they point out, it is important to live one's life in accord with this divinely ordained plan. Only by living a moral life, it is said, can people live in harmony with the larger, divinely created order.

The first claim, then, is that religion is necessary to provide moral motivation. The problem with that argument, however, is that religious motives are far from the only ones people have. For most of us, a decision to do the right thing (if that is our decision) is made for a variety of reasons: "What if I get caught? What if somebody sees me—what will he or she think? How will I feel afterwards? Will I regret it?" Or maybe the thought of cheating just doesn't arise. We were raised to be a decent person, and that's what we are—period. Behaving fairly and treating others well is more important than whatever we might gain from stealing or cheating, let alone seriously harming another person. So it seems clear that many motives for doing the right thing have nothing whatsoever to do with religion. Most of us, in fact, do worry about getting caught, being blamed, and being looked down on by others. We also may do what is right just because it's right, or because we don't want to hurt others or embarrass family and friends. To say that we need religion to act morally is mistaken; indeed it seems to me that many of us, when it really gets down to it, don't give much of a thought to religion when making moral decisions. All those other reasons are the ones which we tend to consider, or else we just don't consider cheating and stealing at all. So far, then, there seems to be no reason to suppose that people can't be moral yet irreligious at the same time.

A second argument that is available for those who think religion is necessary to morality, however, focuses on moral guidance and knowledge rather than on people's motives. However much people may want to do the right thing, according to this view, we cannot ever know for certain what is right without the guidance of religious teaching. Human understanding is simply inadequate to this difficult and controversial task; morality involves immensely complex problems, and so we must consult religious revelation for help.

Again, however, this argument fails. First, consider how much we would need to know about religion and revelation in order for religion to provide moral guidance. Besides being sure that there is a God, we'd also have to think about which of the many religions is true. How can anybody be sure his or her religion is the right one? But even if we assume the Judeo-Christian God is the real one, we still need to find out just what it is He wants us to do, which means we must think about revelation.

Revelation comes in at least two forms, and not even all Christians agree on which is the best way to understand revelation. Some hold that revelation occurs when God tells us what he wants by providing us with His words: The Ten Commandments are an example. Many even believe, as evangelist Billy Graham once said, that the entire *Bible* was written by God using 39 secretaries. Others, however, doubt that the "word of God" refers literally to the words God has spoken, but believe instead that the *Bible* is an historical document, written by human beings, of the events or occasions in which God revealed Himself. It is an especially important document, of course, but nothing more than that. So on this second view revelation is not understood as *statements* made by God but rather as His *acts* such as leading His people from Egypt, testing Job, and sending His son as an example of the ideal life. The *Bible* is not itself revelation, it's the historical account of revelatory actions.

If we are to use revelation as a moral guide, then, we must first know what is to count as revelation—words given us by God, historical events, or both? But even supposing that we could somehow answer those questions, the problems of relying on revelation are still not over since we still must interpret that revelation. Some feel, for example, that the *Bible* justifies various forms of killing, including war and capital punishment, on the basis of such statements as "An eye for an eye." Others, emphasizing such sayings as "Judge not lest ye be judged" and "Thou shalt not kill," believe the *Bible* demands absolute pacifism. How are we to know which interpretation is correct? It is likely, of course, that the answer people give to such religious questions will be influenced in part at least by their own moral beliefs: if capital punishment is thought to be unjust, for example, then an interpreter will seek to read the *Bible* in a way that is consistent with that moral truth. That is not, however, a happy conclusion for those wishing to rest morality on revelation, for it means that their understanding of what God has revealed is itself dependent on their prior moral views. Rather than revelation serving as a guide for morality, morality is serving as a guide for how we interpret revelation.

So my general conclusion is that far from providing a short-cut to moral understanding, looking to revelation for guidance often creates more questions and problems. It seems wiser under the circumstances to address complex moral problems like abortion, capital punishment, and affirmative action directly, considering the pros and cons of each side, rather than to seek answers through the much more controversial and difficult route of revelation.

The Divine Command Theory

It may seem, however, that we have still not really gotten to the heart of the matter. Even if religion is not necessary for moral motivation or guidance, it is often claimed, religion is necessary in another more fundamental sense. According to this view, religion is necessary for morality because without God there could BE no right or wrong. God, in other words, provides the foundation or bedrock on which morality is grounded. This idea was expressed by Bishop R. C. Mortimer:

> "God made us and all the world. Because of that He has an absolute claim on our obedience. . . . From [this] it follows that a thing is not right simply because we think it is. It is right because God commands it."[1]

What Bishop Mortimer has in mind can be seen by comparing moral rules with legal ones. Legal statutes, we know, are created by legislatures; if the state assembly of New York had not passed a law limiting speed people can travel, then there would be no such legal obligation. Without the statutory enactments, such a law simply would not exist. Mortimer's view, the *divine command theory,* would mean that God has the same sort of relation to moral law as legislature has to statutes it enacts: without God's commands there would be no moral rules, just as without a legislature there would be no statutes.

Defenders of the divine command theory often add to this a further claim, that only by assuming God sits at the foundation of morality can we explain the objective difference between right and wrong. This point was forcefully argued by F. C. Copleston in a 1948 British Broadcasting Corporation radio debate with Bertrand Russell.

Copleston: . . . The validity of such an interpretation of man's conduct depends on the recognition of God's existence, obviously. . . . Let's take a look at the Commandant of the [Nazi] concentration camp at Belsen. That appears to you as undesirable and evil and to me too. To Adolf Hitler we suppose it appeared as something good and desirable. I suppose you'd have to admit that for Hitler it was good and for you it is evil.

Russell: No, I shouldn't go so far as that. I mean, I think people can make mistakes in that as they can in other things. If you have jaundice you see things yellow that are not yellow. You're making a mistake.

Copleston: Yes, one can make mistakes, but can you make a mistake if it's simply a question of reference to a feeling or emotion? Surely Hitler would be the only possible judge of what appealed to his emotions.

Russell: . . . You can say various things about that; among others, that if that sort of thing makes that sort of appeal to Hitler's emotions, then Hitler makes quite a different appeal to my emotions.

Copleston: Granted. But there's no objective criterion outside feeling then for condemning the conduct of the Commandant of Belsen, in your view. . . . The human being's idea of the content of the moral law depends certainly to a large extent on education and environment, and a man has to use his reason in assessing the validity of the actual moral ideas of his social group. But the possibility of criticizing the accepted moral code presupposes that there is an objective standard, that there is an ideal moral

order, which imposes itself. . . . It implies the existence of a real foundation of God.[2]

Against those who, like Bertrand Russell, seek to ground morality in feelings and attitudes, Copleston argues that there must be a more solid foundation if we are to be able to claim truly that the Nazis were evil. God, according to Copleston, is able to provide the objective basis for the distinction, which we all know to exist, between right and wrong. Without divine commands at the root of human obligations, we would have no real reason for condemning the behavior of anybody, even Nazis. Morality, Copleston thinks, would then be nothing more than an expression of personal feeling.

To begin assessing the divine command theory, let's first consider this last point. Is it really true that only the commands of God can provide an objective basis for moral judgments? Certainly many philosophers have felt that morality rests on its own perfectly sound footing, be it reason, human nature, or natural sentiments. It seems wrong to conclude, automatically, that morality cannot rest on anything but religion. And it is also possible that morality doesn't have any foundation or basis at all, so that its claims should be ignored in favor of whatever serves our own self-interest.

In addition to these problems with Copleston's argument, the divine command theory faces other problems as well. First, we would need to say much more about the relationship between morality and divine commands. Certainly the expressions "is commanded by God" and "is morally required" do not *mean* the same thing. People and even whole societies can use moral concepts without understanding them to make any reference to God. And while it is true that God (or any other moral being for that matter) would tend to want others to do the right thing, this hardly shows that being right and being commanded by God are the same thing. Parents want their children to do the right thing, too, but that doesn't mean parents, or anybody else, can make a thing right just by commanding it!

I think that, in fact, theists should reject the divine command theory. One reason is what it implies. Suppose we were to grant (just for the sake of argument) that the divine command theory is correct, so that actions are right just because they are commanded by God. The same, of course, can be said about those deeds that we believe are wrong. If God hadn't commanded us not to do them, they would not be wrong.

But now notice this consequence of the divine command theory. Since God is all-powerful, and since right is determined solely by His commands, is it not possible that He might change the rules and make what we now think of as wrong into right? It would seem that according to the divine command theory the answer is "yes": it is theoretically possible that tomorrow God would decree that virtues such as kindness and courage have become vices while actions that show cruelty and cowardice will henceforth be the right actions. (Recall the analogy with a legislature and the power it has to change law.) So now rather than it being right for people to help each other out and prevent innocent people from suffering unnecessarily, it would be right (God having changed His mind) to create as much pain among innocent children as we possibly can! To adopt the divine command theory therefore commits its advocate to the seemingly absurd position that even the greatest atrocities might be not only acceptable but morally required if God were to command them.

Plato made a similar point in the dialogue *Euthyphro*. Socrates is asking Euthyphro what it is that makes the virtue of holiness a virtue, just as we have been asking what makes kindness and courage virtues. Euthyphro has suggested that holiness is just whatever all the gods love.

Socrates: Well, then, Euthyphro, what do we say about holiness? Is it not loved by all the gods, according to your definition?

Euthyphro: Yes.

Socrates: Because it is holy, or for some other reason?

Euthyphro: No, because it is holy.

Socrates: Then it is loved by the gods because it is holy: it is not holy because it is loved by them?

Euthyphro: It seems so.

Socrates: . . . Then holiness is not what is pleasing to the gods, and what is pleasing to the gods is not holy as you say, Euthyphro. They are different things.

Euthyphro: And why, Socrates?

Socrates: Because we are agreed that the gods love holiness because it is holy: and that it is not holy because they love it.[3]

This raises an interesting question: Why, having claimed at first that virtues are merely what is loved (or commanded) by the gods, would Euthyphro so quickly contradict this and agree that the gods love holiness *because* it's holy, rather than the reverse? One likely possibility is that Euthyphro believes that whenever the gods love something they do so with good reason, not without justification and arbitrarily. To deny this, and say that it is merely the gods' love that makes holiness a virtue, would mean that the gods have no basis for their attitudes, that they are arbitrary in what they love. Yet—and this is the crucial point—it's far from clear that a religious person would want to say that God is arbitrary in that way. If we say that it is simply God's loving something that makes it right, then what sense would it make to say God wants us to do right? All that could mean, it seems, is that God wants us to do what He wants us to do; He would have no reason for wanting it. Similarly "God is good" would mean little more than "God does what He pleases." The divine command theory therefore leads us to the results that God is morally arbitrary, and that His wishing us to do good or even God's being just mean nothing more

than that God does what He does and wants whatever He wants. Religious people who reject that consequence would also, I am suggesting, have reason to reject the divine command theory itself, seeking a different understanding of morality.

This now raises another problem, however. If God approves kindness because it is a virtue and hates the Nazis because they were evil, then it seems that God discovers morality rather than inventing it. So haven't we then identified a limitation on God's power, since He now, being a good God, must love kindness and command us not to be cruel? Without the divine command theory, in other words, what is left of God's omnipotence?

But why, we may ask, is such a limitation on God unacceptable? It is not at all clear that God really can do anything at all. Can God, for example, destroy Himself? Or make a rock so heavy that He cannot lift it? Or create a universe which was never created by Him? Many have thought that God cannot do these things, but also that His inability to do them does not constitute a serious limitation on His power since these are things that cannot be done at all: to do them would violate the laws of logic. Christianity's most influential theologian, Thomas Aquinas, wrote in this regard that "whatever implies contradiction does not come within the scope of divine omnipotence, because it cannot have the aspect of possibility. Hence it is more appropriate to say that such things cannot be done than that God cannot do them."[4]

How, then, ought we to understand God's relationship to morality if we reject the divine command theory? Can religious people consistently maintain their faith in God the Creator and yet deny that what is right is right because He commands it? I think the answer to this is "yes." Making cruelty good is not like making a universe that wasn't made, of course. It's a moral limit on God rather than a logical one. But why suppose that God's limits are only logical?

One final point about this. Even if we agree that God loves justice or kindness because of their nature, not arbitrarily, there still remains a sense in which God could change morality even having rejected the divine command theory. That's because if we assume, plausibly I think, that morality depends in part on how we reason, what we desire and need, and the circumstances in which we find ourselves, then morality will still be under God's control since God could have constructed us or our environment very differently. Suppose, for instance, that he created us so that we couldn't be hurt by others or didn't care about freedom. Or perhaps our natural environment were created differently, so that all we have to do is ask and anything we want is given to us. If God had created either nature or us that way, then it seems likely our morality might also be different in important ways from the one we now think correct. In that sense, then, morality depends on God whether or not one supports the divine command theory.

"Morality Is Social"

I have argued here that religion is not necessary in providing moral motivation or guidance, and against the divine command theory's claim that God is necessary for there to be morality at all. In this last section, I want first to look briefly at how religion and morality sometimes *do* influence each other. Then I will consider the development of moral conscience and the important ways in which morality might correctly be thought to be "social."

Nothing I have said so far means that morality and religion are independent of each other. But in what ways are they related, assuming I am correct in claiming morality does not *depend* on religion? First, of course, we should note the historical influence religions have had on the development of morality as well as on politics and law. Many of the important leaders of the abolitionist and civil rights movements were religious leaders, as are many current members of the pro-life movement. The relationship is not, however, one-sided: morality has also influenced religion, as the current debate within the Catholic church over the role of women, abortion, and other social issues shows. In reality, then, it seems clear that the practices of morality and religion have historically each exerted an influence on the other.

But just as the two have shaped each other historically, so, too, do they interact at the personal level. I have already suggested how people's understanding of revelation, for instance, is often shaped by morality as they seek the best interpretations of revealed texts. Whether trying to understand a work of art, a legal statute, or a religious text, interpreters regularly seek to understand them in the best light—to make them as good as they can be, which requires that they bring moral judgment to the task of religious interpretation and understanding.

The relationship can go the other direction as well, however, as people's moral views are shaped by their religious training and beliefs. These relationships between morality and religion are often complex, hidden even from ourselves, but it does seem clear that our views on important moral issues, from sexual morality and war to welfare and capital punishment, are often influenced by our religious outlook. So not only are religious and moral practices and understandings historically linked, but for many religious people the relationship extends to the personal level—to their understanding of moral obligations as well as their sense of who they are and their vision of who they wish to be.

Morality, then, is influenced by religion (as is religion by morality), but morality's social character extends deeper even than that, I want to argue. First, of course, we possess a socially acquired language within which we think about our various choices and the alternatives we ought to follow, including whether a possible course of action is the right thing to do. Second, morality is social in that it governs relationships among people, defining our responsibilities to others and theirs to us. Morality provides the standards we rely on in gauging our interactions with family, lovers, friends, fellow citizens, and even strangers. Third, morality is social in the sense that we are, in fact, subject to criticism by others for our actions. We discuss with others what we should do, and often hear from them concerning whether our decisions were acceptable. Blame and praise are a central feature of morality.

While not disputing any of this, John Dewey has stressed another, less obvious aspect of morality's social character. Consider then the following comments regarding the origins of morality and conscience in an article he titled "Morality Is Social":

> In language and imagination we rehearse the responses of others just as we dramatically enact other consequences. We foreknow how others will act, and the foreknowledge is the beginning of judgment passed on action. We know *with* them; there is conscience. An assembly is formed within our breast which discusses and appraises proposed and performed acts. The community without becomes a forum and tribunal within, a judgment-seat of charges, assessments and exculpations. Our thoughts of our own actions are saturated with the ideas that others entertain about them. . . . Explicit recognition of this fact is a prerequisite of improvement in moral education. . . . Reflection is morally indispensable.[5]

To appreciate fully the role of society in shaping morality and influencing people's sense of responsibility, Dewey is arguing, requires appreciating the fact that to think from the moral point of view, as opposed to the selfish one, for instance, means rejecting our private, subjective perspective in favor of the view of others, envisioning how they might respond to various choices we might make. Far from being private and unrelated to others, moral conscience is in that sense "public." To consider a decision from the moral perspective, says Dewey, requires that we envision an "assembly of others" that is "formed within our breast." In that way, our moral conscience cannot be sharply distinguished from our nature as social beings since conscience invariably brings with it, or constitutes, the perspective of the other. "Is this right?" and "What would this look like were I to have to defend it to others?" are not entirely separable questions.[6]

It is important not to confuse Dewey's point here, however. He is *not* saying that what is right is finally to be determined by the reactions of actually existing other people, or even by the reaction of society as a whole. What is right or fair can never be finally decided by a vote, and might not meet the approval of any specific others. But what then might Dewey mean in speaking of such an "assembly of others" as the basis of morality? The answer is that rather than actual people or groups, the assembly Dewey envisions is hypothetical or "ideal." The "community without" is thus transformed into a "forum and tribunal within, a judgment seat of charges, assessments and exculpations." So it is through the powers of our imagination that we can meet our moral responsibilities and exercise moral judgment, using these powers to determine what morality requires by imagining the reaction of Dewey's "assembly of others."

Morality is therefore *inherently* social, in a variety of ways. It depends on socially learned language, is learned from interactions with others, and governs our interactions with others in society. But it also demands, as Dewey put it, that we know "with" others, envisioning for ourselves what their points of view would require along with our own. Conscience demands we occupy the positions of others.

Viewed in this light, God would play a role in a religious person's moral reflection and conscience since it is unlikely a religious person would wish to exclude God from the "forum and tribunal" that constitutes conscience. Rather, for the religious person conscience would almost certainly include the imagined reaction of God along with the reactions of others who might be affected by the action. Other people are also important, however, since it is often an open question just what God's reaction would be; revelation's meaning, as I have argued, is subject to interpretation. So it seems that for a religious person morality and God's will cannot be separated, though the connection between them is not the one envisioned by defenders of the divine command theory.

Which leads to my final point, about moral education. If Dewey is correct, then it seems clear there is an important sense in which morality not only can be taught but must be. Besides early moral training, moral thinking depends on our ability to imagine others' reactions and to imaginatively put ourselves into their shoes. "What would somebody (including, perhaps, God) think if this got out?" expresses more than a concern with being embarrassed or punished; it is also the voice of conscience and indeed of morality itself. But that would mean, thinking of education, that listening to others, reading about what others think and do, and reflecting within ourselves about our actions and whether we could defend them to others are part of the practice of morality itself. Morality cannot exist without the broader, social perspective introduced by others, and this social nature ties it, in that way, with education and with public discussion, both actual and imagined. "Private" moral reflection taking place independent of the social world would be no moral reflection at all; and moral education is not only possible, but essential.

Notes

1. R. C. Mortimer, *Christian Ethics* (London: Hutchinson's University Library, 1950), pp. 7–8.
2. This debate was broadcast on the "Third Program" of the British Broadcasting Corporation in 1948.
3. Plato, *Euthyphro,* tr. H. N. Fowler (Cambridge, MA: Harvard University Press, 1947).
4. Thomas Aquinas, *Summa Theologica,* Part I, Q.25, Art. 3.
5. John Dewey, "Morality Is Social" in *The Moral Writings of John Dewey,* revised edition, ed. James Gouinlock (Amherst, NY: Prometheus Books, 1994), pp. 182–184.
6. Obligations to animals raise an interesting problem for this conception of morality. Is it wrong to torture animals only because other *people* could be expected to disapprove? Or is it that the animal itself would disapprove? Or, perhaps, duties to animals rest on sympathy and compassion while human moral relations are more like Dewey describes, resting on morality's inherently social nature and on the dictates of conscience viewed as an assembly of others?

John Arthur (1946–2007) created and served as Director of the Institute for Philosophy, Politics, and Law at Binghamton University. He published three books: *Words That Bind: Judicial Review and the Grounds of Modern Constitutional Practice* (Westview Press, 1995), *The Unfinished Constitution: Philosophy and Constitutional Practice* (1989), and *Race, Equality, and the Burdens of History* (Cambridge University Press, 2007). He was also the editor or co-editor of more than 8 other books and authored over 25 articles addressing issues of public concern.

EXPLORING THE ISSUE

Does Morality Need Religion?

Critical Thinking and Reflection

1. In what sense can we say that it "pays" to behave morally in today's society? Can you think of any additional examples in which acting morally means acting against your own self-interest? In such cases, should people behave morally? Why or why not?
2. Do you think that religion is needed to provide a motivation to do the right thing? What other possible motivations do people have to do the right thing?
3. The problem raised by Plato and mentioned by Arthur with regard to Divine Command theory is an important one: is something good because God commands it, or does God command it because it is good? How would you resolve this question?

Is There Common Ground?

Layman's argument that the secular viewpoint provides inadequate grounds for morality conflicts directly with Arthur's argument that morality does not depend on religion. Arthur does, however, discuss ways in which morality and religion are related, while Layman attempts to describe hypothetical, if incomplete, secular justifications for morality.

A position that neither philosopher explicitly addresses that might bring them into some agreement is the view known as *etiamsi daremus* (Latin for "even if we should grant"). This is a view held by many theistic philosophers that even if we should grant that there is no God, we would still be able to derive moral principles by which to lead our lives from observation and analysis of human nature and the world around us. Natural law ethics, for example, has an *etiamsi daremus* basis; although it is a system of ethics often followed by believers, it does not rely on religious belief for its foundation. Natural law provides an ethics that is consistent with ethics derived from religious faith, and that can be accounted for within a theistic metaphysical system as being "built into" the way God created the world. In such a system, Layman could find a morality with an ultimate theistic basis, while Arthur could find a morality that does not require religious belief.

Create Central

www.mhhe.com/createcentral

Additional Resources

E. M. Adams, *Religion and Cultural Freedom* (Temple University Press, 1993)

Paul Chamberlain, *Can We Be Good Without God? A Conversation About Truth, Morality, Culture, and a Few Other Things That Matter* (InterVarsity Press, 1996)

Richard J. Mouw, *The God Who Commands: A Study in Divine Command Ethics* (University of Notre Dame Press, 1990)

D. Z. Phillips, ed., *Religion and Morality* (St. Martin's Press, 1996)

Glenn Tinder, "Can We Be Good Without God? On the Political Meaning of Christianity," *The Atlantic Monthly* (December 1989)

Internet References . . .

Council for Secular Humanism

www.secularhumanism.org/

Ontario Consultants on Religious Tolerance: Ethics and Morality

www.religioustolerance.org/morality.htm

Philosophy Links: Philosophy of Religion

http://users.ox.ac.uk/~worc0337/
phil_topics_religion.html

Society of Christian Philosophers

www.societyofchristianphilosophers.com/

Unit 2

Sex, Marriage, and Reproduction

*S*exuality is an important, powerful dimension of being human. It is therefore important to have an understanding of the moral permissibility or impermissibility of certain types of sexual activity. The role of government in sexual matters also becomes a matter for moral judgment, as people must decide which types of marriage should be recognized and encouraged by the state. Finally, medical and technological advances raise a host of moral questions about reproductive matters. The issues in this section do not question the morality of sexual activity itself, but they do raise questions about the moral judgments we should make about controversial topics involving human sexuality.

Selected, Edited, and with Issue Framing Material by:
Owen M. Smith, *Stephen F. Austin State University*
and
Anne Collins Smith, *Stephen F. Austin State University*

ISSUE

Must Sex Involve Commitment?

YES: Steven E. Rhoads, from "Hookup Culture: The High Costs of a Low 'Price' for Sex," *Society* (December 2012)

NO: Raja Halwani, from "Casual Sex," in *Sex from Plato to Paglia: A Philosophical Encyclopedia* (Greenwood Press, 2005)

Learning Outcomes

After reading this issue, you will be able to:

- Describe the purported evolutionary origins for the mating preferences of men and women.
- Explain how casual sex frustrates these evolved preferences, especially for women.
- Offer a general definition of casual sex, and explain why it is difficult to define it precisely.
- Formulate your own position on the morality of casual sex and identify evidence supporting your position.
- Identify the main objections to your position and formulate responses to these objections.

ISSUE SUMMARY

YES: Steven Rhoads offers evidence drawn from a variety of sources, including surveys of sexually active college students as well as research in evolutionary anthropology, to support his two main contentions: (a) casual sex is bad for society in general, and (b) casual sex is especially emotionally damaging for women.

NO: Raja Halwani first discusses the difficulties involved in defining casual sex precisely. He next examines a number of objections to casual sex, and concludes that casual sex need not be morally wrong because each of these objections involves factors that are not, for the most part, specifically intrinsic to casual sex.

For many people, sex and morality are interconnected. Yet, with the exception of specialized issues such as sexual harassment, most contemporary moral philosophers have very little to say about sexual morality. This silence may, in part, be due to the view that many traditional views about sex are outdated and have little relevance to the world in which we now live.

During the ancient and medieval period, moral philosophy was integrated into a larger framework of philosophical theories about the structure of reality and the role of humans within that structure. Ancient Greek philosophers developed elaborate metaphysical theories, which were in turn adapted by medieval philosophers and theologians. According to these theories, humans were different from animals, and in general from the rest of the natural world, because they were rational and were thus thought to have an immaterial or spiritual dimension that was not possessed by other purely material beings. The special metaphysical or supernatural status of humans had consequences for the moral assessment of sexual actions. To the extent that the certain sexual actions, like casual sex, failed to express, or even undermined, the immaterial or spiritual dimension of humanity, they were morally wrong.

Belief in an immaterial or spiritual dimension to humanity, however, has waned in recent decades, and it is now more common to view humans as purely material beings that form part of the natural world, without any special metaphysical or supernatural status. The view that humans are purely material beings, like animals, has had an influence on contemporary attitudes toward sexual activity. Sexual desires are now considered to be simply a part of our physical nature, like our eating preferences. This view, however, does not automatically mean that it is morally right to indulge these sexual desires, such as an urge for casual sex. After all, we have natural desires to eat certain foods, but that does not mean that eating these foods is good for us. We cannot simply eat whatever we feel like whenever we want to; we must curb our desires and use our reason to choose the correct foods from a nutritional standpoint. Traditionalists take a similar approach to natural sexual desires.

It is not moral to indulge in all our sexual desires. Rather, we must exercise self-control regarding our sexual urges, and use our reason to determine when, and with whom, sexual activity is appropriate. Of course, some modernists disagree, arguing that the analogy between eating and sexual activity is flawed in many ways, not least because eating habits were only minimally affected by cultural attitudes, whereas cultural attitudes greatly affected sexual practices.

Today, we are left with a mixed view toward sexual activity, composed of elements drawn from ancient, medieval, and modern thought. It is clear that we cannot disregard modern views about human sexuality and simply return to a traditional approach to sexual morality. However, the precise role that modern views should play in sexual morality is not yet clear.

In the following selections, Steven Rhoads argues that our contemporary culture's support for casual sex has had significant negative repercussions, especially for young women. Raja Halwani, on the other hand, argues that casual sex itself is not morally problematic, rather the immorality of certain casual sexual acts stems from factors other than its casualness.

YES

Steven E. Rhoads

Hookup Culture: The High Costs of a Low "Price" for Sex

In his piece, "Contemporary Mating Market Dynamics, Sex-Ratio Imbalances, and Their Consequences," Mark Regnerus is right to emphasize that sex ratios are extremely important in determining whether men's or women's mating preferences are more likely to be honored. Now that women outnumber men on college campuses, they must compete among themselves by giving men more of what men want if they expect to find male companionship on Saturday night. Women are still the gatekeepers who determine how physical things will get, but, as Regnerus says, they have much more limited choices these days.

But Regnerus points out that even non-college men and post-college men get sex with more women than they used to. Sex ratios in the broader society are not so skewed as they are in college; so, why do men have more relationship power everywhere these days? Maybe there are also more marriageable men than women in the broader society once one subtracts all the disproportionately male homeless and criminal. But the homeless and criminal were *always* disproportionately male. What has changed? Why did women used to get wooed far more than they are today?

In his conclusion, Regnerus says "what scholars and journalists have described as the 'hook-up culture' that has emerged both on and off (and after) college campuses today, I assert, has little to do with sexual culture change, and far more to do with the bifurcated mating market and the sex-ratio imbalances that have emerged therein." But wasn't there always a bifurcated mating market? Collegiate men in the fifties would have been interested in sleeping with a variety of women on weekends just as they are today, but few attractive, educated women were available for those sorts of encounters. Now they are. The sexual culture *has* changed. The collegiate women are available because most of the women's movement has insisted that sexual liberation is an important part of women's liberation and because the Pill seemed to make sexual liberation costless.

If equal proportions of men and women were interested in casual sex on the one hand and in committed sex on the other, the bifurcated markets would not be problematic for women. The problem is not the new arrival of bifurcated markets, but rather the enduring fact that, despite all the huffing and puffing of androgynous feminists, casual sex is not a good fit for women's natures.

For the past 14 years, I have taught a college course on sex differences to juniors and seniors. When we talk about relationships and sex, the vast majority of the women seem very unhappy with the dominant hookup culture. In their papers and in class, time and again, they talk about their girlfriends' post-hookup traumas, even if they manage to avoid them themselves. If the men who these women hook up with do call again, they often only want more hookups, and, as soon as the women push for a real relationship, the men break it off.

I asked one senior who had been a resident advisor for freshmen for two academic years to write up her observations about the college hookup culture. She thought one of her friend's observations echoed many of the chastened freshmen women when she told her, "I hate this feeling—the pressure to sell my body to men, to dress scandalously just to get their attention, just to get them to notice me. Then all they want is a one night stand; they will use me for sex and don't give a shit about me as a person. They don't want to get to know me at all! I keep getting into it, I keep thinking I'll find someone this way—but I only get used every time."

The resident advisor concluded, "even females who try very hard to follow the male example with regard to sex are at a loss. . . . Most of my female friends have tried being in purely physical relationships; not one of them lasted for more than a month. However, we are constantly told that we should be able to enjoy our sexuality with or without a relationship, just like men. When it comes to sex we are encouraged to do what we want, provided we protect ourselves from STDs and pregnancy. Yet we are not taught how to protect ourselves emotionally."

In 2010, together with two college female seniors, I wrote an article for the *Chronicle* (the online version of the *Chronicle of Higher Education*) that presented evidence showing that my female students' reactions to casual sex were not idiosyncratic. What is remarkable is that even women who write books about their sexual adventures and want to defend or even tout their sexual freedom end up telling the same story. In *The Morning After: Sex, Fear, and Feminism* (1994), Katie Roiphe speaks of feeling "almost sick with the accumulated anonymity of it, the haphazardness, the months and months of toweled men." In *Lip Service* (1997), Kate Fillion recounts how she retroactively decided she was in love with every man she had

had sex with and how the power she got from sex "was the power to cause myself emotional pain." Cindy Chupack, an executive producer and writer for the HBO series "Sex and the City," gives us the details of her sexual escapades in *The Between Boyfriends Book* (2004), but confesses that she wants to be more than "a notch in somebody's bedpost"; she is looking for a husband.

None of this would surprise John Townsend, an evolutionary anthropologist whose extensive research has led him to conclude that women often go through an experimental stage where they try casual sex, but they almost always end up rejecting it. According to Townsend, for women, intercourse produces feelings of "vulnerability" and of being used when they cannot get the desired emotional investment from their partners. In Townsend's studies, these feelings occur even in the most sexually liberated women. Despite this group's free-thinking attitudes, their emotions make it impossible for them to enjoy casual sex.

Like other evolutionists, Townsend hypothesizes that men are more eager for sex than women because eons ago men with powerful sexual urges passed on their genes in greater numbers than men with moderate or low inclinations for sex. Men back then also would want sex with lots of mates because more mates would mean more offspring. In contrast, women who took advantage of any and every sexual opportunity would not produce children who thrived as well as choosier women. Women who mated with unusually strong or healthy men or men willing to commit ample resources to their children's needs would increase their children's likelihood of survival. Thus, through the ages, women with such tastes would be more apt to reproduce and rear their offspring successfully. Although some of the tastes and preferences that enhanced the survival of our ancestors in the past make less sense today, according to evolutionary psychology, these same tastes and preferences remain part of our genetically inherited psychological makeup and affect our decisions even when we are unaware of them.

Other social scientists report the same sex differences that Townsend does. Edward S. Herold and Dawn-Marie Mewhinney found that females who hook up get less enjoyment and feel more guilt than men do. Denise Hallfors and colleagues found that female teens are many times more likely than male teens to become depressed after sexual encounters with multiple partners. Catherine Grello, a clinical psychologist, and colleagues found that the college men who sleep around the most are the least likely to report symptoms of depression whereas female college students who engage in casual sex the most are the most likely to report depression.

In their book, *Premarital Sex in America*, Regnerus and coauthor Jeremy Uecker report that having more sexual partners is associated with "poorer emotional states in women, but not in men." The more lifetime partners the women have, the more likely they are to be depressed, the more likely they are to cry almost every day and the

more likely they are to report relatively low satisfaction with their life as a whole. Paul Chara and Lynn Kuennen's research seems to support the female souring effect that Townsend found. Chara and Kuennen asked young women and men in high school and college whether they would be willing to engage in sex after a wonderful first date. On average, college seniors are certainly more sexually experienced than ninth graders. Yet 30% of the ninth grade women said they would be game for sex after that great first date while only 5% of college senior women said they would be. The trend for young men was the opposite. About 30% of the ninth grade boys said they would have sex after the great first date, but fully 60% of the college senior men said they would do so.

My female students tell me that the emotional pain that casual sex causes women goes largely unreported because the women are often ashamed that they care about men who treat them like strangers the next morning. These women don't want the men involved or the rest of the campus to know about their tears.

Our *Chronicle* article prompted some private correspondence with a sociologist who thought the magnitude of the gender differences in emotional costs of casual sex was relatively small. More generally, she thought, "in the industrialized West we may be nearing the very first point in human history [when] social and physical costs associated with women's promiscuity are lowered enough to actually get a chance to see what women would do and like if not constrained by fears of pregnancy, childbearing or social stigma."

So, we know that since the beginning of recorded history, it is men not women who are eager enough to have sex with a variety of women that they hire prostitutes. We know that in the privacy of their bedrooms, men consume pornography presenting a variety of quasi-anonymous female bodies, while women consume romance novels in which sex occurs with a special man who feels an all-consuming love for the heroine. We know that, if space allowed, there is far more research that could be offered supporting the position that men like casual sex more than women. Some of this research is so cross-cultural that it bears titles such as "Universal Sex Differences in the Desire for Sexual Variety: Tests from 52 Nations, 6 Continents, and 13 Islands." Moreover, we now have had three generations of young women come of age since the sexual revolution. But still, we are told, it is too soon to come to any conclusions about women's sexual nature. We need more time. Such is the power of the dominant paradigm—sex differences are to be seen as gender differences, small and socially constructed.

I wish Regnerus had qualified his argument less broadly. He writes: "many, many women don't mind this new sexual economy" and "plenty of them like to spend some time in less-serious relationships." "Plenty" in absolute terms or relative terms? It's a big country. There could be plenty, and it could still be only a small fraction of the number of men who like casual sex.

Testosterone raises the libido, and there is reason to think that, on average, women who are the most attracted to casual sex have above average testosterone for their sex. The women Townsend studied who had the most casual sex experience had characteristics that have been associated with high testosterone. They competed in traditionally male sports and rejected traditional female roles and sexual morality. Because they found "sex outside of marriage totally acceptable," they were "shocked by their intense emotional reactions to their experiences. They honestly believed that they could enjoy sexual relations that involved little investment from their partners. They did not expect these emotions, could not understand them, and were surprised and disturbed by their inability to control them. These feelings were not part of their sex-role ideology and that is why the women were caught off guard."

Regnerus says, "It's not true, of course, that starry-eyed women are now simply being more efficiently duped or hoodwinked by skirt-chasing, commitment-phobic men." Does he really know from his findings that the women who have had the most lifetime partners and who are now crying almost every day did not begin with high hopes for romance with the men they spent time with? The Hallfors study, mentioned previously finds in its sample of pre-college youth that sleeping with multiple men comes first and depression second. At the University of Virginia, my classes tell me that freshmen women are more likely to participate in the hookup scene than upper class women. I'm told that some frat boys call the freshmen coeds "fresh meat" and think they are more easily charmed into bed.

When Regnerus says "most women tend to prefer (and are more apt to enjoy) sex in stable, committed, romantic relationships," does he mean "most" or a "very large majority"? If "most" women prefer committed sex, but "plenty" prefer less serious sex, it's hard to see why the bifurcated markets are the grim problem for women that he says they are. Regnerus believes that as women age, they become concerned about commitment phobic men and their declining fecundity. This makes it sound as if women are not troubled by casual sex until they are in their thirties. Townsend and I believe instead that women are troubled by the time they are college seniors—or before if they have had many sexual partners. It is past time to repeat Townsend's research—to see whether casual sex is only attractive to a substantial proportion of women during an experimental period.

Regnerus says that "the sky is not falling"; it is true that the hookup culture will not lead to a cosmological catastrophe. But is it a "big deal"? I think it is. I suspect that Regnerus does as well, but an exceedingly cautious tone on this subject is necessary for a young scholar trying to make his way in sociology.

Regnerus is right to link the hookup culture with non-marital child births and to argue that women would not choose an ever lengthening and circuitous journey to marriage. Since children brought up by their biological parents tend to fare much better than with other arrangements, our society should want the mating market to reflect women's preferences far more than it does now.

In what follows, I will have more to say about how casual sex affects women. But when considering here broader societal effects, it is important to talk about how the hookup culture affects men. There is much discussion these days about young men's failure to thrive. But the discussions rarely mention sex.

We know that young men used to be willing to settle down with one woman and raise a family. They used to be willing to answer to a boss for 40 to 50 hours a week for 40 to 50 years. But men hate to be told what to do. Why, then, did they become reliable partners and providers often answering to their wives as well as their bosses? Perhaps because they could not get appealing women to pay attention to them unless they had "prospects." Men had to be marriageable and ready to commit or most women would not have sex with them. Most men still want marriage in a distant future, but they see no reason not to partake of the bodily charms of many attractive women in the meantime. To bed these women at their age in this age, men find that good pectoral muscles (thus time in the gym) are at least as useful as good career prospects (time in the library).

It will not be easy to weaken the casual sex culture. But here are some places to start:

Sex Education

Women in my classes do know that they are more likely than male peers to have an unwanted pregnancy after sexual intercourse! But it seems half or more have never been told of other relevant facts about sex—and not just about the emotional costs of casual sex. They generally do not know that they're much more likely than men to get a sexually transmitted disease from contact with an infected partner, that they're much more likely than males to become infertile if they are infected; that the birth control pill dampens their sexual interest and pleasure; or that the Pill scrambles sensory (sub-conscious smell) messages, making them more attracted to men with immune systems similar to theirs rather than immune systems unlike theirs. The scrambled signals are a risk factor should one fall in love with a man while on birth control pills. If a woman marries the man and tries to have children with him, she will have somewhat higher odds of repeated miscarriages and perhaps of having more vulnerable offspring. Current "just the facts" sex education ignores important facts that young women have a right to know.

Student Health Services

As explained in the book *Unprotected,* the student health services on most college campuses do a woefully bad job of addressing the problems for women arising from casual sex.

Women's Centers

There are few questions that college women ponder with more concern than what to do about invitations to have sex. Women's Centers could provide an invaluable service if they provided forums and counseling addressing the subject. On a number of occasions I've asked my classes whether it would be good or bad for women if their percentage on campuses went from 57 to 60 as seems possible in the not too distant future. The vast majority of my female students think it would be terrible. They know that more women and fewer men will make it still harder for them to find a good man ready to commit. Women still want to marry, and they want to marry men who are *at least* as educationally and professionally accomplished as they are. Perhaps we could encourage Women's Centers interested in outside the box thinking to sponsor forums on ways to get a higher proportion of men prepared for and interested in a college education. Leonard Sax and Christina Hoff Sommers could be asked to help on this project.

Religious Institutions

The historic teachings of Christianity, Judaism and Islam all include a belief in sex differences, and their doctrines about sexuality are unfriendly to casual sex. Their institutions could do more than they now do to teach young women and young men about how casual sex harms both sexes, particularly women.

Parents

It is with reluctance that I make unsolicited suggestions for what parents might say to their daughters about their relationships with men. Young women will have differing life plans and may or may not have boyfriends. Still, I wonder about the advice that parents give their graduating daughters who have boyfriends of whom the parents approve. My students tell me that the parents often advise their daughters to "not even think about getting married until you have a graduate degree and have begun your profession. With a 50% divorce rate it is too risky to get married right out of college." The first problem is that these parents have some facts wrong. The divorce rate for all Americans is not 50%; it is more like 43%. More importantly, it is much less for college graduates—about 33% of marriages to those without college degrees end in 10 years, while only 11% to those with college degrees end in 10 years. The median duration of marriages for those who end up divorcing is 8 years, so that 11% is not likely to be doubled over the college graduates' lifetimes.

Marriages of couples who marry in their thirties *are* more likely to last than those that commence at an earlier age. But later marriage does not necessarily mean happier marriages. Husbands and wives who marry in their mid to late twenties are more likely to report that they are very happy than are those who marry at a later age. And marriages that are *both* stable and very happy are more likely to commence in the couple's early to mid-twenties than later. Moreover, the 22-year-old woman in love with a boyfriend with "prospects" might not get another attractive proposal later. About fifty-seven percent of college graduates are women. This means that about 14 out of every 57 graduate women (just under 25%) will not be able to marry a man who is also a college graduate, at least one who has not previously been divorced. And many women who don't marry until their early thirties will have sexual relations with and cohabit with men who will break up with them. The therapist Patricia Dalton has written of the difficulties she has with thirtyish female clients who are "acting like a wife" while their partners are "acting like a boyfriend."

Dalton is convinced that sex makes the breakups much harder on women. She acknowledges that, though she can perhaps help these women in some ways, "the emotional costs of breaking up over and over . . . are hard to calculate." Dalton says she "can't magically restore the hope, optimism and innocence that these world-weary women have lost."

I wonder whether parents who advise their daughters to avoid marriage soon after college think about what dating and mating is likely to be like for their daughters between, say, 22 and 32. And, they may or may not think about the fertility pressures that the later marriage brings with it.

Women are deeply relational. Ninety percent of married women say their marriage makes them happy all or most of the time; only 60% say the same about their job.

Young Women

Economists assume that we can tell what people like by their revealed preferences. Most of the time we can. If people take up tennis or softball and begin playing more, we can fairly assume that it is because they have come to enjoy those activities more. As argued above, this assumption doesn't work with casual sex for women. Townsend finds that adventurous, untraditional women who are initially attracted to casual sex, in time find that their feelings will not cooperate. It does not make them happy, and they become less and less inclined to participate as time goes by. Moreover, as unfair as it may seem, men who enjoy sex with lots of women usually prefer to marry women who have not had lots of sex with lots of men. (Evolutionists argue that men's aversion toward wives with promiscuous pasts runs deep because the aversion makes it more likely that they will not end up unwittingly raising other men's children).

Women who conclude that casual sex does or would make them unhappy can choose not to participate. But to get a more female friendly mating culture, they will need to unite with other women. Danielle Crittenden has argued that "if women *as a group* cease to be readily available—if they begin to demand commitment (and real commitment, as in marriage) in exchange for sex—market conditions, will shift in favor of women."

Women who participate in casual sex make it harder for the majority of women to get dates and committed sex. They make it harder for women to live in a world where they are courted and respected. We live in a very tolerant age, but this majority of women should feel free to try to protect their interests. Women who participate in casual sex impose external costs on the majority who would prefer a dating culture to a hookup one.

The majority are free to choose their friends from among their peers who do not impose costs on them. They should not feel guilty about protecting their interests, even if the women participating in serial hookups are making themselves happy (which seems unlikely given what I present above).

Groups that try to combat the hookup culture and create a more female friendly dating culture already exist on many campuses. I'm thinking of the Network of Enlightened Women (NeW) and the Love and Fidelity network. NeW, for example, tries to encourage the better side of men by sponsoring a Gentlemen's Showcase, in which chapters nominate and campaign for their nominees to become the national network's outstanding gentleman of the year. The Love and Fidelity Network sponsors national and regional conferences where speakers and students discuss the benefits of love and fidelity.

These sorts of groups could do more. For example, during orientation week they could sponsor forums where upper class women explain the hookup culture to entering freshmen females. They could also approach women's centers in a friendly way, presenting the evidence about the effects of casual sex on young women. If women's centers refuse to take the issue seriously, the groups could picket the centers and take their concerns to the media or state legislatures.

Sexual mores are a "big deal." As Regnerus argues, the current ones lead to late marriages in which women cannot have as many healthy children as they would prefer. And, they also lead to too many children raised without the benefits of stable marriages of parents biologically connected to them.

STEVEN E. RHOADS is a Professor of Government and Foreign Affairs at the University of Virginia. His publications include the books *Taking Sex Seriously* and *The Economist's View of the World*.

Raja Halwani

 **NO**

Casual Sex

Casual sex is often characterized as sex for the sake of sexual pleasure itself, rather than, say, for procreation, and is often contrasted with sex that expresses **love** or is done in a loving context. It involves **sexual desire** alone rather than sexual desire *and* love. Men, generally, engage in casual sex, or would like to, more than women—excluding female sex workers (for an evolutionary account of this difference, see Buss). When gay men engage in it, they often keep it impersonal, especially when otherwise involved in (nonmonogamous) relationships (Blumstein and Schwartz, 295–97). Types of casual sex include one-night stands, orgiastic and "swinging" sex, anonymous encounters in bathhouses and the backrooms of bars (usually between gay men), encounters in Internet chat rooms (**cybersex**), and **prostitution**. Casual sex admits of both conceptual and normative questions. I start with the conceptual. It might seem easy to define "casual sex," but it is not. This, however, does not mean that "there is no such thing as a casual . . . sexual act" (Anscombe, 24).

No definition that relies only on behavioral criteria will work. Such a definition might capture some sexual acts that are casual, such as orgies, sex with animals (**bestiality**), and sex with human corpses (necrophilia), but it would not capture the difference between two couples, one that engages in oral sex casually and the other noncasually. There might be no behavioral differences between them. Beliefs or other mental states must figure in the definition.

One might define "casual sex" as "sexual activity for the sake of sexual pleasure only." It is not sex intended for procreation or the communication of love but solely for pleasure, as in recreational sex. This will not do. We can describe sex for pleasure as recreational if it occurs between two people in a loving relationship, but here it is not casual. Anthony Ellis defines "casual sex" as sex between partners who have no deep or substantial relationship (157). This definition does not specify the type of prior relationship that exists between the parties: that they are strangers, acquaintances, or friends. This is good because not only strangers engage in casual sex. Acquaintances sometimes do, and friends. But the definition fails. Suppose both parties believe that their sex will lead to a committed relationship. Even in the presence of these beliefs, the sexual act, on Ellis's definition, would still be casual. But it is plausible that the presence of these beliefs renders their sex not

(fully) casual. It is likely a mark of casual sex that it be done without any beliefs that it be anything more than a sexual encounter.

Let us try this definition: "Casual sex is sexual activity engaged in with the understanding or belief that it will not lead to emotional commitments." One good thing about this definition is that it includes only "negative" mental states as necessary for sex to be casual. The inclusion of "positive" states leads to counterintuitive results. For example, suppose the positive intention "for the sake of sexual pleasure" is necessary. This yields the result that **sexual activity** between a prostitute and her client is not casual, because prostitutes typically are not motivated to engage in sex for their own pleasure. Thus, the motives and intentions of the parties must be left open: We should stipulate only that the parties understand that there is no future commitment.

"Understanding" is important. Suppose Monica has sex with Bill, hoping or desiring that it will lead to a love relationship. However, Monica understands that Bill has no such hope and that he does not desire to be in a relationship with her. Thus, Monica realizes that Bill is about to engage in casual sex, yet nevertheless hopes, against the odds, that it will lead somewhere. Despite her hopes, the sex between them is casual, for both realize that it is engaged in only for the sake of sex. Thus, while mental states are crucial for defining casual sex, we must carefully choose which ones to include. Certain hopes and desires should not factor into the definition.

This definition faces problems. First, must both parties involved have the above understanding? What if one person understands that the sexual encounter will not lead to a future commitment, while the other does not, or believes the opposite? Indeed, how would we describe a sexual encounter in which the parties, or at least one, have no beliefs one way or the other? Should we require that the parties *have* the belief that their sex will not lead to any commitment or that the parties have *no* belief that there will be a commitment? If the former, how strong must the belief be? Should the parties believe that their sex *will not,* or *probably* will not, lead to a commitment? Further, must these beliefs be genuine or veridical, or could they be self-deceptive or false? And how should we describe sex occurring between a person and an entity that cannot have beliefs: an animal, an inflated doll, a cadaver? Perhaps these sexual acts are not casual; at least the latter two are cases of **masturbation**, and masturbation might not be casual sex, due to the absence of a partner. But sex with an animal could not be dismissed so easily.

Second, the definition does not reflect the understanding of most people that casual sex involves one important positive motive, the desire for sexual pleasure. The definition does not mention this motive. However, there are many motives for casual sex, and thus most people's understanding might be mistaken. Third, the definition applies to a sexual act, **rape**, that might be, strictly speaking, casual, yet is not the first case that comes to mind when we think of casual sex. Marital and **date rape** (perhaps) aside, the rapist does not think of himself as forcing sex on a person while believing that this will lead to a committed relationship. Even if rape is casual sex because of this fact, this is not the way we usually think of rape or of casual sex. Fourth, it is worthwhile to reconsider whether it is necessary that a definition of "casual sex" refers to mental states. If the parties to a casual encounter do believe it will lead to an emotional commitment, but it does not, that failure would seem to be sufficient to describe their sex as casual.

Thus, the above definition does not capture *exactly* what we mean by "casual sex." Perhaps "casual sex" is too vague for precise analysis, and pinning down a definition might come at the cost of jettisoning some of our intuitions about it. There is, of course, the danger of confusing the concept of casual sex with promiscuity. Any definition of promiscuity must assert that it is sexual activity with different partners over time (Frederick Elliston [1944–1987], 225–26). Because casual sex does not entail multiple partners (a single one-night stand in a person's life might be casual), it is not the same as promiscuity. It might even be that promiscuity does not entail casual sex. Suppose one has sex with many partners while believing that this is the best way to secure a committed relationship. This person's sexual behavior is promiscuous, but because of the intention we would not necessarily describe it as casual. (Benatar [193–94] equates promiscuity and casual sex, but this is because he defines promiscuity as sex lacking romantic or emotional significance instead of in terms of sex with multiple partners.)

I turn, now, to normative issues. These can arise along three logically different axes: the moral versus the immoral, the sexually pleasurable versus the not pleasurable, and the normal versus the perverted.

Sometimes casual sex is morally wrong for reasons having nothing to do with its being casual. If two married people engage in casual sex (with persons other than their spouses), each also commits **adultery**. Insofar as adultery is wrong, their casual sex is wrong as adultery. Casual sex might also be wrong because it involves deception or coercion. If Tom falsely promises Nicole **marriage** if Nicole were to have sex with him, Nicole's **consent** is not genuine because it relies on false information. Tom has deceived her, and the ensuing sex would be morally wrong. If Sally tells the destitute Mark, who does not desire Sally, that she will not evict him and his children from their apartment

if he were to have sex with her, the ensuing sex would be coerced and hence wrong (see Mappes, 180–83). Again, it is not wrong just because it is casual. Casual sex might also be wrong due to a lack of adequate communication. Suppose Edna and Skinner are about to have sex. Edna does not desire that it be more than casual but is unsure of Skinner's intentions. It might even be uncommon that the parties, excited by desire, know each other's intentions. If there is a moral obligation to disclose one's intentions, failure to do so would make casual sex wrong—although not because it is casual. Note that unclarity about intentions might be gendered; women, more than men, often use sexual encounters as preludes to relationships (Blumstein and Schwartz, 297).

Even if casual sex involves no deception or coercion, is not adulterous, and the parties clearly communicate their intentions, it still might be wrong in virtue of its consequences (an "external" reason for its wrongfulness), that is, harm to the parties involved and harm to other people. Two possible bad consequences of casual sex are contracting disease and unwanted pregnancy. These are consequences to the parties to the sexual act, but they might also affect other persons and society in general. Anthony Ellis claims that these effects are not morally relevant because they are "medical problems" (166). This is not exactly true. Some **sexually transmitted diseases** (e.g., HIV [human immunodeficiency virus]) present serious moral problems. Unwanted pregnancies also change one's life drastically, as pregnant teenage girls know. The parties to the sexual act should, morally and pragmatically, take precautions against disease and pregnancy. But that casual sex that leads to unwanted pregnancy or disease might be morally wrong does not show that casual sex itself is wrong.

It is not obvious what other bad consequences casual sex has. One possibility is that insofar as society applies a double standard to men and women, women who accept casual sex are seen as cheap ("sluts"), while men are not (Blumstein and Schwartz, 297). Such negative views about women might be a form of harm (for example, a blow to their "reputation"). However, the double standard is only a contingent and perhaps disappearing feature of our society. This may be why casual sex does not always cause negative judgments. Many female college students who engage in casual sex are not viewed negatively and so escape the double standard. Further, whether some people's judging a woman a "slut" harms her depends on how it affects her psychologically: Some woman can brush it off easily or even laugh at it. Moreover, the argument does not tell against casual sex between men.

Another possibility was suggested by **G.E.M. Anscombe** (1919–2001) in claiming that casual sex makes one "shallow" (24), perhaps by making practitioners incapable of forming meaningful, loving relationships (see Kristjansson). However, this argument applies primarily to promiscuous sex, not casual sex. It is difficult to see why a few casual sexual events in one's life would make one incapable of forming loving relationships. Further, the argument depends on the assumption that love relationships are crucial in a person's leading a good life. This might not be true. It seems that one can, logically and psychologically, lead a good life without such relationships (though perhaps not without **friendship**; Halwani, chaps. 2, 3). Indeed, **Albert Ellis** argues that "personality growth"—an increase in enlightened self-interest, self-acceptance, tolerance, flexibility, and acceptance of ambiguity and uncertainty—is "abetted and enhanced by sexual adventuring" (95). Casual sex, as a form of "sexual adventuring," might have these benefits. However, whether healthy or successful sexual adventuring *presupposes* these admirable personality traits, instead of enhancing them, is unclear. Further, the list of traits praised by Ellis is obviously value-laden and might not be fully accepted by other psychologists.

Casual sex might also be morally wrong for "internal" reasons. Some motives could make a casual sex act morally wrong. Having a one-night stand with a monk to humiliate him afterward about his lax virtue is wrong, since it is done out of the vicious intention to demean. Having sex with a teenage girl or a married woman to blackmail her is also wrong. But such motives are not part of casual sex itself. Some motives are, of course, good. A nurse or a friend might masturbate a willing quadruple amputee to orgasm out of kindness. Most casual sex is not done from such motives. Tpically, it is done for sexual pleasure. What needs to be shown, to make the moral case against casual sex, is that the motive to achieve sexual pleasure is morally bad. Perhaps this motive leads one to neglect the needs of one's partner. If this refers to the partner's needs outside the context of the sexual act, then further argument must be provided to explain why this is morally objectionable; for in most of our dealings with people, we do not consider all their other needs. If, however, the needs are sexual and pertain to the casual sex event itself, the argument is likely unsound. It involves misunderstanding what a person typically feels in casual sex. He or she does not usually want another to be a passive body but wants full sexual interaction with that person. This usually takes the form of tending to the partner's sexual needs, even if partly for one's own sake (Goldman, 268–71; Soble, "Sexual Use," 229–32). Prostitution might be an exception, casual sex in which the client does not typically go out of his way to please the prostitute.

The crucial accusation on the grounds of base motives might be that sexual desire leads one to treat one's partner as less than fully human; desire focuses on one aspect of a person, his or her body, and on the sexual organs in particular. This is the accusation of **sexual objectification.** Note that to claim that casual sex is objectifyingly immoral need not turn on issues of motive. Casual sex might be objectifyingly immoral even if done out of non-lustful motives, as when a prostitute engages in sex with a client for the money. **Immanuel Kant** (1724–1804) claimed that whenever we sexually desire another, we do not desire the person as such but only his or her sexual parts (*Lectures*, 162–68). This leads to a problem: On this account of sexual desire, it is difficult for sexuality to satisfy Kant's Second

Formulation of the Categorical Imperative: "Act in such a way that you treat humanity, whether in your own person or in the person of any other, always at the same time as an end and never simply as a means" (*Grounding*, Ak 4:429). Casual sex, from a Kantian perspective, involves one person's not only treating another as an object but also treating oneself the same way. Kant thought the only time that sexual activity was permissible, despite its objectification, was when it occurs within marriage.

In contemporary discussions of objectification (unlike Kant's), the focus is not on the agent's objectifying himself in the sexual act but on the agent's objectifying the other. Prostitution, **pornography**, and casual sex have been judged immoral because they involve objectification, that is, treating a person as an object. This is wrong because persons are not, or not *just*, objects. The main problem with objectification is that it reduces a person to the status of something less than human, like an animal or inanimate object. But we are not animals or objects, since we possess something special—rationality, inherent worth, dignity, autonomy, or an immaterial and eternal soul. But here we must be cautious. These attributions are not empirical in any straightforward way. For we find many humans to be irrational, lacking worth, or undignified. The claim that humans have a special ontological and hence moral status needs cogent defense. If it is false, casual sex would not be objectifying, because it could not reduce us to something we are not or fail to respect a status we do not have (see Soble, *Pornography*, chap. 2).

The second normative issue concerns the nonmoral goodness of casual sex. Is casual sex pleasurable? It might seem that a positive answer to this question is obvious, for people find a large, indefinite number of people desirable. Sexual activity is, under certain "normal" conditions, enjoyable. However, this does not mean that casual sex is always pleasurable. Just because the prospect of sex is exciting, it need not turn out satisfying and pleasurable. One might want to distinguish the pleasure that regular sexual partners experience and the pleasure that casual sex partners experience (see Moulton, 538–39; Soble, *Sexual Investigations*, 87–89). The sexuality of regular partners might be routine, but the parties know what to expect and can count on some satisfaction. Casual sex partners, however, do not know what to expect. While they might approach the encounter with anticipatory excitement (and indeed experience the pleasure of making contact with a new person), the ensuing sex might not be as satisfying as imagined: The partners do not know how to satisfy each other's particular needs or desires. Nevertheless, some types of casual sex might have higher probabilities of yielding satisfaction. Two examples are anonymous sex and sex within purely sexual relationships (say, between "fuck buddies")— the former because the expectations are minimal to begin with, the latter because the expectations are known. Note that **Sigmund Freud** (1856–1939) once speculated that both men (183) and women (186), for different psychological reasons, had some difficulty achieving full sexual satisfaction with their spouses, someone they loved. Men, in particular, often find casual sexual encounters more satisfying than sexual activity with their beloved and loving wives. This division between the sexual and the affectionate psychological currents implies a sexual problem with or disadvantage of marriage and long-term relationships (which, of course, may still offer other benefits). What Kant thought was terribly morally suspicious about sexuality Freud identifies as an important factor in satisfaction.

The third normative issue about casual sex concerns psychological normality and **sexual perversion**. There are some types of casual sex that might qualify as also being perverted, just like some casual sex is adulterous, harmful, and so forth. *If* shoe or panty fetishism is perverted, then any coupled casual sex involving gratification with shoes or panties will be perverted, but not because it is casual. A more interesting question is whether casual sex might be psychologically abnormal, even when it is morally permissible or pleasurable (or even *because* it is pleasurable). If the natural or normal way that sexual desire and activity progress is by aiming at or culminating in love (see **Roger Scruton**, chaps. 4, 10), then casual sex, perhaps by definition, would not be normal. However, given that we very often experience sexual desire directed at various people without love entering the scene at all (not even unconsciously), it seems that the very common event of casual sex is perfectly within the bounds of the psychologically normal. It is implausible to analyze the sexually normal so that many people turn out to be abnormal or perverted. Perhaps the philosopher who argues that casual sex is abnormal is not, after all, offering a psychological thesis but is telling us how he or she would *like* things to be (Primoratz, chap. 3).

Casual sex is difficult to define. We know that it has much to do with the lack of an emotional or loving commitment and much to do with seeking pleasure for its own sake. Other than that, a plausible definition immune to counterexamples is elusive. Casual sex does not seem to be morally wrong as such. The one plausible case to be made revolves around objectification. But there is room for dissent, and if casual sex is faulted for being objectifying, much else in the sexual domain must also be faulted. It might even be that some casual sex is "an act of charity which proclaims the glory of God" (Williams, 81–82).

References

Anscombe, G.E.M. "Contraception and Chastity." *The Human World*, no. 7 (1972), 9–30; Benatar, David. "Two Views of Sexual Ethics: Promiscuity, Pedophilia, and Rape." *Public Affairs Quarterly* 16:3 (2002), 191–201; Blumstein, Philip, and Pepper Schwartz. *American Couples: Money, Work, Sex.* New York: Morrow, 1983; Buss, David M. "Casual Sex." In *The Evolution of Desire: Strategies of Human Mating.* New York: Basic Books, 1994, 73–96; Ellis, Albert. "Sexual Adventuring and Personality Growth." In Herbert A. Otto, ed., *The New Sexuality.* Palo Alto, Calif.: Science and Behavior Books, 1971, 94–109; Ellis, Anthony. "Casual Sex." *International Journal of Moral and Social Studies* 1:2 (1986), 157–69; Elliston, Frederick. "In Defense of Promiscuity." In Robert Baker and Frederick Elliston, eds., *Philosophy and Sex*, 1st ed. Buffalo, N.Y.: Prometheus, 1975, 223–43; Freud, Sigmund. (1912) "On the Universal Tendency to Debasement in the Sphere of Love." In James Strachey, ed. and trans., *The Standard Edition of the Complete Psychological Works of Sigmund Freud,* vol. 11. London: Hogarth Press, 1953–1974, 177–90; Goldman, Alan. "Plain Sex." *Philosophy and Public Affairs* 6:3 (1977), 267–87; Halwani, Raja. *Virtuous Liaisons: Care, Love, Sex, and Virtue Ethics.* Chicago, Ill.: Open Court, 2003; Kant, Immanuel. (1785) *Grounding for the Metaphysics of Morals.* Trans. James Ellington. Indianapolis, Ind.: Hackett, 1993; Kant, Immanuel. (ca. 1780) *Lectures on Ethics.* Trans. Louis Infield. New York: Harper and Row, 1963; Kristjansson, Kristjan. "Casual Sex Revisited." *Journal of Social Philosophy* 29:2 (1998), 97–108; Mappes, Thomas A. "Sexual Morality and the Concept of Using Another Person." In Thomas A. Mappes and Jane S. Zembaty, eds., *Social Ethics: Morality and Social Policy*, 6th ed. Boston, Mass.: McGraw-Hill, 2002, 170–83; Moulton, Janice. "Sexual Behavior: Another Position." *Journal of Philosophy* 73:16 (1976), 537–46; Primoratz, Igor. *Ethics and Sex.* New York: Routledge, 1999; Scruton, Roger. *Sexual Desire: A Moral Philosophy of the Erotic.* New York: Free Press, 1986; Soble, Alan. *Pornography, Sex, and Feminism.* Amherst, N.Y.: Prometheus, 2002; Soble, Alan. *Sexual Investigations.* New York: New York University Press, 1996; Soble, Alan. "Sexual Use and What to Do about It: Internalist and Externalist Sexual Ethics." In Alan Soble, ed., *The Philosophy of Sex*, 4th ed. Lanham, Md.: Rowman and Littlefield, 2002, 225–58; Williams, Harry Abbott. "Theology and Self-Awareness." In A. R. Vidler, ed., *Soundings: Essays Concerning Christian Understanding.* Cambridge: Cambridge University Press, 1963, 67–101.

Raja Halwani is a Professor of Philosophy at the School of the Art Institute of Chicago. His publications include the books *Philosophy of Love, Sex, and Marriage: An Introduction* and *Virtuous Liaisons: Care, Love, Sex, and Virtue Ethics.*

EXPLORING THE ISSUE

Must Sex Involve Commitment?

Critical Thinking and Reflection

1. How is casual sex different from sex in a committed relationship? In what ways do you think it might be better? In what ways do you think it might be worse?
2. Are there ways in which men, as well as women, are negatively affected by casual sex?
3. In what way(s) do people engaged in casual sex objectify themselves? In what way(s) do they objectify their partners? Do you think it is always wrong to treat yourself or someone else as an object rather than as a person? Why or why not?

Is There Common Ground?

It is clear that Rhoads and Halwani differ fundamentally in their approach to sex and commitment. Rhoads considers our culture's embrace of casual sex to have been a mistake with serious detrimental consequences; Halwani, by contrast, considers casual sex to be essentially morally neutral.

One area of commonality between the two philosophers, however, involves the differing responses of men and women to casual sex. In his article, Rhoads emphasizes strongly that even women who engage in casual sex do not really "buy into" the notion of sex without commitment, and that many are actually hoping for genuine relationships with the men with whom they have casual sex. Halwani agrees, noting that while casual sex may be defined as sex that is not intended to lead to a further relationship, there are women who nonetheless hope and desire that a casual sexual act will lead to a relationship. In discussing the importance of clarifying the intentions of each sexual partner, he also cites research saying that women, more often than men, tend to view sex as leading to a relationship.

While Halwani only considers casual sex to be morally wrong when one of the parties lies to the other, or when intentions are not made clear, Rhoads might argue that casual sex is always morally wrong because the tendency of women to connect sexual intimacy with emotional intimacy is intrinsic to female sexuality and not simply an external problem with casual sex that can be overcome by truth-telling and clarification.

Create Central

www.mhhe.com/createcentral

Additional Resources

Thomas A. Mappes, "Sexual Morality and the Concept of Using Another Person," in Thomas A. Mappes and Jane S. Zembaty, eds., *Social Ethics: Morality and Social Policy*, 8th edn. (McGraw-Hill, 2011)

Alan Soble, *The Philosophy of Sex and Love* (Paragon House, 2008)

John M. Townsend, *What Women Want—What Men Want: Why the Sexes Still See Love and Commitment so Differently* (Oxford University Press, 1998)

Internet References . . .

Internet Encyclopedia of Philosophy: Philosophy of Sexuality

www.iep.utm.edu/sexualit/

The Society for the Philosophy of Sex and Love: Resources

http://philosophyofsexandlove.wordpress.com/resources/

Women's History Sourcebook

www.fordham.edu/halsall/women/womensbook.asp

Selected, Edited, and with Issue Framing Material by:
Owen M. Smith, *Stephen F. Austin State University*
and
Anne Collins Smith, *Stephen F. Austin State University*

ISSUE

Is Abortion Immoral?

YES: **Mary Meehan**, from "Why Liberals Should Defend the Unborn," *Human Life Review* (Summer 2011)

NO: **Amy Borovoy**, from "Beyond Choice: A New Framework for Abortion?" *Dissent* (Fall 2011)

Learning Outcomes

After reading this issue, you will be able to:

- Explain the stages of development in a normal human pregnancy and identify common reasons why a spontaneous abortion (miscarriage) might terminate a pregnancy.
- Explain the difference between a legal judgment about the permissibility of induced abortion and a moral judgment about the permissibility of induced abortion.
- Explain the importance of the concept of personhood to both legal and moral judgments about the permissibility of induced abortion.
- Formulate your own position on abortion and identify evidence supporting your position
- Identify the main objections to your position and formulate responses to these objections.

ISSUE SUMMARY

YES: Meehan argues that the unborn are exactly the kind of vulnerable population traditionally defended by liberals. She discusses a number of factors in support of this connection, such as scientific claims about when life begins, the obligations that arise from the act of conception, the disproportionate impact of abortion on poor women and women of color, and issues relating to disability rights and the environment.

NO: Borovoy argues that the traditional defense of abortion, which opposes the choice of the woman against the life of the fetus, does not effectively capture the unique experience of pregnancy, and finds inspiration for a more satisfying approach in Japanese culture, where the decision whether or not to have an abortion is contextualized in the woman's responsibility not only to her fetus but to her family.

Abortion is a divisive topic, and discussions concerning abortion can easily become polarized. Rational discourse about this topic, then, should begin by establishing a neutral set of facts about pregnancy and abortion based on scientific and medical research. Moral principles can then be applied to these facts to reach moral judgments about the circumstances, if any, under which abortion may be moral.

The life of a human being begins when the reproductive cell from a female (the ovum or egg) unites with the reproductive cell from a male (the spermatozoon or sperm). Each type of reproductive cell has 23 chromosomes, and once mature, these cells have a very brief life span. Reproductive cells cannot divide and have no potential to develop to a rational being. The fusion of the two reproductive cells forms a fertilized ovum or zygote with 46 chromosomes, which then begins to divide and has the potential to develop into a rational being. The fertiliza-

tion of the ovum normally occurs in one of the female's fallopian tubes; during the course of the pregnancy, the zygote travels through the fallopian tube, enters the female's uterus, and implants itself in the uterine wall. The implanted zygote, now generally referred to as an embryo, continues to develop, along with a placenta and umbilical cord, which nourish and protect it. Once the basic structural plan of the embryo is complete, the developing organism is called a fetus, a designation it retains until birth.

From fertilization of the ovum until the birth of the fetus, the human pregnancy lasts an average of 38 weeks (266 days). The precise date of the fertilization of the ovum can be difficult to determine, and so the length of the human pregnancy is usually measured from the first day of the woman's last menstrual period. Since fertilization typically takes place about 2 weeks after this date, the length of a human pregnancy is normally considered to be 40 weeks (280 days). This period is traditionally divided into three approximately equal periods, known as trimesters. The first trimester consists of the period from the fertilization of the ovum to the twelfth week of development, during which the developing organism is called first a zygote and then an embryo. The second trimester consists of the period from the thirteenth week to the twenty-fifth week of development, during which the developing organism is known as a fetus. The final stages of fetal development occur during the third trimester, which covers the period from the twenty-sixth week of fetal development until birth.

During the course of a normal human pregnancy, the developing organism passes a number of significant milestones. While still a zygote, the developing organism may split into two or more groups of cells. These groups may then refuse into a single zygote or continue separate development; in the latter case, the multiple organisms become identical siblings. It is possible for a woman's reproductive tract to contain more than one zygote, each resulting from the fusion of separate pairs of reproductive cells. If the development of the zygotes proceeds in parallel, the developing organisms become fraternal multiples. Occasionally, however, two separate zygotes will fuse into a single being, known as a chimera, with two distinct sets of genetic material. At a certain stage of development, however, the zygote loses the ability to split and refuse, leaving a single organism to continue its development. The embryo becomes sufficiently developed to generate brain waves and a heartbeat during the first trimester, after about six weeks of development. Spontaneous movement of the fetus can first be felt at about 14 or 15 weeks of development; this event is traditionally known as the quickening of the fetus. The age at which the fetus attains viability, or the ability to live independently of the woman's body (albeit with assistance), depends on many factors, including the current state of medical technology. Infants have survived birth as early as the second trimester, during the twentieth week of pregnancy after 18 weeks of fetal development.

Human pregnancy is a complex process, and many events can occur that cause the death of the developing organism and terminate the pregnancy. The zygote may never implant itself in the lining of the uterus and die as it passes out of the woman's body. This event is far from infrequent; research involving assisted reproduction technologies such as *in vitro* fertilization has yielded estimates that 30–70 percent of all zygotes fail to implant themselves in the uterus. Alternately, the zygote may implant itself somewhere other than in the uterus, resulting in an ectopic pregnancy; the developing organism is not normally able to proceed to term in an ectopic pregnancy, and the condition can cause potentially fatal blood loss in the woman if the pregnancy is not terminated. Chromosomal abnormalities may halt the development of the organism and cause its death. Problems with the woman's reproductive system may also prevent a pregnancy from proceeding to term and result in the death of the developing organism. The rate at which these events occur is difficult to measure, since the death of the organism can occur while it is still a zygote, before the woman even suspects she is pregnant. If the death of the developing organism occurs before the twentieth week of pregnancy, the termination of the pregnancy is known as a spontaneous abortion or miscarriage. According to some estimates, as many as half of all pregnancies end in spontaneous abortion. About 15 percent of all recognized pregnancies end in spontaneous abortion, usually within the first trimester. It is relatively uncommon for pregnancies that have lasted 20 weeks or more to terminate on their own; such events are termed late miscarriages. The termination of pregnancy at any stage by artificial methods that are intended to cause the death of the developing organism is generally termed induced abortion.

In order to address the issue of abortion clearly, it is important to distinguish between moral judgments and legal judgments. A moral judgment is a conclusion about the morality of an action that is reached by applying a moral rule of behavior (moral standard) to a specific set of circumstances. In contrast, a legal judgment is a conclusion about the legality of an action that is reached by applying a law (legal standard) to a specific set of circumstances. Since moral rules of behavior do not have the same status as laws, moral judgments are not the same as legal judgments. The distinction between moral judgments and legal judgments is central to the issue of abortion because the assertion that abortion is legal is not the same thing as the assertion that abortion is moral.

In its landmark 1973 ruling in *Roe v. Wade,* the Supreme Court ruled that a human being comes to have the legal status of a person only upon birth. Therefore, developing human beings such as fetuses does not have the legal rights and protections according to persons, be they natural persons such as human beings or artificial entities such as corporations that have been legally granted this status. As a consequence, while the state has a legitimate interest in protecting the potentiality of human life, laws restricting induced abortion in the early stages of pregnancy, coinciding approximately with the first trimester, is an unconstitutional restriction upon the freedom of the pregnant woman. In later stages of pregnancy, coinciding approximately with the second and third trimesters, the state may protect its interest in the woman's health by appropriate regulation of induced abortions. However, once the fetus achieves viability, the state may regulate or prohibit induced abortions "except where it is necessary, in appropriate medical judgment, for the preservation of the life or health of the mother" (410 U.S. 113, 93 S. Ct. 705 [1973]). In a companion decision, *Doe v. Bolton,* the Supreme Court made it clear that the medical grounds warranting the induced termination of a pregnancy, even after the fetus becomes viable, are at the complete discretion of the woman and her physician, effectively permitting induced abortion on demand at any time during pregnancy. In subsequent decades, various states have attempted to exercise their authority to regulate induced abortion and, subject to certain restrictions, even prohibit the practice, with varying degrees of success.

Traditional arguments about the morality of abortion also turn on the issue of the personhood of a zygote, embryo, or fetus. According to most philosophers, persons may not ethically be treated in the same way as nonpersons. In particular, they must be recognized as having intrinsic value, and so cannot morally be treated merely as means to another person's end. If these entities are persons in the ethical sense, most induced abortions would be morally impermissible. If not, the moral status of induced abortions is relatively unproblematic, save for the moral obligations to protect the welfare of the woman and to treat the unborn human being in humane fashion, like any sentient, non-personal entity such as an animal.

In the following selections, Mary Meehan constructs an argument based on liberal principles to support a pro-life position. She focuses on the liberal tradition of protecting the most vulnerable members of society, which, she argues, should include the unborn. Amy Borovoy finds traditional arguments that attempt to justify abortion on the basis of a woman's right to choose unsatisfactory, and looks beyond Western culture to gain a more holistic understanding of the issues that underlie the decision whether to have an abortion.

YES ←

Mary Meehan

Why Liberals Should Defend the Unborn

Why does the warm heart of liberalism turn to ice on the subject of unborn children? Why do so many liberals support abortion and *Roe v. Wade*? These are not easy questions to answer, given liberal convictions that should instead lead them to oppose abortion. As someone with an early background in antiwar politics, and who lived through the legalization of abortion, I will suggest reasons why so many liberals support it. Then I will offer many reasons why they should, instead, defend the unborn. Most of those reasons should also appeal to radicals and libertarians. I hope that all will consider my case, both in their personal lives and in thinking about public policy.

Whatever Happened to the Joy of Life?

In 1973, when the U.S. Supreme Court issued its decision in *Roe v. Wade*, liberals still revered the Court for its defense of civil rights and civil liberties in the 1950s and 1960s. They trusted the Court, and especially the three liberal justices who bore much responsibility for *Roe*: William Brennan, William O. Douglas, and Thurgood Marshall. They also had faith in the American Civil Liberties Union, which supported legal abortion. Led astray by institutions and people they relied on, many liberals did not follow their own better instincts. Nor did they do the hard thinking they should have done on a matter of life or death. . . .

There is a great need to engage liberals intellectually—and press them hard—on the ways that abortion breaks faith with basic liberal principles and traditions. We need the kind of robust dialogue and debate that should have occurred decades ago.

Back to Basics

Liberals respect science, and science confirms that a new human life begins at fertilization.[1] Each of us started as a tiny embryo: the President of the United States, every justice of the Supreme Court, every member of Congress, the window-washer on a skyscraper, the teacher in the classroom, the lawyer in the courtroom, the farmer in the fields, the truck driver on the highways. We should think about our own humble origins, rather than disdain the tiny size of the newest humans. That tiny size is deceptive, for the embryo is a *"self-assembler"*[2] who grows by leaps

and bounds. We should view the complexity and rapid development of human embryos with awe and respect.

Defending those who cannot defend themselves has long been the pride of the left. When no one else would do it, liberals and radicals stood up for the little guys and the little gals: day laborers and domestic workers, abused children, African Americans and other minorities, elderly patients with dementia, the poor, the unloved and unwanted, the down-and-outers. The unborn are the most defenseless members of the human community. Others can cry out for help, and some can defend themselves, but unborn children cannot. To abandon them is to abandon the heart and honor of the left. . . .

Another liberal tradition, much neglected now, is optimism about the future and the possibility of progress. A gloomy and pessimistic view of life never characterized liberals at their best. Nor did they view children as liabilities, or as predestined for bad outcomes by poverty or disability. Instead, liberals saw children as a sign of hope. And progressives used to be the can-do people of our politics. They used to say, "Let's change conditions that keep people down. *Right now!*" The anti-slavery movement, early feminism, the labor movement, and the civil rights movement did not begin in pessimism and despair—and certainly did not end there. Liberals and radicals *belong* on the side of life. . . .

The right to life underlies and sustains every other right we have. To destroy human beings at the beginning of their lives is to destroy, with just one blow, all of their rights and liberties. Deprived of their entire future, the aborted unborn will never exercise the rights to free speech or a free press. They will never organize, vote, or run for office. They will never pursue or enjoy happiness. Civil libertarians who support abortion are profoundly wrong and are actually attacking their own principles. By undermining the right to life at its beginning, they endanger that right—and all other rights—for humans of all ages and conditions. Thus, within a dozen years of *Roe v. Wade*, many Americans supported the denial of lifesaving surgery for handicapped newborns. *Roe* also emboldened advocates of euthanasia for adults.

It is a mistake to argue that abortion must be legal because some disagree about when each human life begins. The scientific evidence for fertilization as the starting point is overwhelming. It is reactionary to appeal, as some abortion advocates do, to the mistaken embryology

---

of Aristotle or medieval philosophers in order to promote doubt on the matter. In his *Roe v. Wade* opinion, Justice Harry Blackmun acknowledged that briefs in the case had outlined "at length and in detail the well-known facts of fetal development." Then he proceeded to ignore those facts, saying the Court "need not resolve the difficult question of when life begins." Yet that question had been resolved by science long before Blackmun wrote.[3] All the Court had to do was take judicial notice of a fact already known and accepted. Liberals, given their respect for science, should be dismayed by the Court's failure on this key point.

Intellectual Chaos

Some liberals claim that one can be a human being without being a person and that we have a right to kill "non-persons." They fail to realize what a heavy burden of proof they must meet here, especially since they cannot even agree among themselves on when personhood begins. (Some favor weeks after fertilization, while others say months later, or even at birth.) Restating a classic ethical case in the plural: Hunters notice movement in a thicket, but don't know whether it is caused by a deer or another human being. If they shoot without determining the facts, and kill a human, they are guilty of homicide. Many abortion supporters say they cannot find out, yet they are willing to shoot anyway.

Libertarians for Life founder Doris Gordon comments: "Abortion choicers try to get around the intellectual chaos on their side by saying, 'Let the woman decide.' If one is free to decide whether another is a person, then whoever is strongest will do the deciding, and we all had better be thinking about our own prospects." She also notes: "No sperm or ovum can grow up and debate abortion; they are not 'programmed' to do so. What sets the *person* aside from the *non-person* is the root capacity for reason and choice. If this capacity is not in a being's nature, the being cannot develop it. We had this capacity on Day One, because it came with our human nature."[4]

One could even contend that it is worse to kill human beings before, rather than after, they develop the potential their nature gives them. At least the rest of us have the chance to use our potential. Whether we use it well or poorly, we have our day in the sun. As a recent March for Life sign asked: "You got a chance/Why can't they?" And if we discriminate against others on the basis of intellectual ability, we reject the principle of equal rights. We establish two classes of humanity—those who have rights and those who do not. That dangerous precedent places many other people at risk: newborn babies, stroke survivors, people who are retarded or demented, accident survivors who have severe brain injuries. Liberals should ponder the words of the late Dr. Bernard Nathanson, who said that our era keeps "defining personhood upward so that fewer and fewer of us make the cut." He warned that "everything, including your life, my friend, is up for discussion."[5]

"All I Can Believe in Is Life"

The right to life is a bedrock right for secular people as well as religious believers. Perhaps non-believers should defend life even more ardently than believers do. Existence on earth should be more precious, not less, to those who believe it's the only one we have. Nat Hentoff, the noted author and civil libertarian, said that "it's a lot easier for an atheist—at least, this atheist—to be against abortion because all I have is life, this life. All I can believe in is life." As Hentoff and others realize, attacking the right to life of a whole class of humans undermines that right—and thus all other rights—for everyone else as well. Non-believers also can rely on the Golden Rule, "Do unto others as you would have them do unto you," which has been honored through the centuries by both religious and secular people. Bernard Nathanson, once an abortion doctor, was an atheist when he joined the pro-life side. He described the Golden Rule as "a statement of innate human wisdom" and applied it to abortion. "Looked at this way," he said, "the 'sanctity of life' is not a theological but a secular concept, which should be perfectly acceptable to my fellow atheists." A group called SecularProLife.org notes that the "human right to life is affirmed in the Declaration of Independence, the fourteenth amendment of the United States Constitution, and many other human rights documents. . . . You don't have to be religious to join one of today's most important human rights movements![6]

Religious people have done most of the organizing and speaking against abortion, and those opposed to them claim that they are trying to impose their religious beliefs on others. Yet most great movements for social change in American history, although separately justifiable on secular grounds, have been deeply rooted in the religious community. Quakers and evangelical Protestants led the anti-slavery movement.[7] "Labor priests" were important to the rise of the labor movement. Quakers, Mennonites, mainline Protestants, Catholics, and Jews have provided much leadership for the peace movement. Religious people have been deeply involved in efforts to abolish the death penalty. Dr. Martin Luther King, Jr., and other ministers made the African American churches the backbone of the civil rights movement in the 1950s and 1960s. No one suggests that civil rights laws passed in that era are invalid because their advocates had religious motivation for their work. There should not be a different standard today for the religious motivation of many pro-lifers. The right to life is not the private property of any church. It is a universal human right.

Don't Shove Her Out in Mid-flight!

Abortion is an escape from an obligation that parents owe their children. By bringing a child into existence, Doris Gordon notes, the parents place her in a state of dependence with a need for care. "Liberals believe we have enforceable obligations toward strangers, including other people's children. Why not our own?" she asks. She says that conceiving and then aborting one's child "could be compared to capturing someone, placing her on one's airplane, and then shoving her out in mid-flight without a parachute."[8]

Roe v. Wade does not acknowledge the obligation of parents to protect from harm the human beings they bring into existence. It ignores the father's obligation. It treats the mother as having no responsibility for the child before birth, yet virtually total responsibility if she decides against abortion. "Maternity, or additional offspring, may force upon the woman a distressful life and future. . . . Mental and physical health may be taxed by child care," the *Roe* justices declared. Nothing there about the father's joint responsibility for children and child care. If the justices were determined to act as a legislature rather than a court, they at least should have called for *more* male responsibility, not less.

They were remarkably negative toward parenting and children, referring to "the distress, for all concerned, associated with the unwanted child."[9] As the late Hispanic activist Grace Olivarez once said, 'Those with power in our society cannot be allowed to 'want' and 'unwant' people at will. . . . I believe that, in a society that permits the life of even one individual (born or unborn) to be dependent on whether that life is 'wanted' or not, all its citizens stand in danger."[10] The *Roe* justices also ignored the preamble to the Constitution, which speaks of securing "the blessings of liberty to ourselves and our posterity." Posterity means *all* descendants. Our Founders were deeply concerned about posterity, and they did not make deadly distinctions between wanted and unwanted children, nor between born children and "fetuses." General George Washington, when perplexed about a problem during the American Revolution, said that what Congress wanted him to do, "I know no more than the child unborn and beg to be instructed."[11] This was just ten years before Washington presided over our Constitutional Convention.

"We Created a Monster"

The *Roe* justices should have upheld the right to life guaranteed by the Constitution's Fifth and Fourteenth Amendments: that no person may be deprived of "life, liberty, or property, without due process of law." Instead, *Roe* pushed local and federal governments into defending abortion clinics with police, federal court injunctions, and federal marshals. That is governmental action to deprive unborn human beings of their lives. So is the subsidy of abortion that many states provide. The governments involved do not hold trials to give due process to the unborn. After all, of what crime could they be accused? The crime of existing?

The *Roe* justices dealt briefly and unconvincingly with the Fourteenth Amendment, claiming that its use of "person" does not cover the unborn. This is where they established a legal policy of two classes of humanity. Under the 1857 *Dred Scott* decision, African American slaves were the non-citizens of our Constitution, but the *Dred Scott* majority

at least called them a "class of persons." Southern state laws offered slaves some protection. Although those laws were often ignored in practice, a few whites were sentenced to death for killing slaves.[12] Under *Roe,* however, unborn children are non-persons, lacking even the right not to be killed.

Roe places women in an adversarial position toward their own children and, in a real sense, toward themselves. This is what Joan Appleton faced when she saw women go through emotional trauma over abortion. As head nurse of an abortion clinic in Virginia, Appleton was a committed feminist who saw her clinic work as a chance to help other women. Although she counseled women carefully, she saw many go through emotional ordeals over abortion. She said some came back to her, months or even years later, as "psychological wrecks." This and other evidence led her to conclude: "We created a monster, and now we don't know what to do with it." Like Dr. Nathanson, Appleton joined the pro-life side.[13]

When young men face a draft in wartime, this forces them to start adult life by deciding whether to kill other human beings. There is never a good time to make such a decision, but the volatile teen years are an especially bad time. Now young women face the same decision in their teens, often under strong pressure from others to destroy their own children. This sets them up for psychological problems. Dr. David Fergusson, a New Zealand professor, has led major studies of abortion's psychological effects on a group of young New Zealand women. In 2006 he and his colleagues reported that those who had abortions had higher rates of depression, anxiety, and thoughts of suicide than other women in the group. The rates were especially high for those who were 15 to 18 years old. Fergusson, who described himself as pro-choice and "an atheist and a rationalist," acknowledged on a television program that he was surprised by results of his study. Another Fergusson-led study in 2008 found that women in the group who had abortions "had rates of mental health problems that were about 30% higher than rates of disorder in other women."[14]

Pro-Life Feminists, Then and Now

But what about the argument that women need abortion availability in order to have true equality with men? This was not the view of American feminists of the 1800s such as Susan B. Anthony, Elizabeth Cady Stanton, and Elizabeth Blackwell. Writer Mary Krane Derr and her colleagues show that early feminists thought men—through unreasonable sexual demands, abandonment, or outright coercion—bore the greatest responsibility for abortion. But they also show that those feminists did not condone abortion or see it as a good for women. Nor did they say it should be legalized. . . .

The early feminists thought equality, both within marriage and in society, was the best preventive of abortion. Today's pro-life feminists carry on that tradition when they say we should change society to accommodate mothers, rather than vice-versa. Serrin Foster, president of Feminists for Life of America, works hard to spread this view around the country and on Capitol Hill. She is keenly aware of economic pressures that push women toward abortion. She knew that such pressures resulted in abortion for Kate Michelman, former president of NARAL Pro-Choice America. That knowledge, Foster said, "inspired me personally to work for child-support enforcement" when Congress debated welfare reform some years ago.[15] Her group works to make college life easier for women who are pregnant and students who are caring for small children. The Feminists for Life have a can-do approach, and they are willing to work with people on all sides of the abortion issue to make life better for women and their children. . . .

Why should we worship at the shrine of choice? "Abortion" is a terrible word, and a terrible reality, so we should not be surprised that its advocates prefer to say "freedom of choice," "pro-choice," and "the choice issue." Yet the glory of humanity does not consist in making choices as such, but in making them wisely and well and in a way that avoids harming other people. We should not fear being called "anti-choice" when we support laws that are needed to prevent great harm to others, especially when that harm will end their lives. Ginny Desmond Billinger, a pro-life feminist, once wrote an essay called "Confessions of an Anti-Choice Fanatic." She was anti-choice not only on abortion , but also on spousal and child abuse, drunk driving, unsafe disposal of hazardous wastes, and more.[16] A little reflection shows that liberals are anti-choice on many issues. They should add abortion to the list. . . .

Targeting Poor Children and Minorities

Anyone concerned about civil rights should be alarmed by abortion as lethal discrimination against poor people and ethnic minorities. Eugenicists long have targeted both groups for population control. The 1956 membership list of the American Eugenics Society could have been called *Who's Who in Population Control*. It included sociologist Kingsley Davis, ethicist Joseph Hetcher, biologist Bentley Glass, birth-control leader Margaret Sanger, physician Alan Guttmacher, and other movers and shakers in public policy. Some of them later suggested coercive population control, and many supported abortion as a quick way to reduce birthrates. Most were white males who didn't care about adverse health effects on women of the early birth control pill, IUDs, and surgical abortion. They were not worried about women's health or about ethics; they just wanted to get the numbers down. Some had major influence on the legalization of abortion.[17]

But where eugenicists of the 1920s were blunt about their disdain for the poor, their heirs of the 1970s presented abortion as a *good* for poor women. In 1971 Dr. Guttmacher (by then the president of Planned Parenthood) wrote Governor Nelson Rockefeller of New York to support Medicaid funding of abortion for poor women. Guttmacher said a recent cut-back of such funding was

"grossly discriminatory against the least privileged citizens of this State." He asked, "What are such poor souls to do in the future?" Then he added, as abortion advocates often did—and many still do—an economic argument for eliminating poor children: "To save a few million dollars now the State must pay far more eventually for prenatal care and delivery and the eighteen-year annual upkeep of children likely to become financial burdens of the State."[18]

Planned Parenthood leaders fought hard in Congress and the federal courts for subsidized abortion. When they lost at the federal level, they fought and often won in state courts. Naive liberals did much to aid those fights. So did the American Civil Liberties Union. Aryeh Neier, who was the ACLU executive director in 1970–78, later referred to "whites who were eager to eliminate or limit the number of welfare mother babies out of an anti-black feeling" and acknowledged that "I dealt with some supporters of abortion who are very much in favor of abortion for exactly that reason." Interviewed by one of his law students at New York University, Prof. Neier said two foundations, one in Pittsburgh and one in Missouri, supported abortion efforts because of such racist views. "I don't regard it as dirty money," he said, "so long as people don't try to impose conditions on what you can do with the money. . . . So as long as they don't try to impose restrictions, I will always take the money."[19]

The abortion rate for poor women is far higher than the rate for middle-class and upper-class women. In the year 2000, the abortion rate for African American women was nearly four times that for white women, according to a survey report by—ironically—the Alan Guttmacher Institute. The authors estimated that of all pregnancies among black women in 2000, 43 percent led to abortion.[20] Civil rights activist Dick Gregory was right, many years earlier, when he called abortion "a death sentence upon us." The late Fannie Lou Hamer, a great civil rights activist in Mississippi, shared his view.[21] Many African American women have suffered bitter regret and depression as a result of abortion. Pamela Carr had one when she was just 17 and headed toward college. "The anguish and guilt I felt were unbelievable," she wrote later in *Ebony*. "I became deeply depressed. . . . Over time I was able to forgive myself and go on with my life, but always with the knowledge that I had swept away a part of my future which could never be recovered." Her question about the unborn: "How many more of them have to die before we realize that abortion is not a solution but another, more troubling, problem plaguing our community?" Arlene Campbell had a legal abortion that nearly killed her: "Depression became a major part of my daily existence. . . . I now speak of life, but for many years all I could think of was death."[22]

Disability Rights for the Unborn

Abortion also involves lethal discrimination against children with disabilities. Some writers suggest that a "new eugenics" produced prenatal testing and abortion of the handicapped unborn. Actually, it was the same old eugenics that for decades supported compulsory sterilization of the "feebleminded." After the Nazi era, though, U.S. eugenics leaders realized they had to be more subtle. Frederick Osborn, the shrewd chief of the American Eugenics Society, was co-founder and first administrator of the Population Council. He used the Council to advance all of his eugenic interests. In addition to other population-control programs, the Council funded medical-genetics fellowships for students who were recommended by a committee of Osborn's eugenics society. His society also promoted heredity counseling, which it called "the opening wedge in the public acceptance of eugenic principles."[23]

Osborn supported the new American Society of Human Genetics (ASHG), which other eugenicists had started, and served as that group's vice president in 1958. Many other ASHG leaders and members were deeply involved in developing or advocating prenatal testing for fetal handicaps such as Down Syndrome and spina bifida. But prenatal testing would have meant little had abortion remained illegal. Big money took care of that problem: In 1962 a project to develop a Model Penal Code for the states, funded by the Rockefeller Foundation, proposed the legalization of abortion for fetal disability and other hard cases.[24] Several states followed its advice; then *Roe* made special exceptions unnecessary.

It is tragic that the disability rights movement was still getting off the ground in the 1970s. Had it become a major force decades earlier, eugenics might not have developed into such a powerful monster. But the disability rights movement came of age after *Roe v. Wade,* and it includes both people who support *Roe* and people who oppose abortion and are appalled by its use as a tool of eugenics. Joseph P. Shapiro, who authored a history of the movement, said it has dealt with abortion "largely by keeping its distance."[25]

Liberals usually side with people who have disabilities, insisting that they have equal rights. That's where liberals and disability rights activists should be on the issue of eugenic abortion. They should remind everyone that most of us have one or more disabilities, ranging from poor eyesight to severe problems, and that we will have more as we grow older. As disability rights activist Mary Jane Owen has said, "developing a few glitches, developing impairments, is *not* the end of the joy of life," and "we can enjoy life learning new functions and new ways of being."[26]

Protect the Children, and "Live Lightly on the Earth"

Liberals should realize, too, that abortion harms children who are not aborted, but hear about abortion when they are very young. One psychiatrist reported, "I have had children who suffer from night terrors and who fear to

fall asleep because they overheard their parents discussing an abortion they had or planned to have. These children fear they may be gotten rid of the next time they make their parents angry."[27] Drs. Philip G. Ney and Marie A. Peeters-Ney wrote that some children suffer from "survivor guilt" because they know that one or more siblings were aborted. Children who know their parents considered aborting *them,* the doctors suggested, tend to be fearful and over-eager to please. And the Neys quoted someone who had cancer at the age of twelve: "My mother told me she was going for prenatal diagnosis to make sure the baby was alright [sic]. I knew what would happen if the baby wasn't. One night I thought perhaps if I did not get better the doctors would get rid of me too. I never trusted my mother after that. In actual fact I never trusted anybody after that."[28]

Abortion also goes against the harmony with nature that environmentalists celebrate and encourage. Childbirth, after all, is the natural way to end a pregnancy. Why, then, do so many environmentalists promote abortion? Many do so because they see all human beings—except, perhaps, themselves and those they love—as threats to the natural environment. They assume that the fewer people there are, the less pollution and resource exhaustion we will have. Some of their messages make people feel guilty to be alive or to have children. Yet environmentalists over look what seems to be a perverse result of population control: The fewer people there are, the more *things* each person wants. Despite today's norm of two children per family, American houses are larger than ever before. Many tiny families rattle around in mini-castles—and drive huge, gas-guzzling vans and SUVs. Where a family used to have one television, many now have one per bedroom, plus others scattered around the home. Has all of this led to greater happiness? That seems doubtful, given how hard people work to buy all their stuff, to take care of it, and then to buy even bigger houses to store it all. "Live lightly on the earth" is a splendid environmental slogan, and that is where our emphasis should be. Instead of eliminating people, we should return to simpler and less stressful lifestyles.

Liberals, like most Americans, tend to acquire too much stuff. They also have inherited much ideological debris from recent generations of the left. Neither kind of junk makes them happy. If they discard both, they will have plenty of room for children and for life. Then they might, like Lucinda Matlock, shout to the wooded hills and sing to the green valleys.

Notes

1. In the case of identical twins, a second human life begins when the first embryo divides. Triplets and higher multiples can be identical, fraternal, or a combination. See Keith L. Moore and others, *Before We Are Born,* 7th ed. (Philadelphia: Saunders/Elsevier , 2008), 2 & 88–90.

2. John Walker, "Power and Act: Notes Towards Engaging in a Discussion of One of the Underlying Questions in the Abortion Debate," *International Journal of Sociology and Social Policy* 19, nos. 3/4 (1999), 54–64, 57 (available at www.141.org; go to "Library").

3. *Roe v. Wade*, 410 U.S. 113 at 156 & 159 (1973); Alan Frank Guttmacher with Ellery Rand, *Life in the Making* (New York: Viking , 1933), 3; and George W. Comer, *Ourselves Unborn: An Embryologist's Essay on Man* (New Haven: Yale, 1944; reprint, Hamden, Conn.: Archon Books/Shoe String Press, 1972), 1. Comer wrote, "When a man is born, he is already nine months old."

4. Doris Gordon, "Abortion and Rights: Applying Libertarian Principles Correctly," *International Journal of Sociology and Social Policy* 19, nos. 3/4 (1999), 97–127, 112 & 111. This is the best, richest, and clearest philosophical article on abortion that I have ever read. It is available on the Libertarians for Life website, www.141.org (go to "Library").

5. "March for Life 2011 Photos," www.meehanreports.com, accessed 28 March 2011; and Bernard Nathanson, *The Hand of God* (Washington: Regnery, 1996), 4 & 5.

6. Nat Hentoff, "You Don't Have to Believe in God to Be Prolife," *U.S. Catholic,* March 1989, 28–30, 28; and Bernard N . Nathanson with Richard N. Ostling, *Aborting America* (Garden City, N.Y.: Doubleday, 1979), 227. (Nathanson eventually joined the Catholic Church.) See, also: "Is Abortion a Religious Issue?" www.secularprolife.org (under "Publications"), accessed 30 March 2011.

7. On evangelicals' role in the anti-slavery movement, see Benjamin P. Thomas, *Theodore Weld, Crusader for Freedom* (New Brunswick, N.J.: Rutgers, 1950); Henry Mayer, *All on Fire: William Lloyd Garrison and the Abolition of Slavery* (New York: St. Martin's, 1998); and Bertram Wyatt-Brown, *Lewis Tappan and the Evangelical War Against Slavery* (Cleveland: Case Western Reserve, 1969).

8. Doris Gordon, telephone conversation with the author, 15 April 2011; and Gordon (n. 11), 120.

9. *Roe v. Wade* (n. 10) at 153.

10. "Separate Statement of Grace Olivarez" in U.S. Commission on Population Growth and the American Future, *Population and the American Future* (Washington: U.S. Government Printing Office, 1972), 160–64, 161 & 163.

11. George Washington to Benjamin Harrison, 19 Aug. 1777, in John C. Fitzpatrick, ed., *The Writings of George Washington* (Washington: U.S. Government Printing Office, 1931–44), vol. 9, 95–96.

12. *Roe v. Wade* (n. 10) at 156–59; *Dred Scott v. Sandford,* 60 U.S. (19 Howard) 393 at 403, 404, 407, 409, 411 & 422 (1857); and Kenneth M. Stampp, *The Peculiar Institution* (New York: Knopf, 1956), 217–24.

13. Joan Appleton, Remarks at "Meet the Abortion Providers" conference, 3 April 1993, sponsored by the Pro-Life Action League, Chicago, Ill., audio recording.

14. David M. Fergusson and others, "Abortion in Young Women and Subsequent Mental Health," *Journal of Child Psychology and Psychiatry* 47, no. 1 (2006), 16–24, 19; Australian Broadcasting Corporation, "Higher Risk of Mental Health Problems After Abortion: Report," transcript of 3 Jan. 2006 broadcast; and David M. Fergusson and others, "Abortion and Mental Health Disorders: Evidence from a 30–Year Longitudinal Study," *British Journal of Psychiatry* (2008), 444–51, 449.

15. Serrin Foster, interview by author, 22 Jan. 1998, Washington, D.C., transcript.

16. Ginny Desmond Billinger, "Confessions of an Anti-Choice Fanatic," in Gail Grenier Sweet, ed., *Pro-Life Feminism: Different Voices* (Toronto: Life Cycle Books, 1985), 77–78.

17. American Eugenics Society, "Membership List, 1956," *Eugenics Quarterly* 3, no. 4 (Dec. 1956), 243–52 (Margaret Sanger listed under her married name of Margaret Sanger Slee, 249); Meehan, "The Road to Abortion" (n. 3); and Rebecca Messall, ''The Long Road of Eugenics: From Rockefeller to *Roe v. Wade*," *Human Life Review* 30, no. 4 (Fall 2004), 33–74.

18. Alan F. Guttmacher to Nelson Rockefeller, 12 April 1971 [mimeographed copy distributed to media], Alan Frank Guttmacher Papers, HMS c155, box 4, f. 45, Harvard Medical Library in the Francis A. Countway Library of Medicine, Boston, Mass.

19. Aryeh Neier, interview with Thomas J. Balch, 3 Nov. 1979, in Balch's "Convincing the Courts on Abortion," a paper for Prof. Neier's "Litigation and Public Policy" course [New York University School of Law], Fall 1979, appendix, 12–13. See, also, Mary Meehan, "ACLU v. Unborn Children," *Human Life Review* 27, no. 2 (Spring 2001), 49–73.

20. Rachel K. Jones and others, "Patterns in the Socioeconomic Characteristics of Women Obtaining Abortions in 2000–2001," *Perspectives on Sexual and Reproductive Health* 34, no. 5 (Sept.–Oct. 2002), 226–35, 228.

21. Barry Farrell, "Running with Dick Gregory," *Ramparts,* Aug.–Sept. 1975, 26 ff., 54; and Kay Mills, *This Little Light of Mine: The Life of Fannie Lou Hamer* (New York: Dutton/Penguin, 1993), 260–61 & 274.

22. Pamela Carr, "Which Way Black America? Anti-Abortion," *Ebony* 44, no. 12 (Oct. 1989), 134 ff., 138; and Arlene Campbell, "A Shattered Life," Black Americans for Life newsletter, Washington, D.C., Spring 2005 [3].

23. American Eugenics Society, *Five-Year Report of the Officers: 1953–1957* (New York, n.d.), 9–11, 10.

24. Mary Meehan, "The Triumph of Eugenics in Prenatal Testing," *Human Life Review* 35, no. 3 (Summer 2009), 28–40, 33–36.

25. Joseph P. Shapiro, *No Pity* (New York: Times Books/Random House, 1993), 278.
26. Mary Jane Owen, telephone interview by author, 31 July 1992, transcript.
27. Edward J. Sheridan, interview by John G. Gatewood, *Georgetown University Right to Life Journal* 2 (Fall 1981), 1–5, 1.
28. Philip G. Ney and Marie A. Peeters-Ney, *Abortion Survivors* (Victoria, B.C., Canada: Pioneer Publishing, 1998), 26–27 & 33.

MARY MEEHAN is a writer and speaker who links a consistent pro-life ethic to a number of issues, including stances against war and the death penalty as well as suicide prevention strategies.

Amy Borovoy

Beyond Choice: A New Framework for Abortion?

Every year I teach a class called "Mind, Body, and Bioethics in Japan" to a group of Princeton undergraduates made up of students drawn to ethical dilemmas—aspiring doctors, scientists, and lawyers. The class departs from typical approaches to bioethics. Instead of attempting to arrive logically at the "right" or "best" answer to the human dilemmas posed by modern medicine, we take an anthropological approach, asking how the dilemmas themselves are shaped by and understood through the context of culture.

The unit focusing on pregnancy, prenatal care, and attitudes toward abortion and human life, in particular, provokes some of the most passionate discussion. The topic is fraught in any context, but given the polarized politics of "life" vs. "choice" to which U.S. students have been exposed, Japan reveals intriguing contradictions. Japanese obstetricians do not practice aggressive prenatal screening; women are encouraged to accept the baby that is born, and fetal selection for birth abnormalities or sex is regarded as unethical. A fetus is humanized—so much so that obstetricians routinely hail their clients as "Mom," even from the early stages of the pregnancy. At the same time, terminating a pregnancy is accepted as a morally sound means of preventing a situation in which a child would go uncared for. Small statues commemorating the unborn at Buddhist temples mark an institutionalized space in which women mourn their aborted fetuses.

Teaching the class has sharpened my feelings that there is something missing from the traditional "pro-choice" stance on abortion. The position is an heir of *Roe v. Wade*'s legal framework of the right to privacy and, also, of 1960s and 1970s liberal feminism, with its emphasis on women's autonomy. When I started teaching, I had no children. Now, as a parent, even though I support the right to abortion, when I see T-shirts on college campuses emblazoned with "My body, my choice," I feel that they are glib and vaguely irresponsible, an attitude I know I share with others who also support abortion rights. Successful campaigns against legitimating abortion primarily in terms of "choice" and "rights" have led to such bipartisan initiatives as the Prevention First Act, the Pregnant Women Support Act, and the Reducing the Need for Abortion and Supporting Parents Act. Many Democrats have backed away from aggressive promotion of "rights" and

"choice." Barack Obama's 2010 reassertion of Bill Clinton's statement that we should make abortion "safe, legal, and rare" reflects a liberal attempt to recognize the moral dimension of the problem while holding on to a "right" that in many places in the United States is a "right" in name only.

Meanwhile, anthropologists and sociologists who study reproductive health care on the ground, in clinics, note how the discourse of "choice" offers little space to recognize the conflicted feelings often associated with terminating a pregnancy on the part of women, abortion rights advocates, and even health care practitioners themselves. Jeannie Ludlow, in a powerful essay entitled, "Sometimes, It's a Child *and* a Choice," has written about women's attachments to what the majority refer to as their "baby," despite their decision to terminate the pregnancy, and about committed abortion providers' private confusion about the status of the fetus. Most women seeking abortions must balance demanding work schedules while caring for other dependents. Some 61 percent of American women getting abortions today are already mothers of one or more children; 69 percent are economically disadvantaged. Only 18 percent of women obtaining abortions are teenagers. Concern about their ability to adequately care for an additional child is central to their decision.

The Japanese example offers a window into the particularities of the American debate and the limits of each position. As here, the fetus is humanized in many contexts, and yet abortion is ethically acceptable. Even second trimester abortions are legal in Japan. The question of when life begins, central to U.S. abortion politics, is less important to the Japanese ethical framework. The focus is neither on the rights of the mother nor on the personhood of the fetus, but rather on the social life of the child, the welfare of the family, and the question of the social good more broadly. Although teenage abortion rates are rising, the majority of women seeking abortions are in their thirties and forties. The strong sense that these are decisions made by parents out of concern for family welfare undercuts the logic of opposing abortion based on the fetus's humanity alone. In Japan, as elsewhere, a mother is trusted to make the decision about the fate of her fetus not because she has freedom of "choice" but rather because she is its trusted caregiver; a parent alone can provide her child with an appropriate environment. Japanese parents do live with deep psychic tensions between the acceptance of the humanity of the fetus and the pervasive practice of abortion. This tension is easily exploited by Buddhist sects harboring marginal views, and images of the innocent, child-like fetuses make their appearance in comics and other forms of popular culture that treat the issue of abortion and women's inner conflict. Still, the logic is that child rearing and a mother's health (both physical and emotional) are central to producing a good society, and that children respond to the resources and care they receive. This notion of abortion as a social necessity differs from the notion of abortion as a "right" and deemphasizes the dividing lines between "life" and "choice."

Japanese school textbooks treat the issue of birth control and abortion in required courses on home economics. A common middle-school textbook explains the procedure under a section entitled, "Deciding when and when not to give birth." It begins by stating that "as an individual human being, a child has the right to be raised in an appropriate environment." The passage suggests that a parent should be concerned foremost with appropriate upbringing and socialization of a child, and should thus practice birth control rigorously. While the textbook reassures its readers that abortion as a last resort is safe and legal, it cautions that such a measure constitutes "the termination of a life that one has cultivated," and also that "the hardship for a woman, physically and emotionally, is large." Thus, while the passage explicitly imagines the fetus as a life, the ethical focus is not on the fetus but rather on a mother's welfare and the future child's environment. The entire section appears in a chapter on "Childrearing."

As such stories suggest, family has hardly been regarded as a "private sphere" in modern Japan. The status of abortion as a family matter must be seen in the context of social policy that has historically regarded strong families as integral to a successful society. In fact, the history of abortion is closely entwined with platforms for social betterment—producing a "planned family," a strong society, and powerful nation. Infanticide was a common practice throughout the seventeenth and eighteenth centuries in many parts of Japan for reasons of poverty and food shortage. In prosperous areas, such "weeding" (*mabiki*, as it was called) was carried out by midwives at the behest of the family with the objective of creating "small, healthy, and economically productive families"—while the state looked away. Abortion was banned at the turn of the century in order to encourage population growth and fuel Japan's imperial ambitions.

Despite citizens' activism toward legalization in the 1920s and 1930s, the government did not officially legalize abortion until 1948, in the context of postwar devastation and starvation, out of concern for population control. At the height of the eugenic policies that influenced the industrialized world, the bill emphasized the priority of population quality, permitting abortion if there was evidence of a hereditary condition that might be transmitted to a child and compelling sterilization in certain instances. The law, the National Eugenic Protection Law (*Nihon Yūsei Hogo-Hō*), included a list of specific hereditary conditions that legitimized abortion. In the context of the postwar baby boom, many women began to take advantage of the law, and a clause was added permitting abortion for reasons of economic hardship.

After decades of opposition by human rights activists, the eugenic clause was eventually deleted in a 1996 law, which was re-titled, "The Maternal Body Protection Law" (*Botai Hogo Hō*). The economic necessity clause remains (in addition to rape, incest, or possible harm to the mother), and is the primary legal recourse for abortion. Abortion as a means of fetal selection is undoubtedly still practiced under the cloak of economic need, but it is regarded warily by obstetricians and families alike.

Still, family continues to be the primary prism through which decisions to terminate a pregnancy are viewed. The anthropologist Margaret Lock, who has studied Japanese attitudes toward fetal selection and new reproductive technologies, suggests that the ethical question of whether to terminate a problematic pregnancy hinges foremost on its consequences for family life. One mother whom she interviewed, who was raising a child with Down Syndrome, expressed the view that terminating a first pregnancy for reasons of the discovery of a chromosomal abnormality would be "selfish." However, terminating a second abnormal pregnancy that could jeopardize family life and the quality of parenting for the first child would more likely be regarded as acceptable. Japanese obstetricians have steadfastly declined to conduct proactive prenatal testing, even tests that are considered routine in the United States. Instead they direct their focus to the mother's behavior and the "environment" she creates for her fetus. As eugenic practices have come to be regarded as taboo among obstetricians, what has replaced them is a strong commitment to the power of motherhood, which is thought to begin with pregnancy. A recent ethnography of prenatal care by Israeli anthropologist Tsipy Ivry demonstrates the burden but also the pride that such practices confer on Japanese women. Ivry's book, *Embodying Culture*, draws a striking contrast with Israel, where concern for birth outcomes results in more aggressive prenatal testing, trivializing the mother and the pregnancy itself as an influence on the baby.

During Japan's decades of rapid economic growth in the sixties, seventies, and eighties, the government, together with Japanese enterprise, subsidized middle-class women to stay at home, protecting the family wage system through mutual corporate shareholding and bank loans for companies that buffered employees from economic volatility. The middle-class housewives of this era, while economically dependent on their husbands, enjoyed a good deal of economic stability and social security and regarded the work of raising children as socially important, skilled labor. Suzanne Vogel, one of the first Western scholars of the Japanese family, remarked that one rarely hears a Japanese woman refer to herself as "just a housewife."

In some ways, the family values that have defined the discourse on pregnancy and abortion have recently come to dissuade women from having children—an irony that is visible in other "family friendly" nations, such as Italy, Spain, and South Korea. Ideals concerning motherhood are so high that it is difficult to combine them with women's advancement in the labor force, and economic instability has made the single wage-earner model less viable for many. While it is tempting to see the low fertility rate as evidence of "women's liberation" or a rebellion from traditional roles, there is evidence, in Japan at least, that it marks a continuing conservatism in what constitutes an ideal child-rearing environment.

Japan stands out, for example, for its low incidence of children born out of wedlock—despite the conditions of urbanization and rising rates of education for women that made illegitimacy more common in other industrialized nations. In Japan, more than half of all premarital pregnancies to women aged fifteen to twenty-nine between the years 2000 and 2004 were aborted; 38 percent of pregnancies to this age group ended up as marital births. Only 4 percent led to non-marital births. (In the United States, almost 50 percent of non-maritally conceived children result in nonmarital births.) Oxford University sociologist Ekaterina Hertog interviewed sixty-eight women from the small population of women in their thirties and forties who decided to give birth outside of marriage. All emphasized the difficulty of their decision. Her recent book, *Tough Choices,* demonstrates the preference among women to raising children within a dual-parent household, preferably with a primary wage-earner. Single motherhood almost always compels Japanese women to work outside the home. Japanese social support for single mothers is not generous, though it is somewhat more expansive than in the United States, and the women whom Hertog interviewed told her that having a father and breadwinner in the house allows women to be more present mothers—although such a father may be remote from the daily goings-on of family life. For many women in such circumstances, abortion is deemed the "responsible" choice, despite the often powerful desire to have a child.

Japan's entrenched division of labor and conservative ideals about family are hardly enviable, and we might argue that Japan's liberal policy around abortion helps to reinforce those ideals. Although Japan was one of the first nations to permit legal abortion, the law was passed from on high and reflects less concern with women's "choice" or sexual freedom than with producing appropriate mothers and children, as some feminists have pointed out.

There are other reasons not to envy Japan. Japanese women have a high abortion rate. Abortion has continued to be the predominant form of birth control in Japan well after the invention and legalization of birth control medication in many other industrialized countries. A revealing study by political scientist Tiana Norgren showed how a cluster of professional groups with a vested interest in defending access to abortion (midwives, ob-gyns, and even feminists who worried about the pill's health effects) obstructed the legalization of the birth control pill until 1999—more than forty years after Food and Drug Administration approval of the first pill in the United States. Given the political and economic conflicts in the country, there is no cause to celebrate the normalcy of abortion.

Still, to the extent that termination of pregnancy is inevitable in some cases, can we not find something useful in the ability to cast this decision in terms of its consequences for social stability and care for others? And should we not envy this society's recognition and value of the dignity and importance of parenting? Japanese attitudes toward pregnancy are fully entwined with an appreciation for the importance of parenthood, an ideal celebrated in popular U.S. culture but disdained in social and economic policy and at the workplace. Can we not find here a way around the discourse that currently pits a woman's "choice" against the sanctity of a fetus's "life"?

In regarding abortion as an aspect of social welfare, health, and family, Japan is not unusual among social democracies. Germany, the United Kingdom, Switzerland, Canada, and many of the East European post-socialist societies harbor similar politics and trade-offs. In Germany, abortion has been legally sanctioned as a matter of "protection"— the responsibility of the welfare state to care for German families. The 1994 law that went into effect after German unification legalized women's rights to terminate a pregnancy within the first trimester; it linked this with state-funded abortions for women on welfare and promises to increase state support for kindergartens and other aid for childcare. In essence, the German courts weighed the potential hardship of the mother against their emphasis on the sanctity of human life. While the state requires counseling which must be "pro-life oriented but outcome-open," the law defines its responsibility as being to "help not punish" the pregnant woman.

In Canada, just across the U.S. border, law and court deliberations on abortion led to allowing abortion largely as a matter of universal provision of health care (with health defined as emotional, physical, or psychological). Although some Canadian pro-choice feminists have expressed envy of the protection of abortion as a woman's private right in the United States, there is a reluctance to regard the matter of abortion as a "private" matter. Abortions are financed by public insurance in Canada—a provision that was excluded from *Roe v. Wade* and remains one of the most contentious issues in U.S. social policy. As William Saletan and others have noted, *Roe v. Wade*'s protection of abortion through women's right to privacy set the stage for the retrenchment of abortion services across the country; states may not interfere with a woman's right to an early abortion, but they are under no legal responsibility to provide them.

What makes the German and Canadian legislation stand out in contrast to *Roe v. Wade*, is their focus on protection. German law, like West European law more broadly, emphasizes public health and humanitarian justifications for the practice of abortion: the social costs of unwanted pregnancy, health risks to women, the psychic toll of raising unwanted children, and the state's positive obligation to protect women. In contrast, *Roe v. Wade* defined the right to first-trimester abortion primarily in terms of negative liberty—the right of the individual to decide for herself whether abortion is appropriate; it deliberately and explicitly excluded the possibility of the state's consideration for women's broader social circumstances.

These comparisons help us frame a bigger picture: nations that see abortion in terms of social welfare are paternalistic, "nannying," and often socially conservative, viewing motherhood as women's primary role. Concerns for "quality" of population and family values are sometimes uncomfortably close to concerns for social homogeneity, elitism, and what could potentially become intolerance. A woman's right to a first-trimester abortion on any grounds in the United States is envied by many women around the world. But, as many other commentators on the debate in the United States have asked, to what extent are we protecting women's "freedom," "choice," or "autonomy" when we focus on abortion as a right in the absence of other social protections for women and families: subsidized day care, job security, a family wage, quality public education, and universal health care?

Roe v. Wade created the possibility for women to have control over their lives and choices. But the discourse of "choice" alone has not provided a sustaining moral framework for handling the necessity of abortion, which will always be a final recourse. What is needed is a framework that can simultaneously be compatible with liberal and feminist values.

In fact, the inadequacy of our current categories has been known for some time. In the early 1980s, in a study widely known among anthropologists, Faye D. Ginsburg (*Contested Lives: The Abortion Debate in an American Community*) listened to women in Fargo, North Dakota, after the opening of the controversial Fargo Women's Health Center. The pro-life activists remembered their mothers' suffering in raising children they could not afford; the pro-choice activists described what they called their "Midwestern feminism," rooted in responsibility to kin, community, and a larger social order. Both saw reproductive decision-making as an opportunity to affirm the importance of family and nurturance in the context of a society that they perceived as increasingly committed to rationalism and personal fulfillment.

Yet it is surprising how little the current discourse on either side of the abortion debate is connected to family and social welfare (although in the United States, too, the promotion of birth control was linked to eugenic concerns through the mid-twentieth century). It is a pattern that differentiates American feminism from many industrial democracies, as Eastern Europeanist Kristen Ghodsee and I have noted in an unpublished essay, "Is Individual Liberation Good for Women?" arguing that feminism in the social democracies and post-socialist East Europe has emphasized a better life for women through securing social and economic security, even at the cost of individual liberties.

Perhaps the hesitation to address abortion rights in the context of family is also because the Left has had to respond to an increasingly extremist Right. The conservative judges who dissented in *Roe v. Wade* worried that the decision disempowered individual states from wrestling with the "relative importance of the continued existence and development of the fetus . . . against a spectrum of possible impacts on the mothers." These judges recognized the need to balance competing needs within the family. However, the humanization of the fetus in today's political environment feels threatening rather than considerate, as conservatives push to use ultrasound images to change the minds of women who seek to terminate their pregnancies. And then there are cases of women who have been prosecuted for unhealthy practices such as smoking or other drug abuse while pregnant.

How can liberals include a concern for family in their discourse, so as not to cede this issue to the Right? Some thinkers, such as the communitarian moral philosopher Michael J. Sandel, have suggested that liberals must take a position on the life of the fetus; they can no longer ignore the issue. Feminist provocateur Naomi Wolf wrote in the *New Republic* several years ago that liberals must recognize abortion's inhumanity. Others, such as the moral philosopher Judith Jarvis Thompson, have made the case that even if we grant the humanity of the fetus, a woman is still not ethically obliged to keep it. All these interventions are helpful. But what I am suggesting here is slightly different; it is a greater focus on the dignity and importance of parenthood.

From a medical standpoint, some have begun to question whether obstetrical practices that are rooted in the view of the fetus as autonomous constitute "best practices." In a recent issue of *Obstetrics and Gynecology*, a group of medical sociologists, philosophers, and ethicists founded by Anne D. Lyerly and Maggie Little, who focus on the issue of risk in obstetrical practice, expressed concern with obstetrical practices that are rooted in the view of the fetus as autonomous. They explore, for instance, how obstetricians should ethically balance a mother's need for antidepressants or asthma medications against the small likelihood of risk to the fetus. Should not physicians take into account the indisputable truth that the welfare and empowerment of the mother are also related to the outcome of the pregnancy?

As pundits, politicians, physicians, and others grapple for some vocabulary to enter into this new terrain, popular culture is already moving out in front. The 2007 film *Juno,* for example, captured pregnancy in a way that was startlingly fresh, highlighting the inadequacy of the standard "pro-choice" rhetoric, while remaining firmly in the liberal camp. *Juno* plays with all the tropes of "pro-life" and "pro-choice" discourse, tossing them aside like so many clichés. Upon learning that she is pregnant from a sexual encounter with her high school boyfriend, Juno, a slacker-type who lives with her father and step mother, dutifully phones a clinic she finds in the yellow pages ("Women Now"), telling them in dead-pan fashion that she wishes to "procure a hasty abortion." (She reassures her boyfriend that she intends to "nip it in the bud.") In front of the clinic, Juno finds her high-school friend Su-Chin, carrying placards and chanting perfunctorily, "All babies want to get born!" Juno shrugs off her friend and proceeds into the clinic. In the end, however, she is unable to go through with the procedure. She leaves the clinic and, after deliberating with another friend, instead decides to seek a family to adopt the baby, consulting the classifieds in the local paper. Amid the advertisements, Juno finds an elegant, loving, stable young couple who, she decides, will be the perfect parents, and, in what follows, Juno cultivates a deep attachment to the new parents.

Through her connection to them, Juno experiences many parent-like moments, sharing images of the ultrasound, imagining names, and visiting the home during the daytime to bond over music and horror films with the husband. In one scene, Juno and the husband begin to dance, listening to oldies, and, as Juno rests her head on the husband's shoulder, her pregnant stomach protruding between them, one senses that Juno has fallen in love with him—but less as an object of erotic desire and more as the father of her imagined child. In another scene, Juno encounters the wife at a shopping mall and beams as the prospective mother is able to feel the baby kick.

Through this romantic fantasy, the movie offers a different approach to the politics of pregnancy. Liberals can be moved by Juno's decision to carry the baby to term, because it is rooted in something different from the inherent personhood of the fetus ("the right to life"). At the same time, Juno's "choice" is not constructed in terms of autonomy or freedom but rather in the context of Juno's growing relationships to others: the new mother Juno chooses to adopt the baby; Juno's old-fashioned working-class dad, who, despite what he might consider a source of "shame," supports her decision; and, in particular, one of the film's heroes, Juno's imperfect stepmother, a hard-bitten woman who becomes Juno's champion and caregiver during her pregnancy, but who doesn't hesitate to remind Juno of the sacrifices she has made to help raise her and her sister. The handsome husband of the young couple (the prospective father) who, through Juno, clings to his fantasy of remaining young and unburdened is the one figure regarded with disdain. What Juno's pregnancy affirms is neither the autonomy of fetus or woman but the value of committed social relationships, the desire to make a social contribution, and the struggle to care for those one is responsible for.

Policy analysts, moral philosophers, and social scientists—all have expressed dissatisfaction with the stale terms of the debate on abortion and the fetus. As the debate unfolds, encumbered by the language of autonomy and rights that both sides marshal to make their case, it is worth remembering that the United States looks unusual in the context of other industrial democracies, and that elsewhere it is more intuitive for liberals as well as conservatives to see pregnancy—and abortion—in terms of family.

AMY BOROVOY is an Associate Professor of East Asian Studies at Princeton University. Her research focuses on Japanese culture, including issues of public health and women's roles; she has published a number of articles as well as a book, *The Too-Good Wife: Alcohol, Codependency, and the Politics of Nurturance in Postwar Japan* (University of California Press, 2005).

EXPLORING THE ISSUE

Is Abortion Immoral?

Critical Thinking and Reflection

1. Proponents of legalized abortion typically prefer the term "pro-choice" rather than "pro-abortion." Based on the arguments presented by Borovoy in favor of abortion, which term do you think is more accurate? Explain your answer.
2. Opponents of legalized abortion typically prefer the term "pro-life" rather than "anti-abortion." Based on the arguments presented by Meehan against abortion, which term do you think is more accurate? Explain your answer.
3. Because human pregnancy is a complex process, many factors must be considered in determining whether a zygote, embryo, or fetus should be accorded the moral status of a person. Which factors about human pregnancy are morally relevant to this determination? Do these factors support or undermine the assertion that an unborn human should be morally regarded as a person? Explain your answer.
4. What alternative solutions can be found to the problems that typically lead women to consider abortion?
5. What impact would the development of a safe, reliable, easily accessible method for transferring a human embryo from one uterus to another (either natural or artificial) have on the morality of abortion? Explain your answer.

Is There Common Ground?

Meehan and Borovoy are both dissatisfied with the traditional positions usually staked out by conservatives and liberals in the abortion debate. Meehan believes that a genuinely pro-life attitude has much in common with liberal rather than conservative values. Her position is in agreement with ideas expressed by groups such as Feminists for Life, who contend that it is essential to resolve the problems that lead women to consider abortion, such as employers and schools that are hostile to the needs of pregnant workers and students.

Borovoy is part of a movement within feminism to situate the abortion decision not within an opposition between the interests of the woman and the embryo or fetus, but within the special relationship that a woman has with her embryo or fetus. Some contemporary feminists claim that this relationship entails both rights and responsibilities, including the right—or even the responsibility—to abort under certain circumstances. While this position is still squarely in the pro-choice camp, it assigns a much greater value to the unborn child than traditional pro-choice arguments that compare an embryo or fetus to a mere clump of cells to be removed, or to an unrelated intruder to be evicted.

Create Central

www.mhhe.com/createcentral

Additional Resources

David Boonin, *A Defense of Abortion* (Cambridge University Press, 2002)

Anne Hendershott, *The Politics of Abortion* (Encounter Books, 2006)

Louis Pojman and Francis J. Beckwith, *The Abortion Controversy: 25 Years after Roe vs. Wade, a Reader* (Wadsworth, 1998)

Laurie J. Schrage, *Abortion & Social Responsibility: Depolarizing the Debate* (Oxford University Press, 2003)

Internet References . . .

Ethics Updates: Internet Resources on Abortion

http://ethics.sandiego.edu/Applied/Abortion/index.asp

Feminists for Life

www.feministsforlife.org

NARAL Pro Choice America

www.naral.org

National Right to Life

www.nrlc.org/

Selected, Edited, and with Issue Framing Material by:
Owen M. Smith, *Stephen F. Austin State University*
and
Anne Collins Smith, *Stephen F. Austin State University*

ISSUE

Is It Morally Right to Prohibit Same-Sex Marriage?

YES: Helen M. Alvaré, from "Brief of Amicus Curiae Helen M. Alvaré in Support of Hollingsworth and Bipartisan Legal Advisory Group" in *Hollingsworth v. Perry, U.S. v. Windsor,* Supreme Court of the United States (2013)

NO: The American Psychological Association et al., from "Brief of Amici Curiae in Support of Affirmance" in *Hollingsworth v. Perry,* Supreme Court of the United States (2013)

Learning Outcomes

After reading this issue, you will be able to:

- Understand social changes with regard to marriage over the past century.
- Describe the role of government in defining marriage and determining/restricting the eligibility of certain people to enter into a marriage.
- Formulate your own position on same-sex marriage and identify evidence supporting your position.
- Identify the main objections to your position and formulate responses to these objections.

ISSUE SUMMARY

YES: Law professor Helen Alvaré argues that the state's interest in promoting opposite-sex marriage stems from its interest in the procreation of children by opposite-sex married couples. Moreover, Alvaré traces the decline of marriage to the loss of traditional connections among marriage, sex, and children. State recognition of same-sex marriage would further undermine these connections and thus contribute to the destabilization of marriage, with negative repercussions to society, especially among the poor. Therefore, she argues, the state has an interest in prohibiting same-sex marriage.

NO: The American Psychological Association joins together with a number of other groups to argue that the substantial benefits that accrue to married couples should not be denied to same-sex couples. Citing evidence in favor of the ability of same-sex couples to form stable, long-lasting, committed relationships, they argue that denying marriage to same-sex couples unfairly stigmatizes and discriminates against them.

In the United States, individual states and Native American jurisdictions have the authority to determine eligibility requirements for marriage licenses. Until recently, eligibility for marriage was either explicitly or presumptively restricted to opposite-sex couples. Over the last several decades, the movement to broaden these eligibility requirements to include same-sex couples has achieved significant success, both in terms of legislative initiatives establishing the right of same-sex couples to marry and legal challenges to laws that prohibit same-sex marriage. Currently, approximately one-third of the population of the United States lives in areas that permit same-sex couples to marry. Furthermore, when the Supreme Court declared a key provision of the Defense of Marriage Act (DOMA) unconstitutional in 2013, the federal government was required to recognize same-sex married couples as spouses for purposes of all federal laws.

Eligibility for marriage confers important practical advantages upon a couple. The government of the United States offers its citizens a vast array of incentives to marry, including tax advantages, access to a spouse's Social Security and veteran's benefits, health care decision-making privileges, family leave, and laws designed to protect spouses' interests in case of separation or divorce. These benefits have long been available to heterosexual couples, and access to these benefits by same-sex couples is a principal goal of those who wish to gain legal recognition of/ for same-sex marriage.

Nevertheless, for many same-sex couples, the right to marry is fundamentally an issue of fairness, not benefits. In their view, there are no relevant differences between people who desire to marry members of their own sex and people who desire to marry members of the opposite sex. In the absence of relevant differences between the two groups, they argue, the two groups should have the same rights and privileges, including the right to marry the spouse of their choice. Denying them this right, they insist, is unfair and immoral.

Opponents of the legalization of same-sex marriages typically seek to frame the debate carefully. The morality (and legality) of same-sex marriages, they insist, is distinct from issues concerning homosexual orientation and homosexual activity. They do not deny that same-sex couples and opposite-sex couples are being treated differently under the law. Rather, they point to differences between same-sex couples and opposite-sex couples and assert that these differences are relevant to the issue of whether same-sex marriage is moral and should receive government approval.

Helen Alvaré is an opponent of the legalization of same-sex marriage. She first addresses the basis for governmental interest in marriage. Since the state would cease to exist unless current citizens reproduced and brought new generations of citizens into existence, she argues, the state has a legitimate interest in promoting marriages in which children can be produced. Opposite-sex couples are able to procreate and contribute directly to the next generation of citizens, while same-sex couples are not. For this reason, the state has a legitimate interest in promoting the marriage of opposite-sex couples, not same-sex couples.

While this argument may provide support for governmental recognition of opposite-sex marriage, it is neutral toward governmental recognition of same-sex marriage; there may be reasons other than the production of new citizens that justify bestowing the right to marry on same-sex couples. Therefore, Alvaré offers an additional argument that the state actually has an interest in opposing same-sex marriage. Alvaré observes that our society has, over the past several decades, experienced a decrease in the stability of marriage and the nuclear family: fewer people are getting married and staying married, and more children are being born out of wedlock. Moreover, this decrease is not spread evenly across society; it is disproportionately found among the poor. The combination of poverty and single parenthood is associated with a multitude of problems both for the poor themselves and for society as a whole, not the least of which is a greater probability of poverty and single parenthood in subsequent generations. Alvaré traces the destabilization of marriage to the delinking of marriage, sex, and procreation, which were formerly closely connected to one another in our society. She argues that sanctioning same-sex marriage will contribute to this delinking, thereby worsening the decline of marriage and, as a consequence, the plight of the poorest members of society. In order to promote the welfare of its poorest citizens, she concludes, the state should prohibit same-sex marriage.

In January, 2013, the American Psychological Association (APA), together with other organizations, filed a brief with the U.S. Supreme Court supporting the legality of same-sex marriage. This brief begins with an explanation by the APA regarding scientific research; it is especially important to note the APA does not reject studies simply because they disagree with the conclusion. Based on the research they have examined, the APA makes two key assertions: (1) same-sex couples are capable of forming stable, long-lasting relationships similar to those formed by opposite-sex couples, and (2) children raised by same-sex parents in stable, committed relationships are as healthy and well-adjusted as children raised by opposite-sex parents. Moreover, they point to research conducted among opposite-sex couples showing that those who are married are generally happier and healthier than unmarried opposite-sex couples who live together. Thus, there appear to be significant psychological and physical health benefits of marriage. If same-sex couples are not allowed to marry, the APA argues, they will be deprived of these benefits. Since this deprivation is not justified by any research findings, the APA concludes that it can only be based on unfair discrimination.

YES

Helen M. Alvaré

Brief of Amicus Curiae Helen M. Alvaré in Support of Hollingsworth and Bipartisan Legal Advisory Group

I. The State Has at Least a Legitimate, But More Likely a Compelling, Interest in Singling Out Opposite-Sex Marriage for Protection, Sufficient to Satisfy the Equal Protection Clause

Plaintiffs[1] in these cases claim that the Equal Protection Clause of the Fourteenth Amendment prohibits states from defining marriage as the union of a man and a woman. In addition to the many contrary arguments asserted by the *Hollingsworth* Petitioners, this *amicus* adds that this Court should recognize that states have governmental interests sufficient to justify their recognizing opposite-sex but not same-sex partnerships as "marriages."

States are constitutionally permitted in legislation to classify people into groups that "possess distinguishing characteristics relevant to interests the State has the authority to implement."[2]

Even more relevant to the question of same-sex marriage, this Court has affirmed the constitutionality of state classifications where recognizing or benefitting one group "promotes a legitimate governmental purpose, and the addition of other groups would not."[3]

As described in Section III below, recognizing same-sex marriage as the institution defined by Plaintiffs—as an adult-centered, emotion-based accomplishment—would not only fail to promote the government's substantial interest in opposite-sex marriages, but contradict that interest in ways likely to harm the segment of society already suffering the most from a retreat from marriage.

In *Perry*, the Ninth Circuit held that California's Proposition 8 "operates with no apparent purpose but to impose on gays and lesbians . . . a majority's private disapproval of them and their relationships."[4] The district

court concluded similarly, partially relying on the fact that "California, like every other state, has never required that individuals entering a marriage be willing or able to procreate."[5] Yet the lack of a pre-marital "procreation test" does not undermine the legitimacy of the state's classifying couples as same-sex or opposite-sex, and offering marriage only to the latter.

This Court has repeatedly stated that "[t]he rationality commanded by the Equal Protection Clause does not require States to match . . . distinctions and the legitimate interests they serve with razorlike precision"[6] or "mathematical nicety."[7] Rather, classifications that neither involve fundamental rights nor suspect classifications are "accorded a strong presumption of validity."[8] For such classifications, the government is not required to "actually articulate at any time the purpose or rationale supporting its classification,"[9] and a court should uphold it against an Equal Protection challenge "if there is any reasonably conceivable state of facts that could provide a rational basis for the classification."[10]

Moreover, even if intermediate scrutiny applies (as for gender-based classifications) an exact fit is not required. Intermediate scrutiny mandates only a "substantial relation" between the classification and the underlying objective, not a perfect fit.[11] "None of our gender-based classification equal protection cases have required that the statute . . . be capable of achieving its ultimate objective in every instance."[12]

In *Perry*, the voters of the State of California drew a distinction between same-sex and opposite-sex couples that is rationally and substantially related to California's interests in preserving the link between sex, marriage, and procreation. In *Windsor*, Congress made the same calculation in enacting the Defense of Marriage Act. No same-sex couples can procreate; the vast majority of opposite-sex couples can and do. According to the Census Bureau, by the age of 44, over 80% of married couples have children in the household. This figure does not even include couples whose children are older or have moved away from home.[13]

Given the invasions of privacy that would certainly be involved in ascertaining couples' procreative willingness and capacities prior to marriage, the possibility of unintended pregnancies, and couples' changing intentions, it would be impossible for states, effectively, to determine the procreative potential of any particular opposite-sex couple. Drawing a line between same-sex and opposite-sex couples is rationally related to the state's interests in maintaining in the public mind the links between sex, marriage, and children.

II. This Court Has Regularly and Frequently Recognized with Approval the Importance of States' Interests in the Procreative Aspects of Opposite-Sex Marriage. While It Has Also Recognized That Marriage Serves Adults' Interests in Happiness and Stability, the Court Has Not Isolated These from the Procreative Aspects of Marriage

Supreme Court decisions from the early nineteenth to the late twentieth century have repeatedly recognized, with approval, states' interests in the procreative features of marriage: childbirth and childrearing by the adults who conceived them, and the contribution of that childrearing to a stable democratic society.

The Court has written a great deal on the nature of the states' interests in the context of evaluating state laws affecting entry into or exit from marriage, or concerning parental rights and obligations. Typically, these statements recognize that states are vitally interested in marriage because of the advantages not only to adults but also to children and to the larger society. Children replenish communities, and communities benefit when children are reared by their biological parents because parents best assist children to grow to become well-functioning citizens. The Court does not give special attention to adults' interests nor accord them extra weight. Nor are the interests of some children vaulted over the interests of all children generally.

The material below considers the various manners in which this Court has, in the past, discoursed approvingly about marriage and parenting as expressing states'

interwoven interests in the flourishing of adults, children, and society.

A. States have substantial interest in the birth of children.

While it is difficult to disentangle completely the Court's language recognizing a legitimate state interest in the very birth of children from the state's interest in the healthy *formation* of children within marriage, still it is possible to discern it.

In the case refusing to allow polygamy on the grounds of the Free Exercise Clause, *Reynolds v. United States*, this Court explained states' interests in regulating marriage with the simple declaration: "Upon [marriage] society may be said to be built."[14] Nearly 100 years later in *Loving v. Virginia,* striking down a state's anti-miscegenation law, the Court referred to marriage as "fundamental to our very existence and survival," necessarily endorsing the role of marriage in propagating society through childbearing.[15]

Even in cases where *only* marriage or childbearing was at issue, but not both, the Court has referred to "marriage and childbirth" together in the same phrase, nearly axiomatically. The following cases illustrate:

- In *Meyer v. Nebraska*, which vindicated parents' constitutional right to have their children instructed in a foreign language, this Court referred not merely to parents' rights to care for children but to citizens' rights "to marry, establish a home and bring up children."[16]
- In *Skinner v. Oklahoma ex rel. Williamson*, concerning a law punishing certain classifications of felons with forced sterilization, the Court opined: "Marriage and procreation are fundamental to the very existence and survival of the race."[17]
- In *Zablocki v. Redhail*, which struck down a Wisconsin law restricting marriage for certain child support debtors, the Court wrote: "[I]t would make little sense to recognize a right of privacy with respect to other matters of family life and not with respect to the decision to enter the relationship that is the foundation of the family in our society."[18] As in *Loving, Zablocki* reiterated that marriage is "fundamental to our very existence and survival,"[19] and recognized, additionally the right to "deci[de] to marry and raise the child in a traditional family setting."[20]
- The 1977 opinion in *Moore v. City of East Cleveland,* announcing a blood-and-marriage-related family's constitutional right to co-reside, nonetheless referenced the procreative aspect of family life stating: "the institution of the family is deeply rooted in this Nation's history and tradition. It

is through the family that we inculcate and pass down many of our most cherished values, moral and cultural."[21]

- Similarly, in *Parham v. J.R.*, a case treating parents' rights to direct their children's health care, the Court stated: "Our jurisprudence historically has reflected Western civilization concepts of the family as a unit with broad parental authority over minor children."[22]

B. States have substantial interest in the way marriage socializes children.

A second prominent theme in this Court's prior cases touching upon marriage is the unique importance of the marital family for forming and educating citizens for the continuation of a free, democratic society.

Preliminarily, in cases in which natural parents' interests in directing children's upbringing have conflicted with the claims of another, this Court has approvingly noted the importance of the bond between parents and their natural children. This is found in its observations that states presume that biological parents' "natural bonds of affection" lead them to make decisions for their children that are in the children's best interests. Statements in this vein have been made in *Parham v. J.R.* ("historically [the law] has recognized that natural bonds of affection lead parents to act in the best interests of their children"[23]), in *Smith v. Organization of Foster Families for Equality & Reform* (families' "blood relationship" forms part of the "importance of the familial relationship, to the individuals involved and to the society"[24]), and in the "grandparents' rights" case of *Troxel v. Granville* ("there is a presumption that fit parents act in the best interests of their children"[25]). . . .

Reflecting upon states' continual interest in marriage legislation, in a case concerning the affordability of divorce process, Justice Black's dissenting opinion (objecting to the expansion of the contents of the federal Due Process Clause) in *Boddie v. Connecticut,* asserted that: "The States provide for the stability of their social order, for the good morals of all their citizens and for the needs of children from broken homes. The States, therefore, have particular interests in the kinds of laws regulating their citizens when they enter into, maintain and dissolve marriages."[26]

In the 1977 case in which this Court refused to extend equal parental rights to foster parents, the court wrote about the relationships between family life and the common good stating: "Thus the importance of the familial relationship, to the individuals involved and to the society, stems from the emotional attachments that derive from the intimacy of daily association, and from

the role it plays in 'promot[ing] a way of life' through the instruction of children, as well as from the fact of blood relationship."[27]

As recently as 1983, in the single father's rights case, *Lehr v. Robertson,* the Court referenced the social purposes of the family quite explicitly in terms of states' legitimate interest in maintaining the link between marriage and procreation. Refusing to treat an unmarried father identically to a married father with respect to rights concerning the child, the Court wrote: "marriage has played a critical role . . . in developing the decentralized structure of our democratic society. In recognition of that role, and as part of their general overarching concern for serving the best interests of children, state laws almost universally express an appropriate preference for the formal family."[28]

In summary, it is fair to conclude, upon a review of this Court's family law jurisprudence, that states' interests in the procreational aspects of marriage have been both recognized by this Court and affirmed to be not only legitimate, but essential.

C. The view of marriage advocated by Plaintiffs in *Perry* and *Windsor* ignores children and society.

Undoubtedly the state also values adults' interests in marriage: adult happiness, mutual commitment, increased stability, and social esteem. Yet a view of marriage that focuses solely on these adult-centric interests is incomplete and denies the Court's decisions affirming the states' interests in procreation and healthy childrearing by stably linked, biological parents. It also risks institutionalizing, in law and culture, a notion of marriage that is at the core of an alarming "retreat from marriage" among disadvantaged Americans. (See, *infra,* Section III.)

Same-sex marriage proponents take great pains to excise references to children when quoting this Court's family law opinions. In their Complaint and Trial Memorandum in *Perry,* for example, Plaintiffs reference from *Loving v. Virginia* only the language about marriage as a "basic civil right" of adults, or a "vital personal right essential to the orderly pursuit of happiness by free men," leaving out *Loving's* immediately adjoining reference to marriage as the fount of society.[29] Plaintiffs similarly quote *Cleveland Board of Education v. La Fleur*[30] without noting that the freedom at issue there was a married teacher's "deciding to bear a child."[31]

Perhaps the most egregious example of Plaintiffs' selectively quoting from this Court's opinions addressing the meaning of marriage is their misuse of *Turner v. Safley,* the case in which this Court held that certain prisoners were required to have access to state-recognized marriage.[32] Plaintiffs cite *Turner* for the proposition that civil marriage is an "'expression . . . of emotional support and public commitment,'" and "an exercise in spiritual unity, and a fulfillment of one's self."[33] The district court's Findings of Fact and Conclusions of Law does likewise, selectively quoting only the adult-related aspects of this Court's statements about the meaning of marriage and excising references to procreation.[34]

However, *Turner* explicitly acknowledged, in two ways, both the adults' *and* the procreative interests in marriage. . . . *Turner* concluded that adults' interests were only "elements" or "an aspect" of marriage,[35] and that marriage had other "incidents" that prisoners would eventually realize, referring specifically to consummation, *i.e.* heterosexual intercourse with a spouse.[36] . . .

In reality, proponents of same-sex marriage ask this Court to insist that every state enact and convey a *new* understanding of marriage. This new understanding would signify that what the state values about sexually intimate couples is their emotional happiness and willingness to commit to one another, exclusively, for a long time.[37] In the case of same-sex couples, marriage would additionally connote that the state and society are sorry for past discrimination and stigmatizing of gays and lesbians.[38] However, this understanding completely disregards the procreative aspects of marriage which this Court has recognized as essential. At the same time, it paints a picture of marriage closely associated with a retreat from marriage among the most vulnerable Americans.

Notably, proponents of same-sex marriage acknowledge the power of marriage laws to affect citizens' perceptions and behavior. Indeed, a change of perceptions and behaviors is precisely what the Plaintiffs sought in bringing suit,[39] and what the courts below attempted to achieve in upholding the Plaintiffs' claims.[40] Plaintiffs specifically urge that marriage *not* be understood to imply procreation. . . .

Importantly, same-sex marriage proponents' attempt to redefine "marriage" to excise childbearing, and childrearing comes at a time in history when new empirical data shows that childbearing and childrearing in marriage is threatened—a threat disproportionately visited upon the most vulnerable populations. (See Section III.) States have responded to the data. In fact, over the past 20 years, the legislatures in all 50 states have introduced bills to reform their marriage and divorce laws precisely to better account for children's interests in their parents' marriages.[41] The federal government has done the same, particularly via the marriage-promotion sections of the landmark "welfare reform" law passed in 1996 by bipartisan majorities,

and signed into law by President Clinton.[42] Furthermore, Presidents Bush and Obama, in particular, have promoted extensive federal efforts on behalf of marriage and fatherhood.[43]

In sum, the Court should reaffirm its many prior statements supporting the interests of states in childbearing, childrearing, and social stability that are advanced by opposite-sex marriages. It should resist Plaintiffs' effort to redefine marriage. That states and the federal government may have ignored children's interests too much in the past, is not a reason why states may not choose, and are not choosing today, to legislate to better account for both children's and society's robustly and empirically supported interests in marriage.

III. Redefining Marriage in a Way That De-links Sex, Marriage and Children Can Harm the Most Vulnerable Americans and Exacerbate the "Marriage Gap," Which Is Responsible for Increasing Levels of Social Inequality in America

The disappearing of children's interests in marriage, both at law and in culture, and the vaulting of adults' emotional and status interests, are, today, associated with a great deal of harm, particularly among the most vulnerable Americans. This, in turn, has led to a growing gap between the more and less privileged in the United States, threatening our social fabric. Recognizing same-sex marriage would confirm and exacerbate these trends. Consequently, states legitimately may wish to reconfirm their commitment to opposite-sex marriage on the grounds of its procreative aspects, and refuse to grant marriage recognition to same-sex couples. Speaking quite generally, law and culture before the 1960s normatively held together sex, marriage, and children. Obviously, this was not true in the life of every citizen or family, but social and legal norms widely reflected it. In the ensuing decades, however, these links deteriorated substantially.

First, the link between sex and children weakened with the introduction of more advanced birth control technology and abortion, both of which came to fore in the 1960s and were announced to be constitutional rights by this Court in the 1960s and 1970s. Then, the link between marriage and children was substantially weakened by the passage of no-fault divorce laws during the 1970s. The transcripts of debates concerning the uniform no-fault divorce law reveal the degree to which children's interests were minimized in favor of adult interests, sometimes with mistaken beliefs about children's resiliency and sometimes on the false assertion that most failing marriages were acrimonious such that divorce would benefit, not harm children.[44]

New reproductive technologies further separated children from marriage and sex from children. Since the creation of the first "test tube baby" in 1978, which spawned a billion dollar industry in the United States, neither the federal government nor any states have passed meaningful restraints on such practices. There are today, still, almost no laws affecting who may access these technologies or obtain "donor" sperm, oocytes, or embryos.[45] This persists despite troubling indications that "donor children" experience an enhanced risk of physical or psychological difficulties.[46]

Interwoven with these developments is the declining stigma of nonmarital sex, and even nonmarital pregnancies and births, which further separate sex from marriage, but not always from children.

The effects of these legal and social developments are not evenly distributed across all segments of the population. In fact, a robust and growing literature indicates that more privileged Americans—*i.e.* non-Hispanic Whites, and Americans with a college education—are economically and educationally pulling away from other social classes to an alarming degree.[47] In the words of prominent sociologists W. Bradford Wilcox and Andrew J. Cherlin:

> In the affluent neighborhoods where many college-educated American [s] live, marriage is alive and well and stable families are the rule . . . . [T]he divorce rate in this group has declined to levels not seen since the early 1970s. In contrast, marriage and family stability have been in decline in the kinds of neighborhoods that we used to call working class . . . . More . . . of them are having children in brittle cohabiting unions. . . . [T]he risk of divorce remains high. . . . The national retreat from marriage, which started in low-income communities in the 1960s and 1970s, has now moved into Middle America.[48]

By the numbers, Americans with no more than a high school degree, African Americans, and some groups of Hispanic Americans cohabit more, marry less often, divorce more, have lower marital quality, and have more nonmarital births than those possessing a college degree, sometimes by very large margins. The situation for those with less than a high school degree is even more dire. A few comparisons portray the situation.

- Among Americans with a college degree or more, the nonmarital birth rate is a mere 6%. Among those with only a high school degree, the rate is 44%, and among those without a high school degree, the rate is 54%.[49]
- Poor men and women are only half as likely to marry as those with incomes at three or more times the poverty level.[50]
- The children of these less-privileged groups are far less likely to be living with both their mother and their father, more likely to have a nonmarital pregnancy, and less likely to graduate college or to obtain adequate employment as an adult.[51] . . .

What best explains these trends among the disadvantaged are changes in norms regarding the relationships between sexual activity, births and marriage. Among these, researchers note legal changes emphasizing parenthood but not marriage (*e.g.* strengthened child support enforcement laws), and emphasizing individual rights as distinguished from marriage. They also point to the declining stigma of nonmarital sex, particularly among the lesser educated, and the availability of the pill for separating sex and children.[52] Professor Cherlin writes that law and culture made other ways of living, as distinguished from marriage, not only more acceptable, but also more practically feasible.[53]

Among the lesser privileged, stable employment for the man and a love relationship are the precursors for marriage. The disadvantaged are far less concerned than the more privileged about having children without marriage. To them, marriage is not about children, and children do not necessarily indicate the wisdom of marrying.

And there is further evidence that this trend away from linking children's well-being to a stable home with both a mother and a father is becoming characteristic not only of the disadvantaged, but also of the "millennial generation" as well.[54] Professor Cherlin confirms that among young adults who are not necessarily poor, the idea of "soulmate" marriage is spreading. Never-married Millennial report at a rate of 94% that "when you marry, your [sic] want your spouse to be your soul mate, first and foremost." They hope for a "super relationship," an "intensely private, spiritualized union, combining sexual fidelity, romantic love, emotional intimacy, and togetherness."[55] . . .

Professor Cherlin points to an emphasis on emotional satisfaction and romantic love and an "ethic of expressive individualism that emerged around the 1960s." There is a focus on bonds of sentiment, and the emotional satisfaction of spouses becomes an important criterion for marital success.[56] Professor Cherlin continues, stating that in the later 20th century, "an even more individualistic perspective on the rewards of marriage took root." It was about the "development of their own sense of self and the expression of their feelings, as opposed to the satisfaction they gained through building a family and playing the roles of spouse and parent. The result was a transition from the companionate marriage to what we might call the individualized marriage."[57] . . .

Notwithstanding these troubling trends, Professor Wax concludes that a "strong marriage norm" is an opportunity to "shape the habits of mind necessary to live up to its prescriptions, while also reducing the need for individuals to perform the complicated calculations necessary to chart their own course."[58] Of course, individuals' decisions will be influenced by individual characteristics and circumstances, but "nonetheless, by replacing a complex personal calculus with simple prudential imperatives, a strong expectation of marriage will make it easier . . . for individuals to muster the restraint necessary to act on long-term thinking."[59]

A strong prescription in favor of marriage as the gateway to adult responsibilities and to caring for the next generation would therefore again likely influence behavior in favor of bearing and rearing children by stably linked, biological parents, ready and able to prepare children for responsible citizenship. Simple rules and norms "place less of a burden on the deliberative capacities and will of ordinary individuals." If, however, individuals are left to guide sexual and reproductive choices in a culture of individualism, "people faced with a menu of options engage in a personal calculus of choice. Many will default to a local [short-term, personal gain] perspective."[60]

The "retreat from marriage" and marital childbearing affects not only individuals and their communities. There is evidence that its problematic effects are being felt even at the national level. Largely as a consequence of changes to family structure, including the inter-generational effects of the absence or breakdown of marriage, there is a growing income and wealth gap in the United States among the least educated, the moderately educated, and the college educated. According to a leading study of this phenomenon, family structure changes accounted for 50% to 100% of the increase in child poverty during the 1980s, and for 41% of the increase in inequality between all Americans between 1976 and 2000.[61] The National Marriage Project even suggests that "it is not too far-fetched to imagine that the United States could be heading toward a 21st century version of a traditional Latin American model of family life, where only a comparatively small oligarchy enjoys a stable married and family life."[62]

In conclusion, marriage historian John Witte Jr. has observed that:

> The new social science data present older prudential insights about marriage with more statistical precision. They present ancient avuncular observations about marital benefits with more inductive generalization. They reduce common Western observations about marital health into more precise and measurable categories. These new social science data thus offer something of a neutral apologetic for marriage.[63]

The notion of marriage that same-sex advocates are describing, and demanding from this Court and from every state, closely resembles the adult-centric view of marriage associated with the "retreat from marriage" among disadvantaged Americans. It would intrinsically and overtly separate sex and children from marriage, for every marriage and every couple and every child. It promotes a meaning of marriage that empties it of the procreative interests understood and embraced by this Court (and every prior generation). Rather, as redefined by Plaintiffs, marriage would merely become a reparation, a symbolic capstone, and a personal reward, not a gateway to adult responsibilities, including childbearing, childrearing, and the inculcating of civic virtues in the next generation for the benefit of the larger society.

Of course, it is not solely the fault of same-sex marriage proponents that we have come to a "tipping point" regarding marriage in the United States, where if the procreational aspects of marriage are not explicitly preserved and highlighted, additional harm will come upon vulnerable Americans and our social fabric itself. The historic institution of marriage was already weakened, likely emboldening same-sex marriage advocates to believe that a redefinition of marriage was only a step, not a leap away. But in its essence, and in the arguments used to promote it, same-sex marriage would be the *coup de grâce* to the procreative meanings and social roles of marriage. It is hoped that the necessary movement for equality and non-discrimination for gays and lesbians will choose a new path, and leave marriage to serve the crucial purposes it is needed to serve.

Conclusion

For the foregoing reasons, the Court should reverse the judgments in both these cases.

Notes

1. For simplicity, *amicus* refers to all proponents of same-sex marriage in *Perry, Hollingsworth,* and *Windsor* as "Plaintiffs."
2. *Bd. of Trs. of the Univ. of Ala. v. Garrett,* 531 U.S. 356, 366 (2001) (quotation marks omitted).
3. *Johnson v. Robison,* 415 U.S. 361, 383 (1974).
4. *Perry v. Brown,* 671 F.3d 1052, 1095 (9th Cir. 2012).
5. *Perry v. Schwarzenegger,* No. 3:09-2292-VRW (N.D. Cal.), Findings of Fact and Conclusions of Law 60, ECF No. 708 [hereinafter Findings of Fact; docket entries for court documents electronically filed under No. 3:09-2292-VRW shall be referred to only by their names and ECF numbers].
6. *Kimel v. Fla. Bd. of Regents,* 528 U.S. 62, 63–64 (2000) (age discrimination action brought by university employees).
7. *Dandridge v. Williams,* 397 U.S. 471, 485 (1970) (quoting *Lindsley v. Natural Carbonic Gas Co.,* 220 U.S. 61, 78 (1911)).
8. *Heller v. Doe,* 509 U.S. 312, 319 (1993).
9. *Id.* at 320 (quoting *Nordlinger v. Hahn,* 505 U.S. 1, 15 (1992)).
10. *Id.* (quoting *Federal Commc'ns Comm'n v. Beach Commc'ns, Inc.,* 508 U.S. 307, 313 (1993)).
11. *See Califano v. Webster,* 430 U.S. 313, 318 (1977) (per curiam) (upholding statute providing higher Social Security benefits for women than men because "women *on the average* received lower retirement benefits than men;" *id.* n.5 (emphasis added)).
12. *Tuan Anh Nguyen v. Immigration and Naturalization Serv.,* 533 US. 53, 70 (2001); *see Metro Broad., Inc. v. Federal Commc'ns Comm'n,* 497 U.S. 547, 579, 582–83 (1990), overruled on other grounds, *Adarand Constructors, Inc. v. Peña,* 515 U.S. 200, 227 (1995) (holding that classification need not be accurate "in every case" if, "in the aggregate," it advances the objective).
13. U.S. Census Bureau, *Family Households with Own Children Under Age 18 by Type of Family, 2000 and 2010, and by Age of Householder, 2010,* The 2012 Statistical Abstract: The National Data Book, Table 65, http://www.census.gov/compendia/statab/2012/tables/12s0065.pdf (last visited Jan. 24, 2013).
14. 98 U.S. 145, 165 (1879).
15. 388 U.S. 1, 12(1967).
16. 262 U.S. 390, 399 (1923).
17. 361 U.S. 535, 541 (1942).
18. 434 U.S. 374, 386 (1978).
19. *Id.* at 383.
20. *Id.* at 386.
21. 431 U.S. 494, 503–04 (1977).
22. 442 U.S. 584, 602 (1979).
23. *Id.* at 602.
24. 431 U.S. 816, 844 (1977).
25. 530 U.S. 57, 68 (2000).
26. 401 U.S. 371, 389 (1971) (Black, J., dissenting).
27. *Org. of Foster Families,* 431 U.S. at 844 (citation omitted).
28. 463 U.S. 248, 257 (1983).
29. Compl. for Declaratory, Injunctive, or other Relief 1, E.C.F. No 1 [hereinafter Compl.]; Pls.' & Pl.-Intervenor's Trial Mem. 3, ECF. No. 281 [hereinafter Trial Mem.]. As noted, *Loving* concludes that marriage and family are "fundamental to our very existence and survival." 388 U.S. at 12.
30. Trial Mem. 3–4, ECF. No. 281 (quoting *Cleveland Bd. of Educ. v. LaFleur,* 414 U.S. 632, 639 (1974) ("personal choice in matters of marriage and family life")).
31. 414 U.S. at 640.
32. 482 U.S. 78 (1987).
33. Trial Mem. 6, ECF No. 281 (citing *Turner v. Safley,* 482 U.S. 78, 95–96).
34. See Findings of Fact 110, ECF No. 708. This approach of Plaintiffs and the courts below is not unique. The plaintiffs in the Massachusetts same-sex marriage case similarly affirmed the ability of the law to affect social perceptions, and requested same-sex marriage recognition in order to attain "social recognition and security" for themselves and their daughter. *Goodridge v. Dep't of Pub. Health,* No. 01–1647 (Superior Court, Cnty. of Suffolk, MA (Aug. 2001), Mem. in Supp. of Pls.' Mot. for Summ. J. 1). They stated that marriage recognition would take away a social "badge of inferiority" and instead "instantly" communicate "their relationship . . . to third parties." *Id.* at 19. And the Massachusetts Supreme Court, like Judge Walker and the Ninth Circuit below, excised children from *Zablocki* and *Loving* and *Skinner* and misused *Turner* similarly. *See Goodridge v. Dep't of Pub. Health,* 798 N.E.2d 941, 970 (Mass. 2003).
35. 482 U.S. at 95–96.
36. *See id.* at 96.
37. *See* Compl. 2, 7, ECF No. 1; Findings of Fact 67, ECF No. 708; *Perry v. Brown,* 671 F.3d 1052, 1078 (9th Cir. 2012). The *Goodridge* court and well-known same-sex marriage advocates urge a similar meaning for marriage. *See Goodridge,* 798 N.E.2d at 948 (Marriage is the "exclusive commitment of two individuals to each other."); *see, e.g.,* Andrew Sullivan, *Here Comes the Groom: A (Conservative) Case for Gay Marriage,* New Republic (Aug. 28, 1989, 1:00 AM), http://www.tnr.com/article/79054/here-comes-the-groom# (describing marriage as a "deeper and harder-to-extract-yourself from commitment to another human being"); *Talking about Marriage*

Equality with Your Friends and Family, Human Rights Campaign, www.hrc.org/resources/entry/talking-about-marriage-equality-with-your-friends-and-family (last visited Jan. 24, 2013) (describing marriage as "the highest possible commitment that can be made between two adults").

38. Several times in Plaintiffs' Complaint in *Perry,* they refer to the theme of "gay and lesbian individuals['] . . . long and painful history of societal and government-sponsored discrimination," or to "stigma." Compl. 1, 4, 7–8, ECF No. 1.

39. *See, e.g.,* Compl. 9–10, ECF No. 1 (asserting that recognition of same-sex marriage would produce the result of "hav[ing] society accord their unions and their families the same respect and dignity of opposite-sex unions and families"); Compl. 8, ECF No. 1 (ameliorate the "stigmatizing" gays and lesbians experience and affect their "stature" in the community).

40. *See* Findings of Fact 86–87, ECF No. 708 (marriage recognition would convey that gays and lesbians partake of the "most socially valued form of relationship"); *Perry v. Brown,* 671 F.3d 1052, 1078 (9th Cir. 2012) (suggesting that the state's designation of a relationship as a "marriage," by itself "expresses validation, by the state and the community," and is "a symbol. . . of something profoundly important").

41. *See, e.g.,* Lynn D. Wardle, *Divorce Reform at the Turn of the Millennium: Certainties and Possibilities,* 33 Fam. L.Q. 783, 790 (1999); Karen Gardiner et al., *State Policies to Promote Marriage: Preliminary Report,* The Lewin Group (Mar. 2002).

42. The Personal Responsibility and Work Opportunity Reconciliation Act of 1996, Pub. L. No. 104–193 (1996).

43. *See* Helen M. Alvaré, *Curbing Its Enthusiasm: U.S. Federal Policy and the Unitary Family,* 2 Int'l J. Jurisprudence Fam. 107, 121–24 (2011).

44. *See* Helen M. Alvaré, *The Turn Toward the Self in Marriage: Same-Sex Marriage and Its Predecessors in Family Law,* 16 Stan. L. & Pol'y Rev. 101, 137–53 (2005).

45. *See* The President's Council on Bioethics, *Reproduction and Responsibility: The Regulation of New Biotechnologies* 8–12 (2003).

46. *See* Elizabeth Marquardt et al., *My Daddy's Name Is Donor: A New Study of Young Adults Conceived through Sperm Donation,* Commission on Parenthood's Future (2010); Jennifer J. Kurinczuk & Carol Bower, *Birth defects in infants conceived by intracytoplasmic sperm injection: an alternative explanation,* 315 Brit. Med. J. 1260 (1997).

47. *See, e.g., The Decline of Marriage and Rise of New Families,* Pew Research Center (Nov. 18, 2010),

http://www.pewsocialtrends.org/2010/11/18/the-decline-of-marriage-and-rise-of-newfamilies/; Richard Fry, No *Reversal in Decline of Marriage,* Pew Research Center (Nov. 20, 2012), http://www.pewsocialtrends.org/2012/11/20/no-reversal-in-decline-of-marriage/; Pamela J. Smock & Wendy D Manning, *Living Together Unmarried in the United States: Demographic Perspectives and Implications for Family Policy,* 26 Law & Pol'y 87 (2004); The National Marriage Project and the Institute for American Values, *When Marriage Disappears: The Retreat from Marriage in Middle America,* State of Our Unions (2010), http://stateofourunions.org/2010/when-marriage-disappears.php (last visited Jan. 24, 2013).

48. W. Bradford Wilcox & Andrew J. Cherlin, *The Marginalization of Marriage in Middle America,* Brookings, Aug. 10, 2011, at 2.

49. *Id.*

50. Kathryn Edin & Joanna M. Reed, *Why Don't They Just Get Married? Barriers to Marriage among the Disadvantaged,* The Future of Children, Fall 15(2)2005, at 117–18.

51. Wilcox & Cherlin, *supra,* at 6; The National Marriage Project, *supra,* at 10–11,17 (citing Ron Haskins & Isabel Sawhill, *Creating an Opportunity Society* (2009); Nicholas H. Wolfinger, *Understanding the Divorce Cycle: The Children of Divorce in Their Own Marriages* (2005)).

52. Wilcox & Cherlin, *supra,* at 3–4.

53. Andrew J. Cherlin, *American Marriage in the Early Twenty-First Century,* The Future of Children, Fall 15(2) 2005, at 41.

54. *See* Wendy Wang & Paul Taylor, *For Millennials, Parenthood Trumps Marriage,* Pew Research Center, 2 (Mar. 9, 2011), http://www.pewsocial-trends.org/2011/03/09/for-millennialsparenthood-trumps-marriage/ (on the question of a child's need for two, married parents, 51% of Millennials disagreed in 2008, compared to 39% of Generation Xers in 1997).

55. Andrew J. Cherlin, *The Deinstitutionalization of American Marriage,* 66 J. of Marriage & Fam. 848, 856 (2004).

56. Cherlin, *The Deinstitutionalization of American Marriage, supra,* at 851.

57. *Id.* at 852.

58. *Id.*

59. *Id.*

60. *Id.* at 61.

61. Molly A. Martin, *Family Structure and Income Inequality in Families with Children, 1976–2000,* 43 Demography 421, 423–24, 440 (2006).

62. The National Marriage Project and the Institute for American Values, *supra,* at 17.

63. John Witte, Jr., *The Goods and Goals of Marriage*, 76 Notre Dame L. Rev. 1019, 1070 (2001).

Bibliography

Cases

Adarand Constructors, Inc. v. Peña, 515 U.S. 200 (1995)

Bd. of Trs. of the Univ. of Ala. v. Garrett, 531 U.S. 356 (2001)

Boddie v. Connecticut, 401 U.S. 371 (1971)

Butler v. Wilson, 415 U.S. 953 (1974)

Califano v. Webster, 430 U.S. 313 (1977)

Cleveland Bd. of Educ. v. LaFleur, 414 U.S. 632 (1974)

Dandridge v. Williams, 397 U.S. 471 (1970)

Federal Commc'ns Comm'n v. Beach Commc'ns, Inc., 508 U.S. 307 (1993)

Goodridge v. Dep't of Pub. Health, 798 N.E.2d 941 (Mass. 2003)

Heller v. Doe, 509 U.S. 312 (1993)

Johnson v. Robison, 415 U.S. 361 (1974)

Johnson v. Rockefeller, 365 F. Supp. 377 (S.D.N.Y. 1973)

Kimel v. Fla. Bd. of Regents, 528 U.S. 62 (2000)

Lehr v. Roberston, 463 U.S. 248 (1983)

Lindsley v. Natural Carbonic Gas Co., 220 U.S. 61 (1911)

Loving v. Virginia, 388 U.S. 1 (1967)

Maynard v. Hill, 125 U.S. 190 (1888)

Metro Broad., Inc. v. Federal Commc'ns Comm'n, 497 U.S. 547 (1990)

Meyer v. Nebraska, 262 U.S. 390 (1923)

Moore v. City of East Cleveland, 431 U.S. 494 (1977)

Murphy v. Ramsey, 114 U.S. 15 (1885)

Nordlinger v. Hahn, 505 U.S. 1 (1992)

Parham v. J.R., 442 U.S. 584 (1979)

Perry v. Brown, 671 F.3d 1052 (9th Cir. 2012)

Prince v. Massachusetts, 321 U.S. 158 (1944)

Reynolds v. United States, 98 U.S. 145 (1879)

Skinner v. Oklahoma ex rel. Williamson, 361 U.S. 535 (1942)

Smith v. Org. of Foster Families for Equal. & Reform, 431 U.S. 816 (1977)

Troxel v. Granville, 530 U.S. 57 (2000)

Tuan Anh Nguyen v. Immigration and Naturalization Serv., 533 US. 53 (2001)

Turner v. Safley, 482 U.S. 78 (1987)

Zablocki v. Redhail, 434 U.S. 374 (1978)

Statutes

The Personal Responsibility and Work Opportunity Reconciliation Act of 1996, Pub. L. No. 104–193 (1996).

Other Authorities

Amy L. Wax, *Diverging family structure and "rational" behavior: the decline in marriage as a disorder of choice*, in Research Handbook on the Economics of Family Law (Lloyd R. Cohen & Joshua D. Wright, eds., 2011)

Andrew J. Cherlin, *The Deinstitutionalization of American Marriage*, 66 J. of Marriage & Fam. 848 (2004)

Andrew Sullivan, *Here Comes the Groom: A (Conservative) Case for Gay Marriage*, New Republic (Aug. 28, 1989, 1:00 AM), http://www.tnr.com/article/79054/here-comes-the-groom# (describing marriage as a "deeper and harder-to-extract-yourself from commitment to another human being")

Elizabeth Marquardt et al., *My Daddy's Name Is Donor: A New Study of Young Adults Conceived through Sperm Donation*, Commission on Parenthood's Future (2010)

Garry J. Gates, *Family Focus on . . . LGBT Families: Family Formation and Raising Children among Same-Sex Couples*, National Council on Family Relations Report, Issue FF51, 2011

Helen M. Alvaré, *Curbing Its Enthusiasm: U.S. Federal Policy and the Unitary Family*, 2 Int'l J. Jurisprudence Fam. 107 (2011)

Helen M. Alvaré, *The Turn Toward the Self in Marriage: Same-Sex Marriage and Its Predecessors in Family Law*, 16 Stan. L. & Pol'y Rev. 101 (2005)

Jennifer J. Kurinczuk & Carol Bower, *Birth Defects in Infants Conceived by Intracytoplasmic Sperm Injection: an Alternative Explanation*, 315 Brit. Med. J. 1260 (1997)

John Witte, Jr., *Response to Mark Strasser*, in Marriage and Same-Sex Unions (Lynn Wardle et al., eds., 2003)

John Witte, Jr., *The Goods and Goals of Marriage*, 76 Notre Dame L. Rev. 1019 (2001)

Karen Gardiner et al., *State Policies to Promote Marriage: Preliminary Report*, The Lewin Group (Mar. 2002)

Kathryn Edin & Joanna M. Reed, *Why Don't They Just Get Married? Barriers to Marriage among the Disadvantaged*, The Future of Children, Fall 15(2) 2005

Lynn D. Wardle, *Divorce Reform at the Turn of the Millennium: Certainties and Possibilities*, 33 Fam. L.Q. 783 (1999)

Mark Regnerus, *How Different Are the Adult Children of Parents Who Have Same-Sex Relationships? Findings from the New Family Structures Study*, 41 Soc. Sci. Research 752 (2012)

Molly A. Martin, *Family Structure and Income Inequality in Families with Children, 1976–2000*, 43 Demography 421 (2006)

Nicholas H. Wolfinger, *Understanding the Divorce Cycle: The Children of Divorce in Their Own Marriages* (2005)

Pamela J. Smock & Wendy D. Manning, *Living Together Unmarried in the United States: Demographic Perspectives and Implications for Family Policy*, 26 Law & Policy 87 (2004)

Pamela J. Smock, *The Wax and Wane of Marriage: Prospects for Marriage in the 21st Century*, 66 J. of Marriage & Fam. 966 (2004)

Ron Haskins & Isabel Sawhill, *Creating an Opportunity Society* (2009)

Talking about Marriage Equality with Your Friends and Family, Human Rights Campaign, www.hrc.org/resources/entry/talking-about-marriage-equality-with-your-friends-and-family (last visited Jan. 24, 2013)

The National Marriage Project and the Institute for American Values, *When Marriage Disappears: The Retreat from Marriage in Middle America*, State of Our Unions (2010), http://stateofourunions.org/2010/when-marriage-disappears

The President's Council on Bioethics, *Reproduction and Responsibility: The Regulation of New Biotechnologies* (2003)

U.S. Census Bureau, *Family Households with Own Children Under Age 18 by Type of Family, 2000 and 2010, and by Age of Householder, 2010*, The 2012 Statistical Abstract: The National Data Book, Table 65, http://www.census.gov/compendia/statab/2012/tables/12s0065.pdf (last visited Jan. 24, 2013)

W. Bradford Wilcox & Andrew J. Cherlin, *The Marginalization of Marriage in Middle America*, Brookings, Aug. 10, 2011

Wendy Wang & Paul Taylor, For *Millennials, Parenthood Trumps Marriage*, Pew Research Center (Mar. 9, 2011), http://www.pewsocialtrends.org/2011/03/09/formillennials-parenthood-trumps-marriage/

HELEN M. ALVARÉ is a Professor of Law at George Mason University School of Law, where she teaches Family Law, Law and Religion, and Property Law. She has published in law reviews and other academic journals on matters concerning marriage, parenting, non-marital households, abortion and the First Amendment religion clauses.

**The American Psychological
Association et al.**

 **NO**

Brief of Amici Curiae in Support of Affirmance in *Hollingsworth v. Perry*

Introduction and Summary

As the Ninth Circuit noted, "Proposition 8 had one effect," to "strip[] same-sex couples" of "the right to obtain and use the designation of 'marriage.'" Perry v. Brown, 671 F.3d 1052, 1063 (9th Cir. 2012). By so doing, the initiative withholds from gay men and lesbian women an important symbol of "state legitimization and societal recognition." Id. Some proponents of the initiative claim that this exclusion merely reflects meaningful differences between same-sex and heterosexual relationships, or between the parenting abilities of same-sex and heterosexual couples. The scientific research does not justify those claims.

Rather, scientific evidence strongly supports the conclusion that homosexuality is a normal expression of human sexuality; that most gay, lesbian, and bisexual adults do not experience their sexual orientation as a choice; that gay and lesbian people form stable, committed relationships that are equivalent to heterosexual relationships in essential respects; and that same-sex couples are no less fit than heterosexual parents to raise children and their children are no less psychologically healthy and well-adjusted than children of heterosexual parents. In short, the claim that official recognition of marriage for same-sex couples undermines the institution of marriage and harms their children is inconsistent with the scientific evidence.

The body of research presented below demonstrates that the discrimination effected by Proposition 8 unfairly stigmatizes same-sex couples.

Argument

I. The Scientific Evidence Presented in This Brief

Representing the leading associations of psychological, psychiatric, medical, and social work professionals, Amici have sought in this brief to present an accurate and responsible summary of the current state of scientific and professional knowledge concerning sexual orientation and families relevant to this case.

In drawing conclusions, Amici rely on the best empirical research available, focusing on general patterns rather than any single study. Before citing a study herein, Amici have critically evaluated its methodology, including the reliability and validity of the measures and tests it employed, and the quality of its data-collection procedures and statistical analyses.

Scientific research is a cumulative process and no empirical study is perfect in its design and execution. Even well-executed studies may be limited in their implications and the generalizability of their findings.[1] Accordingly, Amici base their conclusions as much as possible on general patterns rather than any single study.

All scientific studies can be constructively criticized, and scientists continually try to identify ways to improve and refine their own work and that of their colleagues. Thus, many studies cited herein discuss their limitations and provide suggestions for further research. This is consistent with the scientific method and does not impeach the overall conclusions.

Most of the studies and literature reviews cited herein have been peer-reviewed and published in reputable academic journals. In addition, other academic books, book chapters, and technical reports, which typically are not subject to the same peer-review standards as journal articles, are included when they report research employing rigorous methods, are authored by well-established researchers, and accurately reflect professional consensus about the current state of knowledge. Amici have made a good faith effort to include all relevant studies and have not excluded any study because of its findings.

I. Homosexuality Is a Normal Expression of Human Sexuality, Is Generally Not Chosen, and Is Highly Resistant to Change

Sexual orientation refers to an enduring disposition to experience sexual, affectional, and/or romantic attractions to one or both sexes. It also encompasses an individual's sense of personal and social identity based on those attractions, on behaviors expressing those attractions, and on membership in a community of others who share those attractions and behaviors.[2] Although sexual orientation ranges along a continuum from exclusively heterosexual to exclusively homosexual, it is usually discussed in three categories: heterosexual (having sexual and romantic attraction primarily or exclusively to members of the other sex), homosexual (having sexual and romantic attraction primarily or exclusively to members of one's own sex), and bisexual (having a significant degree of sexual and romantic attraction to both sexes).

Although homosexuality was classified as a mental disorder when the American Psychiatric Association published the first Diagnostic and Statistical Manual of Mental Disorders in 1952, only five years later a study sponsored by the National Institute of Mental Health found no evidence to support the classification.[3] On the basis of that study and others demonstrating that the original classification reflected social stigma rather than science,[4] the American Psychiatric Association declassified homosexuality as a mental disorder in 1973. In 1974, the American Psychological Association adopted a policy reflecting the same conclusion. For decades, then, the consensus of mental health professionals and researchers has been that homosexuality and bisexuality are normal expressions of human sexuality and pose no inherent obstacle to leading a happy, healthy, and productive life, and that gay and lesbian people function well in the full array of social institutions and interpersonal relationships.[5]

Most gay men and lesbians do not experience their sexual orientation as resulting from a voluntary choice. In a U.S. national probability sample of 662 self-identified lesbian, gay, and bisexual adults, 88% of gay men and 68% of lesbians reported feeling they had no choice at all about their sexual orientation, while another 7% of gay men and 15% of lesbians reported only a small amount of choice. Only 5% of gay men and 16% of lesbians felt they had a fair amount or a great deal of choice.[6]

Several amici supporting Proposition 8 challenge the conclusion that for most people sexual orientation is not a matter of choice, but they offer no credible scientific support for their position.[7] Moreover, although some groups and individuals have offered clinical interventions that purport to change sexual orientation from homosexual to heterosexual—sometimes called "conversion" therapies—these interventions have not been shown to be effective or safe. A review of the scientific literature by an American Psychological Association task force concluded that sexual orientation change efforts are unlikely to succeed and indeed can be harmful.[8]

All major national mental health organizations—including Amici—have adopted policy statements cautioning the profession and the public about treatments that purport to change sexual orientation.[9]

II. Sexual Orientation and Relationships

Sexual orientation is commonly discussed as a characteristic of the individual, like biological sex or age. This perspective is incomplete because sexual orientation necessarily involves relationships with other people. Sexual acts and romantic attractions are categorized as homosexual or heterosexual according to the biological sex of the individuals involved in them, relative to each other. Indeed, it is only by acting with another person—or desiring to act—that individuals express their heterosexuality, homosexuality, or bisexuality. Thus, sexual orientation is integrally linked to the intimate personal relationships that human beings form with others to meet their deeply felt needs for love, attachment, and intimacy. One's sexual orientation defines the universe of persons with whom one is likely to find the satisfying and fulfilling relationships that, for many individuals, comprise an essential component of personal identity.

A. Gay Men and Lesbian Women Form Stable, Committed Relationships That Are Equivalent to Heterosexual Relationships in Essential Respects

Like heterosexuals, most gay and lesbian people want to form stable, long-lasting relationships,[10] and many of them do: numerous studies using nonprobability samples of gay and lesbian people have found that the vast majority of participants have been in a committed relationship at some point in their lives, that large proportions are currently in such a relationship (40–70% of gay men and 45–80% of lesbian women), and that many of those couples have been together 10 or more years.[11] Survey data from probability samples support these findings.[12] Data from the 2010 US Census show that same-sex couples headed more than 600,000 US households and more than 90,000 in California.[13]

Empirical research demonstrates that the psychological and social aspects of committed relationships between same-sex partners largely resemble those of heterosexual partnerships. Like heterosexual couples, same-sex couples form deep emotional attachments and commitments. Heterosexual and same-sex couples alike face similar issues concerning intimacy, love, equity, loyalty, and stability, and they go through similar processes to address those issues.[14] Empirical research also shows that gay and lesbian couples have levels of relationship satisfaction similar to or higher than those of heterosexual couples.[15]

B. The Institution of Marriage Offers Social, Psychological, and Health Benefits That Are Denied to Same-Sex Couples

Marriage as a social institution has a profound effect on the lives of the individuals who inhabit it. The sociologist Emile Durkheim observed that marriage helps to protect the individual from "anomy," or social disruption and breakdowns of norms.[16] Twentieth-century sociologists advised that marriage creates order[17] and "provides a strong positive sense of identity, self-worth, and mastery."[18] Empirical research demonstrates that marriage has distinct benefits that extend beyond the material necessities of life.[19] These intangible elements of the marital relationship have important implications for the physical and psychological health of married individuals and for the relationship itself.

Because marriage rights have been granted to same-sex couples only recently and only in a few jurisdictions, no empirical studies have yet been published that compare married same-sex couples to unmarried same-sex couples, or those in civil unions. Based on their scientific and clinical expertise, Amici believe it is appropriate to extrapolate from the empirical research literature for heterosexual couples—with qualifications as necessary—to anticipate the likely effects of marriage for same-sex couples.[20]

Married men and women generally experience better physical and mental health than their unmarried counterparts.[21] These health benefits do not appear to result simply from being in an intimate relationship, for most studies have found that married heterosexual individuals generally manifest greater well-being than those of comparable cohabiting couples.[22] Of course, marital status alone does not guarantee greater health or happiness. People who are unhappy in marriage often manifest lower levels of well-being than the unmarried, and marital discord and dissatisfaction is often associated with negative health effects.[23] Nevertheless, satisfied married couples consistently manifest higher levels of happiness, psychological well-being, and physical health than the unmarried.

Being married also is a source of stability and commitment. Marital commitment is a function not only of attractive forces (i.e., rewarding features of the partner or

relationship) but also of external forces that serve as constraints on dissolving the relationship. Barriers to terminating a marriage include feelings of obligation to one's family members; moral and religious values; legal restrictions; financial concerns; and the anticipated disapproval of others.[24] In the absence of adequate rewards, the existence of barriers alone is not sufficient to sustain a marriage in the long term. Perceiving one's intimate relationship primarily in terms of rewards, rather than barriers to dissolution, is likely to be associated with greater relationship satisfaction.[25] Nonetheless, perceived barriers are negatively correlated with divorce and thus the presence of barriers may increase partners' motivation to seek solutions for problems, rather than rushing to dissolve a salvageable relationship.[26]

Lacking access to legal marriage, the primary motivation for same-sex couples to remain together derives mainly from the rewards associated with the relationship rather than from formal barriers to separation.[27] Given this fact, and the legal and prejudicial obstacles that same-sex partners face, the prevalence and durability of same-sex relationships are striking.

Amici emphasize that the abilities of gay and lesbian persons as parents and the positive outcomes for their children are not areas where credible scientific researchers disagree.[28] Thus, after careful scrutiny of decades of research, the American Psychological Association concluded in 2004 that (a) "there is no scientific evidence that parenting effectiveness is related to parental sexual orientation: Lesbian and gay parents are as likely as heterosexual parents to provide supportive and healthy environments for their children" and (b) that "research has shown that the adjustment, development, and psychological well-being of children are unrelated to parental sexual orientation and that the children of lesbian and gay parents are as likely as those of heterosexual parents to flourish." Am. Psychol. Ass'n, Resolution on Sexual Orientation, Parents, and Children (2004), available at http://www.apa.org/about/governance/council/policy/parenting.pdf.

Similarly, the American Academy of Pediatrics has recently adopted a policy statement which states: "Scientific evidence affirms that children have similar developmental and emotional needs, and receive similar parenting, whether they are raised by parents of the same or different genders. If a child has 2 living and capable parents who choose to create a permanent bond by way of civil marriage, it is in the best interests of their child(ren) that legal and social institutions allow and support them to do so, irrespective of their sexual orientation." Am. Acad. of Pediatrics, Committee on Psychosocial Aspects of Child and Family Health, Policy Statement: Promoting the

Well-Being of Children Whose Parents Are Gay or Lesbian, 131 Pediatrics (forthcoming 2013).

NASW has similarly determined that "[t]he most striking feature of the research on lesbian mothers, gay fathers, and their children is the absence of pathological findings. The second most striking feature is how similar the groups of gay and lesbian parents and their children are to heterosexual parents and their children that were included in the studies." Nat'l Ass'n of Soc. Workers, Policy Statement: Lesbian, Gay, and Bisexual Issues, in Social Work Speaks 193, 194 (4th ed. 1997). See also Nat'l Ass'n of Soc. Workers, Policy Statement: Family Planning and Reproductive Choice, in Social Work Speaks 129, 132 (9th ed. 2012).

The American Psychoanalytic Association has likewise determined that "[t]here is no credible evidence that shows that a parent's sexual orientation or gender identity will adversely affect the development of the child." Am. Psychoanalytic Ass'n, Position Statement: Parenting (2012), available at http://www.apsa.org/about_apsaa/position_statements/parenting.aspx.

In adopting an official Position Statement in support of legal recognition of same-sex civil marriage, the American Psychiatric Association observed that "no research has shown that the children raised by lesbians and gay men are less well adjusted than those reared within heterosexual relationships." Am. Psychiatric Ass'n, Position Statement: Support of Legal Recognition of Same-Sex Civil Marriage (2005), available at http://www.psych.org/Departments/EDU/Library/APAOfficialDocumentsandRelated/Position Statements/200502.aspx.

Finally, the American Medical Association likewise has adopted a policy supporting legislative and other reforms to allow adoption by same sex partners.[29]

III. Denying the Status of Marriage to Same-Sex Couples Stigmatizes Them

The foregoing shows that the beliefs about gay men and lesbian women advanced to support Proposition 8—about their capacity for committed, long lasting relationships, and their ability to raise healthy well-adjusted children—are contradicted by the scientific evidence and instead reflect an unreasoned antipathy towards an identifiable minority. In depriving gay men and lesbian women of membership in an important social institution, Proposition 8 conveys the state's judgment that committed intimate relationships between people of the same sex are inferior to heterosexual relationships. This is the essence of stigma.

A stigmatized condition or status is negatively valued by society, defines a person's social identity, and thus disadvantages that person.[30] A classic work in this area characterized stigma as "an undesired differentness."[31] It can be manifested both in social institutions, such as the law, and in individual behaviors. Laws that accord majority and minority groups differing status highlight the perceived "differentness" of the minority and thereby tend to legitimize prejudicial attitudes and individual acts against the disfavored group, including ostracism, harassment, discrimination, and violence. Large numbers of lesbian, gay, and bisexual people experience such acts of prejudice because of their sexual orientation.[32]

Proposition 8 is an instance of institutional stigma. It conveys the government's judgment that, in the realm of intimate relationships, a legally united same-sex couple is inherently less deserving of society's full recognition than are heterosexual couples. As the Ninth Circuit correctly recognized, Proposition 8 "lessen[s] the status and human dignity of gays and lesbians in California." Perry, 671 F.3d at 1063. By devaluing and delegitimizing the relationships that constitute the very core of a homosexual orientation, Proposition 8 compounds and perpetuates the stigma historically attached to homosexuality. This Court has repeatedly recognized the unconstitutional nature of stigmatizing legislation based on stereotypic classifications. See Heckler v. Mathews, 465 U.S. 728, 739–40 (1984) ("[A]s we have repeatedly emphasized, discrimination itself, by perpetuating 'archaic and stereotypic notions' or by stigmatizing members of the disfavored group as 'innately inferior' and therefore as less worthy participants in the political community* * * can cause serious non-economic injuries to those persons who are personally denied equal treatment solely because of their membership in a disfavored group.") (footnote and citations omitted).

Conclusion

The judgment below should be affirmed.

Notes

1. For example, to confidently describe the prevalence or frequency with which a phenomenon occurs in the population at large, it is necessary to collect data from a "probability" or "representative" sample. A probability sample consists of individuals selected from the study population through a process that gives each member of the population a calculable chance of being included. Nonprobability samples do not give all members of the study population a chance of being included—such as, for example, a study of voters

that relies on volunteers who phone in to a telephone number advertised in a newspaper. Case studies and nonprobability samples can be used to document the existence of a phenomenon in the study population. For studies of groups that constitute a relatively small proportion of the population, obtaining a probability sample can be extremely expensive or otherwise not feasible. Consequently, researchers studying such groups may rely on nonprobability samples. If they wish to compare members of the smaller group with members of the majority group (e.g., lesbian mothers with heterosexual mothers), they may recruit nonprobability samples of both groups that are matched on relevant characteristics (e.g., educational level, age, income). Regardless of the sampling method used, greater confidence can be placed in findings that have been replicated by others using different samples.

2. See A.R. D'Augelli, Sexual Orientation, in 7 Am. Psychol. Ass'n, Encyclopedia of Psychology 260 (A.E. Kazdin ed., 2000); G.M. Herek, Homosexuality, in 2 The Corsini Encyclopedia of Psychology 774–76 (I.B. Weiner & W.E. Craighead eds., 4th ed. 2010); Institute of Medicine, The Health of Lesbian, Gay, Bisexual, and Transgender People: Building a Foundation for Better Understanding (2011).

3. E. Hooker, The Adjustment of the Male Overt Homosexual, 21 J. Projective Techs. 18 (1957).

4. B.F. Riess, Psychological Tests in Homosexuality, in Homosexual Behavior: A Modern Reappraisal 296 (J. Marmor ed., 1980); J.C. Gonsiorek, The Empirical Basis for the Demise of the Illness Model of Homosexuality, in Homosexuality: Research Implications for Public Policy 115 (J.C. Gonsiorek & J.D. Weinrich eds., 1991).

5. See, e.g., Am. Psychiatric Ass'n, Position Statement: Homosexuality and Civil Rights (1973), in 131 Am. J. Psychiatry 497 (1974); Am. Psychol. Ass'n, Minutes of the Annual Meeting of the Council of Representatives, 30 Am. Psychologist 620, 633 (1975).

6. G. Herek et al., Demographic, Psychological, and Social Characteristics of Self-Identified Lesbian, Gay, and Bisexual Adults in a US Probability Sample, 7 Sexuality Res. & Soc. Pol'y 176 (2010). See also G. Herek et al., Internalized Stigma Among Sexual Minority Adults: Insights From a Social Psychological Perspective, 56 J. Counseling Psychol. 32 (2009).

7. See Amicus Br. of Liberty Counsel, at 35; Amicus Br. of Parents and Friends of Ex-Gays and Gays, passim; Amicus Br. of Family Research Council, at 27–28; Amicus Br. of Dr. Paul McHugh, at 14–28.

8. Am. Psychol. Ass'n, Report of the American Psychological Association Task Force on Appropriate Therapeutic Responses to Sexual Orientation (2009); see also Am. Psychol. Ass'n, Resolution on Appropriate Affirmative Responses to Sexual Orientation Distress and Change Efforts (2009), both available at http://www.apa.org/pi/lgbt/resources/sexual-orientation.aspx.

9. See Am. Psychol. Ass'n, Resolution, supra note 9; Am. Psychiatric Ass'n, Position Statement: Psychiatric Treatment and Sexual Orientation (1998), available at http://www.psych.org/Departments/EDU/Library/APAOfficialDocumentsandRelated/PositionStatements/199820.aspx; Am. Ass'n for Marriage & Fam. Therapy, Reparative/Conversion Therapy (2009), available at http://www.aamft.org/iMIS15/AAMFT/MFT_Resources/Content/Resources/Position_On_Couples.aspx; Am. Med. Ass'n, Policy H-160.991, Health Care Needs of the Homosexual Population, available at http://www.ama-assn.org/ama/pub/about-ama/our-people/member-groups-sections/glbt-advisory-committee/ama-policy-regarding-sexual-orientation.page; Nat'l Ass'n of Soc. Workers, Position Statement: "Reparative" and "Conversion" Therapies for Lesbians and Gay Men (2000), available at http://www.naswdc.org/diversity/lgb/reparative.asp; Am. Psychoanalytic Ass'n, Position Statement: Attempts to Change Sexual Orientation, Gender Identity, or Gender Expression (2012), available at http://www.apsa.org/about_apsaa/position_statements/attempts_to_change_sexual_orientation.aspx; B.L. Frankowski, Sexual Orientation and Adolescents, 113 Pediatrics 1827 (2004).

10. In a 2005 U.S. national probability sample of 662 self-identified lesbian, gay, and bisexual adults, of those who were currently in a relationship, 78% of the gay men and 87% of the lesbian women said they would marry their partner if it was legal, and, of those not currently in a relationship, 34% of gay men and 46% of lesbian women said that they would like to marry someday. Herek et al., Demographic, supra note 7. See also Henry J. Kaiser Fam. Found., Inside-OUT: A Report on the Experiences of Lesbians, Gays and Bisexuals in America and the Public's Views on Issues and Policies Related to Sexual Orientation 31 (2001), available at http://www.kff.org/kaiserpolls/upload/New-Surveys-on-Experiences-of-Lesbians-Gays-and-Bisexuals-and-the-Public-s-Views-Related-to-Sexual-Orientation-Report.pdf; A.R. D'Augelli et al., Lesbian and Gay Youth's Aspirations for Marriage and Raising Children, 1 J. LGBT Issues Counseling 77 (2007).

11. See A.W. Fingerhut & L.A. Peplau, Same-Sex Romantic Relationships, in Handbook of Psychology and Sexual Orientation 165 (C.J. Patterson & A.R. D'Augelli eds., 2013); L.A. Peplau & A.W. Fingerhut, The Close Relationships of Lesbians and Gay Men, 58 Ann. Rev. Psychol. 405 (2007); L.A. Peplau & N. Ghavami, Gay, Lesbian, and Bisexual Relationships, in Encyclopedia of Human Relationships (H.T. Reis & S. Sprecher eds., 2009).

12. Herek et al., Demographic, supra note 7; T.C. Mills et al., Health-Related Characteristics of Men Who Have Sex with Men: A Comparison of Those Living in "Gay Ghettos" with Those Living Elsewhere, 91 Am. J. Pub. Health 980, 982 (Table 1) (2001); S.D. Cochran et al., Prevalence of Mental Disorders, Psychological Distress, and Mental Services Use Among Lesbian, Gay, and Bisexual Adults in the United States, 71 J. Consulting & Clinical Psychol. 53, 56 (2003); Henry J. Kaiser Fam. Found., supra note 11.

13. Same-Sex Unmarried Partner or Spouse Households by Sex of Householder by Presence of Own Children: 2010 Census and 2010 American Community Survey, available at http://www.census .gov/hhes/samesex/files/supp-table-AFF.xls.

14. L.A. Kurdek, Change in Relationship Quality for Partners from Lesbian, Gay Male, and Heterosexual Couples, 22 J. Fam. Psychol. 701 (2008); L.A. Kurdek, Are Gay and Lesbian Cohabiting Couples Really Different from Heterosexual Married Couples?, 66 J. Marriage & Fam. 880 (2004); G.I. Roisman et al., Adult Romantic Relationships as Contexts for Human Development: A Multimethod Comparison of Same-Sex Couples with Opposite-Sex Dating, Engaged, and Married Dyads, 44 Developmental Psychol. 91 (2008); see generally L.A. Kurdek, What Do We Know About Gay and Lesbian Couples?, 14 Current Directions Psychol. Sci. 251 (2005); Peplau & Fingerhut, supra note 12; Peplau & Ghavami, supra note 12.

15. K.F. Balsam et al., Three-Year Follow-Up of Same-Sex Couples Who Had Civil Unions in Vermont, Same-Sex Couples Not in Civil Unions, and Heterosexual Married Couples, 44 Developmental Psychol. 102 (2008); Kurdek, Change in Relationship Quality, supra note 15; L.A. Peplau & K.P. Beals, The Family Lives of Lesbians and Gay Men, in Handbook of Family Communication 233, 236 (A.L. Vangelisti ed., 2004).

16. E. Durkheim, Suicide: A Study in Sociology 259 (J.A. Spaulding & G. Simpson trans., Glencoe, Ill.: Free Press 1951) (original work published 1897).

17. P. Berger & H. Kellner, Marriage and the Construction of Reality: An Exercise in the Microsociology of Knowledge, 12 Diogenes 1 (1964).

18. W.R. Gove et al., The Effect of Marriage on the Well-Being of Adults: A Theoretical Analysis, 11 J. Fam. Issues 4, 16 (1990).

19. See S. Stack & J.R. Eshleman, Marital Status and Happiness: A 17-Nation Study, 60 J. Marriage & Fam. 527 (1998); R.P.D. Burton, Global Integrative Meaning as a Mediating Factor in the Relationship Between Social Roles and Psychological Distress, 39 J. Health & Soc. Behav. 201 (1998); Gove et al., supra note 19, at 5.

20. Researchers recognize that comparisons between married and unmarried heterosexual couples are complicated by the possibility that observed differences might be due to self-selection. After extensive study, however, researchers have concluded that benefits associated with marriage result largely from the institution itself rather than self-selection. See, e.g., Gove et al., supra note 19, at 10; J.E. Murray, Marital Protection and Marital Selection: Evidence from a Historical-Prospective Sample of American Men, 37 Demography 511 (2000). It is reasonable to expect that same-sex couples who choose to marry, like their heterosexual counterparts, will benefit from the institution of marriage itself.

21. See N.J. Johnson et al., Marital Status and Mortality: The National Longitudinal Mortality Study, 10 Annals Epidemiology 224 (2000); C.E. Ross et al., The Impact of the Family on Health: The Decade in Review, 52 J. Marriage & Fam. 1059 (1990); R.W. Simon, Revisiting the Relationships Among Gender, Marital Status, and Mental Health, 107 Am. J. Soc. 1065 (2002).

22. See supra note 20; see also S.L. Brown, The Effect of Union Type on Psychological Well-Being: Depression Among Cohabitors Versus Marrieds, 41 J. Health & Soc. Behav. 241 (2000). But see, e.g., C.E. Ross, Reconceptualizing Marital Status as a Continuum of Social Attachment, 57 J. Marriage & Fam. 129 (1995) (failing to detect significant differences in depression between married heterosexuals and comparable cohabiting heterosexual couples).

23. See W.R. Gove et al., Does Marriage Have Positive Effects on the Psychological Well-Being of the Individual?, 24 J. Health & Soc. Behav. 122 (1983); K. Williams, Has the Future of Marriage Arrived? A Contemporary Examination of Gender, Marriage, and Psychological Well-Being, 44 J. Health & Soc. Behav. 470 (2003); J.K. Kiecolt-Glaser & T.L. Newton, Marriage and Health: His and Hers, 127 Psychol. Bull. 472 (2001).

24. See G. Levinger, Marital Cohesiveness and Dissolution: An Integrative Review, 27 J. Marriage & Fam. 19 (1965); J.M. Adams & W.H. Jones,

The Conceptualization of Marital Commitment: An Integrative Analysis, 72 J. Personality & Soc. Psychol. 1177 (1997).

25. See, e.g., D. Previti & P.R. Amato, Why Stay Married? Rewards, Barriers, and Marital Stability, 65 J. Marriage & Fam. 561 (2003).

26. See T.B. Heaton & S.L. Albrecht, Stable Unhappy Marriages, 53 J. Marriage & Fam. 747 (1991); L.K. White & A. Booth, Divorce Over the Life Course: The Role of Marital Happiness, 12 J. Fam. Issues 5 (1991).

27. L.A. Kurdek, Relationship Outcomes and Their Predictors: Longitudinal Evidence from Heterosexual Married, Gay Cohabiting, and Lesbian Cohabiting Couples, 60 J. Marriage & Fam. 553 (1998).

28. One unreplicated 1996 Australian study purports to show deficits in lesbian and gay parents and their children. See S. Sarantakos, Children in Three Contexts: Family, Education and Social Development, 21 Child. Australia 23 (1996). But the anomalous Sarantakos results are likely the result of multiple methodological problems, especially confounding the effects of parental sexual orientation with the effects of parental divorce, which is known to correlate with poor adjustment and academic performance. See, e.g., Amato, supra note 34. Some commentators have cited publications by Paul Cameron, but his work has been repeatedly discredited for bias and inaccuracy. See G.M. Herek, Bad Science in the Service of Stigma: A Critique of the Cameron Group's Survey Studies, in Stigma and Sexual Orientation: Understanding Prejudice Against Lesbians, Gay Men, and Bisexuals 223 (G.M. Herek ed., 1998); Baker v. Wade, 106 F.R.D. 526, 536 (N.D. Tex. 1985) (ruling that Cameron made "misrepresentations" to the court).

29. See Am. Med. Ass'n, Policy H-60.940, Partner Co-Adoption, available at http://www.ama-assn.org/ama/pub/about-ama/our-people/member-groups-sections/glbt-advisory-committee/ama-policy-regarding-sexual-orientation.page.

30. See E. Goffman, Stigma: Notes on the Management of Spoiled Identity (1963); B.G. Link & J.C. Phelan, Conceptualizing Stigma, 27 Ann. Rev.

Soc. 363 (2001); J. Crocker et al., Social Stigma, in 2 The Handbook of Social Psychology 504 (D.T. Gilbert et al. eds., 4th ed. 1998); Am. Med. Ass'n, Policy H- 65.973, Health Care Disparities in Same-Sex Partner Households, available at http://www.ama-assn.org/ama/pub/about-ama/our-people/member-groups-sections/glbt-advisory-committee/ama-policy-regarding-sexual-orientation.page (recognizing that "exclusion from civil marriage contributes to health care disparities affecting same-sex households").

31. Goffman, supra note 65, at 5.

32. A national survey of a representative sample of gay, lesbian, and bisexual adults found that 21% of them had been the target of a physical assault or property crime since age 18 because of their sexual orientation. Thirty-eight percent of gay men had been the target of assault or property crime because of their sexual orientation. Eighteen percent of gay men and 16% of lesbians reported they had experienced discrimination in housing or employment. G.M. Herek, Hate Crimes and Stigma-Related Experiences Among Sexual Minority Adults in the United States: Prevalence Estimates from a National Probability Sample, 24 J. Interpersonal Violence 54 (2009); see also G.M. Herek et al., Psychological Sequelae of Hate-Crime Victimization Among Lesbian, Gay, and Bisexual Adults, 67 J. Consulting & Clinical Psychol. 945, 948 (1999); M.V.L. Badgett, Money, Myths, and Change: The Economic Lives of Lesbians and Gay Men (2001).

THE AMERICAN PSYCHOLOGICAL ASSOCIATION is the largest scientific and professional organization representing psychology in the United States. They are joined in this brief by the American Medical Association, the American Academy of Pediatrics, the California Medical Association, the American Psychiatric Association, the American Psychoanalytic Association, the American Association for Marriage and Family Therapy, the National Association of Social Workers and its California chapter, and the California Psychological Association.

EXPLORING THE ISSUE

Is It Morally Right to Prohibit Same-Sex Marriage?

Critical Thinking and Reflection

1. Do you believe that the morality of homosexual activity is relevant to governmental recognition of same-sex marriage? Why or why not?
2. The debate over same-sex marriage is often framed in terms of the competing interests of the individual, who wishes to exercise the freedom to choose a spouse, and the state, which seeks to promote the welfare of its citizens. How would you balance these interests? Do these interests really conflict?
3. What actions, if any, do you recommend the government take to reduce the negative impact of single parenthood on society? Do these actions include a specific governmental policy regarding marriage, either same-sex marriage or opposite-sex marriage? Why or why not?
4. How might the arguments in favor of same-sex marriage be extended to polygamy or other non-traditional forms of marriage? Should the government recognize or prohibit these forms of marriage?

Is There Common Ground?

The authors draw different conclusions regarding same-sex marriage in part because their arguments emphasize different issues. It would be interesting to reflect on each author's attitude toward the central issues raised by the other. What would Alvaré say about discrimination against homosexuals? What would the APA say about the desirability of linking marriage, sex, and procreation? There could well be agreement between the authors on the legitimacy of these interests, even if this agreement does not result in a consensus on same-sex marriage.

One position that neither author addresses is the belief that government should not be involved in marriage at all. Proponents of this view focus on the distinction between a civil union and a marriage. They assert that the state should authorize civil unions for both opposite-sex and same-sex couples who desire the advantages of a publicly recognized relationship. Couples who further desire that their union be called a marriage would be free to have their relationship blessed by the faith community of their choice. In this way, same-sex couples would have the freedom to marry in any amenable faith community and the state would protect its interests by providing incentives for couples to remain in long-term stable relationships.

Another argument that may have the potential to create common ground on the issue of same-sex marriage has to do with the interests of society in fostering stable

households. While same-sex couples do not procreate directly, recent developments in reproductive technology, such as surrogate pregnancy and in-vitro fertilization, can enable them to become parents; they can also offer two-parent homes to children in need of foster care or adoption. Offering same-sex couples the option of long term, publicly recognized relationships can help the state address its interest in the generation of new citizens. Moreover, by permitting same-sex couples to marry, the state might help restore, rather than threaten, the stability of marriage and thereby promote the welfare of its poorest citizens.

Additional Resources

Geroge Chauncey, *Why Marriage? The History Shaping Today's Debate over Gay Equality* (Basic Books, 2004)

David Moats, *Civil War: A Battle for Gay Marriage* (Harcourt, 2004)

The TFP Committee on American Issues, *Defending a Higher Law: Why We Must Resist Same-Sex "Marriage" and the Homosexual Movement* (The American Society for the Defense of Tradition, Family and Property, 2004)

Evan Wolfson, *Why Marriage Matters: America, Equality, and Gay People's Right to Marry* (Simon & Schuster, 2004)

Internet References . . .

Ethics Updates: Sexual Orientation

http://ethics.sandiego.edu/Applied
/SexualOrientation/index.asp

Should Gay Marriage Be Legal?

http://gaymarriage.procon.org/

The Pew Research Center: Gay Marriage and Homosexuality

www.pewresearch.org/topics/gay-marriage
-and-homosexuality/

Selected, Edited, and with Issue Framing Material by:
Owen M. Smith, *Stephen F. Austin State University*
and
Anne Collins Smith, *Stephen F. Austin State University*

ISSUE

Should Human Cloning Be Banned?

YES: Michael J. Sandel, from "The Ethical Implications of Human Cloning," *Perspectives in Biology and Medicine* (Spring 2005)

NO: John A. Robertson, from "Human Cloning and the Challenge of Regulation," *The New England Journal of Medicine* (July 9, 1998)

Learning Outcomes

After reading this issue, you will be able to:

- Explain the benefits that may be provided by new developments in human cloning.
- Explain the dangers that may be posed by new developments in human cloning.
- Formulate your own position on human cloning and identify evidence supporting your position.
- Identify the main objections to your position and formulate responses to these objections.

ISSUE SUMMARY

YES: Political philosopher Michael J. Sandel argues that much of the talk about cloning revolves around a few limited concepts (e.g., rights, autonomy, and the supposed unnaturalness of asexual reproduction) that are inadequate and fail to express what is really wrong with cloning. We need, instead, to address fundamental questions about our stance toward nature.

NO: Law professor John A. Robertson maintains that there should not be a complete ban on human cloning but that regulatory policy should be focused on ensuring that it is performed in a responsible manner.

The issue of human cloning requires careful consideration. Each person is believed to be uniquely valuable. Also, many prefer to differentiate humans from animals. If it is accepted that the same technology that allows for the cloning of sheep can also be applied to the cloning of humans, both of these ideas are brought into question. In light of animal cloning, the existence of humans seems to be based on the very same biological processes that exist in sheep and other animals. And if there can be such a thing as human cloning, what happens to the idea that we are all unique? What happens to the idea that we all have our individual lives to lead, and that each person is responsible for his or her own choices?

Moreover, cloning can change ideas about reproduction. In cloning, no male is required. Consider the case of Dolly, the sheep cloned from the cell of an adult ewe. An egg cell, taken from a female sheep, had its nucleus removed; this was replaced with the nucleus of a cell taken from another female sheep. Then the result was implanted and grew in the uterus of a third female sheep, who eventually gave birth to Dolly. Normally, a newborn has genetic input from both the father's side and the mother's side, with the mother supplying the egg cell. But the original egg cell that was used in Dolly's case contributed almost nothing in this regard. The nucleus from the cell of the other sheep contained virtually all of the genetic input for Dolly.

Identical twins are familiar cases of human beings who, like clones, share a common genetic input. When environmental factors connected with identical twins are closely the same, and when they have similar clothes, haircut, etc., they can be difficult to tell apart. But when the environmental factors that impinge on their lives are quite different—as in the case of twins separated at birth—the twins can be quite different in obvious physical ways.

Physical aspects such as height have both genetic and environmental inputs; two people with the same genetic input can have quite different heights if environmental conditions (e.g., their diets) are different.

In some ways, clones are like identical twins, but in many cases there would be far less resemblance between clones than between identical twins, since they would be subject to very different environmental factors. Being conceived and born at different times—perhaps years or even decades apart from each other—they may have radically different environmental input.

Human cloning can be seen as beneficial. Cloning may provide another way for people to utilize technological assistance in reproduction. For example, a couple who could not have children naturally might consider a range of options, including cloning. Some maintain that is a relatively innocent use of human cloning, and can benefit those who are infertile.

Some object to cloning by citing other possible scenarios. Suppose a person wanted numerous clones of himself or herself. Suppose a sports star desired a clone who would then be expected to achieve greatness in sports. Suppose parents wanted a replacement for a child that they had lost, or want a child who could serve as a bone marrow or organ donor. These cases may give some pause, since the motivation for cloning appears to be questionable.

To counter this argument, it is stated that proper regulation would prevent these types of scenarios from occurring. Instead, cloning would be performed only under the correct circumstances, and would promote individual happiness.

In the following selections, Michael Sandel argues that there is something deeply wrong with human cloning. What is wrong goes beyond questions of rights, autonomy, and cloning's supposed "unnaturalness." It involves our fundamental attitudes toward nature and human existence. John A. Robertson counters that human cloning, if properly regulated, need not and would not be sinister. Properly regulated, human cloning should be permitted.

YES ↩

Michael J. Sandel

The Ethical Implications of Human Cloning

In this essay, I will consider the ethics of reproductive and therapeutic cloning. But I want also to advance a more general claim: that the cloning issue, and related debates about genetic engineering, will change the way philosophers think about their subject. Much of the debate about cloning and genetic engineering is conducted in the familiar language of autonomy, consent, and individual rights. Defenders of "liberal eugenics" argue that parents should be free to enhance the genetic traits of their children for the sake of improving their life prospects (Agar 1999; Buchanan et al. 2000; Dworkin 2000). Ronald Dworkin, for example argues that there is nothing wrong with the ambition "to make the lives of future generations of human beings longer and more full of talent and hence achievement." In fact, he maintains, the principle of ethical individualism makes such efforts obligatory (Dworkin 2000, p. 452). Many opponents of cloning and genetic engineering also invoke the language of autonomy and rights. For example, Jurgen Habermas (2003) worries that even favorable genetic enhancements may impair the autonomy and individuality of children by pointing them toward particular life choices, hence violating their right to choose their life plans for themselves.

But talk of autonomy and rights does not address the deepest questions posed by cloning. In order to grapple with the ethical implications of cloning and genetic engineering, we need to confront questions largely lost from view in the modern world—questions about the moral status of nature and about the proper stance of human beings toward the given world. Since questions such as these verge on theology, or at least involve a certain view of the best way for human beings to live their lives, modern philosophers and political theorists tend to shrink from them. But our new powers of biotechnology make these questions unavoidable.

In the United States today, no federal law prohibits human cloning, either for purposes of reproduction or for purposes of biomedical research. This is not because most people favor reproductive cloning. To the contrary, public opinion and almost all elected officials oppose it. But there is strong disagreement about whether to permit cloning for biomedical research. And the opponents of cloning for biomedical research have so far been unwilling to support a separate ban on reproductive cloning, as Britain has enacted. Because of this stalemate, no federal ban on cloning has been enacted.

The Ethics of Reproductive Cloning

I turn first to the ethics of reproductive cloning, and then to cloning for biomedical research. The case for banning human reproductive cloning is not difficult to make, at least for now. Most scientists agree that it is unsafe and likely to lead to serious abnormalities and birth defects. But suppose that, one day, producing a baby through cloning were no more risky than natural reproduction. Many believe—and I agree—that it would still be ethically objectionable. But it is not easy to say why.

The autonomy argument against cloning is not persuasive, for it wrongly implies that, absent a genetically designing parent, children can choose their physical characteristics for themselves. But none of us has a right to choose our genetic inheritance. The alternative to a cloned or genetically enhanced child is not an autonomous one, but a child at the mercy of the genetic lottery.

Some argue that cloning is wrong because it departs from natural, sexual procreation (Kass and Wilson 1998). But this objection also fails to reach the heart of the matter. What makes reproductive cloning morally troubling is that its primary purpose is to create children of a certain kind. In this respect, it is similar to other forms of genetic engineering by which parents seek to choose the traits of their children—sex, eye color, perhaps one day even their intellectual attributes, athletic prowess, and musical ability. Although a few eccentric narcissists might aspire to create genetic replicas of themselves, the real market for designer children lies elsewhere, in the desire of parents to produce children with genetic traits superior to their own.

The desire to control the genetic characteristics of one's offspring points to the heart of the ethical issue. The moral problem with reproductive cloning lies not in its asexual character, but in its assault on the understanding of children as gifts rather than possessions, or projects of our will, or vehicles for our happiness.

It might be replied that cloning and genetic engineering are in principle no different from other ways in which parents go to great lengths to produce children of a certain kind, or "designer children." But rather than giving us reason to embrace cloning, this observation

Sandel, Michael J. As seen in *Perspectives in Biology and Medicine*, Spring 2005, pp. 241–247. Original to *Jahrbuch für Wissenschaft und Ethik 8* (December 2003), pp. 5–10. Copyright © 2003 by Walter de Gruyter GmbH. Reprinted by permission.

may give us reason to worry about existing practices of childrearing.

What is most troubling about human cloning and bioengineering is not that they represent a radical departure, but that they carry to full expression troubling tendencies already present in our culture, especially in the way we regard and treat children. We have already traveled some distance down the path of regarding children as vehicles for our own ambitions or fulfillment. Consider the chilling discrepancy in sex ratios in China, South Korea, and parts of India, where boys now outnumber girls by up to 30% (Eberstadt 2002). But think also of the enormous pressure parents put on children in the United States and many other Western societies to qualify for admission to the best schools—not only at the university level, but even, in Manhattan at least, at the preschool level. Sometimes, the drive to produce successful children begins even earlier. The Harvard college newspaper recently carried an advertisement from a couple seeking an egg donor. They did not want just any egg donor. The ad specified that the donor should be attractive, athletic, at least 5 feet, 10 inches tall, and with a college entrance exam score of 1400 or above. For an egg from a donor meeting these stringent qualifications, the couple was offering a payment of $50,000 (Kolata 1999).

The notion that the project of mastery and choice is subject to certain limits is at odds with the spirit of contemporary liberalism. That is why many who are uneasy with human cloning try to cast their objections in the language of autonomy and rights, arguing that choosing the traits of one's children, by cloning or otherwise, violates their rights. The European Assembly has maintained, for example, that human cloning is wrong because it is a violation of human rights. But the language of rights misses the point. The problem is not that parents usurp the autonomy of the child they design: it is not as if the child could otherwise choose her gender, height, and eye color for herself. The problem lies in the hubris of the designing parents, in their drive to master the mystery of birth. Even if this hubris does not make parents tyrants to their children, it disfigures the relation of parent and child. It deprives the parents of the humility and enlarged human sympathies that an openness to the unbidden "otherness" of our progeny can cultivate.

Like the autonomy objection, the argument that focuses on the asexual character of reproductive cloning misses the point. Understood simply as a departure from sexual procreation, cloning would not represent a serious threat. Sex will survive perfectly well on its own—without the help of federal legislation. By contrast, the sense of life as a gift we cannot summon or control is fragile and vulnerable. In the face of the Promethean drive to mastery that animates modern societies, an appreciation of the giftedness of life is in constant need of support.

The Ethics of Cloning for Biomedical Research

I turn now to the ethics of cloning for biomedical research. It is here that the greatest disagreement prevails. The U.S. Senate is split between those who want to ban all cloning and those who want to ban reproductive cloning but not cloning for stem cell research and regenerative medicine. (For the American debate on cloning, see President's Council 2002.) As in the case of reproductive cloning, the concepts of autonomy and rights cannot by themselves resolve the moral question. In order to assess the moral permissibility of cloning for stem cell research, we need to determine the moral status of the early embryo. If the six-day, pre-implantation embryo (or blastocyst) is morally equivalent to a person, then it is wrong to extract stem cells from it, even for the sake of curing devastating diseases such as Parkinson's, Alzheimer's, or diabetes. If the embryo is a person, then not only should all therapeutic cloning be banned, so also should all embryonic stem cell research.

Before turning to the moral status of the embryo, I would like to consider one influential argument against cloning for biomedical research that stops short of opposing embryonic stem cell research as such. Some opponents of research cloning, troubled by the deliberate creation of embryos for research, support embryonic stem cell research, provided it uses "spare" embryos left over from fertility clinics (Sandel 2002). Since in vitro fertilization (IVF) clinics (at least in the United States) create many more fertilized eggs than are ultimately implanted, some argue that there is nothing wrong with using those spares for research: if excess embryos would be discarded anyway, why not use them (with donor consent) for potentially life-saving research?

This seems to be a sensible distinction. But on closer examination, it does not hold up. The distinction fails because it begs the question whether the "spare" embryos should be created in the first place. If it is immoral to create and sacrifice embryos for the sake of curing or treating devastating diseases, why isn't it also objectionable to create and discard spare IVF embryos in the course of treating infertility? Or, to look at the argument from the opposite end, if the creation and sacrifice of embryos in IVF is morally acceptable, why isn't the creation and sacrifice of embryos for stem cell research also acceptable? After all, both practices serve worthy ends, and curing diseases such as Parkinson's is at least as important as enabling infertile couples to have genetically related children.

Of course, bioethics is not only about ends, but also about means. Those who oppose creating embryos for research argue that doing so is exploitative and fails to accord embryos the respect they are due. But the same argument could be made against fertility treatments that create excess embryos bound for destruction. In fact, a recent study found that some 400,000 frozen embryos are languishing in American fertility clinics, with another 52,000 in the United Kingdom and 71,000 in Australia (Wade 2003).

If my argument is correct, it shows only that stem cell research on IVF spares and on embryos created for research (whether natural or cloned) are morally on a par. This conclusion can be accepted by people who hold very different views about the moral status of the embryo. If cloning for stem cell research violates the respect the embryo is due, then so does stem cell research on IVF spares, and so does any version of IVF that creates and discards excess embryos. If, morally speaking, these practices stand or fall together, it remains to ask whether they stand or fall. And that depends on the moral status of the embryo.

The Moral Status of the Embryo

There are three possible ways of conceiving the moral status of the embryo: as a thing, as a person, or as something in between. To regard an embryo as a mere thing, open to any use we may desire or devise, is, it seems to me, to miss its significance as nascent human life. One need not regard an embryo as a full human person in order to believe that it is due a certain respect. Personhood is not the only warrant for respect: we consider it a failure of respect when a thoughtless hiker carves his initials in an ancient sequoia, not because we regard the sequoia as a person, but because we consider it a natural wonder worthy of appreciation and awe—modes of regard inconsistent with treating it as a billboard or defacing it for the sake of petty vanity. To respect the old growth forest does not mean that no tree may ever be felled or harvested for human purposes. Respecting the forest may be consistent with using it. But the purposes should be weighty and appropriate to the wondrous nature of the thing.

One way to oppose a degrading, objectifying stance toward nascent human life is to attribute full personhood to the embryo. I will call this the "equal moral status" view. One way of assessing this view is to play out its full implications, in order to assess their plausibility. Consider the following hypothetical: a fire breaks out in a fertility clinic, and you have time to save either a five-year-old girl or a tray of 10 embryos. Would it be wrong to save the girl?[1]

A further implication of the equal moral status view is that harvesting stem cells from a six-day-old blastocyst is as morally abhorrent as harvesting organs from a baby. But is it? If so, the penalty provided in the proposed U.S. anti-cloning legislation—a $1 million fine and 10 years in prison—is woefully inadequate. If embryonic stem cell research is morally equivalent to yanking organs from babies, it should be treated as a grisly form of murder, and the scientist who performs it should face life imprisonment or the death penalty.

A further source of difficulty for the equal moral status view lies in the fact that, in natural pregnancies, at least half of all embryos either fail to implant or are otherwise lost. It might be replied that a high rate of infant mortality does not justify infanticide. But the way we respond to the natural loss of embryos or even early miscarriages suggests that we do not regard these events as the moral or religious equivalent of infant mortality. Otherwise, wouldn't we carry out the same burial rituals for the loss of an embryo that we observe for the death of a child?

The conviction that the embryo is a person derives support not only from certain religious doctrines but also from the Kantian assumption that the moral universe is divided in binary terms: everything is either a person, worthy of respect, or a thing, open to use. But this dualism is overdrawn.

The way to combat the instrumentalizing impulse of modern technology and commerce is not to insist on an all-or-nothing ethic of respect for persons that consigns the rest of life to a utilitarian calculus. Such an ethic risks turning every moral question into a battle over the bounds of personhood. We would do better to cultivate a more expansive appreciation of life as a gift that commands our reverence and restricts our use. Human cloning to create designer babies is the ultimate expression of the hubris that marks the loss of reverence for life as a gift. But stem cell research to cure debilitating disease, using six-day-old blastocysts, cloned or uncloned, is a noble exercise of our human ingenuity to promote healing and to play our part in repairing the given world.

Those who warn of slippery slopes, embryo farms, and the commodification of ova and zygotes are right to worry but wrong to assume that cloning for biomedical research necessarily opens us to these dangers. Rather than ban stem cell cloning and other forms of embryo research, we should allow it to proceed subject to regulations that embody the moral restraint appropriate to the mystery of the first stirrings of human life. Such regulations should include licensing requirements for embryo research projects and fertility clinics, restrictions on the commodification of eggs and sperm, and measures to prevent proprietary interests from monopolizing access to stem cell lines. This approach, it seems to me, offers the best hope of avoiding the wanton use of nascent human life and making these biomedical advances a blessing for health rather than an episode in the erosion of our human sensibilities.

Note

1. I am indebted to George Annas for this hypothetical (see Annas 1989).

References

Agar, N. 1999. Liberal eugenics. In *Bioethics*, ed. H. Kuhse and P. Singer. Oxford: Blackwell.

Annas, G. J. 1989. A French homunculus in a Tennessee court. *Hastings Cent Rep* 19(6): 20–22.

Buchanan, A., et al. 2000. *From chance to choice: Genetics and justice.* Cambridge: Cambridge Univ. Press.

Dworkin, R. 2000. Playing God: Genes, clones, and luck. In *Sovereign virtue: The theory and practice of equality*, 427–52. Cambridge: Harvard Univ. Press.

Eberstadt, N. 2002. Testimony to President's Council on Bioethics, Oct. 17. . . .

Habermas, J. 2003. *The future of human nature.* Cambridge, UK: Polity Press.

Kass, L. R., and J. Q. Wilson. 1998. *The ethics of human cloning.* Washington, DC: AEI Press.

Kolata, G. 1999. $50,000 offered to tall, smart egg donor. *NY Times,* March 3.

President's Council on Bioethics. 2002. *Human cloning and human dignity: The report of the President's Council on Bioethics.* Washington, DC: President's Council on Bioethics. Repr. New York: Public Affairs, 2002. . . .

Sandel, M. J. 2002. The anti-cloning conundrum. *NY Times,* May 28.

Wade, N. 2003. Clinics hold more embryos than had been thought. *NY Times,* May 9.

Michael J. Sandel is the Anne T. and Robert M. Bass Professor of Government at Harvard University, where he has taught political philosophy since 1980. He is the author of *Liberalism and the Limits of Justice* (Cambridge University Press, 1982, 2nd edition, 1997; translated into eight foreign languages), *Democracy's Discontent: America in Search of a Public Philosophy* (Harvard University Press, 1996), *Public Philosophy: Essays on Morality in Politics* (Harvard University Press, 2005), *The Case Against Perfection: Ethics in the Age of Genetic Engineering* (Harvard University Press, 2007), and *Justice: What's the Right Thing to Do?* (Farrar, Straus and Giroux, 2009).

John A. Robertson

 **NO**

Human Cloning and the Challenge of Regulation

The birth of Dolly, the sheep cloned from a mammary cell of an adult ewe, has initiated a public debate about human cloning. Although cloning of humans may never be clinically feasible, discussion of the ethical, legal, and social issues raised is important. Cloning is just one of several techniques potentially available to select, control, or alter the genome of offspring.[1-3] The development of such technology poses an important social challenge: how to ensure that the technology is used to enhance, rather than limit, individual freedom and welfare.

A key ethical question is whether a responsible couple, interested in rearing healthy offspring biologically related to them, might ethically choose to use cloning (or other genetic-selection techniques) for that purpose. The answer should take into account the benefits sought through the use of the techniques and any potential harm to offspring or to other interests.

The most likely uses of cloning would be far removed from the bizarre or horrific scenarios that initially dominated media coverage.[4] Theoretically, cloning would enable rich or powerful persons to clone themselves several times over, and commercial entrepreneurs might hire women to bear clones of sports or entertainment celebrities to be sold to others to rear. But current reproductive techniques can also be abused, and existing laws against selling children would apply to those created by cloning.

There is no reason to think that the ability to clone humans will cause many people to turn to cloning when other methods of reproduction would enable them to have healthy children. Cloning a human being by somatic-cell nuclear transfer, for example, would require a consenting person as a source of DNA, eggs to be enucleated and then fused with the DNA, a woman who would carry and deliver the child, and a person or couple to raise the child. Given this reality, cloning is most likely to be sought by couples who, because of infertility, a high risk of severe genetic disease, or other factors, cannot or do not wish to conceive a child.

Several plausible scenarios can be imagined. Rather than use sperm, egg, or embryo from anonymous donors, couples who are infertile as a result of gametic insufficiency might choose to clone one of the partners. If the husband were the source of the DNA and the wife provided the egg that received the nuclear transfer and then gestated the fetus, they would have a child biologically related to each of them and would not need to rely on anonymous gamete or embryo donation. Of course, many infertile couples might still prefer gamete or embryo donation or adoption. But there is nothing inherently wrong in wishing to be biologically related to one's children, even when this goal cannot be achieved through sexual reproduction.

A second plausible application would be for a couple at high risk of having offspring with a genetic disease.[5] Couples in this situation must now choose whether to risk the birth of an affected child, to undergo prenatal or preimplantation diagnosis and abortion or the discarding of embryos, to accept gamete donation, to seek adoption, or to remain childless. If cloning were available, however, some couples, in line with prevailing concepts of kinship, family, and parenting, might strongly prefer to clone one of themselves or another family member. Alternatively, if they already had a healthy child, they might choose to use cloning to create a later-born twin of that child. In the more distant future, it is even possible that the child whose DNA was replicated would not have been born healthy but would have been made healthy by gene therapy after birth.

A third application relates to obtaining tissue or organs for transplantation. A child who needed an organ or tissue transplant might lack a medically suitable donor. Couples in this situation have sometimes conceived a child coitally in the hope that he or she would have the correct tissue type to serve, for example, as a bone marrow donor for an older sibling.[6, 7] If the child's disease was not genetic, a couple might prefer to clone the affected child to be sure that the tissue would match.

It might eventually be possible to procure suitable tissue or organs by cloning the source DNA only to the point at which stem cells or other material might be obtained for transplantation, thus avoiding the need to bring a child into the world for the sake of obtaining tissue.[8] Cloning a person's cells up to the embryo stage might provide a source of stem cells or tissue for the person cloned. Cloning might also be used to enable a couple to clone a dead or dying child so as to have that child live on in some closely related form, to obtain sufficient numbers of embryos for transfer and pregnancy, or to eliminate mitochondrial disease.[5]

From *The New England Journal of Medicine,* vol. 339, no. 2, July 9, 1998, pp. 119–121. Copyright © 1998 by Massachusetts Medical Society. All rights reserved. Reprinted by permission.

Most, if not all, of the potential uses of cloning are controversial, usually because of the explicit copying of the genome. As the National Bioethics Advisory Commission noted, in addition to concern about physical safety and eugenics, somatic-cell cloning raises issues of the individuality, autonomy, objectification, and kinship of the resulting children.[5] In other instances, such as the production of embryos to serve as tissue banks, the ethical issue is the sacrifice of embryos created solely for that purpose.

Given the wide leeway now granted couples to use assisted reproduction and prenatal genetic selection in forming families, cloning should not be rejected in all circumstances as unethical or illegitimate. The manipulation of embryos and the use of gamete donors and surrogates are increasingly common. Most fetuses conceived in the United States and Western Europe are now screened for genetic or chromosomal anomalies. Before conception, screening to identify carriers of genetic diseases is widespread.[9] Such practices also deviate from conventional notions of reproduction, kinship, and medical treatment of infertility, yet they are widely accepted.

Despite the similarity of cloning to current practices, however, the dissimilarities should not be overlooked. The aim of most other forms of assisted reproduction is the birth of a child who is a descendant of at least one member of the couple, not an identical twin. Most genetic selection acts negatively to identify and screen out unwanted traits such as genetic disease, not positively to choose or replicate the genome as in somatic-cell cloning.[3] It is not clear, however, why a child's relation to his or her rearing parents must always be that of sexually reproduced descendant when such a relationship is not possible because of infertility or other factors. Indeed, in gamete donation and adoption, although sexual reproduction is involved, a full descendant relation between the child and both rearing parents is lacking. Nor should the difference between negative and positive means of selecting children determine the ethical or social acceptability of cloning or other techniques. In both situations, a deliberate choice is made so that a child is born with one genome rather than another or is not born at all.

Is cloning sufficiently similar to current assisted-reproduction and genetic-selection practices to be treated similarly as a presumptively protected exercise of family or reproductive liberty?[10] Couples who request cloning in the situations I have described are seeking to rear healthy children with whom they will have a genetic or biologic tie, just as couples who conceive their children sexually do. Whether described as "replication" or as "reproduction," the resort to cloning is similar enough in purpose and effects to other reproduction and genetic-selection practices that it should be treated similarly. Therefore, a couple should be free to choose cloning unless there are compelling reasons for thinking that this would create harm that the other procedures would not cause.[10]

The concern of the National Bioethics Advisory Commission about the welfare of the clone reflects two types of fear. The first is that a child with the same nuclear DNA as another person, who is thus that person's later-born identical twin, will be so severely harmed by the identity of nuclear DNA between them that it is morally preferable, if not obligatory, that the child not be born at all.[5] In this case the fear is that the later-born twin will lack individuality or the freedom to create his or her own identity because of confusion or expectations caused by having the same DNA as another person.[5, 11]

This claim does not withstand the close scrutiny that should precede interference with a couple's freedom to bear and rear biologically related children.[10] Having the same genome as another person is not in itself harmful, as widespread experience with monozygotic twins shows. Being a twin does not deny either twin his or her individuality or freedom, and twins often have a special intimacy or closeness that few non-twin siblings can experience.[12] There is no reason to think that being a later-born identical twin resulting from cloning would change the overall assessment of being a twin.

Differences in mitochondria and the uterine and childhood environment will undercut problems of similarity and minimize the risk of overidentification with the first twin. A clone of Smith may look like Smith, but he or she will not be Smith and will lack many of Smith's phenotypic characteristics. The effects of having similar DNA will also depend on the length of time before the second twin is born, on whether the twins are raised together, on whether they are informed that they are genetic twins, on whether other people are so informed, on the beliefs that the rearing parents have about genetic influence on behavior, and on other factors. Having a previously born twin might in some circumstances also prove to be a source of support or intimacy for the later-born child.

The risk that parents or the child will overly identify the child with the DNA source also seems surmountable. Would the child invariably be expected to match the phenotypic characteristics of the DNA source, thus denying the second twin an "open future" and the freedom to develop his or her own identity?[5, 11, 13] In response to this question, one must ask whether couples who choose to clone offspring are more likely to want a child who is a mere replica of the DNA source or a child who is unique and valued for more than his or her genes. Couples may use cloning in order to ensure that the biologic child they rear is healthy, to maintain a family connection in the face of gametic infertility, or to obtain matched tissue for transplantation and yet still be responsibly committed to the welfare of their child, including his or her separate identity and interests and right to develop as he or she chooses.

The second type of fear is that parents who choose their child's genome through somatic-cell cloning will view the child as a commodity or an object to serve their own ends.[5] We do not view children born through coital or assisted reproduction as "mere means" just because people reproduce in order to have company in old age, to fulfill what they see as God's will, to prove their virility, to have heirs, to save a relationship, or to serve other selfish purposes.[14] What counts is how a child is treated after birth. Self-interested motives for having children do not prevent parents from loving children for themselves once they are born.

The use of cloning to form families in the situations I have described, though closely related to current assisted-reproduction and genetic-selection practices, does offer unique variations. The novelty of the relation—cloning in lieu of sperm donation, for example, produces a later-born identical twin raised by the older twin and his spouse—will create special psychological and social challenges. Can these challenges be successfully met, so that cloning produces net good for families and society? Given the largely positive experience with assisted-reproduction techniques that initially appeared frightening, cautious optimism is justified. We should be able to develop procedures and guidelines for cloning that will allow us to obtain its benefits while minimizing its problems and dangers.

In the light of these considerations, I would argue that a ban on privately funded cloning research is unjustified and likely to hamper important types of research.[8] A permanent ban on the cloning of human beings, as advocated by the Council of Europe and proposed in Congress, is also unjustified.[15, 16] A more limited ban—whether for 5 years, as proposed by the National Bioethics Advisory Commission and enacted in California, or for 10 years, as in the bill of Senator Dianne Feinstein (D-Calif.) and Senator Edward M. Kennedy (D-Mass.) that is now before Congress—is also open to question.[5, 17, 18] Given the early state of cloning science and the widely shared view that the transfer of cloned embryos to the uterus before the safety and efficacy of the procedure has been established is unethical, few responsible physicians are likely to offer human cloning in the near future.[5] Nor are profit-motivated entrepreneurs, such as Richard Seed, likely to have many customers for their cloning services until the safety of the procedure is demonstrated.[19] A ban on human cloning for a limited period would thus serve largely symbolic purposes. Symbolic legislation, however, often has substantial costs.[20, 21] A government-imposed prohibition on privately funded cloning, even for a limited period, should not be enacted unless there is a compelling need. Such a need has not been demonstrated.

Rather than seek to prohibit all uses of human cloning, we should focus our attention on ensuring that cloning is done well. No physician or couple should embark on cloning without careful thought about the novel relational issues and child-rearing responsibilities that will ensue. We need regulations or guidelines to ensure safety and efficacy, fully informed consent and counseling for the couple, the consent of any person who may provide DNA, guarantees of parental rights and duties, and a limit on the number of clones from any single source.[10] It may also be important to restrict cloning to situations where there is a strong likelihood that the couple or individual initiating the procedure will also rear the resulting child. This principle will encourage a stable parenting situation and minimize the chance that cloning entrepreneurs will create clones to be sold to others.[22] As our experience grows, some restrictions on who may serve as a source of DNA for cloning (for example, a ban on cloning one's parents) may also be defensible.[10]

Cloning is important because it is the first of several positive means of genetic selection that may be sought by families seeking to have and rear healthy, biologically related offspring. In the future, mitochondrial transplantation, germ-line gene therapy, genetic enhancement, and other forms of prenatal genetic alteration may be possible.[3, 23, 24] With each new technique, as with cloning, the key question will be whether it serves important health, reproductive, or family needs and whether its benefits outweigh any likely harm. Cloning illustrates the principle that when legitimate uses of a technique are likely, regulatory policy should avoid prohibition and focus on ensuring that the technique is used responsibly for the good of those directly involved. As genetic knowledge continues to grow, the challenge of regulation will occupy us for some time to come.

References

1. Silver LM. Remaking Eden: cloning and beyond in a brave new world. New York: Avon Books, 1997.
2. Walters L, Palmer JG. The ethics of human gene therapy. New York: Oxford University Press, 1997.
3. Robertson JA. Genetic selection of offspring characteristics. Boston Univ Law Rev 1996;76:421–82.
4. Begley S. Can we clone humans? Newsweek. March 10, 1997:53–60.
5. Cloning human beings: report and recommendations of the National Bioethics Advisory Commission. Rockville, Md.: National Bioethics Advisory Commission, June 1997.
6. Robertson JA. Children of choice: freedom and the new reproductive technologies. Princeton, N.J.: Princeton University Press, 1994.
7. Kearney W, Caplan AL. Parity for the donation of bone marrow: ethical and policy considerations. In: Blank RH, Bonnicksen AL, eds. Emerging issues in biomedical policy: an annual review. Vol. 1. New York: Columbia University Press, 1992:262–85.
8. Kassirer JP, Rosenthal NA. Should human cloning research be off limits? N Engl J Med 1998;338:905–6.
9. Holtzman NA. Proceed with caution: predicting genetic risks in the recombinant DNA era. Baltimore: Johns Hopkins University Press, 1989.
10. Robertson JA. Liberty, identity, and human cloning. Texas Law Rev 1998; 77:1371–456.
11. Davis DS. What's wrong with cloning? Jurimetrics 1997;38:83–9.
12. Segal NL. Behavioral aspects of intergenerational human cloning: what twins tell us. Jurimetrics 1997;38:57–68.

13. Jonas H. Philosophical essays: from ancient creed to technological man. Englewood Cliffs, N.J.: Prentice-Hall, 1974:161.
14. Heyd D. Genethics: moral issues in the creation of people. Berkeley: University of California Press, 1992.
15. Council of Europe. Draft additional protocol to the Convention on Human Rights and Biomedicine on the prohibition of cloning human beings with explanatory report and Parliamentary Assembly opinion (adopted September 22, 1997). XXXVI International Legal Materials 1415 (1997).
16. Human Cloning Prohibition Act, H.R. 923, S. 1601 (March 5, 1997).
17. Act of Oct. 4, 1997, ch. 688, 1997 Cal. Legis. Serv. 3790 (West, WESTLAW through 1997 Sess.).
18. Prohibition on Cloning of Human Beings Act, S. 1602, 105th Cong. (1998).
19. Stolberg SG. A small spark ignites debate on laws on cloning humans. New York Times. January 19, 1998:A1.
20. Gusfield J. Symbolic crusade: status politics and the American temperance movement. Urbana: University of Illinois Press, 1963.
21. Wolf SM. Ban cloning? Why NBAC is wrong. Hastings Cent Rep 1997;27(5):12.
22. Wilson JQ. The paradox of cloning. The Weekly Standard. May 26, 1997:23–7.
23. Zhang J, Grifo J, Blaszczyk A, et al. In vitro maturation of human preovulatory oocytes reconstructed by germinal vesicle transfer. Fertil Steril 1997; 68:Suppl:S1. abstract.
24. Bonnicksen AL. Transplanting nuclei between human eggs: implications for germ-line genetics. Politics and the Life Sciences. March 1998:3–10.

John A. Robertson holds the Vinson and Elkins Chair at The University of Texas School of Law at Austin. He has written and lectured widely on law and bioethical issues. He is the author of two books in bioethics: *The Rights of the Critically Ill* (1983) and *Children of Choice: Freedom and the New Reproductive Technologies* (1994), and numerous articles on reproductive rights, genetics, organ transplantation, and human experimentation. He has served on or been a consultant to many national bioethics advisory bodies, and is currently Chair of the Ethics Committee of the American Society for Reproductive Medicine.

EXPLORING THE ISSUE

Should Human Cloning Be Banned?

Critical Thinking and Reflection

1. What, according to Sandel, is the true difficulty with the concept of "designer children" (and indeed, with our contemporary attitude toward children in general)? How is this difficulty related to the morality of human reproductive cloning?
2. How does the moral status of a human embryo affect the morality of human reproductive cloning? How does it affect the morality of human cloning for biomedical research? Can the answers to these two questions be different? Why or why not?
3. Explain whether human reproductive cloning is morally permissible in each of the following situations: (a) infertile couples; (b) couples at high risk for having offspring with a genetic disease; (c) parents of a child in need of a compatible tissue donor. Are there any other cases in which you think that human reproductive cloning is permissible?
4. How is human reproductive cloning different from current methods of assisted reproduction and genetic selection? What is the moral significance, if any, of these differences?

Is There Common Ground?

As much as Sandel and Robertson disagree, neither would think it advisable for human cloning to proceed in a totally free and unregulated way. In addition to the difficulties they raise, others have also come to light.

One problem that might seem small at first, but is actually quite serious, is that we do not have a good way of assimilating the new ideas of cloning into our vocabulary and thought. For example, since a clone's genes come from a single original person, we may speak of the single original person as the clone's sole parent—or as the clone's identical twin. The parents of the original person are genetically the parents of the clone, which means that people can have children in this sense when they are very old or even after their death. Meanwhile, the woman who gives birth to the clone is not the clone's genetic mother, since her egg has its nuclear material entirely replaced by that of the original person.

Some say that the fact that cloning doesn't fit into our normal system for making sense of family relationships is due to the fact that cloning upsets the system in a fundamental way. But others say that the fact that our traditional vocabulary is inadequate to the system shows only that we are unprepared for this new situation, not that human cloning should be totally banned.

Create Central

www.mhhe.com/createcentral

Additional Resources

Cloning Human Beings: Report and Recommendations of the National Bioethics Advisory Commission (Gem Publications, 1998)

Michael C. Brannigan, ed., *Ethical Issues in Human Cloning: Cross-Disciplinary Perspectives* (Seven Bridges Press, 2000)

Leon R. Kass, *Human Cloning and Human Dignity: The Report of the President's Council on Bioethics* (Public Affairs, 2002)

Aaron D. Levine, *Cloning: A Beginner's Guide* (Oneworld Publications, 2007)

Ian Wilmut and Roger Highfield, *After Dolly: The Promise and Perils of Cloning* (2007)

Internet References . . .

Ethics Updates: Bioethics, Cloning, and
Reproductive Technologies

http://ethics.sandiego.edu/Applied/Bioethics/index.asp

The American Medical Association:
Human Cloning

www.ama-assn.org//ama/pub/physician-resources
/medical-science/genetics-molecular-medicine
/related-policy-topics/stem-cell-research
/human-cloning.page

The Center for Ethics in Science and
Technology

www.ethicscenter.net/

Unit 3

UNIT

Law and Society

*A*ristotle *famously asserted that humans are social animals. The social dimension of being human requires that we have rules that govern our behavior and interpersonal interactions. The issues addressed in this section have strongly divided our own society and challenge existing social institutions and practices.*

Selected, Edited, and with Issue Framing Material by:
Owen M. Smith, *Stephen F. Austin State University*
and
Anne Collins Smith, *Stephen F. Austin State University*

ISSUE

Is It Moral to Buy and Sell Human Organs?

YES: Michael B. Gill and Robert M. Sade, from "Paying for Kidneys: The Case Against Prohibition," *Kennedy Institute of Ethics Journal* (2002)

NO: Kishore D. Phadke and Urmila Anandh, from "Ethics of Paid Organ Donation," *Pediatric Nephrology* (2002)

Learning Outcomes
After reading this issue, you will be able to: • Understand the basic medical issues involved in kidney transplantation.   • Explain the potential impact of paid organ donation on the supply of organs available for transplantation.   • Explain the relevance of the concept of human dignity to paid organ donation.   • Formulate your own position on paid organ donation and identify evidence supporting your position.   • Identify the main objections to your position and formulate responses to these objections.

ISSUE SUMMARY

YES: Michael Gill and Robert Sade argue that since there are no moral prohibitions against donating kidneys for transplantation or selling blood plasma, there should be no moral prohibition against selling kidneys for transplantation. They further argue that selling a kidney does not violate a person's dignity and that a system in which a person can receive payment for a kidney is not inherently exploitive.

NO: Kishore D. Phadke and Urmila Anandh argue that the commodification of human organs in the developing world has led not only to exploitation of the poor who sell their organs, but to impaired outcomes for the wealthy recipients. Moreover, the availability of organs for sale actually reduces the availability of organs from other sources.

An informed moral judgment about the sale of human organs for transplantation must be based on accurate medical information. In order to facilitate discussion of this issue, we will focus on one type of organ transplantation, the transplantation of kidneys to prevent or relieve kidney failure.

Kidneys function to remove waste and excess water from the blood, which are then excreted as urine. Humans are normally born with two kidneys, but as long as kidney function is stable, humans need only one kidney to survive. Serious health problems will arise when, owing to injury or disease, kidney function falls below a certain

threshold, usually 20 percent of full kidney function. If kidney function ceases and waste products are allowed to build up in the blood, death will inevitably result. Fortunately, there are therapies to treat kidney failure. In a process known as dialysis, waste products are artificially removed from the body. The most common form of dialysis is hemodialysis, in which blood is removed from the body and passed through a machine that removes waste products; the cleansed blood is then returned to the body. Patients undergoing hemodialysis must usually go to a dialysis center three times per week for the procedure, which typically requires three or four hours to complete. Another form of dialysis does not require patients to visit a dialysis center. In peritoneal dialysis, a fluid that absorbs waste products is introduced into the body and then drained away; patients can learn to perform this procedure on themselves, although in continuous ambulatory peritoneal dialysis (CAPD), the most common form of peritoneal dialysis, patients must change the fluid four times per day.

Dialysis is an effective, although burdensome method for treating kidney failure. For many patients, kidney transplantation is a preferable solution because it cures the underlying problem and eliminates the need for dialysis. In a kidney transplant, a kidney is taken from a donor and surgically implanted in a patient who suffers or is about to suffer kidney failure; waste products and excess water are then removed from the patient by the new kidney. There must be a good tissue match between the donated kidney and the recipient, and recipients of kidney transplants are required to take medication for the rest of their lives to prevent their immune system from attacking and destroying the transplanted organ. Typically, kidneys used in transplantation are taken from anonymous donors who have recently died, although transplants from living donors known to the recipient are becoming more frequent.

Kidney transplantation is a common, relatively safe procedure both for the recipient and for a living donor, although there are always risks associated with major surgery. Moreover, most kidney transplants are successful, with more than 90 percent of transplanted kidneys functioning a year after the transplant surgery. In order to qualify for a transplant, a person must contact a transplant center and be evaluated by a transplant team. Patients who qualify for transplant surgery are placed on a waiting list, which in the United States is maintained by the United Network for Organ Sharing (UNOS). The number of patients on the waiting list vastly outstrips the supply of kidneys from deceased donors. When a donated organ becomes available, transplantation surgery can cost thousands of dollars, including organ procurement fees, physicians' fees, hospital and laboratory fees, and medications. In general, the costs of donating a kidney are borne not by the donor, but by the transplant center and the recipient. Since the passage of the National Organ Transplant Act (NOTA) in 1984, it has been a federal offense to buy or sell human organs for transplantation in the United States, punishable by imprisonment for up to five years, a fine of $50,000, or both.

There are two primary moral considerations associated with the proposal to permit organ donors to receive compensation for their organs, one practical and the other theoretical. The first concerns the impact of this proposal on the availability of organs for transplant. Given the benefits of organ transplantation in general, and kidney transplantation in particular, proposals that increase the number of organs available for transplant have a moral advantage over proposals that only maintain or even decrease this number. Consequently, the authors of both the selections below address the topic of organ supply.

The second consideration deals with human dignity. Philosophers have traditionally distinguished between two types of value: instrumental value and intrinsic value. Instrumental value is the value that a thing possesses as a means to an end. The value of an ordinary lead pencil is primarily instrumental—it enables a person to write words or make a sketch, and when it is too worn down to perform these tasks, it is discarded. Intrinsic value is the value that a thing possesses in and of itself. The value of a novel or a drawing is primarily intrinsic—it does nothing, but is worth having just to read or look at. It is possible for a thing to possess both instrumental value and intrinsic value. Since college graduates frequently earn more than those without college degrees, a college education may be considered to have instrumental value. But for many, the knowledge and skills learned in college have a value apart from the earning potential they confer on a college graduate. Thus, a college education may be considered to have intrinsic value as well as instrumental value.

The relevance of this distinction to the issue of payment for human organs involves the type of value that should be accorded to the human beings who donate the organs. Regarded simply as the source of organs for transplant, donors can be considered as having instrumental value. However, human beings are commonly regarded as also having intrinsic value, and an action that does not acknowledge this intrinsic value is regarded as an immoral affront to human dignity. Stealing an organ from an unwilling donor reduces the donor to a thing possessed merely of instrumental value, and so the theft of an organ is not compatible with human dignity.

Accepting an organ given freely by a donor recognizes the donor as a thing possessed of intrinsic value, worthy of praise for an act of generosity and courage, and so the uncompensated donation of an organ is compatible with human dignity. When payment for a donated organ is considered, however, the issue becomes more complex. Does paying for an organ acknowledge or deny the intrinsic value of the donor? Does it uphold or undermine human dignity? Answers to these questions are provided by the authors of both selections excerpted below.

In the first of these two selections, Michael Gill and Robert Sade argue that the United States should permit kidney donors to be paid for their organs. Since people are more likely to perform an act if they get paid for it, Gill and Sade argue that this policy would increase the available supply of kidneys. Moreover, since it is considered morally acceptable to donate a kidney and to sell body tissues such as plasma, they argue that it should be morally acceptable to sell a kidney. They explicitly address the topic of human dignity and conclude that payment for organ donation is compatible with the intrinsic value of human beings. They also address concerns that offering payment for organs will unfairly exploit the poor.

Kishore Phadke and Urmila Anandh, in contrast, argue against all forms of buying and selling organs. They describe the exploitation and corruption that have resulted in countries where paid organ donation is practiced and explain how payment for organs reduces the supply of altruistic donations and hampers efforts to promote other solutions. They propose that the availability of organs would be increased by fostering altuistic donations, donations from the deceased, and nonhuman transplantation.

YES ⬑

**Michael B. Gill and
Robert M. Sade**

Paying for Kidneys: The Case Against Prohibition

Our society places a high priority on value pluralism and individual autonomy. With few constraints, people make personal decisions regarding what they wish to buy and sell based on their own values. There are laws prohibiting certain kinds of trade; these laws are generally aimed at preventing commercial interactions that are associated with serious harms. Payment to living organ donors has been perceived to be just such a harmful transaction.[1]

. . .

We believe that possible harms arising from allowing payment for organs have been overstated, and that healthy people should be allowed to sell one of their kidneys while they are alive—that kidney sales by living people ought to be legal. In what follows, we will present the case for the legalization of live kidney sales and answer objections to it. We confine our discussion to kidneys because the kidney is a paired organ that can be removed safely with little impact on the health of the donor. Kidney transplantation, moreover, is by far the most common of all transplants, and the discrepancy between kidney supply and need is the greatest. (Our argument does, however, bear on the sale of parts of other, nonpaired, organs, as we discuss in the section entitled "The *Prima Facie* Case for Kidney Sales.")

In presenting our case, we start by making several important preliminary points. We then present an initial argument for allowing healthy people to sell one of their kidneys. This initial argument is not conclusive in itself, but we think that it constitutes a powerful *prima facie* or presumptive case for not prohibiting kidney sales. Next we address the view that kidney sales are intrinsically wrong. Finally, we address the objection that kidney sales are wrong because paying for organs is exploitative. We hope to show that there are very good reasons for overturning the prohibition on payment for kidneys, and that neither the "intrinsically wrong" objections nor the worries about exploitation withstand careful scrutiny.

Preliminary Points

First, we are arguing for the claim that it ought to be legal for a person to *be paid* for one of his or her kidneys. We are not arguing that it ought to be legal for a potential recipient to *buy* a kidney in an open market. We propose that the buyers of kidneys be the agencies in charge of kidney procurement or transplantation; that is, we propose that such agencies should be allowed to use financial incentives to acquire kidneys. We assume that allocation of kidneys will be based on medical criteria, as in the existing allocation system for cadaveric organs. Kidneys will not be traded in an unregulated market.[2] A similar system is currently in place for blood products: a person can receive money for providing blood products, but one's chances of receiving blood are distinct from one's financial status. We further note that transplant recipients or their agents—e.g., insurance companies, Medicaid—pay for organs now, compensating the organ procurement organization that organizes the organ retrieval, the surgeon who removes the organ, the hospital where the organ is procured, and so forth. The only component of the organ procurement process not currently paid is the most critical component, the possessor of the kidney, who is *sine qua non* for organ availability.

Second, we believe the legalization of kidney sales will increase the number of kidneys that are transplanted each year and thus save the lives of people who would otherwise die. We base this belief on two views that seem to us very plausible: first, that financial incentives will induce some people to give up a kidney for transplantation who would otherwise not have done so; and second, that the existence of financial incentives will not decrease significantly the current level of live kidney donations. The first view seems to us to follow from the basic idea that people are more likely to do something if they are going to get paid for it. The second view seems to us to follow from the fact that a very large majority of live kidney donations occur between family members and the idea that the motivation of a sister who donates a kidney to a brother, or a parent who donates a kidney to a child, will not be altered by the existence of financial incentives. Although we think these views are plausible, we acknowledge that there is no clear evidence that they are true. If subsequent research were to establish that the legalization of kidney sales would lead to a decrease in the number of kidneys that are transplanted each year, some of the arguments we make would be substantially weakened.[3]

Third, we are arguing for allowing payment to living kidney donors, but many of the kidneys available for transplantation come from cadavers. We believe that payment for cadaveric organs also ought to be legalized, but we will not discuss that issue here. If we successfully make the case for allowing payment to living donors, the case for payment for cadaveric kidneys should follow easily.

The *Prima Facie* Case for Kidney Sales

With these preliminary points in mind, we will proceed to the initial argument for permitting payment for kidneys.[4] This argument is based on two claims: the "good donor claim" and the "sale of tissue claim."

The good donor claim contends that it is and ought to be legal for a living person to donate one of his or her kidneys to someone else who needs a kidney in order to survive. These donations typically consist of someone giving a kidney to a sibling, spouse, or child, but there are also cases of individuals donating to strangers. Such donations account for about half of all kidney transplants.[5] Our society, moreover, does not simply *allow* such live kidney donations. Rather, we actively praise and encourage them.[6] We typically take them to be morally unproblematic cases of saving a human life.

The sale of tissue claim contends that it is and ought to be legal for living persons to sell parts of their bodies. We can sell such tissues as hair, sperm, and eggs, but the body parts we focus on here are blood products. A kidney is more like blood products than other tissues because both are physical necessities: people need them in order to survive. Our proposed kidney sales are more like the sale of blood products in that both involve the market only in acquisition and not in allocation: the current system pays people for plasma while continuing to distribute blood products without regard to patients' economic status, just as we propose for kidneys. We do not typically praise people who sell their plasma as we do people who donate a kidney to save the life of a sibling. At the same time, most people do not brand commercial blood banks as moral abominations. We generally take them to be an acceptable means of acquiring a resource that is needed to save lives.[7] It is doubtful, for instance, that there would be widespread support for the abolition of payment for plasma if the result were a reduction in supply so severe that thousands of people died every year for lack of blood products.

If both the good donor claim and the sale of tissue claim are true, we have at least an initial argument, or *prima facie* grounds, for holding that payment for kidneys ought to be legal. The good donor claim implies that it ought to be legal for a living person to decide to transfer one of his or her kidneys to someone else, while the sale of tissue claim implies that it ought to be legal for a living person to decide to transfer part of his or her body to someone else for money. It thus seems initially plausible to hold that the two claims together imply that it ought to be legal for a living person to decide to transfer one of his or her kidneys to someone else for money.

Of course, there seems to be an obvious difference between donating a kidney and selling one: motive. Those who donate typically are motivated by benevolence or altruism, while those who sell typically are motivated by monetary self-interest.[8] The sale of tissue claim suggests, however, that this difference on its own is irrelevant to the question of whether kidney sales ought to be legal, because the sale of tissue claim establishes that it ought to be legal to transfer a body part in order to make money. If donating a kidney ought to be legal (the good donor claim), and if the only difference between donating a kidney and selling one is the motive of monetary self-interest, and if the motive of monetary self-interest does not on its own warrant legal prohibition (the sale of tissue claim), then the morally relevant part of the analogy between donating and selling should still obtain and we still have grounds for holding that selling kidneys ought to be legal.

There is also an obvious difference between selling a kidney and selling plasma: the invasiveness of the procedure. Phlebotomy for sale of plasma is simple and quick, with no lasting side effects, while parting with a kidney involves major surgery and living with only one kidney thereafter. It is very unlikely, however, that there will be any long-term ill effects from the surgery itself or from life with a single kidney.[9] Indeed, the laws allowing live kidney donations presuppose that the risk to donors is very small and thus morally acceptable. The good donor claim implies, then, that the invasiveness of the procedure of transferring a kidney is not in and of itself a sufficient reason to legally prohibit live kidney transfer. If the only difference between selling plasma and selling a kidney is the risk of the procedure, and if that risk does not constitute grounds for prohibiting live kidney transfers, then the morally relevant part of the analogy between selling plasma and selling a kidney still should obtain and we still have grounds for holding that kidney sales ought to be legal.

The point of the preceding two paragraphs is this: if we oppose the sale of kidneys because we think it is too dangerous, then we also should oppose live kidney donations. But we do not oppose live kidney donations because we realize that the risks are acceptably low and worth taking in order to save lives. So, it is inconsistent to oppose selling kidneys because of the possible dangers while at the same time endorsing the good donor claim. Similarly, if we oppose kidney sales because we think people should not sell body parts, then we should also oppose commercial blood banks. But most people do not oppose blood banks because they realize that the banks play an important role in saving lives. So, it is inconsistent to oppose selling kidneys because it involves payment while at the same time endorsing the sale of tissue claim.[10]

. . .

Many people continue to oppose kidney sales, however, and some do so directly in the face of the good donor claim and the sale of tissue claim. For them, there are two possible methods of attack. First, they can argue that there *is* a morally relevant intrinsic difference between kidney sales and both kidney donations and plasma sales, the considerations offered above notwithstanding. Second, they can argue that while there might be nothing intrinsically wrong with selling kidneys considered in isolation, the real world circumstances under which these sales would take place would inevitably lead to exploitation. In the next section, we will examine the view that selling kidneys is intrinsically wrong, and, in the subsequent section, the view that kidney sales lead to exploitation.

The Intrinsic Immorality of Selling Organs

The Kantian View

The most common reason offered for the intrinsic wrongness of paying people for kidneys is that doing so violates the dignity of human beings or is incompatible with proper respect for persons. This opposition to kidney sales is usually grounded in the second formulation of Kant's categorical imperative, which tells us that we should never treat humanity, whether in ourselves or in others, merely as a means (Kant 1983, p. 36). But by selling a kidney, according to this Kantian reasoning, we are treating humanity in ourselves merely as a means. Mario Morelli (1999, p. 320) summarizes the position in this way:

> The question that needs to be addressed is why, on a Kantian view, selling a body part is not respecting one's humanity, whereas donating a kidney may not be objectionable, at least sometimes. The short answer is, I think, that selling oneself or part of oneself is always treating oneself as a mere means. It is treating oneself as an object with a market price, and thus a commodity. The transaction, the selling, is done for the receipt of the money to be obtained. One's humanity, one's body, is being treated only as a means and not as an end in itself. It is not simply the giving up of a body part that is objectionable: it is giving it up for the reason of monetary gain. However, there are forms of alienation of the body, such as donation of a kidney to save another's life, that would not violate the principle. . . . One is not using oneself as a mere means if one donates a kidney for such beneficent purposes.

In the Kantian view, then, to sell one's kidney is to violate a duty to oneself; it is to violate the duty not to treat the humanity in oneself merely as a means (see Chadwick 1989, pp. 131–34; Kass 1992, p. 73). . . .

The Flaws in the Kantian View

There are two problems with this approach. First, even if selling a kidney does violate a Kantian duty to oneself, this still would not justify a legal prohibition on kidney sales; second, it is doubtful that selling a kidney does violate a Kantian duty to oneself.

Even if selling a kidney does violate a Kantian duty to oneself, it is still far from clear that we are justified in having laws and public policies against payment for kidneys. We generally do not use the law to enforce duties to oneself, and the Kantian opponents of kidney sales have not explained why we should use the law to enforce a duty to oneself in this particular case (see Dworkin 1994, pp. 155–61; Radcliffe-Richards 1996, pp. 384–87). . . .

But that is not the worst of it for the Kantian opposition to selling kidneys. The worst of it is that there is no good reason to think that selling a kidney violates the Kantian sense of autonomy.[11]

Kant says that we ought not to treat humanity in ourselves merely as a means. But my kidney is not my humanity. Humanity—what gives us dignity and intrinsic value—is our ability to make rational decisions (see Hill 1992, pp. 38–41), and a person can continue to make rational decisions with only one kidney. Thus, Cohen's distinction between essential and nonessential parts does not help her case, for a person can function perfectly well with a single kidney and so a second kidney cannot be essential to personhood. Selling a kidney does not destroy or even seriously compromise what Kant says is intrinsically valuable and dignified (see Nelson 1991, p. 69).

The problem with the Kantian opposition shows up clearly when we consider the claim by Morelli (1999, pp. 318–24) and Cohen (1999, pp. 292–95) that kidney sales are immoral because they violate "bodily integrity." If we take "bodily integrity" in its most literal sense, then selling a kidney clearly violates it. But such literal violations occur whenever a person sells or donates plasma or gives a kidney to a relative, so opponents must not be claiming that it is wrong to engage in any activity that breaks the surface of the flesh and extracts a part of the body. What, then, is the sense in which selling a kidney violates "bodily integrity" but selling other body parts does not? As Morelli (1999, p. 321) tries to explain it,

> . . . a reasonably strong case can be made for the value of bodily integrity in terms of the Kantian principle of respect for the persons, insofar as human persons are embodied. After all, it is undeniable that our existence as rational and autonomous beings and the exercise of our powers of rationality and autonomy are dependent to a considerable extent on our physical well-being. . . . [But] what we do to or with our bodies can . . . constitute or contribute to the impairment of our capacities for rationality and autonomy.

The underlying moral idea is that it violates one's humanity to engage in activities that "impair" one's "rationality and autonomy." That is why suicide and excessive drug use are wrong. There is, however, no reason to believe that selling a kidney impairs one's rationality and autonomy in any significant respect. The medical data provide no evidence that individuals who have given away a kidney suffer any grave limitations or restrictions on their future decision making.

The reason that even a Kantian should accept kidney sales stands out sharply when we contrast that activity with suicide and selling oneself into slavery. Suicide and selling oneself into slavery clearly violate the Kantian duty to oneself. They violate this duty by destroying one's humanity through annihilation of the ability to make rational decisions. But while death and slavery are incompatible with rational decision making, selling a kidney is not. A kidney seller may be incapacitated while recovering from surgery, but many acceptable activities (such as contracted labor and military service) involve giving up deci-

sion making in the short term for long-term benefit. Nor are the kidney seller's future options significantly limited: there are few, if any, intellectual side effects or physical sequelae. And the fact that two athletes (Sean Elliot and Pete Chilcutt) have played in the National Basketball Association with only one kidney makes it difficult to argue that having one kidney compromises the normal range of physical activity.

There is, moreover, an additional problem facing those who would try to find Kantian grounds for opposing kidney sales while allowing kidney donations. Kant argued that the moral status of an action was based entirely on the motive behind it. A person who sells a kidney, however, may have motives that do much better on the Kantian scale than those of a person who donates a kidney. A living donor, for instance, could be motivated entirely by illogical guilt and an irrationally low estimation of self-worth, or by an emotional need for grateful adoration, or by a desire to indebt and manipulate someone else. A kidney seller, by contrast, may be motivated by the idea that he ought to save someone else's life if it is in his power and that he ought to earn the money necessary to pay for his child's education. Needless to say, we do not mean to cast aspersions on the motives of those who donate their kidneys, nor to suggest that all those who sell their kidneys will have morally admirable motives. We mean merely to highlight another way in which Kantian moral theory fails to justify both the practice of kidney donation and the prohibition on kidney sales. Kant's moral theory, concerned as it is with motive, has its place in the first-person deliberations of moral agents; it is ill-equipped to draw the third-person legal distinctions that the opponents of kidney sales want to maintain. . . .

Exploitation

Much of the opposition to payment for kidneys is based not simply on Kantian duties to self but on the real-world circumstances in which such a practice would occur. A market in kidneys, it is said, will inevitably be exploitative, and for this reason it should be prohibited.[12] Some of the worries about exploitation are fueled by stories in the popular press of the international black market in kidneys. Such stories typically involve desperately poor people from underdeveloped countries selling their kidneys to wealthy individuals from developed countries. The wealthy individuals pay very large sums for an uncertain product; the poor people receive their payment and are hastily returned to their desperate lives, with poor medical follow-up and without one of their kidneys (see Finkel 2001, pp. 28–31).

The international black market in kidneys is worthy of moral condemnation, and the popular press has been right to expose it. But the horrible stories do not constitute justification for a blanket rejection of payment for kidneys in this country because there are two crucial differences between the international black market and the legal domestic program we propose.

First, in our proposal the medical setting in which legal kidney transfer would take place is that of contemporary transplantation, safe and medically sophisticated. Screening would select only potential kidney sellers whose kidneys are suitable for transfer and whose medical condition predicts minimal risk. Follow-up care would be scrupulous. Sellers would receive exactly the same medical attention and treatment that living kidney donors now receive in this country. The people to whom the kidneys are transferred will also receive the same medical attention and treatment that kidney recipients currently receive.

Second, the domestic program we propose involves money only in the acquisition of kidneys, unlike the international black market. Allocation of kidneys would be based on medical criteria, as it is today. No private individual would be able to buy a kidney outside the system. Poor individuals will have just as much chance of receiving one of the kidneys.

Disproportionate Burden

These two differences between an international black market and a legal domestic program will not, however, alter everyone's belief that payment for kidneys is exploitative. The problem, as some will continue to believe, is that even if the *benefits* are spread evenly across the economic spectrum, the *burdens* will still fall disproportionately on the poor. For it is the poor who will sell, not the rich, and there has to be something deeply morally wrong with a proposal that results in the neediest parting with a kidney while the fortunate do not.

Though this objection seems solid, the reasoning behind it is vague. When the ideas underlying the objection are clarified, it turns out to be much less substantive than it initially appears.

There are two ways of understanding the objection. First, one can hold that kidney sales are morally unacceptable no matter who does the selling and that the proposal to legalize such sales is especially pernicious because the poor will be disproportionately affected. Second, one can hold that kidney sales *per se* are morally unobjectionable, but that we know in the real world the sellers will be disproportionately poor, and this economic disproportionality makes the proposal morally unacceptable. We will examine these two versions of the objection in order.

If payment for kidneys were morally unacceptable no matter who did the selling, then it would be especially offensive that the sellers are disproportionately poor; an activity that victimizes everyone it touches is made worse when those affected are especially vulnerable. The problem with this objection, however, is that it assumes without argument that such payments are morally unacceptable and thus ought to be illegal, when the moral and legal status of kidney sales is just what is under dispute. The objection thus begs the question. Of course, many people believe there are independent reasons for thinking that paying for kidneys is immoral and ought to be illegal, regardless of who receives the payment. But they have to articulate and defend those reasons before they can legitimately claim that economic factors will make matters worse. Pointing out that most kidney sellers will be poor will not on its own strengthen a weak argument for the intrinsic wrongness of allowing kidney sales.

The second way of understanding the objection contends that paying for kidneys might not be intrinsically wrong, but such sales ought not be allowed because the resulting situation in which the poor sell and the rich do not would be morally unacceptable. Some people might be drawn to this objection by a concern for equality, believing that it is morally unacceptable to implement any policy that widens the gap between rich and poor. An egalitarian principle of this sort requires argument, but even if we grant for the moment the essential importance of equality, it still does not speak against paying for kidneys. If paying for kidneys is legalized, the ratio of poor people with only one kidney to rich people with only one kidney probably will increase. The kind of equality that matters to egalitarians, however, concerns not the presence of one kidney versus two but economic and political power. There is no reason to think that allowing payment for kidneys will worsen the economic or political status of kidney sellers in particular or of poor people in general. To equate the selling of a kidney with being worse off is to beg the question once again.

It might seem more promising to cast this objection in terms of consent and coercion. No one should give up a kidney without freely consenting to do so. According to this objection, however, the people who sell their kidneys will be so desperate that their decision to sell will be neither reasonable nor rational and therefore should not be counted as instances of free consent. Poverty will, in effect, coerce people into selling their kidneys, and it is clearly immoral to take advantage of others' poverty in this way. The fact that we can find people desperate enough for money to do something they would not otherwise do is no justification for allowing them to do it (Abouna et al. 1990, p. 166).

In this view, the amount of money involved is what vitiates true consent to sell a kidney.[13] This concern about money could come in two guises. One could claim that paying for kidneys will be coercively exploitative because the sellers will be paid too little money, or one could claim that paying for kidneys will be coercively exploitative because the sellers will be paid too much.

Those who hold that the payment will be too low point to the international black market, where payment for a kidney is often five thousand dollars or less (see Finkel 2001, pp. 28–31). Considering the surgery the sellers must undergo, this is taken to be a relative pittance, and certainly not enough to alter in any serious and long-lasting way the dire circumstances that force people to sell their kidneys in the first place. In this view, selling a kidney for five thousand dollars is so manifestly unreasonable that anyone who agrees to do it must be too desperate to give truly informed consent.

One way of responding to this concern is to mandate that kidney sellers receive a much higher sum. Some may object, however, that if the sum is too high, it will unfairly manipulate people into making irrational decisions. Large sums of money can tempt people to do what is wrong to do (Sells 1991, p. 20).[14]

Clearly, though, the concern that people will be paid too little or too much for a kidney is not fatal to the case for payment. There are two ways to view this element of the exploitation issue. First, there is a certain amount of money that is universally too much to pay for a kidney, and a certain amount that is too little. Second, there is no objective way to decide universally the question of the monetary value of a kidney. In the first case, a universally nonexploitative payment can be established by setting the fee so that sellers are reasonably compensated without being unduly tempted to abandon their principles. We are not arguing that kidney sales be left entirely up to an unregulated market, so we do not rule out the idea that the price could be adjusted to ensure fairness and consent. The second case holds that personal values and circumstances make it impossible to set a single dollar amount for a kidney that would be reasonable and nonexploitative for all potential sellers of kidneys. Personal needs and values, regional economy, and numerous other factors will create wide variations in the payment level at which a person will choose to part with a kidney. The best one can do, such a position suggests, is to set the price of a kidney at a level that would persuade a sufficient number of sellers to

relieve the kidney shortage (Barnett, Blair, and Kaserman 1992, pp. 373–74).

These solutions, however, will leave unsatisfied some of those who believe selling kidneys to be coercively exploitative. The decision to sell a kidney, these people will argue, is always unreasonable or irrational, no matter what the price, and so no one can ever truly and freely consent to do it. There is something crucially wrong with the decision to sell a kidney, regardless of whether one is paid one thousand dollars or one million. But to hold that it is irrational or unreasonable to sell a kidney no matter what the price is to revert once again to the view that selling a kidney is intrinsically wrong. It is asserting that kidney sales would be wrong even if practiced by people across the economic spectrum and abandoning the idea that what would make kidney sales wrong is that only poor people will sell. Now many people do believe that it would be wrong to allow kidney sales no matter who engages in them. As we have argued above, however, that belief requires justification, and until that justification is provided, the fact that poor people would be more likely than rich people to sell their kidneys does not on its own constitute a moral objection to the legalization of kidney sales.

Moreover, the good donor claim makes it very difficult to show that it will always be irrational or unreasonable to sell a kidney, no matter who does the selling. If it can be rational and reasonable for a person to decide to donate a kidney to a relative or to a stranger, it is difficult to imagine why it must always be irrational and unreasonable to sell a kidney. It seems plausible that a live seller can gain from the sale something intangible that is equal in value to what a live donor gains. Indeed, it is quite plausible that a living seller can gain exactly what a living donor gains—the satisfaction of saving a life, or of significantly improving the life prospects of another—plus a financial reward. If it is rational or reasonable for a living person to donate a kidney, then it seems that it would also be rational or reasonable for a living person to sell a kidney when the seller receives from the transaction the same benefit as the donor plus more.

Perhaps some opponents will continue to maintain that the mere fact that only the poor will sell is clear evidence of the coercively exploitative nature of paying for kidneys, the considerations above notwithstanding. Such opponents might base their argument on the idea that an act that no wealthy person would ever agree to must have some essentially rebarbative quality that always makes it wrong to inflict on the poor. The opposition might, in other words, hold this principle: if the only people who will agree to X are poor, then X must be an activity to which no one can truly and freely consent.

The problem with this principle is that it is inconsistent with many of the jobs that employ a large percentage of our population. A wealthy person rarely will choose to clean toilets for a living, or to pick strawberries. But this does not prove that it is immoral to allow people to do these jobs. Of course we should be concerned about the wages and conditions of custodians and field hands. But the solution is to take measures to ensure fair wages and tolerable conditions, not to ban public toilets and commercially grown strawberries. Similarly, if we are concerned about the price and safety of kidney sales and removal, then the answer is not to ban them but to make them as fair and safe as possible.

Can the surgical procedure associated with kidney sales ever truly be safe? We think it can be. There are risks, to be sure, but they can be minimized so that the procedure will pose less of a threat to the seller than do many jobs and activities that our society currently allows. Live kidney donation is now not merely allowed but actively encouraged precisely because these risks can be minimized. In our proposal, potential sellers will be screened and monitored just as carefully as potential donors are, so that the risks to the former should be no greater than the risks to the latter. . . .

Conclusion

Undoubtedly, many people will continue to oppose kidney sales, regardless of the arguments we have offered. Many people will continue to find the sale of a kidney repugnant, a feeling that rational argumentation alone may be incapable of dislodging (Kass 1992, pp. 84–85). But we should not let this feeling of repugnance hold hostage our moral thinking. For a great many things we now hold in the highest esteem—including organ transplantation itself—occasioned strong repugnance in times past.

Still, it is there in our psyche and hard to shake—the sense that there is something unsavory, something sharply distasteful, about paying perfectly healthy individuals to submit to a major operation and to live thereafter without one of their internal organs. The mind flinches at the thought of what such individuals will endure for money. This reaction, however, may be the result of restricted vision, for there is another part of the story, another image that we must attend to before we can honestly say that we are responding to the matter in its entirety. The other part of the story is the people waiting for kidneys—the people who will live if they receive a kidney or die, or at least suffer needlessly, if they do not. A complete emotional response requires that we frame in our mind an image of these sick people, as well as of their families and friends,

that is just as vivid as our image of the healthy kidney sellers.

When we complete the picture, we may find that our feelings of repugnance begin to soften, and perhaps to dissipate. Such imaginative exercises should not substitute for rational moral arguments, but they may help pave the way for a fair consideration of those arguments.

Notes

1. We intentionally use the term "donor" to refer to those selling as well as those freely giving organs and tissues, in keeping with the common usage of the term with respect to other paid givers of biological materials, such as commercial blood donors, donors to sperm banks, and human egg donors.
2. This is an example of what Margaret Jane Radin (1987, p. 1919) has helpfully labeled "incomplete commodification."
3. In the early 1970s, Titmuss (1971) and Singer (1973) argued that the existence of financial incentives for blood products would decrease the amount of blood products overall, and some people might believe that the same argument can be extended to financial incentives for kidneys, leading to the conclusion that payment for kidneys will decrease the overall number of kidneys available for transplant. Singer and Titmuss's criticisms of payment for blood products are consequentialist—they argue that such payment is wrong because it would reduce the amount of blood for people who needed it. We believe, first of all, that their consequentialist arguments against payment for blood products have turned out to be inconclusive at best—that the available evidence does not support the conclusion that payment for blood products has reduced blood supply in the United States. And we believe, secondly, that because live kidney donations are usually between family members, there is a significant difference between blood and kidneys that makes it illegitimate to transfer Titmuss and Singer's conclusions to the kidney debate. We do, however, remain open to the possibility that future evidence may vitiate our belief that payment for kidneys will increase supplies. For discussion of Titmuss and Singer in relation to kidney sales, see Campbell (1992, pp. 41–42); Cherry (2000, pp. 340–41); and Harvey (1999, p. 119).
4. Similar arguments occur in Radcliffe-Richards (1996, pp. 375–416); Nelson (1991, pp. 63–78); Tilney (1998, p. 1950); and Dworkin (1994, pp. 155–61). See also Brecher (1990, pp. 120–23).

5. As Laura Meckler (2001) reports, "Organ donations from the living jumped by 16 percent last year, the largest increase on record, as the waiting list for transplants grew much faster than donations from people who had died. More than 5,500 people gave a kidney or, less commonly, a piece of the liver, accounting for nearly half the nation's donors in 2000, said the Department of Health and Human Services. . . . The number of living donors has been growing more quickly than the number of cadaveric donors for a decade, but the gap was particularly striking in 2000. While the number of living donors jumped 16.5 percent, donations from the dead edged up by just 2.7 percent. At this rate, living donors will outnumber cadaveric donors within a year or two."

6. The New England Medical Center currently has a program to encourage organ donation. As Jay Lindsay (2001) reports, "Susan Stephens helped her 13-year-old son get a kidney transplant by giving up one of her own—to a stranger in Greece. A new kidney exchange program at the New England Medical Center allowed Stephens to donate her kidney, which wasn't a match for her son. In exchange, her son, Corey, was moved to the top of the kidney waiting list. Corey received his new kidney last month, after his mother's donation reduced a possible 18-month wait to a few weeks. Meanwhile, Stephens' kidney ended six years on a dialysis machine for Evangelos Natsinas, 36, of the Greek village Palamas. Doctors say the program will increase the critically small organ donor pool, while allowing willing donors to help loved ones, regardless of whether their organs match. So far, the program only includes kidneys."

7. As we point out in note 3, some people (Titmuss, Singer, and others) have opposed commercial blood banks. Does that opposition constitute a threat to our position? It depends upon the reasons for the opposition. If one's reasons for opposing such blood banks are (like Singer's) consequentialist—i.e., if the only reason one has for opposing blood banks is that one thinks they will lead to lower blood supplies—then one is committed to opposing the legalization of kidney sales only if legalization will lead to fewer kidneys for transplant. But this purely consequentialist reasoning may also commit one to *supporting* the legalization of kidney sales if legalization will lead to more kidneys for transplant (although the pure consequentialist would consider other effects of legalization as well; we address some of these other possible effects in our discussion of exploitation, slippery slopes, and commodification). If one's reasons for opposing commercial blood banks are

nonconsequentialist—if one thinks there is something wrong with blood banks distinct from how they affect the blood supply—then those reasons have to be defended and evaluated on their own merits. (We evaluate the Kantian class of nonconsequentialist reasons in our discussion of the objection that selling kidneys is intrinsically wrong.)

8. As we note later in the article, the difference between the motivations of a donor and a seller may not be as clear and simple as opponents of kidney sales suggest, for a donor could have selfish motives and a seller could have altruistic ones. But even if we grant for the moment that all donors will be altruistic and all sellers will be selfish, the argument presented here still seems to constitute a strong initial case for kidney sales.

9. As Andrews (1996, p. 32; in part citing Caplan (1985)) writes, "Physicians have adopted an odd view of risks to organ donors. Transplants surgeons traditionally have maintained that removing a kidney from a live donor presents minimal health risks. 'However,' Arthur Caplan points out, 'when the proposal was made to buy and sell kidneys what had historically been deemed "minimal risks" suddenly escalated into intolerable dangers when profit became an obvious motive?'" Or, as Tilney (1998, p. 1950) puts it, "The risk involved in nephrectomy is not in itself high, and most people regard it as acceptable for living related donors. . . . [T]he exchange of money cannot in itself turn an acceptable risk into an unacceptable one . . . ."

10. Some might try to counter the initial argument for kidney sales by employing an analogy to prostitution. Prostitution, they may say, consists of an act that is morally acceptable when money is not involved but morally unacceptable when money is involved. One can, of course, hold that prostitution is morally unacceptable while also holding that many other acts that involve money are morally acceptable. The example of prostitution, then, shows that the fact that a particular activity, A, is acceptable when money is not involved, and the fact that other activities are acceptable when money is involved, do not together imply that activity A is acceptable when money is involved. But if the prostitution analogy is going to bolster opposition to payment for kidneys, we have to know first of all why prostitution is wrong. Now there are two ways in which prostitution could be wrong: because it has unacceptable consequences, or because it is wrong in itself. If prostitution is wrong because of its consequences, the analogy between prostitution and kidney sales will support opposition to the latter only if it can be shown that kidney sales

have unacceptable consequences similar to those of prostitution. We will address consequentialist arguments of this sort later in the article in the section on exploitation and commodification. What of the other possibility, that prostitution is wrong in itself, distinct from its consequences? Does this argument establish that payment for kidneys is wrong? On its own, it does not. For the bare claim that prostitution is intrinsically wrong does not show that payment for kidneys is wrong as well. What we need is an explanation of the wrongness of prostitution that enables us to draw an analogy to payment for kidneys. It is not enough for opponents of kidney sales simply to point to the prohibition on prostitution; they also must show that the features of prostitution that make it wrong are shared by kidney sales. They have not done this, to our knowledge. In addition to prostitution, we have been asked at various points about a number of other things that are legal to give but not to sell. One example is selling oneself into slavery; we explain the crucial disanalogy between selling a kidney and selling oneself into slavery in our discussion of the Kantian objection below. Two other examples are buying one's way out of the military draft and selling one's body for medical experiments, both of which we discuss below in our section on the additional flaws in the exploitation argument. Our general rejoinder to all these putative counterexamples is this: our argument does not depend on the absolutist claim that everything that it is legal to give should also be legal to sell. Our view, rather, is that the fact that something is legal to give constitutes *prima facie* grounds for thinking that it should be legal to sell—that the burden of proof falls on those who would argue that something should be legal to *give* but not legal to *sell*. In the parts of this paper that follow our *prima facie* case, we address attempts to meet that burden of proof with regard to kidney transfer and try to explain why we think those attempts fail.

11. Kant himself seems to have been opposed to the selling of any body part. Even the selling of one's hair, he says, "is not entirely free from blame" (Kant 1983, p. 84). As we argue in this section, however, it is difficult to see how such opposition follows from Kant's fundamental moral principle of respect for humanity. It is worth noting, as well, that the circumstances of kidney transplantation could hardly have been anticipated by Kant, and so one must proceed with great caution when trying to draw moral conclusions about kidney transplantation (not simply from Kant's fundamental moral principles but also) from his specific judgments of practices particular to his day, such as his condemnation of one's submitting "oneself to castration in order to gain an easier livelihood as a singer" (Kant 1983, p. 84).

12. This kind of argument is made by Morelli (1999, p. 323); Chadwick (1989, pp. 137–38); Essig (1993, p. 65); and Sells (1993). This kind of argument is criticized by Andrews (1986); Cherry (2000); Harvey (1990); and Radcliffe-Richards (1996, pp. 378–84).

13. For criticism of this claim, see Radcliffe-Richards (1986, pp. 380–84); Cherry (2000, pp. 345–49); Tadd (1991, p. 97*)*; and Nelson (1991, p. 74–75).

14. Faden and Beauchamp (1986, p. 340) criticize the idea that an offer can be coercive because it is irresistibly attractive. We agree with Faden and Beauchamp's view that the prospect of financial reward cannot in and of itself constitute coercion.

References

Abouna, G. M.; Sabawi, M. M.; Kumar, M. S. A.; and Samhan, M. 1991. The Negative Impact of Paid Organ Donation. In *Organ Replacement Therapy: Ethics, Justice, Commerce: First Joint Meeting of ESOT and EDTA/ERA, Munich, December 1990*, ed. W. Land and J. B. Dossetor, pp. 164–72. New York: Springer-Verlag.

Andrews, Lori B. 1986. My Body, My Property. *Hastings Center Report* 16 (5): 28–38.

Barnett, Andrew H.; Blair, Roger D.; and Kaserman, David L. 1992. Improving Organ Donation: Compensation Versus Markets. *Inquiry 29*: 372–78.

Brecher, Bob. 1990. The Kidney Trade: Or, the Customer Is Always Wrong. *Journal of Medical Ethics* 16:120–23.

Campbell, Courtney S. 1992. Body, Self, and the Property Paradigm. *Hastings Center Report* 22 (5): 34–42.

Caplan, Arthur L. 1985. Blood Sweat, Tears, and Profits: The Ethics of the Sale and Use of Patient Derived Materials in Biomedicine. *Clinical Research* 33: 448–451.

Chadwick, Ruth E. 1989. The Market for Bodily Parts: Kant and Duties to Oneself. *Journal of Applied Philosophy* 6: 129–39.

Cherry, Mark J. 2000. Is a Market in Human Organs Necessarily Exploitative? *Public Affairs Quarterly* 14: 337–60.

Cohen, Cynthia B. 1999. Selling Bits and Pieces of Humans to Make Babies. *Journal of Medicine and Philosophy* 24: 288–306.

Dworkin, Gerald. 1994. Markets and Morals: The Case of Organ Sales. In *Morality, Harm and the Law,* ed. Gerald Dworkin, pp. 155–61. Boulder, CO: Westview Press.

Essig, Beth. 1993. Legal Aspects of the Sale of Organs. *Mount Sinai Journal of Medicine* 60: 64–65.

Faden, Ruth R., and Beauchamp, Tom L., in collaboration with Nancy M. P. King. 1986. *A History and Theory of Informed Consent.* New York: Oxford University Press.

Finkel, Michael. 2001. This Little Kidney Went to Market. *New York Times Magazine* (27 May): 26–59 passim.

Harvey, J. 1990. Paying Organ Donors. *Journal of Medical Ethics* 16: 117–19.

Hill, Thomas E. 1992. *Dignity and Practical Reason in Kant's Moral Theory.* Ithaca: Cornell University Press.

Kant, Immanuel 1983. *Ethical Philosophy: The Complete Texts of Grounding for the Metaphysics of Morals, and Metaphysical Principles of Virtue, Part II of The Metaphysics of Morals,* trans. James W. Ellington. Indianapolis: Hackett Publishing.

Kass, Leon R. 1992. Organs for Sale? Propriety, Property, and the Price of Progress. *Public Interest* 107 (Spring): 72–85.

Lindsay, Jay. 2001. Program Allows Donors to Indirectly Donate Organs to Loved Ones. The Associated Press State & Local Wire, filed 11 April. Available on Lexis-Nexis Wire Service Reports.

Meckler, Laura. 2001. Living Organ Donations Jump in 2000. Associated Press Online, posted 16 April. Available on Lexis-Nexis Wire Service Reports.

Morelli, Mario. 1999. Commerce in Organs: A Kantian Critique. *Journal of Social Philosophy* 30: 315–24.

Nelson, Mark T. 1991. The Morality of a Free Market for Transplant Organs. *Public Affairs Quarterly* 5: 63–78.

Radcliffe-Richards, Janet. 1996. Nephrarious Goings On. *Journal of Medicine and Philosophy* 21: 375–416.

Radin, Margaret Jane. 1987. Market-Inalienability. *Harvard Law Review* 100: 1849–1937.

Sells, R. A. 1991. Voluntarism of Consent. In *Organ Replacement Therapy: Ethics, Justice, Commerce: First Joint Meeting of ESOT and EDTA/ERA, Munich, December 1990,* ed. W Land and J. B. Dossetor, pp. 18-24. New York: Springer-Verlag.

_____. 1993. Resolving the Conflict in Traditional Ethics Which Arises from Our Demand for Organs. *Transplantation Proceedings* 25: 2983–84.

Singer, Peter. 1973. Altruism and Commerce: A Defense of Titmuss Against Arrow. *Philosophy and Public Affairs 2:* 312-20.

Tadd, G. V. 1991. The Market for Bodily Parts: A Response to Chadwick. *Journal of Applied Philosophy* 8: 95–102.

Tilney, Nicholas. 1998. The Case for Allowing Kidney Sales. *Lancet* 351: 1950–51.

Titmuss, Richard M. 1971. *The Gift Relationship: From Human Blood to Social Policy.* New York: Pantheon Books.

MICHAEL B. GILL is an associate professor of philosophy at the University of Arizona. He has published numerous articles in the areas of history of ethics, medical ethics, and contemporary meta-ethics, as well as the book *The British Moralists on Human Nature and the Birth of Secular Ethics* (Cambridge University Press, 2006).

ROBERT M. SADE is a professor of surgery at the Medical University of South Carolina, where he also serves as director of Institute of Human Values in Health Care and the Clinical Research Ethics Program of the South Carolina Clinical and Translational Research Institute, and the Head of the Bioethics Section of the Division of Cardiothoracic Surgery. He has organized nearly 20 conferences and has edited over 15 special issues of peer-reviewed journals on medical/surgical and bioethical topics.

Kishore D. Phadke and
Urmila Anandh

Ethics of Paid Organ Donation

Introduction

Paid organ donors are the most prevalent source of kidney donors in India at present. Though no official transplant registries exist, it is estimated that more than 60% of kidney donations are paid. Organ donation, specifically paid organ donation, in a developing country such as India raises many ethical and moral issues. It also hampers the development of a viable living-related and cadaver organ donor program. In India, where there are strong family ties, organ donation, especially for children from living relatives, is negatively influenced by the availability of paid donors. India, which is on the threshold of scientific and medical achievements, is a country of many contrasts—the most striking being the stark financial and social inequalities. Because of this, organ donation is often unrelated and paid for despite the legislation banning "Commerce in Transplantation" (Human Organ Transplantation Act, Government of India, 1994), making it a criminal offense. There are instances of alleged removal of organs without the knowledge of the donor and exploitation of the donor by the "middleman" [1]. Also, there have been reports in the medical literature of multiple complications in the recipients, including life threatening infection [2]. By and large, unrelated donors are commercial paid donors. Often the true history of these donors is hidden. Their general health is poorer. Reliable data about these transplants do not exist. Despite the existing problems, there have always been strong proponents of paid organ donation, often raising issues of great concern [3]. The concept of paid organ donation is not limited to India, but is prevalent in many other developing countries. The developed world is also witnessing a tendency towards drifting into the marketing of organs [4, 5].

There is a universal consensus that in living-related organ donation, the benefits of organ donation far outweigh the risk to the donor. There has been adequate evidence to suggest that kidney donation is medically safe [6]. Although there is pain, anxiety and some risk involved with the nephrectomy procedure, the benefits to the recipient and the psychological, spiritual, and emotional advantage to the donor, along with the fact that kidney donation increases self-esteem [7], justify the act of kidney donation. What is more important, is that the donor has made an informed decision, with a clear understanding of the risks and benefits, to donate his/her kidney, based on altruistic motives and not on coercion. Thus, in living-related kidney donation, the principle of non-maleficence is outweighed by other tenets of ethics, namely autonomy and beneficence.

The perspective changes when we talk about selling or vending the organ, considering the organ as a marketable commodity in contrast to giving the organ as a gift. As the waiting list of patients requiring organ transplantation grows, there is a subtle but noticeable shift in society towards accepting organs as a commodity, which can be paid for. In the next few paragraphs, we discuss arguments for and against paid organ donation.

The Issue of Altruism and Autonomy

It is argued that as altruism has failed to supply enough organs, resulting in many patients waiting for a kidney, the option of paid organ donation should be explored. Maybe the sale of body parts is a necessary social evil and hence our concerns should focus not on some philosophic imperative such as altruism, but on our collective responsibility of maximizing life-saving organ recovery [8].

However, the above argument appears at once as an easy way out with tremendous moral and ethical implications for society. By advocating financial incentives (it is difficult to fix a price), a deliberate conflict is created between altruism and self-interest, reducing freedom to make a gift. The concept that human organs are spare parts that can be bought and sold can adversely influence respect for the human body and human dignity. It puts organ sale in the same category of paid human body transactions as prostitution and slavery [9]. When organs are "thingified" these marketing practices can lead to serious erosion of cherished values in society. This issue has been highlighted in Iran, where the selling of organs is allowed. It has been shown that in almost all instances, the donor-recipient relationship becomes pathological. Fifty-one percent of donors hated the recipients and 82% were unsatisfied with their behavior [10]. Some sections of society may be treated as saleable commodities rather than as human beings. The medical profession compromises its deontological commitments (that all individuals have a value beyond price) by adopting a mainly utilitarian ethic (maximizing the good for the largest number) [11]. The medical profession also has a moral obligation to use its influence to change the cultural behavior of society. For example, if female feticide is the cultural behavior of society, the medical profession, instead of accepting it, should make active efforts to bring about a behavioral change in society. It should be remembered that, once a moral barrier is broken, it is difficult to contain abuses in society, even by regulation or law.

On the face of it, the act of selling an organ may seem justifiable on the principle of autonomy. However, it should be noted that human autonomy has limitations. This is because "no man is an island entire of itself; every man is a piece of the continent, a part of the main." The act of selling should be considered as arising out of narcissism—too much self-focussing rather than mere execution of autonomy.

It is usually the poor who donate and poverty is perhaps the most significant factor in making a person vulnerable to coercion [12].

Since the consent for kidney sale can be considered to be under coercion, it cannot be accepted as a valid consent.

Can and Should Paid Organ Donation Be Regulated?

It has been suggested that the concerns relating to malfunction of the organ trade, such as exploitation by middlemen or brokers, may be addressed organizationally through a centralized coordinated organ bank or "National Commission for Kidney Purchase—NCKP" [7].

Rewarded gifting or compensation (tax rebates, burial grants, future medical coverage, tuition subsidies for children) to the donors has been suggested. Although paid organ donation in an ideal situation (i.e. without exploitation, with justice to everyone and transparent) may be acceptable, we have reservations as to whether the regulation and implementation of regulatory law on this subject is a possibility at all in a developing country such as India. In many developing countries, including India, a great degree of societal and governmental dysfunction exists. Rampant corruption colors almost every monetary transaction.

Vigilance against wrong and unjust practices in relation to the existent laws is grossly inadequate. Sufficient legal resources, checks, controls and balances for such a system to keep it from getting on the slippery slope of commercialism do not exist. The boundaries between pure compensation and incentives for organ donation with potential for inducement, manipulation, coercion and exploitation will be difficult to define and monitor in developing countries. Only the rich who can afford to buy kidneys will derive benefits, thus violating the principle of justice. Organ donation will be practiced with a neglect of beliefs, sentiments and emotions. It will be practiced in backstreet clinics without adequate facilities for postoperative care [13]. This practice will only enhance high morbidity and mortality among recipients who have bought living-unrelated donor kidneys [14]. The slippery slope of commercialism is no ethical illusion but a recurrent reality in India.

Cadaver organ transplantation is in its infancy in the developing world, and, legalizing paid organ donation will kill the cadaver program without any increase in the number of transplants [15, 16].

Also, paid organ donation should not be looked upon as a measure of alleviating the poverty of individuals. There are 3.5 billion poor people worldwide and there are better ways to address poverty issues, which include providing fresh drinking water, adequate sewage facilities, and immunization programs.

Are the Issues Different in the Developed World?

We feel it is logical to think that universalistic ethics promoting human life and dignity transcend time, space, national boundaries and boundaries of social circumstances. The differences in expression of fundamental ethical principles merely reflect inequities in resources between first and third world countries. Complex modes of moral reasoning and considerations of ethics of rights, as well as social responsibilities, should guide the practice of modern medicine everywhere. The regulatory forces may be considered to be better developed in the developed world, making regulated sale of organs an achievable proposition. It is suggested though, that the principle of minimizing ethical risk should be pursued, wherein, promotion of living-related donor programs, cadaver programs and xenotransplantation should be explored to the fullest extent before embarking on commercialization of transplantation. The business nature of organ donation and neglect of altruism will alter the attitudes of society towards medical professionals, with the development of suspicion and loss of respect. This may be considered an unhealthy trend.

Conclusions

The question of organ shortage and the problem of patients awaiting the availability of organs will continue to exist. Offering paid organ donation as a solution to this problem raises many ethical and moral issues. WHO guidelines issued in 1989 clearly state that "commercialization of human organs and tissues should be prevented, if necessary by penal sanctions. National and International measures should be adopted to prevent the utilization of organs and tissues obtained through the exploitation of the economic needs of the donor or their relatives." As of now, no regulatory body has endorsed paid organ donation. The organ trade is likely to take unfair advantage of poor people and poor countries. Paid organ donation will exploit the poor, commercialize the human body, deter altruism, and retard the progress of living-related, cadaver and animal organ donor programs. In a society that acknowledges gift giving and resource sharing, there is no place for organ marketing. "Even if it is banned, it will go on anyway" is a very inadequate reason to support it. It is high time that health professionals stop turning a blind eye, becoming accomplices to the unscrupulous and illegal organ trade. It is our plea that the medical community, ethicists, etc., address the issue in its totality before they think of legalizing the organ trade.

References

[1]. Chugh KS, Jha V (1996) Commerce in transplantation in third world countries. Kidney Int 49:1181–1186

[2]. Sever MS, Ecder T, Ayedin AE, Turkman A, Kallicallan I, Uysal V, Erakay H, Calangu S, Carin M, Eldegez U (1994) Living unrelated (paid) kidney transplantation in third world countries: high risk of complications besides the ethical problem. Nephrol Dial Transplant 9:350–354

[3]. Radcliffe R, Daar AS, Guttman RD, Hoffenberg R, Kennedy I. Lock M, Sells RA, Tilney N (1998) The case for allowing kidney sales: International forum for transplant ethics. Lancet 351:1951–1952

[4]. Cameron JS, Hoffenberg R (1999) Ethics and the International Society of Nephrology: paid organ donation and the use of executed prisoners as donors. Kidney Int 55:724–732

[5]. Miller RB (1999) Ethics of paid organ donation and the use of executed prisoners as donors: a dialectic with Professors Cameron and Hoffenberg. Kidney Int 55:733–737

[6]. Ferhman-Ekholm I, Elinder C, Stenbeck M, Tyden G, Growth C (1997) Kidney donors live longer. Transplantation 64:976–978

[7]. Wesley L, Fauchald P, Talseth T, Jacobson A, Flatmark A (1993) Donors enjoy more self-esteem. Nephrol Dial Transplant 8:1146–1148

[8]. Thomas GP (1991) Life or death: the issue of payment in cadaver organ donation. JAMA 265:1302–1305

[9]. Levine DJ (2000) Kidney vending: yes or no: Nephrology Ethics Forum. Am J Kidney Dis 35:1002–1018

[10]. Zargooshi J (2001) Iranian kidney donors: motivations and relations with recipients. J Urol 165:386–392

[11]. Veatch RM (2000) An ethical framework. In: Veatch RM (ed) Transplantation ethics. Georgetown University Press, Washington, USA, pp 28–39

[12]. Marshall PA, Thomasma DC, Daar AS (1996) Market human organs: the autonomy paradox. Theor Med 17:1–18

[13]. Chugh KS, Jha V (2000) Problems and outcome of living unrelated donor transplants in the developing countries. Kidney Int 57: Suppl 74:S131–S135

[14]. Salahudeen AK, Woods HF, Pingle A, Nur-El-Huda-Suleyman A, Shakuntal K, Nandakumar M, Yahya TM, Daar AS (1990) High mortality among recipients of bought living unrelated donor kidneys. Lancet 336:725–728

[15]. Thiel G (1997) Emotionally related living kidney donation: pros and cons. Nephrol Dial Transplant 12:1820–1824

[16]. Braumand B (1999) Living donors: the Iran experience. Nephrol Dial Transplant 12:1830–1831

Kishore D. Phadke is an expert in pediatric nephrology at the St. John's Medical College Hospital in Bangalore, India. He has written and coauthored over 50 articles in his field and coauthored the *Manual of Pediatric Nephrology*.

Urmila Anandh is a nephrologist at St. John's Medical College Hospital in Bangalore, India and a member of the editorial board of the *Indian Journal of Peritoneal Dialysis*.

EXPLORING THE ISSUE

Is It Moral to Buy and Sell Human Organs?

Critical Thinking and Reflection

1. Would you consider donating a kidney to a family member? Would you consider donating a kidney to a stranger? Are your answers to these questions different? Why or why not?
2. Would an offer of payment increase your willingness to donate a kidney to a stranger? Why or why not?
3. Would an offer of payment for your kidney offend your human dignity? Why or why not?
4. Besides payment, can you think of any other ways to encourage more people to donate organs? Are these ways compatible with human dignity?

Is There Common Ground?

Whether they favor or oppose payment for human organs, all the authors in this section recognize the immense medical benefits provided by organ transplantation, and they all seek ways to increase the number of organs available for transplant. They differ on the likelihood that offering payment for organs would succeed in increasing their supply, and they disagree on the compatibility of paid organ donation with the human dignity of the donors.

Contemporary research may hold out a solution that will increase the number of organs available for transplant without compromising the human dignity of donors. The advent of stem cell technology and 3-D printers may soon make it possible to construct replacement organs from a patient's own cells. There would then be no need to harvest organs from recently deceased anonymous donors or induce living donors to provide organs. Unfortunately, it will be at least ten or fifteen years before this technology is developed to the level required to provide large numbers of organs for transplant. Until that time, patients will still need to wait and hope for donated organs. The debate about payment for organs may not last much longer, but it is still a critical issue for people who need organs now.

Additional Resources

Sunil Shroff, "Legal and ethical aspects of organ donation and transplantation," *Indian Journal of Urology* 25:3 (July–September 2009)

Mark J. Cherry, *Kidney for Sale by Owner: Human Organs, Transplantation, and the Market* (Georgetown University Press, 2005)

Lesley A. Sharp, *Bodies, Commodities, and Biotechnologies: Death, Mourning, and Scientific Desire in the Realm of Human Organ Transfer* (Columbia University Press, 2006)

Rohan J. Hardcastle, *Law and the Human Body: Property Rights, Ownership and Control* (Hart Publishing, 2007)

Donna Dickenson, *Body Shopping: The Economy Fuelled by Flesh and Blood* (Oneworld Publications, 2008)

Internet References . . .

Bioethics.net: Organ Transplant & Donation

http://www.bioethics.net/topics/organ-transplant
-donation/

U.S. Department of Health and Human Services Organ Procurement and Transplantation Network

http://optn.transplant.hrsa.gov/resources/bioethics
.asp?index=10

The Hastings Center: Organ Transplantation

http://www.thehastingscenter.org/Publications
/BriefingBook/Detail.aspx?id=2198

Selected, Edited, and with Issue Framing Material by:
Owen M. Smith, *Stephen F. Austin State University*
and
Anne Collins Smith, *Stephen F. Austin State University*

ISSUE

Do Anti-Smoking Policies Violate Smokers' Autonomy?

YES: Lewis Maltby, from "Whose Life Is It Anyway? Employer Control of Off-Duty Smoking and Individual Autonomy" *William Mitchell Law Review* (2008)

NO: C. R. Hooper and C. Agule, from "Tobacco Regulation: Autonomy Up in Smoke?" *Journal of Medical Ethics* (2009)

Learning Outcomes

After reading this issue, you will be able to:

- Distinguish between first-order and second-order (or "critical") autonomy.
- Describe the regulations that the World Health Organization wishes to impose on advertisement, sale, and consumption of tobacco products.
- Formulate your own position on smoking restrictions and identify evidence supporting your position.
- Identify the main objections to your position and formulate responses to these objections.

ISSUE SUMMARY

YES: Lewis Maltby analyzes the growing trend among employers to reduce health care costs by regulating their employees' off-duty behavior, including requiring employees not to smoke. He argues that this trend is intrusive and unfair, and links it to national anti-smoking policies, which, he also believes, intrude on people's right to do what they want in their own homes.

NO: Hooper and Agule address the question of whether global tobacco regulation violates the autonomy of those who choose to smoke. They argue that regulating the tobacco industry actually protects people's autonomy, since higher-order autonomy requires conditions that are only available under regulation. Indeed, they argue, nicotine addiction itself is a threat to autonomy.

If you visit an online archive of 20th century advertisements, you may be astonished by early-to-mid 20th century cigarette advertisements. As you might expect, tobacco companies attempted to create an atmosphere of glamour and sophistication associated with smoking; in this way, tobacco advertising has not changed all that much. Rather, what may surprise you is that tobacco companies also attempted to associate smoking with good health. Glossy advertisements, some with testimonials from medical professionals, claimed that smoking was beneficial to the throat and soothing to the digestion. Influenced by such misleading and inaccurate statements, many people chose to smoke, unaware of the health risks associated with smoking. Eventually, scientific research began to link tobacco use with a host of illnesses, and the purported health benefits of smoking were dropped from tobacco advertising campaigns. Finally, in 1964, the Surgeon General issued a report explicitly linking tobacco use with bronchitis, emphysema, low infant birth weight, heart disease, and lung cancer, effectively shattering the illusion that smoking would not only embellish your image, but improve your health.

Subsequent reports by Surgeons General have continued to publicize the health risks of tobacco use. Smoking tobacco is the leading cause of preventable death in the United States; the Centers for Disease Control (CDC) state that cigarette smoking causes 1 in 5 deaths annually. Even Lewis Maltby, who vigorously defends the freedom of American consumers to choose to purchase and use tobacco products, describes tobacco as "by far the most dangerous consumer substance available in America." Nevertheless, the CDC estimates that in 2012, 18.1 percent of all adults (42.1 million people) in the United States regularly smoked cigarettes; worldwide, the number of smokers is about 1 billion people.

While it may seem tempting, from a public health standpoint, simply to ban smoking altogether, proponents of the freedom to purchase and use tobacco products argue that such a ban would be an immoral violation of the freedom of adults to make personal choices. The foundation for this argument is the Principle of Autonomy, which states that adults should be accorded the dignity of making decisions about their conduct, even if those decisions imperil their health. Since a ban on smoking would restrict the ability of adults to make personal choices, such a ban would constitute a violation of the Principle of Autonomy, and hence would be immoral.

Proponents of strict regulation of tobacco products respond to this argument not by denying the Principle of Autonomy, but by presenting a more nuanced application of this principle to the decision to use tobacco products. The Principle of Autonomy flows from the inherent dignity of human beings, which requires that they be recognized as having intrinsic value, not merely instrumental value. In other words, human beings are valuable in and of themselves, and it would be wrong to treat them as mere objects, whose value derives from their usefulness in achieving a desired goal. In the context of tobacco use, the Principle of Autonomy requires companies that manufacture and sell tobacco products to respect the intrinsic value of the consumers who purchase and consume their products, and not treat them merely as means to generate profit.

Does the inherent dignity of human beings preclude any activity that uses human beings as a means to an end? How then can tobacco companies, or any company for that matter, make a profit? The answer to these questions lies in recognizing that it is moral to treat human beings in an instrumental fashion as long as this treatment also respects their intrinsic value. In practical terms, this respect must be demonstrated by obtaining a person's voluntary, informed consent to be treated as a means to an end. Let us take each component of this requirement separately. First, human beings must give their consent to be treated as a means to an end; if no consent is obtained,

this treatment does not respect their intrinsic value and is immoral. Second, they must be in possession of all relevant facts before giving their consent; if not, their consent is uninformed and morally invalid. Finally, they must give their consent freely and without coercion; if not, their consent is involuntary and morally invalid. In the absence of voluntary, informed consent, it is immoral to treat a person as a means to an end.

In the context of tobacco use, a tobacco company must demonstrate its respect for the intrinsic value of its customers by obtaining their voluntary, informed consent to purchase and consume tobacco products. Proponents of strict regulation of tobacco products acknowledge that many people do, in fact, give their consent to purchase and consume tobacco products. However, they deny that this consent is always informed and voluntary.

In the decades before the first Surgeon General's report on the adverse health effects of smoking, people did not have a full understanding of the significance of their choice to use tobacco; indeed, tobacco advertising misled consumers by promoting the health benefits of tobacco! As a result, their choice was uninformed, and therefore morally invalid. As a consequence of the Surgeon General's report, strict warning labels were required on tobacco products to address this problem. As tobacco companies expand into markets around the world, the World Health Organization wants to regulate advertising and requires public health education to prevent people from making uninformed decisions about smoking. Thus, strict regulation of tobacco products may be seen as protecting, rather than violating the autonomy of the people who choose to purchase and consume tobacco products.

In addition, tobacco products contain a highly addictive substance, nicotine. Indeed, research suggests that the majority of smokers want to quit but find themselves unable to do so because of their addiction to nicotine. Once people have become addicted to nicotine, however, their addiction compels them to continue to use tobacco products. As a result, their consent to purchase and consume tobacco products becomes involuntary, and therefore morally invalid. Because tobacco products are inherently addictive, mere regulation may not be sufficient to protect the autonomy of potential tobacco consumers; an outright ban on tobacco products may be necessary.

In the following selections, Maltby argues that autonomy must be defended by allowing people to make the personal choice to assume the risks of smoking, so long as they do so in ways that do not harm others (for example, by exposing them to secondhand smoke). In his opinion, anti-smoking restrictions that are not specifically aimed at preventing harm to nonsmokers violate the principle of autonomy.

Hooper and Agule, on the other hand, make an important distinction between two types of autonomy: first-order autonomy, which is the ability to satisfy one's immediate desires, and second-order (or "critical") autonomy, which is the ability to satisfy the desires that arise from mature, informed reflection on one's first-order desires. In regard to the purchase and consumption of tobacco, many smokers have an immediate (and in fact, overwhelming) desire to continue smoking because of their addiction to nicotine, while they have a reflective desire to quite smoking because of the health risks posed by smoking. Their inability to fulfill the latter desire indicates that their second-order autonomy has been compromised. In order to support this second-order autonomy, Hooper and Agule argue, regulations on the tobacco industry are needed to prevent deceptive advertising and provide education on the true risks of smoking.

YES

Lewis Maltby

Whose Life Is It Anyway? Employer Control of Off-Duty Smoking and Individual Autonomy

Henry Ford had his own private police force.[2] If you worked for Ford Motor Company, its officers could show up at your door at any hour of the day or night and search your entire home.[3] If they found anything Henry Ford disapproved of, you were fired.[4] If you were drinking, you were fired.[5] If there was someone upstairs at night that you were not married to, you were fired.[6] If you were playing cards for money, you were fired.[7] If you had books Ford did not like, you were fired.[8]

Today, we know that this was wrong. The fact that Henry Ford signed people's paychecks did not give him the right to control their private lives.

But we are in danger of slipping back into this kind of world. Many employers are beginning to take control of employees' private lives in the name of reducing health care costs.[9]

The most common example of this trend involves employers who prohibit employees from smoking in their private lives.[10] The Administrative Management Society has estimated that six percent of all employers in the United States discriminate against off-duty smokers.[11] These employers argue that smokers incur higher medical costs that adversely affect profitability.[12] This is clearly correct. While the magnitude by which smokers' medical costs exceed those of other employees has not been precisely measured, nor the amount of these higher costs that fall on a particular employer, there is no question that smokers cost their employers more money for medical care.[13]

But smoking is not the only behavior that increases medical costs. Alcohol isn't good for you.[14] Neither is junk food, red meat, too much coffee, lack of exercise, or lack of sleep.[15] Many forms of recreation have medical risks, including skiing, scuba diving, and riding motorcycles. Getting to work by bicycle may be good exercise, but it increases the risk of being hurt in a traffic accident. Even your sex life has health care cost implications. People with multiple sexual partners have a greater risk of acquiring STDs than those who are monogamous.[16] If it is acceptable for employers to ban off-duty smoking because it increases costs, it is equally acceptable for employers to control all of these other types of behavior. The more we learn about the relationships between behavior and health, the more we realize that everything we do in our private lives affects our health. If employers are permitted to control private behavior when it is related to health, virtually every aspect of our private lives is subject to employer control.

Some people argue this isn't really a slippery slope—employers wouldn't try to control other aspects of people's private lives, only smoking.[17] These people don't understand business. Employers don't ban off-duty smoking because they are anti-smoking; they ban off-duty smoking to increase the bottom line. To an employer, a dollar saved by forcing an employee to give up junk food and lose weight is just as valuable as a dollar saved by forcing an employee to quit smoking. Recent studies from the Centers for Disease Control show that obesity is rapidly overtaking smoking as the leading cause of preventable death in the United States.[18] Cost-conscious employers will soon have more incentive to regulate diet and exercise than smoking.

In fact, some employers have banned other forms of private behavior. Multi-Developers, a real estate development company, prohibits employees from skiing, riding a motorcycle, or engaging in any other risky hobby.[19] The Best Lock Corporation, in Indiana, prohibits the consumption of alcohol at any time.[20] Best Lock fired Daniel Winn after eight years of good performance because Mr. Winn went out for a few beers with some friends after work.[21] The city of Athens, Georgia, required all municipal employees to take cholesterol tests—if your cholesterol was too high, you were fired.[22]

Other employers have gone further. Lynne Gobbell lost her job at an Alabama insulation company because she had a "Kerry for President" bumper sticker on her car.[23] Glen Hiller, from West Virginia, was fired because his boss didn't like a question he asked a candidate at a political rally.[24] Laurel Allen, from New York, was fired by Wal-Mart because it disapproved of her boyfriend.[25] Kimberly Turic, from Michigan, was fired for telling her supervisor that she was considering having an abortion.[26]

Virtually all of these terminations were legal. Under American law, an employer has the right to fire an employee at any time, for any reason, unless there is a statute prohibiting a specific reason for termination.[27] A variety of federal and state laws prohibit discrimination based on race, age, gender, religion, disability, and (in some jurisdictions) sexual orientation.[28] However, in other than a handful of states,[29] there is no law against being fired because your employer disapproves of your private life.

Employment decisions should be based on how well you do your job, not on your private life. Most successful companies operate on this principle. There is no reason all companies shouldn't follow it.

Where does this leave employers who don't want to absorb the additional health care costs created by employee smoking? One option is for employers to require a higher personal contribution to the health care plan for employees who smoke.[30] There is nothing wrong with this in principle. We may all have the right to conduct our private lives as we choose, but we do not have the right to make other people take responsibility for the consequences of our behavior. If people choose to smoke, there is nothing unfair about requiring them to take financial responsibility for the health care costs this behavior creates. Employers could determine the amount by which health care costs of smokers exceed those of non-smokers and require smoking employees to contribute this amount personally.

Employers that choose this policy need to ensure that their surcharge is actuarially correct. While there is no question that smokers have higher health care costs, the actual cost differential is not entirely clear.[31] Moreover, most of the published estimates come from advocates and not from neutral experts.[32] Employers need to check their sources and consult with independent actuaries before determining the amount of the surcharge.

To be completely fair, employers should also analyze the amount of smokers' higher health care charges that the company will pay. For example, one of the largest components of smokers' health care costs is cancer treatment.[33] In many cases, smoking-related cancers occur later in life, after the person has retired, with the majority of that person's medical costs paid by Medicare.[34] Such

factors should be included in calculating an employee's surcharge.

Even if actuarially correct, however, there are other concerns about surcharges. To be fair, surcharges should apply to all health-related off-duty behavior. Some non-smokers have higher health risks than some smokers. Someone who eats lunch at McDonald's seven days a week, never exercises, and drinks a six-pack of beer every day probably has greater health risks than a light smoker who does everything else right. Since the justification for the surcharge is the higher cost that the employee's behavior creates, in such cases the non-smoker should pay a higher surcharge. To be fair, a surcharge program needs to contain penalties for poor diet, lack of exercise, risky hobbies, risky sex, and anything else that affects health. This may not be unfair from the standpoint of personal responsibility, but from the perspective of individual autonomy it is "Henry Ford-light."

There are also privacy concerns implicated in such surcharges. For an employer to establish a comprehensive surcharge program, it needs comprehensive knowledge of its employees' private lives. It needs to know how much employees drink, what they eat, what they do in their spare time, and how many sexual partners they have. Do we really want to reveal this information to our employers? Employers' poor historical record of maintaining the privacy of personal information increases the level of concern about surrendering our privacy to this degree.[35]

Enforcement of surcharge programs also raises privacy issues. Many employees will misrepresent their private behavior in order to avoid penalties. To protect the integrity of the program, employers will need programs to detect such deception. One method is urine testing. Cotinine, the most common metabolite of nicotine, can be detected in smokers' urine, just as THC metabolites are detected in the urine of marijuana users.[36] Before initiating such a program, however, employers need to consider how employees will react. While Americans have generally become accustomed to one-time pre-employment urine tests, random testing of incumbent employees is relatively rare, in part because of employee resistance. Such programs could also run afoul of the Americans with Disabilities Act's prohibition of medical testing that is not job-related.[37]

Another method is to encourage employees who know another employee is secretly smoking off-duty (or secretly riding a motorcycle) to inform management. This approach, however, seems even more likely to cause conflict. What happens to the working relationship between two people when one has turned the other in for smoking or drinking off-duty?

In short, surcharge programs may well create more problems than their cost savings justify.

It might be far more productive for employers to approach employee medical costs from a helpful perspective rather than a punitive one. Very few of us are proud of our bad habits. Surveys repeatedly show that most smokers want to quit.[38] Millions of us make New Year's resolutions to eat less, go to the gym more often, and cut down on our drinking.[39] Employers could do a great deal to help us follow through on these good intentions. For example, employers could pay for smoking cessation programs for employees who want to quit.[40] They could even offer a modest incentive for employees who are successful, such as an extra vacation day or a small amount of money. Such programs are highly cost-effective.[41] The same approach could be equally effective in helping employees who want to lose weight. A more ambitious program would make medical personnel available for voluntary consultations with employees about how to improve their health. This type of program not only avoids the legal and morale problems of the punitive approach but would be perceived as an added benefit by employees.

The fact that so many employers are approaching this issue in a punitive fashion reflects that we have lost our way on smoking in the United States. Our goals should be:

1. Protecting non-smokers from second-hand smoke;
2. Keeping tobacco out of the hands of minors; and
3. Helping smokers who want to quit.

Our actual policy, however, has become eliminating smoking by any means necessary.

You can see this in our official national policy on smoking. The Healthy People Initiative, a program of the Federal Department of Health and Human Services, has a goal of cutting adult smoking in half by the year 2010.[42] Not to protect non-smokers, not to help smokers who want to quit, but to eliminate smoking, period.

This mistake is not merely verbal; it shows in actions as well. Legislation has been enacted in most states prohibiting companies from terminating employees based on off-duty smoking.[43] Such laws do not expose employees to second-hand smoke—they simply protect peoples' right to behave as they want in their own home. Employers can still restrict or ban tobacco use on company property. Anti-smoking groups consistently and vigorously opposed the enactment of these laws.[44] When challenged, they claimed that such laws give undeserved special protection to smokers.[45] But when bills were introduced protecting all forms of legal off-duty conduct, the anti-smoking establishment opposed them too.[46] The only policy consistent with the actions of the anti-smoking establishment is prohibition.

The prohibitionist mentality is not confined to tobacco regulation. Kelly Brownell of Yale University is one of the leading thinkers of the health community. She has proposed that the government create a special tax on junk food so that people will be encouraged to eat less of it.[47] According to Brownell, "the government needs to regulate food as it would a potentially dangerous drug."[48]

This is a serious error. Not only is it wrong for any of us to try to tell the rest of us how to live in our own homes, prohibition is unworkable in practice.

America has tried prohibition. In 1919 the Volstead Act prohibited the production or consumption of alcohol.[49] Alcohol production didn't stop; it merely went underground as legitimate companies were replaced by criminals like Al Capone.[50] Nor did Americans stop drinking. They just turned to illegal bars and homemade liquor. This required us to devote vast amounts of our criminal justice resources searching for underground bars and ordinary citizens brewing beer in their bathtubs. Only fourteen years later, Prohibition was universally rejected as a colossal failure and the law was repealed.[51] One definition of insanity is to keep repeating the same behavior expecting different results.

A comprehensive proposal for an alternative national policy is beyond the scope of this paper, but a good first step would be to give the Food and Drug Administration (FDA) jurisdiction over tobacco products. Tobacco is by far the most dangerous consumer substance available in America. To fail to regulate it is indefensible. We regulate air conditioners, hammocks, and even coffee mugs in the interest of public safety.[52] It is absurd not to regulate tobacco. Giving the FDA jurisdiction would also establish that tobacco is a legitimate consumer product that needs to be regulated, not prohibited.[53]

We need to follow a similar regulatory policy regarding other forms of risky behavior; one that focuses on protecting other people from the risks we choose to take.

Notes

1. Attributed to Justice Oliver Wendell Holmes.
2. See Henry Ford & Samuel Crowther, My Life and Work 128–29 (1922). Ford employed as many as fifty investigators in his "social welfare department" who looked into the private lives of Ford Motor Company employees. Id. The Social Department was originally instituted to evaluate each

employee's eligibility for a "prosperity-sharing" program. Id. at 129.

3. See Keith Sward, The Legend of Henry Ford 59 (1948).

4. Id.

5. Id.

6. Id.

7. Id.

8. Id.

9. See generally Jeremy W. Peters, Company's Smoking Ban Means Off-Hours, Too, N.Y. Times, Feb. 8, 2005, at C5.

10. See, e.g., Peters, supra note 9.

11. Nat'l Workrights Inst., Lifestyle Discrimination: Employer Control of Legal Off-Duty Employee Activities 2, http://www.workrights.org/issue lifestyle/ldbrief2.pdf [hereinafter NWI on Lifestyle Discrimination].

12. In 2002, the Centers for Disease Control and Prevention estimated that, on average, each adult smoker in the United States cost their employer $3391 in additional health care and productivity losses annually. Annual Smoking-Attributable Mortality, Years of Potential Life Lost, and Economic Costs—United States, 1995–1999, Apr. 12, 2002, http://www.cdc.gov/mmwr/preview/mmwrhtml/mm5114a2.htm [hereinafter CDC Report].

13. See id. The CDC, along with other individuals and organizations, has estimated the costs of smoking to employers. Id. See also Am. Cancer Soc'y, Smoking in the Workplace Costs You Money, http://www.cancer.org/downloads/COM/ Smoking in the Workplace Costs You Money.pdf. However, all of these estimates have methodological problems that are beyond the scope of this article.

14. A recent study by the National Institute of Health found that how much and how often people consume alcohol independently influences the risk of death from a number of causes. Nat'l Inst. on Alcohol Abuse and Alcoholism, Quantity and Frequency of Drinking Influence Mortality Risk, http://www.niaaa.nih.gov/NewsEvents/NewsReleases/mortalityrisk.htm.

15. See, e.g., Rob Stein, Scientists Finding Out What Losing Sleep Does to a Body, Wash. Post, Oct. 9, 2005, at A01, available at http://www.washingtonpost.com/wp-dyn/content/article/2005/10/08/AR2005100801405.html.

16. The CDC states that "the most reliable way to avoid transmission of STDs is to abstain from sex or to be in a long-term, mutually monogamous relationship with an uninfected partner." Ctrs. for Disease Control & Prevention, Sexually Transmitted Diseases; Treatment Guidelines: 2006; Clinical Prevention Guidance, http://www.cdc.gov/std/treatment/2006/clinical.htm#clinical1.

17. See Micah Berman & Rob Crane, Mandating a Tobacco-Free Workforce; A Convergence of Business and Public Health Interests, 34 Wm. Mitchell L. Rev 1653, 1672 (2008) (arguing that tobacco use is distinguishable from other potentially hazardous activities and that "slippery slope concerns are entirely speculative"); Michele L. Tyler, Blowing Smoke: Do Smokers Have a Right? Limiting the Privacy Rights of Cigarette Smokers, 86 Geo. L.J. 783, 794–95(1998) (discussing the slippery slope doctrine and concluding that a smoking ban is unlikely to result in further invasions of other privacy rights because of economic factors); Christopher Valleau, If You're Smoking, You're Fired: How Tobacco Could Be Dangerous To More Than Just Your Health, 10 DePaul J. Health Care L. 457, 490-92 (2007) (concluding that the slippery slope doctrine fails because smoking is inherently different than other lifestyle behaviors).

18. Ali H. Mokdad et al., Actual Causes of Death in the United States, 2000, 291 J. Am. Med. Ass'n 1238–45 (Mar. 10, 2004), available at http://www.csdp.org/research/1238.pdf.

19. Zachary Schiller et al., If You Light Up on Sunday, Don't Come in on Monday, Bus. Wk., Aug. 26, 1991, at 68. Multi-Developers, Inc.'s policy prohibits employees from engaging in "'hazardous activities and pursuits including such things as skydiving, riding motorcycles, piloting private aircraft, mountain climbing, motor vehicle racing, etc." Id. To the author's knowledge, this is still the policy at Multi-Developers, Inc.

20. Best Lock Corp. v. Review Bd., 572 N.E.2d 520, 521 (Ind. Ct. App. 1991). Best Lock Corporation's tobacco, alcohol, and drug use rule (TAD Rule) states: "The use of tobacco, the use of alcohol as a beverage, or the use of drugs by an employee shall not be condoned. . . . Any employee violating this policy, at work or away from the plant, will be summarily terminated." Id.

21. See id. (Winn admitted under oath, in a proceeding involving the termination of his brother from Best Lock Corporation, that he had consumed alcohol on several social occasions while employed at Best Lock Corporation).

22. Schiller et al., supra note 19. The city of Athens, Georgia, for a short period of time, required job applicants to submit to a cholesterol test. Id. Applicants whose cholesterol levels ranked in the top 20% of all applicants were eliminated from consideration for employment. Id. Local protests led to elimination of the policy. Id.

23. Paola Singer, Fired Over Kerry Sticker; Her Loss Is Their Gain, Newsday, Sept. 17, 2004, at A33.

24. Jessica Valdez, Frederick Company Fires Employee Who Taunted Bush, Wash. Post, Aug. 22, 2004, at C06.

25. Dottie Enrico, When Office Romance Collides With the Corporate Culture, Newsday, Aug. 1, 1993, at 70. Allen was dating a fellow employee while she was still married to her husband, although they were separated. Id.

26. Pregnancy Bias Case Costs a Hotel $89,000, Chi. Trib., Mar. 16, 1994, at M3. Turic later won a lawsuit for wrongful termination and was awarded $89,000. Id.

27. See generally 27 Am. Jur. 2d Employment Relationship § 10 (2008).

28. See, e.g., 42 U.S.C. § 2000e-2 (2000) (making it illegal for an employer to discriminate on the basis of race, color, religion, sex, or national origin); Minn. Stat. § 363A.08 subdiv. 2 (Supp. 2007) (listing sexual orientation as a class protected from employment discrimination).

29. New York, Colorado, North Dakota, and Montana offer broad protection of legal off-duty behavior. See NWI on Lifestyle Discrimination, supra note 11, at 11–13 (citing 2004 State by State Guide to Human Resources Law (John F. Buckley & Ronald M. Green eds., 2004)).

30. See Peters, supra note 9 (describing the $50 fee charged by one employer to all smokers to cover increased healthcare costs associated with smoking-related illnesses).

31. See CDC Report, supra note 12; see also Kate Fitch et al., American Legacy Foundation, Covering Smoking Cessation as a Health Benefit: A Case for Employers 11 (2007), http://www.americanlegacy .org/PDFPublications/ Milliman report ALF—3.15.07 .pdf (estimating that employees who suffer strokes or develop coronary artery disease can cost their employers upwards of $ 65,000 per year in medical expenses).

32. Two of the most active of these advocates are The American Cancer Society, http://www.cancer.org, and The American Legacy Foundation, http://www .americanlegacy.org.

33. See Am. Cancer Soc'y, Cancer Facts & Figures 2008, at 48-51, http://www.cancer.org/downloads/STT /2008CAFFfinalsecured.pdf.

34. See News Release, U.S. Dep't of Health & Human Servs., Medicare Will Help Beneficiaries Quit Smoking: New Proposed Coverage for Counseling as Medicare Shifts Focus to Prevention (Dec. 23, 2004), available at http://www.hhs.gov/news/press/2004pres /20041223a.html (stating that "in 1993, smoking cost the Medicare program about $ 14.2 billion, or approximately 10 percent of Medicare's total budget").

35. See, e.g., Rita Tehan, Cong. Research Serv. Report for Cong., Data Security Breaches: Context and Incident Summaries tbl. 1 (May 7, 2007), available at http://ftp.fas.org/sgp/crs/misc/RL33199.pdf.

36. Found. for Blood Research, Important Patient Information About . . . Cotinine Testing, http://www .fbr.org/publications/pamphlets/cotinine.html (last visited Apr. 10, 2008).

37. See Americans with Disabilities Act, 42 U.S.C. § 12112 (d)(4)(A) (2000). This provision of the ADA states:

A covered entity shall not require a medical examination and shall not make inquiries of an employee as to whether such employee is an individual with a disability or as to the nature or severity of the disability, unless such examination or inquiry is shown to be job-related and consistent with business necessity.
Id.

38. See, e.g., Jonathan Lynch, Survey Finds Most Smokers Want to Quit, CNN.com, July 25, 2002, http://archives.cnn.com/2002/HEALTH/07/25/cdc .smoking/index.html (citing a CDC survey that found that 70% of the 32,374 smokers surveyed responded that they wanted to quit smoking).

39. See, e.g., RIS Media.com, The Top New Year's Resolutions for 2008 and How to Keep Them (Dec. 20, 2007), http://rismedia.com/wp/2007-12-19/the-top-new-years-resolutions-for-2008-and-how-to-keep-them/.

40. See, e.g., Milt Freudenheim, Seeking Savings, Employers Help Smokers Quit, N.Y. Times, Oct. 26, 2007, at A1 (citing U.P.S. and Union Pacific Railroad as companies that offer smoking cessation programs).

41. See Free & Clear, Inc., Reducing the Burden of Smoking on Employee Health and Productivity, http:// www.freeclear.com/case for cessation/library/studies /burden.aspx?nav section=2 ("There is much evidence to support that paying for tobacco cessation treatment is the single, most cost-effective health insurance benefit for adults and is the benefit that has the greatest positive impact on health.") (citing Nat'l Bus. Group on Health, Reducing the Burden of Smoking on Employee Health and Productivity, Vol. 1, No. 5 (2003), available at http://www.business-grouphealth.org/pdfs/issuebrief cphssmoking.pdf).

42. Healthy People 2010 Volume II, Tobacco Use, http://www .healthypeople.gov/Document/HTML/Volume2/27Tobacco .htm# Toc489766214 (last visited Apr. 6, 2008).

43. Thirty states and the District of Columbia have lifestyle discrimination statutes that prohibit employers from firing employees for certain legal, private activities, including smoking. These states include: Arizona, California, Colorado, Connecticut, Illinois, Indiana, Kentucky, Louisiana, Maine, Minnesota,

Mississippi, Missouri, Montana, Nevada, New Hampshire, New Jersey, New Mexico, New York, North Carolina, North Dakota, Oklahoma, Oregon, Rhode Island, South Carolina, South Dakota, Tennessee, Virginia, West Virginia, Wisconsin, and Wyoming. NWI on Lifestyle Discrimination, supra note 11, at 11–13.

44. See, e.g., Samantha K. Graff, Tobacco Control Legal Consortium, There is no Constitutional Right to Smoke: 2008, at 3 (2d ed. 2008) (arguing that off-duty restrictions on smoking are not precluded by an employee's right to privacy), available at http://tobaccolawcenter.org/documents/constitutional-right.pdf.

45. See, e.g., Matthew Reilly, Florio Urged to Provide Smokers Bias Protection, Star-Ledger (Newark, N.J.), Jan. 4, 1991 (quoting Regina Carlson, executive director of the New Jersey Group Against Smoking Pollution (GASP), as stating that the passage of a bill that protects the privacy rights of smokers "would elevate drug addiction to civil rights status, along with race and sex").

46. See, e.g., Graff, supra note 44, at 5 (stating that "smoker protection laws," including laws protecting all off-duty legal conduct, are a "barrier to a smoke-free agenda").

47. Is it Time for a Fat Tax?, Psychol. Today, Sept.–Oct. 1997, at 16.

48. Id.

49. Darryl K. Brown, Democracy and Decriminalization, 86 Tex. L. Rev. 223, 238 (2007).

50. See, e.g., Chi. Historical Soc'y, History Files—Al Capone, http://www.chicagohs.org/history/capone/cpn1a.html (last visited Apr. 6, 2008).

51. See Brown, supra note 49, at 238.

52. See, e.g., 67 Fed. Reg. 36368-01 (Aug. 6, 2002) (to be codified at 10 C.F.R. pt. 430) (concerning the regulation of energy conservation standards for central air conditioners); Christopher D. Zalesky, Pharmaceutical Marketing Practices: Balancing Public Health and Law Enforcement Interests; Moving Beyond Regulation-Through-Litigation, 39 J. Health L. 235, 252 (2006) (discussing the FDA's regulation of the advertisement of prescription drugs, including the imprinting of prescription drug names on items such as coffee mugs).

53. A bipartisan group of legislators proposed legislation in February 2007 that would give the FDA regulatory power over tobacco. See Christopher Lee, New Push Grows for FDA Regulation of Tobacco, Wash. Post, Feb. 17, 2007, at A08. The Bush administration and the FDA's skepticism of such a regulatory measure appear to have stalled the movement for now. See Marc Kaufman, Decades-Long U.S. Decrease in Smoking Rates Levels Off, Wash. Post, Nov. 9, 2007, at A07.

Lewis Maltby is a president of the National Workrights Institute, a research and advocacy organization specializing in employment issues; he is also a faculty member of the Rutgers School of Management and Labor Relations. His publications include the book *Can They Do That? Reclaiming Our Fundamental Rights at Work* as well as a number of scholarly articles.

C. R. Hooper and C. Agule

 **NO**

Tobacco Regulation: Autonomy Up in Smoke?

The incidence of smokers in the developing world has increased exponentially over the past few *decades* and is now approaching epidemic proportions.[1] This momentous change has *come* about for one main reason: "Big Tobacco" has moved in. Phillip Morris, RJ Reynolds, British American Tobacco and other large tobacco companies have been targeting the emerging markets of the developing world for years and it is these companies that are primarily responsible for driving up the numbers of smokers in poor countries.[2,3]

The World Health Organization (WHO) *stepped* in a few years ago to try to contain the contagious spread of tobacco. To this end, the WHO drafted a tobacco control treaty in 2003 and then published a special report on tobacco control in 2008.[4,5] Both the treaty and the report set out a series of regulations to control the tobacco industry, and in this article *we* aim to show that these regulations can *be* defended by appeal to the principles of autonomy and liberty. Our motivation for defending the regulation in this way is simple: tobacco companies may appeal to liberal principles to defend the liberty rights of consumers to purchase their products without regulation.[6] This appeal to freedom to oppose regulation fails, however, because real freedom (understood as "critical autonomy") is enhanced rather than limited by regulation.

Now this latter claim stands in need of *some* defence, because it may *seem* paradoxical to claim that regulation, which invariably involves state interference in the voluntary transactions of producers and consumers, actually increases rather than decreases people's autonomy. However, *we* will argue in the third section of this paper that autonomy involves far more than the simple ability to make choices for oneself, which means that simply letting *people* engage in unregulated transactions will not protect their critical autonomy. Rather, regulation is needed to set up and maintain the conditions necessary for critical autonomy to flourish.

Smoking, Disease, and Statistics: Big Tobacco's Metastasis into the Developing World

The association between smoking and disease has been well known for over half a century.[7] Tobacco is a risk factor for six of the eight leading causes of death; it causes at least 10 different kinds of cancers; and it is implicated in the development of a number of serious respiratory and cardiovascular diseases.[8,9] Furthermore, an estimated 100 million deaths were caused by tobacco in the 20th century and if current trends continue a billion more people will die of tobacco-related diseases in the 21st century.[8]

The global *distribution* of smokers, meanwhile, has changed rapidly over the past few decades. In the developed world there has been a steep decrease in the number of smokers, while in the developing world there has been an explosive increase in the number of tobacco users.[10] Indeed, of the 1.8 billion smokers worldwide, around 84% live in the developing world, and over 70% of smoking-related deaths now occur in poor rather than rich countries.[11,12]

This change in the distribution of smokers is deeply worrying. Smoking tends to kill *people* at the height of their productivity and thus causes substantial economic hardship in poor countries.[12] Smoking also causes a range of chronic diseases that place substantial strains on healthcare resources. Poor countries cannot *cope* with this increased pressure, as they are already overtaxed by an inequitable distribution of the global disease burden. Thus, the globalisation of smoking will make the worst-off members of our global society even more badly off than they already are.

Counterattack: The Policies of Victory

In 2003, the World Health Assembly adopted the WHO Framework Convention on Tobacco Control.[4] This tobacco control treaty was the first global treaty attempting to regulate the tobacco industry, and it has now been signed by 168 states, making it the most widely accepted in UN history.[4]

The treaty *set* out a programme to reduce the number of smokers worldwide by reducing tobacco supply and demand. In particular the treaty advocated preventing sales to minors; banning smoking in public places; providing education aimed at increasing public awareness about the dangers of smoking; regulating tobacco marketing and advertising; and taxing tobacco products to reduce demand.[4]

In 2008, the WHO published another report, called the MPOWER report, which supplemented the original treaty by advocating the implementation of six cost-effective solutions previously shown to be highly successful in reducing tobacco use.[5]

Importantly, both the treaty and the report aim to curb the spread of smoking through *regulation*. This inevitably means that the WHO's recommendations will come under fire from liberals, libertarians and tobacco executives who will decry paternalistic state interference in the lives of citizens. However, we argue that that these regulations, which we outline in the next section, can be justified even on liberal grounds.

A Liberal Defence of Tobacco Regulation

Liberals are committed to some form of Mill's harm principle, which states that interference in someone's affairs is justified only if it prevents harms to others, never for paternalistic reasons.[13] Of course, smoking can cause harm to other people, but it does not always do so, and therefore a blanket ban is unacceptable.

However, though total prohibition cannot be defended from a liberal position, the kind of partial regulation of the tobacco industry advocated by the WHO can be defended from such a perspective. This is possible because some regulation is required to properly protect people's *higher-order* autonomy.

This may seem a surprising claim, because autonomy is commonly understood as the ability to make one's *own* decisions about what to do and how to do it. Given this understanding, it makes sense to argue that regulation can only interfere with people's freedom to choose. However, although we accept that the ability to choose for oneself is necessary for autonomy, we also suggest that it is not sufficient for higher-order autonomy. The point is that people who have the ability to make their own decisions, but who do not possess other important capacities, will achieve only an "uncritical," or first-order, type of autonomy.[14]

In order to achieve "critical," or second-order, autonomy people must certainly be able to make their own decisions, but they also need to have access to relevant information so that they can make informed decisions; they need to achieve a basic level of intellectual maturity so that they can come to some kind of reasoned decision; and, finally, they need to be able to reflect upon their first-order desires and be able to act upon their second-order desires. Second-order desires are preferences about first-order desires, and our claim is that people can be truly autonomous only if they can decide, at a "higher" level, whether to follow or to banish their more primitive preferences. Following one's first-order desires is not enough; control over one's first-order desires is also crucial for critical autonomy. It could also be argued that people can really achieve *full* critical autonomy only if they have the added ability to question and modify the contextual rules within which choices are made.[14]

Given this more extensive account of autonomy, it should be clear why some regulation can be defended from a liberal point of view. Government regulation is needed to ensure that people's critical autonomy is suitably protected and nurtured. If the free market reigns supreme, people may well achieve some basic or uncritical level of autonomy, but they will not achieve the fuller kind of autonomy that most liberals care about.

With this in mind, we can now examine some of the WHO's specific regulatory suggestions to see how these contribute to the protection and nurturing of people's critical autonomy. However, we should first note that *all* of the regulatory measures discussed below could be defended by a general, autonomy-based, argument, because tobacco products contain an addictive substance. The key point is that many smokers have second-order desires *not* to smoke, but they are unable to act on these desires because they have an overpowering first-order desire to smoke. This overpowering desire is generated by nicotine and there can be no doubt that this addictive substance frustrates people's ability to act on their second-order desires. This matters because, as we have argued above, critical autonomy cannot be achieved unless people have the capacity to act on their second-order desires. Thus, the addictive nature of tobacco provides the ammunition required for a quite general autonomy-based argument in defence of *all* tobacco regulations.

Regulation on the Sale of Tobacco to Children

The WHO argues that governments and tobacco companies alike have a duty to ensure that children do not get access to tobacco. The autonomy concern arises here because children do not have the capacity to make informed decisions about whether they wish to engage in a risky, expensive and potentially life-threatening activity. Nor, indeed, do they have the capacity to understand the nature of addiction. Of course children have the ability to make their own choices, but, as we have argued above, this does not mean that they have the intellectual maturity to make *critically autonomous* choices. Thus, in order to protect their future autonomy, they must be prevented from smoking until they become adults.

However, a blanket ban on the sale of tobacco to children will be insufficient to protect these autonomy interests, because no such law is likely to be very effective. Thus, further measures might be needed. For example the sale of sweets, snacks and toys in the form of tobacco could be prohibited, as could the sale of individual cigarettes and the distribution of free cigarettes to minors.[4]

The impact of these regulations on the autonomy of other smokers and potential smokers is limited. Adults may find themselves having to offer some proof of age in order to purchase cigarettes (especially if they are young adults), and they may be required to purchase a pack of cigarettes instead of purchasing single cigarettes. However, these restrictions will put only the slightest of stumbling blocks in the path of an adult who wishes to smoke.

Regulation on Smoking in Public Places: Protecting Others

A ban on smoking in public places appeals to concern about the serious health risks posed by passive or second-hand smoking to third parties who may not have consented to be exposed to the smoke. However, we cannot prohibit every activity that poses a risk to others in the absence of consent, because many every-day activities pose such a risk. What is more, garnering consent for everyone who might be exposed to the risk is often incredibly expensive and in some cases it is impossible (perhaps because the potential exposure class cannot be usefully identified in advance).[15]

The autonomy critique of smoking bans is usually that, if such bans were desirable, then the market would bring them about. However, there is a host of reasons why markets may not operate perfectly, especially with regard to tobacco. For example, many members of the public may under-appreciate the harms of secondary smoke inhala-

tion and so may unintentionally risk significant long-term health costs in order to garner relatively moderate short-term wage gains. Though such a trade-off is not necessarily irrational, if the market participants have imperfect information, their choices will not serve their reflective interests. Permitting a market failure is not respecting autonomy. In the context of a market failure, perhaps the best way to respect autonomy is to attempt to discern what the result of a perfectly functioning market would be and then to implement that result. It is certainly plausible that a perfectly functioning market would yield predominantly tobacco-free public spaces. That mistakes could be made in the course of this process does not mean that it is not autonomy-enhancing.

There are two negative impacts on autonomy posed by such regulation. First, those individuals who wish to work, live or participate in an environment where tobacco smoke is permitted will be denied that choice. This may seem like an unlikely choice, but if, for example, more alcohol is consumed when tobacco smoking is permitted, hospitality employees might prefer to work in tobacco-permitting establishments in order to receive a greater income. If the market failure argument is compelling, however, one side or the other will have to give way, and aggregate measures of autonomy are fraught with difficulty. Second, if bans on public smoking become the norm, then public smoking bans may approach a total smoking ban in effect.

Regulation on the Marketing and Advertising of Tobacco

The WHO also argues that tobacco companies should be prohibited from advertising their products through direct advertising or through sponsorship. The tobacco companies' business can survive restrictions on marketing to children and restrictions on smoking in certain public places. Nevertheless, a blanket ban on advertising and sponsorship is likely to severely restrict the companies' ability to market and distribute their wares. However desirable this might be from a public health standpoint, preventing the tobacco companies from marketing their products is also preventing their potential consumers from making their own decisions about consuming tobacco.

So, whether this restriction can be justified on purely liberal grounds is unclear. There is no question that governments can prohibit misleading advertising and that they can require tobacco advertising and cigarette packaging to contain overt references to the addictive nature and health risks of tobacco. Likewise, governments can proscribe advertising that might appeal to children. These restrictions can be defended by appeal to the autonomy of potential smokers, because each measure ensures that those who smoke are able to make an *informed* choice about doing so.

It could also be argued that more stringent restrictions are justifiable on the grounds of autonomy. For example, a case could be made in favour of banning all tobacco advertising because advertising undermines the autonomy of people whose real autonomy is already being subverted by the addictive nature of nicotine. We have already noted that the addictive nature of nicotine provides a general defence of all tobacco regulation on the basis of autonomy. However, this argument has special resonance in the case of advertising precisely because advertising has the specific ability to further undermine rational choice.

Taxing to Reduce Consumption

The WHO also recommends taxing tobacco in order to reduce consumption. In general, taxes have a complicated relationship with autonomy. The popular response is to note that taxation represents government arrogation of the freedom to determine what to do with private money. While that complaint has a kernel of truth, it is often predicated upon the assumption that the greatest freedom would be the least government interference- that is, the notion that we have the most freedom if the government takes none of our resources. This, however, is not the case. In the absence of a properly functioning government of some form, there would be no security to enable private citizens to make use of the resources at their disposal, and properly functioning government requires taxation. While taxation may reduce the taxpayers' autonomy, it is often a necessary component of programmes that, on the whole, increase autonomy.

How, then, are we to understand the taxation of tobacco? We should look to autonomy-increasing programmes of which taxation is a necessary component. If the money is used to fund educational initiatives that increase public awareness of the dangers of smoking, to set up programmes to help tobacco addicts quit or to enforce tobacco regulations, then the loss of taxpayer autonomy may be offset by the increase in autonomy caused by those policies, as discussed earlier. Moreover, although such programmes could probably be funded by general taxation spread over the entire population, tobacco-specific taxation allows the taxpayers a greater degree of volition in the matter.

Taxation can also be used to directly dissuade people from using tobacco. If cigarettes are more expensive, fewer people will smoke, and some who continue will smoke

less.[16] This use of taxpayers' money seems harder to justify from the liberal point of view in light of the harm principle. At least some smokers are informed, competent adults, and their ability to smoke as they elect is undeniably restricted by such taxation.

Two responses can be made to this point. First, taxation to dissuade people from smoking may help to offset the threat to autonomy engendered by the addictive nature of nicotine. This, of course, would involve a delicate balancing act between protecting people's freedom to smoke and protecting their freedom to give up smoking when they are addicted. Consequently, this argument could only be used to defend *limited* taxation to dissuade people from smoking.

Second, the standard response to this argument is that smoking has tremendous negative externalities, such as the social cost of disease, and forcing others to bear the cost of those externalities impinges upon their autonomy. Hence, taxing tobacco in order to reduce use does not violate the harm principle, as the interest being served is not that of the smoker, but that of the rest of society forced to bear some of the costs of the smoker's choices. For example, when a worker contracts a tobacco-related illness, he may be forced (via insurance and healthcare policies) to bear his personal healthcare costs. However, other people will be forced to bear lost productivity costs. Similarly, the costs of the regulatory scheme to address tobacco and the social costs of the diversion of medical research from other ailments to tobacco-related problems are borne socially. Addressing these social burdens via taxation protects the autonomy of those who would otherwise be forced to bear the costs of smokers' personal decisions.

The externality argument is a powerful one, and although many find it persuasive in the context of tobacco regulation, it is not clear that an argument solely from autonomy concerns can provide a reasoned distinction between risk-causing activity we wish to regulate (eg, tobacco use) and risk-causing activity we think should be left free of regulatory burden (eg, playing football in a park).[15] Where the line should be drawn is not self-evident, but we are confident that tobacco regulation will fall on the "right" side of this line.

Conclusion

The WHO's regulations are aimed at stopping the spread of Big Tobacco through the developing world. We have argued in this paper that these regulatoiy policies can be defended on the grounds of autonomy because regulation can ensure that only competent, rational and informed adults become smokers. Our argument neuters the ability of tobacco companies to attack the WHO's suggestions by appealing to the rights of consumers to consume what they wish. Of course, there are limitations to the legitimate regulation that the international community can impose on the production, sale and consumption of tobacco if the defence of the regulation is based on autonomy alone. Nonetheless, we hope that we have helped arm the WHO's tobacco control regulations against Big Tobacco's potential libertarian counterarguments and we hope that our arguments encourage national governments to continue their regulatory fight against the tobacco epidemic.

References

1. Action on Smoking and Health (ASH). *Essential information on tobacco and the developing world.* London: ASH, 2007. http://www.ash.org.uk/files /documents/ASH 126.pdf (accessed 28 Apr 2009).
2. Lovell G. *You are the target. Big tobacco: lies, scams— now the truth.* Vancouver: Chryan Communications, 2002.
3. Saffer H. *Economics of tobacco control: tobacco advertising and promotion.* Washington, DC: The World Bank Group, 2000. http://www1.worldbank.org /tobacco/tcdc/215T0236.PDF (accessed 28 Apr 2009).
4. World Health Organization (WHO). *WHO framework convention on tobacco control.* Geneva: WHO, 2003. http://www.who.int/fctc/text_download/en/index .html (accessed 28 Apr 2009).
5. World Health Organization (WHO). *WHO report on the global tobacco epidemic, 2008. the MPOWER package.* Geneva: WHO, 2008. http://www.who.int /tobacco/mpower/mpower_report_full_2008.pdf (accessed 28 Apr 2009).
6. Taylor P. *Smoke ring; the politics of tobacco.* London: Bodley Head, 1984.
7. Doll R, Hill A. Smoking and carcinoma of the lung: preliminary report. *BMJ* 1950;2:739–48.
8. World Health Organization. *Tobacco free initiative (TFI): tobacco facts.* Geneva: WHO, 2008. http:// www.who.int/tobacco/mpower/tobacco_facts/en/index .html (accessed 28 Apr 2009).
9. Cancer Research UK. CancerStats key facts on lung cancer and smoking. London: Cancer Research UK, 2007. http://info.cancerresearchuk.org /cancerstats/types/lung/ (accessed 28 Apr 2009).
10. Food and Agriculture Organization of the United Nations (FAO). *Projections of tobacco production, consumption and trade to the year 2010.* Rome: FAD, 2003. http://www.fao.org/docrep/006/Y4956E/y4956e00 .HTM (accessed 28 Apr 2009).
11. Triggle N. Smoking gets own "Kyoto treaty." *BBC News UK version* 27 Feb 2005. http://news.bbc.co.uk/1 /hi/health/4295845.stm (accessed 28 Apr 2009).
12. World Health Organization (WHO). O&A: tobacco. Online O&A 7 Feb 2006. http:// www.who.int/topics /tobacco/qa/en/index.html (accessed 28 Apr 2009).
13. Mill J. *On liberty.* London: Longman, 2007.
14. Doyal L, Gough I. *A theory of human need.* London: Macmillan. 1991.
15. Nozick R. *Anarchy, state, and utopia.* Oxford: Basic Books, 1974.
16. van Walbeek C. *Tobacco excise taxation in South Africa: tools for advancing tobacco control in the XX/st century: success stories and lessons learned.* Geneva: World Health Organization, 2003.

C.R. Hooper is a senior lecturer in medical ethics and law at St George's, University of London. His current research interests span global bioethics, political philosophy as applied to health and the use of novel e-Learning materials in the teaching and assessment of medical and healthcare ethics and law.

EXPLORING THE ISSUE

Do Anti-Smoking Policies Violate Smokers' Autonomy?

Critical Thinking and Reflection

1. Explain why employers wish to prohibit risky off-duty behavior, such as smoking, among their employees. Do such restrictions respect the autonomy of employees? Why or why not?
2. Do you think that a person who is addicted to nicotine is able to give voluntary consent to the purchase and use of tobacco products? Why or why not? If not, is the addictiveness of nicotine grounds for banning the purchase and use of tobacco products?
3. Select another aspect of life in which people are addicted to an activity or are obsessed with an activity. What regulations do you think should be imposed on that activity?
4. Would you accept a position working for a company that produces, sells, or advertises tobacco products? Why or why not?

Is There Common Ground?

Superficially, there is a great deal of agreement between the authors. All are in agreement that autonomy is an extremely important moral value and that efforts to violate the Principle of Autonomy should be resisted. Moreover, they also agree that tobacco is a highly dangerous substance that poses significant health risks not only to the people who directly use tobacco products, but also to people who are exposed to secondhand smoke. As a result, all support some form of regulation of tobacco products.

The dispute among the authors arises from their application of the Principle of Autonomy to tobacco regulation. Maltby writes primarily about tobacco use in the United States, which has already imposed strict restrictions on tobacco advertising and publicizes widely the health risks associated with tobacco use. Hooper and Agule are concerned about the expansion of tobacco use into markets without strict restrictions on tobacco advertising and among people without an accurate understanding of the health risks of smoking. There would seem to be agreement on the need to protect the autonomy of consumers

by ensuring they make informed decisions on tobacco use, free from the influence of deceptive advertising and in full knowledge of the detrimental effect of tobacco use on health. With regard to protecting the autonomy of consumers by ensuring they make voluntary decisions on tobacco use, the authors are in more direct conflict. Presumably, however, both would support reseach into safe, effective methods of ending addiction to nicotine, so that any use of tobacco products be truly voluntary, and not the result of an addictive compulsion.

Additional Resources

Robert Goodin, *No Smoking: The Ethical Issues* (University of Chicago Press, 1990)

J.E. Katz, "Individual rights advocacy in tobacco control policies: An assessment and recommendation," *Tobacco Control 14* (2005)

Thaddeus Mason Pope, "Balancing public health against individual liberty: The ethics of smoking regulations," *University of Pittsburgh Law Review* (2000)

Internet References . . .

The Tobacco Institute Document Site

http://www.tobaccoinstitute.com/

Centers for Disease Control and Prevention: Smoking & Tobacco Use

http://www.cdc.gov/tobacco/index.htm

Smoking, Liberty, and Health Fascism

http://www.pierrelemieux.org/re-smoking.html

Selected, Edited, and with Issue Framing Material by:
Owen M. Smith, *Stephen F. Austin State University*
and
Anne Collins Smith, *Stephen F. Austin State University*

ISSUE

Should Drugs Be Legalized?

YES: Vanessa Baird, from "Legalize Drugs—All of Them!" *New Internationalist* (2012)

NO: Theodore Dalrymple, from "Don't Legalize Drugs," *City Journal* (1997)

Learning Outcomes

After reading this issue, you will be able to:

- Explain the benefits that proponents of drug legalization claim would follow from decriminalizing drugs that are now illegal.
- Explain the harms that opponents of drug legalization claim would follow from decriminalizing drugs that are now illegal.
- Formulate your own position on drug legalization and identify evidence supporting your position.
- Identify the main objections to your position and formulate responses to these objections.

ISSUE SUMMARY

YES: Vanessa Baird argues that the legalization of drugs would provide many sorts of benefits: for example, crime would fall, the quality of life in inner cities would rise, and taxpayers would no longer have to pay for an unwinnable "war on drugs." Legalizing drugs would also benefit countries where cocaine and heroin production are currently controlled by organized crime.

NO: Theodore Dalrymple stresses the harm that drugs can do and the danger of "giving up" in the "war on drugs." He takes issue with most of the claims of the supporters of legalization, and more generally with Mill's "harm principle": the idea that in a free society, adults should be permitted to do whatever they please (provided that they are willing to accept the consequences of their own actions, and those actions don't cause harm to others).

Among the most contentious political issues confronting the United States, and indeed the entire world, is the use of psychoactive drugs for recreational purposes. In the early part of the 20th century, the federal government began to implement legislation to address the growing number of citizens who had become addicted to such drugs. By 1970, however, alarm at the proliferation of new psychoactive drugs fueled the development of a wide-ranging set of policies regarding the manufacture, importation, distribution, possession, and consumption of these drugs. This set of policies, soon dubbed the "war on drugs," has had a tremendous impact on contemporary society, not only in

terms of the immense amount of money spent each year to enforce these policies, but also in terms of the human cost suffered by those who abuse these drugs, along with their families, friends, and indeed society at large.

In the decades since the inauguration of the "war on drugs," criticism of these policies has become more and more strident. To what extent has the "war on drugs" been effective in reducing the availability and use of psychoactive drugs?

Has the "war on drugs" been unnecessarily counterproductive, both in the expansion of the criminal justice system and the development of organized crime? Is it time to approach the recreational use of psychoactive drugs in a radically different way? If so, which policies should be adopted by the government to reduce the abuse of psychoactive drugs? Before answering these questions, let us briefly examine current federal drug policy and address recent developments in the "war on drugs."

A psychoactive drug is a substance whose use affects the mind of the user, including alterations in mood (feeling), perception, thought processes (cognition), and/or behavior. For millennia, psychoactive drugs have been used in religious or spiritual contexts by numerous cultures throughout the world. Many psychoactive drugs have medicinal uses, including treatment for pain management and psychiatric disorders. The principal focus of this investigation, however, is the recreational use of psychoactive drugs.

Current federal drug policy is based on the Controlled Substances Act (CSA), which formed part of the Comprehensive Drug Abuse Prevention and Control Act of 1970. This legislation created five classifications (schedules) of controlled substances based on three factors: the potential for abuse of the drug, the presence or absence of current accepted medical uses for the drug in treatment in the United States, and the safety with which the drug may be used, including the degree to which use of the drug will lead to physical or psychological dependence. Each schedule is associated with a different degree of regulation, including restrictions on the production and prescription of the controlled substances. The Administrator of the Drug Enforcement Administration (DEA) is primarily responsible for determining whether or not a substance should be controlled as well as making changes in the classification of a controlled substance.

The most dangerous psychoactive drugs are placed within Schedule I. These drugs are considered to have a high potential for abuse, no currently accepted medical use in treatment in the United States, and a lack of safety standards for use of the drug under medical supervision. Included among Schedule I drugs are marijuana and its cannabinoids, heroin, LSD (lysergic acid diethylamide), mescaline (the main psychoactive constituent of peyote), psilocybin (the main psychoactive constituent of "magic mushrooms"), DMT (dimethyltryptamine, a constituent of ayahuasca), and MDMA (also known as "ecstasy"). Strict religious exemptions for use of Schedule I drugs have been extended for peyote and DMT. Criminal penalties for violations of the federal laws and regulations regarding Schedule I drugs can be severe.

The use of recreational drug classifications such as those found in the CSA is controversial, as is the placement of specific drugs within this classification system. In particular, the placement of marijuana and hallucinogenic drugs such as LSD and psilocybin in Schedule I is coming under increasing criticism. Researchers in Great Britain have developed alternative drug classification systems that focus more precisely on the harm posed by specific psychoactive drugs; these systems indicate that marijuana, LSD, and MDMA pose less threat than do tobacco or alcohol, and therefore should be regulated less strictly than under current law. The Netherlands, Portugal, and Uruguay have been at the forefront of an international movement to legalize the sale, possession, and use of marijuana for recreational purposes.

In the United States, there have been a number of successful initiatives in past two decades on the state level to remove or modify the penalties associated with the possession and use of marijuana. The original thrust of these initiatives was to legalize the use of marijuana for the treatment of medical conditions. Since 1996, 20 states and Washington, D.C., have enacted a variety of "medical marijuana" laws that provide protection from state arrest and prosecution for the possession of a small amount of marijuana for personal medical use; in addition, these laws frequently authorize the establishment of marijuana growers or dispensaries to provide marijuana for medical use. In 2012, Colorado and Washington became the first two states to legalize the recreational use of marijuana by adults aged 21 and older, and voters in Alaska, Oregon, and Washington, D.C. passed similar initiatives in 2014. Despite these measures, marijuana still remains a Schedule I drug, and use of marijuana, even for medical purposes, still remains a violation of federal law.

In moral terms, the recreational use of marijuana may initially be expressed in terms of the Principle of Autonomy, which states that adults are moral agents and should be accorded the dignity of making decisions about their conduct, including the use of psychoactive substances. Moral theorists as diverse as Immanuel Kant and John Stuart Mill, however, assert that indulgence in idle pleasure, especially pleasure that impairs the use of mental faculties, is morally objectionable; arguments on both deontological and utilitarian grounds might therefore be made not only against addiction to psychoactive drugs, but also against their regular use.

The issue here, however, is not whether the use of psychoactive drugs is immoral. Rather, the issue is the morality of legalizing the use of such drugs for recreational purposes. The principal moral foundation for this issue is therefore not the Principle of Autonomy, but another principle—the Principle of Harm. According to this principle, the primary moral justification for restricting individual autonomy is the reduction of the harm produced by action, both to the moral agent and to others affected by the action. This principle lends itself to consequentialist analysis, in which the consequences of an action (such as legalizing the recreational use of psychoactive substances) are predicted and assessed for the amount and type of benefit and harm they produce. The moral debate, and in many cases the legal debate as well, is thus reduced to duelling accounts of the relative benefits and harms that would result from reduced regulation, or even legalization, of the recreational use of psychoactive drugs, primarily marijuana.

Proponents of the legalization of psychoactive drugs for recreational purposes propose a variety of plans for establishing legal marketplaces for these substances, with greater or lesser degrees of government regulation and control. In general, however, they assert that these marketplaces would offer an opportunity for monitoring the quality of psychoactive drugs available for public consumption, reduce the role of criminal organizations in supplying controlled substances, and generate revenue for the government through the imposition of taxes and fees.

Each of these claims, however, is disputed by opponents of the legalization of psychoactive drugs for recreational purposes. Moreover, these opponents argue for a degree of governmental paternalism, in which policies on the regulation and control of psychoactive substances can provide incentives for individuals to exercise their autonomy in ways that do not diminish their personal development.

In the following selections, Vanessa Baird and Theodore Dalrymple present radically different views on the legalization of psychotropic drugs. Baird argues that government programs meant to control the use of these substances are misguided; in fact, these efforts are themselves responsible for much drug-related crime, and both drug users and the general public would benefit from the legalization of drugs. In contrast, Dalrymple argues that the use of psychoactive drugs is harmful in itself, and any proposal short of full legalization would be impractical, since drug dealers would continue to undermine any remaining restrictions on the sale of restricted drugs. Furthermore, he contends, the legalization of drugs would reap far fewer benefits that legalization proponents predict and would lead to an increase in drug abuse and drug addiction, with a worsening of the social ills associated with these problems.

YES ⤶

Vanessa Baird

Legalize Drugs—All of Them!

We were sitting in a café drinking cola. My two companions, drug enforcement soldiers, kept their guns resting across their knees. Fingers not quite on triggers but close enough for rapid response. They were smiling.

The woman running the café was not. Her face was closed, expressionless. Through the open window we could hear the almost constant sound of light aircraft taking off and landing somewhere in the thick greenery of Peru's Upper Huallaga Valley. When, earlier, I had innocently asked a local mayor whether such planes were carrying drugs, he had smiled and equally innocently replied: "They are air taxis. That's how people get about here."

Later I went out with soldiers on patrol. Running through the jungle, we spotted coca plants being grown between generous banana leaves. Finally we came upon a lab for making coca paste. It was a simple affair—two big piles of coca leaves, a trough made out of wood and plastic sheeting, and some cans of kerosene.

"It's been abandoned," remarked one of the soldiers. He didn't seem surprised or disappointed. "Will they be back?" I asked.

"Probably not. They won't use this one again if they know we have been here. They will make another lab somewhere else. It's easy."

This was 27 years ago, early days in the "war on drugs." And already then it seemed hopeless.

Steps to Showdown

"They used to laugh at us," says Danny Kushlick of Transform, a British drug policy reform group.

Today he and his colleagues are regularly called upon to make the case for ending the prohibitionist policy that has dominated the world since the UN Single Convention on Narcotic Drugs was put in place in 1961.

They have been researching other possibilities, including an idea that until recently was pretty much taboo—making all drugs legal.

The list of high-profile figures supporting the cause for reform is growing by the minute, and ranges from Nobel laureate economists and police chiefs to stand-up comedians and drug activists.

Serving politicians have tended to be cautious, fearing voter backlash. Before coming to power, both Barack Obama and David Cameron indicated that they were in favour of reform, including some degree of legalization. Once in high office, they fell silent. Mexico's former leader Vicente Fox, now a leading advocate of "legalization all the way," waited until he was safely out of office.

But today, even incumbent leaders are sticking their heads above the parapet. "That's something new," says Kushlick.

In the past few months, President Juan Manuel Santos of Colombia, for example, has initiated a global taskforce for a total rethink of drug policy. Costa Rica's Laura Chinchilla has said the consumption of drugs should be a matter of health, not law. Guatemalan President Otto Pérez Molina is calling for legalization of the use and sale of drugs. While in Uruguay, President José Mujica has proposed a groundbreaking law that would enable the state to sell marijuana to its people and derive tax revenue from it. "Someone has to be first," he commented.

The US is not immune to the whiff of drug revolution. In November three states—Washington, Oregon and Colorado—will vote on legalization of marijuana for adult recreational use. This would directly contravene both federal law and the UN Convention. "We're heading for a showdown," says Sanho Tree of the Institute for Policy Studies in Washington. "It's hard to talk about tipping points but I think we are close to one with regard to cannabis. This is a clear sign that people are looking for a different paradigm."

War on Drugs

From a country like Mexico, where ever-deepening drug-related violence claims 33 lives a day, the global "war on drugs" declared by President Nixon 40 years ago can be seen for what it is—a colossal failure. Costing more than a trillion dollars, this "war" has involved hundreds of thousands of military personnel, customs officers, enforcement agents, crop eradicators, police and prison staff. But still the illegal narcotics trade flourishes—worth about $320 billion a year—and drug use keeps growing.

Worse, the war on drugs has unleashed a deadly set of "unintended consequences."

It's "like trying to put out an electrical fire by dousing it with water," says Sanho Tree.

Crackdowns on drug cartels have increased the huge profits bestowed by illegality. Violence has surged as rival groups jockey to fill the vacuum left when a major cartel has been hammered by government forces.

The global war is militarizing societies and tearing up democratic rights. It also enables illegal drug money to flow into the coffers of Al Qaeda, the Taliban, and the Colombian FARC, ELN, AUC and others.[1,2] Meanwhile, punishing drug users and sellers has filled prisons and increased addiction.

Something needs to be done.

"It is the biggest, most complex challenge facing us today," says Mauricio Rodríguez, Colombian ambassador in London and a close ally of President Santos, whose proposed taskforce of global experts is already at work under the auspices of the Inter-American Drug Abuse Control Commission (CICAD), expected to report within 12 months.

Colombians know better than most the cost of the war on drugs. They have been on the frontline of the US-designed Plan Colombia, a $7 billion anti-narcotics and military aid drive also used to tackle leftwing insurgency. In 2002 the conflict was claiming some 28,000 Colombian lives a year.[3]

Today, violence is down by about a third and coca production has declined by 58 percent. "But any improvements in Colombia have meant serious deterioration in other parts of Latin America and the world," says Rodríguez. "Production has gone to Peru and Bolivia and traffic has gone mostly to Central America, West Africa, and islands of the Caribbean."

This is the so-called balloon effect, where action taken in one place simply pushes the illegal drug problem into another.

Latin Americans, the ambassador says, are fed up with drug-related violence. "Why do we have to pay such a price for a problem that is essentially not ours? We are not big consumers; it's unfair that tens of thousands of Mexicans or Colombians or Guatemalans have to lose their lives because of consumption in the US. Who is really responsible? The consumers are and so are those who have

created this model of illegality. Either consuming nations need to reduce their consumption or they need to help us to change this model."

The Damage Done?

Many people in those major consuming nations would agree. In recent months opinion polls have shown remarkable upswings in people supporting legalization of some drugs at least. A survey in Colorado showed 61 percent of the population supported legalization of cannabis. Polls in Britain, Australia and Canada show similar seismic shifts in public attitude.

The number of people who have never tried an illegal recreational drug is dwindling and with it the hysteria that surrounds narcotics. Psychoactive—mind-altering—substances have always been a part of human experience. And other animal experience too, if you count elephants bingeing on fermenting fruit and goats getting high on coffee beans.

The effects of different drugs and their wider impacts vary enormously. But for many people, current legal classification of drugs seems divorced from the reality they know, especially in relation to cannabis or "party drugs" like ecstasy.

There is also a growing awareness that some legal drugs—alcohol and tobacco, for example—are much more harmful than many currently illegal ones. Some illicit substances have medically therapeutic benefits, such as cannabis (to alleviate the symptoms of multiple sclerosis) and ecstasy or magic mushrooms (for treating post-traumatic stress disorder), that cannot be properly researched or exploited by medical professionals and patients.

But what about the hard stuff?

Heroin and crack cocaine are high on the scientific list of harmful illegal drugs. The 27 million "problem drug users" in the world tend to be addicted to these or related substances. The proliferation of drugs like krokodil (a cheaper heroin derivative that gets its name from the skin damage it causes and its flesh-devouring tendencies) in Russia compounds fear of drugs and what they can do.

Andria Efthimiou-Mordaunt is a Harm Reduction activist and former heroin addict living in London. She sees addiction as a disease to be treated. She also thinks that legal regulation and control is the only way to go. "I don't say it fearlessly though, because I think that, at least temporarily, there will be an increase in drug use. But I don't think that will be sustained."

In 2001, Portugal embarked on one of the most daring and progressive actions in recent times: it effectively decriminalized the personal use of all drugs, including the hard ones.

The results were interesting. Drug use carried on increasing but at a slower rate than in Spain or France. But, significantly, addiction to hard drugs fell by half, from an estimated 100,000 addicts before decriminalization to 40,000 in 2011. Opiate-related deaths and HIV infection were also down—the latter by 17 percent.[4,5] This is partly because Portugal coupled decriminalization with a well-funded public health programme to help people get off drugs.

Counter-intuitive as it may seem, the evidence suggests that criminalization does not deter use—but decriminalization does.

It makes perfect sense to Andria Efthimiou-Mordaunt. "I have now heard thousands of stories of people who have become dependent on heroin, cocaine and so on. Most of us were most interested because these drugs were forbidden.

"Also we were a bit vulnerable, didn't have much love for ourselves, and therefore we put ourselves in danger. We don't care that it's a crime and we could go to jail. We just want to use this drug that we have found is comforting or exciting or pleasurable."

She explains: "People aren't wilfully creating havoc: they are doing something that they find will assist them in their lives, even if it's temporary and it gets them into all sorts of other problems. But for the majority of us, it is clear that the prohibitive punitive system has actually been the cause of most of our other problems—like poverty, homelessness, sex work, shoplifting, dealing."

These problems in turn intensify the need for the drug and make it harder to stop.

"What saddens me is that some of the people who are most punitive and intolerant are those who are directly affected. One of our arguments needs to be that just because you are legalizing the drug does not mean that you are promoting it. You can say: look, we are not changing the laws because we want everyone to take these substances, but because they're currently bloody dangerous because of where you get them from."

There are many good models for reducing harm, through a combination of *de facto* decriminalization and supportive treatment. "In Switzerland they found that people would come off heroin faster because there was nothing to fight against any more; they still had their addictions but once the other bits of their lives had been sorted to some degree, there wasn't this huge monster that needed to be medicated every day."

In Vancouver, Canada, the response to a high level of drug deaths was the creation of a "consumption room" where users can safely inject legal or illegal drugs. They call it "the demilitarized zone." Similar initiatives have been developed in Australia, Spain, Germany, Portugal and the Netherlands.

Decriminalize or Legalize?

So why not go down the Portuguese route and decriminalize the use of all drugs?

It is, to varying degrees, already happening in practice in around 25 countries, mainly in Europe and Latin America, where people found in possession may simply have their drugs confiscated but will not be prosecuted.[5]

However, decriminalization does not deal with the supply side—and the deadly nexus of money and violence.

Drugs have little intrinsic value. It's prohibition that gives an astronomical "price support" to traffickers. The profits are extreme and so are the violence and corruption needed to protect them. Hence the grotesquely cruel methods used by the gangs, making simple decapitation a blessing.

Only legalization and regulation can break the hold of the criminals. Legal drugs could be taxed. The corrupt network of tax-evading banks and front companies that support the industry by laundering drug money would have to start paying their way. "The war on drugs I would like to see is the war on laundering drug money," says ambassador Rodríguez. And some of the criminals might even be caught. It's worth remembering that only when the prohibition of alcohol ended in the US was Al Capone finally apprehended—on a charge of tax evasion in 1933.

Making drugs legal has many potential benefits. It could interrupt the flow of money to warlords, corrupt officials and the Taliban that is ensuring continuing instability in Afghanistan and other parts of the world. This is highlighted in a recent study by the former MI6 director of operations Nigel Inkster and Virginia Comolli, a research analyst at the International Institute of Strategic Studies.[6]

It could dramatically reduce prison populations. The billions the world spends on the global war on drugs could instead go towards health, addiction treatment and prevention, and other socially useful things. It would lower the risk of death by overdose because the strength and quality of drugs would be marked and controlled.

But one of the biggest impacts would be on HIV/AIDS. Contrary to global trends, infection through injecting drug use is on the rise and now accounts for a third of all new HIV infections outside sub-Saharan Africa. Punitive policies are fuelling the AIDS pandemic in the US, Thailand, China and especially the former soviet states. In Russia violent police attacks on drug users are commonplace, opiate substitutes are outlawed, and needle exchange programmes non-existent. "Refusing to reduce HIV infection and protect people who have a drug problem is criminal," said entrepreneur Richard Branson at the launch of a hard-hitting report by the Global Commission on Drugs, a collection of ex-drug tsars, former leaders and experts who are calling upon current world leaders to decriminalize drug use and to invest in harm reduction.[7]

In a world where drug taking was not a crime, addicts would be less likely to go underground, less likely to share needles and more likely to test for HIV. Millions of new HIV infections could be averted.

Other human rights abuses generated by prohibition could be reduced, such as capital punishment in Iran. This is mainly used against people found in possession of drugs and is effectively being funded by Britain, Ireland and others through a UN anti-drug smuggling programme.[8]

Finally, legalization would provide a decent living, without fear, for thousands of poppy and coca farmers in some of the world's poorest countries.

What Next?

What happens in the US, the world's premier drugs consumer and also the most ardent guardian of the UN Convention, is critical. In the lead-up to November's elections, President Obama is in ultra-cautious mode. He has said he is "critical" of legalization but is prepared to consider whether Washington policies are "doing more harm than good in certain places."

The US drug warriors in Congress and in the military are entrenched and still have international clout, as Bolivia saw when it tried to legalize production of coca for traditional use.

In theory, the US can act against countries that depart from the UN Convention by blocking loans from financial institutions such as the IMF or the World Bank. But when there is a regional uprising, with one country after another saying they want to legalize, be it Belize or Uruguay or Argentina, it may get harder to do.

In the US itself Sanho Tree reckons that: "Once we have a regulated model for cannabis, it will show voters that the sky didn't fall, life did not grind to a halt. That will help. On the hard drugs, examples from Europe of

successful harm reduction programmes will show people in the US that another way is possible."

But he adds that the main political work will be in public education. This is because drugs policy is, by its nature, counter-intuitive; being tough is the opposite of being effective.

Prohibition is a simplistic solution to a complex problem that simply does not work. At no time or place in history has it ever worked. Sue Pryce, an academic and mother of a drug addict, observes: "There is an uncomfortable similarity between the drug addict and those who support drug prohibition. The addict comes to see a fix as the solution to life's problems; the prohibitionists have come to see prohibition as the fix for the drug problems which are also part of life itself."[9]

Even if the world, or even a part of it, comes to accept that legalization is the way forward, the devil will be in the detail. Pricing, for example, is a tricky issue—too cheap and use may rocket; too expensive and the rationale for a criminal market is re-ignited.

Antonio Maria Costa, former UN drug tsar and a leading prohibitionist, warns that multinational corporations will muscle in if drugs are legalized. Steve Rolles from Transform, however, presents a model that involves considerable state control and a ban on advertising.[10]

In an ideal world the UN would replace the prohibitionist conventions with a new progressive policy that all countries could sign up to together. Perhaps President Santos' global taskforce process will produce a blueprint for such a policy. But it's questionable how radical it will be if it has to have US and Canadian approval. UN-watcher Damon Barrett of Harm Reduction International thinks that real change is more likely to come "from below." Social and harm reduction activists, public educators and just ordinary people opening their minds will be the key players in this revolution.

People have and always will take intoxicants that provide pleasure and harm. But there are ways in which we can make that activity safer, less damaging to individuals, to society, to the world.

It may sound paradoxical, but ridding ourselves of prohibition could be the best way of getting a grip.

Notes

1. Gretchen Peters, *Seeds of Terror: How heroin is bankrolling the Taliban and Al Qaeda,* Oneworld Publications, 2009.
2. BBC nin.tl/OqjN6j.
3. *Los Angeles Times* nin.tl/MptbV8.

4. *Forbes* nin.tl/OqkDQx.
5. Transform, "The Alternative World Drugs Report," 2012 nin.tl/Oqp0Lf.
6. Nigel Inkster and Virginia Comolli *Drugs, Insecurity and Failed States: the Problems of Prohibition,* IISS, 2012.
7. Global Commission on Drugs, "The War on Drugs and HIV/AIDS," globalcommissionondrugs.org.
8. Harm Reduction International, "Partners in Crime," 2012 nin.tl/MpuQtS.
9. Sue Pryce, *Fixing Drugs: the Politics of Drug Prohibition,* Palgrave Macmillan, 2012.
10. Intelligence Squared, "It's time to end the war on drugs," nin.tl/OqvtG5.

VANESSA BAIRD joined *New Internationalist* as a coeditor in 1986 and since then has written on everything from migration, money, religion, and equality to indigenous activism, climate change, feminism, and global LGBT rights. Her books include *The Little Book of Big Ideas* (2009), *People First Economics* (2010), and *The No-Nonsense Guide to World Population* (2011). In 2012 she won a prestigious Amnesty International Human Rights Media award for her work publicizing the struggle for autonomy of indigenous peoples in the Peruvian Amazon.

Theodore Dalrymple  **NO**

Don't Legalize Drugs

There is a progression in the minds of men: first the unthinkable becomes thinkable, and then it becomes an orthodoxy whose truth seems so obvious that no one remembers that anyone ever thought differently. This is just what is happening with the idea of legalizing drugs: it has reached the stage when millions of thinking men are agreed that allowing people to take whatever they like is the obvious, indeed only, solution to the social problems that arise from the consumption of drugs.

Man's desire to take mind-altering substances is as old as society itself—as are attempts to regulate their consumption. If intoxication in one form or another is inevitable, then so is customary or legal restraint upon that intoxication. But no society until our own has had to contend with the ready availability of so many different mind-altering drugs, combined with a citizenry jealous of its right to pursue its own pleasures in its own way.

The arguments in favor of legalizing the use of all narcotic and stimulant drugs are twofold: philosophical and pragmatic. Neither argument is negligible, but both are mistaken, I believe, and both miss the point.

The philosophic argument is that, in a free society, adults should be permitted to do whatever they please, always provided that they are prepared to take the consequences of their own choices and that they cause no direct harm to others. The locus classicus for this point of view is John Stuart Mill's famous essay On Liberty: "The only purpose for which power can be rightfully exercised over any member of the community, against his will, is to prevent harm to others," Mill wrote. "His own good, either physical or moral, is not a sufficient warrant." This radical individualism allows society no part whatever in shaping, determining, or enforcing a moral code: in short, we have nothing in common but our contractual agreement not to interfere with one another as we go about seeking our private pleasures.

In practice, of course, it is exceedingly difficult to make people take all the consequences of their own actions—as they must, if Mill's great principle is to serve as a philosophical guide to policy. Addiction to, or regular use of, most currently prohibited drugs cannot affect only the person who takes them—and not his spouse, children, neighbors, or employers. No man, except possibly a hermit, is an island; and so it is virtually impossible for Mill's principle to apply to any human action whatever, let alone shooting up heroin or smoking crack. Such a principle is virtually useless in determining what should or should not be permitted.

Perhaps we ought not be too harsh on Mill's principle: it's not clear that anyone has ever thought of a better one. But that is precisely the point. Human affairs cannot be decided by an appeal to an infallible rule, expressible in a few words, whose simple application can decide all cases, including whether drugs should be freely available to the entire adult population. Philosophical fundamentalism is not preferable to the religious variety; and because the desiderata of human life are many, and often in conflict with one another, mere philosophical inconsistency in policy—such as permitting the consumption of alcohol while outlawing cocaine—is not a sufficient argument against that policy. We all value freedom, and we all value order; sometimes we sacrifice freedom for order, and sometimes order for freedom. But once a prohibition has been removed, it is hard to restore, even when the newfound freedom proves to have been ill-conceived and socially disastrous.

Even Mill came to see the limitations of his own principle as a guide for policy and to deny that all pleasures were of equal significance for human existence. It was better, he said, to be Socrates discontented than a fool satisfied. Mill acknowledged that some goals were intrinsically worthier of pursuit than others.

This being the case, not all freedoms are equal, and neither are all limitations of freedom: some are serious and some trivial. The freedom we cherish—or should cherish—is not merely that of satisfying our appetites, whatever they happen to be. We are not Dickensian Harold Skimpoles, exclaiming in protest that "Even the butterflies are free!"

We are not children who chafe at restrictions because they are restrictions. And we even recognize the apparent paradox that some limitations to our freedoms have the consequence of making us freer overall. The freest man is not the one who slavishly follows his appetites and desires throughout his life—as all too many of my patients have discovered to their cost.

We are prepared to accept limitations to our freedoms for many reasons, not just that of public order. Take an extreme hypothetical case: public exhibitions of necrophilia are quite rightly not permitted, though on Mill's principle they should be. A corpse has no interests and cannot be harmed, because it is no longer a person; and no member of the public is harmed if he has agreed to attend such an exhibition.

Our resolve to prohibit such exhibitions would not be altered if we discovered that millions of people wished to attend them or even if we discovered that millions already were attending them illicitly. Our objection is not based upon pragmatic considerations or upon a head count: it is based upon the wrongness of the would-be exhibitions themselves. The fact that the prohibition represents a genuine restriction of our freedom is of no account.

It might be argued that the freedom to choose among a variety of intoxicating substances is a much more important freedom and that millions of people have derived innocent fun from taking stimulants and narcotics. But the consumption of drugs has the effect of reducing men's freedom by circumscribing the range of their interests. It impairs their ability to pursue more important human aims, such as raising a family and fulfilling civic obligations. Very often it impairs their ability to pursue gainful employment and promotes parasitism. Moreover, far from being expanders of consciousness, most drugs severely limit it. One of the most striking characteristics of drug takers is their intense and tedious self-absorption; and their journeys into inner space are generally forays into inner vacuums. Drug taking is a lazy man's way of pursuing happiness and wisdom, and the shortcut turns out to be the deadest of dead ends. We lose remarkably little by not being permitted to take drugs.

The idea that freedom is merely the ability to act upon one's whims is surely very thin and hardly begins to capture the complexities of human existence; a man whose appetite is his law strikes us not as liberated but enslaved. And when such a narrowly conceived freedom is made the touchstone of public policy, a dissolution of society is bound to follow. No culture that makes publicly sanctioned self-indulgence its highest good can long survive: a radical egotism is bound to ensue, in which any limitations upon personal behavior are experienced as infringements of basic rights. Distinctions between the important and the trivial, between the freedom to criticize received ideas and the freedom to take LSD, are precisely the standards that keep societies from barbarism.

So the legalization of drugs cannot be supported by philosophical principle. But if the pragmatic argument in favor of legalization were strong enough, it might overwhelm other objections. It is upon this argument that proponents of legalization rest the larger part of their case.

The argument is that the overwhelming majority of the harm done to society by the consumption of currently illicit drugs is caused not by their pharmacological properties but by their prohibition and the resultant criminal activity that prohibition always calls into being. Simple reflection tells us that a supply invariably grows up to meet a demand; and when the demand is widespread, suppression is useless. Indeed, it is harmful, since—by raising the price of the commodity in question—it raises the profits of middlemen, which gives them an even more powerful incentive to stimulate demand further. The vast profits to be made from cocaine and heroin—which, were it not for their illegality, would be cheap and easily affordable even by the poorest in affluent societies—exert a deeply corrupting effect on producers, distributors, consumers, and law enforcers alike. Besides, it is well known that illegality in itself has attractions for youth already inclined to disaffection. Even many of the harmful physical effects of illicit drugs stem from their illegal status: for example, fluctuations in the purity of heroin bought on the street are responsible for many of the deaths by overdose. If the sale and consumption of such drugs were legalized, consumers would know how much they were taking and thus avoid overdoses.

Moreover, since society already permits the use of some mind-altering substances known to be both addictive and harmful, such as alcohol and nicotine, in prohibiting others it appears hypocritical, arbitrary, and dictatorial. Its hypocrisy, as well as its patent failure to enforce its prohibitions successfully, leads inevitably to a decline in respect for the law as a whole. Thus things fall apart, and the center cannot hold.

It stands to reason, therefore, that all these problems would be resolved at a stroke if everyone were permitted to smoke, swallow, or inject anything he chose. The corruption of the police, the luring of children of 11 and 12 into illegal activities, the making of such vast sums of money by drug dealing that legitimate work seems pointless and silly by comparison, and the turf wars that make poor neighborhoods so exceedingly violent and dangerous, would all cease at once were drug taking to be decriminalized and the supply regulated in the same way as alcohol.

But a certain modesty in the face of an inherently unknowable future is surely advisable. That is why prudence is a political virtue: what stands to reason should happen does not necessarily happen in practice. As Goethe said, all theory (even of the monetarist or free-market variety) is gray, but green springs the golden tree of life. If drugs were legalized, I suspect that the golden tree of life might spring some unpleasant surprises.

It is of course true, but only trivially so, that the present illegality of drugs is the cause of the criminality surrounding their distribution. Likewise, it is the illegality of stealing cars that creates car thieves. In fact, the ultimate cause of all criminality is law. As far as I am aware, no one has ever suggested that law should therefore be abandoned. Moreover, the impossibility of winning the "war" against theft, burglary, robbery, and fraud has never been used as an argument that these categories of crime should be abandoned. And so long as the demand for material goods outstrips supply, people will be tempted to commit criminal acts against the owners of property. This is not an argument, in my view, against private property or in favor of the common ownership of all goods. It does suggest, however, that we shall need a police force for a long time to come.

In any case, there are reasons to doubt whether the crime rate would fall quite as dramatically as advocates of legalization have suggested. Amsterdam, where access to drugs is relatively unproblematic, is among the most violent and squalid cities in Europe. The idea behind crime—of getting rich, or at least richer, quickly and without much effort—is unlikely to disappear once drugs are freely available to all who want them. And it may be that officially sanctioned antisocial behavior—the official lifting of taboos—breeds yet more antisocial behavior, as the "broken windows" theory would suggest.

Having met large numbers of drug dealers in prison, I doubt that they would return to respectable life if the principal article of their commerce were to be legalized. Far from evincing a desire to be reincorporated into the world of regular work, they express a deep contempt for it and regard those who accept the bargain of a fair day's work for a fair day's pay as cowards and fools. A life of crime has its attractions for many who would otherwise lead a mundane existence. So long as there is the possibility of a lucrative racket or illegal traffic, such people will find it and extend its scope. Therefore, since even legalizers would hesitate to allow children to take drugs, decriminalization might easily result in dealers turning their attentions to younger and younger children, who—in the permissive atmosphere that even now prevails—have already been inducted into the drug subculture in alarmingly high numbers.

Those who do not deal in drugs but commit crimes to fund their consumption of them are, of course, more numerous than large-scale dealers. And it is true that once opiate addicts, for example, enter a treatment program, which often includes maintenance doses of methadone, the rate at which they commit crimes falls markedly. The drug clinic in my hospital claims an 80 percent reduction in criminal convictions among heroin addicts once they have been stabilized on methadone.

This is impressive, but it is not certain that the results should be generalized. First, the patients are self-selected: they have some motivation to change, otherwise they would not have attended the clinic in the first place. Only a minority of addicts attend, and therefore it is not safe to conclude that, if other addicts were to receive methadone, their criminal activity would similarly diminish.

Second, a decline in convictions is not necessarily the same as a decline in criminal acts. If methadone stabilizes an addict's life, he may become a more efficient, harder-to-catch criminal. Moreover, when the police in our city do catch an addict, they are less likely to prosecute him if he can prove that he is undergoing anything remotely resembling psychiatric treatment. They return him directly to his doctor. Having once had a psychiatric consultation is an all-purpose alibi for a robber or a burglar; the police, who do not want to fill in the 40-plus forms it now takes to charge anyone with anything in England, consider a single contact with a psychiatrist sufficient to deprive anyone of legal responsibility for crime forever.

Third, the rate of criminal activity among those drug addicts who receive methadone from the clinic, though reduced, remains very high. The deputy director of the clinic estimates that the number of criminal acts committed by his average patient (as judged by self-report) was 250 per year before entering treatment and 50 afterward. It may well be that the real difference is considerably less than this, because the patients have an incentive to exaggerate it to secure the continuation of their methadone. But clearly, opiate addicts who receive their drugs legally and free of charge continue to commit large numbers of crimes. In my clinics in prison, I see numerous prisoners who were on methadone when they committed the crime for which they are incarcerated.

Why do addicts given their drug free of charge continue to commit crimes? Some addicts, of course, continue to take drugs other than those prescribed and have to fund their consumption of them. So long as any restriction whatever regulates the consumption of drugs, many addicts will seek them illicitly, regardless of what they receive legally. In addition, the drugs themselves exert a long-term effect on a person's ability to earn a living and severely limit rather than expand his horizons and mental repertoire. They sap the will or the ability of an addict to make long-term plans. While drugs are the focus of an addict's life, they are not all he needs to live, and many addicts thus continue to procure the rest of what they need by criminal means.

For the proposed legalization of drugs to have its much vaunted beneficial effect on the rate of criminality, such drugs would have to be both cheap and readily available. The legalizers assume that there is a natural limit to the demand for these drugs, and that if their consumption were legalized, the demand would not increase substantially. Those psychologically unstable persons currently taking drugs would continue to do so, with the necessity to commit crimes removed, while psychologically stabler people (such as you and I and our children) would not be enticed to take drugs by their new legal status and cheapness. But price and availability, I need hardly say, exert a profound effect on consumption: the cheaper alcohol becomes, for example, the more of it is consumed, at least within quite wide limits.

I have personal experience of this effect. I once worked as a doctor on a British government aid project to Africa. We were building a road through remote African bush. The contract stipulated that the construction company could import, free of all taxes, alcoholic drinks from the United Kingdom. These drinks the company then sold to its British workers at cost, in the local currency at the official exchange rate, which was approximately one-sixth the black-market rate. A liter bottle of gin thus cost less than a dollar and could be sold on the open market for almost ten dollars. So it was theoretically possible to remain dead drunk for several years for an initial outlay of less than a dollar.

Of course, the necessity to go to work somewhat limited the workers' consumption of alcohol. Nevertheless, drunkenness among them far outstripped anything I have ever seen, before or since. I discovered that, when alcohol is effectively free of charge, a fifth of British construction workers will regularly go to bed so drunk that they are incontinent both of urine and feces. I remember one man who very rarely got as far as his bed at night: he fell asleep in the lavatory, where he was usually found the next morning. Half the men shook in the mornings and resorted to the hair of the dog to steady their hands before they drove their bulldozers and other heavy machines (which they frequently wrecked, at enormous expense to the British taxpayer); hangovers were universal. The men were either drunk or hung over for months on end.

Sure, construction workers are notoriously liable to drink heavily, but in these circumstances even formerly moderate drinkers turned alcoholic and eventually suffered from delirium tremens. The heavy drinking occurred not because of the isolation of the African bush: not only did the company provide sports facilities for its workers, but there were many other ways to occupy oneself there. Other groups of workers in the bush whom I visited, who did not have the same rights of importation of alcoholic drink but had to purchase it at normal prices, were not nearly as drunk. And when the company asked its workers what it could do to improve their conditions, they unanimously asked for a further reduction in the price of alcohol, because they could think of nothing else to ask for.

The conclusion was inescapable: that a susceptible population had responded to the low price of alcohol, and the lack of other effective restraints upon its consumption, by drinking destructively large quantities of it. The health of many men suffered as a consequence, as did their capacity for work; and they gained a well-deserved local reputation for reprehensible, violent, antisocial behavior.

It is therefore perfectly possible that the demand for drugs, including opiates, would rise dramatically were their price to fall and their availability to increase. And if it is true that the consumption of these drugs in itself predisposes to criminal behavior (as data from our clinic suggest), it is also possible that the effect on the rate of criminality of this rise in consumption would swamp the decrease that resulted from decriminalization. We would have just as much crime in aggregate as before, but many more addicts.

The intermediate position on drug legalization, such as that espoused by Ethan Nadelmann, director of the Lindesmith Center, a drug policy research institute sponsored by financier George Soros, is emphatically not the answer to drug-related crime. This view holds that it should be easy for addicts to receive opiate drugs from doctors, either free or at cost, and that they should receive them in municipal injecting rooms, such as now exist in Zurich. But just look at Liverpool, where 2,000 people of a population of 600,000 receive official prescriptions for methadone: this once proud and prosperous city is still the world capital of drug-motivated burglary, according to the police and independent researchers.

Of course, many addicts in Liverpool are not yet on methadone, because the clinics are insufficient in number to deal with the demand. If the city expended more money on clinics, perhaps the number of addicts in treatment could be increased five- or tenfold. But would that solve the problem of burglary in Liverpool? No, because the profits to be made from selling illicit opiates would still be large: dealers would therefore make efforts to expand into parts of the population hitherto relatively untouched, in order to protect their profits. The new addicts would still burgle to feed their habits. Yet more clinics dispensing yet more methadone would then be needed. In fact Britain, which has had a relatively liberal approach to the prescribing of opiate drugs to addicts since 1928 (I myself have prescribed heroin to addicts), has seen an explosive increase in addiction to opiates and all the evils associated with it since the 1960s, despite that liberal policy. A few hundred have become more than a hundred thousand.

At the heart of Nadelmann's position, then, is an evasion. The legal and liberal provision of drugs for people who are already addicted to them will not reduce the economic benefits to dealers of pushing these drugs, at least until the entire susceptible population is addicted and in a treatment program. So long as there are addicts who have to resort to the black market for their drugs, there will be drug-associated crime. Nadelmann assumes that the number of potential addicts wouldn't soar under considerably more liberal drug laws. I can't muster such Panglossian optimism.

The problem of reducing the amount of crime committed by individual addicts is emphatically not the same as the problem of reducing the amount of crime committed by addicts as a whole. I can illustrate what I mean by an analogy: it is often claimed that prison does not work because many prisoners are recidivists who, by definition, failed to be deterred from further wrongdoing by their last prison sentence. But does any sensible person believe that the abolition of prisons in their entirety would not reduce the numbers of the law-abiding? The murder rate in New York and the rate of drunken driving in Britain have not been reduced by a sudden upsurge in the love of humanity, but by the effective threat of punishment. An institution such as prison can work for society even if it does not work for an individual.

The situation could be very much worse than I have suggested hitherto, however, if we legalized the consumption of drugs other than opiates. So far, I have considered only opiates, which exert a generally tranquilizing effect. If opiate addicts commit crimes even when they receive their drugs free of charge, it is because they are unable to meet their other needs any other way; but there are, unfortunately, drugs whose consumption directly leads to violence because of their psychopharmacological properties and not merely because of the criminality associated with their distribution. Stimulant drugs such as crack cocaine provoke paranoia, increase aggression, and promote violence. Much of this violence takes place in the home, as the relatives of crack takers will testify. It is something I know from personal acquaintance by working in the emergency room and in the wards of our hospital. Only someone who has not been assaulted by drug takers rendered psychotic by their drug could view with equanimity the prospect of the further spread of the abuse of stimulants.

And no one should underestimate the possibility that the use of stimulant drugs could spread very much wider, and become far more general, than it is now, if restraints on their use were relaxed. The importation of the mildly stimulant khat is legal in Britain, and a large proportion of the community of Somali refugees there devotes its entire life to chewing the leaves that contain the stimulant, miring these refugees in far worse poverty than they would otherwise experience. The reason that the khat habit has not spread to the rest of the population is that it takes an entire day's chewing of disgustingly bitter leaves to gain the comparatively mild pharmacological effect. The point is, however, that once the use of a stimulant becomes culturally acceptable and normal, it can easily become so general as to exert devastating social effects. And the kinds of stimulants on offer in Western cities—cocaine, crack, amphetamines—are vastly more attractive than khat.

In claiming that prohibition, not the drugs themselves, is the problem, Nadelmann and many others—even policemen—have said that "the war on drugs is lost." But to demand a yes or no answer to the question "Is the war against drugs being won?" is like demanding a yes or no answer to the question "Have you stopped beating your wife yet?" Never can an unimaginative and fundamentally stupid metaphor have exerted a more baleful effect upon proper thought.

Let us ask whether medicine is winning the war against death. The answer is obviously no, it isn't winning: the one fundamental rule of human existence remains, unfortunately, one man one death. And this is despite the fact that 14 percent of the gross domestic product of the United States (to say nothing of the efforts of other countries) goes into the fight against death. Was ever a war more expensively lost? Let us then abolish medical schools, hospitals, and departments of public health. If every man has to die, it doesn't matter very much when he does so.

If the war against drugs is lost, then so are the wars against theft, speeding, incest, fraud, rape, murder, arson, and illegal parking. Few, if any, such wars are winnable. So let us all do anything we choose.

Even the legalizers' argument that permitting the purchase and use of drugs as freely as Milton Friedman suggests will necessarily result in less governmental and other official interference in our lives doesn't stand up. To the contrary, if the use of narcotics and stimulants were to become virtually universal, as is by no means impossible, the number of situations in which compulsory checks upon people would have to be carried out, for reasons of public safety, would increase enormously. Pharmacies, banks, schools, hospitals—indeed, all organizations dealing with the public—might feel obliged to check regularly and randomly on the drug consumption of their employees. The general use of such drugs would increase the locus standi of innumerable agencies, public and private, to interfere in our lives; and freedom from interference, far from having increased, would have drastically shrunk.

The present situation is bad, undoubtedly; but few are the situations so bad that they cannot be made worse by a wrong policy decision.

The extreme intellectual elegance of the proposal to legalize the distribution and consumption of drugs, touted as the solution to so many problems at once (AIDS, crime, overcrowding in the prisons, and even the attractiveness of drugs to foolish young people) should give rise to skepticism. Social problems are not usually like that. Analogies with the Prohibition era, often drawn by those who would legalize drugs, are false and inexact: it is one thing to attempt to ban a substance that has been in customary use for centuries by at least nine-tenths of the adult population, and quite another to retain a ban on substances that are still not in customary use, in an attempt to ensure that they never do become customary. Surely we have already slid down enough slippery slopes in the last 30 years without looking for more such slopes to slide down.

THEODORE DALRYMPLE is a retired prison psychiatrist and writer. He is the author of numerous books; his most recent works include the essay collections *Not With a Bang But a Whimper* and *Second Opinion* (both in 2009).

EXPLORING THE ISSUE

Should Drugs Be Legalized?

Critical Thinking and Reflection

1. In what sense does prohibiting the recreational use of psychoactive drugs deprive human beings of their freedom (autonomy)? Do you think that governments should use laws, such as those discouraging the recreational use of psychoactive drugs, to provide incentives for individuals to exercise their autonomy in ways that do not diminish their personal development? Why or why not?
2. Explain the effects on society of each of the following scenarios: (a) the legalization of marijuana; (b) the legalization of hallucinogenic drugs such as Ecstasy, psilocybin, and LSD; (c) the legalization of "hard" drugs such as heroin, cocaine, and methamphetamine? In your view, do these scenarios provide a moral justification for legalizing these psychoactive drugs?
3. Numerous states have experimented with legalizing the use of marijuana for medical purposes. Do you think that these experiments provide relevant information concerning the legalization of marijuana for recreational purposes? If so, does this information support or undermine the case for legalizing marijuana, and other psychoactive drugs, for reactional purposes?
4. Several foreign countries, as well as two states (Colorado and Washington), have legalized the use of marijuana for recreational purposes. Have the results of this legalization come closer to the predictions of the proponents of drug legalization or the opponents of drug legalization? Can these results be extrapolated to the legalization of other restricted substances?
5. What regulations, if any, do you think are appropriate for the use of psychoactive drugs? What consequences do you think that these regulations will have regarding the benefits and harms of legalizing the use of psychoactive drugs for recreational purposes?

Is There Common Ground?

None of the authors on this issue claim that recreational drugs are beneficial in themselves or that drug addiction is a good thing. Rather, they disagree on the best way for society to handle the situation. Baird states that governmental efforts to control drug use create serious social problems, including the often violent criminal activity associated with international trafficking in illegal drugs; consequently, social conditions would be much improved if drugs were legalized.

In contrast, Theodore Dalrymple is skeptical of the claims of the proponents of drug legalization. His position is not merely a blind rejection of their views; in many cases, it is supported by his extensive experience working with drug users. He notes, for example, that even those who are provided with drugs seek other drugs that they cannot have, while those who have unlimited access tend to overindulge to an extreme extent. Legalization of drugs, he argues, would lead to many more users and many more social problems.

The concerns of both authors might be combined in a hybrid approach to the regulation of psychoactive drugs. It might well be possible to formulate a distinction between "hard" psychoactive drugs, such as heroin, and "soft" psychoactive drugs, such as marijuana and LSD. Strict regulation could then be maintained for the former group, while the latter group could become available under more relaxed regulation, such as the restrictions currently imposed on the purchase of alcohol or tobacco, or perhaps the more rigorous restrictions imposed on the purchase of products containing pseudoephedrine. Neither author would be completely satisfied, but such a proposal might well produce many of the benefits associated with legalizing the recreational use of psychoactive drugs without incurring the more serious society ills associated with the current "war on drugs."

Additional Resources

Margaret J. Goldstein, *Legalizing Drugs: Crime Stopper or Social Risk?* (Twenty-First Century, 2010)

Douglas Husak, *Drugs and Rights* (Cambridge University Press, 2002)

Peggy J. Parks, *Drug Legalization* (ReferencePoint Press, 2008)

Doris M. Provine, *Unequal Under Law: Race in the War on Drugs* (University of Chicago, 2007)

Internet References . . .

National Institute on Drug Abuse

www.drugabuse.gov/

RAND Drug Policy Research Center

www.rand.org/multi/dprc.html

The Drug Reform Coordination Network Online Library of Drug Policy

www.druglibrary.org/

Selected, Edited, and with Issue Framing Material by:
Owen M. Smith, *Stephen F. Austin State University*
and
Anne Collins Smith, *Stephen F. Austin State University*

ISSUE

Is Affirmative Action Fair?

YES: **Albert G. Mosley,** from "Affirmative Action: Pro," in *Affirmative Action: Social Justice or Unfair Preference?* (Rowman & Littlefield, 1996)

NO: **Roger Clegg,** from "Affirmative Discrimination and the Bubble," *Academic Questions* (December 2011)

Learning Outcomes

After reading this issue, you will be able to:

- Explain how fairness is not equivalent to equality.
- Explain how affirmative action is intended to remedy the effects of historical discrimination.
- Explain how affirmative action might lead to increased prejudice against minorities.
- Formulate your own position on affirmative action and identify evidence supporting your position.
- Identify the main objections to your position and formulate responses to these objections.

ISSUE SUMMARY

YES: Professor of philosophy Albert G. Mosley argues that affirmative action is a continuation of the history of black progress since the *Brown v. Board of Education* desegregation decision of 1954 and the Civil Rights Act of 1964. He defends affirmative action as a "benign use of race."

NO: Roger Clegg argues that affirmative action as it is now practiced—which he calls "affirmative discrimination"—has contributed to unsustainable rapid growth ("the bubble") in higher education as well as the reduction in quality of college education. Affirmative action in the form of preferences for minority groups, he argues, is a form of discrimination that is unfair, has negative consequences for both white and minority students, and fails to address the true problems that challenge minority students today.

T he basic moral principle involved in discrimination is fairness. Initially, it may appear that fairness means the same thing as equality or sameness: two people are treated fairly when both receive the same treatment. Upon futher reflection, however, it becomes clear that fairness is not equivalent to equality or sameness. When two people are different in significant ways, it is fair to treat them differently, although the difference in treatment must be directly related to the differences between the people. An example that is not does not involve racial or sexual discrimination would be heating water for tea. Let us consider two pots, one containing 10 ounces of water and the other containing 20 ounces of water. If we apply the same amount of heat to both pots, the one with 10 ounces of water will boil more quickly than the pot with 20 ounces of water. If our goal is to have both pots of water boil at the same time, more heat will have to be applied to the larger pot than to the smaller pot. The two pots are being treated differently, but the difference in treatment is directly related to the difference in size between the two pots. When considering discrimination and affirmative action, our focus must be not only upon equality or sameness of treatment, but also upon the differences between people, the relevance of these differences to the specific type of treatment under consideration, and the degree to which these differences require different treatment for the goal of fairness to be achieved.

As a result of the civil rights movement and women's rights movement, the United States has begun to confront a history of discrimination in which women and members of racial and ethnic minorities were deprived of equal opportunities to participate in social, economic, and political activities. It might be difficult for those who did not personally witness the overt discrimination of past decades to appreciate the many ways in which discrimination was embedded in American culture, but a recognition of past injustices is essential in making judgments about the current morality of affirmative action programs.

With respect to racial and ethnic discrimination, the most blatant example of unfair treatment was slavery.

Slaves were considered to be property, without the status accorded to persons under law. Slaves were bought and sold as commodities, and there were few legal restrictions on slaveholders' treatment of their slaves. Accounts of the maltreatment of slaves are as common as they are horrific, and even considerate slaveholders accorded their slaves different treatment than their white, freeborn associates. Many slaveholders considered similarities and differences between whites and people of color to be of little importance; slaves were an economic necessity for large agrarian landowners, especially in the South. Others rationalized the difference in treatment accorded to slaves on the basis of perceived, but unfounded differences in ability between whites and people of color, differences that they believed prevented members of racial and ethnic minorities from governing their own affairs properly. For some, these differences were thought to be the result of a lack of civilization or deficiency in culture, which in time might be remedied through proper stewardship by the white majority. For others, these differences were thought to be intrinsic, precluding the possibility of equal treatment of whites and racial minorities. For decades after the abolition of slavery, overt discrimination against people of color was widespread throughout the country, and while strides have been made against this disparity in treatment, especially in legal contexts, it has not yet been eliminated in all aspects of life.

With respect to discrimination against women, an excerpt from a nineteenth century court opinion illustrates the attitudes on the differences between males and females that long influenced the disparate treatment accorded the sexes:

> [T]he civil law, as well as nature herself, has always recognized a wide difference in the respective spheres and destinies of man and woman. Man is, or should be, woman's protector and defender. The natural and proper timidity and delicacy which belongs to the female sex evidently unfits it for many of the occupations of civil life. . . . The paramount destiny and mission of woman are to fulfill the noble and benign offices of wife and mother.

On this basis, Justice Joseph Bradley voted with a majority of the U.S. Supreme Court in *Bradwell v. Illinois* (1873) to deny Myra Bradwell a license to practice law on the grounds that she was a woman. While this opinion no longer carries legal weight, the views it expresses were sufficiently widespread to deny women equal treatment with men for decades. The contemporary struggles of many women to balance career and family obligations, struggles not incumbent upon men to nearly the same degree, bear witness that the disparity in treatment between men and women are not merely an historical curiosity.

Even if overt discrimination against women and racial and ethnic minorities were eradicated from this country, the effects of decades of discrimination would still have to be addressed in order to determine whether equality in treatment constitutes fairness.

Some consequences of past discrimination are systemic, resulting in continuing disparities in housing, education, and economic status. For example, black parents who attended substandard schools during the period of racial segregation did not receive the same quality of education as the parents of their children's white classmates. This makes it harder for them to prepare their children to enter school, to help them with their homework, and to interact effectively with teachers and school administrators. In this way, the legacy of black children suffering an educational disadvantage compared to white children can perpetuate itself despite laws intended to prevent discrimination.

Affirmative action policies are designed primarily to redress systemic disadvantages that are currently being suffered by women and members of racial and ethnic minorities. Advocates of affirmative action, like Albert G. Mosely, assert that relevant differences still exist between these groups and majority white males, and because of these differences, the goal of fairness can only be achieved by treating these groups differently. In support of his views, Mosley places controversies surrounding affirmative action in a historical context and considers the justification of affirmative action both from the "backward-looking" perspective of corrective justice and from the "forward-looking" perspective of the social distribution of harms and benefits.

Opponents of affirmative action, like Roger Clegg, counter that the goal of fairness is no longer being served by these programs. Clegg examines the results of affirmative action in college admissions, including the role of affirmative action in contributing to the higher education bubble, a term used by economists to describe a temporary boom in demand and price that must ultimately collapse, and ultimately concludes that affirmative action programs as they are now practiced are harmful to everyone, especially to the minority groups they were intended to benefit.

YES

Albert G. Mosley

Affirmative Action: Pro

Legislative and Judicial Background

In 1941, Franklin Roosevelt issued Executive Order 8802 banning discrimination in employment by the federal government and defense contractors. Subsequently, many bills were introduced in Congress mandating equal employment opportunity but none were passed until the Civil Rights Act of 1964. The penalty for discrimination in Executive Order 8802 and the bills subsequently proposed was that the specific victim of discrimination be "made whole," that is, put in the position he or she would have held were it not for the discriminatory act, including damages for lost pay and legal expenses.

The contemporary debate concerning affirmative action can be traced to the landmark decision of *Brown v. Board of Education* (1954), whereby local, state, and federal ordinances enforcing segregation by race were ruled unconstitutional. In subsequent opinions, the Court ruled that state-mandated segregation in libraries, swimming pools, and other publicly funded facilities was also unconstitutional. In *Swann v. Charlotte-Mecklenburg* (1971), the Court declared that "in order to prepare students to live in a pluralistic society" school authorities might implement their desegregation order by deciding that "each school should have a prescribed ratio of Negro to White students reflecting the proportion for the district as a whole."[1] The ratio was not to be an inflexible one, but should reflect local variations in the ratio of Whites to Blacks. But any predominantly one-race school in a district with a mixed population and a history of segregation was subject to "close scrutiny." This requirement was attacked by conservatives as imposing a "racial quota," a charge that reverberates in the contemporary debate concerning affirmative action.

With the Montgomery bus boycotts of the mid-1950s, Blacks initiated an era of nonviolent direct action to publicly protest unjust laws and practices that supported racial discrimination. The graphic portrayals of repression and violence produced by the civil rights movement precipitated a national revulsion against the unequal treatment of African Americans. Blacks demanded their constitutional right to participate in the political process and share equal access to public accommodations, government-supported programs, and employment opportunities. But as John F. Kennedy stated in an address to Congress: "There is little value in a Negro's obtaining the right to be admitted to hotels and restaurants if he has no cash in his pocket and no job."[2]

Kennedy stressed that the issue was not merely eliminating discrimination, but eliminating as well the oppressive economic and social burdens imposed on Blacks by racial discrimination.[3] To this end, he advocated a weak form of affirmative action, involving eliminating discrimination and expanding educational and employment opportunities (including apprenticeships and on-the-job training). The liberal vision was that, given such opportunities, Blacks would move up the economic ladder to a degree relative to their own merit. Thus, a principal aim of the Civil Rights Act of 1964 was to effect a redistribution of social, political, and economic benefits and to provide legal remedies for the denial of individual rights.

The Civil Rights Act of 1964

The first use of the phrase "affirmative action" is found in Executive Order 10952, issued by President John F. Kennedy in 1961. This order established the Equal Employment Opportunity Commission (EEOC) and directed that contractors on projects funded, in whole or in part, with federal funds "take affirmative action to ensure that applicants are employed, and employees are treated during their employment, without regard to the race, creed, color, or national origin."

As a result of continuing public outrage at the level of violence and animosity shown toward Blacks, a stronger version of the Civil Rights Bill was presented to the Congress than Kennedy had originally recommended. Advocates pointed out that Blacks suffered an unemployment rate that was twice that of Whites and that Black employment was concentrated in semiskilled and unskilled jobs. They emphasized that national prosperity would be improved by eliminating discrimination and integrating Black talent into its skilled and professional workforce.[4]

Fewer Blacks were employed in professional positions than had the requisite skills, and those Blacks who did occupy positions commensurate with their skill level had half the lifetime earnings of Whites. Such facts were introduced during legislative hearings to show the need to more fully utilize and reward qualified Blacks throughout the labor force, and not merely in the unskilled and semiskilled sectors. . . .

Conceptual Issues

There are many interests that governments pursue—maximization of social production; equitable distribution of rights, opportunities, and services; social safety and cohesion; restitution—and those interests may conflict in various situations. In particular, governments as well as their constituents have a prima facie obligation to satisfy the liabilities they incur. One such liability derives from past and present unjust exclusionary acts depriving minorities and women of opportunities and amenities made available to other groups.

"Backward looking" arguments defend affirmative action as a matter of *corrective justice*, where paradigmatically the harmdoer is to make restitution to the harmed so as to put the harmed in the position the harmed most likely would have occupied had the harm not occurred. An important part of making restitution is the acknowledgment it provides that the actions causing injury were unjust and such actions will be curtailed and corrected. In this regard Bernard Boxill writes:

> Without the acknowledgement of error, the injurer implies that the injured has been treated in a manner that befits him. . . . In such a case, even if the unjust party repairs the damage he has caused . . . nothing can be demanded on legal or moral grounds, and the repairs made are gratuitous. . . . [J]ustice requires that we acknowledge that this treatment of others can be required of us; thus, where an unjust injury has occurred, the injurer reaffirms his belief in the other's equality by conceding that repair can be demanded of him, and the injured rejects the allegation of his inferiority . . . by demanding reparation.[5]

This view is based on the idea that restitution is a basic moral principle that creates obligations that are just as strong as the obligations to maximize wealth and distribute it fairly.[6] If x has deprived y of opportunities y had a right not to be deprived of in this manner, then x is obligated to return y to the position y would have occupied had x not intervened; x has this obligation irrespective of other obligations x may have. . . .

[An] application of this principle involves the case where x is not a person but an entity, like a government or a business. If y was unjustly deprived of employment when firm F hired z instead of y because z was White and y Black, then y has a right to be made whole, that is, brought to the position he/she would have achieved had that deprivation not occurred. Typically, this involves giving y a position at least as good as the one he/she would have acquired originally and issuing back pay in the amount that y would have received had he/she been hired at the time of the initial attempt.

Most critics of preferential treatment acknowledge the applicability of principles of restitution to individuals in specific instances of discrimination. The strongest case is where y was as or more qualified than z in the initial competition, but the position was given to z because y was Black and z was White.[7] Subsequently, y may not be as qualified for an equivalent position as some new candidate z', but is given preference because of the past act of discrimination by F that deprived y of the position he or she otherwise would have received.

Some critics have suggested that, in such cases, z' is being treated unfairly. For z', as the most qualified applicant, has a right not to be excluded from the position in question purely on the basis of race; and y has a right to restitution for having unjustly been denied the position in the past. But the dilemma is one in appearance only. For having unjustly excluded y in the past, the current position that z has applied for is not one that F is free to offer to the public. It is a position that is already owed to y, and is not available for open competition. Judith Jarvis Thomson makes a similar point:

> suppose two candidates [A and B] for a civil service job have equally good test scores, but there is only one job available. We could decide between them by coin-tossing. But in fact we do allow for declaring for A straightway, where A is a veteran, and B is not. It may be that B is a non-veteran through no fault of his own. . . . Yet the fact is that B is not a veteran and A is. On the assumption that the veteran has served his country, the country owes him something. And it is plain that giving him preference is not an unjust way in which part of that debt of gratitude can be paid.[8]

In a similar way, individual Blacks who have suffered from acts of unjust discrimination are owed something by the perpetrator(s) of such acts, and this debt takes precedence over the perpetrator's right to use his or her options to hire the most qualified person for the position in question.

Many White males have developed expectations about the likelihood of their being selected for educational, employment, and entrepreneurial opportunities that are realistic only because of the general exclusion of women and non-Whites as competitors for such positions. Individuals enjoying inflated odds of obtaining such opportunities because of racist and sexist practices are recipients of an "unjust enrichment."

Redistributing opportunities would clearly curtail benefits that many have come to expect. And given the frustration of their traditional expectations, it is understandable that they would feel resentment. But blocking traditional expectations is not unjust if those expectations conflict with the equally important moral duties of restitution and just distribution. It is a question, not of "is," but of "ought": not "Do those with decreased opportunities as a result of affirmative action feel resentment?" but "Should those with decreased opportunities as a result of affirmative action feel resentment?". . .

Since Title VII [of the Civil Rights Act of 1964] protects bona fide seniority plans, it forces the burden of rectification to be borne by Whites who are entering the labor force rather than Whites who are the direct beneficiaries of past discriminatory practices. Given this limitation placed on affirmative action remedies, the burden of social restitution may, in many cases, be borne by those who were not directly involved in past discriminatory practices. But it is generally not true that those burdened have not benefited at all from past discriminatory practices. For the latent effects of acts of invidious racial discrimination have plausibly bolstered and encouraged the efforts of Whites in roughly the same proportion as it inhibited and discouraged the efforts of Blacks. Such considerations are also applicable to cases where F discriminated against y in favor of z, but the make-whole remedy involves providing compensation to y' rather than y. This suggests that y' is an *undeserving beneficiary* of the preferential treatment meant to compensate for the unjust discrimination against y, just as z' above appeared to be the innocent victim forced to bear the burden that z benefited from. Many critics have argued that this misappropriation of benefits and burdens demonstrates the unfairness of compensation to groups rather than individuals. But it is important that the context and rationale for such remedies be appreciated.

In cases of "egregious" racial discrimination, not only is it true that F discriminated against a particular Black person y, but F's discrimination advertised a general disposition to discriminate against any other Black person who might seek such positions. The specific effect of F's unjust discrimination was that y was refused a position he or she would otherwise have received. The latent (or dispositional) effect of F's unjust discrimination was that many Blacks who otherwise would have sought such positions were discouraged from doing so. Thus, even if the specific y actually discriminated against can no longer be compensated, F has an obligation to take affirmative action to communicate to Blacks as a group that such positions are indeed open to them. After being found in violation of laws prohibiting racial discrimination, many agencies have disclaimed further discrimination while in fact continuing to do so.[9] In such cases, the courts have required the discriminating agencies to actually hire and/or promote Blacks who may not be as qualified as some current White applicants until Blacks approach the proportion in F's labor force they in all likelihood would have achieved had F's unjust discriminatory acts not deterred them.

Of course, what this proportion would have been is a matter of speculation. It may have been less than the proportion of Blacks available in the relevant labor pool from which applicants are drawn if factors other than racial discrimination act to depress the merit of such applicants. This point is made again and again by critics. Some, such as Thomas Sowell, argue that cultural factors often mitigate against Blacks meriting representation in a particular labor force in proportion to their presence in the pool of candidates looking for jobs or seeking promotions.[10]

Others, such as Michael Levin, argue that cognitive deficits limit Blacks from being hired and promoted at a rate proportionate to their presence in the relevant labor pool.[11] What such critics reject is the assumption that, were it not for pervasive discrimination and overexploitation, Blacks would be equally represented in the positions in question. What is scarcely considered is the possibility that, were it not for racist exclusions, Blacks might be over rather than under represented in competitive positions.

Establishing Blacks' presence at a level commensurate with their proportion in the relevant labor market need not be seen as an attempt to actualize some valid prediction. Rather, given the impossibility of determining what level of representation Blacks would have achieved were it not for racist discrimination, the assumption of proportional representation is the only *fair* assumption to make. This is not to argue that Blacks should be maintained in such positions, but their contrived exclusion merits an equally contrived rectification.[12]

Racist acts excluding Blacks affected particular individuals, but were directed at affecting the behavior of the group of all those similar to the victim. Likewise, the benefits of affirmative action policies should not be conceived as limited in their effects to the specific individuals receiving them. Rather, those benefits should be conceived as extending to all those identified with the recipient, sending the message that opportunities are indeed available to qualified Black candidates who would have been excluded in the past. . . .

Forward-Looking Justifications of Affirmative Action

. . . [Some] have defended preferential treatment but denied that it should be viewed as a form of reparation. This latter group rejects "backward looking" justifications of affirmative action and defends it instead on "forward-looking" grounds that include distributive justice, minimizing subordination, and maximizing social utility.

Thus, Ronald Fiscus argues that backward-looking arguments have distorted the proper justification for affirmative action policies.[13] Backward-looking arguments depend on the paradigm of traditional tort cases, where a specific individual x has deprived another individual y of a specific good t through an identifiable act a, and x is required to restore y to the position y would have had, had a not occurred. But typically, preferential treatment requires that x' (rather than x) restore y' (instead of y) with a good t' that y' supposedly would have achieved had y not been deprived of t by x. The displacement of perpetrator (x' for x) and victim (y' for y) gives rise to the problem of (1) White males who are innocent of acts having caused harm nonetheless being forced to provide restitution for such acts; and (2) Blacks who were not directly harmed by those acts nonetheless becoming the principal beneficiaries of restitution for those acts. . . .

Fiscus argues that the backward-looking argument reinforces the perception that preferential treatment is unfair to innocent White males, and so long as this is the case, both the courts and the public are likely to oppose strong affirmative action policies such as quotas, set-asides, and other preferential treatment policies.

In contrast, Fiscus recommends that preferential treatment be justified in terms of distributive justice, which as a matter of equal protection, "requires that individuals be awarded the positions, advantages, or benefits they would have been awarded under fair conditions," that is, conditions under which racist exclusion would not have precluded Blacks from attaining "their deserved proportion of the society's important benefits." Conversely, "distributive justice also holds that individuals or groups may not claim positions, advantages, or benefits that they would not have been awarded under fair conditions."[14] These conditions jointly prohibit White males from claiming an unreasonable share of social benefits and protects White males from having to bear an unreasonable share of the redistributive burden.

Fiscus takes the position that any deviation between Blacks and Whites from strict proportionality in the distribution of current goods is evidence of racism. Thus, if Blacks were 20 percent of a particular population but held no positions in the police or fire departments, that is indicative of past and present racial discrimination. . . .

Because the Equal Protection Clause of the Fourteenth Amendment protects citizens from statistical discrimination on the basis of race, the use of race as the principal reason for excluding certain citizens from benefits made available to other citizens is a violation of that person's constitutional rights. This was one basis for [Alan] Bakke's suit against the UC-Davis medical school's 16 percent minority set-aside for medical school admission. There were eighty-four seats out of the one hundred admission slots that he was eligible to fill, and he was excluded from competing for the other sixteen slots because of his race. On the basis of the standard criteria (GPA, MCAT scores, etc.), Bakke argued that he would have been admitted before any of the Black applicants admitted under the minority set-aside. He therefore claimed that he was being excluded from the additional places available because he was White.

Currently, Blacks have approximately 3.25 times fewer physicians than would be expected given their numbers in the population. Native Americans have 7 times fewer physicians than what would have been expected if intelligent, well-trained, and motivated Native Americans had tried to become physicians at the same rate as did European Americans.

For Fiscus, the underrepresentation of African and Native Americans among physicians and the maldistribution of medical resources to minority communities is clearly the effect of generations of racist exclusions. . . . Not only are qualified members of the oppressed group harmed by . . . prejudice, but even more harmed are the many who would have been qualified but for injuries induced by racial prejudice.

For Fiscus, individuals of different races would have been as equally distributed in the social body as the molecules of a gas in a container and he identifies the belief in the inherent equality of races with the Equal Protection Clause of the Fourteenth Amendment.[15] In a world without racism, minorities would be represented among the top one hundred medical school applicants at UC-Davis in the same proportion as they were in the general population. Accordingly, because Bakke did not score among the top eighty-four Whites, he would not have qualified for admission. Thus, he had no right to the position he was contesting, and indeed if he were given such a position in lieu of awarding it to a minority, Bakke would be much like a person who had received stolen goods. "Individuals who have not personally harmed minorities may nevertheless be prevented from reaping the benefits of the harm inflicted by the society at large."[16]

Justice O'Connor has voiced skepticism toward the assumption that members of different races would "gravitate with mathematical exactitude to each employer or union absent unlawful discrimination."[17] She considers it sheer speculation as to "how many minority students would have been admitted to the medical school at Davis absent past discrimination in educational opportunities."[18] I likewise consider it speculative to assume that races would be represented in every area in proportion to their proportion of the general population. But because it is impossible to reasonably predict what that distribution would have been absent racial discrimination, it is not mere speculation but morally fair practice to assume that it would have been the same as the proportion in the general population. Given the fact of legally sanctioned invidious racism against Blacks in U.S. history, the burden of proof should not be on the oppressed group to prove that it would be represented at a level proportionate to its presence in the general population. Rather, the burden of proof should be on the majority to show why its overrepresentation among the most well off is not the result of unfair competition imposed by racism. We are morally obligated to assume proportional representation until there are more plausible reasons than racism for assuming otherwise. . . .

Thus, it should be the responsibility of the Alabama Department of Public Safety to show why no Blacks were members of its highway patrol as of 1970, even though Blacks were 25 percent of the relevant workforce in Alabama. It should be the responsibility of the company and the union to explain why there were no Blacks with seniority in the union at the Kaiser plant in Louisiana, although Blacks made up 39 percent of the surrounding population. Likewise, it should be the responsibility of the union to explain why no Blacks had been admitted to the Sheet Metal Workers' Union in New York City although minorities were 29 percent of the available workforce. If no alternative explanations are more plausible, then the assumption that the disparity in representation is the result of racism should stand.

The question should not be whether White males are innocent or guilty of racism or sexism, but whether they have a right to inflated odds of obtaining benefits relative to minorities and women. A White male is innocent only up to the point where he takes advantage of "a benefit he would not qualify for without the accumulated effects of racism. At that point he becomes an accomplice in, and a beneficiary of, society's racism. He becomes the recipient of stolen goods."[19] . . .

Cass Sunstein also argues that the traditional compensation model based on the model of a discrete injury caused by one individual (the tort-feasor or defendant) and suffered by another individual (the plaintiff) is inadequate to capture the situation arising from racial and sexual discrimination.[20] With the traditional tortlike model, the situation existing prior to the injury is assumed to be noncontestable, and the purpose of restitution is to restore the injured party to the position that party would have occupied if the injury had not occurred. But in cases where the injury is not well defined, where neither defendant nor plaintiff are individuals connected by a discrete event, and where the position the injured party would have occupied but for the injury is unspecifiable, then in such cases dependence on the traditional model of compensatory justice is questionable.[21]

In contrast to the position taken by Fiscus, Sunstein argues that the claim that affirmative action and preferential treatment is meant to put individuals in the position they would have occupied had their groups not been subject to racial and sexual discrimination is nonsensical: "What would the world look like if it had been unaffected by past discrimination on the basis of race and sex? . . . the question is unanswerable, not because of the absence of good social science, but because of the obscure epistemological status of the question itself."[22]

Affirmative action must be justified in terms of alternative conceptions of the purpose of legal intervention, and Sunstein recommends instead the notion of "risk management" (intended to offset increased risks faced by a group rather than compensate the injuries suffered by a particular individual) and the "principle of nonsubordination" (whereby measures are taken to reverse a situation in which an irrelevant difference has been transformed by legally sanctioned acts of the state into a social disadvantage). The notion of risk management is meant to apply to cases where injuries are "individually small but collectively large" so that pursuing each case individually would be too costly both in terms of time and effort.[23] In such cases, those harmed may be unable to establish a direct causal link between their injuries and the plaintiff's actions. Thus, a person who develops a certain type of cancer associated with a toxin produced by a particular company might have developed that condition even in the absence of the company's negligent behavior. At most, they can argue that the company's actions caused an increased risk of injury, rather than any specific instance of that injury.

Harms suffered in this way systematically affect certain groups with higher frequency than other groups, without it being possible to establish causal links between the injuries of specific plaintiffs and the actions of the defendant. Regulatory agencies should be designed to address harms that are the result of increased risks rather than of a discrete action.[24] One of their principal aims should be not to compensate each injured party (and only injured parties), "but instead to deter and punish the risk-creating behavior" by redistributing social goods.[25] . . .

The principle of nonsubordination is meant to apply to cases where the existing distribution of wealth and opportunities between groups are the result of law rather than natural attributes.[26] The purpose of affirmative action from a forward-looking perspective should be to end social subordination and reverse the situation in which irrelevant differences have been, through social and legal structures, turned into systematic disadvantages operative in multiple spheres that diminish participation in democratic forms of life.[27] . . .

> affirmative action does not appear an impermissible 'taking' of an antecedent entitlement. Because the existing distribution of benefits and burdens between Blacks and Whites and men and women is not natural . . . and because it is in part a product of current laws and practices having discriminatory effects, it is not decisive if some Whites and men are disadvantaged as a result.[28]

A central question in the debate over affirmative action is the extent to which racial classifications are important in accomplishing the goal of relieving the subordinate status of minorities and women. Given the aim of improving safety in transportation, classifying people in terms of their race is rationally irrelevant, while classifying them in terms of their driving competency, visual acuity, and maturity is essential. On the other hand, given the aim of improving health care in Black neighborhoods, classifying applicants for medical school in terms of their race is, in addition to their academic and clinical abilities, a very relevant factor.

To illustrate, African Americans, Hispanics, and Native Americans make up 22 percent of the population but represent only 10 percent of entering medical students and 7 percent of practicing physicians. A number of studies have shown that underrepresented minority physicians are more likely than their majority counterparts to care for poor patients and patients of similar ethnicity. Indeed, "each ethnic group of patients was more likely to be cared for by a physician of their own ethnic background than by a physician of another ethnic background."[29] This suggests that sociocultural factors such as language, physical identity, personal background, and experiences are relevant factors in determining the kinds of communities in which a physician will establish a practice. If this is the case, then the race of a medical school applicant would be an important factor in providing medical services to certain underrepresented communities. Thus, while there might be some purposes for which race is irrelevant, there might be other purposes in which race is important (though perhaps not necessary) for achieving the end in view.[30] The remedy targets Blacks as a group because racially discriminatory practices were directed against Blacks as a group.[31]

. . . Preferential treatment programs are meant to offset the disadvantages imposed by racism so that Blacks are not forced to bear the principal costs of that error.

. . . To condemn polices meant to correct for racial barriers as themselves erecting barriers is to ignore the difference between action and reaction, cause and effect, aggression and self-defense. . . .

Conclusion

Racism was directed against Blacks whether they were talented, average, or mediocre, and attenuating the effects of racism requires distributing remedies similarly. Affirmative action policies compensate for the harms of racism (overt and institutional) through antidiscrimination laws and preferential policies. Prohibiting the benign use of race as a factor in the award of educational, employment and business opportunities would eliminate compensation for past and present racism and reinforce the moral validity of the status quo, with Blacks overrepresented among the least well off and underrepresented among the most well off.

It has become popular to use affirmative action as a scapegoat for the increased vulnerability of the White working class. But it should be recognized that the civil rights revolution (in general) and affirmative action (in particular) has been beneficial, not just to Blacks, but also to Whites (e.g., women, the disabled, the elderly) who otherwise would be substantially more vulnerable than they are now.

Affirmative action is directed toward empowering those groups that have been adversely affected by past and present exclusionary practices. Initiatives to abolish preferential treatment would inflict a grave injustice on African Americans, for they signal a reluctance to acknowledge that the plight of African Americans is the result of institutional practices that require institutional responses.

Notes

1. Kent Greenawalt, *Discrimination and Reverse Discrimination* (New York: Alfred A. Knopf, 1983), 129 ff.
2. Kathanne W. Greene, *Affirmative Action and Principles of Justice* (New York: Greenwood Press, 1989), 22.
3. Kennedy stated: "Even the complete elimination of racial discrimination in employment—a goal toward which this nation must strive—will not put a single unemployed Negro to work unless he has the skills required." Greene, *Affirmative Action*, 23.
4. Greene, *Affirmative Action*, 31.
5. Bernard Boxill, "The Morality of Reparation" in *Social Theory and Practice*, 2, no. 1, Spring 1972: 118–119. It is for such reasons that welfare programs are not sufficient to satisfy the claims of Blacks for restitution. Welfare programs contain no admission of the unjust violation of rights and seek merely to provide the basic means for all to pursue opportunities in the future.
6. I am presuming that most of us would recognize certain primae facie duties such as truth telling, promise keeping, restitution, benevolence, justice, nonmalficience as generally obligatory. See W. D. Ross, *The Right and the Good* (Oxford: Clarendon Press, 1930).
7. Even in the case where y was only as qualified as z, a fair method of choice between candidates should produce an equitable distribution of such positions between Blacks and Whites in the long run if not in the short.
8. Judith Jarvis Thompson, *Philosophy and Public Affairs*, 2 (Summer 1973): 379–380.
9. *Sheet Metal Workers v. EEOC* (1986); *United States v. Paradise* (1987).
10. Thomas Sowell, *Ethnic America* (New York: Basic Books, 1981); *Preferential Policies: An International Perspective* (New York: William Morrow, 1990); For a recent critique of Sowell's position, see Christopher Jencks, *Rethinking Social Policy: Race, Poverty, and the Underclass* (New York: Harper, 1993), chap. 1.
11. Michael Levin, "Race, Biology, and Justice" in *Public Affairs Quarterly*, 8, no. 3 (July 1994). There are many good reasons for skepticism regarding the validity of using IQ as a measure of cognitive ability. See *The Bell Curve Wars* ed. Steven Fraser (New York: Basic Books, 1995); *The Bell Curve Debate*, ed. by Russell Jacoby and Naomi Glauberman (New York: Times Books, 1995); Allan Chase, *The Legacy of Malthus* (Urbana: University of Illinois Press, 1980); Steven J. Gould, *The Mismeasure of Man* (New York: Norton, 1981); R. C. Lewontin, S. Rose, L. J. Kamin, *Not in Our Genes* (New York: Pantheon Books, 1984).
12. See Robert Fullinwider, *The Reverse Discrimination Controversy: A Moral and Legal Analysis* (Totowa, N.J.: Rowman & Littlefield, 1980), 117. Ronald Fiscus, *The Constitutional Logic of Affirmative Action* (Durham, N.C.: Duke University Press, 1992).
13. Ronald J. Fiscus, *The Constitutional Logic of Affirmative Action* (Durham, N.C.: Duke University Press, 1992).
14. Fiscus, *Constitutional Logic*, 13.
15. Fiscus, *Constitutional Logic*, 20–26.
16. Fiscus, *Constitutional Logic*, 38.
17. *Sheet Metal Workers v. EEOC*, 478 US 421, 494 (1986); Fiscus, *Constitutional Logic*, 42.
18. *City of Richmond v. J. A. Croson Co.*, 109 S.Ct. at 724 (1989); Fiscus, *Constitutional Logic*, 42.

19. Fiscus, *Constitutional Logic*, 47. With regard to the problem of so-called "undeserving beneficiaries" of affirmative action Fiscus writes: "When the rightful owner of stolen goods cannot be found, the law . . . may or may not award possession to the original but wrongful claimant; but if it does not, if it awards possession to a third party whose claim is arguable, the original claimant cannot justifiably feel morally harmed. And the government's action cannot be said to be arbitrary unless it awards the goods to an individual whose claim is even less plausible than that of the original claimant" (49).

20. Cass Sunstein, "Limits of Compensatory Justice" in *Nomos* 33, *Compensatory Justice*, ed. John Chapman (New York: New York University Press, 1991), 281–310.

21. "It is not controlling and perhaps not even relevant that the harms that affirmative action attempts to redress cannot be understood in the usual compensatory terms. . . . [T]he nature of the problem guarantees that the legal response cannot take the form of discrete remedies for discrete harms" (Sunstein, "Limits," 297).

22. Sunstein, "Limits," 303.

23. The orientation of the EEOC toward investigating individual cases of alleged discrimination is one explanation of its extraordinary backlog of over 80,000 cases. This orientation precludes it from focusing on systemic practices that affect many individuals, and instead forces it to expend resources dealing with particular instances. See "The EEOC: Pattern and Practice Imperfect" by Maurice Munroe in *Yale Law and Policy Review*, 13, no. 2, (1995): 219–80.

24. Sunstein, "Limits," 292.

25. Sunstein, "Limits," 289.

26. "The current distribution of benefits and burdens as between blacks and whites and women and men is not part of the state of nature but a consequence of past and present social practices" (Sunstein, "Limits," 294).

27. See also Thomas H. Simon, *Democracy and Social Justice* (Lanham, Md.: Rowman & Littlefield, 1995), chap. 5.

28. Sunstein, "Limits," 306.

29. Gang Xu, Sylvia Fields, et al., "The Relationship between the Ethnicity of Generalist Physicians and Their Care for Underserved Populations," Ohio University College of Osteopathic Medicine, Athens, Ohio, 10.

30. Of course, we may ask whether the use of race is necessary for the achievement of the end in view or whether it is one among alternative ways of achieving that end. For instance, it might be possible to induce doctors to practice in Black neighborhoods by providing doctors, irrespective of their race, with suitable monetary incentives. But given the importance of nonmonetary factors in physician-patient relationships, it is doubtful that purely monetary rewards would be sufficient to meet the needs of underserved populations.

31. Remedial action based on the imbalance between blacks in the available work force and their presence in skilled jobs categories presumes that imbalance is caused by racial discrimination. This assumption has been challenged by many who cite cultural and cognitive factors that might equally be the cause of such imbalances. See Thomas Sowell, *Markets and Minorities* (New York: Basic Books, 1981); Richard Herrenstein and Charles Murray, *The Bell Curve* (New York: The Free Press, 1994). This literature has itself been subject to critique: for Sowell, see Christopher Jencks, *Rethinking Social Policy* (New York: Harper, 1993); for Herrenstein and Murray, see *The Bell Curve Wars*, ed. Steven Fraser (New York: Basic Books, 1995).

ALBERT G. MOSLEY, philosopher and musician, is currently a Professor of Philosophy at Smith College in Massachusetts. He is the Editor of *African Philosophy: Selected Readings* (Pearson Education, 1995), and coauthor, with Nicholas Capaldi, of *Affirmative Action* (Rowman & Littlefield, 1996). He has written a number of articles on racial issues, African philosophy, and music.

Roger Clegg  **NO**

Affirmative Discrimination and the Bubble

Introduction

If the higher education bubble deflates or bursts, what will be the fate of affirmative action in the shrinking academic world?

Before addressing that question, let me define some terms. I will be talking only about programs that discriminate or grant preference on the basis of race, ethnicity, or sex—"affirmative discrimination," to borrow Nathan Glazer's felicitous phrase. Sometimes—indeed, typically—"affirmative action" and "diversity" programs involve such discrimination, but not always. The original meaning of affirmative action, for example, as President Kennedy used it in an executive order involving government contractors in 1961, meant taking positive steps, proactive measures—affirmative action, get it?—to ensure that discrimination was *not* occurring. Measures like that raise no moral or legal problems today, and their economic costs are likely to be less as well. In fact, to the extent that racial discrimination is inefficient and irrational—and it is— avoiding it will save colleges money.

But the kind of discrimination and preference that I *am* talking about is widely used against students as well as faculty, and it is found in admissions and hiring and in the privileges and opportunities available after initial selection—for example, scholarships and internships for students, and promotion and funding sources for faculty. As a general matter, for both students and faculty, African Americans receive the most preferential treatment, followed by Latinos. Whites are discriminated against, and often Asians are discriminated against even more, at least in admissions. Racial and ethnic groups receiving preferences are frequently labeled "underrepresented minorities," or URMs.

Interestingly, while women are commonly given preferential treatment for faculty positions, this is less true with respect to student admissions; in fact, it is likely that in undergraduate admissions to many liberal arts schools, women are now discriminated against. But that's a story for another day.

In this essay, I will offer some tentative answers to a series of questions, which I have tried to arrange in a logical sequence. Did affirmative action help cause the higher education bubble in the first place? What are the costs of preferences? Will the purported benefits of preferences diminish if the bubble bursts? Does the outcome of a cost-benefit analysis really matter; that is, even if preferential

programs cost money, will they likely be scaled back as money becomes scarcer, or is the commitment to these programs so stubborn that they will be defended at all costs? Finally, with or without a burst bubble, where are racial preferences likely headed?

Did Preferences Help Cause the Bubble?

To what extent did affirmative discrimination help inflate the bubble in the first place?

It is likely that the turn the civil rights movement took in the 1960s—away from equal opportunity and toward equal results—caused a lowering of academic standards and helped inflate the bubble.

Here's how: Education as an important pathway out of poverty and into the good life has long been part of the American dream. So it was natural that those seeking to improve the lot of African Americans would also seek to improve their education—first by desegregating it so that they had the same opportunities, and also by raising the number of African Americans entering higher education. But the focus on numbers rather than nondiscrimination meant, inevitably, a lowering of academic standards, since simple nondiscrimination would not lead to the numbers desired, at least not immediately.

More students ended up going to college—and going to particular, selective colleges—than their academic qualifications would merit. At the same time, the education offered to them declined in quality. This was due to affirmative action in faculty hiring and a decline in the academic qualifications of the students. Further, the curricula were watered down, since both students and faculty were not up to the rigors of the old curricula. And even with the watered down curricula, students were less likely to graduate, particularly because they were "mismatched" to the school attended, and surely a student who does not complete college cannot claim to have received just as good an education as a student who has graduated.

So: more and more students getting a worse and worse education. Hmmm, yes, that would help inflate the bubble, all right.

By the way, studies conducted by the Center for Equal Opportunity over the years have documented the extent of preferences at schools all over the country and the mismatch effect on graduation rates.[1] And others—on both sides of the aisle—have likewise confirmed the extent of preferences and the presence of a mismatch effect.[2]

Are There Costs to Preferences?

Now that we've established that preferences helped create the bubble, the next obvious question to ask is: Are there continuing costs of preferences so that the post-bubble, sobered-up, cost-cutting academy will want to eliminate them?

Yes. There are economic costs to "diversity," and there are more intangible costs to the university, too, which may ultimately lead to financial costs.

The economic costs are direct and indirect. For starters, it costs money to staff an office for diversity. And the more complicated the selection process, the more time and money it costs to insert extraneous considerations into it. Another expense: the use of racial and ethnic preferences and discrimination keeps the university's lawyers busy, and may result in lawsuits that necessitate hiring high-priced outside counsel.

And consider this. If a company does not produce the best product it can, then it will sell less of that product. Note that it cannot be argued persuasively that this is not so if *all* companies are hampered in the same way, because the demand for any good is not inelastic. Thus, if universities produce an inferior product by hiring other than the most qualified teachers, then there will be less demand for that product. Students are getting less of what they would like, and those who fund the university for its research capability (government, industry, etc.) get less, too. So preferences have this additional, somewhat more indirect cost.

And then there are the less tangible costs of such discrimination. Consider this list for student and faculty discrimination: It is personally unfair, passes over better qualified students and faculty, and sets a disturbing legal, political, and moral precedent in permitting racial discrimination; it creates resentment; it stigmatizes the so-called beneficiaries in the eyes of their classmates and colleagues, teachers and deans, and themselves, as well as future employers, clients, and patients; it fosters a victim mindset, removes the incentive for academic excellence, and encourages separatism; it compromises the academic mission of the university and lowers the overall academic quality of the student body and faculty; it creates pressure to discriminate in grading and graduation, and promotion and tenure; it breeds hypocrisy within the school; it encourages a scofflaw attitude among college officials; it mismatches students and faculty with institutions, guaranteeing failure for many of the former; it papers over the real social problem of why so many African Americans and Latinos are academically uncompetitive; and it gets states and schools involved in unsavory activities like deciding which racial and ethnic minorities will be favored and which ones will not, and how much blood is needed to establish group membership.

Finally, the costs that are less tangible can also translate ultimately into more tangible ones. For example, the mismatching of individuals and institutions also has economic costs. It's a waste of tuition money for the student, and a waste of resources for the school, when an underqualified student fails to graduate, especially if he likely would have graduated had he attended a school where his qualifications were on par with the other students.

One would suppose, in the bursting-bubble world, that students who are most likely to stop going to a particular school are the ones who would likely not graduate if they did attend. If indeed the evidence is correct that racial preferences lead to a "mismatch effect" that in turn leads to lower graduation rates for members of "preferred" racial and ethnic groups, there ought to be some reluctance among such individuals to accept the preferences being afforded them (at least to the extent that they are aware of the preferences and the mismatch effect, which, sadly, is often not the case).

Here's another angle: How will URMs behave and how will they be treated in the post-bubble world? Now, just because there are fewer URMs, net, interested in going to school doesn't necessarily mean there will be less affirmative discrimination, because those going will still be sought after, and those who opt out may be going to less selective schools that are less likely to use preferences. But URMs *are* more likely to avoid mismatching and worthless majors in the post-bubble world, and there are reasons to suppose that universities *will* be more wary of mismatching and offering worthless majors—to anyone—in that world, too. In particular, the phenomenon of switching from STEM majors to, say, ethnic studies—or dropping out altogether—will become less common and accepted, and if a higher percentage of URMs have as a goal actually graduating with a STEM degree, they are more likely to refuse affirmative action.[3]

Will the Purported Benefits Diminish If the Bubble Bursts?

So there *are* costs to affirmative discrimination. But we must also consider the purported benefits, and the effect of a bubble-burst on these benefits, and how they are assessed.

The remedial rationale for racial preferences is the only one that anyone really believes in. America has a long, sad, tragic history of discrimination against African Americans, in particular, and there is a visceral feeling that somehow we would like to make up for it. Addressing this feeling through affirmative discrimination is not logical—slavery and legal discrimination are long past, while today's recipients of university admission preferences were born around 1993—and the Supreme Court has rejected it. The feeling survives, however. But if universities are scaled back financially, it is less likely that they will be seen as the logical vehicle for redressing historical and societal discrimination.

Even the diversity rationale is weakening as it becomes harder and harder to use race and ethnicity as a proxy for the experiences individuals have had or the perspectives they have gained. What's more, if schools return to offering more rigorous curricula, the "educational benefits" from having random conversations with someone who happens to have a different skin color will likely be discounted as well.

And as for the "role model" justification for faculty hiring preferences, not only has the Supreme Court rejected it, but the rationale for it will weaken as our society becomes increasingly multiracial. Besides, if there are fewer students of X race, then logically there is also less need to provide such students with faculty role models of X race.[4]

Do the Costs and Benefits Really Matter?

Of course, the fact that a rational person would conclude that the costs of racial preferences outweigh the benefits is not dispositive if nonrational people are making the decisions. To the extent that the academics who defend preferences are nonrational, the preferences will remain hard to dislodge.

This may well be the case, and one suspects that a strong ideological bias ensures that preferences will have to be pried out of the cold, dead fingers of many academics. Moreover, much of the defense is perfectly rational, at least from the standpoint of the defender, who may owe his position to that ideology. This can be so in three ways: (a) the individual's job exists only because of the diversity aim (e.g., vice dean for diversity); (b) the individual knows that his having been hired is likely owed in part to racial preferences, as are future promotions and tenure; and (c) the individual's academic specialty is nurtured by diversity politics (e.g., some ethnic studies programs and certain approaches to other disciplines—say, in sociology).

That said, it is also likely that these folks will have the hardest time defending their net benefit to the university in a post-bubble world. And if *they* go, gone too, of course, is their effectiveness in defending preferential programs, which also might embolden the remaining academics enough to point out the emperor's nakedness, since most of them have their own misgivings about such programs.[5]

The departments that lead to less remunerative majors (for example, women's studies) are the ones more likely to be cut back, and they are also the ones that are most likely to use preferences. These departments are also often less rigorous and, therefore, are the ones most likely to engage in discriminatory faculty hiring. Likewise, if the bubble-burst results in schools changing curricula so that they better prepare students for jobs, this is likely to result in less politically correct curricula.[6] On this point, if schools go back to teaching—that is, focusing on professors telling students things they need to know and then testing them to see if they have learned those things—then the "educational benefits" of a racially and ethnically diverse student body become less plausibly a "compelling" interest for the school.

Where Are Preferences Headed Anyway?

Another way to approach the problem is to ask where preferences are headed even if the bubble doesn't burst, and then to ask what effect a bubble-burst would have on this trend. The bubble-burst will cause soul-searching about all kinds of things, and that soul-searching will likely involve a reconsideration of pervasive preferences—especially if, at the same time, other pressures against their use are reaching a critical mass. If the momentum is away from affirmative discrimination to begin with, a bubble-burst would further lead to its diminished support.

Those pressures and that momentum are indeed building. Preferences are unpopular with most Americans, as is evidenced by the fact that when put to a popular vote, red and blue states alike have rejected them: California, Michigan, Washington, Arizona, and Nebraska. Only in Colorado did they escape—and by just a razor-thin margin. A similar ballot initiative will be placed before Oklahoma and likely Utah voters in 2012; and its governor ended admission preferences in Florida as a means of avoiding a ballot initiative there. To this list of states we can add two others that, for a period of time as a result of court decisions in recent years, did not engage in racial admissions discrimination at their top state schools: Texas and Georgia. In light of this list, which represents about 37 percent of the U.S. population, how plausible is it that the Supreme Court will now find that higher education demands the use of such discrimination? A Texas case representing this issue is headed to the Supreme Court—a Court in which Justice O'Connor will not be able, again, to cast the fifth vote for racial preferences. She has been replaced by Justice Alito.[7]

The latest census data also undercut the case for preferences. The fastest growing groups are Latinos and Asians, and Latinos now outnumber blacks. What claim do recent immigrants and their children have on remedial preferences? What is the historical justification, indeed, for giving Latinos an admission preference not only over whites but also Asians, as many schools do? Is there a history of Asian subjugation of Latinos in this country?

More fundamentally, in an increasingly multiracial and multiethnic society—one in which, indeed, the census also tells us that individual Americans (beginning with our president) are themselves multiracial and multiethnic—it is simply untenable for our institutions to sort Americans by skin color and the birthplace of their ancestors, and to treat some better than others depending on which little box is checked on an admissions application or employment form.

By the way, 2012 will also see the publication of at least two important books that are likely to challenge the continued use of racial preferences in higher education: one by Stuart Taylor and Richard Sander, and the other by Russell K. Nieli. Prof. Sander continues to build the case that racial preferences in admissions have actually hurt rather than helped African Americans as a result of the mismatch effect. If preferences are not even helping their principal "beneficiary," then how can they possibly be defended?

Conclusion

The bottom line is that there are lots of reasons why the bubble-burst may be bad for preferences, and few if any that would be good for preferences. If the bubble deflates, it is likely that affirmative discrimination will diminish.

Notes

1 These studies are posted on the Center for Equal Opportunity website at http://www.ceousa.org/content/blogcategory/78/100/.

2 See, for example, William Bowen and Derek Bok, *The Shape of the River: Long-Term Consequences of Considering Race in College and University Admissions* (Princeton, NJ: Princeton University Press, 1998), chaps. 2 and 3; Richard H. Sander, "A Systemic Analysis of Affirmative Action in American Law Schools," *Stanford Law Review* 57, no. 2 (November 2004): 367–473; and Stephen Cole and Elinor Barber, *Increasing Faculty Diversity: The Occupational Choices of High-Achieving Minority Students* (Cambridge, MA: Harvard University Press, 2003).

3 On the connection between STEM majors and mismatch, see Gail Heriot, "Want to Be a Doctor? A Scientist? An Engineer? An Affirmative Action Leg Up May Hurt Your Chances," *Engage* 11, no. 3 (December 2010): 18–25. A slightly revised version of this piece appears in this issue of *Academic Questions*.

4 See Wygant v. Jackson Board of Education, 476 U.S. 267 (1986); Roger Clegg, "Martin Luther King vs. Role Model Nonsense," *Inside Higher Ed*, January 19, 2006, http://www.insidehighered.com/views/2006/01/19/clegg; and Elia Powers, "Faculty Gender and Student Performance," *Inside Higher Ed*, June 21, 2007, http://www.insidehighered.com/

news/2007/06/21/gender, which discusses a University of Toronto study that found that "a student's performance and interest in a given subject are not affected much by the professor's gender."

5 Nearly a decade ago I wrote in "When Faculty Hiring Is Blatantly Illegal," which appeared in the November 1, 2002, *Chronicle of Higher Education*:

> A 1996 national study conducted by the Roper Center for Public Opinion Research found that 60 percent of professors surveyed felt their institutions "should not grant preference to one candidate over another in faculty employment decisions on the basis of race, sex, or ethnicity." In 2000, the Connecticut Association of Scholars commissioned the Center for Survey Research and Analysis at the University of Connecticut to conduct a survey of the respective faculties at UConn, the Connecticut State University System, and the state's community-college system. Majorities at all three (52, 61, and 75 percent, respectively) said their institution "should not grant preference" on the basis of race, ethnicity, or sex in faculty employment decisions.

6 See Walter Olson, *Schools for Misrule: Legal Academia and an Overlawyered America* (New York: Encounter Books, 2011), which is reviewed in this issue of *Academic Questions*.

7 I have written frequently on the legal vulnerabilities of universities' affirmative discrimination. See, for example, "Attacking 'Diversity,'" *Journal of College and University Law* 31, no. 2 (2005): 417–36; and "A Half-Dozen Push-Backs for Faculty Hiring Committee Meetings," National Association of Scholars, March 22, 2010; reposted March 17, 2011, http://www.nas.org/polArticles.cfm?doc_id=1872.

ROGER CLEGG, a graduate of Yale University Law School, is President and General Counsel of the Center for Equal Opportunity. He focuses on legal issues arising from civil rights laws, including the regulatory impact on business and the problems in higher education created by affirmative action.

EXPLORING THE ISSUE

Is Affirmative Action Fair?

Critical Thinking and Reflection

1. Consider the meaning of the term "discrimination." What concepts does this term convey besides differences in treatment? Keeping these concepts in mind, is it correct to describe affirmative action as a form of discrimination?
2. Affirmative action programs frequently mandate preferential treatment for minorities based on membership in a group. However, not all members of a minority group have suffered from discrimination in the past or currently experience the systemic consequences of past discrimination. Should people who have not personally suffered from historical discrimination in this country, such as recent immigrants, benefit from affirmative action programs?
3. Can you think of strategies other than affirmative action to bring about a fair treatment of different groups of people and a more just society?
4. Do you consider a racially diverse student population to be a valuable asset for a college or university? Why or why not? How do your views on this issue affect your endorsement or rejection of affirmative action programs?

Is There Common Ground?

The goal of fair treatment of all persons, members of minority groups and majority groups alike, is shared by all parties in this debate. Moreover, past unjust discrimination in this country on the basis of sex and membership in racial and ethnic minorities is a matter of historical record. Mosley and Clegg further agree that inequities based on membership in minority groups still remain in this country and action must be taken to address these inequalities.

The primary disagreement between Mosley and Clegg revolves around the proper means to achieve the goal of fair treatment of all persons. Mosley is concerned that a case-by-case approach to eliminating unjustified differences in the treatment of minorities is not adequate to the task of achieving this goal, and without affirmative action programs that apply to disadvantaged minority groups, members of these groups will be frozen in an unfair *status quo.* Clegg, on the other hand, is concerned that affirmative action programs as they are now practiced are not able to achieve this goal, but only perpetuate unequal and unfair treatment of minorities and impose "reverse discrimination," a modern form of unjust discrimination against members of majority groups.

Create Central

www.mhhe.com/createcentral

Additional Resources

Susan D. Clayton and Faye J. Crosby, *Justice, Gender, and Affirmative Action* (University of Michigan Press, 1992)

Charles V. Dale, *Affirmative Action Revisited* (Nova Science Publishers, 2002)

Samuel Leiter and William M. Leiter, *Affirmative Action in Antidiscrimination Law and Policy: An Overview and Synthesis* (State University of New York Press, 2002)

Paul D. Moreno, *From Direct Action to Affirmative Action: Fair Employment Law and Policy in America, 1933–1972* (Louisiana State University Press, 1999)

Fred L. Pincus, *Reverse Discrimination: Dismantling the Myth* (Lynne Rienner Publishers, 2003)

Internet References . . .

American Association for Affirmative Action

www.affirmativeaction.org/

Ethics Updates: Race, Ethnicity, and Multiculturalism

ethics.sandiego.edu/Applied/Race/index.asp

Public Administration: Affirmative Action and Diversity Resources

www.publicadministration.net/resources/affirmative-action-and-diversity-resources/

The Center for Equal Opportunity

www.ceousa.org

Selected, Edited, and with Issue Framing Material by:
Owen M. Smith, *Stephen F. Austin State University*
and
Anne Collins Smith, *Stephen F. Austin State University*

ISSUE

Should the Death Penalty Be Abolished?

YES: Robert Grant, from "Capital Punishment and Violence," *The Humanist* (2004)

NO: Ernest van den Haag, from "The Death Penalty Once More," *U.C. Davis Law Review* (1985)

Learning Outcomes

After reading this issue, you will be able to:

- State and briefly explain the two most common justifications for the death penalty.
- Explain the apparent connection between the death penalty and the escalation of violence in society.
- Explain the apparent connection, described by van den Haag, between the death penalty and deterrence.
- Formulate your own position on the death penalty and identify evidence supporting your position.
- Identify the main objections to your position and formulate responses to these objections.

ISSUE SUMMARY

YES: Robert Grant, an attorney and history instructor, argues that the death penalty does not discourage violence but instead contributes to it an escalating cycle. Retributive justice, Grant asserts, should be replaced by restorative justice in order to heal the disease of violence that afflicts our society.

NO: Professor of law Ernest van den Haag argues that the death penalty is entirely in line with the U.S. Constitution and that although studies of its deterrent effect are inconclusive, the death penalty is morally justified and should not be abolished.

Since punishment involves the intentional infliction of harm upon another person, and since the intentional infliction of harm is generally wrong, the idea of punishment itself is somewhat problematic. Punishment requires a strong rationale if it is not to be just another form of wrongdoing; capital punishment, also known as the death penalty, requires an especially strong rationale. The rationale for capital punishment usually rests on one of two different lines of reasoning. One is based on the idea of retribution, the other on the idea of deterrence.

The justification for capital punishment based on retribution rests on the claim that justice demands that people who have committed certain criminal acts deserve to die, because these crimes must be paid for by death.

One of the most important objections to this view focuses on the idea of a person "paying" for a crime by death (or even by some other form of punishment). What concept of "paying" is being used here? It does not seem like an ordinary case of paying a debt. It sounds more like a kind of personal vengeance, as when one person says to another, "I'll make you pay for that," meaning, "I'll make you suffer because you did that." Yet one of the ideas behind state-inflicted punishment is that it is supposed to be very official, even bureaucratic, and certainly not personal. The state, in a civilized society, is not supposed to be motivated by a desire for revenge.

In response, proponents of capital punishment argue that enacting retributive justice is an essential role of the state in order to channel citizens' personal desire for retribution into an institutional form. If the state does not punish criminals, this argument goes, individuals will seek to do so themselves, leading to vigilanteism and chaos. Thus, capital punishment is intended not only to punish a criminal who deserves death, but to institutionalize retribution and thereby eliminate personal vengeance and private vendettas.

The justification for capital punishment based on deterrence rests on the claim that the threat of death as a punishment will prevent crimes that would not be prevented by lesser threats. An old joke reflects this view: A Texan tells a visitor that in the old days, the local punishment for horse-stealing was hanging. The visitor is shocked. "You used to hang people just for taken horses?" "Nope," says the Texan, "horses never got stolen."

Unlike the arguing about "paying," the logic behind deterrence is clear. If we look at it from the point of view of the duties of the state, we may reason thus: if by killing a few murderers now and then to make an example, the state can prevent many murders in the future, the net result appears to be a positive benefit for society. It even seems logical from the point of view of criminals, who may be more reluctant to commit murder if they know they will be executed, rather than merely imprisoned.

However, this argument only works if capital punishment really does deter more crimes than other punishments. We can easily think of examples, however, where it would not. Consider a scenario in which two people get into an argument while drinking. In the heat of the moment, one of them pulls a gun and shoots the other, who dies. It is unlikely that the killer, acting in a drunken rage, was deterred by—or even thinking about—the punishment for murder. Another less common scenario concerns people who commit crimes in order to seek notoriety, and may deliberately choose to commit murder so as to gain even more attention by being executed. In general, there is considerable debate concerning the unique effectiveness of capital punishment as a deterrent, which may not be clearly borne out by actual statistics and empirical evidence.

In the following selections, Robert Grant argues for the abolition of the death penalty. He refers to its role in maintaining and increasing a cycle of violence in our society and to the racially skewed way in which it is practiced. Then Ernest van den Haag argues against its abolition, discussing the constitutionality, possible deterrent effect, and moral justification of the death penalty.

YES

Robert Grant

Capital Punishment and Violence

To understand the debate over capital punishment, it is necessary to identify the purpose of the criminal justice system. To a majority of Americans it is, essentially, to retaliate and punish those who commit crimes, especially brutal and vicious murders, thus balancing the scales of justice. To others its goal is to reduce violence overall. The question of capital punishment, then, pits two great demands of society against each other: the demand for retribution for violating the most basic duty of the social contract—the duty not to murder another—and the need to eliminate, or at least minimize, society's culture of violence.

In the United States, capital punishment was adopted from British common law. Then, from the time of the American Revolution through the Civil War, degrees of murder were developed, dividing the crime into first degree premeditated murder, to which the death penalty applied, and a second degree crime of impulse or passion. This was a compromise between those (mostly Quakers) who wanted to abolish the death penalty entirely and those who wished to keep the law essentially unchanged. From the Civil War until the 1960s many states first abolished and then reinstated capital punishment.

But by the 1960s the role of the federal appellate courts had greatly expanded as they applied the federal Bill of Rights to state criminal proceedings in capital cases, especially the prohibition against cruel and unusual punishment and the requirements for due process and equal protection of the law. This coincided with an increased public demand for an end to capital punishment. As a result, capital punishment laws were repealed in several states and no executions were carried out anywhere in the country from 1968 to 1976.

These changes led in June 1972 to the U.S. Supreme Court decision in *Furman v. Georgia*. The Court ruled that the way in which capital punishment statutes were administered was unconstitutional. After reviewing the statistics from the 1920s through the 1960s, the majority concluded: "The death sentence is disproportionately imposed and carried out on the poor, the Negro, and the members of unpopular groups." The conviction and execution of blacks were particularly disparate when the murder victim was white and especially when a white woman was raped. Justice William J. Brennan observed. "When a country of over 200 million people inflicts an unusually severe punishment no more than 50 times a year, the inference is strong that the punishment is not being regularly and fairly applied." The Court also found that excessive punishments are prohibited and concluded that, since life imprisonment is as effective a deterrent as execution, capital punishment was excessive. Justice Thurgood Marshall added, " I cannot believe that at this stage in our history, the American people would ever knowingly support purposeless vengeance."

In response to the decision in *Furman,* the state of Georgia amended its law to provide for capital punishment of certain crimes in a way designed to eliminate excessive penalties as well as discrimination and arbitrariness in deciding who will die. The amended law was then used to convict and sentence to die Troy Gregg for the 1973 murder of two men during his theft of their car. The case, *Gregg v. Georgia,* was appealed to the U.S. Supreme Court, which determined in 1976 that the defendants had been accorded due process of law and that the death penalty in this case didn't constitute cruel and unusual punishment. The Court thus reinstated capital punishment on the ground that the practice wasn't unconstitutional per se.

This decision was reached on the following two bases. First, the Fifth Amendment to the U.S. Constitution expressly recognizes and, to that extent, authorizes the death penalty when it states. "No person shall . . . be deprived of life . . . without due process of law." This is because, by implication, a person may indeed be deprived of life *with* due process of law. Second, regarding the matter of cruel and unusual punishment, the majority stated that "the petitioners on *Furman* and its companion cases predicated their argument primarily upon the asserted proposition that standards of decency had evolved to the point where capital punishment no longer could be tolerated" and that the Eighth Amendment prohibiting cruel and unusual punishment could now be construed "as prohibiting capital punishment." However, "developments during the four years since *Furman* have undercut substantially" that proposition. The majority referred to new death penalty laws that had been enacted in at least thirty-five states in response to *Furman,* and to Congress' 1974 passage of a law "providing the death penalty for aircraft piracy that results in death." The majority of justices concluded that all of these "post-*Furman* statutes make clear that capital punishment itself has not been rejected by the elected representatives of the people." Therefore the social evolution in which Justice Marshall had previously placed his belief didn't actually appear evident.

Today it seems even less evident. Many in U.S. society demand vengeance and retribution for violent criminal conduct. Retributive justice means that the criminal must be made to pay for the crime by a crude mathematics that demands the scales of justice be balanced; this appeals to humanity's basest animal instincts and ancient demands for an eye for an eye, a life for a life. Retributive justice is fueled by hatred and satisfied only with full and complete revenge—the more cruel, the more satisfying. Civil liberties defender and lawyer Clarence Darrow observed that the state "continues to kill its victims, not so much to defend society against them . . . but to appease the mob's emotions of hatred and revenge." After Oklahoma City bomber Timothy McVeigh was executed amid wide television coverage, over 80 percent of the viewers polled said that he deserved to die; many said his death was too clinical and he should have died more painfully. One man said that McVeigh should have been stoned to death. Others were willing to forego his execution because they thought that life behind bars with no possibility of parole would be a greater punishment.

Retributive justice has a bad history, however, as it has historically been used to enforce a class society by oppressing the poor and protecting the rich. It has been used to impose racism by applying the law in an unfairly heavy-handed way upon African-American citizens and in a lenient manner upon white Americans. The U.S. justice system has imprisoned more that two million people; about half are black, although African-Americans constitute only 12 percent of the total population. The prison system has been likened to a twenty-first century form of slavery.

More astonishing, perhaps, is that execution statistics from 1977 through 2002 show that capital punishment isn't so much a national problem as it is a problem local to the South. Nationally, 563 executions occurred during this period and the eleven states of the old Confederacy account for about 87.5 percent of these. Texas is way ahead of the pack, having performed about one-third of all executions. In 2002 Texas alone killed thirty-three death row prisoners. Ifs no coincidence that the South is also the most violent region of the country. However as more and more death row prisoners in other states exhaust their appeals, capital punishment will become more of a national problem.

Of those who favor capital punishment, not all would agree that retribution is their motive. Many argue that it is a deterrent to murder. But is it? Think of the troubled boys at Columbine High School who killed a teacher and students first and then committed suicide. Many violent people—particularly violent adolescents—resort to violence toward others only as an alternative to suicide and, in many cases, kill themselves anyway after killing others. Capital punishment wouldn't be a deterrent to them.

If these might be viewed as exceptional circumstances, then a way of covering all circumstances would be to compare statistics between states and nations with and without capital punishment. However, the majority of the justices in *Gregg,* after reviewing the evidence, concluded, "Statistical attempts to evaluate the worth of the death penalty as a deterrent to crimes by potential offenders have occasioned a great deal of debate. The results simply have been inconclusive." This may be because whatever deterrence factor exists for capital punishment probably exists almost equally for life imprisonment.

A far greater deterrent than either, however, would be more efficient police investigation. An average of twenty-two thousand murders and non-negligent manslaughters are committed annually in the United States but only two-thirds, or fifteen thousand, suspects are arrested. And only 45 percent, or about ten thousand, of all accused killers are convicted.

So, in the end, there is only one purpose, one motive, one true reason for demanding death over life imprisonment; revenge. The issue isn't whether the state has the right to execute those who commit premeditated murder; it has. The issue is whether the state *ought* to execute convicted murders.

The U.S. justice system has reverted to a strictly punitive method in order to prove it is "tough on crime" and in the hope that stronger punishment will somehow deter future criminal activity. But the reality is that severe punishment isn't working. Kids and petty offenders under the current system become hardened, violent, and persistent criminals. The present punitive and retaliatory justice system is unworthy of the American people's high standard of justice, which values the individual and demands equal justice for all.

Many who seek to eliminate the culture of violence in society assert that capital punishment actually exacerbates the level and intensity of violence in the community. They observe that the state is backwardly killing people in order to teach others not to kill. They search for ways to heal the effects of crime upon society, the victim, and the offender. Restorative justice seeks to eliminate violence from the community and heal the harm done to the extent possible.

Violence is a highly contagious social disease that causes emotional, psychological, and physical damage and turns a peaceful person into a hostile one. The essence of violence is hatred, anger, rage, and desire for revenge caused by an act of wrongful violence internalized by the victim. When one allows oneself to be filled with these emotions in response to a violent attack, it allows the attacker to do more than just cause physical injuries. The attacker then does emotional and psychological damage as well. She or he has destroyed the victim's sense of inner tranquility and stability—a destruction that remains long after the physical injuries have healed. When anger, rage, hatred, and vengeance fill that space, the victim is turned from a peaceful to a violent person. This violence is the self-inflicted destruction of one's inner peace.

And violence begets more violence. It is a contagion spreading hatred, anger, rage, and desire for revenge to others out of empathy for the victim. Moreover, a violent victim may seek revenge against the original perpetrator and can be tempted to take out that anger on family members and friends when emotional triggers enflame the violent condition. Violent people don't have ample social skills to resolve differences peacefully and thus the contagion spreads. Each time a person commits a violent act with the intent to injure or kill, the attacker not only causes physical, emotional, and psychological injury to the victim but becomes a more violent person as well. Every act of violence makes the perpetrator more violent—whether the person is someone assaulting an innocent shopkeeper, acting in self-defense, performing a state execution, or soldiering in war. The contagious nature of violence infects the morally righteous police officer as well as the brutal lawbreaker. In his study of young murderers, Cornell University human development professor James Garbarino observes:

Epidemics tend to start among the most vulnerable segments of the population and then work their way outward, like ripples in a pond. These vulnerable populations don't cause the epidemic. Rather, their disadvantaged position makes them a good host for the infection. . . . The same epidemic model describes what is happening with boys who kill.

Horrifically, this is a social disorder that can turn innocent people against each other.

A productive way to react to an act of violence is to have the courage to resist the normal impulse for revenge and punishment, to refrain from allowing anger, hatred, rage, and vengeance to destroy one's inner peace. Civil rights activist Martin Luther King Jr. observed:

Returning violence for violence only multiplies violence, adding deeper darkness to a night already devoid of stars. Darkness cannot drive out darkness, only light can do that. Hate cannot drive out hate; only love can do that.

On the day of McVeigh's execution, a pastor at a memorial service for some of the victims' families asked, "Is there another way we can respond to this violence without doing violence ourselves?" Restorative justice doesn't promote anger, hatred, rage, or revenge by society or by the victim but offers a nonviolent response to the violence done. The focus of restorative justice isn't the punishment of the offender; it is the separation of the violent person from peaceful society for the protection of law-abiding citizens. With a peaceful attitude and conscious decision to choose a nonviolent and nonvengeful response, the cycle of violence can be broken and the contagion stopped. It is all a matter of attitude and the realization that violence should be countered in a mature and rational manner in order to protect society without doing damage to its citizens.

So we need to approach the problem of capital punishment not as a legal matter determining the rights and duties of the parties but as if we were treating a disease—the disease of violence. The past one hundred years have comprised the most violent century in human history. That violence is reflected in our television programs, movies, video games, literature, political attitudes, militaristic paranoia, the alarming abuse toward children, pervasive domestic violence, hostility toward the genuinely poor and helpless, the persistence of racism and intolerance, the way we treat petty juvenile offenders, and the mistreatment of prisoners. When we impose severe and excessive punishment, when we seek an eye for an eye, a tooth for a tooth, a life for a life, when we seek revenge on lawbreakers by some clumsy arithmetic we call justice, we become violent law abiders. We become what we say we abhor—more like criminals—more violent people. And the contagion spreads.

Every time we send a criminal to jail, especially a juvenile offender, it is a failure of society; every time that we execute a murderer, it is another failure of society. Where were the caring family members, helpful friends, concerned teachers, and supportive social workers when that criminal was a child being abused and neglected? Who loved that child? Who educated that child so that he or she could succeed in this world? Who demeaned that child because his or her skin color or religion or ethnicity was different from the majority in the community? Who did violence to that child by relegating him or her to poverty and then hating that child because he or she was poor? Generally speaking, children who are loved and cared for don't become criminals. Family and community violence toward children, including top-down governmental violence, turns some of them into criminals. Ethical communities don't need a police officer on every street corner because ethical communities care for all their children. Criminals aren't born; they are made.

And once made, society gives little thought to rehabilitating the offender, since the purpose of retributive justice is to punish. Or they view punishment as itself rehabilitative. Americans pretend that state-inflicted cruelty will somehow teach a violent felon *not* to be cruel and violent; and then 97 percent of these "rehabilitated" violent criminals are released into civil society. The theory seems to be that punishment teaches one how to become a good and respected member of the community. Yet the current punishments only succeed in destroying an offender's self-esteem by imprisoning that person and separating him or her from family and friends, then dehumanizing the prisoner by referring to him or her by a number instead of a name. Prisoners also become victims of the internal violence of prison life and, when not building up resentments, become schooled by other inmates

in the techniques of crime—aware that society's rejection will continue once they are released.

In order to foster a less violent society, the treatment of the offender should be as humane and non-violent as forcible incarceration can allow. Rehabilitation of the offender ought to be a necessary condition of parole. Life imprisonment without the possibility of parole ought to be the alternative to capital punishment.

Restorative justice seeks to eliminate the culture of violence in U.S. society and replace it with a culture of caring. It's a matter of attitude. We must not allow our hearts to be filled with hatred, anger, rage, and the desire for revenge. It's hard to put aside such feelings when a child or loved one is murdered, especially if the killing is particularly brutal or cruel. This is why violence is so hard to subdue. Look at the difficulties in restoring peace in countries like Northern Ireland, Israel, Bosnia, and India and Pakistan which have engaged in civil wars. Similarly, if we don't find a way to break the cycle of violence we will never be able to end the culture of violence that infects the United States.

Restorative justice doesn't ask that we "turn the other cheek." Restorative justice doesn't seek mercy or forgiveness for those who, by the calculus of duties and rights, deserve to die. Rather, it asks us to protect ourselves from the disease of violence by *not* killing the despised one. Someone must go first to stop the cycle of violence; the obvious candidate is the state. The words of John Donne from his poem "No Man Is an Island" seem particularly appropriate when we execute a condemned prisoner: "Ask not for whom the bell tolls; it tolls for thee!"

ROBERT GRANT is a U.S. attorney and former judge, who teaches history at Oglethorpe University. He is the author of *American Ethics and the Virtuous Citizen: Basic Principles* as well as *American Ethics and the Virtuous Citizen: The Right to Life.*

Ernest van den Haag

 **NO**

The Death Penalty Once More

People concerned with capital punishment disagree on essentially three questions: (1) Is it constitutional? (2) Does the death penalty deter crime more than life imprisonment? (3) Is the death penalty morally justifiable?

Is the Death Penalty Constitutional?

The fifth amendment, passed in 1791, states that "no person shall be deprived of life, liberty, or property, without due process of law." Thus, with "due process of law," the Constitution authorizes depriving persons "of life, liberty or property." The fourteenth amendment, passed in 1868, applies an identical provision to the states. The Constitution, then, authorizes the death penalty. It is left to elected bodies to decide whether or not to retain it.

The eighth amendment, reproducing almost verbatim a passage from the English Bill of Rights of 1689, prohibits "cruel and unusual punishments." This prohibition was not meant to repeal the fifth amendment since the amendments were passed simultaneously. "Cruel" punishment is not prohibited unless "unusual" as well, that is, new, rare, not legislated, or disproportionate to the crime punished. Neither the English Bill of Rights, nor the eighth amendment, hitherto has been found inconsistent with capital punishment.

Evolving Standards

Some commentators argue that, in *Trop v. Dulles,* the Supreme Court indicated that "evolving standards of decency that mark the progress of a maturing society" allow courts to declare "cruel and unusual," punishments authorized by the Constitution. However, *Trop* was concerned with expatriation, a punishment that is not specifically authorized by the Constitution. The death penalty is. *Trop* did not suggest that "evolving standards" could de-authorize what the Constitution repeatedly authorizes. Indeed, Chief Justice Warren, writing for the majority in *Trop,* declared that "the death penalty . . . cannot be said

to violate the constitutional concept of cruelty."[1] Furthermore, the argument based on "evolving standards" is paradoxical: the Constitution would be redundant if current views, enacted by judicial fiat, could supersede what it plainly says. If "standards of decency" currently invented or evolved could, without formal amendment, replace or repeal the standards authorized by the Constitution, the Constitution would be superfluous.

It must be remembered that the Constitution does not force capital punishment on the population but merely authorizes it. Elected bodies are left to decide whether to use the authorization. As for "evolving standards," how could courts detect them without popular consensus as a guide? Moral revelations accepted by judges, religious leaders, sociologists, or academic elites, but not by the majority of voters, cannot suffice. The opinions of the most organized, most articulate, or most vocal might receive unjustified deference. Surely the eighth amendment was meant to limit, but was not meant to replace, decisions by the legislative branch, or to enable the judiciary [to] do what the voters won't do.[2] The general consensus on which the courts would have to rely could be registered only by elected bodies. They favor capital punishment. Indeed, at present, more than seventy percent of the voters approve of the death penalty. The state legislatures reflect as much. Wherefore, the Supreme Court, albeit reluctantly, rejected abolition of the death penalty by judicial *fiat.* This decision was subsequently qualified by a finding that the death penalty for rape is disproportionate to the crime,[3] and by rejecting all mandatory capital punishment.

Caprice

Laws that allowed courts too much latitude to decide, perhaps capriciously, whether to actually impose the death penalty in capital cases also were found unconstitutional. In response, more than two-thirds of the states have modified their death penalty statutes, listing aggravating and mitigating factors, and imposing capital punishment only when the former outweigh the latter. The Supreme Court is satisfied that this procedure meets the constitutional requirements of non-capriciousness. However, abolitionists are not.

In *Capital Punishment: The Inevitability of Caprice and Mistake,*[4] Professor Charles Black contends that the death penalty is necessarily imposed capriciously, for irremediable reasons. If he is right, he has proved too much, unless capital punishment is imposed more capriciously now than it was in 1791 or 1868, when the fifth and fourteenth amendments were enacted. He does not contend that it is. Professor Black also stresses that the elements of chance, unavoidable in all penalizations, are least tolerable when capital punishment is involved. But the irreducible chanciness inherent in human efforts does not constitutionally require the abolition of capital punishment, unless the framers were less aware of chance and human frailty than Professor Black is. (I shall turn to the moral as distinguished from the legal bearing of chanciness anon.)

Discrimination

Sociologists have demonstrated that the death penalty has been distributed in a discriminatory pattern in the past: black or poor defendants were more likely to be executed than equally guilty others. This argues for correction of the distributive process, but not for abolition of the penalty it distributes, unless constitutionally excessive maldistribution ineluctably inheres in the penalty. There is no evidence to that effect. Actually, although we cannot be sure that it has disappeared altogether, discrimination has greatly decreased compared to the past.[5]

However, recently the debate on discrimination has taken a new turn. Statistical studies have found that, *ceteris paribus,* a black man who murders a white has a much greater chance to be executed than he would have had, had his victim been black.[6] This discriminates against black *victims* of murder: they are not as fully, or as often, vindicated as are white victims. However, although unjustified per se, discrimination against a class of victims need not, and here does not, amount to discrimination against their victimizers. The pattern discriminates *against* black murderers of whites and *for* black murderers of blacks. One may describe it as discrimination for, or discrimination against, just as one may describe a glass of water as half full or half empty. Discrimination against one group (here, blacks who kill whites) is necessarily discrimination in favor of another (here, blacks who kill blacks).

Most black victims are killed by black murderers, and a disproportionate number of murder victims is black. Wherefore the discrimination in favor of murderers of black victims more than offsets, numerically, any remaining discrimination against other black murderers.[7]

Comparative Excessiveness

Recently lawyers have argued that the death penalty is unconstitutionally disproportionate if defendants, elsewhere in the state, received lesser sentences for comparable crimes. But the Constitution only requires that penalties be appropriate to the gravity of the crime, not that they cannot exceed penalties imposed elsewhere. Although some states have adopted "comparative excessiveness" reviews, there is no constitutional requirement to do so.

Unavoidably, different courts, prosecutors, defense lawyers, judges and juries produce different penalties even when crimes seem comparable. Chance plays a great role in human affairs. Some offenders are never caught or convicted, while others are executed; some are punished more than others guilty of worse crimes. Thus, a guilty person, or group of persons, may get away with no punishment, or with a light punishment, while others receive the punishment they deserve. Should we let these others go too, or punish them less severely? Should we abolish the penalty applied unequally or discriminatorily?[8]

The late Justice Douglas suggested an answer to these questions:

> A law that . . . said that blacks, those who never went beyond the fifth grade in school, those who made less than $3,000 a year, or those who were unpopular or unstable should be the only people executed [would be wrong]. A law which in the overall view reaches that result in practice has no more sanctity than a law which in terms provides the same.[9]

Justice Douglas' answer here conflates an imagined discriminatory law with the discriminatory application of a non-discriminatory law. His imagined law would be inconsistent with the "equal protection of the laws" demanded by the fourteenth amendment, and the Court would have to invalidate it *ipso facto.* But discrimination caused by uneven application of non-discriminatory death penalty laws may be remedied by means other than abolition, as long as the discrimination is not intrinsic to the laws.

Consider now, albeit fleetingly, the moral as distinguished from the constitutional bearing of discrimination. Suppose guilty defendants are justly executed, but only if poor, or black and not otherwise. This unequal justice would be morally offensive for what may be called tautological reasons:[10] if any punishment for a given crime is just, then a greater or lesser punishment is not. Only one punishment can be just for all persons equally guilty of the same crime.[11] Therefore, different punishments for equally guilty persons or group members are unjust: some offenders are punished more than they deserve, or others less.

Still, equality and justice are not the same. "Equal justice" is not a redundant phrase. Rather, we strive for two distinct ideals, justice and equality. Neither can replace the other. We want to have justice and, having it, we want to extend it equally to all. We would not want equal injustice. Yet, sometimes, we must choose between equal injustice and unequal justice. What should we prefer? Unequal justice is justice still, even if only for some, whereas equal injustice is injustice for all. If not every equally guilty person is punished equally, we have unequal justice. It seems preferable to equal injustice—having no guilty person punished as deserved.[12] Since it is never possible to punish equally all equally guilty murderers, we should punish, as they deserve, as many of those we apprehend and convict as possible. Thus, even if the death penalty were inherently discriminatory—which is not the case—but deserved by those who receive it, it would be morally just to impose it on them. If, as I contend, capital punishment is just and not inherently discriminatory, it remains desirable to eliminate inequality in distribution, to apply the penalty to all who deserve it, sparing no racial or economic class. But if a guilty person or group escaped the penalty through our porous system, wherein is this an argument for sparing others?

If one does not believe capital punishment can be just, discrimination becomes a subordinate argument, since one would object to capital punishment even if it were distributed equally to all the guilty. If one does believe that capital punishment for murderers is deserved, discrimination against guilty black murderers and in favor of equally guilty white murderers is wrong, not because blacks receive the deserved punishment, but because whites escape it.

Consider a less emotionally charged analogy. Suppose traffic police ticketed all drivers who violated the rules, except drivers of luxury cars. Should we abolish tickets? Should we decide that the ticketed drivers of non-luxury cars were unjustly punished and ought not to pay their fines? Would they become innocent of the violation they are guilty of because others have not been ticketed? Surely the drivers of luxury cars should not be exempted. But the fact that they were is no reason to exempt drivers of nonluxury cars as well. Laws could never be applied if the escape of one person, or group, were accepted as ground for not punishing another. To do justice is primarily to punish as deserved, and only secondarily to punish equally.

Guilt is personal. No one becomes less guilty or less deserving of punishment because another was punished leniently or not at all. That justice does not catch up with all guilty persons understandably is resented by those caught. But it does not affect their guilt. If some, or all, white and rich murderers escape the death penalty, how does that reduce the guilt of black or poor murderers, or make them less deserving of punishment, or deserving of a lesser punishment?

Some lawyers have insisted that the death penalty is distributed among those guilty of murder as though by a lottery and that the worst may escape it.[13] They exaggerate, but suppose one grants the point. How do those among the guilty selected for execution by lottery become less deserving of punishment because others escaped it? What is wrong is that these others escaped, not that those among the guilty who were selected by the lottery did not.

Those among the guilty actually punished by a criminal justice system unavoidably are selected by chance, not because we want to so select them, but because the outcome of our efforts largely depends on chance. No murderer is punished unless he is unlucky enough both to be caught and to have convinced a court of his guilt. And courts consider evidence not truth. They find truth only when the evidence establishes it. Thus they may have reasonable doubts about the guilt of an actually guilty person. Although we may strive to make justice as equal as possible, unequal justice will remain our lot in this world. We should not give up justice, or the death penalty, because we cannot extend it as equally to all the guilty as we wish. If we were not to punish one offender because another got away because of caprice or discrimination, we would give up justice for the sake of equality. We would reverse the proper order of priorities.

Is the Death Penalty More Deterrent Than Other Punishments?

Whether or not the death penalty deters the crimes it punishes more than alternative penalties—in this case life imprisonment with or without parole—has been widely debated since Isaac Ehrlich broke the abolitionist ranks by finding that from 1933–65 "an additional execution per year . . . may have resulted on the average in seven or eight fewer murders."[14] Since his article appeared, a whole cottage industry devoted to refuting his findings has arisen.[15] Ehrlich, no slouch, has been refuting those who refuted him.[16] The result seems inconclusive.[17] Statistics have not proved conclusively that the death penalty does or does not deter murder more than other penalties.[18] Still, Ehrlich has the merit of being the first to use a sophisticated statistical analysis to tackle the problem, and of defending his analysis, although it showed deterrence. (Ehrlich started as an abolitionist.) His predecessors cannot be accused of mathematical sophistication. Yet the academic community uncritically accepted their abolitionist results. I myself have no contribution to make to the mathematical analyses of deterrent effects. Perhaps this is why I have come to believe that they may becloud the issue, leading us to rely on demonstrable deterrence as though decisive.

Most abolitionists believe that the death penalty does not deter more than other penalties. But most abolitionists would abolish it, even if it did.[19] I have discussed this matter with prominent abolitionists such as Charles Black, Henry Schwarzchild, Hugo Adam Bedau, Ramsey Clark, and many others. Each told me that, even if every execution were to deter a hundred murders, he would oppose it. I infer that, to these abolitionist leaders, the life of every murderer is more valuable than the lives of a hundred prospective victims, for these abolitionists would spare the murderer, even if doing so would cost a hundred future victims their lives.

Obviously, deterrence cannot be the decisive issue for these abolitionists. It is not necessarily for me either, since I would be for capital punishment on grounds of justice alone. On the other hand, I should favor the death penalty for murderers, if probably deterrent, or even just possibly deterrent. To me, the life of any innocent victim who might be spared has great value; the life of a convicted murderer does not. This is why I would not take the risk of sacrificing innocents by not executing murderers.

Even though statistical demonstrations are not conclusive, and perhaps cannot be, I believe that capital punishment is likely to deter more than anything else. They fear most death deliberately inflicted by law and scheduled by the courts. Whatever people fear most is likely to deter most. Hence, I believe that the threat of the death penalty may deter some murderers who otherwise might not have been deterred. And surely the death penalty is the only penalty that could deter prisoners already serving a life sentence and tempted to kill a guard, or offenders about to be arrested and facing a life sentence. Perhaps they will not be deterred. But they would certainly not be deterred by anything else. We owe all the protection we can give to law enforcers exposed to special risks.

Many murders are "crimes of passion" that, perhaps, cannot be deterred by any threat. Whether or not they can be would depend on the degree of passion; it is unlikely to be always so extreme as to make the person seized by it totally undeterrable. At any rate, offenders sentenced to death ordinarily are guilty of premeditated murder, felony murder, or multiple murders. Some are rape murderers, or hit men, but, to my knowledge, no one convicted of a "crime of passion" is on death row. Whatever the motive, some prospective offenders are not deterrable at all, others are easily deterred, and most are in between. Even if only some murders were, or could be, deterred by capital punishment, it would be worthwhile. . . .

Almost all convicted murderers try to avoid the death penalty by appeals for commutation to life imprisonment. However, a minuscule proportion of convicted murderers prefer execution. It is sometimes argued that they murdered for the sake of being executed, of committing suicide via execution. More likely, they prefer execution to life imprisonment. Although shared by few, this preference is not irrational per se. It is also possible that these convicts accept the verdict of the court, and feel that they deserve the death penalty for the crimes they committed, although the modern mind finds it hard to imagine such feelings. But not all murderers are ACLU humanists. . . .

Is the Death Penalty Moral? Miscarriages

Miscarriages of justice are rare, but do occur. Over a long enough time they lead to the execution of some innocents.[20] Does this make irrevocable punishments morally wrong? Hardly. Our government employs trucks. They run over innocent bystanders more frequently than courts sentence innocents to death. We do not give up trucks because the benefits they produce outweigh the harm, including the death of innocents. Many human activities, even quite trivial ones, forseeably cause wrongful deaths. Courts may cause fewer wrongful deaths than golf. Whether one sees the benefit of doing justice by imposing capital punishment as moral, or as material, or both, it outweighs the loss of innocent lives through miscarriages, which are as unintended as traffic accidents.

Vengeance

Some abolitionists feel that the motive for the death penalty is an un-Christian and unacceptable desire for vengeance. But though vengeance be the motive, it is not the purpose of the death penalty. Doing justice and deterring crime are the purposes, whatever the motive. Purpose (let alone effect) and motive are not the same.

The Lord is often quoted as saying "Vengeance is mine." He did not condemn vengeance. He merely reserved it to Himself—and to the government. For, in the same epistle He is also quoted as saying that the ruler is "the minister of God, a revenger, to execute wrath upon him that doeth evil." The religious notion of hell indicates that the biblical God favored harsh and everlasting punishment for some. However, particularly in a secular society, we cannot wait for the day of judgment to see murderers consigned to hell. Our courts must "execute wrath upon him that doeth evil" here and now.

Charity and Justice

Today many religious leaders oppose capital punishment. This is surprising, because there is no biblical warrant for their opposition. The Roman Catholic Church and most Protestant denominations traditionally have supported capital punishment. Why have their moral views changed? When sharing secular power, the churches clearly distinguished between justice, including penalization as deserved, a function of the secular power, and charity, which, according to religious doctrine, we should feel for all those who suffer for whatever reasons. Currently, religious leaders seem to conflate justice and charity, to conclude that the death penalty and, perhaps, all punishment, is wrong because uncharitable. Churches no longer share secular power. Perhaps bystanders are more ready to replace justice with charity than are those responsible for governing.

Human Dignity

Let me return to the morality of execution. Many abolitionists believe that capital punishment is "degrading to human dignity" and inconsistent with the "sanctity of life." Justice Brennan, concurring in *Furman*, stressed these phrases repeatedly.[21] He did not explain what he meant.

    Why would execution degrade human dignity more than life imprisonment? One may prefer the latter; but it seems at least as degrading as execution. Philosophers, such as Immanuel Kant and G. F. W. Hegel, thought capital punishment indispensable to redeem, or restore, the human dignity of the executed. Perhaps they were wrong. But they argued their case, whereas no one has explained why capital punishment degrades. Apparently those who argue that it does degrade dignity simply define the death penalty as degrading. If so, degradation (or dehumanization) merely is a disguised synonym for their disapproval. Assertion, reassertion, or definition, do not constitute evidence or argument, nor do they otherwise justify, or even explain, disapproval of capital punishment.

    Writers, such as Albert Camus, have suggested that murderers have a miserable time waiting for execution and anticipating it.[22] I do not doubt that. But punishments are not meant to be pleasant. Other people suffer greatly waiting for the end, in hospitals, under circumstances that, I am afraid, are at least as degrading to their dignity as execution. These sufferers have not deserved their suffering by committing crimes, whereas murderers have. Yet, murderers suffer less on death row, unless their consciences bother them.

Lex Talionis

Some writers insist that the suffering the death penalty imposes on murderers exceeds the suffering of their victims. This is hard to determine, but probably true in some cases and not in other cases. However, the comparison is irrelevant. Murderers are punished, as are all offenders, not just for the suffering they caused their victims, but for the harm they do to society by making life insecure, by threatening everyone, and by requiring protective measures. Punishment, ultimately, is a vindication of the moral and legal order of society and not limited by the *Lex Talionis*, meant to limit private retaliation for harms originally regarded as private.

Sanctity of Life

We are enjoined by the Declaration of Independence to secure life. How can this best be achieved? The Constitution authorizes us to secure innocent life by taking the life of murderers, so that any one who deliberately wants to take an innocent life will know that he risks forfeiting his own. The framers did not think that taking the life of a murderer is inconsistent with the "sanctity of life" which Justice Brennan champions. He has not indicated why they were wrong.[23]

Legalized Murder?

Ever since Cesare Bonesana, Marchese di Beccaria, wrote *Dei Delitti e Delle Pene*, abolitionists have contended that executing murderers legitimizes murder by doing to the murderer what he did to his victim. Indeed, capital punishment retributes, or pays back the offender. Occasionally we do punish offenders by doing to them what they did to their victims. We may lock away a kidnapper who wrongfully locked away his victim, and we may kill the murderer who wrongfully killed his victim. To lawfully do to the offender what he unlawfully did to his victim in no way legitimizes his crime. It legitimizes (some) killing, and not murder. An act does not become a crime because of its physical character, which, indeed, it may share with the legal punishment, but because of its social, or, better, antisocial, character—because it is an unlawful act.

Severity

Is the death penalty too severe? It stands in a class by itself. But so does murder. Execution is irreparable. So is murder. In contrast, all other crimes and punishments are, at least partly or potentially, reparable. The death penalty thus is congruous with the moral and material gravity of the crime it punishes.[24]

Still, is it repulsive? Torture, however well deserved, now is repulsive to us. But torture is an artifact. Death is not, since nature has placed us all under sentence of death. Capital punishment, in John Stuart Mills' phrase, only "hastens death"—which is what the murderer did to his victim. I find nothing repulsive in hastening the murderer's death, provided it be done in a nontorturous manner. Had he wished to be secure in his life, he could have avoided murder.

To believe that capital punishment is too severe for any act, one must believe that there can be no act horrible enough to deserve death.[25] I find this belief difficult to understand. I should readily impose the death penalty on a Hitler or a Stalin, or on anyone who does what they did, albeit on a smaller scale.

Conclusion

The death penalty has become a major issue in public debate. This is somewhat puzzling, because quantitatively it is insignificant. Still, capital punishment has separated the voters as a whole from a small, but influential, abolitionist elite. There are, I believe, two reasons that explain the prominence of the issue.

First, I think, there is a genuine ethical issue. Some philosophers believe that the right to life is equally imprescriptible for all, that the murderer has as much right to live as his victim. Others do not push egalitarianism that far. They believe that there is a vital difference, that one's right to live is lost when one intentionally takes an innocent life, that everyone has just the right to one life, his own. If he unlawfully takes that of another he, *eo ipso,* loses his own right to life.

Second, and perhaps as important, the death penalty has symbolic significance. Those who favor it believe that the major remedy for crime is punishment. Those who do not, in the main, believe that the remedy is anything but punishment. They look at the causes of crime and conflate them with compulsions, or with excuses, and refuse to blame. The majority of the people are less sophisticated, but perhaps they have better judgment. They believe that everyone who can understand the nature and effects of his acts is responsible for them, and should be blamed and punished, if he could know that what he did was wrong.

Human beings are human because they can be held responsible, as animals cannot be. In that Kantian sense the death penalty is a symbolic affirmation of the humanity of both victim and murderer.

Notes

1. 356 U.S. 99 (1958).
2. The courts have sometimes confirmed the obsolescence of non-repealed laws or punishments. But here they are asked to invent it.
3. In *Coker v. Georgia,* 433 U.S. 584, 592 (1977), the Court concluded that the eighth amendment prohibits punishments that are "'excessive' in relation to the crime committed." I am not sure about this disproportion. However, threatening execution would tempt rapists to murder their victims who, after all, are potential witnesses. By murdering their victims, rapists would increase their chances of escaping execution without adding to their risk. Therefore, I agree with the court's conclusion, though not with its argument.
4. C. BLACK, CAPITAL PUNISHMENT: THE INEVITABILITY OF CAPRICE AND MISTAKE (2d ed. 1981).
5. Most discrimination occurred in rape cases and was eliminated when the death penalty for rape was declared unconstitutional.
6. For a survey of the statistical literature, see, e.g., Bowers, *The Pervasiveness of Arbitrariness and Discrimination under Post-Furman Capital Statutes,* 74 J. CRIM. L. & CRIMINOLOGY 1067 (1983). His article is part of a "Symposium on Current Death Penalty Issues" compiled by death penalty opponents.
7. Those who demonstrated the pattern seem to have been under the impression that they had shown discrimination against black murderers. They were wrong. However, the discrimination against black victims is invidious and should be corrected.
8. The capriciousness argument is undermined when capriciousness is conceded to be unavoidable. But even when capriciousness is thought reducible, one wonders whether releasing or retrying one guilty defendant, because another equally guilty defendant was not punished as much, would help reduce capriciousness. It does not seem a logical remedy.
9. *Furman v. Georgia,* 408 U.S. 238, 256 (1971) (Douglas, J., concurring).
10. I shall not consider here the actual psychological motives that power our unending thirst for equality.

11. If courts impose different punishments on different persons, we may not be able to establish in all cases whether the punishment is just, or (it amounts to the same) whether the different persons were equally guilty of the same crime, or whether their crimes were identical in all relevant respects. Thus, we may not be able to tell which of two unequal punishments is just. Both may be, or neither may be. Inequality may not entail more injustice than equality, and equality would entail justice only if we were sure that the punishment meted out was the just punishment.

12. Similarly, it is better that only some innocents suffer undeserved punishment than that all suffer it equally.

13. It would be desirable that all of the worst murderers be sentenced to death. However, since murderers are tried in different courts, this is unlikely. Further, sometimes the testimony of one murderer is needed to convict another, and cannot be obtained except by leniency. Morally, and legally it is enough that those sentenced to death deserve the penalty for their crimes, even if others, who may deserve it as much, or more, were not sentenced to death.

14. Ehrlich, *The Deterrent Effect of Capital Punishment: A Question of Life or Death,* 65 AM. ECON. REV. 397, 414 (1975).

15. *See, e.g.,* Baldus & Cole, *A Comparison of the Work of Thorsten Sellin and Isaac Ehrlich on the Deterrent Effect of Capital Punishment,* 85 YALE L. J. 170 (1975); Bowers & Pierce, *Deterrence or Brutalization: What Is the Effect of Executions?,* 26 CRIME & DELINQ. 453 (1980); Bowers & Pierce, *The Illusion of Deterrence in Isaac Ehrlich's Research on Capital Punishment,* 85 YALE L. J. 187 (1975).

16. Ehrlich, *Fear of Deterrence,* 6 J. LEGAL STUD. 293 (1977); Ehrlich & Gibbons, *On the Measurement of the Deterrent Effect of Capital Punishment and the Theory of Deterrence,* 6 J. LEGAL STUD. 35 (1977).

17. At present there is no agreement even on whether the short run effects of executions delay or accelerate homicides. *See* Phillips, *The Deterrent Effect of Capital Punishment: New Evidence on an Old Controversy,* 86, AM. J. SOC. 139 (1980).

18. As stated in *Gregg v. Georgia,* 428 U.S. 153, 185 (1976), "Although some of the studies suggest that the death penalty may not function as a significantly greater deterrent than lesser penalties, there is no convincing empirical evidence either supporting or refuting this view."

19. Jeffrey Reiman is an honorable exception. *See* Reiman, *Justice, Civilization, and the Death Penalty: Answering van den Haag,* 14 PHIL. & PUB. AFF. 115 (1985).

20. Life imprisonment avoids the problem of executing innocent persons to some extent. It can be revoked. But the convict also may die in prison before his innocence is discovered.

21. "[T]he Cruel and Unusual Punishments Clause prohibits the infliction of uncivilized and inhuman punishments. The State, even as it punishes, must treat its members with respect for their intrinsic worth as human beings." *Furman v. Georgia,* 408 U.S. 238, 270 (1972) (Brennan, J., concurring). "When we consider why [certain punishments] have been condemned, . . . we realize that the pain involved is not the only reason. The true significance of these punishments [that have been condemned] is that they treat members of the human race as nonhumans, as objects to be toyed with and discarded." *Id.* at 272–73.

> In determining whether a punishment comports with human dignity, we are aided also by a second principle inherent in the Clause—that the State must not arbitrarily inflict a severe punishment. This principle derives from the notion that the State does not respect human dignity when, without reason, it inflicts upon some people a severe punishment that it does not inflict upon others.

Id. at 274. "Death is truly an awesome punishment. The calculated killing of a human being by the State involves, by its very nature, a denial of the executed person's humanity." *Id.* at 290. "In comparison to all other punishments today, then, the deliberate extinguishment of human life by the State is uniquely degrading to human dignity." *Id.* at 291.

22. In *Reflections on the Guillotine,* Camus stated that "[t]he parcel [the condemned person] is no longer subject to the laws of chance that hang over the living creature but to mechanical laws that allow him to foresee accurately the day of his beheading. . . . The Greeks, after all, were more humane with their hemlock." A. CAMUS, RESISTANCE, REBELLION AND DEATH 175, 202 (1960).

23. "Sanctity of life" may mean that we should not take, and should punish taking innocent life: *"homo homini res sacra."* In the past this meant that we should take the life of a murderer to secure innocent life, and stress its sacredness. Justice Brennan seems to mean that the life of the murderer should be sacred too—but no argument is given for this premise.

24. Capital punishment is not inconsistent with *Weems v. United States,* 217 U.S. 349 (1910),

which merely held that punishment cannot be excessive, that is, out of proportion to the gravity of the crime. Indeed, if life imprisonment suffices for anything else, it cannot be appropriate for murder.

25. The notion of deserving is strictly moral, depending exclusively on our sense of justice, unlike the notion of deterrence, which depends on the expected factual consequences of punishment. Whilst deterrence alone would justify most of the punishments we should impose, it may not suffice to justify all those punishments that our sense of justice demands. Wherefore criminal justice must rest on desert as well as deterrence, to be seen as morally justified.

Ernest van den Haag (1914–2002) was a distinguished lecturer at Columbia University, Yale University, and Harvard University. For many years, he was John M. Olin Professor of Jurisprudence at Fordham University and also a scholar at the Heritage Foundation. Van den Haag was both a psychoanalyst and a criminologist. He is coauthor, with John P. Conrad, of *The Death Penalty: A Debate* (Plenum, 1983).

EXPLORING THE ISSUE

Should the Death Penalty Be Abolished?

Critical Thinking and Reflection

1. Does the continued use of the death penalty violate or uphold the principle of the sanctity of life? Explain your response.
2. What corrective action might be taken to eliminate the disproportionate administration of the death penalty to black killers of white victims? In your opinion, would these measures be effective? If not, should the death penalty be abolished?
3. Is the use of the death penalty justified on the grounds of retribution, that is, the principle of making the criminals pay for their crimes? Why or why not?

Is There Common Ground?

One of the major points on which Grant and van den Haag differ is the extent to which we can separate and correct negative features such as racial bias from the death penalty itself. Van den Haag would argue that these negative features can be addressed without the moral acceptability of the death penalty being brought into question. Grant might very well respond that the moral acceptability of the death penalty must be determined not in an ideal world but in the real world that we live in.

However, the conflict between Grant and van den Haag runs deeper than their disagreement over the significance of imperfections in the administration of the death penalty. Grant argues that the death penalty encourages rather than deters violence and that it is partially respon-

sible for an epidemic of violence in our society today. Van den Haag argues that the death penalty is an appropriate and constitutional practice that is the most, and sometimes the only, correct punishment for certain crimes. Thus, they differ on whether the death penalty should be part of our legal system at all.

Additional Resources

Hugo Bedau and Paul Cassell, eds., *Debating the Death Penalty: Should America Have Capital Punishment?* (Oxford University Press, 2004) Mark Grossman, *Encyclopedia of Capital Punishment* (ABC-CLIO, 1998)

Bill Kurtis, *The Death Penalty on Trial: Crisis in American Justice* (Public Affairs, 2004)

Internet References . . .

Death Penalty Information Center

www.deathpenaltyinfo.org/

Ethics Updates: The Death Penalty and Punishment

http://ethics.sandiego.edu/Applied/DeathPenalty/
index.asp

The Death Penalty: Specific Issues

http://justice.uaa.alaska.edu/death/issues.html

Selected, Edited, and with Issue Framing Material by:
Owen M. Smith, *Stephen F. Austin State University*
and
Anne Collins Smith, *Stephen F. Austin State University*

ISSUE

Is Torture Ever Justified?

YES: Mirko Bagaric and Julie Clarke, from "Not Enough Official Torture in the World? The Circumstances in Which Torture Is Morally Justifiable" *University of San Francisco Law Review* (Spring 2005)

NO: Christopher Kutz, from "Torture, Necessity, and Existential Politics," *California Law Review* (February 2007)

Learning Outcomes

After reading this issue, you will be able to:

- Explain the difference between a legal judgment and a moral judgment, and explain why legal judgments do not always correspond with moral judgments in a society.
- Identify significant factors that limit the acceptable use of torture, and explain how these factors should be applied in specific circumstances.
- Distinguish between institutional (legal) and pre-institutional (moral) rights, and explain why the necessity defense cannot override pre-institutional rights.
- Formulate your own position on the morality of torture and identify evidence supporting your position.
- Identify the main objections to your position and formulate responses to these objections.

ISSUE SUMMARY

YES: Bagaric and Clarke remind us, first of all, that torture, although prohibited by international law, is nevertheless widely practiced. A rational examination of torture and a consideration of hypothetical (but realistic) cases show that torture is justifiable in order to prevent great harm. Torture should be regulated and carefully practiced as an information-gathering technique in extreme cases.

NO: Christopher Kutz examines the reasoning intended to justify torture in a memo produced by the Bush administration and concludes that even in extreme hypothetical cases, such reasoning is not valid because the right not to be tortured is a pre-institutional right that cannot be revoked under any circumstances.

The morality of torture was brought to the attention of the American people in a new and urgent way because of the terror attacks on 9/11. Prior to these events, philosophers had been discussing this issue primarily in a theoretical context. Afterwards, when torture was first proposed, and then adopted by the American government as a method to combat terror attacks, the issue moved from the realm of theory to practical urgency.

In order to address this issue clearly, it is important to distinguish between moral judgments and legal judgments. A moral judgment is a conclusion about the morality of an action that is reached by applying a moral rule of behavior (moral standard) to a specific set of circumstances. In contrast, a legal judgment is a conclusion about the legality of an action that is reached by applying a law (legal standard) to a specific set of circumstances. Since moral rules of behavior do not have the same status as laws, moral judgments are not the same as legal

judgments. It is true that moral judgments and legal judgments often coincide: killing someone for entertainment is regarded by most people as immoral and is illegal in most societies, while donating canned food to a food bank is regarded by most people as moral and is legal in most societies. However, moral judgments and legal judgments do not always coincide: lying about one's plans in order to avoid a social obligation, while considered immoral by many people, is usually legal, while breaking the speed limit in order to get a severely injured person to the hospital is considered moral by most people, but is technically illegal. There are many reasons why a moral judgment may not correspond with a legal judgment:

- A society may not wish to devote the extensive resources needed to investigate, prosecute, and punish all immoral actions as crimes;
- A society may reject the extensive governmental intrusion required to treat all immoral actions as crimes; and

- Laws without a basis in morality, such as driving on the right side of the road, are necessary to prevent confusion and foster efficient interactions among citizens.

The distinction between moral judgments and legal judgments is central to the issue of torture because the assertion that torture is legal is not the same thing as the assertion that torture is moral. A governmental authority, such as a legislature, attorney general, or court, may determine that torture is legal under certain circumstances, but torture is not thereby made moral. Indeed, many societal advances in the United States and around the world have occurred because conscientious people have concluded that certain actions, while legal, are nevertheless immoral or unjust, and as result of this conclusion, have chosen to challenge, and if necessary to violate, the immoral laws of their society and work for their repeal or amendment.

In examining the morality of torture, both sides frequently make use of hypothetical scenarios. Those who hold the view that torture can be morally justified construct scenarios in which a person has information that can prevent a great harm, but chooses not to divulge the information to the appropriate authorities. They advocate the use of torture, that is, the deliberate infliction of pain, to induce that person to reveal the information and thus prevent or mitigate the great harm. The moral reasoning behind such a scenario is essentially utilitarian in nature: the benefit to the persons escaping the great harm is sufficiently greater than the harm inflicted on the person being tortured as to make the torture morally justified. This argument is enhanced if the harm involves irreparable injury or death to innocent parties and the torture inflicts no lasting damage on the guilty party.

Those who hold the view that torture cannot be morally justified criticize these scenarios on several grounds. One ground concerns the reliability of the information extracted by torture. The harm suffered by the person being tortured is morally justified on utilitarian grounds only if it results in the production of reliable information that can sufficiently benefit others. If the information is not reliable, then the benefit to others may not be realized, and the harm inflicted through torture would not therefore be morally justified. Another ground for rejecting the morality of torture is based not on utilitarianism, but on a different approach to ethics called deontology. An important principle of deontology is that persons should never be treated merely as a means to an end; rather, persons should always be valued as end in themselves. According to this ethical theory, torture is fundamentally immoral because it treats the person being tortured merely as a means to gaining information. As such, torture is morally wrong, no matter how important the information is or how much harm the information can prevent.

In the first reading, Bagaric and Clarke present such a scenario and advance a utilitarian argument to support their assertion that torture is sometimes justified. They further argue that torture is already being practiced widely—although unmonitored and "underground." Their idea is to acknowledge it, endorse it to some extent, but draw lines to regulate and limit its use.

In the second reading, Christopher Kutz does not wish to condone torture at all. He argues from a deontological perspective that we must maintain our commitment to human rights even in a scenario such as the one proposed by Bagaric and Clarke. On his view, the gravest danger in the war on terror is the damage that we ourselves may do to our own most deeply held principles about human rights.

YES ↵

Mirko Bagaric and Julie Clarke

Not Enough Official Torture in the World? The Circumstances in Which Torture Is Morally Justifiable

Recent events stemming from the "war on terrorism" have highlighted the prevalence of torture, both as an interrogation technique and as a punitive measure. Torture is almost universally deplored. It is prohibited by international law and is not officially sanctioned by the domestic laws of any state. The formal prohibition against torture is absolute—there are no exceptions to it. This is not only pragmatically unrealistic, but unsound at a normative level. Despite the absolute ban on torture, it is widely used. Contrary to common belief, torture is not the preserve of despot military regimes in third world nations. For example, there are serious concerns regarding the treatment by the United States of senior Al Qaeda leader Khalid Shaikh Mohammad. There is also irrefutable evidence that the United States tortured large numbers of Iraqi prisoners, as well as strong evidence that it tortured prisoners at Guantanamo Bay prison in Cuba, where suspected Al Qaeda terrorists are held. More generally Professor Alan Dershowitz has noted, "[C]ountries all over the world violate the Geneva Accords [prohibiting torture]. They do it secretly and hypothetically, the way the French did it in Algeria."

Dershowitz has also recently argued that torture should be made lawful. His argument is based on a harm minimization rationale from the perspective of victims of torture. He said, "Of course it would be best if we didn't use torture at all, but if the United States is going to continue to torture people, we need to make the process legal and accountable." Our argument goes one step beyond this. We argue that torture is indeed morally defensible, not just pragmatically desirable. The harm minimization rationale is used to supplement our argument.

While a "civilized" community does not typically condone such conduct, this Article contends that torture is morally defensible in certain circumstances, mainly when more grave harm can be avoided by using torture as an interrogation device. The pejorative connotation associated with torture should be abolished. A dispassionate analysis of the propriety of torture indicates that it is morally justifiable. At the outset of this analytical discussion, this Article requires readers to move from the question of whether torture is *ever* defensible to the issue of the circumstances in which it is morally permissible.

Consider the following example: A terrorist network has activated a large bomb on one of hundreds of commercial planes carrying over three hundred passengers that is flying somewhere in the world at any point in time. The bomb is set to explode in thirty minutes. The leader of the terrorist organization announces this intent via a statement on the Internet. He states that the bomb was planted by one of his colleagues at one of the major airports in the world in the past few hours. No details are provided regarding the location of the plane where the bomb is located. Unbeknown to him, he was under police surveillance and is immediately apprehended by police. The terrorist leader refuses to answer any questions of the police, declaring that the passengers must die and will do so shortly.

Who in the world would deny that all possible means should be used to extract the details of the plane and the location of the bomb? The answer is not many. The passengers, their relatives and friends, and many in society would expect that all means should be used to extract the information, even if the pain and suffering imposed on the terrorist resulted in his death.

Although the above example is hypothetical and is not one that has occurred in the real world, the force of the argument cannot be dismissed on that basis. As C.L. Ten notes, "fantastic examples" that raise fundamental issues for consideration, such as whether it is proper to torture wrongdoers, play an important role in the evaluation of moral principles and theories. These examples sharpen contrasts and illuminate the logical conclusions of the respective principles to test the true strength of our commitment to the principles. Thus, fantastic examples cannot be dismissed summarily merely because they are "simply" hypothetical.

Real life is, of course, rarely this clear cut, but there are certainly scenarios approaching this degree of desperation, which raise for discussion whether it is justifiable to inflict harm on one person to reduce a greater level of harm occurring to a large number of blameless people. Ultimately, torture is simply the sharp end of conduct whereby the interests of one agent are sacrificed for the greater good. As a community, we are willing to accept this principle. Thus, although differing in degree, torture is no

From *University of San Francisco Law Review,* vol. 39, Spring 2005, pp. 581–616. Copyright © 2005 by University of San Francisco Law Review. Reprinted by permission.

different in nature from conduct that we sanction in other circumstances. It should be viewed in this light.

Given this, it is illogical to insist on a blanket prohibition against torture. Therefore, the debate must turn to the circumstances when torture is morally appropriate. This is the topic of this Article.

International law defines torture as severe pain and suffering, generally used as an interrogation device or as a punitive measure. This Article focuses on the use of torture as an interrogation device and poses that the device is only permissible to prevent significant harm to others. In these circumstances, there are five variables relevant in determining whether torture is permissible and the degree of torture that is appropriate. The variables are (1) the number of lives at risk; (2) the immediacy of the harm; (3) the availability of other means to acquire the information; (4) the level of wrongdoing of the agent; and (5) the likelihood that the agent actually does possess the relevant information.

This Article analyzes the meaning of torture and the nature and scope of the legal prohibition against torture [and] examines whether torture is morally defensible. It is argued that torture is no different than other forms of morally permissible behavior and is justifiable on a utilitarian ethic. It is also argued that, on close reflection, torture is also justifiable against a backdrop of a non-consequentialist rights-based ethic, which is widely regarded as prohibiting torture in all circumstances. Thus, the Article concludes that torture is morally justifiable in rare circumstances, irrespective of which normative theory one adopts. [We] examine the circumstances in which torture is justifiable. Finally, [we] debunk the argument that torture should not be legalized because it will open the floodgates to more torture.

Torture: Reality and Legal Position

The Law on Torture

Pursuant to international law, "torture" is defined as:

> Any act by which severe pain or suffering, whether physical or mental, is intentionally inflicted on a person for such purposes as obtaining from him or a third person information or a confession, punishing him for an act he or a third person has committed or is suspected of having committed, or intimidating or coercing him or a third person, or for any reason based on discrimination of any kind, when such pain or suffering is inflicted by or at the instigation of or with the consent or acquiescence of a public official or other person acting in an official capacity. It does not include pain or suffering arising only from, inherent in or incidental to lawful sanctions.

Torture is prohibited by a number of international documents. It is also considered to carry a special status in customary international law, that of *jus cogens,* which is a "peremptory norm" of customary international law. The

significance of this is that customary international law is binding on all states, even if they have not ratified a particular treaty. At the treaty level, there are both general treaties that proscribe torture and specific treaties banning the practice.

In terms of general treaties, torture is prohibited by a number of international and regional treaties. . . .

The rigidity of the rule against torture is exemplified by the fact that it has a non-derogable status in human rights law. That is, there are no circumstances in which torture is permissible. This prohibition is made clear in Article 2(2) of the U.N. Convention Against Torture, which states, "No exceptional circumstances whatsoever, whether a state of war or a threat of war, internal political instability or any other public emergency, may be invoked as a justification of torture." Thus, the right not to be tortured is absolute. . . .

This absolute prohibition is frequently highlighted by Amnesty International and other human rights organizations. For example, Amnesty International states, "The law is unequivocal—torture is absolutely prohibited in all circumstances. . . . The right to be free from torture is absolute. It cannot be denied to anyone in any circumstances."

Torture is also prohibited as a war crime, pursuant to humanitarian law. In addition, torture is considered to be a crime against humanity when the acts are perpetrated as part of a widespread or systematic attack against a civilian population, whether or not they are committed in the course of an armed conflict.

The Reality of Torture

As with many legal precepts, the black letter law must be considered against the context of reality. As this part shows, various forms of torture are used despite the legal prohibition of it.

1. Forms of Torture

As is noted by Dershowitz, torture comes in many different forms and intensities:

> Torture is a continuum and the two extremes are on the one hand torturing someone to death— that is torturing an enemy to death so that others will know that if you are caught, you will be caused excruciating pain—that's torture as a deterrent. . . . At the other extreme, there's non-lethal torture which leaves only psychological scars. The perfect example of this is a sterilised needle inserted under the fingernail, causing unbearable pain but no possible long-term damage. These are very different phenomena. What they have in common of course is that they allow the government physically to come into contact with you in order to produce pain.

Various methods of torture have and continue to be applied in a multitude of countries. The most common methods are beating, electric shock, rape and sexual abuse, mock execution or threat of death, and prolonged solitary confinement. Other common methods include sleep and sensory deprivation, suspension of the body, "shackling interrogees in contorted painful positions" or in "painful stretching positions," and applying pressure to sensitive areas, such as the "neck, throat, genitals, chest and head."

2. The Benefits of Torture: An Effective Information Gathering Device

The main benefit of torture is that it is an excellent means of gathering information. Humans have an intense desire to avoid pain, no matter how short term, and most will comply with the demands of a torturer to avoid the pain. Often even the threat of torture alone will evoke cooperation. To this end, Dershowitz cites a recent kidnapping case in Germany in which the son of a distinguished banker was kidnapped. The eleven-year-old boy had been missing for three days. The police had in their custody a man they were convinced had perpetrated the kidnapping. The man was taken into custody after being seen collecting a ransom that was paid by the boy's family. During seven hours of interrogation the man "toyed" with police, leading them to one false location after another. After exhausting all lawful means of interrogation, the deputy commissioner of the Frankfurt police instructed his officers, in writing, that they could try to extract information "by means of the infliction of pain, under medical supervision and subject to prior warning." Ten minutes after the warning was given the suspect told the police where the boy was; unfortunately the boy was already dead, having been killed shortly after the kidnapping.

3. The Widespread Use of Torture

a. Torture Around the World Despite the contemporary abhorrence against it, dozens of countries continue to use torture. A study of 195 countries and territories by Amnesty International between 1997 and mid-2000 found reports of torture or ill-treatment by state officials in more than 150 countries and in more than seventy countries that torture or ill-treatment was reported as "widespread or persistent." It is also clear that torture is not limited to military regimes in third world nations. Amnesty International recently reported that in 2003 it had received reports of torture and ill-treatment from 132 countries, including the United States, Canada, Japan, France, Italy, Spain, and Germany. . . .

The Circumstances in Which Torture Is Acceptable

The only situation where torture is justifiable is where it is used as an information gathering technique to avert a grave risk. In such circumstances, there are five variables relevant in determining whether torture is permissible and the degree of torture that is appropriate. The variables are (1) the number of lives at risk; (2) the immediacy of the harm; (3) the availability of other means to acquire the information; (4) the level of wrongdoing of the agent; and (5) the likelihood that the agent actually does possess the relevant information. Where (1), (2), (4) and (5) rate highly and (3) is low, all forms of harm may be inflicted on the agent—even if this results in death.

The Harm to Be Prevented

The key consideration regarding the permissibility of torture is the magnitude of harm that is sought to be prevented. To this end, the appropriate measure is the number of lives that are likely to be lost if the threatened harm is not alleviated. Obviously, the more lives that are at stake, the more weight that is attributed to this variable.

Lesser forms of threatened harm will not justify torture. Logically, the right to life is the most basic and fundamental of all human rights—non-observance of it would render all other human rights devoid of meaning. Every society has some prohibition against taking life, and "the intentional taking of human life is . . . the offence which society condemns most strongly." The right to life is also enshrined in several international covenants. For example, Article 2 of the European Convention on Human Rights (which in essence mirrors Article 6 of the International Covenant on Civil and Political Rights) provides that "everyone's right to life shall be protected by law. No one shall be deprived of his life intentionally save in the execution of a sentence of a court following his conviction of a crime for which this penalty is provided by law."

Torture violates the right to physical integrity, which is so important that it is only a threat to the right to life that can justify interference with it. Thus, torture should be confined to situations where the right to life is imperiled.

Immediacy of Harm and Other Options to Obtain Information

Torture should only be used as a last resort and hence should not be utilized where there is time to pursue other avenues of forestalling the harm. It is for this reason that torture should only be used where there is no other means to obtain the relevant information. Thus, where a terrorist has planted a bomb on a plane, torture will not be permissible where, for example, video tapes of international airports are likely to reveal the identity of the plane that has been targeted.

The Likelihood of Knowledge or Guilt

As a general rule torture should normally be confined to people that are responsible in some way for the threatened harm. This is not, however, invariably the case. People who are simply aware of the threatened harm, that is "innocent people," may in some circumstances also be subjected to torture.

Regardless of the guilt of the agent, it is most important that torture is only used against individuals who actually possess the relevant information. It will be rare that conclusive proof is available that an individual does, in fact, possess the required knowledge; for example, potential torturees will not have been through a trial process in which their guilt has been established. This is not a decisive objection, however, to the use of torture. The investigation and trial process is simply one means of distinguishing wrongdoers from the innocent. To that end, it does not seem to be a particularly effective process. There are other ways of forming such conclusions. One is by way of lie-detector tests. The latest information suggests that polygraphs are accurate about eighty to ninety per cent of the time. There has been little empirical research done to ascertain the number of innocent people who are ultimately convicted of criminal offenses. As one example, however, research carried out in the United Kingdom for the Royal Commission on Criminal Justice suggests that up to eleven percent of people who plead guilty claim innocence. The wrongful acquittal rate would no doubt be even higher than this.

Moreover, it is important to note that even without resort to polygraphs there will be many circumstances where guilt or relevant knowledge is patently obvious. A clear example is where a person makes a relevant admission that discloses information that would only be within the knowledge of the wrongdoer. Another example occurred in the recent German kidnapping case, referred to earlier, where the man in custody had been witnessed collecting a ransom and had indicated to the police that the kidnapped boy was still alive. Where lesser forms of evidence proving guilt are available, the argument in favor of torture is lower.

The Formula

Incorporating all these considerations, the strength of the case in favor of torture can be mapped as follows:

$$\frac{W + L + P}{T \times O}$$

Where:
  W = whether the agent is the wrongdoer
  L = the number of lives that will be lost if the information is not provided
  P = the probability that the agent has the relevant knowledge
  T = the time available before the disaster will occur ("immediacy of the harm")
  O = the likelihood that other inquiries will forestall the risk

W is a weighting that is attributable to whether the agent has had any direct connection with the potential catastrophe. Where the person is responsible for the incident—for example, planted or organized the

bomb—more emphasis should be attached. Where the agent is innocent and has simply stumbled on the relevant information—for example, she saw the bomb being planted or overheard the plan to plant the bomb—this should be reduced by a certain amount. The prohibition against inflicting harm on the innocent is certainly strong, but it is not inviolable.

Torture should be permitted where the application of the variables exceeds a threshold level. Once beyond this level, the higher the figure the more severe the forms of torture that are permissible. There is no bright line that can be drawn concerning the point at which the "torture threshold" should be set. More precision can, however, be obtained by first ascribing unit ranges to each of the above variables (depending on their relative importance), then applying the formula to a range of hypothetical situations, and then making a judgment about the numerical point at which torture is acceptable.

There is obviously a degree of imprecision attached to this process and considerable scope for discussion and disagreement regarding the *exact* weight that should be attached to each variable. It is important to emphasize, however, that this is not an argument against our proposal. Rather it is a signal for further discussion and refinement. This is a call that we are confident other commentators will take up. The purpose of this Article is not to set in stone the full range of circumstances where torture is justifiable. Our aim is more modest—to convince readers that torture is justifiable in some circumstances and to set out the variables that are relevant to such an inquiry.

Regulation Better Than Prohibition

In addition to the moral argument for torture as an interrogation device, Dershowitz has argued that torture should be legalized for harm minimization reasons. Dershowitz has pushed for the introduction of "a torture warrant," which would place a "heavy burden on the government to demonstrate by factual evidence the necessity to administer this horrible, horrible technique of torture." He further adds:

> I think that we're much, much better off admitting what we're doing or not doing it at all. I agree with you, it will much better if we never did it. But if we're going to do it and subcontract and find ways of circumventing, it's much better to do what Israel did. They were the only country in the world ever directly to confront the issue, and it led to a supreme court decision, as you say, outlawing torture, and yet Israel has been criticized all over the world for confronting the issue directly. Candor and accountability in a democracy is very important. Hypocrisy has no place.

The obvious counter to this is the slippery slope argument. "If you start opening the door, making a little exception here, a little exception there, you've basically sent the signal that the ends justify the means," resulting in even more torture. The slippery slope argument is often invoked in relation to acts that in themselves are justified, but which have similarities with objectionable practices, and urges that in morally appraising an action we must not only consider its intrinsic features but also the likelihood of it being used as a basis for condoning similar, but in fact relevantly different undesirable practices. The slippery slope argument in the context of torture holds that while torture might be justified in the extreme cases, legalizing it in these circumstances will invariably lead to torture in other less desperate situations.

This argument is not sound in the context of torture. First, the floodgates are already open—torture is widely used, despite the absolute legal prohibition against it. It is, in fact, arguable that it is the existence of an unrealistic absolute ban on torture that has driven torture "beneath the radar screen of accountability" and that the legalization of torture in very rare circumstances would, in fact, reduce the instances of torture because of the increased level of accountability.

Second, there is no evidence to suggest that the *lawful* violation of fundamental human interests will necessarily lead to a violation of fundamental rights where the pre-conditions for the activity are clearly delineated and controlled. Thus, in the United States the use of the death penalty has not resulted in a gradual extension of the offenses for which people may be executed or an erosion in the respect for human life. Third, promulgating the message that the "means justifies the ends [sometimes]" is not inherently undesirable. Debate can then focus on the precise means and ends that are justifiable.

Conclusion

The absolute prohibition against torture is morally unsound and pragmatically unworkable. There is a need for measured discussion regarding the merits of torture as an information gathering device. This would result in the legal use of torture in circumstances where there are a large number of lives at risk in the immediate future and there is no other means of alleviating the threat. While none of the recent high profile cases of torture appear to satisfy these criteria, it is likely that circumstances will arise in the future where torture is legitimate and desirable. A legal framework should be established to properly accommodate these situations.

Mirko Bagaric is a Professor of Law at Deakin University's School of Law in Australia; he is currently Dean and Head of the School of Law. He has published on a wide variety of social issues. His publications include books such as *How to Live: Being Happy and Dealing with Moral Dilemmas* (University Press of American, 2006) and *Future Directions in International Law and Human Rights* (Sandstone Academic Press, 2007).

Christopher Kutz

Torture, Necessity, and Existential Politics

> "[I]f there is something worse than accepting slavery, it consists in defending it."[1]
>
> —Bernard Williams, *Shame and Necessity*

Introduction

The Costs of Rights

Rights have costs—that is their point. The cost of rights is in the coin of foregone welfare gains. No one minds a claim to a particular right when honoring that right simultaneously enhances welfare. For example, the distinctively modern achievement for speech and conscience has been to demonstrate the consilience of rights protecting those domains with the promotion of a flourishing public and private life. As a result, claims of rights to free speech and conscience are among the most easily accepted in U.S. public life. The test of a claim of right, however, comes not when its exercise serves the public good, directly or indirectly, but when it represents a direct hit to welfare. At the level of institutional and philosophical discourse, the United States used to honor the right of individuals to be free of torture in this way. The U.S. government viewed it as justified independently of the costs or gains that might accrue from respecting it.[2] Now things are different. The current administration of George W. Bush has decided not to pay those costs. Instead, it chooses to use coercive interrogation techniques that would conventionally be thought of as straightforwardly torturous, including water-boarding, false burial, "Palestinian hanging" (where the prisoner is suspended by his arms, manacled behind his back), being left naked in a cold cell and doused with cold water, and being made to stand for forty hours while shackled to a cell floor.[3] The override of detainee rights against torture has been justified on grounds of "necessity," i.e., that the welfare cost of observing the right would be too great for the nation rationally to bear. . . .

My aim in this Essay is to take up the question of torture's justification . . . raised by the infamous (and now withdrawn) Office of Legal Counsel (OLC) memorandum of August 1, 2002, which became widely known as the "Torture memo."[4] . . .

I argue that attention to the concept of necessity as a justification for torture, and especially to the limits of that justification, reveals that we make use in legal and political thought of two very different normative concepts of rights. The first concept serves to impose limits on institutional considerations, while the second is far more sensitive to such considerations. Instances of the former are core human rights protections; instances of the latter are rights of disposition over property. Legal and philosophical arguments purporting to justify torture by reference to necessity betray a failure to grasp these distinctions.[5] . . .

[T]he heart of the paper takes up the claim of necessity in ethics, first in relation to the infamous "ticking bomb" example so often put forward to establish a principle of permissibility. The ticking bomb case is a particular example of a general problem for principle-based ("deontological," in philosophers' jargon), rather than welfare-based (or "utilitarian"), ethics, namely making sense of limits to rights claims without giving up the core of deontological theory. I distinguish here between two different, familiar and ubiquitous conceptions of rights: rights inherently sensitive to necessity claims, and those insensitive—of which, I argue, rights against torture are the primary example. . . .

I

Micro- and Macro-Necessity as a Criminal Defense to Torture

As the story is now familiar, I will summarize: In the spring of 2004, the leak of government memoranda creating a legal basis for U.S. personnel to use torture in interrogations was a shock to many outside the administration. The shock lay less in the acknowledgment that the U.S. was deploying torture than in the lawyerly *justification* of torture, particularly because, despite the erratic and frequently cruel course of actual state practice, the eradication of the moral and legal basis for torture has been one of the defining features of post-Enlightenment liberal politics. This moral and legal evolution began with the early polemics of Voltaire and Beccaria[6] and continued with the now-twenty-year-old U.N. Convention against Torture and other Cruel, Inhuman, or Degrading Treatment or Punishment, which has been ratified by sixty-five countries, including all of the most developed nations save Korea.[7] Against growing international consensus, the

Kutz, Christopher. From *California Law Review,* 95 Calif. L. Rev. 235, February 2007, excerpts pp. 235–236, 238–244, 248, 250–254, 256–258, 262–263, 275–276. Copyright © 2007 by California Law Review, Inc. Used with permission.

U.S. administration made clear in the days immediately following the terrorist attacks of September 11th that, in Vice President Dick Cheney's words, "we have to work, though, sort of the dark side."[8] With a political go-ahead, the CIA decided to use a number of formerly proscribed interrogation techniques on "high value" interrogees, notably including "water-boarding," which consists of repeated submersion in cold water to create the impression of drowning.[9] At some point, before or after the interrogations had actually begun, the CIA apparently became worried that its personnel might be subject to the harsh penalties dictated by 18 U.S.C. §§ 2340-2340A, the implementing legislation for the Convention against Torture. Section 2340A authorizes up to twenty years imprisonment for anyone who outside the U.S. "commits or attempts to commit torture," with capital punishment authorized if death results.[10] Insofar as the statutory definition of torture includes acts "specifically intended to inflict severe physical or mental pain or suffering," which pain or suffering can result from "the threat of imminent death," orders to deploy waterboarding (which by design arouses a sensation of imminent death by drowning) would clearly have focused the minds of U.S. personnel on the consequences of the Torture statute.[11]

Prompted by the CIA's request, the OLC, under the signature of Jay Bybee, provided a memorandum to the White House on August 1, 2002.[12] This memorandum, which I will call the Bybee memo, made a number of arguments toward several aims. First, it sought to reduce the potential scope of § 2340 to include only the most heinous forms of torture. Second, it sought to suggest a range of complete criminal defenses U.S. personnel could deploy if charged under the statute. Finally, it sought to establish as a principle of constitutional law that § 2340A could not constitutionally be interpreted to bind the President while exercising his war powers as Commander in Chief.[13]

After giving its restrictive definition of torture, the memo contemplates the case in which U.S. personnel may be found to have engaged in acts within the scope of the statutory prohibition, namely to have inflicted with specific intent or attempted to inflict severe physical or mental pain or suffering.[14] It then argues for the claim that "[s]tandard criminal law defenses of necessity and self-defense could justify interrogation methods needed to elicit information to prevent a direct and imminent threat to the United States and its citizens."[15] As the memo rightly describes the Model Penal Code (MPC), necessity will justify a defendant in violation of a law when he or she engages in conduct that the actor "believes to be necessary to avoid a harm or evil to himself or to another," provided that violating the norm is necessary to avoid a "harm or evil" that is "greater than that sought to be prevented by the law defining the offense charged," but only so long as there is no specific legislation or "legislative purpose" to exclude the justification.[16] Necessity justifies otherwise criminal acts against subjects who do

not directly pose a threat to the actor. In its paradigm applications, for example, necessity justifies sailors jettisoning cargo to save their ship or a hiker breaking into a cabin to escape a sudden storm.[17] Necessity is, therefore, a potential justification for the situation under consideration in the memo: the decision whether to torture a subdued detainee, who may have information that may help avert a threat that may arise.

Specifically, the claim would have to be used to justify an interrogation technique believed to be the sole effective means of avoiding yet worse harms. On its face, then, necessity might provide a good fit for the interrogation practices in question. . . .

As the memo correctly states, the core of self- or other-defense lies in the defender's belief that such force is "immediately necessary" to avoid the harm posed by someone presenting a direct and imminent threat of serious bodily harm to oneself or another.[18] Necessity grounds the permission to use otherwise impermissible force.

So the argument for the justifiability of torture as a matter of criminal law must stand or fall with the force of the general necessity defense and its limitations. Let us return, then, to the general justificatory element of necessity, specifically, the "necessity" of deploying force in order to prevent a more serious harm. Taken literally, the defense is limited to cases in which the use of force is the only possible response to the threat and is sure to be an effective response to the threat. Only when the defendant's act is a necessary element of a set of conditions sufficient to avert the harm can it be said that the defendant acted as he must, in order to minimize evil. It cannot, in other words, be necessary to act when one's act will be ineffective, even if, were other conditions in place, it might have been part of a set of conditions sufficient to avert the harm.[19]

In fact, the criminal defense of "necessity" presents much softer constraints than true, logical "necessity" would indicate, in large part because it is applied relative to the actor's beliefs about the threat and its projected alternatives. Under the MPC, actors can assert the defense so long as they believe in the necessity of their acts, both regarding the likelihood of the threat and the effectiveness of the alternatives, even if in fact there is no threat, or the means chosen could not be effective. Thus, the MPC defense protects actors who believe, however unreasonably, in the necessity of their acts. However, the necessity provision also provides for liability for defendants who are reckless or negligent in either bringing about the conditions demanding their response or in assessing the necessity of the response.[20] The net result, under both common law and the MPC, is that full justification is provided only to actors who reasonably appraise the situation as calling for their violation of the law.[21] But it should be understood that the subjective extension of the defense, to the reasonable but mistaken defendant, clearly gets its justificatory force from the objective situation where, under the circumstances, the defendant performed an act necessary in fact to avert the greater evil.[22] Put otherwise, an actor's *judgment* of necessity can only be exculpatory if, when the factual premises of that judgment are true, the actor really would be justified. If necessity were instead conceived as an excuse, then any belief, however unreasonable, would be sufficient to exculpate. Since common law and the MPC are clear that only reasonable mistake fully exculpates, the underlying principle must be one of objective justification.[23]

Note the slippage in the theory of necessity—a slippage that, as we shall see, plays a role in evaluating the special case of the ticking-bomb hypothetical. The objective situation is posed timelessly, where the antecedent threat can be weighed against the future consequence of the law-breaking response. But in reality, of course, the defense must apply to conduct undertaken before the threat materializes. It is nearly always impossible to know whether the threat really would have been realized—perhaps the attacker would have suddenly run rather than shot, or a rescue ship might have appeared on the horizon, had defendants waited a few more days.[24] Furthermore, it is almost always impossible for anyone, let alone the defendant, to know in advance whether the use of force will be effective in meeting the threat. Defendants cannot perfectly anticipate the consequences of their acts, but must instead calculate the expected value of their responses in relation to the expected disvalue of the threatened harm. This is an elementary point, but, when understood, it means that in practice actual "necessity" almost never exists. The defense must instead be read to justify the rather oxymoronic category of "probabilistic necessity": the defense justifies extralegal acts when and only when they are highly likely to avert a virtually certain threat, and it is also highly likely that there are no other options. The normative force of necessity resides in the epistemic requirement of high certainty—a requirement necessary to foreclose the possibility of defendants taking extremely low-probability gambles on high-payoff results.[25] In sum, it is a form of cost-benefit analysis that justifies criminal acts when, given only two options, good consequences outweigh the bad, restricted to some indeterminate extent by a requirement of substantial certainty as to the relevant gambles.[26] . . .

Thus, whatever might be said on behalf of the Bybee's analysis, a great deal more clearly needs to be said before it could be deemed independently convincing, let alone serve as a foundation stone for an enormously controversial change in the United States' legal conception of its duties to detainees. Yet the memo was influential, serving as the basis for the subsequent and widely disseminated Department of Defense Working Group Report, which set policy for interrogations involving military personnel around the world.[27] . . .

In short, the Bush administration has made two distinct propositions about the justifiability of torture and has supported those propositions with its actions even as it has backed away from its legal claims. Those propositions are:

> (i) Micro-necessity: a governmental actor may use torture in interrogation at least when torture is the only available and a highly likely means of avoiding a near certain threat of harm graver than that incurred by the act of torture.
> (ii) Macro-necessity: the President, pursuing national security or other military objectives, may authorize torture as a necessary response to a threat to national security, irrespective of statutory restrictions.

I turn now to considering these propositions as matters of ethical and political theory.

II

Necessity, Thresholds and Ticking Bombs

[T]he core philosophical notion of a right is that rights provide us with reasons to act (or not act), even when considerations about overall welfare raise morally powerful concerns about the consequences of those acts.[28] There are always illegitimate reasons not to honor a rights claim—my selfish desires give me (illegitimate) reason to take your property or to make you an instrument of my desire. Rights claims do rule out such obviously inappropriate claims, but were their force maintained only in such cases, they would have no distinctive content. Long-run welfare-based considerations ("consequentialist" considerations, in philosophers' jargon) about the general misery of a world lived amid theft and abuse would rule those claims out of bounds as well. For claims of right to have distinctive content, for it to be more than a rule of thumb for maximizing welfare, it must apply even in the face of putatively good reasons, particularly if violating the rule would maximize social welfare.

This is a point about the philosophical concept of right, for that concept to have distinctive content. It is not a general justification of rights—a project far beyond the scope of this Essay—nor even a specification of what rights we humans may be said to have. It is simply a point about what the concept must mean, given the role it is meant to play in arguments about morals, politics, and law. But this descriptive, conceptual point has a consequence: it makes clear why a general ethical defense of micro-necessity and a deontological conception of right are incompatible. The necessity justification proposes precisely what the rights claim denies: that action may be taken when the good pays for the bad, as measured by the "cost" of the rights violation. An unconstrained micro-necessity justification consists, effectively, in the forcible conversion of a deontological ethical framework into utilitarian one. Necessity justifications ignore the concept of right.

The Necessity Defense in Criminal Law: Beyond the Bybee Memo

Criminal law protects individual rights of bodily integrity and security of possession as much as it protects aggregate social interests such as the maintenance of public order or the rendering of just deserts. Given the disparate goals of criminal law, you might think that theoretical discussions of the necessity defense would recognize the inherent limits of any basically utilitarian mode of argument applied to individual rights. On the contrary, Anglo-American criminal law theorists and treatise writers, including the authors of the MPC, are typically critical of the courts for giving the necessity defense so little force beyond its formal recognition. Theorists complain about the failure of common-law courts to extend the justification beyond its well-recognized instances (where it typically justifies regulatory violations, such as speeding en route to the hospital or very local property violations).[29] . . .

The relatively few decisions on the necessity defense meet this pattern: necessity claims usually lose, and when they win, it is for easy cases, which fall far short of the infliction of violence, let alone homicide (excluding self-defense). This statement from a recent California case, *People v. Coffman*, is typical: "It is not acceptable for a defendant to decide that it is necessary to kill an innocent person in order that he [or she] may live."[30] . . .

[T]here are no decisions in Anglo-American law, nor any documented decisions not to prosecute, in which innocents not otherwise in harm's way are assaulted or killed in order to avert harm from others.

The same appears also to be true in European jurisdictions. . . . The standard Continental examples of successful necessity defenses are, in essence, gleaning cases: squatters found justified in taking over abandoned housing, breaking and entering to shelter poor children, and in principle the theft of food (though it is generally impossible to show that theft was the only option).[31]

Necessity in Moral Philosophy

. . . Let us look now at the infamous ticking bomb . . . In the standard story, an interrogator is faced with a terrorist who has planted a bomb that will kill many innocent citizens. Torturing the terrorist is the last, best hope for saving them. The first thing to be said, and the first thing that was said, in Henry Shue's seminal article twenty-five years ago, is that at best the ticking-bomb hypothetical is of virtually no practical significance, and at worst it is utterly corrupt in the illicit conclusions it invites.[32] The example gains its force from its stipulated perfect satisfaction of all the traditional criteria of necessity: the interrogator is certain of the threat and its attendant costs, knows that the person to be tortured is responsible for the bomb, and is reasonably certain that torturing him is the sole means of avoiding catastrophe and is likely to be effective. While under these conditions, there might be widespread consensus that torture would be justifiable, relax any of the dimensions of justification—maybe it's a hoax, maybe

it's the wrong guy, maybe the interrogator has chosen to torture the terrorist's child instead, maybe the suspect will lie—and dissensus emerges immediately.

In the real world, it is most likely that some or all of the traditional criteria will be unsatisfied. Moreover, institutions and institutional actors tend to abuse the limits of their discretion and coerced confessions are demonstrably of inferior intelligence quality to detective work.[33] For all these reasons, attempts to institutionalize any principle of morally permissible torture invariably either (1) define the circumstances under which torture is permissible so *narrowly* that the requisite criteria are virtually never met; or (2) define the circumstances under which torture is permissible so *broadly* that the torture is allowed even when it is not morally justified.[34] To the extent that the Bybee memo goes beyond the hypothetical exploration of an *ex post* defense to a charge of torture and actually lays out *ex ante* an institutional space for torture (grounded in the qualified immunity of officials relying on its legal advice), I believe it is tantamount to criminal complicity.[35]

With all these considerations against it, the persistence of the ticking-bomb hypothetical might seem hard to explain. Since the conditions under which its conclusion results never actually obtain, it might be best to treat it as a kind of ethical "singularity," a black hole that swallows up intuition and lets nothing emerge. But, in fact, the ticking-bomb example is no harmless anomaly. It persists because of a series of related mistakes in thinking about rights under pressure from welfare, and how to conceive the role of necessity in these cases. Necessity really does justify overriding some kinds of rights claims in many instances, but these are rights of a fundamentally different nature from the ones involved in the ticking-bomb example. Criminal theorists have over-generalized the appropriate normative scope of the necessity defense by confusing those rights whose abrogation the defense can legitimately justify with all rights.

Institutional versus Pre-Institutional Rights

Let us put aside, for a moment, the cases of torture and ticking bombs and shift to the law of torts and property. As controversial as a legal decision authorizing homicide or torture would be, so uncontroversial are decisions in tort cases like *Vincent v. Lake Erie Transp. Co.*, or *Ploof v. Putnam*,[36] which involved intentional trespasses upon property clearly justified as necessary under the choices of evils at hand. So clear is the force of the necessity defense in such cases that no prosecutor would consider them, and the question of justice is simply who should pay the costs. As I discussed above, criminal necessity defenses are generally found to lie in affronts to property rights, as well as to violations of regulations that impair no rights.[37] The difference might be thought simply a matter of the relatively weaker interests at play, property versus life, but I think it goes deeper than that, to the kind of right the law of property protects, versus the kind of right protected by homicide law—or, in the instant case, by § 2340 and the body of international treaty and customary law that stands behind it.[38] This is the difference between what I want to call *institutional* and *pre-institutional* rights.[39]

Institutional rights are the rights consequentialists defend: individual claims secured by a general promise that their respect will promote welfare. Pre-institutional rights, by contrast, are claims that institutions must honor, and the institutions' basic justice or legitimacy is assessed by reference to these claims. . . .

A full account of the force of the right against torture would focus on the peculiar horror of torture, the combination of suffering with the deliberate subordination of the victim's consciousness to the will of the interrogator.[40] But it would share with the peacetime right against homicide a commitment to the value of the individual life, a value that cannot be aggregated, or so our legal and moral theories have generally presumed. The scene of torture, in the imagination of those who reject it, makes the nature of this value especially clear: the interrogee is not confronted as a part of an armed host, but as an individual, already disarmed and vulnerable.[41] This is the field of basic, pre-institutional human rights. . . .

Summary

In criminal law, the defense of necessity runs out when it confronts pre-institutional rights, whose value is not the product of an instrumental calculus.[42] My point is not that we could not conceive it in these terms, nor even that we do not, since obviously some people do. My point is that the tradition of criminal law, across the civilian and Anglo-American spectrum, is remarkably fallow ground for justifying acts of violence against individuals, outside either the peculiar space of warfare, or the narrow context of immediate self-defense. While torture and other forms of intentional violence against persons occur on the battlefield as well as in the station house, such acts have received no official legal authorization beyond the awkward discussion in the Israeli Supreme Court and the Bybee memo in the United States. Criminal law theorists have commonly remarked that the near-absolute value of life shows that the law "reflects a moral uneasiness with reliance on a utilitarian calculus."[43] It would be more precise to say that the law responds in a utilitarian fashion to institutional rights and in a non-utilitarian fashion to pre-institutional rights.

III

Necessities at War: Fact versus Justification

I have so far argued that we operate across ethics, politics, and law with two distinct concepts of rights. Institutional, instrumentally justified rights—of which property rights are exemplary—are subject to override by what I have called a micro-necessity justification. But pre-institutional rights, which reflect a conception of the distinct value of individuals, are as a conceptual matter immune to micro-necessity overrides. Assertion of a necessity justification in

their face simply denies their deontological status. Rights against torture are core examples of pre-institutional rights and so it follows logically that they are immune from violation justified by necessity. . . .

Perhaps it is not too overwrought to worry instead that the real existential threat comes from the evisceration of our principles in the name of security. . . .

It does no dishonor to a principled commitment against torture to recognize its limits in the hypothetical of the ticking bomb. Nor do we dishonor a general commitment to life's value by insisting that the hypothetical is imaginary, that we remain outside the state of emergency until we can no longer resist its existential claim. . . .

Conclusion

I have argued that the attempt to justify . . . torture and . . . by reference to necessity fails. It rests upon a conflation of necessity as fact with necessity as justification and on a broad and deep misunderstanding of the nature of pre-institutional rights.

The bedrock principles we have, concerning the dignity of humanity and the limits of legitimate power, are hard-won achievements of the last several centuries. Scrabbled together out of convention, claimed in the shadow of authoritarian power, they have become the marks by which we know our moral identities as both persons and nations. Threats and emergencies demand response, but that response must be grounded in a confidence in our principles' abilities to meet the demands of the world on our own terms. This confidence is equally a form of judgment: the determination that threats to our interests not be confused with threats to our existence. Far more dangerous to us, to who we are, is the threat of finding necessity in every conflict with evil and emergency in every war.

At the level of philosophical reflection, the ticking-bomb example does show something. It shows that we can *imagine* limits to even our most deeply held moral principles. But we should use this realization to strengthen our principles and their application in the world, not to abridge them. Here is how the realization of imagined limits can *strengthen* principles such as the right against torture. By their very divergence from real situations (existential necessity can exist only in a hypothetical world), imagined scenarios like the ticking-bomb example can continually remind us that we have not reached the imagined limits in reality, that we need to push our principles further and ever further, that if we relinquish our deepest precepts in an ideal world of imagined scenarios, there will surely be no hope for them in the real world we all inhabit.

Notes

1. BERNARD WILLIAMS, SHAME AND NECESSITY 111 (1993).
2. I echo here David Luban's claims in his paper, *Liberalism. Torture, and the Ticking Bomb,* in THE

TORTURE DEBATE IN AMERICA 35 (Karen J. Greenberg ed., 2006) [hereinafter THE TORTURE DEBATE]. I am throughout indebted to his discussion.

3. While there is debate over whether some other well-documented techniques (mild assault, sexual humiliation, terrorization with dogs) legally constitute torture or merely "cruel, inhuman, or degrading" treatment, there is no reasonable debate whether water-boarding (whose point is to introduce fear of death), hanging, and induced hypothermia fit within the definition of torture. *See* Brian Ross and Richard Esposito, *CIA's Harsh Interrogation Techniques Described,* ABC NEWS, Nov. 18, 2005, http://abcnews.go.com/WNT/lnvestigation/story?id=1322866&page=1; Michael Hirsh and Mark Hosenball, *The Politics of Torture,* NEWSWEEK, Sept. 25, 2006, http://www.msnbc.msn.com/id/14872708/site/newsweek/; Dana Priest, *CIA Holds Terror Suspects in Secret Prisons,* WASH. POST, Nov. 2, 2005, at Al; Jane Mayer, *A Deadly Interrogation,* THE NEW YORKER, Nov. 14, 2005, at 44, *available at* http://www.newyorker.com/fact/content/articles/051114fa_fact. . . .

4. Bybee memo, *supra* note 7.

5. I discuss examples of this confusion below, in Section III.

6. Voltaire (François Marie Arouet), "Torture," DICTIONNAIRE PHILOSOPHIQUE (1764), *available at* http://www.voltaire-integral.com/Html/20/torture.htm; Cesare Beccaria, "Ch. 16: Of Torture," ON CRIMES AND PUNISHMENTS (Edward D. Ingraham trans., 1778), *available at* http://www.constitution.org/cb/crim_pun.htm.

7. Convention against Torture and other Cruel, Inhuman, or Degrading Treatment or Punishment, June 26, 1987, 1465 U.N.T.S. 85. The Convention was ratified by the U.S. on April 18, 1988.

8. Interview by Tim Russert with Richard Cheney, "Meet the Press" (Sept. 16, 2001) (transcript available at www.whitehouse.gov/vicepresident/news-speeches/speeches/vp20010916.html). As Cofer Black, former Director of CIA Counterterrorist Center, subsequently testified to Congress, "All I want to say is that there was 'before' 9/11 and 'after' 9/11. After 9/11 the gloves come off." Testimony of Cofer Black to Joint House and Senate Select Intelligence Committee, Sept. 26, 2002, *available at* http://www.fas.org/irp/congress/2002_hr/092602black.html.

9. Douglas Jehl and David Johnston, *C.I.A. Expands its Inquiry into Interrogation Tactics,* N.Y. TIMES, Aug. 29, 2004, at Al; Mark Danner, *Abu Ghraib: The Hidden Story,* N.Y. REV. OF BOOKS, Oct. 7, 2004, *available at* http://www.nybooks.com/articles/l7430.

10. 18 U.S.C. § 2340A(a).

11. 18 U.S.C. § 2340(1), (2)(c).

12. Bybee memo, *supra* note 7.

13. I discuss the Bybee memos at greater length, and the specific role of the OLC lawyers, in two papers: *The Lawyers Know Sin,* in THE TORTURE DEBATE, *supra* note 2, at 241-46; and *Causeless Complicity: The Case of the OLC Lawyers,* CRIM. L AND PHIL. (forthcoming 2007).

14. Bybee memo, *supra* note 7, at 27.

15. *Id.* at 39.

16. Model Penal Code § 3.02(1), (l)(a) [hereinafter MPC]. More exactly, § 3.02(1) provides for a defense whenever a defendant believes, even unreasonably, that he or she is in a situation of necessity. Under § 3.02(2), however, reckless or negligent defendants can still be liable for crimes for which recklessness or negligence suffice for culpability. The net result approximates the position at common law, according to which only a reasonable belief as to the necessity of the act serves as a defense.

17. Model Penal Code and Commentaries § 3.02, cmt. 1, at 9–10 [hereinafter MPC Commentaries].

18. Bybee memo, *supra* note 7, at 42–43 (citing MPC § 3.04 and LAFAVE & SCOTT, *supra* note 25, at 649).

19. Logically, if "ought implies can,"—that is, one only has obligations to do what it is possible to do—then "cannot" also implies "not ought." One has no obligation, much less requirement, to do the impossible. My swimming to rescue the drowning swimmer might have been a necessary condition of his being saved, if I am the only one within range; but if I cannot swim, it is not necessary that I try.

20. MPC § 3.02(2) states:
When the actor was reckless or negligent in bringing about the situation requiring a choice of harms or evils or in appraising the necessity for his conduct, the justification afforded by this Section is unavailable in a prosecution for any offense for which recklessness or negligence, as the case may be, suffices to establish culpability.

21. *See* WAYNE R. LAFAVE, CRIMINAL LAW § 10.1(d)(3) (4th ed. 2003).

22. The effect of rendering the justification subjective is to include both objectively unjustified but morally non-culpable actors, and to exclude coincidentally justified but morally culpable actors. The essentially objective character of the justification is evident in LaFave and Scott's treatment, and is manifest in the memo, which discusses the defense as providing a genuine justification, and not just exculpation.

23. As LaFave says,

The rationale of the necessity defense is not that a person, when faced with the pressure of circumstances of nature, lacks the mental element which the crime in question requires. Rather, it is this reason of public policy: the law ought to promote the achievement of higher values at the expense of lesser values, and sometimes the greater good for society will be accomplished by violating the literal language of the criminal law.

LAFAVE, *supra* note 30, at 524.

24. See the famous example of *Regina v. Dudley & Stephens,* 14 Q.B.D. 273 (1884) (upholding rejection of defense of necessity by cannibalistic sailors, in part because the sailors "might possibly have been picked up next day by a passing ship; they might possibly not have been picked up at all.") (Lord Coleridge, C.J.).

25. At common law, self-defenders are not even held to such a high standard. The majority of states do not require defenders to choose to retreat, even when they can do so in safety, and one need never retreat from a home. *See* LaFave & Scott, *supra* note 25, § 10.4(f).

26. Treatises, the MPC Commentaries, and the Bybee memo straightforwardly identify the defense as having utilitarian value. *See* MPC Commentaries, *supra* note 23, §3.02, cmt. 3; LaFave, *supra* note 30, §10.1(a); Bybee memo, *supra* note 7, at 40.

27. Working Group Report on Detainee Interrogations in the Global War on Terrorism: Assessment of Legal, Historical, Policy, and Operational Considerations (Apr. 4, 2003), *reprinted in* The Torture Papers, *supra* note 7, at 241-85. Also available at http://www.gwu.edu/~nsarchiv/NSAEBB/NSAEBB127/03.04.04.pdf.

28. This is, I think, a consensus view of what a deontological conception of rights, or of duties grounding rights, is committed to: a claim of right (or duty not to act in some way) overrides whatever instrumental (welfare-based or other) considerations militate in favor of acting contrary to the right. For its sources in the philosophical literature, see, obviously, Immanuel Kant, Groundwork of the Metaphysics of Morals Bk. II (1785) (our duties as rational agents to treat others as free and equal agents create in them rights not to be used for our purposes, and to be aided in the pursuit of their ends); Robert Nozick, Anarchy, State & Utopia 30-34 (1977) (the function of rights is to limit, as "side constraints," the pursuit of individual or collective welfare gains); Thomas Nagel, *War and Massacre, reprinted in* Mortal Questions 53-74 (1979) (duties to others are deontological constraints which limit the force of consequentialist justifications); Samuel Scheffler, The Rejection of Consequentialism 80-83 (rev. ed. 1994) (duties not to act in certain ways limit the force of consequentialist claims). . . .

29. On the potential justifiability of killing a non-threatening individual, see LaFave, *supra* note 30, § 10.1(a); MPC Commentaries, *supra* note 23, § 3.02, Commentary 3; Glanville Williams, Criminal Law: The General Part § 237 (2d ed. 1961); Sanford H. Kadish, Blame and Punishment 122-23 (1987). George Fletcher is a rare criminal law theorist who explicitly rejects a much less restrictive necessity test. *See* George Fletcher, Rethinking Criminal Law § 10.4 (1978). J.C. Smith notes that if English law does permit application of the defense to cases of homicide

(unclear, given the infamous *R. v. Dudley & Stephens* precedent, 14 Q.B.D. 273 (1884)) the defense does not extend past cases of killing some lest all die. Sir John Smith & Brian Hogan, Criminal Law 271-74 (10th ed. 2003).

30. 34 Cal. 4th 1, 100 (2004), *cert. denied,* 544 U.S. 1063 (2005) (denying necessity defense in robbery-murder where defendant alleged co-perpetrator had threatened her life and the life of her son) (internal quotation marks omitted).

31. *Id.* at § 10.2; Robert, *supra* note 67, at 272.

32. Henry Shue, *Torture,* 7 Phil. & Pub. Aff. 124, 142-43 (1978).

33. John Langbein quotes Sir James FitzJames Stephen's *A History of the Criminal Law of England,* concerning "the proclivity of the native police [in India] for torturing suspects. 'It is far pleasanter to sit comfortably in the shade rubbing red pepper in some poor devil's eyes than to go about in the sun hunting up evidence.'" John H. Langbein, *The Legal History of Torture, in* Torture: A Collection 93, 101 (Sanford Levinson ed., 2004). Notably, Justice Frankfurter also quotes Stephen in *McNabb v. United States,* 318 U.S. 332, 343 (1943), an important coerced-confession case in which the Court asserted its inherent authority to regulate federal investigatory authority.

34. There is no way to institutionalize any principle of permissible torture without falling into the swamp of Abu Ghraibs and Bagrams, in which innocents are routinely subjected to abuse for the amusement of sadists playing "intelligence" games. On the abuses at Bagram, see Tim Golden's exposé, *In U.S. Report. Brutal Details Of 2 Afghan Inmates' Deaths,* N.Y. Times, May 20, 2005, at A1.

35. I defend these claims in *The Lawyers Know Sin, supra* note 19, at 241. Briefly, there exists a basis for accomplice liability for any purposefully abetted acts of assault or torture, and for purposefully abetting acts, in reckless disregard of the risks, that through recklessness or negligence led to the deaths of some of the detainees.

36. 124 N.W. 221, 222 (Minn. 1910) (holding boat operator acted justifiably, but still liable for damage to dock incurred during unconsented use during storm); 81 Vt. 471, 474-75 (1908) (plaintiff had right to compensated use of defendant's dock during storm).

37. Arguably, this is not quite right. If one accepts a right to be free from certain degrees of ex ante risk, then a speeding driver on the way to the hospital may be violating the rights of those he endangers. French criminal law explicitly treats the issue in this way, and deems it a matter of justified necessity. Robert, *supra* note 67, at 273-77 (citing CA Metz, 8 mars 1990, Dr. pén., 1991, comm. 49).

38. Apart from the Convention against Torture, torture is categorically prohibited by the

International Covenant on Civil and Political Rights, 999 U.N.T.S. 171 (Dec. 16, 1966); by all four Geneva Conventions, through both Common Article 3 and through specific articles: Geneva Convention for the Amelioration of the Condition of the Wounded and Sick in Armed Forces in the Field, 75 U.N.T.S. 31; Geneva Convention for the Amelioration of the Condition of Wounded, Sick and Shipwrecked Members of Armed Forces at Sea, 75 U.N.T.S. 85; Geneva Convention Relative to the Treatment of Prisoners of War, 75 U.N.T.S. 135 [hereinafter GC III]; Geneva Convention Relative to the Protection of Civilian Persons in Time of War, 75 U.N.T.S. 287 [hereinafter GC IV]. All were signed 12 Aug. 1949. The rule against torture is also seen as a non-derogable, *jus cogens* norm of customary international law. *See, e.g.*, REST. (THIRD) OF FOREIGN RELATIONS LAW OF THE UNITED STATES, § 702, and Reporter's Note 5.

39. I borrow the idea of the institutional vs. pre-institutional distinction from John Rawls, though he uses it to discuss the related issue of desert. JOHN RAWLS, THEORY OF JUSTICE § 48 (2d ed. 1999).

40. For excellent discussions, see Luban, *supra* note 2; David Sussman, *What's Wrong With Torture?,* 33 PHIL. & PUB. AFF. 1(2005).

41. Of course, from the perspective of the interrogators, it is this scene that renders the victim least human, as Hannah Arendt observed of the concentration camp inmates. HANNAH ARENDT, THE ORIGINS OF TOTALITARIANISM, 284 (1973).

42. I want to put aside the very different case of knowingly running ex ante risks of statistical deaths, even risks up to a moral certainty. Such risks can, I think, be justified on a basis consistent with individual rights. I discuss this briefly in *Self-Defense and Political Justification,* 88 CALIF. L. REV. 751, 751-58 (2000).

43. *See, e.g.*, KADISH, *supra* note 61, at 123.

CHRISTOPHER KUTZ is a Professor of Law at University of California-Berkeley. His publications include the book *Complicity: Ethics and Law for a Collective Age* as well as articles on ethics, criminal law, and legal and political philosophy.

EXPLORING THE ISSUE

Is Torture Ever Justified?

Critical Thinking and Reflection

1. Bagaric and Clarke assert that torture is already being practiced widely. If true, does this fact affect the morality of torture? Why or why not?
2. While Bagaric and Clarke argue that torture can be both moral and legal, they nevertheless advocate that limits be placed on torture. What is the moral justification for these limits? Can limits on torture address the deontological concerns raised by Kutz?
3. How useful is the formula proposed by Bagaric and Clarke for justifying torture? Can precise data ever be identified for insertion into the formula, especially in light of Kutz's discussion of real-life situations? Is precise data even needed for this formula to be useful?
4. If you were placed in a hypothetical situation like the one described by Bagaric and Clarke, would you authorize the use of torture to gain information that might prevent a terrorist attack? What considerations influence you most in making your decision? Why are these the most important considerations for you?

Is There Common Ground?

The authors of these articles agree on one fundamental issue: torture is inherently evil and repulsive. In ideal world, there would be no need for torture, and questions about the morality and legality of torture would not arise. However, we do not live in an ideal world. We live in a world where torture is a tempting method for gaining information that might eliminate threats to the social order and prevent grievous harm to innocent people.

The question, therefore, is not how best to use torture, but whether we can circumscribe the use of torture in a way that sufficiently mitigates its inherent evil. Our authors have diametrically opposed responses to this question. Kutz answers in the negative, and so concludes that torture is morally wrong, no matter how it is used. Bagaric and Clarke answer in the affirmative, and so propose limitations and regulations for the use of torture. These differences stem from a basic incompatibility in the fundamental principles of utilitarian and deontological ethics, and there appears to be no way to resolve this dispute.

Create Central

www.mhhe.com/createcentral

Additional Resources

Philip E. Devine, "What's Wrong with Torture?" *International Philosophical Quarterly* (vol. 49, September 2009)

Karen J. Greenberg, *The Torture Debate in America* (Cambridge University Press, 2005)

Sanford Levinson, *Torture: A Collection* (Oxford University Press, 2006)

Jeff McMahan, "Torture, Morality, and Law," *Case Western Reserve Journal of International Law* (vol. 37, 2006)

Darius Rejali, *Torture and Democracy* (Princeton University Press, 2009)

Internet References . . .

Amnesty International: Torture

www.amnestyusa.org/our-work/issues/torture

Ethics Updates—Philosophers Speak Out about War, Terrorism, and Peace

http://ethics.sandiego.edu/Resources/PhilForum /Terrorism/index.asp

Political Concepts: Torture

www.politicalconcepts.org/issue1/torture/

The Stanford Encyclopedia of Philosophy: Torture

http://plato.stanford.edu/entries/torture/

Selected, Edited, and with Issue Framing Material by:
Owen M. Smith, *Stephen F. Austin State University*
and
Anne Collins Smith, *Stephen F. Austin State University*

ISSUE

Is Physician-Assisted Suicide Wrong?

YES: Richard Doerflinger, from "Assisted Suicide: Pro-Choice or Anti-Life?" *Hastings Center Report* (January/February 1989)

NO: Anthony Back, Robert Baker, et al., from *Appellate Brief of* Amicus Curiae *Supporting Respondents in* Vacco v. Quill, WL 709337, Supreme Court of the United States (1996)

Learning Outcomes

After reading this issue, you will be able to:

- Distinguish physician-assisted suicide from other forms of suicide.
- State the Principles of Autonomy, Nonmaleficence, and Beneficence.
- Explain how assisting someone to commit suicide may or may not conflict with the moral obligations imposed on physicians by these principles.
- Formulate your own position on physician-assisted suicide and identify evidence supporting your position.
- Identify the main objections to your position and formulate responses to these objections.

ISSUE SUMMARY

YES: Admitting that religiously based grounds for the wrongness of killing an innocent person are not convincing to many people, Doerflinger argues on mainly secular grounds having to do with inconsistencies in the arguments of supporters of physician-assisted suicide. He examines the idea of autonomy, and the tendency for something like physician-assisted suicide to spread once it becomes initially accepted in a limited way.

NO: Back, Baker, and their co-authors argue that the physician's ethical duty to relieve pain and respect patient autonomy not only justifies, but sometimes even requires, physician-assisted suicide. In order to avoid negative connotations associated with the term "suicide," they propose using the term "physician-assisted death." Physician-assisted death, they claim, is a right that should be available to mentally competent, terminally ill patients, while safeguards must be enacted to ensure that it is not practiced on anyone else.

When end-of-life issues arise, especially in cases where medical intervention is ineffective in curing the patient or relieving the patient's pain and suffering, physicians face a tangled web of moral responsibilities. Because of the vulnerability of their patients, physicians are held to a rigorous set of professional obligations designed to ensure that they do not misuse their authority and abuse the extraordinary trust placed in them by their patients. In antiquity, these obligations were codified into the Hippocratic Oath, in which physicians swore to a variety of gods to follow a specific set of ethical practices. In the twentieth century, various alterations were proposed to the Hippocratic Oath, and while the oath is not required of physicians who practice in the United States, the vast majority of new physicians take some form of the oath before beginning to practice medicine.

Modern versions of the Hippocratic Oath embody several important ethical principles regarding the practice of medicine. First is the Principle of Autonomy, which states that patients are moral agents and should be accorded the dignity of making decisions about their own treatment. The Principle of Autonomy flows from the recognition that a patient is a human being, with intrinsic value, and not merely an object or thing. If doctors were to impose their judgment on patients and administer treatment without consulting them or in defiance of their wishes, they would be treating their patients as mere things, objects on which to practice medicine, not human beings. Consequently, this principle requires physicians to obtain a patient's voluntary informed consent before beginning medical treatment. Even when patients are unable to give consent, as for example when an unconscious person arrives in an emergency room in need of treatment, the physician is to take only those actions that are in the patients' best interest and would reasonably be approved by the patients, were they able to give consent.

Another ethical principle governing the practice of medicine is the Principle of Nonmaleficence. This principle obligates physicians to avoid exposing their patients to the unnecessary risk of needless harm. This principle does not enjoin physicians from causing harm to their patients, since medical treatment may at times require harming a patient, as when a surgeon cuts into a patient's body to repair an injured organ. This principle only forbids physicians from performing harmful actions that are not necessary for the accomplishment of a greater good, such as curing a patient or relieving a patient's pain and suffering. Moreover, it is not necessary for a physician to cause actual harm to a patient to violate this principle. Simply exposing a patient to needless harm, for example by acting in a careless or negligent fashion, violates this principle.

A third ethical principle governing the practice of medicine is the Principle of Beneficence. This principle imposes on physicians the moral obligation to help their patients when they are able to do so. Although philosophers differ whether there is a general moral obligation to help other people (as opposed to not hurting them), a fundamental aspect of the relationship between physician and patient is the dependence of the patients on their physicians to supply the knowledge, skill, and experience they lack in diagnosing and treating their medical conditions. This dependence requires physicians not merely to avoid harming their patients unnecessarily, but to act to promote their patients' welfare. This obligation applies not merely to physicians, but to the members of all the helping professions, such as nurses, therapists, and social workers. While it is difficult to circumscribe the extent of this positive duty precisely, this principle has led many physicians and health care workers to expose themselves to injury and infection on behalf of their patients, sometimes at the cost of their own lives.

While these principles provide physicians with clear and concise guidance in the practice of medicine, the compatibility of these principles, and the moral obligations they impose on physicians, may become problematic when a patient wishes to die and requests the assistance of a physician in performing this act. A simple appeal to the Principle of Autonomy is not sufficient to resolve the problem. Physicians as well as patients are moral agents and must be accorded the dignity of choosing how to act. The mere fact that a patient desires a medical treatment does not obligate a physician to provide the treatment, although the physician may be obligated to direct the patient to a physician who will provide the treatment. An appeal to the Principle of Beneficence may suffice to justify a physician prescribing treatment to relieve the pain and suffering of a patient, but if a patient faces the prospect of an extended period of pain and suffering, especially if the patient has a terminal illness and hence no hope of recovery or cure, the welfare of the patient may well be served by ending the life of the patient, and with it all pain and suffering. The Principle of Nonmaleficence is often considered the determining principle—causing the death of a patient is unambiguously an act of harming the patient, and thus would seem to be clearly prohibited by the Principle of Nonmaleficence. However the Principle of Nonmaleficence prohibits only needless harm, and if the pain of the patient can only be ended by the patient's death, causing the death of the patient may not qualify as needless harm.

In this circumstance, the requirements imposed on a physician by the Principle of Nonmaleficence might be addressed in another way. While this principle may prohibit the physician from taking direct action to cause the death of a patient, it does not clearly enjoin a physician from assisting a patient to achieve this goal. The knowledge, skill, and experience that enable a physician to treat illnesses and injuries can also be used to cause illness, injury, and even death; the Hippocratic Oath and the principles it embodies originated precisely to prevent unscrupulous physicians from acting in this way. A physician is in an excellent position to provide advice to a person who wishes to commit suicide, for example by identifying the appropriate drugs and providing directions on how they might effectively be used to provide a painless death. Since death is the result of the patient's own actions, not those of the physician, it can be argued that a physician who assists a patient to commit suicide does not actually kill the patient, and so does not violate the Principle of Nonmaleficence. By providing this type of assistance, a physician might also be praised for respecting the autonomy of the patient and for promoting the patient's welfare by bringing an end to the patient's pain and suffering.

Care would have to be taken, however, so that the reasoning used to circumvent the Principle of Nonmaleficence is applied only in appropriate circumstances, and not to the detriment of patients or the medical profession as a whole. The strongest case for physician-assisted suicide is a terminally ill patient undergoing extensive pain and suffering. If physician-assisted suicide is permitted in this case, however, the practice of physician-assisted suicide might expand to other cases where the justification is far less clear. A person with a terminal illness, but who is not yet in pain, may seek the assistance of a physician to avoid the pain that would inevitably arise. A person who is not terminally ill, but who experiences chronic pain and suffering might also seek such help. So might a person who is not terminally ill and not in chronic pain, but who suffers discomfort or embarrassment from a physical or mental disability. Even more disturbing, a person might request physician-assisted suicide on behalf of another who is unable to make such a request or even give an opinion on the matter. A person might be pressured by family members or government officials to request physician-assisted suicide in order to avoid expensive medical bills, even though this person does not want to die. Such cases form a slippery slope in which the rationale for physician-assisted suicide can be used to attack the very principles on which the ethical practice of medicine is based. Such a slippery slope, moreover, is not merely theoretical. Cases such as these have been reported in countries where the practice of physician-assisted suicide is legal.

These issues are addressed in greater detail in the selected excerpts below. Richard Doerflinger opposes physician-assisted suicide and argues that the whole idea of "rational suicide" is flawed. In contrast, a group of bioethicists use an *amicus curiae* ("friend of the court") brief in a case involving physician-assisted suicide to argue that the term "suicide" is misleading in this circumstance and that physicians should engage in this practice in order to prevent suffering and protect patient autonomy.

YES ⤶

Richard Doerflinger

Assisted Suicide:
Pro-Choice or Anti-Life?

The intrinsic wrongness of directly killing the innocent, even with the victim's consent, is all but axiomatic in the Jewish and Christian worldviews that have shaped the laws and mores of Western civilization and the self-concept of its medical practitioners. This norm grew out of the conviction that human life is sacred because it is created in the image and likeness of God, and called to fulfillment in love of God and neighbor.

With the pervasive secularization of Western culture, norms against euthanasia and suicide have to a great extent been cut loose from their religious roots to fend for themselves. Because these norms seem abstract and unconvincing to many, debate tends to dwell not on the wrongness of the act as such but on what may follow from its acceptance. Such arguments are often described as claims about a "slippery slope," and debate shifts to the validity of slippery slope arguments in general.

Since it is sometimes argued that acceptance of assisted suicide is an outgrowth of respect for personal autonomy, and not lack of respect for the inherent worth of human life. I will outline how autonomy-based arguments in favor of assisting suicide do entail a statement about the value of life. I will also distinguish two kinds of slippery slope argument often confused with each other, and argue that those who favor social and legal acceptance of assisted suicide have not adequately responded to the slippery slope claims of their opponents.

Assisted Suicide versus Respect for Life

Some advocates of socially sanctioned assisted suicide admit (and a few boast) that their proposal is incompatible with the conviction that human life is of intrinsic worth. Attorney Robert Risley has said that he and his allies in the Hemlock Society are "so bold" as to seek to "overturn the sanctity of life principle" in American society. A life of suffering, "racked with pain," is "not the kind of life we cherish."[1]

Others eschew Risley's approach, perhaps recognizing that it creates a slippery slope toward practices almost universally condemned. If society is to help terminally ill patients to commit suicide because it agrees that death is objectively preferable to a life of hardship, it will be difficult to draw the line at the seriously ill or even at circumstances where the victim requests death.

Some advocates of assisted suicide therefore take a different course, arguing that it is precisely respect for the dignity of the human person that demands respect for individual freedom as the noblest feature of that person. On this rationale a decision as to when and how to die deserves the respect and even the assistance of others because it is the ultimate exercise of self-determination—"ultimate" both in the sense that it is the last decision one will ever make and in the sense that through it one takes control of one's entire self. What makes such decisions worthy of respect is not the fact that death is chosen over life but that it is the individual's own free decision about his or her future.

Thus Derek Humphry, director of the Hemlock Society, describes his organization as "pro-choice" on this issue. Such groups favor establishment of a constitutional "right to die" modeled on the right to abortion delineated by the U.S. Supreme Court in 1973. This would be a right to choose *whether or not* to end one's own life, free of outside government interference. In theory, recognition of such a right would betray no bias toward choosing death.

Life versus Freedom

This autonomy-based approach is more appealing than the straight-forward claim that some lives are not worth living, especially to Americans accustomed to valuing individual liberty above virtually all else. But the argument departs from American traditions on liberty in one fundamental respect.

When the Declaration of Independence proclaimed the inalienable human rights to be "life, liberty, and the pursuit of happiness," this ordering reflected a long-standing judgment about their relative priorities. Life, a human being's very earthly existence, is the most fundamental right because it is the necessary condition for all other worldly goods including freedom; freedom in turn makes it possible to pursue (without guaranteeing that one will attain) happiness. Safeguards against the deliberate destruction of life are thus seen as necessary to protect freedom and all other human goods. This line of thought is not explicitly religious but is endorsed by some modern religious groups:

> The first right of the human person is his life. He has other goods and some are more precious, but this one is fundamental—the condition of all the others. Hence it must be protected above all others.[2]

On this view suicide is not the ultimate exercise of freedom but its ultimate self-contradiction: A free act that by destroying life, destroys all the individual's future earthly freedom. If life is more basic than freedom, society best serves freedom by discouraging rather than assisting self-destruction. Sometimes one must limit particular choices to safeguard freedom itself, as when American society chose over a century ago to prevent people from selling themselves into slavery even of their own volition.

It may be argued in objection that the person who ends his life has not truly suffered loss of freedom, because unlike the slave he need not continue to exist under the constraints of a loss of freedom. But the slave does have some freedom, including the freedom to seek various means of liberation or at least the freedom to choose what attitude to take regarding his plight. To claim that a slave is worse off than a corpse is to value a situation of limited freedom less than one of no freedom whatsoever, which seems inconsistent with the premise of the "pro-choice" position. Such a claim also seems tantamount to saying that some lives (such as those with less than absolute freedom) are objectively not worth living, a position that "pro-choice" advocates claim not to hold.

It may further be argued in objection that assistance in suicide is only being offered to those who can no longer meaningfully exercise other freedoms due to increased suffering and reduced capabilities and lifespan. To be sure, the suffering of terminally ill patients who can no longer pursue the simplest everyday tasks should call for sympathy and support from everyone in contact with them. But even these hardships do not constitute total loss of freedom of choice. If they did, one could hardly claim that the patient is in a position to make the ultimate free choice about suicide. A dying person capable of making a choice of that kind is also capable of making less monumental free choices about coping with his or her condition. This person generally faces a bewildering array of choices regarding the assessment of his or her past life and the resolution of relationships with family and friends. He or she must finally choose at this time what stance to take regarding the eternal questions about God, personal responsibility, and the prospects of a destiny after death.

In short, those who seek to maximize free choice may with consistency reject the idea of assisted suicide, instead facilitating all choices *except* that one which cuts short all choices.

In fact proponents of assisted suicide do *not* consistently place freedom of choice as their highest priority. They often defend the moderate nature of their project by stating, with Derek Humphry, that "we do not encourage suicide for any reason except to relieve unremitting suffering." It seems their highest priority is the "pursuit of happiness" (or avoidance of suffering) and not "liberty" as such. Liberty or freedom of choice loses its value if one's choices cannot relieve suffering and lead to happiness; life is of instrumental value, insofar as it makes possible choices that can bring happiness.

In this value system, choice as such does not warrant unqualified respect. In difficult circumstances, as when care of a suffering and dying patient is a great burden on family and society, the individual who chooses life despite suffering will not easily be seen as rational, thus will not easily receive understanding and assistance for this choice.

In short, an unqualified "pro-choice" defense of assisted suicide lacks coherence because corpses have no choices. A particular choice, that of death, is given priority over all the other choices it makes impossible, so the value of choice as such is not central to the argument.

A restriction of this rationale to cases of terminal illness also lacks logical force. For if ending a brief life of suffering can be good, it would seem that ending a long life of suffering may be better. Surely the approach of the California "Humane and Dignified Death Act"—where consensual killing of a patient expected to die in six months is presumably good medical practice, but killing the same patient a month or two earlier is still punishable as homicide—is completely arbitrary.

Slippery Slopes, Loose Cannons

Many arguments against sanctioning assisted suicide concern a different kind of "slippery slope": Contingent factors in the contemporary situation may make it virtually inevitable in practice, if not compelling at the level of abstract theory, that removal of the taboo against assisted suicide will lead to destructive expansions of the right to kill the innocent. Such factors may not be part of euthanasia advocates' own agenda; but if they exist and are beyond the control of these advocates, they must be taken into account in judging the moral and social wisdom of opening what may be a Pandora's box of social evils.

To distinguish this sociological argument from our dissection of the conceptual *logic* of the rationale for assisted suicide, we might call it a "loose cannon" argument. The basic claim is that socially accepted killing of innocent persons will interact with other social factors to threaten lives that advocates of assisted suicide would agree should be protected. These factors at present include the following:

The psychological vulnerability of elderly and dying patients. Theorists may present voluntary and involuntary euthanasia as polar opposites; in practice there are many steps on the road from dispassionate, autonomous choice to subtle coercion. Elderly and disabled patients are often invited by our achievement-oriented society to see themselves as useless burdens on younger, more vital generations. In this climate, simply offering the *option* of "self-deliverance" shifts a burden of proof, so that helpless patients must ask themselves why they are *not* availing themselves of it. Society's offer of death communicates the message to certain patients that they *may* continue to live if they wish but the rest of us have no strong interest in their survival. Indeed, once the choice of a quick and painless death is officially accepted as rational, resistance to this choice may be seen as eccentric or even selfish.[3]

The crisis in health care costs. The growing incentives for physicians, hospitals, families, and insurance companies to control the cost of health care will bring additional pressures to bear on patients. Curt Garbesi, the Hemlock Society's legal consultant, argues that autonomy-based groups like Hemlock must "control the public debate" so assisted suicide will not be seized upon by public officials as a cost-cutting device. But simply basing one's own defense of assisted suicide on individual autonomy does not solve the problem. For in the economic sphere also, offering the option of suicide would subtly shift burdens of proof.

Adequate health care is now seen by at least some policymakers as a human right, as something a society owes to all its members. Acceptance of assisted suicide as an option for those requiring expensive care would not only offer health care providers an incentive to make that option seem attractive—it would also demote all other options to the status of strictly private choices by the individual. As such they may lose their moral and legal claim to public support—in much the same way that the U.S. Supreme Court, having protected abortion under a constitutional "right of privacy," has quite logically denied any government obligation to provide public funds for this strictly private choice. As life-extending care of the terminally ill is increasingly seen as strictly elective, society may become less willing to appropriate funds for such care, and economic pressures to choose death will grow accordingly.

Legal doctrines on "substituted judgment." American courts recognizing a fundamental right to refuse life-sustaining treatment have concluded that it is unjust to deny this right to the mentally incompetent. In such cases the right is exercised on the patient's behalf by others, who seek either to interpret what the patient's own wishes might have been or to serve his or her best interests. Once assisted suicide is established as a fundamental right, courts will almost certainly find that it is unjust not to extend this right to those unable to express their wishes. Hemlock's political arm, Americans Against Human Suffering, has underscored continuity between "passive" and "active" euthanasia by offering the Humane and Dignified Death Act as an amendment to California's "living will" law, and by including a provision for appointment of a proxy to choose the time and manner of the patient's death.

By such extensions our legal system would accommodate nonvoluntary, if not involuntary, active euthanasia.

Expanded definitions of terminal illness. The Hemlock Society wishes to offer assisted suicide only to those suffering from terminal illnesses. But some Hemlock officials have in mind a rather broad definition of "terminal illness." Derek Humphry says "two and a half million people alone are dying of Alzheimer's disease."[4] At Hemlock's 1986 convention, Dutch physician Pieter Admiraal boasted that he had recently broadened the meaning of terminal illness in his country by giving a lethal injection to a young quadriplegic woman—a Dutch court found that he acted within judicial guidelines allowing euthanasia for the terminally ill, because paralyzed patients have difficulty swallowing and could die from aspirating their food at any time.

The medical and legal meaning of terminal illness has already been expanded in the United States by professional societies, legislatures, and courts in the context of so-called passive euthanasia. A Uniform Rights of the Terminally Ill Act proposed by the National Conference of Commissioners on Uniform State Laws in 1986 defines a terminal illness as one that would cause the patient's death in a relatively short time if life-preserving treatment is *not* provided—prompting critics to ask if all diabetics, for example, are "terminal" by definition. Some courts already see comatose and vegetative states as "terminal" because they involve an inability to swallow that will lead to death unless artificial feeding is instituted. In the *Hilda Peter* case, the New Jersey Supreme Court declared that the traditional state interest in "preserving life" referred only to "cognitive and sapient life" and not to mere "biological" existence, implying that unconscious patients are terminal, or perhaps as good as dead, so far as state interests are concerned. Is there any reason to think that American law would suddenly resurrect the older, narrower meaning of "terminal illness" in the context of *active* euthanasia?

Prejudice against citizens with disabilities. If definitions of terminal illness expand to encompass states of severe physical or mental disability, another social reality will increase the pressure on patients to choose death: long-standing prejudice, sometimes bordering on revulsion, against people with disabilities. While it is seldom baldly claimed that disabled people have "lives not worth living," able-bodied people often say they could not live in a severely disabled state or would prefer death. In granting Elizabeth Bouvia a right to refuse a feeding tube that preserved her life, the California Appeals Court bluntly stated that her physical handicaps led her to "consider her existence meaningless" and that "she cannot be faulted for so concluding." According to disability rights expert Paul Longmore, in a society with such attitudes toward the disabled, "talk of their 'rational' or 'voluntary' suicide is simply Orwellian newspeak."[5]

Character of the medical profession. Advocates of assisted suicide realize that most physicians will resist giving lethal injections because they are trained, in Garbesi's words, to be "enemies of death." The California Medical Association firmly opposed the Humane and Dignified Death Act, seeing it as an attack on the ethical foundation of the medical profession.

Yet California appeals judge Lynn Compton was surely correct in his concurring opinion in the *Bouvia* case, when he said that a sufficient number of willing physicians can be found once legal sanctions against assisted suicide are dropped. Judge Compton said this had clearly been the case with abortion, despite the fact that the Hippocratic Oath condemns abortion as strongly as it condemns euthanasia. Opinion polls of physicians bear out the judgment that a significant number would perform lethal injections if they were legal.

Some might think this division or ambivalence about assisted suicide in the medical profession will restrain broad expansions of the practice. But if anything, Judge Compton's analogy to our experience with abortion suggests the opposite. Most physicians still have qualms about abortion, and those who perform abortions on a full-time basis are not readily accepted by their colleagues as paragons of the healing art. Consequently they tend to form their own professional societies, bolstering each other's positive self-image and developing euphemisms to blunt the moral edge of their work.

Once physicians abandon the traditional medical self-image, which rejects direct killing of patients in all circumstances, their new substitute self-image may require ever more aggressive efforts to make this killing more widely practiced and favorably received. To allow killing by physicians in certain circumstances may create a new lobby of physicians in favor of expanding medical killing.

The human will to power. The most deeply buried yet most powerful driving force toward widespread medical killing is a fact of human nature: Human beings are tempted to enjoy exercising power over others; ending another person's life is the ultimate exercise of that power. Once the taboo against killing has been set aside, it becomes progressively easier to channel one's aggressive instincts into the destruction of life in other contexts. Or as James Burtchaell has said: "There is a sort of virginity about murder; once one has violated it, it is awkward to refuse other invitations by saying, 'But that would be murder!'"[6]

Some will say assisted suicide for the terminally ill is morally distinguishable from murder and does not logically require termination of life in other circumstances. But my point is that the skill and the instinct to kill are more easily turned to other lethal tasks once they have an opportunity to exercise themselves. Thus Robert Jay Lifton has perceived differences between the German "mercy killings" of the 1930s and the later campaign to annihilate the Jews of Europe, yet still says that "at the heart of the Nazi enterprise . . . is the destruction of the boundary between healing and killing."[7] No other boundary separating these two situations was as fundamental as this one, and thus none was effective once it was crossed. As a matter of historical fact, personnel who had conducted the "mercy killing" program were quickly and readily recruited to operate the killing chambers of the death camps.[8] While the contemporary United States fortunately lacks the anti-Semitic and totalitarian attitudes that made the Holocaust possible, it has its own trends and pressures that may combine with acceptance of medical killing to produce a distinctively American catastrophe in the name of individual freedom.

These "loose cannon" arguments are not conclusive. All such arguments by their nature rest upon a reading and extrapolation of certain contingent factors in society. But their combined force provides a serious case against taking the irreversible step of sanctioning assisted suicide for any class of persons, so long as those who advocate this step fail to demonstrate why these predictions are wrong. If the strict philosophical case on behalf of "rational suicide" lacks coherence, the pragmatic claim that its acceptance would be a social benefit lacks grounding in history or common sense.

References

1. Presentation at the Hemlock Society's Third National Voluntary Euthanasia Conference, "A Humane and Dignified Death," September 25–27, 1986, Washington, DC. All quotations from Hemlock Society officials are from the proceedings of this conference unless otherwise noted.
2. Vatican Congregation for the Doctrine of the Faith, *Declaration on Procured Abortion* (1974), para. 11.
3. I am indebted for this line of argument to Dr. Eric Chevlen.
4. Denis Herbstein, "Campaigning for the Right to Die," *International Herald Tribune,* 11 September 1986.
5. Paul K. Longmore, "Elizabeth Bouvia, Assisted Suicide and Social Prejudice," *Issues in Law & Medicine* 3:2 (1987), 168.
6. James T. Burtchaell, *Rachel Weeping and Other Essays on Abortion* (Kansas City: Andrews & McMeel, 1982), 188.
7. Robert Jay Lifton, *The Nazi Doctors: Medical Killing and the Psychology of Genocide* (New York: Basic Books, 1986), 14.
8. Yitzhak Rad, *Belzec, Sobibor, Treblinka* (Bloomington, IN: Indiana University Press, 1987), 11, 16–17.

Richard Doerflinger is deputy director of the secretariat for Pro-Life Activities at the U.S. Conference of Catholic Bishops in Washington, D.C. He is also adjunct fellow in bioethics and public policy at the National Catholic Bioethics Center in Boston. Speaking on behalf of the Catholic Bishops, he has prepared policy statements and given congressional testimony on abortion, euthanasia, human embryo research, and other bioethical issues.

Anthony Back, Robert Baker, et al.

 **NO**

Appellate Brief of Amicus Curiae *Supporting Respondents in* Vacco v. Quill

. . . The amicus group of bioethicists strongly believes that physicians, in carrying out their ethical duty to relieve the pain and suffering of their terminally-ill patients, should be legally permitted to accede to the desire of a patient to hasten death when the patient's decision is voluntarily reached, a patient is competent to make the decision, and the patient has been fully informed of the diagnosis and prognosis of an incurable, fatal disease which has progressed to the final stages. The amicus group also strongly believes that a physician may decline to honor such a request if it violates the physician's beliefs, morals or scruples or is contrary to the physician's medical judgment. The amicus group believes that the right to physician-assisted suicide should be recognized by this Court as a fundamental right, as the Court of Appeals for the Ninth Circuit ruled in *Glucksberg.* Moreover, the amicus group agrees with the Court of Appeals for the Second Circuit in Quill that the denial of physician-assisted suicide is a denial of equal protection to terminally-ill patients who do not have the option of hastening death by requesting the removal of life support systems.

These views are rooted in the four basic principles of biomedical ethics: autonomy, nonmalfeasance, beneficence, and justice. Beauchamp and Childress, *Principles of Biomedical Ethics* (4th ed. 1994). From these principles, articulated in various ways in differing ethical systems, arise the two considerations most basic in medical care: the patient's fundamental right of self-determination and respect for the patient's interests (President's Commission for the Study of Ethical Problems in Medicine and Biomedical and Behavioral Research, 1983). Ethical requirements of respect for the patient's right of self-determination and respect for the patient's interests appropriately guide all care of patients, including the care of dying patients. (Brock, 1992).

Argument

This Court Should Recognize a Right to Physician-Assisted Suicide for Competent Dying Patients

Petitioners . . . have presented arguments that far exceed the understanding of physician-assisted suicide as approved by the Second and Ninth Circuit Courts. They argue that permitting physician-assisted suicide for terminally-ill patients who seek to end their suffering in the final stages of degenerative diseases will lead to the involuntary killing of terminal patients and the healthy mentally ill and disabled.

These arguments are entirely flawed. The institution of safeguards to prevent abuse is necessary, but there is no basis to conclude that a voluntary practice limited to terminally-ill patients would be involuntarily applied, or that it could be imposed upon incompetents.

Petitioners . . . also attempt to exploit taboos associated with suicide, citing, for example, instances of suicide among the depressed or mentally ill. The cases before this Court, however, do not involve sanctioning suicide of depressed or mentally-ill individuals.

Unlike other cultures, our language has but one word to describe self-inflicted death. The word "suicide" does not differentiate among the deaths of a teenager overcome by the struggles of adolescence, a middle-aged family man facing financial ruin and an eighty-year old cancer patient who seeks to avoid further protracted pain and suffering when her death is near. Unlike the first two tragic illustrations, there can be a sense of meaningfulness, emotional resolution, and communicative culmination, including gratitude for a life now complete, in the "suicide" of the dying patient who seeks both to avoid a bad death and to bring life to an inevitable but appropriate close. The dying patient may act to avoid or relieve suffering, and may also seek to meet death at a time and place of his or her own choosing, surrounded by those whom he or she trusts and loves, while still conscious and still capable of prayer and farewells. The right to seek a death which is both free of pain, but faced while conscious and alert, is not a trivial right, but one of great significance for many people.

The common term "suicide" carries strongly negative associations that have no bearing on the issue before the Court, but are largely derived from medieval attitudes towards violent self-destruction (Battin, 1996). It would have been more accurate if the debate on this issue had been joined on physician-assisted "death" as distinct from physician-assisted "suicide."

Supreme Court of the United States, WL 709337, 1996.

The Prevalence of Death from Degenerative Disease is a Modern Problem Not Addressed by Antiquated Laws

Petitioners stress the long tradition of prohibition against suicide, including penal laws dating to the founding of this country. But such laws derive from a time when death was rarely preceded by long periods of physiologically degenerative suffering. At the time the Constitution and the Bill of Rights were written and throughout the development of English common law, the process of dying was usually quick and more likely to be due to infectious disease. Medical intervention did little to prolong life, or to prolong the process of dying. The cases before the Court, however, involve degenerative death, a creature of modern medicine; they should therefore be decided on an historically clean slate. The Court, in finding for Respondents, would not be judicially mandating social change; it would be applying constitutional doctrines of protected individual rights to a new factual situation.

Epidemiologists identify four distinct periods to describe mortality and longevity in the history of mankind. In the Age of Pestilence and Famine, which extended from the dawn of human existence to approximately 1850, people died primarily from infectious and parasitic diseases, frequently exacerbated by famines and plagues. Advances in public sanitation, immunization and antisepsis in medicine gave rise to the Age of Receding Pandemics, which lasted until approximately 1920 and was accompanied by an increase in life expectancy. In the period from 1920 until 1960, the Age of Degenerative Man-Made Diseases, advanced surgical techniques, antibiotics, techniques for the administration of intravenous fluids and drugs, the development of respiratory support systems and improved therapeutic and diagnostic techniques further increased life expectancy (Omran, 1971). Epidemiologists characterize the current state of mortality and life expectancy, which arose in the mid 1960s, as the Age of Delayed Degenerative Diseases, in which the majority of people die at later ages from degenerative diseases, such as cancer, heart disease, stroke and neurological diseases (Olshansky and Ault, 1987).

These epidemiological changes are partly illustrated by the changes in life expectancy. At the turn of this century, i.e., the 20th, American life expectancy at birth was 46.5 years for males and 49 years for females. Life expectancy at birth is now approximately 72 years for males and 79 years for females (Social Security Administration, SSA Pub. No. 11-11534). But these advances in life expectancy are associated with a fundamental change in the way we die: throughout the developed world of the late 20th century, including the United States, the majority of the population will die of degenerative disease. About a third of deaths are due to circulatory disease; another third are due to cancer; and the remaining third include degenerative conditions like neurological diseases and various forms of organ failure. The modern form of degenerative death is estimated to account for 70–80% of all deaths in the United States (Battin, 1996).

Not only do these deaths from degenerative disease tend to occur at more advanced ages than has been characteristic of earlier periods of human mortality, but particularly in the case of cancer, they are often accompanied by protracted periods of pain and suffering before death, a phenomenon which occurred comparatively rarely until recent years. Prior to the development of modern antibiotics, the patient whose condition deteriorated severely or who became bedridden was likely to contract pneumonia or other infections and die, thus being naturally spared the most difficult phases of end-stage disease.

The issue of physician-assisted suicide should be decided on the basis of present realities and not by reference to antiquated laws and customs adopted long before the modem form of degenerative death became prevalent. Neither the framers of the Constitution, nor any previous legal authorities, could have foreseen the way most people now die.

Classical Medicine Recognized a Patient's Right to Physician-Assisted Suicide

In *Quill*, petitioners cite one version of the Hippocratic Oath which contained the prohibition: "To please no one will I prescribe a deadly drug, nor give advice which may cause his death." Petitioners seem to suggest that the Oath has the force of law, but the version they cite also prohibits a number of medical practices clearly and uncontroversially recognized as legal, including surgery and charging fees for teaching medicine, as well as practices explicitly recognized as legal by this Court, such as abortion.

The Hippocratic Oath can only be understood in its historical context. At the time of Hippocrates, there was no prohibition against physician-assisted suicide in mainstream Greek medicine; the practice was subject to consultation and informed consent similar in intent to the protocols urged by medical professionals and bioethicists today. Thus, at the time of Hippocrates:

> . . . the taking of poison was the most usual means of committing suicide [in terminal illness], and the patient was likely to demand the poison from his physician who was in possession of deadly drugs and knew that which brought about an easy and painless death. On the other hand, such a resolution was not taken without due deliberation, except perhaps in a few cases of great distress or mental strain. The sick man wished to be sure that further treatment would be of no avail, and to render this verdict was the physician's task. The patient, therefore, consulted with him, or urged his friends to speak to the doctor. If the latter, in such a consultation, confirmed the seriousness or hopelessness of the case, he suggested directly or indirectly that the patient commit suicide. . . . [I]n antiquity many physicians actually gave the patients the poisons for which they were asked.

See Edelstein (1967). See also, Amundsen (1978). The Hippocratic Oath is an "esoteric document that is often inconsistent with the larger picture of Greco-Roman medical ethics"; Gourevitch (1969).

The text of the Hippocratic Oath has been modified many times through the ages. Contemporary versions, routinely adopted in medical-school graduation exercises and similar contexts (see text of Oath adopted by World Medical Association in 1948 reproduced at Appendix B), do not contain the prohibitions against surgery, abortion, or accepting fees for teaching medicine, and also omit the prohibition against physician-assisted suicide. In short, neither the Hippocratic Oath nor classical tradition provides a compelling ethical or professional prohibition of physician-assisted suicide.

Petitioners have Not Advanced Sufficient Interests to Overcome the Right of a Terminally-Ill Patient to Assisted Death

The States of New York and Washington argue that the government has an overriding interest in the preservation of life which is not subject to veto by the individual wishes of dying patients. Similarly, the American Medical Association . . . contend(s) that physicians are devoted to the healing arts and should not be involved in the termination of life.

Not only is there no adequate basis for either of these claims, but the AMA's position does not even reflect the views or practices of its constituency. In fact, physicians are divided about this issue, and many support the recognition of a patient's right to assistance and reject state interference in their right to practice medicine in a way they see as humane, compassionate, and respectful of the wishes of their dying patients. As reported in *The New England Journal of Medicine,* 60 percent of doctors in Michigan and 66 percent of doctors in Oregon—two states in which this issue has been very widely discussed—support legalizing assisted suicide for terminally-ill patients (Lee, et al., 1996; Bachman, et al., 1996). In the State of Washington, 12 percent of physicians polled reported that they had been asked by their terminally-ill patients for prescriptions to hasten death, and of these, 24 percent had complied with such a request in the year prior to the study (Bach, et al., 1996).

Assertions that doctors should have no role in death fly in the face of reality. All people eventually die, and the doctor's role appropriately includes ensuring that the patient's death occurs as humanely as possible. As Francis Bacon wrote, the physician's role is to help the patient "make a faire and easie passage."

The humaneness of a death is not only a matter of avoiding pain and physical suffering; it is also a matter of consonance with a patient's most basic values. For some patients, a death softened by the heavy use of painkillers or hastened by withholding or withdrawing life-sustaining treatment will be tolerable; for others such prospects are profoundly repugnant: these patients fear and resent a death preceded by a period of obtundation, or in which their bodies slowly deteriorate from the ravages of a lethal disease. Not all patients will choose to die in the same way, even when death is imminent: some will prefer continued aggressive treatment, in the hope that they can beat the odds; some will prefer withdrawing or withholding specific forms of treatment; others will accept death as a consequence of escalating doses of morphine; still others will choose to forego nutrition and hydration; some will tolerate terminal sedation; but some strongly prefer a peaceful and humane death directly initiated while conscious and alert, facilitated by the assistance of a physician.

Physician-assisted suicide is not an option likely to be chosen by many. In the Netherlands, where assistance in dying is openly practiced and widely accepted, less than 3.5% of patients dying in a given year chose this manner of death. Yet it can be of very great moral and spiritual importance to those who make this choice. It may be the privilege of religious traditions to reject such a practice, . . . but it is not their privilege to assert that such an act on the part of a dying patient must be devoid of personal or spiritual significance.

The state's interest in preservation of life . . . is necessarily subject to careful qualification. Washington and New York have capital punishment statutes, permitting state-sanctioned death of otherwise healthy individuals (Revised Code of Washington 9A.32.030; New York Penal Law Section 60.06). The state, in times of war, sacrifices the lives of its most vital citizens to the national interest. Because the state approves of the deaths of individuals when it serves its interests, the state cannot advance an absolute objection to participation in death as an answer to claims that terminally ill patients have a right to seek and accept assistance from their physicians in suicide. The state clearly does have an interest in preventing suicide that is impulsive, aggressive, irrational, violent, or coerced, or where the suicidal impulse arises from depression or other mental illness; but the state does not have an interest in preventing a competent patient, who is in any case facing death, from rationally and reflectively choosing what to that person is the preferable way of meeting death. It is the overly broad, unwarrantedly negative connotations of the term "suicide" that obscure this crucial distinction.

Virtually all data about the causes and characteristics of suicide and its relationship to mental illness . . . is data only about suicides in the former sense. Although rational, reflective suicides do occur in terminal illness, often assisted by physicians, they are virtually never reported as suicides, and it has thus been impossible to collect reliable data about these latter "suicides." Suicide is often said to be about the choice between life and death. *Glucksberg* and *Quill,* however, are not cases about patients choosing between life and death. They are about patients choosing death in a way that seems to them dignified, humane and more in keeping with their basic values, rather than what seems to them a less desirable and undignified death.

In a lengthy footnote, the Bioethics Professors' Amicus Curiae Brief Supporting Petitioners argues that physicians have no fear of prosecution if they prescribe drugs which a patient subsequently uses to commit suicide, provided the physician is not present when the patient takes the lethal medication (Brief For Bioethics Professors Amicus Curiae Supporting Petitioners at 15–16 n.6)[2]. Even if that were the case, maintaining such a status quo would be unsatisfactory. Physicians do not generally believe that they would be free from prosecution and they are often reluctant to assist patients who wish to die with dignity; it is at best a legally controversial claim. Because current statutes criminalizing assisted suicide contain no exemption for physicians, doctors are often constrained to abandon their patients at their time of greatest need. Even when a doctor prescribes the necessary drugs he or she often refuses to assist the patient in using the drugs. Unaided by professional assistance, an already suffering patient in the process of dying may take the medication improperly, survive, and undergo still more substantial suffering from unwanted, sublethal complications (Shavelson, 1995; Jamison, 1995). Such profoundly unwanted events are not uncommon among "amateur" assisted suicides.

The bioethics professors supporting Petitioners erroneously believe that medical ethics is advanced by a practice where a physician and patient are encouraged to conspire covertly to circumvent the law, but where the patient is then denied medical assistance at the time of death and left to suffer the consequences of inadequate procedures. The bioethicists who are signators of the present brief believe strongly that medical ethics and trust in physicians are better served by physician-assisted suicide where the patient can have the care, comfort and treatment of his or her doctor at the time the patient acts to hasten death.

The argument of the Bioethics Professors in Support of Petitioners also misinterprets the medical facts of dying. Their brief, addressing the equal protection argument in *Quill*, attempts to differentiate between patients on life support and those who are not. Those on life support are different, they argue, because of a bodily intrusion that could only have taken place with their consent, which consent they can withdraw at any time. They further claim that a terminally-ill person who is not on life support is differently situated for equal protection analysis because he or she is not being subjected to an ongoing physical intrusion. But this argument is erroneous. Both types of patients have had bodily intrusions for which they have given consent. A patient gives consent for a ventilator, or a feeding tube, and can then withdraw that consent and the bodily intrusion. Another patient gives consent for chemotherapy, a bodily intrusion which changes him or her unalterably, and ultimately leaves the patient in a condition of dying quite differently from that without the chemotherapy; yet the patient cannot withdraw that bodily intrusion, since it has already irreversibly occurred. Patients not connected to life support are therefore not free from bodily intrusion, and patients who are connected to life support do not die "naturally" if that support is removed. Once life has been prolonged with any sort of therapy, the mode of dying is unnatural; irreversible physical intrusion has already occurred. The Second Circuit Court of Appeals correctly rejected the claim that there is a rational distinction between refusing treatment and suicide.

Protocols and Guidelines may be Imposed to Avoid the "Slippery Slope"

This Court has recognized the rights of individuals to make major life decisions regarding the integrity of their bodies, *Roe v. Wade*, 410 U.S.113 (1973); *Planned Parenthood of Southeastern Pennsylvania v. Casey*, 502 U.S. 1056 (1992), including the right of the terminally-ill to determine the end of their lives. *Cruzan v. Director, Missouri Dept. of Health*, 497 U.S. 261 (1990). In all of these cases, the Court has carefully delineated the rights in question and stated that they are subject to reasonable regulation. *Roe v. Wade, supra,* 410 U.S. at 163 ("a state may regulate the abortion procedure to the extent that the regulation reasonably relates to the preservation and protection of maternal health."); *Planned Parenthood v. Casey, supra,* 505 U.S. at 872 ("Though the woman has a right to choose to terminate or continue her pregnancy before viability, it does not follow at all that the State is prohibited from taking steps to ensure that the choice is thoughtful and informed"); *Cruzan, supra,* 497 U.S. at 281 ("The choice between life and death is a deeply personal decision of obvious and overwhelming finality. We believe Missouri may legitimately seek to safeguard the personal element of this choice through the imposition of heightened evidentiary requirements.").

Despite the history of caution by this Court in delineating rights with respect to life and death decisions, Petitioners . . . contend that the Court's recognition of a right of competent, terminally-ill patients to obtain physician-assisted suicide will lead down a slippery slope such that its holding will lead to involuntary deaths or physician-facilitated deaths of the incompetent.

There is no basis to believe that physician-assisted suicide will lead to such abuses. Safeguards would obviously be devised to protect against abuse. Examples of such safeguards, the details of which are the appropriate concern of the states in regulating the exercise of patients' constitutionally-protected basic rights, are available both in this country and abroad. For example, the Oregon Death With Dignity Act, which by its terms is limited to competent adults who have been determined by the attending physician to be suffering from a terminal disease, requires two oral and one written request from the patient witnessed by two individuals to the effect that the patient is competent, acting voluntarily and is not being coerced to sign the request; requires the physician to inform the patient of his or her medical diagnosis and prognosis, the potential risks in, and probable results from, taking the medication; requires that the physician inform the patient of the feasible alternatives, including comfort care, hospice care, and pain control; requires that the patient be referred to a consulting physician for confirmation of the diagnosis and determination that the patient is competent and acting voluntarily; requires that the patient be referred for counseling if appropriate; imposes a fifteen-day waiting period; and requires that the attending physician provide full documentation demonstrating compliance with the Act. It permits the patient to rescind the request at any time, in any manner.

Similarly, the Dutch guidelines for physician-assisted suicide require that the patient make a voluntary, enduring request; that the patient have adequate information about his or her disease, including alternative methods of treatment; that the patient's suffering be intolerable, in the patient's view, and irreversible, without alternatives for relieving the suffering that are acceptable to the patient; that the attending physician exercise due care in reviewing and verifying the patient's condition; that there be a consultation with a second, independent physician; and that the physician who provides assistance in hastening death file a written report of the death, which may not be reported as a natural death (Battin, 1994 Angel, 1996).

We believe such safeguards will provide patients clearly adequate protection against pursuing physician-assisted suicide from impulse, irrationality, depression, misinformation, manipulation, or coercion. They constitute reasonable means of assuring voluntary choice, of ruling out mental illness, of preventing mistaken diagnoses or faulty prognostications of terminal illness, of detecting familial, professional, or institutional pressures on the patient, of assuring that the practice actually serves the patient's interests, of protecting against the devaluation of members of minorities or disabled or medically dependent people, or in other ways protecting the patient's basic rights. Abuses are equally possible when treatment is withheld or withdrawn, when dosages of painkillers are used which foreseeably depress respiration and so hasten death, when nutrition and hydration are withdrawn, when do-not-resuscitate orders are written, and when other commonplace strategies of "negotiated" death are employed. While there is no credible evidence that these possible abuses are in fact occurring to any significant degree, the safeguards to be erected for the protection of patients in the matter of physician-assisted suicide should operate to provide greater assurance of full voluntariness and full information, and, by requiring reporting, would allow surveillance of the practice to discover and penalize physicians or others who do not adhere to regulatory restrictions (Battin, 1994).

Petitioners and their amici claim that the experience of the Netherlands in permitting physician-performed euthanasia and physician-assisted suicide shows the substantial risks of a "slippery slope," where legalization or legal toleration of directly caused death leads to widespread unacceptable killing. Many of their claims are empirically false and grossly distorted. There is no evidence of conscious, competent patients being euthanased against their will.[3]

The Right of Competent, Dying Patients to Physician-Assisted Suicide is a Negative Right to be Free from State Interference

In *Glucksberg,* the Ninth Circuit Court of Appeals held that physician-assisted suicide is a fundamental liberty right. This right to determine one's own mortality shares one important characteristic with other fundamental rights. Like the rights to vote or to worship, there is no requirement that the right be exercised (Feinberg, 1978).

Similarly, under neither *Glucksberg* nor *Quill* would a physician be required to accede to a request for suicide assistance if the request violates the doctor's personal, medical or religious beliefs. The constitutionally-protected right asserted in these cases is, as bioethicists would put it, a negative right, a right not to be interfered with, a true liberty-right. Neither case asserts a positive right or claim-right, a demand that patients could make upon physicians whether physicians felt it medically or morally appropriate to respond or not. Thus, the full and appropriate scope of a physician's rights as well as a patient's rights would be recognized, since the physician would no longer be legally constricted in caring for a terminally-ill patient where that patient sought help in hastening death, though he or she would not acquire any new or unwanted obligation, and the full range of a patient's traditional, constitutionally-protected liberty rights of self-determination would be recognized in the new factual circumstance of the modern form of degenerative death.

Recognition of a protected right to seek and accept assistance in suicide from a willing physician is not only important for the comparatively small number of terminally-ill patients who might actually use it. Those patients who do not choose to exercise their right to physician-assisted suicide may gain comfort in the knowledge that the option exists if their suffering becomes intolerable. For many, this will make it possible to live fuller, more complete, lives during the process of dying, since they need not fear a bad death (Quill, M.D. 1991). Indeed, the possibility of physician-assisted suicide, even if never used, may contribute positively to the quality of life for those facing death.[4]

The records before this Court contain the testaments of the individual, suffering plaintiff-patients—all of whom died without the desired assistance of their physicians in terminating their pain and suffering and without the knowledge that the Courts of the Ninth and Second Circuits would respond to their anguished pleas. Their tales of agony could be reiterated many thousand times over, but may be summarized by the final note of the Nobel Prize-winning physicist, Percy Bridgman, who nearly 80 years old and suffering from terminal cancer, shot himself. His note stated:

> It isn't decent for society to make a man do this thing himself. Probably this is the last day I will be able to do it myself.

(Delbruck, 1974).

Conclusion

Affirmation of the decisions below will contribute to a more decent society, more respectful of patients' basic rights and interests in the light of the realities of the modem form of degenerative death. We strongly urge that they be affirmed.

Appendix A

Bioethicists Supporting Respondents

Anthony Back, M.D. Assistant Professor University of Washington and VA Puget Sound Health Care System Robert Baker, Ph.D. Professor of Philosophy Union College, Schenectady

Margaret P. Battin, Ph.D. Professor of Philosophy, Adjunct Professor of Internal Medicine University of Utah

Tom L. Beauchamp, Ph.D. Professor of Philosophy, Kennedy Institute of Ethics Georgetown University

Dan W. Brock, Ph.D. Professor of Philosophy and Biomedical Ethics, Brown University

Joan Callahan, Ph.D. Professor of Philosophy University of Kentucky

Marguerite Chapman, J.D., L.L.M. Associate Professor of Law, University of Tulsa, College of Law

R. Alta Charo, J.D. Associate Professor, Law and Medical Ethics University of Wisconsin Law School

Dana S. Davis, J.D., Ph.D. Associate Professor, Cleveland-Marshall College of Law

Gerald Dworkin Professor of Philosophy University of Illinois, Chicago

David J. Green, M.D. Associate Professor of Pediatrics University of Utah School of Medicine

Martin Gunderson, Ph.D., J.D. Associate Professor of Philosophy Macalester College, St. Paul, Minnesota

Robert T. Hall, Ph.D. Professor of Philosophy and Sociology West Virginia State College and Associate Professor of Medicine West Virginia University School of Medicine

James J. Hughes, Ph.D. Dept. of Sociology, University of Connecticut

Daniel L. Icenogle, M.D., J.D. Health Law Consulting, Madison, Wisconsin

C.L. Junkerman, M.D. Emeritus Professor of Medicine; Center for Bioethics Medical College of Wisconsin

Jeffrey P. Kahn, Ph.D., M.P.H. Director, Center for Bioethics Associate Professor of Medicine, Public Health, and Philosophy University of Minnesota

Kenneth Kipnis, Ph.D. Professor of Philosophy, University of Hawaii

Erich Loewy, M.D. Professor of Medicine, Endowed Alumni Association Chair of Bioethics University of California, Davis Ruth Macklin, Ph.D. Professor Albert Einstein College of Medicine

David Mayo, Ph.D. Professor of Philosophy, University of Minnesota, Duluth, and Center for Biomedical Ethics, University of Minnesota, Minneapolis

Ronald Baker Miller, M.D., F.A.C.P. Director, Program in Medical Ethics, University of California, Irvine

Jerry Menikoff, M.D., J.D. Associate Professor of Law University of Akron

Janet Mitchell, M.D., M.P.H. Chairperson, Dept. of OB/GYN, Interfaith Medical Center Brooklyn, New York

Richard Moneyer, Ph.D. Professor of Philosophy, Miami University, Oxford, Ohio

Timothy F. Murphy, Ph.D. Associate Professor of Philosophy of Medicine, University of Illinois, Chicago

Curt Nasser, Ph.D. Department of Philosophy, Fairfield University

Lawrence J. Nelson, Ph.D., J.D. Department of Philosophy; Markkula Center for Applied Ethics Santa Clara University

Robert Pearlman, M.D., M.P.H. Associate Professor of Medicine University of Washington, and Veterans Affairs Puget Sound Health Care System

Gregory Pence, Ph.D. Professor, Schools of Medicine and Humanities, University of Alabama at Birmingham James Rachels, Ph.D. University Professor University of Alabama at Birmingham

Rosamund Rhodes, Ph.D. Associate Professor, Director of Bioethics Education Mount Sinai School of Medicine

John Robertson, J.D. School of Law, University of Texas, Austin

William Ruddick, Ph.D. Professor of Philosophy, Adjunct Professor of Psychiatry New York University Robert

Schwartz, J.D. Professor of Law University of New Mexico

Jeffrey Spike, Ph.D. Assistant Professor of Medical Humanities University of Rochester School of Medicine Director, Ethics Consultation Service, Strong Memorial Hospital

Tom Tomlinson, Ph.D. Center for Ethics and Humanities in the Life Sciences Michigan State University

Benjamin S. Wilfond, M.D. Assistant Professor of Pediatrics, Pediatric Pulmonology and Medical and Molecular Genetics Arizona Respiratory Sciences Center University of Arizona

Peter C. Williams, J.D., Ph.D. Chief, Division of Medicine in Society, Associate Professor of Preventive

Medicine Health Sciences Center, State University of New York, Stony Brook

William Winslade, Ph.D., J.D. James Wade Rockwell Professor of Philosophy in Medicine Institute for the Medical Humanities University of Texas Medical Branch

Ernle Young, Ph.D. Center for Bioethics, Stanford University

Rabbi Noam Zohar, Ph.D. Dept. of Philosophy, Bar Ilan University

Appendix B

The Oath of Hippocrates

I solemnly pledge to consecrate my life to the service of humanity. I will give respect and gratitude to my deserving teachers. I will practice medicine with conscience and dignity. The health and life of my patient will be my first consideration.

I will hold in confidence all that my patient confides in me. I will maintain the honor and the noble traditions of the medical profession.

My colleagues will be as my family. I will not permit considerations of race, religion, nationality, party politics, or social standing to intervene between my duty and my patient. I will maintain the utmost respect for human life.

Even under threat I will not use my knowledge contrary to the laws of humanity. These promises I make freely and upon my honor.

Approved by the World Medicine Association in 1948.

Notes

1. The bioethicists supporting Respondents have received the consent of the parties in *Quill* and *Glucksberg* to file this Amicus Curiae brief. The consents are being filed with the Court simultaneously with this brief.
2. We too, believe that this act should not be regarded as a criminal one, provided the prescription is provided at the voluntary request of a competent, fully informed patient. We particularly welcome these bioethicists' tacit recognition that some dying patients will prefer a directly-caused death and that some physicians will be willing to provide the means for it, since it counters the quite trivializing claim from other amici that the use of opiates, of discontinuing life sustaining treatment, of withholding nutrition and hydration, and of terminal sedation are sufficient answers to the patient's distress.
3. In the majority of cases, a patient's current, explicit request, fitting the guidelines cited above, is in force at the time of assistance in suicide or euthanasia. In a fraction of cases (0.7%), there is no current explicit request; in about half

of these cases (including all competent patients), either the decision was discussed with the patient earlier in the illness or the patient had expressed a wish for euthanasia if suffering became unbearable. In the other cases the patient was incompetent. In 91% of these cases, life was shortened by a week or less (in a third, 24 hours or less), and in the small number with longer life expectancy, the patient was evidently suffering greatly but verbal contact was no longer possible. Van der Maas et al. "Euthanasia, Physician-Assisted Suicide, and Other Medical Practices Involving the End of Life in the Netherlands, 1990–1995," *New England Journal of Medicine* 335:22 (Nov. 28, 1996), 1699, 1701–1702. Loes Pijnenborg et al., "Life-Terminating Acts Without Explicit Request of Patient," *The Lancet* 341 (May 8, 1993) 1196–1199.

New evidence from the Netherlands, based on studies which repeated the initial empirical studies of euthanasia and physician-assisted suicide known as the Remmelink report, show that reporting has increased and the frequency of cases regarded as problematic has decreased. The number of cases has increased in association with the aging of the population and an increase in the proportion of deaths from cancer, a function of the decrease in deaths from ischemic heart disease, but the proportion of requests granted has decreased. (Indeed, most requests for euthanasia or assistance in suicide are not granted.) Physician-assisted death does not involve patients whose illnesses are less severe, nor are there any signs that the decisionmaking has become less careful–rather, there is more frequent consultation and better documentation. Van der Maas, *supra,* at 1703, 1705; Gerrit van der Wal et al., "Evaluation of the Notification Procedure for Physician-Assisted Death in the Netherlands," *New England Journal of Medicine* 335:22 (Nov. 28, 1996), 1706–1711.

In the view of the researchers, "these data do not support the idea that physicians in the Netherlands are moving down a slippery slope," Van der Maas, supra, at 1705, a view echoed by the Executive Editor of the *New England Journal of Medicine.* Marcia Angel, MD., Editorial: "Euthanasia in the Netherlands—Good News or Bad?" *New England Journal of Medicine* 335:22 (Nov. 28, 1996), 1676–1678, at 1677. Physician-assisted death continues to account for less than 3.5 % of all reported deaths: thus the vast majority of patients dying in a given year do not choose it, and even the vast majority of cancer patients— the most frequent diagnosis—do not. Yet it remains widely regarded as an important option even if one rarely needed or utilized.

4. A 1994 Australian study of cancer patients found that those who anticipated a role for the more active options of suicide and/or euthanasia in their own futures, compared to those who anticipated a future possible role for only the more

passive options of wishing death to come early or ceasing all treatment, were more hopeful and reported a higher quality of life than patients who regarded them as out of the question. Owen, et al., "Cancer Patient's Attitudes to Final Events in Life: Wish for Death, Attitudes to Cessation of Treatment, Suicide and Euthanasia," *Psycho-Oncology* 3:1-9 (1994).

Bibliography

Cases

Cruzan v. Director, Missouri Dept. of Health, 497 U.S. 261 (1990)

Planned Parenthood of Southeastern Pennsylvania v. Casey, 502

U.S. 1056 (1992)

Roe v. Wade, 410 U.S.113 (1973).

Statutes

Revised Code of Washington 9A.32.030
New York Penal Law Section 60.06

Books & Articles

Amundsen, "The Physician's Obligation to Prolong Life: A Medical Duty Without Classical Roots," *Hastings Center Report* (August 1978)

Angel, "Euthanasia in the Netherlands—Good News or Bad?" *New England Journal of Medicine* 335:22 (Nov. 28, 1996) 1676

Bach, et al., "Physician Assisted Suicide and Euthanasia in Washington State," *Journal of the American Medical Association* 275:12 (March 27, 1996) 919

Bachman, et al., "Attitudes of Michigan Physicians and of the Public Toward Legalizing Physician Assisted Suicide and Voluntary Euthanasia," *New England Journal of Medicine,* 334:5 (Feb. 1, 1996) 303

Battin, *The Death Debate: Ethical Issues In Suicide* (1996)

Battin, *The Least Worst Death* (1994)

Beauchamp and Childress, *Principles of Biomedical Ethics* (4th ed.1994)

Brock, "Voluntary Active Euthanasia," *Hastings Center Report* 22:2 (March–April 1992) 10

Delbruck, "Education for Suicide," Interview in *Prism,* a publication of the American Medical Association, 2 (1974) 20

Feinberg, "Voluntary Euthanasia and the Inalienable Right to Life,"

Philosophy and Public Affairs 7, no. 2 (Winter, 1978)

Gourevitch, "Suicide Among the Sick in Classical Antiquity," *Bulletin of the History of Medicine* 43 (1969) 501

Jamison, *Final Acts of Love: Families, Friends, and Assisted Dying* (1995)

Lee, et al., "Legalizing Assisted Suicide—Views of Physicians in Oregon," *New England Journal of Medicine* 335:5 (Feb. 1, 1996) 310

Olshansky and Ault, "The Fourth Stage of the Epidemiologic Transition: The Age of Delayed Degenerative Diseases," in Timothy M. Smeeding, et al., eds. *Should Medical Care Be Rationed By Age?* (1987)

Omran, "The Epidemiologic Transition: A Theory of the Epidemiology of Population Change," *Milbank Memorial Fund Quarterly* 49(4):509 (1971)

Owen, et al., "Cancer Patient's Attitudes to Final Events in Life: Wish for Death, Attitudes to Cessation of Treatment, Suicide and Euthanasia," *Psycho-Oncology* 3:1-9 (1994)

Owsei and Temkin, *Ancient Medicine: Selected Papers of Ludwig Edelstein,* (1967) 11

Pijnenborg et al., "Life-Terminating Acts Without Explicit Request of Patient," *The Lancet* 341 (May 8, 1993) 1196

Quill, M.D. "Death and Dignity: A Case of Individualized Decision Making." *The New England Journal of Medicine* 324:10 (March 7, 1991), 691

Shavelson, *A Chosen Death: The Dying Confront Assisted Suicide,*(1995)

Van der Maas et al., "Euthanasia, Physician-Assisted Suicide, and Other Medical Practices Involving the End of Life in the Netherlands, 1990–1995," New England Journal of Medicine 335:22 (Nov. 28, 1996)

Van der Wal et al., "Evaluation of the Notification Procedure for Physician-Assisted Death in the Netherlands," *New England Journal of Medicine* 335:22 (Nov. 28, 1996), 1699

Other Authorities

"Deciding to Forego Life-Sustaining Treatment," President's Commission for the Study of Ethical Problems in Medicine and Biomedical and Behavioral Research, (March 1993)

Life Tables for the United States 1900–2050, Social Security Administration, SSA Pub. No. 11–11534

OXFORD ENGLISH DICTIONARY (new ed.)

Anthony Back is a Professor of Medicine at the University of Washington in Seattle, as well as Director of the Cancer Communication and Palliative Care Programs at the Seattle Cancer Care Alliance and the Fred Hutchinson Cancer Research Center. His primary areas of research are doctor–patient communication and palliative care.

Robert Baker is the William D. Williams Professor of Philosophy at Union College as well as the Founding Director (Emeritus) of the The Union Graduate College-Mount Sinai Bioethics Program. He has written numerous articles on bioethical topics and has co-edited a number of books in the field.

EXPLORING THE ISSUE

Is Physician-Assisted Suicide Wrong?

Critical Thinking and Reflection

1. Under what circumstances, in your opinion, might death be a "necessary harm" in the context of the Principle of Nonmaleficence? How might it be possible to prevent these circumstances so that physician-assisted suicide is unnecessary?
2. Where in the slippery slope of cases listed in the issue introduction would you draw the line between morally acceptable physician-assisted suicide and immoral physician-assisted suicide? What justification can you provide for your answer? Are there any other cases in which you think physician-assisted suicide is moral? Explain your answer.
3. Is there a significant moral difference between a physician assisting a patient to commit suicide and a physician taking direct action to kill a patient? Why or why not?
4. Do you think a physician has an obligation to provide the medical treatment requested by a patient regardless of the physician's own moral view? What impact would your view have on the morality of physician-assisted suicide? What impact would your view have on the morality of other controversial medical treatments?

Is There Common Ground?

The positions taken by the authors of the articles on this issue are fundamentally opposed: Doerflinger considers physician-assisted suicide to be impermissible, while Back, Baker, et al., consider it to be not only permissible but sometimes required. Nonetheless, advocates and opponents of physician-assisted suicides do share some positions in common.

Both advocates and opponents of physician-assisted suicide are concerned about possible expansion of the practice. Doerflinger explores the slippery slope that may result from the legalization of physician-assisted suicide, while Back, Baker, et al., give examples of stringent safeguards that should be implemented to prevent physician-assisted suicide based on "impulse, irrationality, depression, misinformation, manipulation, or coercion." Advocates and opponents of physician-assisted suicide also tend to agree that providing sufficient palliative care to terminal patients, particularly in the form of pain relief, is an essential ethical requirement that can reduce patients' desire for an earlier death.

Create Central

www.mhhe.com/createcentral

Additional Resources

Ian Dowbiggin, *A Merciful End: The Euthanasia Movement in Modern America* (Oxford University Press, 2007)

Gerald Dworkin, R.G. Frey, and Sissela Bok, *Euthanasia and Physician-Assisted Suicide (For and Against)* (Cambridge University Press, 2005)

James H. Ondrey, *Physician-Assisted Suicide* (Greenhaven Press, 2006)

Internet References . . .

Ethics Updates: Euthanasia and End-of-Life Decisions

http://ethics.sandiego.edu/Applied/Euthanasia/index.asp

Euthanasia and Assisted Suicide: Issues and Groups

http://diglib.library.vanderbilt.edu/ginfo-pubpol.pl?searchtext=Euthanasia&Type=LTR&Resource=DB&Website=GOVTINFO

Should Euthanasia or Physician-Assisted Suicide Be Legal?

http://euthanasia.procon.org/

Unit 4

UNIT

Humanity, Nature, and Technology

*W*hen we think about what it means to be human, we cannot help but recognize a paradox. Humans are part of nature, and as such we have certain natural tendencies. One of these natural tendencies is our drive to create technology, which is traditionally considered the opposite of nature. The issues in this unit raise questions about the relationship between humans and the natural world, the relationship between humans and technology, and the relationship between technology and the natural world.

Selected, Edited, and with Issue Framing Material by:
Owen M. Smith, *Stephen F. Austin State University*
and
Anne Collins Smith, *Stephen F. Austin State University*

ISSUE

Does Morality Require Vegetarianism?

YES: Nathan Nobis, from "Vegetarianism and Virtue: Does Consequentialism Demand Too Little?" *Social Theory & Practice* (January 2002)

NO: Beth K. Haile, from "Virtuous Meat Consumption: A Virtue Ethics Defense of an Omnivorous Way of Life," *Logos: A Journal of Catholic Thought and Culture* (Winter 2013)

Learning Outcomes

After reading this issue, you will be able to:

- Use utilitarianism to make a moral argument against the consumption of meat.
- Use virtue ethics to make a moral argument in favor of the consumption of meat.
- Explain how virtue ethics can be combined with utilitarianism to make a moral argument about the consumption of meat.
- Formulate your own position on the consumption of meat and identify evidence supporting your position.
- Identify the main objections to your position and formulate responses to these objections.

ISSUE SUMMARY

YES: Nathan Nobis argues that utilitarianism, an ethical theory in which the moral worth of an action is determined solely by its consequences, requires us to be vegetarians and avoid the consumption of meat. According to Nobis, meat and other animal products are produced under cruel conditions, and utilitarian principles require that we should not participate in or support activities that are cruel or inflict unnecessary pain on animals.

NO: Beth Haile argues that the consumption of meat can be part of a life that seeks to cultivate virtue and avoid vice. Although the way in which our society produces meat for consumption is morally unacceptable, there is nothing intrinsically wrong about the consumption of meat. Once meat is produced in a morally acceptable way, a virtuous life can include the consumption of meat.

Many living beings, especially animals, consume meat or animal products, often in a way that inflicts unnecessary pain and suffering on the animal being consumed. Indeed, some animals kill not only for sustenance, but for reproductive advantage or even as a form of entertainment. Human consumption of meat and animal products, even under cruel conditions, is often justified by terrible examples of "nature, red in tooth and claw."

However, many objections can be raised against the use of animal behavior as a basis for the human consumption of meat and animal products. First, unlike many animals, people do not need to consume meat in order to survive; vegetarianism is a viable method of meeting human nutritional requirements. In addition, humans have the capacity to change their behaviors profoundly in a short period of time. As various cultural practices, such as slavery, have come under rational scrutiny and moral critique, they have been abandoned in favor of less objectionable alternatives. Although human consumption of meat is currently widespread, it is possible for humans to eliminate the practice altogether and obtain the protein they need in other ways. Indeed, vegetarianism is found in most cultures, either as a common practice or as an individual choice. Finally, human beings have the rational capacity not only to choose their goals, but to choose the means by which they achieve these goals. Even if humans choose to continue consuming meat, there is usually no need for that meat to be produced in a way that treats animals cruelly. There exist more humane alternatives to the current methods of factory farming of meat and animal products, although these alternatives may decrease the availability of meat and animal products and increase their cost.

While some people object to the very practice of consuming meat and animal products, a more common objection focuses on the deplorable conditions under which some animals are currently raised and slaughtered. According to this objection, consumers of meat and animal products should be held morally responsible for these conditions because cruel, yet efficient methods are required to produce meat and animal products in the large quantities and at the low prices that consumers demand. Many consumers prefer to remain ignorant of the precise methods by which meat and animal products reach retail outlets so that these products can be enjoyed without the moral qualms that would be raised by their manner of production.

In the following selections, Nathan Nobis argues against the consumption of meat and animal products. He bases his argument on the ethical theory of utilitarianism, noting that it is an important moral principle not to participate in or support morally repugnant practices such as factory farming, regardless of whether our individual actions will bring an end to such practices. Thus, he concludes that a person is still morally obligated to become vegetarian, even if that person's individual choice to avoid the consumption of meat and animal products has no appreciable impact on factory farming.

Beth Haile, in contrast, bases her view on virtue ethics, an approach to ethics that focuses on the character of a moral agent, rather than the morality or immorality of particular actions. She argues that a moral agent must take a number of factors into consideration, including the compassionate treatment of farm animals, fairness toward agricultural workers, and the avoidance of waste. It is possible, she concludes, for a person to be a virtuous moral agent and, under certain circumstances, still consume meat and animal products.

Nathan Nobis

Vegetarianism and Virtue: Does Consequentialism Demand Too Little?

I will argue that each of us personally ought to be a vegetarian.[1]

Actually, the conclusion I will attempt to defend concerns more than one's eating habits in that I will argue that we should be "vegans." Not only should we not buy and eat meat, but we should also not purchase fur coats, stoles, and hats, or leather shoes, belts, jackets, purses and wallets, furniture, car interiors, and other traditionally animal-based products for which there are readily available plant-based or synthetic alternatives. (Usually these are cheaper and work just as well, or better, anyway.) I will argue that buying and eating most eggs and dairy products are immoral as well. (Since it's much easier to avoid all fur, leather, and wool than all eggs and dairy products, I mention those first.) My conclusion might even imply that outfitting one's self in what has been, in recent history, the most "philosophical" of fabrics—tweed—is immoral too!

Many arguments defending the moral obligation to become vegetarian and, to a lesser extent, adopt a vegan lifestyle, have been given, especially in recent decades.[2] While these arguments have convinced many to become vegetarians or vegans, most are still not convinced. My discussion is directed towards those who have not been convinced, especially for these reasons: first, it is often unclear what the argument is for the exact conclusion that *"You, the reader, are morally obligated to be a vegetarian (or a vegan)."* Second, it is often unclear what moral premise is given to justify this conclusion. And, third, it is often especially unclear how this premise might be justified from a broadly consequentialist moral perspective.[3]

This final lack of clarity is somewhat surprising, since much of the contemporary vegetarian movement takes its inspiration from the work of Peter Singer, a self-professed utilitarian consequentialist.[4] He writes, "I am a utilitarian. I am also a vegetarian. I am a vegetarian *because* I am a utilitarian. I believe that applying the principle of utility to our present situation—especially the methods now used to rear animals for food and the variety of foods available to us—leads to the conclusion that we ought to be vegetarians."[5] While a number of non-consequentialist ethical theories can justify a vegetarian or vegan conclusion fairly easily, I will present some doubts that consequentialism can so easily do so. I will then attempt to cast doubts on these doubts.

So my target reader is a consequentialist who denies that she ought to become a vegetarian or vegan. As a consequentialist, she believes this, presumably, because she thinks that her making these changes in her eating habits and lifestyle would result in her bringing about less intrinsic goods into the world than were she to maintain her current omnivorous eating and consumer habits. In effect, she thinks that, in terms of doing what she can to increase the world's overall amount of goodness, there are ways for her to spend her time and resources that are, at least, morally equivalent to becoming a vegetarian, and so it is not obligatory. She must also think that her becoming a vegetarian will prevent her from achieving these other goals that she believes yield equal or, perhaps greater, goods. . . .

I will argue that if consequentialism does not imply or justify a moral principle that *we should not benefit from or (even symbolically) support very bad practices when we can easily avoid doing so*, then consequentialism is mistaken. . . .

This kind of consequentialism is unique in that it takes the instrumental value of having and acting from certain virtues seriously. Some might respond, "So much the worse for consequentialism," but this might be unwise, since, as Henry Sidgwick argued, the theory provides, "a principle of synthesis, and a method for binding the unconnected and occasionally conflicting principles of common moral reasoning into a complete and harmonious system."[6] My discussion is directed towards someone who thinks that consequentialism does this organizing and synthesizing job best, but is skeptical that her seemingly well-confirmed theory implies that she should be a vegetarian or vegan and do her best to develop and act from the virtues that are commonly said to motivate vegetarianism: compassion, caring, sensitivity to cruelty and suffering (both animal and human), resistance to injustice, and integrity, among others.[7]

Contemporary Animal Agriculture and Human Nutrition

First, I will briefly summarize some facts about modern animal agriculture and human nutrition. While this information is readily available, relatively few people are aware of it.

Nobis, Nathan. From *Social Theory and Practice*, January 2002, pp. 135–137, 138–143, 149–156. Copyright © 2002 by Florida State University Dept. of Philosophy. Used with permission.

Many people become vegetarians or vegans when they learn about modem animal agriculture and slaughter techniques, especially "factory farming." In the U.S., each year around nine billion animals live in factory farms where most lead generally miserable lives. Newborns are separated from their mothers hours or days after birth; they are then kept in small cages or crates or confined for most of their lives in extremely cramped, overcrowded pens. Male chicks at egg farms are discarded by the tens of thousands each day into trash bins because their meat is deemed unsuitable for human consumption, or they are ground alive into feed for other animals. Male calves of dairy cows are fed liquid, iron-deficient diets and raised in crates that wholly restrict movement so that their muscles remain weak and tender.

Most animals are confined indoors: very few live "happy lives" in an outdoor barnyard. This confinement results in the animals' basic instinctual urges being frustrated. Many animals become psychotic and exhibit neurotic, repetitive behaviors: many become unnaturally cannibalistic. To ward off death and disease from the stressful and unsanitary conditions, a constant regimen of antibiotics and growth hormones is maintained. On both factory and non-intensive family farms animals are subject to surgical modifications such as beak, toe, and tail removal, ear tagging and clipping, teeth removal, branding, dehorning, castration, and ovary removal. In the interest of containing costs, all these procedures are performed without anesthesia.

Many animals die from starvation and exposure to cold in transport to the slaughterhouse. Those that are unable to walk to slaughter are labeled "downers" and are left to die lying in the yard. Those that remain are slaughtered in extremely painful and inhumane ways. Fur-bearing animals are either trapped in the wild and typically die a slow, painful death, or are raised in small cages, fed each others' remains, and killed by anal electrocution so their pelts are not marred.

Understanding these facts is a common motivation for ethical vegetarianism and adopting a vegan lifestyle: people learn of, especially by *seeing*, the pain, suffering, and death involved in these practices and, at least, simply do not want to be involved with or benefit from it anymore.

One might think that this suffering and death is justified because we need to eat meat and other animal products, but, clearly, nobody needs to eat meat to survive. In fact, the common diet in the U.S. and Europe, a meat-based diet, is strongly correlated with such health problems as heart disease, stroke, diabetes, obesity, stroke, and various cancers. Vegetarians are far less prone to these chronic diseases and they tend to outlive meat-eaters by seven years.[8] There is strong medical evidence that not eating meat is to one's health advantage: even conservative health organizations encourage people to cut back on their consumption of meat to reduce cholesterol and saturated fat intake; others encourage cutting it out completely.

The same things, in fact, can be said about all animal products: no one needs to eat eggs or milk or cheese. Progressive health organizations that advocate preventative medicine, such as the Physician's Committee for Responsible Medicine, advise eliminating them completely and adopting a vegan diet that contains a wide variety of foods solely from the four new food groups: vegetables, fruits, legumes (beans and nuts), and whole grains.[9] There is ample evidence that people not only survive on such a diet, but that they thrive.[10] The list of world-champion vegan athletes is impressive, so no one can honestly say that vegans can't achieve optimal health or nutrition.[11] And, of course, no one needs to wear fur, leather, or wool, or use products made from these materials.

Thus, no product of factory farming, non-intensive farming or animal slaughter is necessary for human health or survival. Animals' short and often miserable lives and cruel and painful deaths are not outweighed or justified by any human need. As for the aesthetic pleasures of taste and fashion, vegetarian cuisine and cruelty-free clothing and accessories can easily gratify those interests. But even if the pleasures of consuming animal-based dishes uniformly outweighed the pleasures of all vegan alternatives (which they don't), it is exceedingly unlikely that the difference in aesthetic pleasure for us outweighs the great pains, suffering, and death for the animals. Thus, it is quite unlikely that the status quo regarding the use and treatment of animals is justified from a consequentialist perspective.

The "Impotence of the Individual" Objection

. . . A critic might accept that it is likely that if *everyone* became a vegetarian (perhaps gradually, so the economy is not disturbed) utility would be maximized, but object that her *personally* becoming a vegetarian won't make any difference to the overall utility. Because the meat and animal products industry is so huge and markets are too insensitive, no consequence of her becoming a vegetarian, or even a vegan, would be that fewer animals would be raised and killed than if she were to continue in her omnivorous ways. While these industries do exist only because people buy their products, they don't exist because *she* buys their products, and they won't come tumbling down if she divests herself from them. If she is supposed to become a vegetarian or vegan *because* doing so will help the plight of animals, this seems to not be the case.

Call this the "impotence of the individual" objection. It obviously depends on an empirical assumption concerning the failure of an individual's consumer behavior to affect a huge industry. This claim seems plausible; it is even accepted by a number of philosophers who defend vegetarianism.[12] As far as I know, nobody has summoned the empirical data to show that it is false. I will presume it is true and so here's the rub: if an individual's refraining from purchasing animal-based products does not make a difference for the animals, then this critic might think that Singer's argument is sound, but that it just does not imply the relevant conclusion, namely that *she* should become a vegetarian. The conclusion seems to be that it ought to be the case that *we all* become vegetarians, which is importantly different from the conclusion that *she* ought to be vegetarian, irrespective of whether others do the same (for one difference, the critic can make it the case that *she* is vegetarian, but her powers over others are quite limited). A consequentialist case for *personal* vegetarianism or veganism, if it can be made, will thereby have to be made on the *actual* positive consequences of an individual's becoming a vegetarian, and it appears that less animals being raised and killed is, unfortunately, not one of the actual consequences. . . .

Vegetarianism and Virtue

One way . . . is to think of the vegetarian in terms of his or her virtues. While Tardiff does not present his case as a virtue-based one, he does describe the meat eater as "selfish," in that she accepts the system of killing animals for her own pleasure; he also describes the ethical vegetarian as "generous," "compassionate," and "peace-loving."[13] Stephens suspects that a "compassionate person would feel moral discomfort, or even revulsion, enjoying something made possible only by the suffering of another."[14] Dixon argues that an individual who thinks it is wrong to cause animals to suffer and be killed for food yet continues to eat meat "seems to be guilty of a lack of integrity."[15]

The common suggestion is that one should be a vegetarian or a vegan because, given an understanding of the relevant facts about both animal and human suffering, this is just how a virtuous, good person would respond. Since people should be virtuous, and being virtuous entails being caring and compassionate (among having other traits), and these traits entail disassociation from the animal-products industry *even if* doing so won't result in less harm to animals, virtuous people should be vegetarian.

In exploring a virtue-based defense of vegetarianism, Russ Shafer-Landau suggests that meat-eaters may be "condemnable to the extent that they display an indifference to the cruelty that went into the 'production' of their 'goods'," and that "they demonstrate a disregard for the suffering experienced by the animals whose remains one is wearing or eating." He describes fur-wearers as "callous." He writes that "[s]eeking and deriving satisfaction from 'products' that are known to result from cruel practices diminishes one's admirability. This is so even if the practical impact of one's indulgence is nonexistent or negligible." Similar judgments are made outside of the vegetarian context: there is "something morally repugnant about a willingness to utilize or purchase soap made from the bodies of concentration camp victims," even if doing so won't prevent any future harms. Also, voicing one's support for a racist dictator or wearing a fur coat received as a gift both seem objectionable.[16]

From these intuitions, Shafer-Landau formulates a moral principle similar to Curnutt's: "One must refuse (even symbolic) support of essentially cruel practices, if a comparably costly alternative that is not tied to essentially cruel practices is readily available."[17] He suspects that something like this principle offers the best hope for those concerned to defend the existence of an obligation to refrain from animal consumption. The problem here, as he notes, is that it's not easy "to identify the sorts of considerations that can ground such a principle," or to find a general moral theory that would justify such a principle.[18]

One approach would be to go the route of a rule-based non-consequentialist or deontological ethic, and hold that this is one of the rules. However, this probably wouldn't be wise, since an ethic of rules is often thought to be "fundamentally non-explanatory" and "anti-theoretical."[19] Presumably, there is a unifying principle that makes these rules the right rules: if there is such a principle, then this is what justifies the rule and makes it the case that the rule should be followed. This fundamental principle is thereby of theoretical interest, not the mid-level rule.

Another route would be virtue ethics. Virtue ethics says, roughly, that evaluations of character and motive are primary in ethics and that other ethical evaluations—say of actions—are derivative from considerations of character and motive: for example, that an action is right if, and only if, a virtuous person would do it. The morality of an action is to be explained by the character of the agent. If one is interested in defending vegetarianism or veganism (and other intuitions about concerned and responsible consumer behavior in general), and one suspects that non-virtue-based theories have a hard time generating the correct judgments about these cases, then one might have a good reason to take more interest in virtue-based ethical theory. It just seems that a virtuous person would not, in response to an understanding of the facts about animal agriculture and nutrition, think that even though animals suffer greatly and die for these products that she does not need (and, in fact, are sometimes harmful to her) and thus only fulfill aesthetic preferences for her, she is nevertheless justified in consuming and using them, even though she could easily refrain from doing so. Thus, virtue theory seems to provide a ready defense for a general principle, similar to Curnutt's and Shafer-Landau's, that *we shouldn't (even symbolically) support bad practices when good alternatives are readily available*, which we might call the "vegetarian justifying principle."

Virtue theory's greatest "vice," however, is that it simply does not seem to provide much of an explanation for why it's good to be virtuous, for example, why it's good (or virtuous) to be compassionate or why a virtuous person would accept the vegetarian justifying principle. Consequentialists can plausibly argue that it's good to be compassionate because compassionate people tend to bring more happiness into the world. They see the virtues as instrumentally valuable: virtue ethics, at least in its bolder varieties (and the non-bold varieties seem to just be theories *of* the virtues, which don't imply anything about ethical theory), holds that the virtues are intrinsically valuable.

In taking a consequentialist view on the virtues, one attempts to give more basic reasons why someone should be compassionate (assuming compassion is a virtue), not merely asserting, as virtue ethics does, that it's just a brute, unexplained fact that compassion is good. The consequentialist critic, of course, will be more attracted to the option that it's a brute fact that, say, happiness or pleasure is good and that virtues are means to those ends. This seems more likely than the idea that the virtues are ends in themselves or are intrinsically good.

If this criticism of virtue ethics is compelling, then while virtue ethics does readily support vegetarianism, it lacks explanatory power. The theory-minded ethical vegetarian seems to be faced with a dilemma: *either* accept a generally plausible ethical theory (e.g., consequentialism) that gets a broad range of cases right (and for seemingly good reasons) but doesn't seem to do as well with personal vegetarianism or veganism in that it seems to lack a place for concerns about animals to provide reasons for action, *or* adopt a virtue ethics or other non-consequentialist, rule-based perspective that readily supports vegetarianism or veganism but, unfortunately, doesn't amount to much of a general moral theory because it lacks explanatory power.

I suspect that there may be a compromise here, one that will be amenable to consequentialists and help them defend the vegetarian justifying principle. There already are reasons to believe that the locus of evaluation for consequentialism should be broadened beyond individual actions to include the "life histories" of a person. One proposal is to hold that an individual action is right for a person just in case it is part of one of that person's optimal life histories, that is, a life history in which value is maximized over the span of the life.

And here we have a natural place to merge the plausible insights of virtue ethics with consequentialist ethical theory. Pre-theoretically, it seems that, all else equal, a person will bring about more goodness if she has the virtue of compassion, cares about and is sensitive to unnecessary cruelty and suffering (wherever it is found, in humans or animals), opposes injustice and unfairness, and, in general, attempts to have an integrated, coherent moral outlook. These seem to be virtues that we try to instill in our children. And earlier we saw that these virtues (and others) readily support vegetarianism and veganism, as well as a general moral outlook typically associated with them (e.g., deep concerns about human health and the recognition that the most effective ways to promote this are through simple dietary changes and non-animal based medical research,[20] disappointments that people are starving to death while cattle are well-fed, environmental concerns,

concern for public health and safety, concerns for the safety of slaughterhouse workers, and so on).

These virtues have deep implications for how one lives one's life and how one affects others' lives. For each person, it is unclear how their characters would not be improved and how they would fail to bring about more goodness were they to adopt the virtues that commonly motivate vegetarian or veganism. What other better character traits would preclude doing this? Becoming caring and compassionate about animals invariably seems to have "trickle down" positive effects for the rest of one's life. It seems exceedingly unlikely that anyone would, in general, come to treat other humans worse were she to become a vegetarian or vegan out of compassion or sympathy for animals. In fact, the opposite seems likely. One common motive for telling others about the plight of animals, and attempting to persuade them to be vegetarian or vegan, is that others' lives will improve and they will develop these virtues.

One could practice these virtues selectively and not have them affect one's views about animals, or allow one's self to occasionally eat, but probably not buy, meat (whatever amount won't have negative consequences for health, which is unknown). In doing so, however, it seems not unlikely that one would be taking oneself down a life history that would be, on balance, worse than the vegan one. This is because, first, a thoughtful humanist should probably come to conclusions about how to behave that would be very similar to the vegan's (since all their prescriptions promote human well-being anyway) and, second, personal consistency, integrity and commitment typically contribute to better character anyway. It might be difficult to be selectively caring and compassionate: if this would lead one down a slippery slope, the better strategy for doing the best one can with one's life might be to consistently hold these virtues and act in accordance with them. If this is the case, this bridges the gap between the consequentialist case for near-vegetarianism or veganism articulated above and the more consistent outlook, character, and behavior that many vegetarian and vegan philosophers advocate.

Singer states that "becoming a vegetarian [or a vegan, I think he'd agree] is a way of attesting to the depth and sincerity of one's belief in the wrongness of what we are doing to animals."[21] He probably would agree that veganism also is a way to attest to the sincerity of one's belief in the wrongness of what happens to *humans* as a result of how animals are used. I suspect that, in general, a person who has these beliefs and attests to them by becoming a vegetarian or vegan brings more goodness into the world than her non-vegetarian counterpart: some of these ways are more obvious (e.g., health, comparative ability to make financial contributions to good causes), others are less obvious and, of course, harder to evaluate (e.g., consequences of character). If a switch to a vegetarian or vegan lifestyle results in a life history that brings about greater overall value than an omnivorous life history, then this is what consequentialism demands, and, therefore, consequentialism does not demand "too little" because it will require that one conform one's behavior to the "vegetarian justifying principle" (which has implications beyond vegetarianism).

In conclusion, my discussion can be presented as this argument:

1. If consequentialism is true, then S ought to live an optimal life history.
2. If S ought to live an optimal life history, then S ought to have the virtues entailed by an optimal life history.
3. If S ought to have the virtues entailed by an optimal life history, then S ought to be compassionate, sensitive to cruelty (wherever it is found), resist injustice, have moral integrity, etc.
4. If S ought to be compassionate, sensitive to cruelty (wherever it is found), resist injustice, and be morally integrated, etc., then S ought to be a vegetarian or vegan.
5. Therefore, if consequentialism is true, then S ought to be a vegetarian or vegan.

Consequentialists readily accept premise (1) and should accept premise (2) as well, since it explains why it's good to be virtuous. Premise (3) is defended by the quasi-empirical observation that people with these and related virtues tend to, in general and all else being equal, bring about more good in the world than people who lack these virtues. Were major lifestyle changes not at stake, many would probably readily accept this premise: it is difficult to see how people who *lack* compassion, caring, and sensitivity would bring about *more* goods than those who have these traits, or have them to a greater degree.

Premise (4) is obviously difficult, since it concerns empirical matters. It is the claim that people who become vegetarians or vegans in order to more consistently practice virtue produce more overall good than those who dabble in virtue or practice it selectively. Admittedly, this is an exceedingly difficult premise to defend. The data regarding the positive consequences of changing one's character by becoming vegetarian are, for the most part, anecdotal and speculative. However, this is a problem in general for trying to defend any view about personal morality from a consequentialist perspective, since it is very difficult to find any hard data on the consequences of character and lifestyle. Intuitions and impressions are often all we have to go on for such matters, especially those concerning personal choice. But that does not leave us in the dark, since one impression that most of us have is that it is better to be more compassionate and caring, compared to less, unless doing so would be emotionally draining, which being a vegetarian typically isn't (in fact, many find it quite uplifting). Furthermore, whatever other projects we have, it is unclear exactly how becoming a vegetarian could preclude our efforts with them: if our other projects are noble, it is likely that our reasons for doing them would support being a vegetarian as well.

So, while (4) is not easy to defend on consequentialist grounds, it is not easy to deny either. The vegetarian consequentialist typically has some personal experience to justify her sense that her becoming a vegetarian or vegan has resulted in her bringing about better consequences, while the critic typically has little personal experience to think that her being an omnivore has had the best consequences. If this consequentialist strategy for defending personal vegetarianism has promise, further research into the actual consequences of having the kind of character that is receptive to concerns about animal suffering will be necessary. Until then, I hope that some burden has been shifted to those who hold that their becoming vegetarians or vegans would not maximize intrinsic value to explain why this is so and why their characters, and the consequences of their characters, would become worse for their making this change.[22]

Notes

1. My argument is restricted to apply only to people with nutritious and readily available alternatives to meat. I will say nothing about the morality of meat-eating among the relatively few people who, due to insufficient vegetable-food sources, literally *must* eat meat to survive.
2. The recent literature on ethical issues concerning non-human animals is immense, but the writings of Peter Singer and Tom Regan have been most influential. See, e.g., Peter Singer, *Animal Liberation,* 3rd ed. (New York: Ecco Press, 2001), and *Practical Ethics,* 2nd ed. (Cambridge: Cambridge University Press, 1993); Tom Regan, *The Case for Animal Rights* (Berkeley: University of California Press, 1983), *Defending Animal Rights* (Urbana: University of Illinois Press, 2001), and (with Carl Cohen) *Animal Rights: A Debate* (Lanham, Md.: Rowman & Littlefield, 2001). Singer's and Regan's articles are widely reprinted, especially in introductory moral problems texts.
3. Consequentialism is, very roughly, the ethical theory that says the morality of a token action is determined solely by the value of the consequences in terms of the overall balance of intrinsic goods versus evils produced by that action. . . .
4. Utilitarianism is a species of consequentialism that says, roughly, that the only morally relevant consequence is the overall balance of pleasures and pains (or preference satisfactions and dissatisfactions) that come about as a result of the action.
5. Peter Singer, "Utilitarianism and Vegetarianism," *Philosophy and Public Affairs* 9 (1980): 325–37, p. 325 (my emphasis).
6. Henry Sidgwick, *The Methods of Ethics,* 7th ed. (London: Macmillan, 1907), p. 422.
7. For discussion of vegetarianism and these and other virtues, see Nicholas Dixon, "A

Utilitarian Argument for Vegetarianism," *Between the Species* 11 (1995): 90–97, p. 96; Steve Sapontzis, "Everyday Morality and Animal Rights," *Between the Species* 3 (1987): 107–27; Russ Shafer-Landau, "Vegetarianism, Causation and Ethical Theory," *Public Affairs Quarterly* 8 (1994): 85–100, pp. 97–98; William Stephens, "Five Arguments for Vegetarianism," *Philosophy in the Contemporary World* 1 (1994): 25–39, p. 33; and Andrew Tardiff, "Simplifying the Case for Vegetarianism," *Social Theory and Practice* 22 (1996): 299–314, pp. 307, 312.

8. See, e.g., the position paper, "Position of the American Dietetic Association: Vegetarian Diets," *Journal of the American Dietetic Association* 97 (November 1997): 1317–21, p. 1317, where the ADA reports: "Scientific data suggest positive relationships between a vegetarian diet and reduced risk for several chronic degenerative diseases and conditions, including obesity, coronary artery disease, hypertension, diabetes mellitus, and some types of cancer. . . . It is the position of The American Dietetic Association (ADA) that appropriately planned vegetarian diets are healthful, are nutritionally adequate, and provide health benefits in the prevention and treatment of certain diseases." Mylan Engel, in "The Immorality of Eating Meat," summarizes the *extensive* medical literature on the health benefits of vegan and vegetarian diets. See also Mark and Virginia Messina, *The Dietician's Guide to Vegetarian Diets: Issues and Applications,* 2nd ed. (Gaithersburg, Md.: Aspen Publications, 2001); John Robbins, *The Food Revolution* (Berkeley: Conari Press, 2001); and Brenda Davis and Vesanto Melina, *Becoming Vegan: The Complete Guide to Adopting a Healthy Plant-Based Diet* (Summertown, Tenn.: Book Publishing Co., 2000).

9. Available at http://www.pcrm.org/health/VSKNSK9 .htrnl

10. See the references to the nutrition literature above. For a brief review of the medical literature on the benefits of eliminating dairy products, see Robert Cohen, *Milk A-Z* (Englewood Cliffs, N.J.: Argus Publishing, 2001).

11. See Robbins, *The Food Revolution,* pp. 78–79.

12. Hud Hudson, in "Collective Responsbility," writes that he "is persuaded that the [meat] industry is not fine-tuned enough to be affected at all by [his] becoming a [strict] vegetarian," much less be affected by his purchasing a "large basket of extra-hot chicken wings" every two weeks at his favorite restaurant (p. 94). James Rachels, in "The Moral Argument for Vegetarianism," in his *Can Ethics Provide Answers?* (Lanham, Md.: Rowman & Littlefield, 1997), pp. 99–107, notes: "It is discouraging to realize that no animals will actually be helped simply by one person ceasing to eat meat. One consumer's behavior, by itself, cannot have a noticeable impact on an industry as vast as the meat industry" (p. 106). Bart

Gruzalki discusses this objection in his 'The Case Against Raising and Killing Animals for Food," in Harlan Miller and William Williams (eds.), *Ethics and Animals* (Clifton, N.J.: Humana Press, 1983), pp. 251–66, p. 265. His reply focuses on dubious estimations of the probable positive consequences for animals that an individual's becoming a vegetarian would have. In "Opportunistic Carnivorism," *Journal of Applied Philosophy* 17 (2000): 205–11, p. 205, Michael Almeida and Mark Bernstein argue that "insensitivity of the market notwithstanding, consistent consequentialists are morally prohibited from each additional purchase and consumption of meat" because of the very small probability that any individual will purchase the "threshold chicken" (or other animal) that will result in the "increased terror, slaughter, and death of more chickens" (or other animals). The argument is troubled by the dubious empirical assumption that there is such a "threshold chicken" and a wavering back and forth between a subjective or probabilistic consequentialism that judges acts by their expected or probable consequences and an "objective" consequentialism that judges acts by their actual consequences. R.G. Frey raised this objection in his *Rights, Killing, and Suffering: Moral Vegetarianism and Applied Ethics* (Oxford: Basil Blackwell, 1983); Michael Martin raises it in "A Critique of Moral Vegetarianism," *Reason Papers,* No. 3, Fall 1976, pp. 13–43, and his "Vegetarianism, the Right to Life and Fellow Creaturehood," *Animal Regulation Studies* 2 (1979-80): 205–14. This objection is not new. Unfortunately, it seems little has been said to respond to it.

13. Tardiff, "A Catholic Case for Vegetarianism," pp. 307, 312.

14. Stephens, "Five Arguments for Vegetarianism," p. 33.

15. Dixon, "A Utilitarian Argument for Vegetarianism," p. 97.

16. Shafer-Landau, "Vegetarianism, Causation and Ethical Theory," pp. 96–98.

17. Ibid., p. 95. DeGrazia, in *Taking Animals Seriously,* pp. 262, 285.

18. Shafer-Landau, "Vegetarianism, Causation and Ethical Theory," p. 96.

19. See David McNaughton, "Intuitionism," in Hugh LaFollette (ed.), *The Blackwell Guide to Ethical Theory* (Oxford: Blackwell, 2000), pp. 268–87, at pp. 270–71.

20. See Hugh Lafollette and Niall Shanks, *Brute Science: Dilemmas of Animal Experimentation* (London: Routledge, 1997), and Ray and Jean Greek, *Sacred Cows and Golden Geese: The Human Cost of Experiments on Animals* (New York: Continuum, 2001).

21. Singer, "Utilitarianism and Vegetarianism," p. 337.

22. For critical comments that greatly improved this paper, I am grateful to an anonymous

referee and, especially, Christian Basil Mitchell. I am also grateful for comments and discussion from Michael Almeida, Trulie Ankerberg-Nobis, Mark Bernstein, David DeGrazia, Mylan Engel, Bob Holmes, Joel Marks, Gwen Olton, Louis Pojman, Russ Shafer-Landau, Ted Stolze, and Linda Zagzebski. A version of this paper was presented at the Society for the Study of Ethics and Animals at the 2001 meeting of the American Philosophical Association, Pacific Division.

NATHAN NOBIS is an Assistant Professor of Philosophy at Morehouse College. His publications include articles on bioethics, animal rights, and ethical theory.

Beth K. Haile

 **NO**

Virtuous Meat Consumption: A Virtue Ethics Defense of an Omnivorous Way of Life

Contemporary Christian ethicists and moral theologians have not, for the most part, attempted a serious ethical defense of an omnivorous way of life. Those who take the question of eating meat seriously from both an ethical and theological perspective usually do so in order to either oppose eating meat as totally unethical or to defend a vegetarian way of life as more morally sound than an omnivorous way of life. . . .

What does not exist in the literature, however, are any moral theologians offering a moral defense of eating meat, despite the fact that most do. The question of eating meat is an important issue for moral theologians to address, not just in order to defend a vegetarian way of life, but in order to defend an omnivorous one, especially in light of all the moral arguments against eating meat. Working within the Roman Catholic tradition, this paper will attempt to provide a moral defense of an omnivorous way of life by following the principles of virtue ethics. This tradition, as Romano Guardini writes, "seeks to do justice to the living majesty, nobility, and beauty of the good."[1]

The Questionable Ethics of Eating Meat

Many people realize the questionable ethics of eating meat when they learn about modern husbandry and slaughtering techniques.[2] In 2008, 17,328,000 cattle, 4,590,314,000 chickens, and 57,542,000 hogs were slaughtered for food. The factory farm industry uses selective breeding and growth-promoting antibiotics to unnaturally and painfully produce animals ready for slaughter as quickly as possible. Most factory farms house their animals in small, overcrowded confinements, prohibiting the animals from engaging in their natural habits like foraging, nesting, roaming, and running. The slaughtering processes themselves are also quite atrocious, with practices like cutting the beaks off of chickens and the tails off of cows preslaughter commonly utilized. As slaughter lines run at rapid speeds, mistakes are recurrent, with many animals left suffering for long periods of time before slaughter.[3]

The ethical status of factory farms is starting to receive greater media coverage following public health scares such as mad cow disease and more recently, [E.] coli outbreaks from consuming factory farm-produced ground beef.[9] This, along with a greater understanding of the negative impact factory farms have on the environment as major contributors of greenhouse gases and fertilizer runoff, has led many people to forgo eating meat as part of adopting a more environmentally friendly lifestyle.[5] In the midst of all this, those still choosing to practice an omnivorous way of life have been silent about the moral justification for their choice. . . .

There have been few contributions among virtue ethicists on the questionable ethics of eating meat, despite the growing prominence of virtue ethicists in the field. Rosalind Hursthouse briefly defends vegetarianism as a practice of temperance in her book *On Virtue Ethics*.[6] In her book entitled *Ethics: Humans and Other Animals*, Hursthouse illustrates how virtue-based arguments can be used to oppose certain ways of treating animals such as using animals for scientific experiments and fox-hunting for sport.[7]

Despite the relative silence among virtue ethicists on the issue, I argue that virtue ethics is well suited to addressing the ethical concerns of meat consumption. Virtue ethics moves beyond a focus on discrete acts toward a morality concerned rather with a unified life, both personal and communal. From the perspective of virtue ethics, the question is not about whether any specific act of consuming meat is ethical or not, but rather about how meat consumption may or may not fit into a life oriented toward the good.

A Virtue Ethics Approach to an Omnivorous Way of Life

Virtue is a quality of character inclining a person toward the good, or as Aquinas says, "a good quality of the mind, by which we live righteously, of which no one can make bad use" (I-II, Q, 55, art. 4). A virtuous person does not have to think in every discrete circumstance what a good action would be, but rather spontaneously and naturally desires and acts in such a way that is in accordance with the truly good life she is trying to lead. As Jean Porter notes, the human good is attained "by sustaining a life-long course of activity that is determined by our rational grasp of that in which the truly human good consists."[8]

The classical division of the moral virtues that Aquinas adopts identifies four cardinal virtues, which represent four modes of pursuing the good according to the natural inclinations of the human being. Prudence directs the intellect toward the good as the virtue concerning the right choice about things to be done. Justice directs the will toward the good as the virtue concerning right relations with others. Fortitude directs the irascible appetite toward the good as the virtue concerning the pursuit of the arduous good. Temperance directs the concupiscible appetite toward the good as the virtue concerning the pursuit of the simple sensual good.

The virtues are open-ended in the sense that there is no one correct way to exercise them. Through the operation of prudence, a virtuous person is able to discern how to be virtuous given a specific moral context with specific circumstances. In light of the infinite number of contexts and circumstances that can exist "the virtues allow a person to pursue the good in a way that is uniquely suited to her. From the perspective of virtue, the primary question is not whether eating meat is immoral, but rather, how eating meat might be incorporated into a life directed toward the good.

One way to approach this question is to identify individuals who make the conscious choice to consume meat, and yet still seem to lead lives oriented toward the good. One such person is chef, farmer, and writer Hugh Fearnley-Whittingstall, author of *The River Cottage Meat Book,* who is widely known for his commitment to seasonal, sustainable, and ethically produced food. In 2006, Fearnley-Whittingstall organized the "Chicken Out Campaign," producing a series of television shows detailing how commercial breeds of chickens are raised in an effort to encourage people to buy more humanely treated free-range chickens. As part of this campaign, he encouraged activists to purchase shares of Tesco, a major chicken retailer, so they could participate in shareholder meetings encouraging the company to adopt more humane practices toward their chickens, consistent with the Farm Animal Welfare Council's "Five Freedoms."[9] Though unsuccessful at changing Tesco's farming practices, Fearnley-Whittingstall continues to campaign for more responsible and humane farming and consumption practices.

In the introduction to his *The River Cottage Meat Book,* Fearnley-Whittingstall offers a thorough explanation of the morality of eating meat rather than adopting what he calls a "vegetarian utopian" view:

> [The dependency of animals on humans] would not be suspended if we all became vegetarians. If we ceased to kill the domesticated meat species *for* food, then these animals would not revert to the wild. The nature of our relationship would change, but the relationship would not end. We would remain their custodians, with full moral responsibility for their welfare. . . . If we are not to be guilty of great cruelty, we would still have to manage the populations, by veterinary means for

their good health and by culling to avoid population booms and consequent starvation. And wouldn't [we] want to minimize the suffering of old and diseased animals by "putting them down" humanely? Then what happens to the corpses of the deceased? Do we bury them? Are we allowed to feed them to our cats and dogs, or have they become vegetarian too? Or should they just be composted to produce fertilizer for the vegetarian agriculture that is now feeding us? But then wouldn't we sort of end up eating them anyway?[10]

Fearnley-Whittingstall clearly takes the moral implications of meat-eating seriously, yet he has not chosen a vegetarian lifestyle. For meat-eaters looking for ways in which meat consumption can be integrated into a life oriented toward the good, turning to such a person might be a good place to begin, in order to identify specific virtues related to eating meat. Although Fearnley-Whittingstall does not mention virtue ethics specifically in his writing, his book is nevertheless filled with virtue language that virtue ethicists can appropriate into a virtue-based defense of eating meat.

Identifying Virtues for an Omnivorous Way of Life

Although the cardinal virtues give general qualities of character necessary for living a good life, virtues are also context-bound, and for specific questions such as how eating meat may fit into a good life, we need to identify more specific subvirtues that address the question at hand, namely, virtuous consumption of meat. Jean Porter suggests four considerations in the identification of any specific virtue:

> (1) A notion of a particular kind of action that is characteristic 'of the virtue (although not necessarily linked with it in every instance), which will include some idea of the kind of context in which the sort of action would be appropriate; (2) some idea of kinds of actions that are characteristically failures to act well, in the context that provides the setting for the virtue in question; (3) some idea of what it would mean, concretely, for a person to display this virtue through his actions and reactions over a substantial period of time; and finally, (4) some guidelines for distinguishing true from false exemplifications of the virtue in question, guidelines derived from a higher principle that will enable us to say whether in a particular instance this putative virtue is truly being exercised in such a way as to promote the true good of the human person.[11]

Based on these criteria, we can develop a virtue-based approach to the question of meat consumption by examining the example of specific virtuous individuals, in this case, the example set by Fearnley-Whittingstall. We will discuss three specific virtues—responsibility, temperance, and thrift. In each case, we will follow Porter's guidelines, identifying actions constitutive of the virtue, actions that are antithetical to the virtue, how these actions may be manifest over time, and how acts constitutive of the virtue may be distinguished from false manifestations of the virtue.

One virtue identified by Fearnley-Whittingstall is responsibility both in husbandry and in purchasing. Responsible husbandry means "that we embrace, not reject, the moral status of the animals we farm for food. . . . This means among other things, better health, better survival rates, less pain, less stress, more comfort, suitable food and plenty of it."[12] Consumers can practice responsibility by supporting farmers engaged in practices characteristic of this virtue. This means that consumers must research where their meat is coming from, what the animals were fed, how the animals lived and were killed, how their flesh was processed, stored, and shipped: "It's the answers to these questions that tell us whether what we have in front of us is worth taking back to the kitchen. And all too often it's those answers, not the price, that should really make us flinch."[13]

However, if responsibility is a virtue of meat consumption, we must still distinguish true versus false manifestations of this virtue by identifying the end, the *telos,* to which the actions constitutive of this virtue are directed. It is not enough for virtue to simply farm responsibly by avoiding intensive farming practices, nor is it enough for virtue to only buy meat from local farms that practice humane and responsible husbandry. A farmer could engage in humane husbandry because then she may be able to charge more for her meat and bring in a greater profit than if she did not practice humane husbandry. A consumer may buy meat from farms practicing humane husbandry because all her friends buy such meat, and she does not want to be shamed in front of her peers.

Fearnley-Whittingstall says that the end of responsibility, what all the actions constitutive of the virtue of responsibility are directed to, is care for the animals' welfare and recognition that domestic animals raised for meat are still living creatures that need to be cared for, valued, and respected:

> The adjective "happy" is more than a little anthropomorphically loaded. But I don't think it's too much to say that a good extensive livestock system aims to keep its animals at least contented. However, my point is not that the sun always shines as cockerels crow from the gatepost, lambs skip through the meadow, cows called Buttercup mellifluously chew the cud, and pigs romp and root through leafy Arcadian glades. Extensively farmed animals will, from time to time, get cold, muddy, sore, and sick. Occasionally, they will get pushed around and prodded, by the farmer or the vet, and then they may get confused and stressed, for a while. But they will nonetheless spend

almost all of their time—with a bit of luck, day after unmolested day—doing what cows, sheep, pigs, and chickens freely choose to do.[14]

Another virtue Fearnley-Whittingstall identifies is good, or what I will call temperate, meat eating. Temperance is typically used to refer to moderate meat eating, meaning not eating too much (gluttony) or too little (insensibility). Moderation is certainly important in identifying temperance as virtue of meat consumption. However, Fearnley-Whittingstall's virtuous example presents us with a more specific understanding of how moderation in the context of eating meat may be manifested.

Fearnley-Whittingstall points out that temperate meat eating must include eating fat.[15] He notes that although fat gets bad press, the threads of fat running through meat known as "marbling" are a clear indicator that the animal was raised properly. Lean meat comes from animals raised quickly for slaughter that do not have time to develop a stage of maturity in which fat can develop. Marbled meat, on the other hand, comes from animals grown slowly, and generally killed at a proper age and stage of development:

> It is fair to say that a generous layer of external fat, as well as good marbling, occurs in meat that grows naturally, slowly, and predominantly out of doors (the primary function of subcutaneous fat being to insulate the animal against the cold weather). It follows naturally (or unnaturally) enough, that the industrial production of meat, in intensive indoor systems at a speeded-up rate, is well suited to production of lean meat. Certain feeds, and feed additives such as antibiotics, steroids, and hormones, are routinely used in intensive systems, both to speed up the development of muscled (lean meat) and to inhibit the development of fat.[16]

Properly marbled meat not only indicates that an animal was raised correctly, it also makes meat taste better, and makes it more filling, resulting in the need to eat less meat in order to achieve satiation. Fearnley-Whittingstall argues that eating lean meat is not necessarily a way to practice moderation in meat consumption because it takes more lean meat to achieve satiation, and the experience of eating lean meat is less satisfying, leading it to be eaten more quickly rather than savored:

> The critical thing is that many flavor-bearing molecules are soluble in fat but not in water. In addition the flavorful substances incorporated into otherwise dry foods are far more effectively absorbed by the taste buds when combined with or accompanied by fat. It's more or less a straight function of time. Fat effectively slows down the progress of the aromatics over the tongue and across the palate—a sensation you may even be conscious of when you are eating chocolate, for

example—giving us more time to appreciate and enjoy the taste experience.[17]

Temperate—that is, good—meat eating means more than just eating the proper amount of meat from the proper source; it also means deriving the proper pleasure from the experience. It is the job of temperance to regulate this.

Another virtue Fearnley-Whittingstall identifies is thrift. This may come as a surprise to those who are used to the argument for purchasing more organic and humanely raised meat—that it is worth the higher cost. Thrift, as Fearnley-Whittingstall sees it, is just as much about kitchen creativity as it is about economic purchasing. Thrift is more properly understood as "resourcefulness" and "thoroughness," "adjectives that best describe the outlook of the complete meat cook, as he or she assesses the full spectrum of available meat cuts and the endless possibilities they present."[18] Thrift means refusing to waste the animal, as much as is possible. For the home cook, this means using the bones to make stock, and recycling leftover meats in soups and stews and casseroles.

> [Thrift means making] an active commitment to explore those thrifty dishes that have served the "peasants" of the world so well. These are invariably among the most delicious dishes of any food culture—necessity being the mother of invention and all that. Of course, knowledge of such dishes is indispensable to those on a tight budget—it always has been. But these days it is clear that there are two ways of saving money when it comes to buying meat. The modern way is to head straight for the section of the supermarket where low prices reflect low standards and a complete lack of concern for welfare. The old-fashioned approach is to know what to do with certain cuts of meat that are inexpensive even when taken from the best possible carcass. . . . Such thrifty practice has always been in the best interests of good farming, good cooking, and good conscience.[19]

An action not constitutive of thrift is simply buying the cheapest cut of meat available. The way to distinguish true manifestations of thrift from false again resides in the *telos* or purpose to which a person's thrifty actions are directed. The *telos* Fearnley-Whittingstall identifies as critical for truly virtuous thrift is respect for the animals that have died to feed us: "Respect for the farmers who have (assuming you've chosen your meat well) worked tirelessly to keep those animals healthy and contented, so their meat is as good as it can be. And respect for the whole history of animal husbandry and meat gastronomy—endeavors that until recently scorned any practice that was wasteful of the livestock on which they depended."[20]

Thrift also means cooking and eating as much of the animal as possible. Fearnley-Whittingstall dedicates an entire chapter of his book to "offal," known in the United States as variety meats, but meaning essentially the nonmuscle parts of the animals that are frequently discarded as unfit for consumption. This includes organ meat like liver, kidney, spleen, and lights (lungs), as well as tail, trotters (hooves), ear, and tongue.

> Offal offers us a chance to pay our respects, in a full and holistic manner, to the animals we've raised for meat. The nose-to-tail approach to using the animals we kill for food must be a central tenet of the contract of domestication and good husbandry. Waste is not acceptable. It's all or nothing. These are sentiments that have long been readily embraced by cultures more in tune with their environments, and more fully and mutually engaged with their livestock than ours. Sacrifice and libation at the time of slaughter, of an animal's heart, say, or a little of its spilled blood, are not only about thanking your god, they are about thanking an individual animal, by ritually acknowledging the passing of its life.[21] . . .

Conclusion

My goal in writing this article is twofold. First, I want to argue that the decision to eat meat should not be considered a foregone moral choice, simply because it is the norm. In light of all the evidence that an omnivorous way of life is bad for the environment, bad for health, and bad for animals, those who choose to continue eating meat must provide sufficient reasons for their choice. Second, I want to illustrate that one can provide a moral defense of an omnivorous way of life, a task that virtue ethics is particularly suited for, because virtue ethics is not primarily concerned with the intrinsic rightness or wrongness of eating meat, but rather, with how eating meat may be incorporated in a life oriented toward the good.

From the perspective of virtue, both a vegetarian and omnivorous way of life can be oriented toward the good through the cultivation of the appropriate virtues. A vegetarian who cares profoundly for animal welfare but is dismissive of agricultural workers' rights or other aspects of human welfare is not leading a virtuous life. An omnivore who does volunteer social justice work in Latin America but who buys only the cheapest cuts of meat from animals raised intensively on factory farms is also not leading a virtuous life. The virtues I identified in this essay—responsibility, temperance, and thrift (certainly not an exhaustive list)—are not just virtues for an omnivorous way of life, but virtues for consumption in general. As the U.S. bishops wrote in *Renewing the Earth*, human beings are not justified in using any created thing capriciously. Just as Christian charity and justice make a special claim on followers of Christ to care for the poor, so too do these virtues make a claim not just on Christians but on all people of good will to exercise a stewardship that "places upon us responsibility for the well-being of all God's creatures," whether we fulfill that responsibility as a vegetarian or as an omnivore.

Notes

1. Romano Guardini, *The Virtues: On Forms of Moral Life* (Chicago: Henry Regenery Company, 1963), vi.
2. Gail A. Eisnitz, *Slaughterhouse* (Prometheus Books, 1997); Paula Young Lee, *Meat, Modernity, and the Rise of the Slaughterhouse* (UPNE, 2008); Participant Productions and Karl Weber, *Food Inc.: A Participant Guide: How Industrial Food is Making Us Sicker, Fatter, and Poorer—And What You Can Do About It*, 1st ed. (Public Affairs, 2009); Eric Schlosser, *Fast Food Nation: The Dark Side of the All-American Meal*, 1st ed. (Harper Perennial, 2002).
3. "An HSUS Report: The Welfare of Animals in the Meat, Egg, and Dairy Industries," The Humane Society of America, http://www.hsus.org/farm/resources/research/welfare/welfare_overview .html. See also U.S. Department of Agriculture National Agricultural Statistics Service. 2006. Livestock slaughter: 2005 summary. usda. mannlib. cornell. edu I usda/ current/ Live-SlauSu I LiveSlau Su-o3-06-2006_revision. pdf."
4. See Michael Moss, "E. Coli Path Shows Flaws in Beef Inspection," *The New York Times,* October 4, 2009, sec. Health, http:/ /www.nytimes.com/ 2009/10/04/health/ 04meat.html.
5. Ezra Klein, "The Meat of the Problem," *Washington Post,* July 29, 2009. A 2006 UN Report notes that livestock accounts for 18 percent of greenhouse gas emissions across. the globe. The *National Catholic Reporter* has done much to raise awareness among Catholics about the moral implications of their food choices. See Colman McCarthy, "USDA and the Unhealthy Status of Meat," *National Catholic Reporter* 32, issue 27 January 19, 1996); Rich Heffern, "The Ethics of Eating," *National Catholic Reporter* (May 24, 2002); Colman McCarthy, "Think Twice Before Asking 'Where's the Beef?': Amid Mad Cow Disease Alarms We Ignore the Greater Health Dangers Linking Meat to Top Three Killers of Americans," *National Catholic Reporter* 40, issue 23 (April 9, 2004). See also "Catholic Reflections on Food, Farmers, and Farmworkers," United States Catholic Bishops Conference (2003 Statement) http://www.ncrlc .com/Catholic-Reflections-Food.html.
6. Rosalind Hursthouse, *On Virtue Ethics* (Oxford: Oxford University Press, 2002), 2 27.
7. Rosalind Hursthouse, *Ethics, Humans and Other Animals: An Introduction with Readings* (Routledge, 2000).
8. Jean Porter, *Recovery of Virtue* (Presbyterian Publishing Corporation, 1990), 67.
9. See http://www.chickenout.tv I, Steve Hawkes, "Hugh Fearnley-Whittingstall Lobbies Tesco Investors Over Chicken," *The Times,* June 18, 2008; "Five Freedoms," Farm Animal Welfare Council, http://www.fawc.org.uk/freedoms.htm. See also Fearnley-Whittingstall, *The River Cottage Meat Book* (Berkeley, CA: Ten Speed Press, 2004), 54. The five freedoms Fearnley-Whittingstall identifies for domestic animals are (1) freedom from hunger and thirst, (2) freedom from discomfort, (3) freedom from pain, injury, or disease, (4) freedom to perform normal patterns of behavior, and (5) freedom from fear or distress.
10. Fearnley-Whittingstall, *The River Cottage Meat Book,* 17.
11. Porter, *Recovery of Virtue,* 109.
12. Fearnley-Whittingstall, *The River Cottage Meat Book,* 24.
13. Ibid., 28.
14. Ibid., 33.
15. For more on how eating fat from meat is an action constitutive of temperate meat consumption, see Jennifer McLagan, *Fat: An Appreciation of Misunderstood Ingredient, with Recipes* (Ten Speed Press, 2008).
16. Fearnley-Whittingstall, *The River Cottage Meat Book,* 37.
17. Ibid., 36.
18. Ibid., 462.
19. Ibid., 463.
20. Ibid., 462.
21. Ibid., 182.
22. *Renewing the Earth: An Invitation to Reflection and Action on Environment in Light of Catholic Social Teaching,* United States Catholic Conference (November 14, 1991).

Beth K. Haile is an Assistant Professor of Moral Theology at Carroll College. Her research interests include fundamental moral theology, bioethics, moral psychology, and social ethics.

EXPLORING THE ISSUE

Does Morality Require Vegetarianism?

Critical Thinking and Reflection

1. What role should the suffering of animals play in human moral decision making?
2. Is it consistent for a person to be a vegetarian and still permit animals to inflict pain and suffering on each other? Why or why not?
3. Should people be made more aware of the morally objectionable practices of factory farming? If so, how?
4. How might current practices of factory farming be changed to become more humane and still provide meat and animal products in sufficient quantity and at a sufficiently low price?
5. If animals are processed in a human manner, would there still be good reasons to pursue a vegetarian lifestyle? If so, what are they?

Is There Common Ground?

The authors appear to be coming from incompatible theoretical backgrounds, since utilitarianism and virtue ethics are radically different approaches to moral decision making. However both authors acknowledge the role that virtue can play in this moral issue. Haile's entire argument focuses on becoming a moral agent by cultivating virtues. Nobis also argues for the consideration of virtue, since the inclusion of virtues within utilitarianism can be considered a way to ensure choices have the right moral consequences.

The two authors also share a sense of moral horror at the current practices of the meat industry, and both argue that people should not participate in, or support, such abhorrent practices. Nobis argues that the correct response to the meat industry is not to participate in the consumption of meat at all, while Haile argues that the correct response is to support farmers who raise and slaughter animals under humane conditions.

Create Central

www.mhhe.com/createcentral

Additional Resources

Josephine Donovan and Carol Adams, eds., *The Feminist Care Tradition in Animal Ethics* (Columbia University Press, 2007)

Michael A. Fox, "Why We Should Be Vegetarians," *International Journal of Applied Philosophy* (vol. 20, no. 2, 2006)

Steve F. Sapontzis, *Food For Thought: The Debate over Eating Meat* (Prometheus Books, 2004)

Matthew Scully, *Dominion: The Power of Man, the Suffering of Animals, and the Call to Mercy* (St. Martin's Press, 2002)

Internet References . . .

Animal Rights and Vegan Ethics

http://ar.vegnews.org/Animal_Rights.html

The Ethical Omnivore Movement

www.go-eo.org/GoEO/Welcome.html

The Vegetarian Resource Group

www.vrg.org/

Selected, Edited, and with Issue Framing Material by:
Owen M. Smith, *Stephen F. Austin State University*
and
Anne Collins Smith, *Stephen F. Austin State University*

ISSUE

Is It Right to Produce Genetically Modified Food?

YES: Ronald Bailey, from "Dr. Strangelunch—Or: Why We Should Learn to Stop Worrying and Love Genetically Modified Food," *Reason* (January 2001)

NO: Michael W. Fox, from *Killer Foods: When Scientists Manipulate Genes, Better Is Not Always Best* (Lyons Press, 2004)

Learning Outcomes
After reading this issue, you will be able to: • Describe the benefits that could result from the production of genetically modified foods.   • Describe the dangers that could result from the production of genetically modified foods.   • Describe the relationship between biotechnology and economics.   • Formulate your own position on genetically modified food and identify evidence supporting your position.   • Identify the main objections to your position and formulate responses to these objections.

ISSUE SUMMARY

YES: Ronald Bailey is a strong supporter of genetically modified food (GMF). He argues that it is feared by many activists, but there is no strong proof that there are any problems with it. In fact, he suggests that there are great benefits that can be provided by GMFs, especially to the world's poor and to those suffering from natural calamities.

NO: Michael Fox is cautious about the spread of *scientism* and the morally blind push for technological development. This scientism, when combined with an aggressive spirit of enterprise, threatens to upset the balance of nature. We may try to rearrange natural things (including plants and animals) to serve our own purposes, but Fox believes that in this way we end up alienating ourselves from the natural world.

Is it right to produce genetically modified foods (GMFs)? The technology that produces GMFs is a powerful technology that can have effects that are very good and also effects that are very bad. There are two mail sorts of problems here. First, there are the problems that we know about or can reasonably anticipate. Second, there are unanticipated problems that may arise. By way of illustration, consider the idea of environmental impact. We can anticipate certain concerns and make efforts to control them. For example, we may be worried about the cross-pollination of some GMFs with cultivated crops or wild plants. This sort of thing is easily anticipated and maybe controlled or taken into account. On the other hand, the second kind of problem is one that we cannot anticipate. Suppose, for example, that some genetic modification will make an important crop resistant to certain pests. So far, so good. But if the pests don't destroy the genetically

modified plants, they may end up as pests of other plants, plants that were until then relatively safe. In this case, we may have a serious problem on our hands; and it may be too late to do much about it.

Consider an analogous case. There have been problems in the past when a non-native animal was induced into a new environment in order to deal with some problem there. But this non-native species may cause widespread and unanticipated damage. This is exactly what happened with the introduction of European rabbits into Australia. A small group of 12 rabbits were released by an Englishman living in Australia, who thought that he could use them to hunt (as he was used to doing in England) and that in any case 12 rabbits would have no great impact on the land. But these rabbits proliferated at an enormous rate and became pests, eating the very crops that the European settlers were trying to grow in Australia. In addition, the rabbits consumed much of the ground cover and ate the bark around the bases of trees that the settlers tried to plant. The erosion and environmental damage that resulted was huge. Throughout the 1800s, the rabbits continued to spread across Australia. In the early 1900s, a rabbit-proof fence was built, and further fencing was added until the whole fence extended over 2,000 miles. Today, there are hundreds of millions of rabbits in Australia. Estimates of annual damage caused by them in recent times range from $200,000,000 to $600,000,000.

So, a wise choice would be to proceed with caution—perhaps with utmost caution—when it comes to GMF. Supporters of GMF tend to be optimistic, as if the only problems are the kind that we can anticipate. But even if the optimists are correct that these concerns can be addressed, there are still the unanticipated problems. There are really two reasons for proceeding slowly and carefully. One has to do with the unanticipated problems that I have mentioned, but another has to do with people and their having to get used to new ideas—especially when the new ideas have to do with what sort of food they will consume. The problems are connected in this way: if there should arise one of these unanticipated problems, people will be *very* resistant to GMF. Hence, it is in the interest of the optimists themselves to be cautious.

Some critics of GMFs are worried about the powerful connection of capitalism and biological technology. Genetically modified organisms are developed for profit; they are patented. Individuals tend to do what is best for themselves and not necessarily what is best for other people, animals, or the environment. We have already seen how the "family farm" has given way to the "factory farm," in which huge numbers of animals are kept in close quarters, given hormones, and raised and slaughtered as quickly as possible. Some critics worry that the changes made possible by genetic modification would only exacerbate this sort of problem.

In the following readings, we can regard Ronald Bailey as an optimist. He foresees only good results from GMFs. And he is surely correct that there are many good results. But in the next piece, Michael Fox warns us of the dangers of GMFs. These, he would say, are not only of a physical kind, but also spiritual.

YES

Ronald Bailey

Dr. Strangelunch—Or: Why We Should Learn to Stop Worrying and Love Genetically Modified Food

Ten thousand people were killed and 10 to 15 million left homeless when a cyclone slammed into India's eastern coastal state of Orissa in October 1999. In the aftermath, CARE and the Catholic Relief Society distributed a high-nutrition mixture of corn and soy meal provided by the U.S. Agency for International Development to thousands of hungry storm victims. Oddly, this humanitarian act elicited cries of outrage.

"We call on the government of India and the state government of Orissa to immediately withdraw the corn-soya blend from distribution," said Vandana Shiva, director of the New Delhi–based Research Foundation for Science, Technology, and Ecology. "The U.S. has been using the Orissa victims as guinea pigs for GM [genetically modified] products which have been rejected by consumers in the North, especially Europe." Shiva's organization had sent a sample of the food to a lab in the U.S. for testing to see if it contained any of the genetically improved corn and soybean varieties grown by tens of thousands of farmers in the United States. Not surprisingly, it did.

"Vandana Shiva would rather have her people in India starve than eat bioengineered food," says C.S. Prakash, a professor of plant molecular genetics at Tuskegee University in Alabama. Per Pinstrup-Andersen, director general of the International Food Policy Research Institute, observes: "To accuse the U.S. of sending genetically modified food to Orissa in order to use the people there as guinea pigs is not only wrong; it is stupid. Worse than rhetoric, it's false. After all, the U.S. doesn't need to use Indians as guinea pigs, since millions of Americans have been eating genetically modified food for years now with no ill effects."

Shiva not only opposes the food aid but is also against "golden rice," a crop that could prevent blindness in half a million to 3 million poor children a year and alleviate vitamin A deficiency in some 250 million people in the developing world. By inserting three genes, two from daffodils and one from a bacterium, scientists at the Swiss Federal Institute of Technology created a variety of rice that produces the nutrient beta-carotene, the precursor to vitamin A. Agronomists at the International Rice Research Institute in the Philippines plan to crossbreed the variety, called "golden rice" because of the color produced by the beta-carotene, with well-adapted local varieties and distribute the resulting plants to farmers all over the developing world.

Last June, at a Capitol Hill seminar on biotechnology sponsored by the Congressional Hunger Center, Shiva airily dismissed golden rice by claiming that "just in the state of Bengal 150 greens which are rich in vitamin A are eaten and grown by the women." A visibly angry Martina McGloughlin, director of the biotechnology program at the University of California at Davis, said "Dr. Shiva's response reminds me of . . . Marie Antoinette, [who] suggested the peasants eat cake if they didn't have access to bread." Alexander Avery of the Hudson Institute's Center for Global Food Issues noted that nutritionists at UNICEF doubted it was physically possible to get enough vitamin A from the greens Shiva was recommending. Furthermore, it seems unlikely that poor women living in shanties in the heart of Calcutta could grow greens to feed their children.

The apparent willingness of biotechnology's opponents to sacrifice people for their cause disturbs scientists who are trying to help the world's poor. At the annual meeting of the American Association for the Advancement of Science last February, Ismail Serageldin, the director of the Consultative Group on International Agricultural Research, posed a challenge: "I ask opponents of biotechnology, do you want 2 to 3 million children a year to go blind and 1 million to die of vitamin A deficiency, just because you object to the way golden rice was created?"

Vandana Shiva is not alone in her disdain for biotechnology's potential to help the poor. Mae-Wan Ho, a reader in biology at London's Open University who advises another activist group, the Third World Network, also opposes golden rice. And according to a *New York Times* report on a biotechnology meeting held last March by the Organization for Economic Cooperation and Development, Benedikt Haerlin, head of Greenpeace's European anti-biotech campaign, "dismissed the importance of saving African and Asian lives at the risk of spreading a new science that he considered untested."

Shiva, Ho, and Haerlin are leaders in a growing global war against crop biotechnology, sometimes called "green biotech" (to distinguish it from medical biotechnology, known as "red biotech"). Gangs of anti-biotech vandals with cute monikers such as Cropatistas and Seeds of Resistance have ripped up scores of research plots in Europe and the U.S. The so-called Earth Liberation Front burned down a crop biotech lab at Michigan State University on New Year's Eve in 1999, destroying years of work and causing $400,000 in property damage. . . . Anti-biotech lobbying groups have proliferated faster than bacteria in an agar-filled petri dish: In addition to Shiva's organization, the Third World Network, and Greenpeace, they include the Union of Concerned Scientists, the Institute for Agriculture and Trade Policy, the Institute of Science in Society, the Rural Advancement Foundation International, the Ralph Nader–founded Public Citizen, the Council for Responsible Genetics, the Institute for Food and Development Policy, and that venerable fount of biotech misinformation, Jeremy Rifkin's Foundation on Economic Trends. The left hasn't been this energized since the Vietnam War. But if the anti-biotech movement is successful, its victims will include the downtrodden people on whose behalf it claims to speak.

"We're in a war," said an activist at a protesters' gathering during the November 1999 World Trade Organization meeting in Seattle. "We're going to bury this first wave of biotech." He summed up the basic strategy pretty clearly: "The first battle is labeling. The second battle is banning it."

Later that week, during a standing-room-only "biosafety seminar" in the basement of a Seattle Methodist church, the ubiquitous Mae-Wan Ho declared, "This warfare against nature must end once and for all." Michael Fox, a vegetarian "bioethicist" from the Humane Society of the United States, sneered: "We are very clever little simians, aren't we? Manipulating the bases of life and thinking we're little gods." He added, "The only acceptable application of genetic engineering is to develop a genetically engineered form of birth control for our own species." This creepy declaration garnered rapturous applause from the assembled activists.

Despite its unattractive side, the global campaign against green biotech has had notable successes in recent years. Several leading food companies, including Gerber and Frito-Lay, have been cowed into declaring that they will not use genetically improved crops to make their products. Since 1997, the European Union has all but outlawed the growing and importing of biotech crops and food. Last May some 60 countries signed the Biosafety Protocol, which mandates special labels for biotech foods and requires strict notification, documentation, and risk assessment procedures for biotech crops. Activists have launched a "Five-Year Freeze" campaign that calls for a worldwide moratorium on planting genetically enhanced crops. . . .

To decide whether the uproar over green biotech is justified, you need to know a bit about how it works. Biol-

ogists and crop breeders can now select a specific useful gene from one species and splice it into an unrelated species. Previously plant breeders were limited to introducing new genes through the time-consuming and inexact art of crossbreeding species that were fairly close relatives. For each cross, thousands of unwanted genes would be introduced into a crop species. Years of "backcrossing"— breeding each new generation of hybrids with the original commercial variety over several generations—were needed to eliminate these unwanted genes so that only the useful genes and characteristics remained. The new methods are far more precise and efficient. The plants they produce are variously described as "transgenic," "genetically modified," or "genetically engineered."

Plant breeders using biotechnology have accomplished a great deal in only a few years. For example, they have created a class of highly successful insect-resistant crops by incorporating toxin genes from the soil bacterium *Bacillus thuringiensis*. Farmers have sprayed *B.t.* spores on crops as an effective insecticide for decades. Now, thanks to some clever biotechnology, breeders have produced varieties of corn, cotton, and potatoes that make their own insecticide. *B.t.* is toxic largely to destructive caterpillars such as the European corn borer and the cotton bollworm; it is not harmful to birds, fish, mammals, or people.

Another popular class of biotech crops incorporates an herbicide resistance gene, a technology that has been especially useful in soybeans. Farmers can spray herbicide on their fields to kill weeds without harming the crop plants. The most widely used herbicide is Monsanto's Roundup (glyphosate), which toxicologists regard as an environmentally benign chemical that degrades rapidly, days after being applied. Farmers who use "Roundup Ready" crops don't have to plow for weed control, which means there is far less soil erosion.

Biotech is the most rapidly adopted new farming technology in history. The first generation of biotech crops was approved by the EPA, the FDA, and the U.S. Department of Agriculture in 1995, and by 1999 transgenic varieties accounted for 33 percent of corn acreage, 50 percent of soybean acreage, and 55 percent of cotton acreage in the U.S. Worldwide, nearly 90 million acres of biotech crops were planted in 1999. With biotech corn, U.S. farmers have saved an estimated $200 million by avoiding extra cultivation and reducing insecticide spraying. U.S. cotton farmers have saved a similar amount and avoided spraying 2 million pounds of insecticides by switching to biotech varieties. Potato farmers, by one estimate, could avoid spraying nearly 3 million pounds of insecticides by adopting *B.t.* potatoes. Researchers estimate that *B.t.* corn has spared 33 million to 300 million bushels from voracious insects.

One scientific panel after another has concluded that biotech foods are safe to eat, and so has the FDA. Since 1995, tens of millions of Americans have been eating biotech crops. Today it is estimated that 60 percent of the foods on U.S. grocery shelves are produced using ingredients from transgenic crops. In April a National Research Council panel issued a report that emphasized it could not find "any evidence suggesting that foods on the market today are unsafe to eat as a result of genetic modification." *Transgenic Plants and World Agriculture,* a report issued in July that was prepared under the auspices of seven scientific academies in the U.S. and other countries, strongly endorsed crop biotechnology, especially for poor farmers in the developing world. "To date," the report concluded, "over 30 million hectares of transgenic crops have been grown and no human health problems associated specifically with the ingestion of transgenic crops or their products have been identified." Both reports concurred that genetic engineering poses no more risks to human health or to the natural environment than does conventional plant breeding.

As U.C.-Davis biologist Martina McGloughlin remarked at last June's Congressional Hunger Center seminar, the biotech foods "on our plates have been put through more thorough testing than conventional food ever has been subjected to." According to a report issued in April by the House Subcommittee on Basic Research, "No product of conventional plant breeding . . . could meet the data requirements imposed on biotechnology products by U.S. regulatory agencies. . . . Yet, these foods are widely and properly regarded as safe and beneficial by plant developers, regulators, and consumers." The report concluded that biotech crops are "at least as safe [as] and probably safer" than conventionally bred crops. . . .

Activists are also fond of noting that the seed company Pioneer Hi-Bred produced a soybean variety that incorporated a gene—for a protein from Brazil nuts—that causes reactions in people who are allergic to nuts. The activists fail to mention that the soybean never got close to commercial release because Pioneer Hi-Bred checked it for allergenicity as part of its regular safety testing and immediately dropped the variety. The other side of the allergy coin is that biotech can remove allergens that naturally occur in foods such as nuts, potatoes, and tomatoes, making these foods safer.

Even if no hazards from genetically improved crops have been demonstrated, don't consumers have a right to know what they're eating? This seductive appeal to consumer rights has been a very effective public relations gambit for anti-biotech activists. If there's nothing wrong with biotech products, they ask, why don't seed companies, farmers, and food manufacturers agree to label them?

The activists are being more than a bit disingenuous here. Their scare tactics, including the use of ominous words such as *frankenfoods,* have created a climate in which many consumers would interpret labels on biotech products to mean that they were somehow more dangerous or less healthy than old-style foods. Biotech opponents hope labels would drive frightened consumers away from genetically modified foods and thus doom them. Then the activists could sit back and smugly declare that biotech products had failed the market test. . . .

It is interesting to note that several crop varieties popular with organic growers were created through mutations deliberately induced by breeders using radiation or chemicals. This method of modifying plant genomes is obviously a far cruder and more imprecise way of creating new varieties. Radiation and chemical mutagenesis is like using a sledgehammer instead of the scalpel of biotechnology. Incidentally, the FDA doesn't review these crop varieties produced by radiation or chemicals for safety, yet no one has dropped dead from eating them.

Labeling nonbiotech foods as such will not satisfy the activists whose goal is to force farmers, grain companies, and food manufacturers to segregate biotech crops from conventional crops. Such segregation would require a great deal of duplication in infrastructure, including separate grain silos, rail cars, ships, and production lines at factories and mills. The StarLink corn problem is just a small taste of how costly and troublesome segregating conventional from biotech crops would be. Some analysts estimate that segregation would add 10 percent to 30 percent to the prices of food without any increase in safety. Activists are fervently hoping that mandatory crop segregation will also lead to novel legal nightmares: If a soybean shipment is inadvertently "contaminated" with biotech soybeans, who is liable? If biotech corn pollen falls on an organic cornfield, can the organic farmer sue the biotech farmer? Trial lawyers must be salivating over the possibilities.

The activists' "pro-consumer" arguments can be turned back on them. Why should the majority of consumers pay for expensive crop segregation that they don't want? It seems reasonable that if some consumers want to avoid biotech crops, they should pay a premium, including the costs of segregation. . . .

Under the "precautionary principle," regulators do not need to show scientifically that a biotech crop is unsafe before banning it; they need only assert that it has not been proved harmless. Enshrining the precautionary principle into international law is a major victory for biotech opponents. "They want to err on the side of caution not only when the evidence is not conclusive but when no evidence exists that would indicate harm is possible," observes Frances Smith, executive director of Consumer Alert.

Model biosafety legislation proposed by the Third World Network goes even further than the Biosafety Protocol, covering all biotech organisms and requiring authorization "for all activities and for all GMOs [genetically modified organisms] and derived products." Under the model legislation, "the absence of scientific evidence or certainty does not preclude the decision makers from denying approval of the introduction of the GMO or derived products." Worse, under the model regulations "any adverse socio-economic effects must also be considered." If this provision is adopted, it would give traditional producers a veto over innovative competitors, the moral equivalent of letting candlemakers prevent the introduction of electric lighting.

Concerns about competition are one reason European governments have been so quick to oppose crop biotechnology. "EU countries, with their heavily subsidized farming, view foreign agribusinesses as a competitive threat," Frances Smith writes. "With heavy subsidies and price supports, EU farmers see no need to improve productivity." In fact, biotech-boosted European agricultural productivity would be a fiscal disaster for the E.U., since it would increase already astronomical subsidy payments to European farmers.

The global campaign against green biotech received a public relations windfall on May 20, 1999, when *Nature* published a study by Cornell University researcher John Losey that found that Monarch butterfly caterpillars died when force-fed milkweed dusted with pollen from *B.t.* corn. Since then, at every anti-biotech demonstration, the public has been treated to flocks of activist women dressed fetchingly as Monarch butterflies. But when more-realistic field studies were conducted, researchers found that the alleged danger to Monarch caterpillars had been greatly exaggerated. Corn pollen is heavy and doesn't spread very far, and milkweed grows in many places aside from the margins of cornfields. In the wild, Monarch caterpillars apparently know better than to eat corn pollen on milkweed leaves.

Furthermore, *B.t.* crops mean that farmers don't have to indiscriminately spray their fields with insecticides, which kill beneficial as well as harmful insects. In fact, studies show that *B.t.* cornfields harbor higher numbers of beneficial insects such as lacewings and ladybugs than do conventional cornfields. James Cook, a biologist at Washington State University, points out that the population of Monarch butterflies has been increasing in recent years, precisely the time period in which *B.t.* corn has been widely planted. The fact is that pest-resistant crops are harmful mainly to target species—that is, exactly those insects that insist on eating them.

Never mind; we will see Monarchs on parade for a long time to come. Meanwhile, a spooked EPA has changed its rules governing the planting of *B.t.* corn, requiring farmers to plant non-*B.t.* corn near the borders of their fields so that *B.t.* pollen doesn't fall on any milkweed growing there. But even the EPA firmly rejects activist claims about the alleged harms caused by *B.t.* crops. "Prior to registration of the first *B.t.* plant pesticides in 1995," it said in response to a Greenpeace lawsuit, "EPA evaluated studies of potential effects on a wide variety of non-target organisms that might be exposed to the *B.t.* toxin, e.g., birds, fish, honeybees, ladybugs, lacewings, and earthworms. EPA concluded that these species were not harmed."

Another danger highlighted by anti-biotech activists is the possibility that transgenic crops will crossbreed with other plants. At the Congressional Hunger Center seminar, Mae-Wan Ho claimed that "GM-constructs are designed to invade genomes and to overcome natural species barriers."

And that's not all. "Because of their highly mixed origins," she added, "GM-constructs tend to be unstable as well as invasive, and may be more likely to spread by horizontal gene transfer."

"Nonsense," says Tuskegee University biologist C.S. Prakash. "There is no scientific evidence at all for Ho's claims." Prakash points out that plant breeders specifically choose transgenic varieties that are highly stable since they want the genes that they've gone to the trouble and expense of introducing into a crop to stay there and do their work.

Ho also suggests that "GM genetic material" when eaten is far more likely to be taken up by human cells and bacteria than is "natural genetic material." Again, there is no scientific evidence for this claim. All genes from whatever source are made up of the same four DNA bases, and all undergo digestive degradation when eaten. . . .

The environmentalist case against biotech crops includes a lot of innuendo. "After GM sugar beet was harvested," Ho claimed at the Congressional Hunger Center seminar, "the GM genetic material persisted in the soil for at least two years and was taken up by soil bacteria." Recall that the *Bacillus thuringiensis* is a *soil bacterium*—its habitat is the soil. Organic farmers broadcast *B.t.* spores freely over their fields, hitting both target and nontarget species. If organic farms were tested, it's likely that *B.t.* residues would be found there as well; they apparently have not had any ill effects. Even the EPA has conceded, in its response to Greenpeace's lawsuit, that "there are no reports of any detrimental effects on the soil ecosystems from the use of *B.t.* crops."

Given their concerns about the spread of transgenes, you might think biotech opponents would welcome innovations designed to keep them confined. Yet they became apoplectic when Delta Pine Land Co. and the U.S. Department of Agriculture announced the development of the Technology Protection System, a complex of three genes that makes seeds sterile by interfering with the development of plant embryos. TPS also gives biotech developers a way to protect their intellectual property: Since farmers couldn't save seeds for replanting, they would have to buy new seeds each year.

Because high-yielding hybrid seeds don't breed true, corn growers in the U.S. and Western Europe have been buying seed annually for decades. Thus TPS seeds wouldn't represent a big change in the way many American and European farmers do business. If farmers didn't want the advantages offered in the enhanced crops protected by TPS, they would be free to buy seeds without TPS. Similarly, seed companies could offer crops with transgenic traits that would be expressed only in the presence of chemical activators that farmers could choose to buy if they thought they were worth the extra money. Ultimately, the market would decide whether these innovations were valuable.

If anti-biotech activists really are concerned about gene flow, they should welcome such technologies. The pollen from crop plants incorporating TPS would create sterile seeds in any weed that it happened to crossbreed with, so that genes for traits such as herbicide resistance or drought tolerance couldn't be passed on.

This point escapes some biotech opponents. "The possibility that [TPS] may spread to surrounding food crops or to the natural environment is a serious one," writes Vandana Shiva in her recent book *Stolen Harvest*. "The gradual spread of sterility in seeding plants would result in a global catastrophe that could eventually wipe out higher life forms, including humans, from the planet." This dire scenario is not just implausible but biologically impossible: *TPS is a gene technology that causes sterility; that means, by definition, that it can't spread.* . . .

As one tracks the war against green biotech, it becomes ever clearer that its leaders are not primarily concerned about safety. What they really hate is capitalism and globalization. "It is not inevitable that corporations will control our lives and rule the world," writes Shiva in *Stolen Harvest*. In *Genetic Engineering: Dream or Nightmare?* (1999), Ho warns, "Genetic engineering biotechnology is an unprecedented intimate alliance between bad science and big business which will spell the end of humanity as we know it, and the world at large." The first nefarious step, according to Ho, will occur when the "food giants of the North" gain "control of the food supply of the South through exclusive rights to genetically engineered seeds."

Accordingly, anti-biotech activists oppose genetic patents. Greenpeace is running a "No Patents on Life" campaign that appeals to inchoate notions about the sacredness of life. Knowing that no patents means no investment, biotech opponents declare that corporations should not be able to "own" genes, since they are created by nature.

The exact rules for patenting biotechnology are still being worked out by international negotiators and the U.S. Patent and Trademark Office. But without getting into the arcane details, the fact is that discoverers and inventors don't "own" genes. A patent is a license granted for a limited time to encourage inventors and discoverers to disclose publicly their methods and findings. In exchange for disclosure, they get the right to exploit their discoveries for 20 years, after which anyone may use the knowledge and techniques they have produced. Patents aim to encourage an open system of technical knowledge.

"Biopiracy" is another charge that activists level at biotech seed companies. After prospecting for useful genes in indigenous crop varieties from developing countries, says Shiva, companies want to sell seeds incorporating those genes back to poor farmers. Never mind that the useful genes are stuck in inferior crop varieties, which means that poor farmers have no way of optimizing their benefits. Seed companies liberate the useful genes and put them into high-yielding varieties that can boost poor farmers' productivity.

Amusingly, the same woman who inveighs against "biopiracy" proudly claimed at the Congressional Hun-

ger Center seminar that 160 varieties of kidney beans are grown in India. Shiva is obviously unaware that farmers in India are themselves "biopirates." Kidney beans were domesticated by the Aztecs and Incas in the Americas and brought to the Old World via the Spanish explorers. In response to Shiva, C.S. Prakash pointed out that very few of the crops grown in India today are indigenous. "Wheat, peanuts, and apples and everything else—the chiles that the Indians are so proud of," he noted, "came from outside. I say, thank God for the biopirates." Prakash condemned Shiva's efforts to create "a xenophobic type of mentality within our culture" based on the fear that "everybody is stealing all of our genetic material."

If the activists are successful in their war against green biotech, it's the world's poor who will suffer most. The International Food Policy Research Institute estimates that global food production must increase by 40 percent in the next 20 years to meet the goal of a better and more varied diet for a world population of some 8 billion people. As biologist Richard Flavell concluded in a 1999 report to the IFPRI, "It would be unethical to condemn future generations to hunger by refusing to develop and apply a technology that can build on what our forefathers provided and can help produce adequate food for a world with almost 2 billion more people by 2020."

One way biotech crops can help poor farmers grow more food is by controlling parasitic weeds, an enormous problem in tropical countries. Cultivation cannot get rid of them, and farmers must abandon fields infested with them after a few growing seasons. Herbicide-resistant crops, which would make it possible to kill the weeds without damaging the cultivated plants, would be a great boon to such farmers.

By incorporating genes for proteins from viruses and bacteria, crops can be immunized against infectious diseases. The papaya mosaic virus had wiped out papaya farmers in Hawaii, but a new biotech variety of papaya incorporating a protein from the virus is immune to the disease. As a result, Hawaiian papaya orchards are producing again, and the virus-resistant variety is being made available to developing countries. Similarly, scientists at the Donald Danforth Plant Science Center in St. Louis are at work on a cassava variety that is immune to cassava mosaic virus, which killed half of Africa's cassava crop two years ago. . . .

Biotech crops can provide medicine as well as food. Biologists at the Boyce Thompson Institute for Plant Research at Cornell University recently reported success in preliminary tests with biotech potatoes that would immunize people against diseases. One protects against Norwalk virus, which causes diarrhea, and another might protect against the hepatitis B virus which afflicts 2 billion people. Plant-based vaccines would be especially useful for poor countries, which could manufacture and distribute medicines simply by having local farmers grow them. . . .

[O]pponents of crop biotechnology can't stand the fact that it will help developed countries first. New technologies, whether reaping machines in the 19th century or computers today, are always adopted by the rich before they become available to the poor. The fastest way to get a new technology to poor people is to speed up the product cycle so the technology can spread quickly. Slowing it down only means the poor will have to wait longer. If biotech crops catch on in the developed countries, the techniques to make them will become available throughout the world, and more researchers and companies will offer crops that appeal to farmers in developing countries.

Activists like Shiva subscribe to the candlemaker fallacy: If people begin to use electric lights, the candlemakers will go out of business, and they and their families will starve. This is a supremely condescending view of poor people. In order not to exacerbate inequality, Shiva and her allies want to stop technological progress. They romanticize the backbreaking lives that hundreds of millions of people are forced to live as they eke out a meager living off the land.

Per Pinstrup-Andersen of the International Food Policy Research Institute asked participants in the Congressional Hunger Center seminar to think about biotechnology from the perspective of people in developing countries: "We need to talk about the low-income farmer in West Africa who, on half an acre, maybe an acre of land, is trying to feed her five children in the face of recurrent droughts, recurrent insect attacks, recurrent plant diseases. For her, losing a crop may mean losing a child. Now, how can we sit here debating whether she should have access to a drought-tolerant crop variety? None of us at this table or in this room [has] the ethical right to force a particular technology upon anybody, but neither do we have the ethical right to block access to it. The poor farmer in West Africa doesn't have any time for philosophical arguments as to whether it should be organic farming or fertilizers or GM food. She is trying to feed her children. Let's help her by giving her access to all of the options. Let's make the choices available to the people who have to take the consequences."

Ronald Bailey is science editor of *Reason* magazine. He has published articles in *The Washington Post, The Wall Street Journal, Commentary,* and *Forbes*. He has given lectures at many institutions, including Harvard University, Rutgers University, the Cato Institute, and the American Enterprise Institute.

Michael W. Fox

 **NO**

Killer Foods: When Scientists Manipulate Genes, Better Is Not Always Best

Scientific and Bioethical Issues in Genetic-Engineering Biotechnology

> Every creature has its own reason to be. All its parts have a direct effect on one another, a relationship to one another, thereby constantly renewing the circle of life.

—Johann Wolfgang von Goethe

Through genetic-engineering technology, we now have the power to profoundly alter all life forms and the very nature of nature—the natural world, or earth's creation. What are the short- and long-term consequences for humanity, animals, and nature, and what are the ethical principles and boundaries? What risks are justified by what benefits?

This new technology is complex, with many risks, costs, and benefits that need careful consideration because it could permanently and irreversibly alter the biology of life forms, the ecology, and natural evolution.

Through various techniques, the genetic composition of animals, plants, and microorganisms can be altered in ways radically different from those achieved by traditional selective breeding. Genes can be deleted, duplicated, and switched among species. Animal and human genes have been incorporated or "spliced" into the genetic structure or germ plasm of other animals, plants, bacteria, and other microorganisms. Human genes are now present in the genetic makeup of some mice, sheep, pigs, cattle, fish, and other animals.

The creation of transgenic plants, animals, and microorganisms, along with a host of other developments in genetice-ngineering biotechnology, are touted as progressive, if not necessary, and as promising great benefits to society (and investors). Although I have found no coherent argument based on reason, science, or ethics to support any of these claims unconditionally, the biotechnology life-science industry and its supporters, just like the supporters of factory farming and vivisection, give enthusiastic and unconditional endorsement to new developments in biogenetic manipulation and to the industrialization and patent protection of its processes and products. The hyperbole employed on behalf of such

new developments, coupled with a highly competitive and volatile world market, is driven by risk-taking venture capitalists whose cavalier attitude toward such significant risks as socioeconomic inequity, ecological damage, and animal suffering is neither progressive nor visionary. Unfortunately, this attitude is understandably often shared and rarely challenged by bioengineering scientists and academics in their employ, and by politicians and policy makers, who are generally scientifically illiterate.

This is not a good foundation for any new technology, least of all for such a profound and complex one as bioengineering. It is incumbent upon all who do not feel so sanguine about the directions this new technology is taking to challenge its assumptions and presumptions.[1] The doublethink and newspeak logic* of the biotechnocracy evidences some disturbing warning signs, notably of historical amnesia, ecological and biological illiteracy, ethical and moral dyslexia, blind faith, and ideological rigidity.

An international bioethics council within the United Nations would be a beginning to help ensure that this technology is applied with the minimum of harm to further the good of society and the integrity and future of the planetary biosphere. Insofar as its applicability to organic agriculture, biogenetic engineering is, from a philosophical perspective, anathema. It is mechanistic, deterministic, and reductionistic, while organic agriculture is seen as emulating nature—i.e., ecologistic, dynamically indeterminate, holistic, and regenerative. There is also an inimical difference in attitude that separates these two worldviews and in the kinds of medicine, industry, and market economy they aspire to. It has to do with reverential respect for the sanctity and intrinsic value of life, which is more evident on a well-operated (and well-loved) organic farm than in a biotech laboratory or on an industrial farm.

The ideal of value-free objectivity in the method of scientific investigation provides no ethical basis for determining the risks, costs, and benefits in the technology transfer of biotechnical discoveries from the laboratory setting to the real world. A technocratic society runs the risk of serious error in believing that the "truth" of the scientific method is an ethically objective yardstick. This belief system of *scientism*, which is like a religion in the late twentieth century, accounts for the rigid "science-based"

*E.g.: *Knowledge is Power and Science is Truth.* From *1984* by George Orwell.

criteria and policies that corporations and governments—the entwined limbs of the technocracy—so adamantly adhere to. Yet this yardstick is as linear as it is simplistic. A broader bioethical framework is urgently needed in order for society to transcend technological enchantment, so that the fruits of scientific research may be realized for the benefit of the entire life community of the planet. . . .

Two contexts of particular interest to me are agriculture and the use of animals for biomedical research and biopharmaceutical industrial purposes. I am especially concerned about applications of genetic-engineering biotechnology in agriculture, because it is being applied primarily to maintain a dysfunctional system. We have an animal- rather than a plant-based agriculture in the industrial world, which causes much animal suffering and isn't good for the environment, for consumers, or for the social economy of rural communities. And it is now well documented that conventional agricultural practices are ecologically unsound, inhumane, and in the long term unsustainable, even with ever more costly corrective inputs. Some of these are being developed and misapplied by agricultural biotechnologists, who endeavor to maintain and expand globally a bioindustrialized food and drug industry that must be opposed by all because it fails to meet any of the following bioethical criteria of acceptability: that it be humane, ecologically sound, socially just, equitable, and sustainable. Rather, it is a major threat to biodiversity and to the social economies of many more sustainable farming communities.

Now, via GATT, the World Trade Organization, and Codex Alimentarius, the life-science industry, with its new varieties of patented seeds and other bioengineered products and processes, is moving rapidly to a global agricultural and market monopoly.

With regard to the patenting of animals, plants, and other life forms, I believe that it is demeaning to refer to them as "intellectual property" and that there are unresolved questions of ethics and equity over the patenting of life.

The spirit of enterprise and state of mind behind genetic engineering evidences an ethical blindness to the natural integrity, purity, and sanctity of being. Otherwise, how would we ever consider inserting our own and other alien genes into other species, drastically altering their nature and future to make them more useful to us rather than fulfilling their biologically ordained ecological, evolutionary, and spiritual purposes?

The domestication of plants and animals and the transformation of their habitats and ecosystems to serve human ends have had profound consequences on their nature and on the entire natural world. But do thousands of years of domestication and ecosystem alteration provide a historically valid and ethically acceptable precedent for even more profoundly altering the intrinsic nature of other living beings through genetic engineering?

We must ask: Is it necessary? Who are the primary beneficiaries? What are the direct and indirect costs and risks? Are there safer, less invasive and enduring alternatives? Does a cultural history of exploiting life justify its continuation and intensification through genetic-engineering biotechnology?

"Hard" and "Soft" Paths

There are two basic paths that this new technology can take, and I have designated them as "hard" and "soft." The hard path results in permanent physical changes that may be transmissible to subsequent generations. These changes in animals' physiology or anatomy may result in their suffering. For purely ethical, humanitarian reasons, I am opposed to all hard-path applications of genetic-engineering biotechnology of which there is no demonstrable benefit to the animals themselves.

Where such benefits can be demonstrated, as in efforts to conserve endangered species and to prevent or treat various animal diseases of genetic origin, and there are no alternative strategies to achieve the same ends, then I would accept on a case-by-case basis some hard-path applications. But those applications that design animals for purely utilitarian ends should be questioned and opposed in the absence of demonstrable animal benefit.*

Likewise, any nontherapeutic product of genetic-engineering biotechnology, such as recombinant (synthetic) bovine growth hormone (rBGH), that is used to increase animals' utility and can result in animal sickness and suffering, or increase the risk thereof, is not ethically acceptable.

The creation of transgenic plants that are resistant to herbicides and virus infections, or that produce their own insecticides, belong in the hard-path category. They do not accord with accepted standards and principles of organic and sustainable agriculture and are a potential threat to wildlife and nonharmful insects, microorganisms, and biodiversity.

Soft-path developments with this technology include the creation of new-generation vaccines, veterinary pharmaceuticals and diagnostic tests, and genetic screening to identify defective genes and those that convey disease resistance and other beneficial traits. The most promising of these soft-path developments that I would endorse are immunocontraceptives, new-generation contraceptive implants for humans and other mammals.

Soft-path genetically engineered products are acceptable, provided they are safe and effective without side-effects that could cause animal suffering; provided they cannot be transmitted to or harm nontarget species (as with modified live virus vaccines); and provided they are

---

*Utilitarian ends such as to increase appetite, growth, muscle mass, leanness, fertility, or milk or egg production or to deliberately create developmental abnormalities and genetic disorders.

not used to help prevent diseases in animals kept under stressful, inhumane conditions (as on factory farms), rather than changing the conditions that contribute to increased susceptibility to disease. A full socioeconomic and environmental impact assessment is needed prior to approving these soft-path products for animal use. For example, a new vaccine for cattle to combat trypanoso-miasis (to which wild ruminants are immune) could result in an unacceptable loss of biodiversity and an ecologically harmful expansion of livestock numbers. . . .

Genetic Determinism

The broad range of potentially beneficial applications of genetic-engineering biotechnology in agriculture and in veterinary and human medicine are being overshadowed and undermined by an overarching narrowmindedness. This is the reductionist view that since there is a genetic basis to disease, then genetic engineering is the answer to preventing and treating various human, crop, and farm-animal health problems. And that along the way we may even discover ways to genetically engineer (and patent) life forms to enhance their usefulness and "improve" their nature, be it the stature and intelligence of our own species, the growth rates of chickens and pigs, or the herbicide and pest resistance of corn and beans. This simplistic view of genetic determinism is a potentially harmful one because even though it claims to be scientific and objective, i.e., value free, it is extremely subjective and biased since it puts so much value (and faith) in the genetic approach to improving the human condition and the disease resistance and productivity of crops and farm animals.[2]

A more interdisciplinary and holistic approach to human, animal, and crop health and disease prevention is urgently needed. Seeking purely genetic solutions is too narrow and reductionistic, and because of the uncertainty principle inherent in the genotype-environment interface, genetic determinism is unlikely to bring the benefits that its proponents and investors hope and believe are possible.

In its unsubstantiated promises to feed the hungry world, and its promises of great profits for investors, genetic-engineering technology drains human resources from funding more sustainable, eco-friendly, and socially just ways of producing food. It likewise impedes the medical sciences from breaking free of a reductionistic and mechanistic paradigm of human health that blames either nature or our genes for most of our ills. Once people blamed the gods, but as Hippocrates advised, "Physician, do no harm." Conventional medicine has yet to realize this wisdom and put it into practice.

Had the dominant Western culture based its foundation on the worldview of Pythagoras or Plato, rather than that of Aristotle, with his hierarchical, linear thinking, and not on interpreting the book of Genesis as giving man unconditional dominion over God's creation, then our powers over the atoms of matter and the genes of life would probably be applied to very different ends: whole-ness and healing, rather than commodification, monopoly, and selfish exploitation.

The original meaning of *dominion* in the book of Genesis does not rest in the Latin *domino,* to rule over, but in the root Hebrew verb *yorade. Yorade* means to come down to, to have humility, compassion, and communion with all of God's creation. It is an injunction of reverential care, of humane stewardship. Hence, genetic engineering is antithetical to Judeo-Christian tradition and ethics. It also violates the precept of Islam, where it is regarded as a sin to willfully interfere with God's creation, and would be considered a blasphemy of hubris to engage in creating transgenic life forms and then to go and patent them.

Genetic engineering is anathema to Buddhists, Hindus, and Jains, since it is a direct violation of the doctrine of *ahimsa,* of noninterference and nonharming. It is also a fundamental biological interference with the earth's creative process of natural unfoldment and thus a disruption in the spiritual process of incarnation.

One would think that an enlightened biotechnology industry would make every effort to protect the remaining integrity and biodiversity of genetic resources of the first creation—the last of the wild. Future generations, with a more sophisticated understanding of genetic engineering, will need wild places as a source of uncontaminated genetic resources. This "biobank" must be protected now and not ransacked by the industries of timber, mining, real estate, and other business enterprises, and by the millions of poor people who are malnourished and either landless or without sustainable agriculture or way of life. I have seen them in India and Africa leaving an imprint similar to that left by the clear-cutting of old-growth forests and totally obliterated prairies that the U.S. government still permits. To this destruction by the rural poor—especially from grazing too many livestock, plowing marginal land that erodes easily, and killing trees for firewood—we must add industrial and agrochemical pollution in both the "first" and "third" worlds.

An important step to protect the biobank is to eliminate all possibilities of genetic pollution from transgenic crops, bacteria, insects, oysters and other mollusks, shrimp, and other genetically engineered seafoods, which will be the first foods of animal origin on the market.[3] The second step must be to label all foods to indicate whether any product or ingredient has been genetically engineered. To have this information is a consumer's right, on religious and ethical grounds, since many, regardless of assurances as to food quality and safety, would prefer not to unknowingly purchase genetically modified foods. The public has a right to be informed and a right to be able to choose natural foods if they prefer, especially since genetically altered foods violate many people's religious principles.

The third step entails international cooperation on the scale of a United Nations environmental paramilitary police force to help countries protect their wildlife preserves and biodiversity, both aquatic and terrestrial, from further human encroachment, wholesale exploitation, and genetic piracy.

There is no way to collect all potentially useful life forms and store them in culture media, or in seed, sperm, embryo, and cell banks. Many seeds lose their vitality when stored and need to be frequently germinated and harvested, genetic changes due to local environmental influences notwithstanding. They must be protected *in situ* and *in toto*.

The late Professor René Dubos, a renowned biologist from Rockefeller University, said, "An ethical attitude to the scientific study of nature readily leads to a theology of the earth." His concerns, expressed in 1972 in his book *A God Within*, are extremely relevant today with the advent of genetic engineering.[4] He cautioned, "A relationship to the earth based only on its use for economic enrichment is bound to result not only in its degradation but also in the devaluation of human life. This is a perversion which, if not corrected, will become a fatal disease of technological societies." Without an "ethical attitude," beginning with a reverential respect for all life and based on internationally accepted bioethical principles and values, . . . this disease is very likely to be fatal to the dominant culture.

The ethics of preserving the earth's bio-integrity must serve to direct and constrain the emerging biotechnocracy. The biotechnology industry must adopt these ethics; otherwise, the costs and risks to future generations will far outweigh the short-term profits of the present.

Obedience to natural law, which is based on the bioethics of sound science and moral philosophy, must be absolute, like compassion, or else it is not at all. Through science, reason, and reverence, we learn the wisdom of obedience. Industry and commerce must conform to natural law and, like human society, do nothing to jeopardize natural biodiversity, bio-integrity, or the future of earth's creation. The first task of science and of biotechnology is to begin the healing of humanity, which is biologically, economically, and spiritually dependent on the protection and restoration of what is left of the natural world: first creation first!

The application of bioethics, which is the foundation of natural law, to establishing the necessary limits and boundaries of new technologies like genetic engineering is long overdue. Every nation-state needs to have a bioethics council that would function to maximize the benefits and minimize the risks and costs of all new technologies and related commercial activities, and to ensure international harmonization of their policies and guidelines with all countries via the United Nations Council on Sustainable Development.

Beyond Genetic Determinism and Reductionism

Genes "intelligently" organize structural proteins into myriad environmentally co-evolved, living forms. These life forms are variously self-healing, self-replicating, even marginally self-conscious to varying degrees; and they form mutually enhancing or symbiotic communities.

Collectively, for example, they help create and maintain the soil and the atmosphere that sustains the body-earth and life community; much like our digestive, circulatory, and respiratory systems are cellular communities that sustain the body-human. We find phenomenological parallels between the ecological roles of a living forest or a watershed of streams and swamps, and the functions of our own lungs, circulatory system, and kidneys.

In order to know, therefore, *how* genes, organs, and forests function, we must understand their purpose within the larger functional systems in which they participate. Therefore, we must seek to understand the *contexts* in which genes operate, their history (or evolution and development), and their consequences. Such knowledge of temporal and spatial relationships within the intersecting biofields of organisms and their environments is lacking in the reductionistic paradigm of conventional scientific inquiry, and in conventional medical practice, which has been so reticent to recognize the myriad connections between healthy forests and a healthy people. Hence, most of our agricultural, medical, and technological inventions and interventions have caused more harm than good.[5]

The direction being taken by the life-science industrial biotechnocracy today, especially its investment in creating and patenting transgenic life forms that have been engineered to serve narrow human ends, is cause for concern, as the science base is unsound and there is no ethical or ecological framework. . . .

It is unlikely that genetically engineered crops will ever help compensate for nutrient-deficient soils, polluted water, or a contaminated food chain. Using biotechnology to make farm animals more productive and efficient in the context of intensive industrial agriculture will only extend the animals' suffering and prolong the adverse environmental, economic, and consumer health consequences of this kind of agriculture.

Genetic-engineering reductionists might find it advantageous to further reduce life conceptually to its next level—primordial energy, vital force, or chi—and then reflect upon the possibility that the final frontier of materialistic and mechanistic science, molecular genetics, is a grand illusion, a mirage created by a defective worldview and a misconception of human purpose and significance. The antidote is a paradigm shift that broadens our understanding of life by fostering a sense of reverence and awe and a feeling for the spirit or essence of life that is omnipresent in all matter and manifest in all sentient beings.

Ecological and Social Concerns

In relation to ecological concerns, I would concur with Mario Giampietro that:

> Current research on agricultural applications of genetic engineering seems to be heading exactly

in the same direction as the green revolution. The main goal is to provide yet another short-term remedy to sustain, if not increase, the scale of human activity. . . . Genetic engineering aimed only at increasing economic return and technological efficiency is likely to further lower the compatibility of human activity and natural ecosystem processes. . . . Before introducing a massive flow of new transgenic organisms into the biosphere, a better understanding of the endangered equilibrium of the biosphere should be achieved.[6]

Philosopher, scientist, and activist Vandana Shiva eloquently expresses my concerns over the harmful consequences of this new technology and the need for public input to minimize potential harm:

> My major concern these days is with the protection of cultural and biological diversity. I am preoccupied with the ecological and social impacts of globalization of the economy through free trade on the one hand and the colonization of life through genetic engineering and patents on life forms on the other hand. My sense is that unless we can put limits and boundaries on commercial activity and on new technologies, the violence against nature and against people will become uncontrollable. The question I constantly ask myself is, What are the creative catalytic linkages that strengthen community and enable communities of people to exercise social and ecological control of economic and technological processes?[7]

One of the major risks of genetic-engineering biotechnology has a conceptual basis that Craig Holdrege thoroughly dissects in his book *Genetics and the Manipulation of Life*.[8] It stems from scientific reductionism, objectivism, and the mechanomorphizing and reification of genetic and developmental processes and shows no concern and responsibility for effects on the organism and the environment. The belief in genetic determinism is as dangerous ethically as it is flawed scientifically because it is based on the central dogma that genes alone determine how an organism develops and functions.[9] The antidote that Holdrege offers is in seeking an understanding of relationships via contextual thinking, based in part on regarding heredity as potential or plasticity complemented by heredity as limitation or specificity. *Genetics and the Manipulation of Life* is an important book for all students of the biological sciences and for those proponents and critics of biotechnology in particular.

We must be mindful of the fact that nothing that exists originated independently. Therefore, all existences are ultimately interconnected, co-evolved, and interdependent. Genes are not the sole or even the primary controllers and regulators of life processes. It is a product of hubris and reductionism that in isolating and manipulating DNA, we believe we can gain control over life. If we do not act quickly to address all the factors that are leading

to the death of nature, then the virtual reality that the global life-science industrial biotechnocracy is fabricating will collapse. We have neither the wisdom nor the resources to develop a viable analog of the earth's atmosphere, or of an old-growth forest, a mountain stream, or a coral reef. . . .

How then can we expect unnatural, genetically engineered life forms to do any better in the virtual world of global industrialization, even when we too are engineered to withstand the harmful, somatic effects of chemicals, pathogens, and radiation?

Some Bioethical Concerns and Solutions

I am deeply concerned by what I see as a lack of vision in the agricultural biotechnology. industry, which is limiting its benefits to humanity and its potential for profitability and sustainability. The cavalier attitude of corporations, governments, and much of academia toward the release and commercialization of transgenic crops is especially troubling. A related concern is over the fact that agricultural biotechnology is focused primarily on major commodity crops and not linked in any significant way with ecologically sound and sustainable crop and livestock husbandry. It therefore cannot play any significant role in helping relieve world hunger or, especially, in implementing appropriate practices and inputs to restore agricultural and rangelands now sorely degraded worldwide.

Lester Brown writes in *State of the World 1994* that University of Minnesota agricultural economist Vernon Ruttan summarized the feeling of a forum of the world's leading agricultural scientists when he said, "Advances in conventional technology will remain the primary source of growth in crop and animal production over the next quarter century." Biotechnology should not be seen as a panacea, or as a substitute for conventional technologies, the most basic of which are good farming practices in accordance with the land ethic and the principles of humane sustainable agriculture. My opposition to conventional agricultural biotechnology is based on its evident band-aid and high-input roles in conventional, nonsustainable agriculture. As such, it represents a major obstacle to the research, development, and adoption of more sustainable, ecologically sound, and in the long-term more profitable farming practices. . . .

The conservative Hastings Center has published a report that details the complexity of bioethics, especially the creation of genetically engineered animals.[10] This report emphasizes the difficulties of developing a "grand monistic scheme" that "establishes a hierarchy of values and obligations under the hegemony of one ultimate value." Such an approach to dealing with contemporary ethical concerns is dismissed by the authors because, while it "may serve the peace of the soul by reducing internal moral conflict," it would, they believe, work only in relatively small and homogeneous communities. It "invariably is bought at the price of the variety and richness of human experience and significant cultural activity. In this sense it impoverishes the human soul."

I would argue to the contrary. There are moral absolutes such as reverence for life, compassion, and *ahimsa* (nonharmfulness) that can provide both a goal and a common ground for a reasoned and scientific approach to resolving ethical issues. These absolutes are the cornerstones of a monistic hierarchy of human values that could effectively incorporate the plurality of interests of various segments of society and of different cultures. . . .

References

1. *Cancer Weekly Plus,* via News Edge Corp., April 8, 1998.
2. C. McKee et al., "Production of biologically active salmon calcitonin in the milk of transgenic rabbits," *Nature Biotechnology* 16 (1998): 647–49.
3. P. B. Thompson, *Food Biotechnology in Ethical Perspective,* London, England: Chapman Hall, 1997.
4. R. Goldburg, "Something Fishy," *Gene Exchange* (Union of Concerned Scientists), Summer 1998, p. 6.
5. Genetic engineering news email: rwoifson@concentric.net (November 14, 1998).
6. *Eurobarometer Survey,* London, 46.1.
7. See: M. W. Fox, *Eating with Conscience: The Bioethics of Food,* Troutdale, OR: NewSage Press, 1997.
8. V. Shiva, *Biopiracy: The Plunder of Nature and Knowledge,* Boston, MA: South End Press, 1997.
9. *New Scientist,* February 14, 1998, pp. 14–15.
10. S. Nec and R. May, "Extinction and the loss of evolutionary history," *Science* 278 (1997): 692–94.

Michael W. Fox is a well-known veterinarian, the author of over 40 adult and children's books about animal care, animal behavior, and issues in bioethics. He is a long-time activist involved in issues such as the ethical treatment of animals and the protection of the environment.

EXPLORING THE ISSUE

Is It Right to Produce Genetically Modified Food?

Critical Thinking and Reflection

1. How should competing interests related to genetically modified food, such as protecting the environment and providing resources for the poor, be balanced?
2. Are there any possible alternative approaches to solve diseases that afflict food crops, farm animals, and human beings other than genetic modification? What moral problems might arise with these alternative solutions?
3. How are genetically modified organisms similar to and different from those produced naturally? How are they similar to and different from those produced by breeding programs? Do these similarities and differences have any moral relevance? Explain your answer.

Is There Common Ground?

At first sight this dispute might seem hopeless. Ronald Bailey can hardly find a problem with GMF and Michael Fox can hardly find anything good about it. But this conclusion is too strong. Bailey is right that GMFs are widely used and there haven't been the kinds of dire problems that some critics have predicted. In fact, some of the objections of the critics have been shown by Bailey to be based on groundless misunderstandings.

Fox, for all his criticism of GMF, is dismayed that what he calls a "lack of vision" limits the benefits that are possible through genetic modification. We could benefit from genetic modification of living things if, for example, this modification were focused on restoring damaged ecologies, bringing back degraded rangelands, etc. But instead, because of what Fox describes as the "cavalier attitude of corporations, governments, and much of academia," biotechnology is focused on major commodity crops. If the genetic modification of plants leads only to more crowded factory farming conditions, then we are going in the wrong direction. What we really need, in his view, is not a technological fix at all, but a change in attitude.

Create Central

www.mhhe.com/createcentral

Additional Resources

Paul Lurquin, High Tech Harvest: Understanding Genetically Modified Food Plants (Basic Books, 2004)

Michael Ruse and David Castle, eds., Genetically Modified Foods (Prometheus, 2002)

Lisa H. Weasel, Food Fray: Inside the Controversy over Genetically Modified Food (AMACOM, 2009)

Internet References . . .

Genetically Modified Foods: Harmful or Helpful?

www.csa.com/discoveryguides/gmfood/overview.php

Pew Initiative on Food and Biotechnology

www.pewhealth.org/projects/pew-initiative-on-food-and-biotechnology-85899367237

World Health Organization: 20 Questions on Genetically Modified Foods

www.who.int/foodsafety/publications/biotech/20questions/en/

Selected, Edited, and with Issue Framing Material by:
Owen M. Smith, *Stephen F. Austin State University*
and
Anne Collins Smith, *Stephen F. Austin State University*

ISSUE

Are We Morally Obligated to Conserve Resources for Future Generations?

YES: **Ben Dixon**, from "Sustainability and Future Generations," *The Monist* (2014)

NO: **Martin Golding**, from "Limited Obligations to Future Generations," in *Environmental Ethics: Readings in Theory and Application*, Wadsworth (2001)

Learning Outcomes

After reading this issue, you will be able to:

- Describe the basic principles of sustainable development.
- Define the expression "moral community" and explain how the members of a moral community are obligated to one another.
- Explain how the Golden Rule may require us to participate in sustainable development.
- Formulate your own position on our moral obligations to future generations and identify evidence supporting your position.
- Identify the main objections to your position and formulate responses to these objections.

ISSUE SUMMARY

YES: Ben Dixon describes the goals of sustainable development and argues that we are morally obligated to work toward these goals on behalf of future generations by a modified version of the Golden Rule.

NO: Martin Golding argues that obligations to others who are outside our immediate moral community would have to rest on a shared understanding of what constitutes the good. Since we cannot know how future generations will characterize the good, we cannot have obligations toward them.

You may wonder, why is there even a debate about sustainability? Is there any doubt that environmentally responsible behavior is moral? Will any author actually promote the reckless pollution of the environment with toxic waste or the unnecessary destruction of ecologically sensitive areas? Actually, as a moral issue, sustainability has a much broader focus than environmental protection, and even among those who agree about reasonable protections for the environment, sustainability is a complex and disputed topic.

Sustainability, as described by the 2005 World Summit on Social Development, rests on three pillars: environmental protection, social development, and economic development. The inclusion of these latter two elements is a clear indication that sustainability is not simply an environmental movement, but a movement that seeks to accommodate the needs of both developed and developing nations. The goal of sustainable development, however, is the development of policies that will foster the accommodation of these needs not only for the present generation or the next generation, but for all succeeding generations. Thus, the *Brundtland Report*, issued in 1987 by the United Nations World Commission on Environment and Development, defines "sustainable development" as "development that meets the needs of the present without compromising the ability of future generations to meet their own needs." The rationale for the implementation of strategies for sustainable development is the emergence of a peaceful human society free from the threat of resource depletion, and therefore free from the military conflicts and human suffering such depletion would cause.

The search for practical methods of sustainable development is already underway. Experts from a variety of fields are already investigating ways to sustain social and economic development while conserving resources or using renewable resources, including the refinement of alternative fuel sources and the creation of genetically engineered crops.

The theoretical foundation of sustainable development, however, is still quite contested. The extent to which political concepts should form part of the sustainability movement is still under debate, with groups such as the Earth Charter Initiative arguing that the concept of sustainability should be expanded to include the establishment of universal human rights and the elimination of military conflict. Moreover, the precise ethical justification for policies of sustainable development is still unclear. The proponents of sustainability insist that appropriate strategies for social and economic development must be implemented now, with the current generation bearing the costs and sacrifices associated with these strategies. Yet, the beneficial outcomes of these strategies will not be realized until far in the future, if they are even realized at all. Why would we expend the effort and endure the suffering associated with these strategies in order to achieve a result that will not directly benefit us?

The moral dispute about sustainability may thus be framed in terms of the extent to which we (the members of the current generation) are morally obligated to assist others (the members of future generations) when this assistance involves not merely the risk of harm, but the actual imposition of harm. Conceived in this way, the dispute about sustainability is one facet of a larger dispute between two approaches to ethics: egoism and altruism.

A central issue in ethics is the extent to which one person should be concerned with the welfare of other people. Based on their approach to this issue, ethical theories may be divided into two groups:

- Egoistic theories, whose name derives from the Latin term "ego," meaning "I," assert that when I make a moral decision, I should consider only the effects of this decision for my own welfare;

- Altruistic theories, whose name derives from the Latin term "alter," meaning "another," assert that when I make a moral decision, I should give equal consideration to the welfare of everyone affected by this decision.

Since I can directly experience only the benefits and harms my decision causes me, altruism requires me to perform two difficult tasks: I must exercise empathy by identifying the pleasures and pains experienced by other people and I must exercise dispassion by refusing to give my own experiences precedence over the experiences of other people.

Within altruistic ethical theories, the importance of impartiality in moral decision-making is often expressed in terms of a principle known as the Golden Rule. This principle, which appears in both a positive form ("Treat others as you yourself would like to be treated") and a negative form ("Do not treat others in ways that you yourself would not like to be treated"), can be found in sources as diverse as the Analects of Confucius and the Gospel of Matthew.

Ben Dixon argues that our participation in sustainability can be justified by a form of the Golden Rule. When we ordinarily think of the Golden Rule, we apply it to those whose actions are actually capable of having a direct impact on us. Although future generations are not capable of directly affecting us by their actions, Dixon argues for the development of a version of the Golden Rule that still supports the requirement that we consider the impact of our decisions on the welfare of future generations as well as on the welfare of our own.

Martin Golding, on the other hand, argues that our obligations to future generations are limited, and the more distant those generations are from the present, the less we should consider their welfare. His argument rests in part on the recognition that we do not currently know what the needs and wants of future generations will be, and so it is difficult for us to take their welfare into consideration when we make moral decisions in the present.

Indeed, if our attempts to protect their welfare are misguided, we may end up harming the very people whom we wish to benefit. Thus, while a case may be made that sustainable development is not merely desirable, but morally obligatory, this case cannot be based on altruistic considerations for the welfare of future generations.

YES

Ben Dixon

Sustainability and Future Generations

Introduction

Sustainable development or "sustainability" is ethically required because it constitutes fair treatment for those in need of economic development while treating fairly the morally important needs of future generations. In arguing for this conclusion, I'll first discuss, briefly, the idea of fairness. Second, I will argue how sustainable development is in fact rooted in a reasonable idea of fairness. Next, I make a case for how the golden rule—"do to others as you want others to do to you"[1]—can be modified to justify and to guide sustainable thinking and behavior toward future generations. In essence, the golden rule can be "greened" to provide what I am calling "Sustainability's Golden Rule" (cf. Dixon 2012, pp. 37–44). Finally, I will illustrate Sustainability's Golden Rule by applying it to the issue of climate change.

Fairness in Ethical Thinking

The idea of fairness is central to ethics, which is the philosophical study of how we should behave. When determining reasonable behavior, fairness is integral because if there is no relevant moral difference between two different persons, both should receive equal consideration when another person's morally relevant actions would affect them both. Regarding many of our actions, characteristics like gender, race, sexuality, handicap, and religious status are, in themselves, morally unimportant for determining who deserves moral respect. Advocates of sustainable development add to this list the characteristics of being a member of a poor country and being a member of a future generation. In particular, they argue that these persons should be afforded the opportunity to have a materially satisfying life.

Sustainable Development

In 1987 the World Commission on Environment and Development issued what is considered the groundbreaking text on sustainable development. Entitled *Our Common Future*, or sometimes referred to as *The Brundtland Report*, (named after Gro Harlem Brundtland, the commission's chairwoman) this text argues that economic development is good policy, just so long as it does not undermine environmental capacity to provide for future generations. Basically, we ought to pursue "development that meets the needs of the present without compromising the ability of future generations to meet their own needs" (as cited in Holland, 2003, p. 391).

According to estimates by the United Nations, the year 2013 saw Earth's population reach 7.2 billion people (U. N. News Centre: World Population). The U.N. explains some of the consequences for our planet in reaching this milestone: "Human activity has an impact on every inch of the world's surface, every cubic inch of its air and water, and every species that lives on the earth, under the earth or in the sea." Amongst these 7.2 billion persons, those having the greatest effects on Earth's environment are the comparatively affluent—those persons living and consuming in economically developed nations. Everyday, though, more of the world's poor are seeing many of the material benefits economic development provides, swelling the ranks of consumer culture. This, of course, requires from the Earth even more resources. Who can blame the poor, though, for taking advantage of a materially richer life? After all, as the U.N. statement puts it, "the last thing poor countries want is to stay poor" (*United Nations Resources for Speakers on Global Issues: Population*).

Meeting one's basic needs is fundamental to human well-being. Being part of an economic system that readily provides such basic needs, as well as even modest luxuries, appears to be a reasonable desire. Indeed, reflect upon your own considered preferences for a moment: chances are if you are reading this essay, you are amongst those living in the economically developed world or you are a member of the comparatively well-off in a developing country. Thus, you likely value this standard of living. It is arguably a part of what you consider to be a good life. Shouldn't others, then, have the very same opportunity to live as you do?

Of course, as highlighted above, development can have high environmental costs. This is why the idea of sustainable development came about; it provides a framework for incorporating two desired outcomes: (1) fostering development, which makes people economically better-off; and (2) doing so in a way that accommodates future-generations' needs. After all, it is future persons, temporally both near and far, who inherit the world we leave behind and who will need resources to live and to shape their own lives. Thus, it is not only out of a concern for fairness that existing persons are made better off, but a similar concern motivates our doing so without leaving a resource-depleted Earth for future generations. Sustainable development is fair, then, because it represents equality of moral consideration being given to the world's poor and to future generations, and substantively, it cashes this consideration out by urging that they be given the opportunity for a quality of life that is not hindered by a lack of environmental resources.

If fairness in treatment is an inextricable part of sustainable development's logic, then perhaps there is a guiding principle that can capture this idea of fairness and that can provide further help in applying the idea of sustainable development, specifically as it involves far-off, future generations. This principle is a modified version of the golden rule: Do to others as you want others to do unto you. Indeed, I think the logic of golden rule thinking is so exceptionally fitting for the idea of sustainability, and the idea of sustainability to be of such *prima facie* moral importance, that it is actually a test of the intuitive attractiveness of any ethical world-view that it accommodates this modified version of the golden rule or at least its upshot. An additional reason for using the golden rule is that it has cross-cultural currency. Versions of it are found in the philosophies and religions of people all over the world. Because sustainable development is a global endeavor, being able to reason with one's fellow humans, while using values that are important to them, is crucial to sustainability's realization.

Crafting Sustainability's Golden Rule (SGR)

The problem sustainable development seeks to address is that we have an Earth that continues providing for lots of people's needs and desires, but not all our fellow humans benefit in just these ways. So it only seems fair that those lacking material wealth have the chance to develop their economies to increase their own material well-being. The key constraint in pursuit of development is that it is done in such a way that future generations can meet their own needs and satisfy many of their own wants. In order to

adapt the golden rule for application to sustainability, we must first make clear that collective action is necessary. Ultimately, sustainability involves more than just an "I" acting, which is what the original formulation of the golden rule seems to imply.

Next, we must address the "others" to which the golden rule applies. In his reflections on the golden rule, Thomas Hobbes, who considers human psychology to be inescapably egoistic, seemingly requires actual reciprocity from others to be part of golden rule thinking. If Hobbes is correct, this requirement would make the golden rule be an odd choice for guiding sustainability as it applies to future generations, since we do not know who will occupy Earth in the distant future, and thus we do not know who will benefit from our actions or how they will be able to reciprocate our actions. In fact, our interactions with future generations seem limited to what we leave behind, intellectually and materially. Their interactions with us seem similarly limited. They will interact with what we leave, and this provides for their opportunities. But whereas we can only imagine who they will be and what they will exactly be like, they can have more definitive knowledge of who we were through a recorded or otherwise evidence-based history, perhaps remembering us well or poorly, depending upon the future we make possible for them.

Maybe this judgment is too quick. I might imagine future generations remembering me well, say, because I was a proponent of sustainability, and this imagining, in turn, is a happy thought for me, representing a kind of benefit. However, even given strong advocacy for sustainability, the odds of my being remembered, specifically, are miniscule. The working together to promote sustainable development by my generation and those contemporaneous with it is my only reasonable hope for being remembered well, but in this case I would likely be a nameless member of a much larger collectivity. There is, of course, the chance that I might become a noteworthy leader of a sustainability movement, but even this status is only derivable because others were willing to work hard and ultimately be led by me. The basic reality is that whether I am a leader or not, I cannot experience any appreciation by distant, future generations. In other words, there is no intergenerational reciprocity that can help serve as a guide for how I should act toward future generations, given that future generations can do nothing for previous ones. This failure, however, does provide some illumination, as it highlights that whole generations are involved on both the giving and receiving end of sustainability.

The lack of intergenerational reciprocity, however, need not be a fatal objection to adapting the golden rule to sustainability toward future generations. One can reject

Hobbes's view and simply deny the need for any reciprocity at all. In this case, the golden rule would merely require that we imagine ourselves as part of a future generation and ask ourselves what we would have future generations do for us were our roles reversed. Consider an analogous situation. If persons in a far-off, exotic locale were suffering from famine, and we were in the position of offering aid, the golden rule need not paralyze us when deciding how to act, even though most of us are unlikely to interact with these persons ever again. After all, just because we may not benefit from any of these strangers' future actions (i.e., how we want them to treat us), we could still put ourselves in their position and ask ourselves what we would have them do if we were the ones starving. We would almost assuredly help them since we would want them to help us. Moreover, when we think about it, the improbability of reciprocity is a reality for many of us in our day-to-day interactions with others. It is not surprising that some people have interpreted the golden rule as placing ourselves "in the shoes of another," since any reasonable way of moral thinking should guide us in our token interactions with strangers.

A new problem, however, arises when I conceive of myself as a member of a distant, future generation. How do I know their exact needs and wants? My great-grandparents had some very different desires and tastes as compared to those of my own. Many of the technologies I use and all that they make possible were unthinkable to them. Or if I go back even further, say, to my ancestors living in the early 1800s, this brings to mind even more jarring dissimilarities. My modes of travel, how I eat, where and how I purchase things, the levels of education realistically attainable for me, who I am able to interact with—all these would have been unfathomable to them. How do I (we!) realistically know what future generations will need? Indeed, when we craft Sustainability's Golden Rule, must we even worry about what we do to the Earth? Future generations will certainly have better technology than we have now, and perhaps they will simply be able to use their technological advancements to remedy any mistakes we make now and provide whatever resources they need. Thus, we might not need to produce and to consume in ways that the Earth can accommodate; we might not even need the "sustainable" part of sustainable development.

This rejoinder, however, is based on a dangerous assumption. When it comes to future generations' needs, we should not undermine their ability to provide for basic necessities (among them breathable air, clean water, nutrient-rich soils for producing food, and a livable climate), nor should we negatively affect environmental systems that yield these necessities. In fact, it is reasonable

to think that technological advancements in the future are only possible in a world that has these foundational goods. Maybe with these goods established, future generations will, in fact, find ways to clean up environmental messes undermining these very same goods, but current generations must err on the side of caution not to assume as much, lest we seal an unenviable fate for them. Consequently, it is immoral for any of our current actions to risk either these basic goods or the other parts of the environment that make them possible.

The golden rule needs modification if it is to justify sustainable conduct toward future generations and provide further guidance as to the exact nature of that conduct. Based on the considerations we have addressed, I propose the following modifications in the golden rule. First, the rule must be recast in terms of the first person plural ("we") rather than the first person singular ("I"). By doing so, we make it clear that it is collective action that is necessary. As economic development occurs, it must be done in a way that leaves sufficient natural resources both for future persons and other organic life that make up their life support system. Enhanced technologies can also be passed down to allow for a more efficient use of natural resources. And, of course, the scientific knowledge that makes such efficient uses possible should be passed down for future generations to improve upon. Institutions respectful of these efforts and the intellectual material that philosophically justifies them should be handed down as well. Much of this material already represents an inheritance we ourselves benefited from, and it is amongst the best of what we would have had previous generations do unto ours. It is therefore what we should pay forward.

Second, the rule must explicitly recognize the intergenerational aspect of sustainability. The rule must identify future generations as the object of moral concern. Moreover, the test of how we should develop and affect future generations is how we would have wanted previous generations to develop and affect us. Certainly, many of our current concerns are the legacy of the mistakes of previous generations. These mistakes highlight the limitations of our predictive powers and the need to plan prudently for future generations, even with the expectation of vast technological advancements. However, it is important to realize that previous generations did not get everything wrong. We can appreciate much of what they did as being exactly what we would have had them do. Learning from not only their mistakes but also their successes is crucial for us to plan appropriately for future generations.

I therefore formally propose that the golden rule
Do to others as you want others to do to you
be modified to

We should do to future generations what we would have had previous generations do to ours. When the actions under consideration involve supporting or rejecting some form of sustainable development, this modified version can serve as Sustainability's Golden Rule (SGR). At the heart of this rule is the fairness and the impartiality requisite of golden rule thinking. It recognizes the future to be comprised of valuing beings with certain resource requirements that makes that very status as valuing beings possible. Nor should it be thought that this status is limited to just human valuers. Nonhuman valuers should be part of the equation, as they, too, can have their interests positively or negatively affected by our actions. These valuing beings may not be the kind that can think and act on SGR themselves, but they can benefit from it (some humans are like this, too). Every generation of beings capable of moral decision-making has fellow voyagers along with them that have different abilities than they do. However, such beings can still be harmed and benefited in morally relevant ways. Consequently, their well-being must inform how intergenerational behavior proceeds.

Putting Sustainability's Golden Rule to the Test

Let's take SGR for a test run. Consider the problem of climate change.[2] Peering through the lens of science, we see the implications of climate change and consider its causes. Emissions of greenhouse gasses, including carbon dioxide, have a threshold effect that heats up the Earth, making our home more inhospitable to a variety of species, including our own. But if other countries are to continue their development, they will require lots of energy. Although green energy-producing technologies already provide much and promise much more, fossil fuels largely have a cost advantage given current markets. Since the use of fossil fuels produces greenhouse gasses, development for existing persons (a good) is likely to come via global warming both to future generations and to aging contemporaries (a great cost). SGR's use—*We should do to future generations what we would have had previous generations do to ours*—should help us sort out our moral thinking here.

SGR's application to global warming delivers insightful but sobering results. We cannot pass down to future generations a hotter, more biologically inhospitable planet. We would not have wanted our ancestors handing down an Earth exhibiting the full manifestations of global warming. According to SGR, then, doing right by future persons involves not only encouraging development that does not add to the problem, but also having the industrial world modify its behavior to reverse the warming

trend. Sustainable development, that is, can only proceed, morally, with a concomitant reduction in first-world fossil fuel use aided by advances in green energy technologies. Sustainable development consistent with the above requirements has been proposed, for example, in the Kyoto Protocol. The United States, a major polluter, was not a signatory to the treaty, and one of that treaty's pollution reducing mechanisms, cap-and-trade, was rejected as a stand-alone policy by the U.S. Senate.

This is regrettable, because our predecessors demonstrated the efficacy of two major inputs to human behavior, ones that we can put to use creatively: governments and markets. Governments, which provide the rule of law, and markets, which deliver goods and services efficiently, can be used to spur the growth of green-energy producing technologies. Cap-and-trade policies create a market for carbon trading by capping the amount of carbon dioxide emissions, allowing cleaner industrialists to sell pollution credits to dirtier ones. This dynamic can combine with innovations in clean energy technologies to shift the trend toward reduced emissions generally. SGR therefore justifies ethical and creative ways of acting that benefit both those living in the present and those who will live in the remote future.

Conclusion

The unpleasant reality is that we humans can come up with perfectly reasonable moral principles to guide our behavior, even ones having wide cross-cultural appeal, but it is another thing to get persons to do what they know is right. This is especially true when it involves changes to their way of living, changes that involve even modest and reasonable sacrifices. However, an important step is equipping ourselves with the best arguments as to how we should behave. This allows us to put rational pressure on our fellow humans to justify their actions. Correct moral arguments, that is, are essential to public discourse. I believe that SGR provides this rational pressure to shape public discourse, and it should be part of any reasonable moral framework seeking to provide guidance regarding sustainable development.

Notes

1. Jeffery Wattles gives this generic definition of the golden rule (1996, p. v). His book, *The Golden Rule*, is a tremendous resource for the various formulations of the rule, its cross-cultural currency, problems with the rule's use, and a defense of an ethic based upon it.

2. A very accessible breakdown of the evidence for climate change can be found here: <http://climate.nasa.gov/evidence/>

References

Dixon, B. (2012) Sustainability's Golden Rule. In Jerry Williams & Bill Forbes (Eds.), *Toward a More Livable World: Social Dimensions of Sustainability* (pp. 37–44). Nacogdoches, TX: Stephen F. Austin State University Press.

Hobbes, T. (1967) *Leviathan*. Oxford: Clarendon Press.

Holland, A. (2003) Sustainability. In Dale Jamieson (Ed.), *A companion to environmental philosophy* (pp. 390–401). Malden, MA: Blackwell.

National Aeronautics and Space Administration (NASA)—Global Climate Change: Vital Signs of the Planet. Retrieved from <http://climate.nasa.gov/evidence/>

United Nations News Centre: World Population Projected to Reach 9.6 Billion by 2050 Retrieved from <http://www.un.org/apps/news/story.asp?NewsID=45165#.VAYrthwv0dc>

United Nations Resources for Speakers on Global Issues—Population. Retrieved from <http://www.un.org/en/globalissues/briefingpapers/population/>

Wattles, J. (1996) *The golden rule*. Oxford: Oxford University Press.

BEN DIXON is an assistant professor of philosophy at Stephen F. Austin State University where he is also a member of the Center for a Livable World, a research center that explores the human dimensions of sustainable development. He has published articles on environmental ethics and moral progress.

Martin Golding

Limited Obligations to Future Generations

Preliminary Questions

Before I turn to the question of the basis of obligations [to future generations]—the necessity of the plural is actually doubtful—there are three general points to be considered: (1) Who are the individuals in whose regard it is maintained that we have such obligations, to whom do we owe such obligations? (2) What, essentially, do obligations to future generations oblige us to do, what are they aimed at? and (3), To what class of obligation do such obligations belong, what kind of obligation are they? Needless to say, in examining a notion of this sort, which is used in everyday discussion and polemic, one must be mindful of the danger of taking it—or making it out—to be more precise than it is in reality.

1. This cautionary remark seems especially appropriate in connection with the first of the above points. But the determination of the purview of obligations to future generations is both ethically and practically significant. It seems clear, at least, who does not come within their purview. Obligations to future generations are distinct from the obligations we have to our presently living fellows, who are therefore excluded from the purview of the former, although it might well be the case that *what* we owe to future generations is identical with (or overlaps) what we owe to the present generation. However, I think we may go further than this and also exclude our most immediate descendants, our children, grandchildren and great-grandchildren, perhaps. What is distinctive about the notion of obligations to future generations is, I think, that it refers to generations with which the possessors of the obligations cannot expect in a literal sense to share a common life. (Of course, if we have obligations to future generations, understood in this way, we a *fortiori* have obligations to immediate posterity.) This, at any rate, is how I shall construe the reference of such obligations; neither our present fellows nor our immediate posterity come within their purview. What can be the basis of our obligations toward individuals with whom we cannot expect to share a common life is a question I shall consider shortly.

But if their inner boundary be drawn in this way, what can we say about their outer limits? Is there a cutoff point for the individuals in whose regard we have such obligations? Here, it seems, there are two alternatives. First, we can flatly say that there are no outer limits to their purview: all future generations come within their province. A second and more modest answer would be that we do not have such obligations towards any assignable future generation. In either case the referent is a broad and unspecified community of the future, and I think it can be shown that we run into difficulties unless certain qualifications are taken into account.

2. Our second point concerns the question of what it is that obligations to future generations oblige us to do. The short answer is that they oblige us to do many things. But an intervening step is required here, for obligations to future generations are distinct from general duties to perform acts which are in themselves intrinsically right, although such obligations give rise to duties to perform specific acts. Obligations to future generations are essentially an obligation to produce—or to attempt to produce—a desirable state of affairs *for* the community of the future, to promote conditions of good living for future generations. The many things that we are obliged to do are founded upon this obligation (which is why I earlier questioned the necessity of the plural). If we think we have an obligation to transmit our cultural heritage to future generations it is because we think that our cultural heritage promotes, or perhaps even embodies, good living. In so doing we would hardly wish to falsify the records of our civilization, for future generations must also have, as a condition of good living, the opportunity to learn from the mistakes of the past. If, in addition, we believe lying to be intrinsically wrong we would also refrain from falsifying the records; but this would not be because we think we have any special duty to tell the truth to future generations.

To come closer to contemporary discussion, consider, for example, population control, which is often grounded upon an obligation to future generations. It is not maintained that population control is intrinsically right—although the rhetoric frequently seems to approach such a claim—but rather that it will contribute towards a better life for future generations, and perhaps immediate posterity as well. (If population control were intrinsically anything, I would incline to thinking it intrinsically wrong.) On the other hand, consider the elimination of water and air pollution. Here it might be maintained that we have a definite duty to cease polluting the environment on the grounds that such pollution is intrinsically bad or that it violates a Divine command. Given the current mood of neopaganism, even secularists speak of the despoilment of the environment as a sacrilege of sorts. When the building of a new dam upsets the ecological balance and puts the wildlife under a threat, we react negatively and feel that something bad has resulted. And this is not because we necessarily believe that our own interests or those of future generations have been undermined. Both views, but especially the latter (Divine command), represent men as holding sovereignty over nature only as trustees to whom not everything is permitted. Nevertheless, these ways of grounding the duty to care for the environment are distinguishable from a grounding of the duty upon an obligation to future generations, although one who acknowledges such an obligation will also properly regard himself as a trustee to whom not everything is permitted. Caring for the environment is presumably among the many things that the obligation to future generations obliges us to do because we thereby presumably promote conditions of good living for the community of the future.

The obligation—dropping the plural again for a moment—to future generations, then, is not an immediate catalogue of specific duties. It is in this respect rather like the responsibility that a parent has to see to the welfare of his child. Discharging one's parental responsibility requires concern, seeking, and active effort to promote the good *of* the child, which is the central obligation of the parent and out of which grows the specific parental obligations and duties. The use of the term "responsibility" to characterize the parent's obligation connotes, in part, the element of discretion and flexibility which is requisite to the discharging of the obligation in a variety of antecedently unforeseeable situations. Determination of the specific duty is often quite problematic even—and sometimes especially—for the conscientious parent who is anxious to do what is good for his child. And, anticipating my later discussion, this also holds for obligations to future generations. There are, of course, differences, too. Parental responsibility is enriched and reinforced by love, which can hardly obtain between us and future generations. (Still, the very fact that the responsibility to promote the child's good is an obligation means that it is expected to operate even in the absence of love.) Secondly, the parental obligation is always towards assignable individuals, which is not the case with obligations to future generations. There is, however, an additional feature of likeness between the two obligations which I shall mention shortly.

3. The third point about obligations to future generations—to what class of obligation do they belong?—is that they are *owed*, albeit owed to an unspecified, and perhaps unspecifiable, community of the future. Obligations to future generations, therefore, are distinct from a general duty, when presented with alternatives for action, to choose the act which produces the greatest good. Such a duty is not owed to anyone, and the beneficiaries of my fulfilling a duty to promote the greatest good are not necessarily individuals to whom I stand in the moral relation of having an obligation that is owed. But when I owe it to someone to promote his good, he is never, to this extent, merely an incidental beneficiary of my effort to fulfill the obligation. He has a presumptive *right* to it and can assert a claim against me for it. Obligations to future generations are of this kind. There is something which is due to the community of the future from us. The moral relation between us and future generations is one in which they have a claim against us to promote their good. Future generations are, thus, possessors of presumptive rights.

How Can Those Not Yet Born *Now* Have Claims on Us?

This conclusion is surely odd. How can future generations—the not-yet-born—now have claims against us? This question serves to turn us finally to consider the basis of our obligations to future generations. I think it useful to begin by discussing and removing one source of the oddity.

It should first be noticed that there is no oddity in investing present effort in order to promote a future state of affairs or in having an owed obligation to do so. The oddity arises only on a theory of obligations and claims (and, hence, of rights) that virtually identifies them with acts of willing, with the exercise of sovereignty of one over another, with the pressing of demands-in a word, with *making* claims. But, clearly, future generations are not now engaged in acts of willing, are not now exercising sovereignty over us, and are not now pressing their demands. Future generations are not now making claims against us, nor will it be *possible* for them to do so. (Our immediate posterity are in this last respect in a different case.) However, the identification of claims with making claims, demanding, is plausible within the field of rights and obligations because the content of a system of rights is historically conditioned by the making of claims. Individuals and groups put forward their claims to the goods of life, demand them as their right; and in this way the content is increasingly expanded towards the inclusion of more of these goods.

Nevertheless, as suggestive a clue as this fact is for the development of a theory of rights, there is a distinction to be drawn between *having* claims and *making* claims. The mere fact that someone claims something from me is not sufficient to establish it as his right, or that he has a claim relative to me. On the other hand, someone may have a claim relative to me whether or not he makes the claim, demands, or is even able to make a claim. (This is not to deny that claiming plays a role in the theory of rights.) Two points require attention here. First, some claims are frivolous. What is demanded cannot really be claimed as a matter of right. The crucial factor in determining this is the *social ideal,* which we may provisionally define as a conception of the good life for man. It serves as the yardstick by which demands, current and potential, are measured. Secondly, whether someone's claim confers an entitlement upon him to receive what is claimed *from me* depends upon my moral relation to him, on whether he is a member of my *moral community*. It is these factors, rather than any actual demanding, which establish whether someone has a claim relative to me.

Who Are the Members of My Moral Community?

Who are the members of my moral community? (Who is my neighbor?) The fact is that I am a member of more than one moral community, for I belong to a variety of groups whose members owe obligations to one another. And many of the particular obligations that are owed vary from group to group. As a result my obligations are often in conflict and I experience a fragmentation of energy and responsibility in attempting to meet my obligations. What I ought to desire for the members of one of these groups is frequently in opposition to what I ought to desire for the members of another of these groups. Moral communities are constituted, or generated, in a number of ways, one of which is especially relevant to our problem. Yet these ways are not mutually exclusive, and they can be mutually reinforcing. This is a large topic and I cannot go into its details here. It is sufficient for our purpose to take brief notice of two possible ways of generating a moral community so as to set in relief the particular kind of moral community that is requisite for obligations to future generations.

A moral community may be constituted by an explicit contract between its members. In this case the particular obligations which the members have towards each other are fixed by the terms of their bargain. Secondly, a moral community may be generated out of a social arrangement in which each member derives benefits from the efforts of other members. As a result a member acquires an obligation to share the burden of sustaining the social arrangement. Both of these are communities in which entrance and participation are fundamentally a matter of self-interest, and only rarely will there be an obligation of the sort that was discussed earlier, that is, a responsibility to secure the good of the members. In general the obligations will be of more specialized kinds. It is also apparent that obligations acquired in these ways can easily come into conflict with other obligations that one may have. Clearly, a moral community comprised of present and future generations cannot arise from either of these sources. We cannot enter into an explicit contract with the community of the future. And although future generations might derive benefits from us, these benefits cannot be reciprocated. Our immediate posterity, who will share a common life with us, are in a better position in this respect; so that obligations towards our children, born and unborn, conceivably *could* be generated from participation in a mutually beneficial social arrangement. This, however, would be misleading.

It seems, then, that communities in which entrance and participation are fundamentally matters of self-interest, do not fit our specifications. As an alternative let us consider communities based upon altruistic impulses and fellow-feeling. This, too, is in itself a large topic, and I refer to it only in order to develop a single point.

The question I began with was: Who are the members of my moral community? Now it is true that there are at least a few people towards whom I have the sentiments that are identified with altruism and sympathetic concern. But are these sentiments enough to establish for me the moral relationship of owing them an obligation? Are these enough to generate a moral community? The answer, I think, must be in the negative so long as these affections towards others remain at the level of animal feeling. The ancient distinction between mere affection, mere liking, and conscious desire is fundamental here. Genuine concern and interest in the well-being of another must be conscious concern. My desire for another's good must in this event be more than impulsive, and presupposes, rather, that I have a *conception* of his good. This conception, which cannot be a bare concept of what is incidentally a good but which is rather a conception of the good *for* him, further involves that he not be a mere blank to me but that he is characterized or described in some way in my consciousness. It is perhaps unnecessary to add that there is never any absolute guarantee that such a conceived good is not, in some sense, false or fragmentary. Nevertheless, an altruism that is literally mindless—if it can be called "altruism" at all—cannot be the basis of moral community.

But even if it be granted that I have a conception of another's good, I have not yet reached the stage of obligation towards him. We are all familiar with the kind of "taking an interest in the welfare of another" that is gracious and gift-like, a matter of *noblesse oblige*. It is not so much that this type of interest-taking tends to be casual, fleeting and fragmentary and stands in contrast to interest-taking that is constant, penetrating and concerned with the other's total good. It is, rather, a form of interest-taking, however "conceptual," that is a manifestation of an unreadiness or even an unwillingness to recognize the other's claim (as distinct, of course, from his claiming), the other's entitlement, to receive his good from me. An additional step is, therefore, required, and I think it consists in this: that I acknowledge this good as a good, that his good is good-to-me. Once I have made this step, I cannot in conscience deny the pertinence of his demand, if he makes one, although whether I should now act so as to promote his good is of course dependent on a host of factors. (Among these factors are moral considerations that determine the permissibility of various courses of action and priorities of duties.) The basis of the obligation is nevertheless secured. . . .

The structure of the situation is highlighted when a stranger puts forward his demand. The question immediately arises, shall his claim be recognized as a matter of right? Initially I have no affection for him. But is this crucial in determining whether he ought to count as a member of my moral community? The determination depends, rather, on what he is like and what are the conditions of his life. One's obligations to a stranger are never immediately clear. If a visitor from Mars or Venus were to appear, I would not know what to desire for him. I would not know whether my conception of the good life is relevant to him and to his conditions of life. The good that I acknowledge might not be good for him. Humans, of course, are in a better case than Martians or Venusians. Still, since the stranger appears as strange, different, what I maintain in my attempt to exclude him is that my conception of the good is not relevant to him, that "his kind" do not count. He, on the other hand, is in effect saying to me: Given your social ideal, you must acknowledge my claim, for it *is* relevant to me given what I am; your good is my good, also. If I should finally

come to concede this, the full force of my obligation to him will be manifest to me quite independently of any fellow-feeling that might or might not be aroused. The *involuntary* character of the obligation will be clear to me, as it probably never is in the case of individuals who command one's sympathy. And once I admit him as a member of my moral community, I will also acknowledge my responsibility to secure this good for him even in the absence of any future claiming on his part.

With this we have completed the account of the constitution of the type of moral community that is required for obligations to future generations. I shall not recapitulate its elements. The step that incorporates future generations into our moral community is small and obvious. Future generations are members of our moral community because, and insofar as, our social ideal is relevant to them, given what they are and their conditions of life. I believe that this account applies also to obligations towards our immediate posterity. However, the responsibility that one has to see to the welfare of his children is in addition buttressed and qualified by social understandings concerning the division of moral labor and by natural affection. The basis of the obligations is nevertheless the same in both instances. Underlying this account is the important fact that such obligations fall into the area of the moral life which is independent of considerations of explicit contract and personal advantage. Moral duty and virtue also fall into this area. But I should like to emphasize again that I do not wish to be understood as putting this account forward as an analysis of moral virtue and duty in general.

The Inter-Generational Partnership

As we turn at long last specifically to our obligations to future generations, it is worth noticing that the term "contract" has been used to cover the kind of moral community that I have been discussing. It occurs in a famous passage in Burke's *Reflections on the Revolution in France*:

> Society is indeed a contract. Subordinate contracts for objects of mere occasional interest may be dissolved at pleasure-but the state ought not to be considered as nothing better than a partnership agreement in a trade of pepper and coffee, calico or tobacco, or some other such low concern, to be taken up for a little temporary interest, and to be dissolved by the fancy of the parties. It is to be looked upon with other reverence; because it is not a partnership in things subservient only to the gross animal existence of a temporary and perishable nature.

It is a partnership in all science; a partnership in all art; a partnership in every virtue, and in all perfection. As the ends of such a partnership cannot be obtained in many generations, it becomes a partnership not only between those who are living, but between those who are living, those who are dead and those who are to be born.

Each contract of each particular state is but a clause in the great primaeval contract of eternal society, linking the lower with the higher natures, connecting the visible and invisible world, according to a fixed compact sanctioned by the inviolable oath which holds all physical and all moral natures, each in their appointed place.

The contract Burke has in mind is hardly an explicit contract, for it is "between those who are living, those who are dead and those who are to be born." He implicitly affirms, I think, obligations to future generations. In speaking of the "ends of such a partnership," Burke intends a conception of the good life for man—a social ideal. And, if I do not misinterpret him, I think it also plain that Burke assumes that it is relatively the same conception of the good life whose realization is the object of the efforts of the living, the dead, and the unborn. They all revere the same social ideal. Moreover, he seems to assume that the conditions of life and of the three groups are more or less the same. And, finally, he seems to assume that the same general characterization is true of these groups ("all physical and moral natures, each in their appointed place").

Now I think that Burke is correct in making assumptions of these sorts if we are to have obligations to future generations. However, it is precisely with such assumptions that the notion of obligation to future generations begins to run into difficulties. My discussion, until this point, has proceeded on the view that we *have* obligations to future generations. But do we? I am not sure that the question can be answered in the affirmative with any certainty. I shall conclude this note with a very brief discussion of some of the difficulties. They may be summed up in the question: Is our conception—"conceptions" might be a more accurate word—of the good life for man relevant to future generations?

It will be recalled that I began by stressing the importance of fixing the purview of obligations to future generations. They comprise the community of the future, a community with which we cannot expect to share a common life. It appears to me that the more *remote* the members of this community are, the more problematic our obligations to them become. That they are members of

our moral community is highly doubtful, for we probably do not know what to desire for them.

Let us consider a concrete example, namely, that of the maintenance of genetic quality. Sir Julian Huxley has stated:

> [I]f we don't do something about controlling our genetic inheritance, we are going to degenerate. Without selection, bad mutations inevitably tend to accumulate; *in the long run, perhaps 5,000 to 10,000 years from now, we [sic] shall certainly have to do something about it. . . .* Most mutations are deleterious, but we now keep many of them going that would otherwise have died out. If this continues indefinitely . . . then the whole genetic capacity of man will be much weakened.

This statement, and others like it, raises many issues. As I have elsewhere discussed the problems connected with eugenic programs, positive and negative, I shall not go into details here. The point I would make is this: given that we do not know the conditions of life of the very distant future generations, we do not know what we ought to desire for them even on such matters as genie constitution. The chromosome is "deleterious" or "advantageous" only relative to given circumstances. And the same argument applies against those who would promote certain social traits by means of genetic engineering (assuming that social traits are heritable). Even such a trait as intelligence does not escape immune. (There are also problems in eugenic programs having nothing to do with remoteness.) One might go so far as to say that if we have an obligation to distant future generations it is an obligation not to plan for them. Not only do we not know their conditions of life, we also do not know whether they will maintain the same (or a similar) conception of the good life for man as we do. Can we even be fairly sure that the same general characterization is true both of them and us?

The moral to be drawn from this rather extreme example is that the more distant the generation we focus upon, the less likely it is that we have an obligation to promote its good. We would be both ethically and practically well-advised to set our sights on more immediate generations and, perhaps, solely upon our immediate posterity. After all, even if we do have obligations to future generations, our obligations to immediate posterity are undoubtedly much clearer. The nearer the generations are to us, the more likely it is that our conception of the good life is relevant to them. There is certainly enough work for us to do in discharging our responsibility to promote a good life for them. But it would be unwise, both from an ethical and a practical perspective, to seek to promote the good of the very distant.

And it could also be *wrong,* if it be granted—as I think it must—that our obligations towards (and hence the rights relative to us of) near future generations and especially our immediate posterity are clearer than those of more distant generations. By "more distant" I do not necessarily mean "very distant." We shall have to be highly scrupulous in regard to anything we do for any future generation that also could adversely affect the rights of an intervening generation. Anything else would be "gambling in futures." We should, therefore, be hesitant to act on the dire predictions of certain extreme "crisis ecologists" and on the proposals of those who would have us plan for mere survival. In the main, we would be ethically well-advised to confine ourselves to removing the obstacles that stand in the way of immediate posterity's realizing the social ideal. This involves not only the active task of cleaning up the environment and making our cities more habitable, but also implies restraints upon us. Obviously, the specific obligations that we have cannot be determined in the abstract. This article is not the place for an evaluation of concrete proposals that have been made. I would only add that population limitation schemes seem rather dubious to me. I find it inherently paradoxical that we should have an obligation to future generations (near and distant) to determine in effect the very membership of those generations.

A final point. If certain trends now apparent in our biological technology continue, it is doubtful that we should regard ourselves as being under an obligation to future generations. It seems likely that the man—humanoid(?)—of the future will be Programmed Man, fabricated to order, with his finger constantly on the Delgado button that stimulates the pleasure centers of the brain. I, for one, cannot see myself as regarding the good for Programmed Man as a good-to-me. That we should do so, however, is a necessary condition of his membership in our moral community, as I have argued above. The course of these trends may very well be determined by whether we believe that we are, in the words of Burke, "but a clause in the great primaeval contract of eternal society, linking the lower with the higher natures, connecting the visible and invisible world, according to a fixed compact sanctioned by the inviolable oath which holds all physical and all moral natures, each in their appointed place." We cannot yet pretend to know the outcome of these trends. It appears that whether we have obligations to future generations in part depends on what we do for the present.

Martin Golding is a professor of philosophy at Duke University and the author of several works in philosophy of law, including *Philosophy of Law* (1975) for the Prentice-Hall Foundations in Philosophy series.

EXPLORING THE ISSUE

Are We Morally Obligated to Conserve Resources for Future Generations?

Critical Thinking and Reflection

1. Imagine yourself as someone living on Earth one hundred years from now. What criticisms will you make of the actions and decisions of Earth's current inhabitants? In what ways will you be grateful to them? Explain your answers.
2. Do you think past generations had moral obligations to us? If so, what were those obligations? Did they fulfill those moral obligations? Why or why not?
3. Do you think we have moral obligations to future generations? If so, what are these obligations? How should these obligations affect your daily actions?
4. Which of the goals of sustainable development do you consider to be the most important? What actions do you think we should take in the next ten years to achieve these goals? Explain your answers.
5. What technological innovations currently in development might benefit future generations the most? What technological innovations currently in development might harm future generations the most? How important is the impact of these technologies on future generations to our decision whether or not to pursue their development? Explain your answers.

Is There Common Ground?

Dixon and Golding certainly take opposing positions regarding our moral obligations to future generations. Dixon argues that we can use our imagination to place ourselves in their position and thereby gain a reasonable understanding of what they will need and want. In addition, Dixon asserts that it is not prudent to assume that future technological developments will address the social, economic, and environmental concerns of future generations. Consequently, he develops a version of the Golden Rule that imposes on us the moral obligation to take the welfare of future generations into account as we make decisions in the present. Golding, in contrast, argues that technological innovations will have a tremendous impact on the circumstances under which future generations will live, and so it is impossible for us to develop a reasonable understanding of their needs and wants. He thus holds that we do not have a moral obligation to consider the welfare of future generations when we make moral decisions in the present. Moreover, he asserts that attempting to do so might lead to practices, such as population control, that are unjustified and possibly even harmful.

Despite these differences, Dixon and Golding are in agreement on many fundamental issues. Both agree that we have the moral obligation to take into consideration the welfare of our contemporaries and our immediate descendants, such as our children and grandchildren. Since their welfare is dependent on living in a habitable world, both authors acknowledge that it is morally incumbent on us to curb pollution, conserve resources, and restore the environment. Thus, while they differ on the precise theoretical basis of these obligations, their recommendations for moral conduct are remarkably similar.

Additional Resources

W. M. Adams and S. J. Jeanrenaud, "Transition to Sustainability: Towards a Humane and Diverse World," *International Union for Conservation and Nature,* 2008

John Blewitt, *Understanding Sustainable Development,* 2nd ed. (Routledge, 2014)

Bill Devall, *Deep Ecology: Living as if Nature Mattered* (Gibbs Smith, 2001)

World Commission on Environment and Development, *Our Common Future* (Oxford University Press, 1987)

Internet References . . .

The Center for a Livable World

http://www.sfasu.edu/laa/390.asp

Earth Charter International

http://www.earthcharterinaction.org/content/

Ethics Updates: Environmental Ethics

http://ethics.sandiego.edu/Applied/Environment/index.asp

Selected, Edited, and with Issue Framing Material by:
Owen M. Smith, *Stephen F. Austin State University*
and
Anne Collins Smith, *Stephen F. Austin State University*

ISSUE

Is It Ethical to Employ Service Animals?

YES: Nora Wenthold and Teresa A. Savage, from "Ethical Issues with Service Animals," *Topics in Stroke Rehabilitation* (2007)

NO: Randy Malamud, from "Service Animals: Serve Us Animals: Serve Us, Animals," *Social Alternatives* (2013)

Learning Outcomes

After reading this issue, you will be able to:

- Understand the role of service and therapy animals in assisting humans with disabilities.
- Describe specific issues involved in the ethical treatment of such animals.
- Understand the concept of speciesism and speciesist objections to employing service and therapy animals.
- Formulate your own position on employing service and therapy animals and identify evidence supporting your position.
- Identify the main objections to your position and formulate responses to these objections.

ISSUE SUMMARY

YES: Teresa Savage and Nora Wenthold consider the overall use of service animals to be justified. They describe, however, a number of situations in which ethical treatment of service animals requires careful consideration of the animal's strengths, limitations, and well-being. Understanding and respecting the animal's nature is a crucial and sometimes overlooked ethical requirement.

NO: Randy Malamud argues that our current attitudes toward service animals spring from speciesism, an attitude that members of certain species (such as humans) have greater value or more rights than certain other species (such as nonhumans). He is especially concerned about the extension of the practice to animals such as monkeys, parrots, and dolphins, who may derive little benefit to themselves from their association with humans.

Human beings, as Aristotle noted, are social animals, and therefore it is no surprise that most of the contemporary moral problems that occupy our attention involve interactions between humans, whether individually or collectively. This focus, however, should not blind us to the recognition that human beings exist in a much wider context than human society, and thus contemporary moral problems arise as a result of interactions with other beings in our environment, such as plants and animals.

The manifold interactions between human beings and animals, especially domesticated animals, gives rise to a number of ethical issues, especially when these interactions involve inflicting injury on an animal or deliberately causing its death. Yet, even apparently mutually beneficial interactions between animals and humans have recently come under ethical scrutiny, as in the case of employment of service animals.

In order to frame this moral issue, it will be necessary to clarify the notion of a service animal. For millennia, humans have used domesticated animals for a variety of purposes, including providing meat, milk, and fiber for human consumption, assisting humans in the performance of tasks such as hunting and drawing loads, and providing comfort and companionship as pets. It was not until recently, however, that humans began systematically using animals to assist them in overcoming disabilities. The first school devoted to this purpose in the United States was the Seeing Eye, which was established in 1929 to train large dogs such as German shepherds or Labrador retrievers to assist people with visual disabilities. Over the past several decades, similar training regimens have been developed for a wide variety of animals to assist humans in a diverse set of ways. In fact, it may be helpful to distinguish animals that provide assistance to human beings into two groups.

The first group, service animals, are defined under the Americans with Disabilities Act of 1990 as "any guide dog, signal dog, or other animal individually trained to do work or perform tasks for the benefit of an individual with a disability, including but not limited to, guiding individuals with impaired vision, alerting individuals with impaired hearing to intruders or sounds, providing minimal protection or rescue work, pulling a wheelchair, or fetching dropped items." As indicated by this definition, dogs are the most common type of service animal, although miniature horses and capuchin monkeys have also been trained as service animals.

The second group, therapy animals, is less rigorously defined. Any animal that is used to improve a person's quality of life by assisting that person to achieve a therapeutic goal may be considered a therapy animal. Thus, animals that provide a calming presence to patients suffering from stress-induced cardiac problems are therapy animals, as are animals that provide emotional support to individuals suffering from panic disorders and PTSD (post-traumatic stress disorder). The success of therapy animals in helping humans achieve therapeutic goals has led to their widespread utilization in a variety of institutional settings, including nursing homes, rehabilitation centers, and even prisons.

There is no doubt that service animals and therapy animals provide enormous benefit to humans. What basis could there be, then, for raising a moral objection against using animals in this way? The answer lies in the key word "using." In philosophical terms, service animals have instrumental value, rather than intrinsic value. This denial of intrinsic value to animals is at the heart of the moral objection to the use of service animals and therapy animals.

Philosophers have traditionally distinguished between two types of value: instrumental value and intrinsic value. Instrumental value is the value that a thing possesses as a means to an end, while intrinsic value is the value that a thing possesses in and of itself. Traditionally, human beings are regarded as having intrinsic value, and so it would be immoral to use a human being merely as a means to an end, even if that end is improving the life of another human being. Animals, however, are traditionally considered to have only instrumental value. Consequently, there would be no moral objection to using an animal to improve the life of a human being.

There are, however, contemporary challenges to this view of animals. These challenges are based on a principle of critical thinking known as the Universalization Principle. According to this principle, similar cases must be treated similarly. In order for two cases to be treated differently, there must be a morally relevant difference between them; if there is no such morally relevant difference, the two cases must be treated similarly. The Universalization Principle, however, does not tell us which differences are morally relevant and which are not; this determination must be based upon an inquiry into the specific cases under consideration.

The philosopher Peter Singer focuses on the capacity to suffer as the only relevant moral factor in applying the Universalization Principle to humans and animals. Since humans and animals both have the capacity to suffer, they should both be treated similarly; in particular, they both should be accorded intrinsic value. Consequently, assigning service/therapy animals merely instrumental value is a violation of the Universalization Principle, and hence is fundamentally wrong. Indeed, the claim that human beings have a moral status superior to animals is a form of discrimination described by Singer as "speciesism," which, like racism and sexism, would be repugnant because it favors one group over another without any objective, morally relevant justification.

Philosophers who wish to defend the use of service/therapy animals as moral also have recourse to the Universalization Principle. They agree with Singer that service/therapy animals and humans have a common capacity to suffer. Consequently, they propose stringent requirements for protecting the physical and psychological health of these animals, just as they advocate protecting the physical and psychological health of the humans they assist. However, they defend assigning humans a moral status superior to service/therapy animals by asserting a morally relevant difference between them: the ability to reason. Since humans have this ability, and service/therapy animals do not, there is no moral objection to the instrumental use of these animals to assist humans.

In their article, Nora Wenthold and Teresa Savage do not question the morality of using service/therapy animals in general, but raise a number of particular issues that must be considered in the training and employing of these animals. The most important issue to be considered, they assert, is a balance between beneficence (providing benefits to human beings) and nonmaleficence (inflicting harm on the service/therapy animals). They describe a number of situations in which it is crucial to understand and respect the nature of a service/therapy animal in order to treat the animal in an ethical manner.

By describing the many layers of meaning inherent in the language we use to describe service/therapy animals, Randy Malamud points out troubling speciesist attitudes in the use of such animals to benefit humans. He is also concerned about our negative attitude toward animals that are not obedient and useful to us, emphasizing that all animals deserve value and respect. If we can come to understand each animal as it exists in nature, rather than as it can be exploited in our society, we can consider each animal's "service" as the role it plays in contributing to the natural world. Then we will be able to take the next step, which is determining the service that humans can provide to other animals.

YES

Nora Wenthold and Teresa A. Savage

Ethical Issues with Service Animals

Humans have used animals since the beginning of time—for food, clothing, and shelter, as beasts of burden and transportation, for amusement, for medical experimentation, and for companionship. Although their moral status is debated and some philosophers advocate for elevating nonhuman animals to a higher moral status than they currently occupy, animals are treated as property.[1,2] The role of service animal touches on a mutual need of both humans and animals, especially dogs, and that is the need for companionship. Although there are tasks and duties required of the service animal in rehabilitation health care, the service animal brings an acceptance and devotion to their human partners that can surpass a species difference. The bond is as strong as a family bond. Service animals display behaviors often interpreted as caring and loving, but it must be remembered that they are not there by their own volition; they are trained and carefully monitored for any deviations from their trained behavior. They are subject to stresses in their environment and can be harmed or can harm others if not properly managed and cared for. This article will address the ethical issues with service animals.

History

According to the Humane Society of the United States, there are approximately 66 million owned dogs in the United States.[3] A rough estimate is that there are 17,000 assistance dogs currently working in the United States.[4] It is unknown when a dog was used the first time to assist someone with a disability. However, there is evidence such as records of dogs being kept at healing temples in ancient Greece or an illustration on a wooden plaque from medieval times depicting a dog on a leash leading a blind man to suggest that we are simply rediscovering an ancient practice in our use of dogs in rehabilitation. However, more recent records can be found at Les Quinze-Bingts,

a Paris hospital for the blind, that has dated records from 1780 describing systematic attempts to train dogs to aid blind people. From 1788, there are records of a blind sieve-maker from Vienna who trained his spitz (a breed of dog like the husky, malamute, or chow chow) so well that many doubted his disability. A couple decades later, the founder of the Institute for the Education for the Blind in Vienna, Johann Wilhelm Klein, published a book that described his methods on training guide dogs for people with blindness. Unfortunately, there is no evidence of his ideas being realized.

The modern history of the assistance-dog movement began in 1929, with the first guide dog school, The Seeing Eye. This school was inspired by a partnership created between Dorothy Harrison Eustis and Morris Frank. While living in Switzerland, Ms. Eustis observed trained dogs guiding blind veterans. This inspired Ms. Eustis to write an article for the *Saturday Evening Post* describing what she had witnessed and offering to work with an interested blind American. Morris Frank, a young blind man living in Nashville, wrote to Ms. Eustis asking her to train a dog for him and, in return, he would teach others who were blind so that they too could become independent. Morris Frank became the first American to use a dog guide, and Buddy, a female German shepherd, became the pioneer dog guide in America. Morris Frank returned home to Nashville and honored his promise. With $10,000 from Ms. Eustis, he worked to establish the first dog guide school in America.

In contrast to the population of people with visual impairments, Americans with physical disabilities and members of the deaf community have had about 30 years of working with service and hearing dogs in a formalized setting. In the mid-1970s, Bonnie Bergin pioneered the service dog movement and founded Canine Companions for Independence. Agnes McGrath, her contemporary, also pioneered a program to train dogs to assist the hearing impaired and inspired the development of a number of hearing impaired dog training centers.

Assistant Animal Terminology

Although the Americans with Disabilities Act (ADA) defines a service animal, there are many terms for assistant animals. There are three major categories: service animals, therapy animals, and companion animals. The ADA defines a *service animal* as any animal that has been "individually trained to perform tasks for people with disabilities such as guiding people who are blind, alerting people who are deaf, pulling wheelchairs, alerting and protecting a person who is having a seizure, or performing other special tasks."[5] This article will focus primarily on the service group. *Therapy animals* are animals that are used in the course of improving a person's quality of life or in helping the person achieve some therapeutic goal. The Delta Society describes the use of therapy animals in animal-assisted activities, which are opportunities for motivational, educational, recreational, and/or therapeutic benefits to enhance a person's quality of life.[6] Animal-assisted therapy is goal directed in which the animal meeting specific criteria is an integral part of the treatment process.[6] *Companion animal* is another term for a pet, and this animal is usually owned by the person.

Service animals are primarily dogs, so the term *service dog* will be used. Sometimes service dogs are also called assistance dogs. In one particular organization, Paws With a Cause, dogs are rescued from animal shelters, rigorously evaluated for physical attributes and temperament consistent with the duties of a service animal, and then undergo extensive training. The cost of preparing and placing a service or hearing dog with a client exceeds $18,000.[6] The agency will acquire and train the dog to suit the needs of a particular client. A client must be over 14 to get a service dog and over 18 to get a hearing dog.

Hearing dogs are trained to bring their owner (the client) to the source of a noise, such as a ringing doorbell, phone, or smoke alarm. Guide dogs, often bred for the purposes of being service animals, assist persons with blindness to navigate in their home and community.[7] Service dogs perform multiple tasks, such as opening doors, retrieving dropped objects, or turning switches off/on.

There have been studies demonstrating the usefulness of service dogs—the positive economic impact and the positive psychosocial aspects, both to adults and children with disabilities, in using service dogs.[8–11] Little has been written on the ethical issues with service animals. Managing expectations and the workload of the service dog, attending to the physical and psychological needs of the dog, and anticipating separation through retirement or death are all ethical issues to be addressed in this article. Before tackling the ethical issues, certain terminology needs explanation. There are many humans involved with a single service animal. There is the owner of the animal, the leader or handler, the human partner, and patients. Many service animals are trained and owned by an agency that provides the dog to an institution, such as a rehabilitation hospital, through a contractual arrangement. One or two people who undergo special training are designated as the service dog's facilitators. The service dog lives with them, is brought to work by them, and they are responsible for the dog's well-being. The facilitators also act as the service dog's advocate and are pivotal in facilitating communication between the agency that owns the dog, the dog handlers, and the institution where the dog works. Facilitators may or may not be directly involved in the service dog's daily work activities, such as working with the dog during a therapy session, but they are available to the dog or dog's handlers during the day and communicate with dog handlers daily to address pertinent issues. Facilitators provide the constant "behind-the-scenes" care, so the service dog is physically and psychologically ready for work. There are other humans, therapists or other clinicians, who also undergo special training to work with the dog during the day. These are the service dog's handlers. There is oversight of the dog's well-being by the agency owning the service dog. The owner of a service dog assumes ultimate responsibility for the dog. This is done by setting standard guidelines regarding care of the dog that the institute has agreed to uphold, such as the frequency of veterinary visits, the types of toys that the service dog can have, and the equipment that the dog is allowed to wear. This information is communicated to the service dog's owners through site visits, completion of annual progress reports, submission of medical records, and correspondence with the facilitators.

Guide dogs for people who are blind or hearing dogs for people with hearing impairment may be owned by the person with the disability or a service animal agency. Service dogs working in facilities are typically owned by an agency, live with one or two facilitators, and are led by a variety of trained handlers. Inconsistency between humans interacting with the service dog can be a source of ethical problems.

Ethical Issues

The primary ethical issue with service animals is the tension between using the dog to achieve patient or client goals (beneficence) and monitoring the welfare of the dog (nonmaleficence). As an animal, the dog does not have autonomy to choose to be a service animal, but the dog's temperament and response to situations belie the dog's choice. Clarity about who is representing and advocating for the dog's interests is also at issue.

Managing Expectations and the Workload

The role for a service dog in a health care setting is usually defined by patients' needs within the health care institution. This may include game playing, visiting, walking, or grooming activities. Typically, the service dog is asked to participate in activities that he/she enjoys. A select group of handlers, people within an institution who are specially trained to work with a specific service animal within specific guidelines, are the only ones who should direct the service dog's activities. Dogs, like most pack animals, rely on consistency and trust to complete requests made by people. The irregular dynamics of a health care environment can make a seemingly easy request a challenge for the dog. A service dog's performance is strongly impacted by an overstimulating health care environment, so to be successful it is vital that the service dog has complete confidence in his or her dog handler or is known to the dog as the leader. It is critical to have consistency in the people trained to handle the service dog and in the behaviors and signals used to communicate with the dog. Mixed messages, new untrained people, and general confusion can be very stressful for the dog and result in unreliable responses from the dog. The facilitators and handlers must communicate with each other so they know what can be expected from the dog, how to lead and respond to the dog, how to assess the dog for signs of stress, and how to manage the dog's stress.

One of the reasons that dogs have always worked so well with people is that both humans and dogs share a common fundamental need of companionship. However, the companionship that service dogs receive when they are "off-duty" is vastly different from the companionship they receive while "working." Both types of companionship are important to the dog as most service dogs are selected from working breeds that enjoy engaging in task-related duties. However, clear communication is required by the facilitator or handler to ensure the dog reacts appropriately in a given situation. An example of this is how service dogs are trained to greet people in different ways to accommodate various settings. People are always instructed to ask a dog handler if they may pet the dog or many people will ask the question, "Is your dog off duty?" If the dog's facilitator or handler is able to comply, they may look at the dog and give a command such as "release" or "play" and at that point the dog will stand from the seated position to greet the individual

in a similar way that a dog may greet someone walking through the front door. Usually, this greeting includes a wagging tail, kisses, and maybe a small run. A much different reaction is seen from a service dog when the dog is working and the dog handler asks the dog to "visit" or "greet" a patient. When the dog is working, the dog will walk up quietly to a patient, gently rest his/her head on a patient's lap, and wait to receive a pet.

It is crucial that all demands made of a service dog are considered reasonable and appropriate. Failure to do so can result in injury to the dog or to people near the dog. For example, even though a service dog working in a health care setting may be physically able to and enjoy pulling people in a wheelchair, it may not always be appropriate. The tile floors can cause the dog and wheelchair to gain speed quickly and newly waxed floors can prove to be slippery, which can lead to accidents. There are service dogs that pull their human companions in wheelchairs. Typically, these dogs have been trained and conditioned for this specific task and wear proper equipment such as a harness to accomplish this task safely. Most important, these dogs have developed a long-term relationship and trust with the individual using the wheelchair.

Other tasks may be physically appropriate for a service dog but may cause psychological stress. The best way to eliminate psychological stress on a service dog is to provide consistent leadership. Because service dogs are expected to ignore specific survival instincts such as their "flight-or-fight" response, trust in their facilitators and handlers is crucial. Most service dogs only have one or two people that they look to for leadership, and most service dogs have only one home with one set of family dynamics to interpret. However, service dogs working in large facilities may have as many as seven leaders at any given time. In addition, they may live in multiple homes, which require them to adapt to various family dynamics. How can a service dog adapt to this lifestyle successfully and fulfill countless requests from dozens of individuals daily?

The key is consistent leadership. All individuals who handle the service dog must be trained, certified, and have adequate bonding time with the dog. The training and certification process educates the facilitators and handlers on the dog's basic physical and psychological needs. Facilitators and handlers also learn the meaning of all the commands and how to help the service dog to be successful. They learn to interpret the dog's body language and how to lead the dog during situations of unpredictability. All of the facilitators and handlers for the same dog need to work together to mimic each other's behavior. The more similar the leaders' interactions and expectations, the easier the requested tasks are for the dog to understand and perform.

The most important requirement that each facilitator or handler must undergo is to spend bonding time with the service dog. This can be done through the practice of commands, grooming, and spending time "off-duty" together. This helps to build trust between a facilitator or handler and a service dog. If a service dog does not trust his or her facilitator/handler, then it is a set-up for disaster; it will cause psychological stress in the dog, which may lead to injury of the dog or a person.

Addressing the Physical and Psychological Needs of the Dog

Whether a service dog works in a large or small facility, there always needs to be coordination between units and staff to ensure that a dog is not overtaxed. This can be done by setting a schedule for the dog allowing for ample times for breaks between activities and recognizing what a dog would consider a break as opposed to what a person considers a break. For example, being told to sit in a corner of a room while a therapist finishes working with a patient is not a break to a dog as the dog is still "on command" and watching his or her leader for the next command. However, having a dog go into a crate for 15 to 30 minutes in a quiet office gives the dog a clear signal that they are not being expected to respond to commands at the moment and can relax.

In addition to short breaks between tasks at work, service dogs also need breaks on a larger scale. This may include weekend hikes or long walks or breaks from being on a leash. Many service dogs spend a lot of their time active on a leash and following commands; even though they enjoy their work and love being around people, all dogs benefit from time "off leash" and interacting with other dogs. Some service dogs may not be able to fully enjoy this with some of their facilitators or handlers they work with in the health care setting as they are always waiting for the next command. However, these dogs seem to do fine if taken to a dog park with other dogs by a family member of a facilitator or handler. Any facilitator or handler can help his or her service dog enjoy relaxation time in his or her presence by participating in "off-duty" activities, such as taking their service dog to a dog park, on a consistent basis. However, it is important for a facilitator or handler to practice work commands before they reenter the work environment. This provides the service dog with a clear signal that it is time to be "on-duty" and to wait for the next command.

The most important element to remember when working with a service dog is that they are in fact dogs. It sounds silly, but because these dogs perform on a consistent basis and are so well trained it is easy to forget that they can be inconsistent. It is a leader's role to try and interpret the cause of the inconsistency and act appropriately. For example, if a service dog is shying away from a patient who is trying to pet behind the dog's ear, then the leader needs to recognize that behavior and request that the patient refrain from petting the dog behind the ear. Next the leader needs to determine what has caused the dog's resistance. This is usually done by noting the dog's reaction and discussing it with other leaders for the dog. Then it is determined if the problem is physical or psychological. A veterinarian can treat a physical problem, such as an ear infection, and the service dog will refrain from working until the infection is gone. However, the problem may be psychological, such as the previous day a patient grabbed the dog's ear too tightly while petting and now the dog has developed a negative association with having his or her ears petted. This type of problem takes more time to work through as the facilitators and handlers will need to help the service dog develop more positive associations to having his or her ears petted. The facilitators and handlers will need to spend extra time to bond with the dog to reassure him or her that no discomfort will come to the dog while the facilitators and handlers are present. In addition, the facilitators and handlers will advise all patients and staff to refrain from petting the dog's ears until the service dog is comfortable having his or her ears petted by strangers.

Physical and mental capabilities of a service dog are decided by the dog's owners, facilitators, handlers, and veterinarians. Sometimes these decisions are made collectively as a group and sometimes they are individual judgments made as a result of a particular situation. This is why it is so important for each person who handles a service dog in a health care setting to be trained and maintain a certain level of expertise. The popularity of service animals can mean that any given facility may have a number of service animals at any given time. Occasionally, there are some dogs that do not do well around other animals. An important qualification of being a facilitator or handler of a service dog is to know how to lead dogs in an emergency situation, such as if another animal provokes them or is threatening to the facilitator or handler. A qualified facilitator or handler is required to direct the service animal through situations such as these to ensure safety is maintained.

It is ideal for a facilitator or handler to recognize and provide the service dog with a break before common stress signs are apparent. However, if a facilitator or handler notices panting, shedding, or hesitation, it is a sign that the service dog is experiencing stress and needs a break. This may necessitate shortening a session with a patient or moving up the dog's break time. Usually, the service dog will be ready to work again after a 30-minute break that allows for water and a nap in the dog's crate.

A service dog that displays signs of chronic stress such as digestive problems, lack of enthusiasm, or fearfulness/aggression requires more than a 30-minute break. These are signs that something is clearly not working, and a lifestyle change may be required. For a service dog working in a health care facility, chronic stress signs are most likely symptoms caused by a lack of consistency in the dog's lifestyle. Dogs rely on habits, and service dogs rely on the habits of their facilitator or handler to ensure their comfort level. Therefore, a change in the leader's behavior or a 2-week absence from a dog's facilitator or handler can be stress triggers. Stress can also be a sign that the way a facilitator or handler is acting in a situation needs to be changed. An example of the latter occurs frequently when a service dog hesitates. When the dog hesitates, the facilitator or handler will stop walking and face the service dog as if to ask the dog what is wrong. These actions indicate to the service dog that the facilitator or handler is relinquishing the leadership role and this encourages the dog's hesitation further. In a situation like this, the leadership style needs to be altered. The facilitator or handler needs to first identify if there are any obvious reasons for the dog's hesitation, then he or she needs to demonstrate leadership body language and redirect the service dog's focus through treats or additional commands to curb the service dog's hesitation. If these stress signs are not recognized or not properly managed, a service dog may experience chronic stress.

Since service dogs in health care facilities are accustomed to receiving lots of attention, sometimes the lack of attention from an absent leader can cause significant stress. Again, communication between leaders is vital to predict and recognize when a service dog is exhibiting stress signs. The other leaders may need to provide more attention to the service dog or adjust the dog's work schedule to ensure the dog's well-being and prevent the dog from experiencing unnecessary stress.

Facility service dogs are selected specifically because they have a high desire to interact with people. Therefore, many of these dogs are strongly impacted by separation from the facilitators or handlers. Being left alone in a dog crate at work for an afternoon can be just as stressful as working all afternoon without a break. Therefore,

scheduling the duration of break time is just as important as work time. During times when facilities are short staffed, such as over the holidays, it seems to be less stressful for a service dog to stay home in an off-duty mode than to come to work and sit alone for an extended period.

Anticipating Separation Through Retirement or Death

Each agency that owns service dogs has different parameters that address when a dog is ready for retirement. Most service dogs are from work breeds such as German shepherd, Labrador retriever, or golden retriever, which have life expectancies of 12–13 years.[12] Many of these agencies predict a 6–10 year work life for the dog and the majority of service dogs enter the work force around 2 years of age, so they are expected to work until the ages of 8–12 years. The number of years that a service dog is able to work is directly related to the physical and psychological well-being of the service dog. Physical aliments such as arthritis, hip dysplasia, and cataracts and psychological ailments in the form of gastrointestinal problems, hesitation, or fearfulness behavior can all contribute to an earlier retirement.

The agency that owns the service dog makes the final decision of when a service dog is ready to retire. This decision is based on veterinarian medical reports, annual reports submitted by facilitators and handlers, and site visits. The agency also decides the disposition of the dog when the dog retires. Recognizing that consistency is of vital importance in any dog's life, especially in a service dog's life, the facilitator has the first option to keep the retired service dog. Multiple handlers or facilitators may make this situation difficult, but the agency has final say as to who keeps the dog. If the facilitator is unable to take the dog, the dog is typically returned to the agency and an appropriate home for the dog's retirement is found. Usually the individual who raised the dog as a puppy has first option, and most of these agencies have long waiting lists for retired service dogs. If for some reason a home cannot be found, the dog is guaranteed a home at the agency.

When a loss occurs in the life of a service dog, a facilitator, a handler, a frequently seen patient, or another animal that lives with the service dog, the dog may exhibit signs of grief in the form of depression or withdrawal. As with humans, time and understanding may help the dog through this grieving process.[13] During this time, it is important for a service dog to feel secure and successful. This can be done by giving a dog easy commands and adequate praise before having the dog complete more complex commands. It is also always important to make commands and work fun from the dog's perspective. The more fun there is in a service dog and facilitator/handler partnership, the greater the potential for success. The effect of the death of the service animal should not be minimized. Often the service dog is thought of as a friend and companion whose loss is intensely felt.[14] The grief can be as acute as a loss of a family member or close friend. Although grief over the death of an animal is not often recognized in our society, people who work with service animals can appreciate the depth of grief that the animal facilitators, handlers, and patients experience.

Summary

Service animals can fulfill an important role in the lives of people with disabilities. The training, care, and supervision of the animal are extremely important to the animal's success as a service animal. The training and ongoing monitoring of the interactions of facilitators, handlers, and health care professionals with the service animal are also critical to the service animal's success. Managing expectations and the workload of the service dog, attending to the physical and psychological needs of the dog, and anticipating separation through retirement or death raise ethical issues. The ethical issues, from the perspective of the animal's welfare, have been presented with recommendations for resolving the issues.

References

1. Nussbaum MC. The moral status of animals. *Chron Higher Educ.* 2006;52(22): B6–8.
2. Singer P. *Animal Liberation: A New Ethics for Our Treatment of Animals.* New York: Random House; 1975.
3. Humane Society of the United States. Available at: www.hsus.org/pets/issues_affecting_our_pets/pet_overpopulation_and_ownership_statistics/us_pet_ownership_statistics.html. Accessed December 12, 2006.
4. Eames E, Eames T. Bridging differences within the disability community: the assistance dog movement. *Dis Stud Q.* 2001;21(3):55–66.
5. ADA business brief: service animals. Available at: http://www.usdoj.gov/crt/ada/svcanimb.htm. Accessed December 12, 2006.
6. Delta Society. The human-animal health connection. Available at: www.deltasociety.org/ServiceInformationBasic.htm. Accessed December 12, 2006.
7. Guide-dogs for the blind. Available at: www.guidedogs.com/site/PageServer. Accessed December 13, 2006.
8. Mader B, Hart LA, Bergin B. Social acknowledgments for children with disabilities: effects of service dogs. *Child Dev.* 1989;60:1529–1534.
9. Allen K, Blascovich J. The value of service dogs for people with severe ambulatory disabilities: a randomized controlled trial. *JAMA.* 1996;275:1001–1006.
10. Duncan S. The 1997, 1998, 1999 APIC Guidelines Committees: APIC State-of-the-Art Report: the implications of service animals in health care settings. *AJIC.* 2000;28(2):170–180.
11. Eddy J, Hart LA, Boltz RP. The effects of service dogs on social acknowledgments of people in wheelchairs. *J Psych.* 2001;122(1):39–45.
12. Fogle B. *The New Encyclopedia of the Dog.* New York: Dorling Kindersley Publishing, Inc.; 2000.
13. K-State veterinarian says pets can grieve over a loss, too. Available at: http://www.mediarelations.kstate.edu/WEB/News/NewsReleases/listpetgrief.html. Accessed January 9, 2007.
14. Schneider KS. The winding valley of grief: when a dog guide retires or dies. *J Visual Impairment Blindness.* 2005;99(6):368–370.

NORA WENTHOLD is a research administrator at the Rehabilitation Institute of Chicago and a Certified Canine Facilitator with Canine Companions for Independence, Chicago, Illinois.

TERESA A. SAVAGE is a clinical assistant professor in the Department of Women, Children & Family Health Science at the University of Illinois College of Nursing. She has written and coauthored several articles as well as four books addressing ethical issues in nursing.

Randy Malamud

 **NO**

Service Animals: Serve Us Animals: Serve Us, Animals

The term "service animals" describes animals who render assistance of some sort to people with disabilities. I am interested in the boundaries of this concept of service animals, and also the blurriness around the edges; this blurriness surfaces when we consider service animals in relation to companion animals (the animals formerly known as "pets"), working animals, military animals, pack animals, harness animals, prison animals, comfort animals.

"Comfort animals" evokes the term "comfort women," who were forced into sexual slavery, raped and horribly abused by the Japanese military during World War II. Comfort animals are in fact not at all like comfort women—they may provide comfort, as we snuggle with them, to people who are for some reason uncomfortable, somehow afflicted. But the commonality is the idea of "comfort," that is, of course, our comfort—the human's comfort in relation to comfort animals, the man's comfort in relation to comfort women. The World War II term, with its insidiously exploitative, Orwellian connotations wrapped around the simple, pleasant word 'comfort', fuels my anthrozoological[1] cynicism; the idea of "service," too, carries a polyvalence that begs investigation.

Though my definition seems concisely focused— "service animals render assistance to people with disabilities"—consider the proposition that, in some sense, all people have disabilities: none of us is perfect. Everyone could be more *able*, more *enabled*, more fully *capable*, of doing something. Every person lacks, for example, a dog's keen senses of smell and hearing, or a bird's highly-refined sensitivity to a threatening predator, or a horse's bulk and strength, or a seal's ability to insulate against extreme cold. There are a range of 'animal powers' that people do not have as keenly as other animals do: sight, smell, speed—all the senses which facilitate a better attunement to one's environment and a better ability to prosper, safely and powerfully in that environment: flight, camouflage and disguise, hibernation, toxic defense—powers of adaptation and survival.

In taking on animal strengths, can we take without taking? "Taking" the sightedness and instincts of a German Shepherd, training and transforming that animal into a guard dog, or a guide dog, is one way of appropriating animal powers. With comfort animals, people take the serenity of a cat or dog or gerbil (who seems unaware of how anxiety-filled the human world is) and harvest some of the animals' gentleness, their sanity, their happiness, their coping-skills. Do people "take" the serenity of these animals, or "share" their serenity? Probably it varies according to the specific situation, the specific person, and the specific animal.

This sense of the animal strengths that humans lack (the dog's powerful sense of smell, the horse's strength, and so on) combined with a sense of entitlement means that in our perennial disability we are inclined to harvest, or co-opt, or borrow, or steal some aspect of those abilities, that able-ness, from other creatures. This paradigm offers an interesting way to think about our own sense of limit, our own sense of inferiority to other animals; and it may suggest dynamics by which that able-ness may be shared between two species, between a human and another animal. It may suggest ecologically interesting moments of trans-species harmony, coexistence, mutual support. Or we may see the foundation of a relationship that, while predicated upon people's sense of inferiority to other animals' talents and abilities, manifests itself in a trope of jealousy, denial, and imperialism. That is, humans may decide to take, abrogate, exploit, animals' abilities for their own benefit, in which case the ecological equanimity described above would instead manifest as usurping and controlling whatever animal strengths we desire and need for our human progress.

"Service" is etymologically related to "subservience," calling attention to the dynamics and consequences of hierarchy. The *OED* defines "service" as the condition of being a servant; the fact of serving a master (as a servant or as a slave) ("service" *OED*). There's a religious sense of the word—one does God's service, one serves God, by obedience, piety, and good works. The ritual of public worship itself is called a service. A devout person's service denotes her service to God (so perhaps, by implication, an animal in service to people analogously evokes a person's service to God, suggesting that we are to service animals as God is to us).

A soldier is "in the service," as is a public employee—we speak of the diplomatic service, the civil service, Her Majesty's secret service—so by this association, the service animal may be regarded as a participant and supporter of some larger civic mission. Other civic services are provided not just by people but also by technology: telephone service, electric service, broadcasting service, internet service.

We fill cars with gas at service stations. There is a supra-human (posthuman) sense in which anything that adds to the benefit, the infrastructure, of our society comes under the heading of service. The designation of 'service animal' fits into this space, this custom, this ideology, of expecting support for our systems and pleasures and needs. We are used to being serviced.

Going back further into the word's history, "service" describes feudal allegiance, fealty, homage. We see a trace of this in the deference of the polite assistant or clerk who announces that she's "happy to be of service." The *OED* sends one off in myriad directions, stirring up a bundle of provocative associations, explicit and subliminal, lurking in the language. I want to unpack the word to reinforce the point of the pun, the echolalia, in my title: "Service animals; serve us animals; serve us, animals."

The first iteration of "service animals" is meant to be merely descriptive of this topic, this category, this class of animals, though at the same time, the category is not as simple and straightforward as it seems. We can detect and deconstruct a wealth of subtextually derogatory characterisations lurking here, and despite the seeming terminological precision, there's some fuzzy imprecision—therapy animals, harness animals, *et al.*: where do we draw the line? The second iteration conveys the demand of the imperial consumer (in which the empire is the dominion of humanity, and the subalterns are, as described in Genesis, the other animals who exist for people to use as we see fit). *Serve us animals*. We want animals . . . on platters, in cages, on leashes, wherever. And finally, the third iteration is meant as a direct address, a command, a fiat, from the oppressor to the oppressed: serve us, animals. Jump. Entertain. Guide. Protect. Carry. Die. Interestingly, people do not often actually verbalise this command to

other animals: we don't have to, because it goes without saying that we expect animals' service, and in any case, they don't understand us: most of them don't speak English. We don't tell seals to serve us their pelts, or pigs to serve us their ribs, or elephants to serve us their tusks. We just take—perhaps the command would be superfluous, or perhaps the command is inherent in the taking. But we do, actually, tell dogs to serve us—Fetch! Heel! Come! Good dog! It is because dogs are so readily trainable to "serve us" in these ways that they have become the prototypical service animal, which is the guide dog.

The Animal as Guide

Today guide dogs are often called "seeing eye dogs," a phrase originating in a specific business, The Seeing Eye, the oldest extant dog training school. Located now in Morristown, NJ, it was founded in 1929 by Dorothy Harrison Eustis who had been a dog trainer in Switzerland, training police dogs, when she learned about a German school that was training dogs to help German soldiers blinded by mustard gas in the Great War. She wrote an article about it in the Saturday Evening Post, and was besieged by blind American soldiers who wanted her to create a similar facility for them (The Seeing Eye, Inc., n.d.).

Today, people who come to The Seeing Eye are assigned a dog and a trainer. Over a month-long course, they learn how to navigate the world around them with their dogs. The most common breeds are German Shepherds, Labrador Retrievers and Golden Retrievers, though other breeds include Poodles, Collies, Dobermans, Rottweilers, Boxers, and Airedale Terriers.

In the last few decades, the service animal rubric has expanded to include many other animals besides dogs for many other disabilities besides visual impairment. Miniature horses have been impounded into duty to perform services similar to guide dogs. Some people find them more trainable, more mild-mannered, and less threatening than large dogs—and they can live and serve for as long as 30 years, significantly longer than a guide dog. Monkeys are used by people who are quadriplegic or agoraphobic; goats by people with muscular dystrophy; and people with anxiety disorders have conscripted cats, ferrets, pigs, iguanas, and ducks as service animals. There are parrots for people with psychosis. It may seem counterintuitive to put a parrot on the shoulder of a psychotic person, but one such person profiled in the *New York Times* credited his parrot with helping him to keep from snapping, or exploding. Sadie the parrot accompanied him in a backpack-cage, and when she sensed him getting agitated, she would "talk him down," saying, "It's ok, Jim. Calm down, Jim. You're all right, Jim. I'm here, Jim" (Skloot 2008 n.p.).

When animals help us by doing things we cannot do for ourselves, this probably makes people appreciate more keenly the value of other animals, the importance of animals, and maybe even, in a larger sense, the ethical desirability of a more egalitarian, even-handed, respectful relationship with other animals. It seems likely that a person using a guide dog or a service parrot develops a profound appreciation for how smart, loyal, and supportive another animal can be. Certainly, the people who use these service animals are prone to this enlightenment, and possibly even those who simply see people using service animals develop a heightened respect for the animals' powers and their value.

But what is in it for the animals? Maybe the dogs and parrots come to appreciate the intense inter-species bond that they are involved in, and value the feelings of their human companion's dependence, and appreciation. Or perhaps parrots don't like zipping around town in a psychotic person's backpack. Included in the recent trend of more variegated service animals, we see comfort animals for old and disabled people; prison animals (a variant of comfort animals) who help mitigate the violent atmosphere of incarceration.

Military animals include bomb-sniffing dogs and patrol dogs. In the past, armies have used horses and mules in a variety of ways, as well as carrier pigeons. Hannibal used elephants to cross the Alps. It is not a stretch to regard such animals as service animals. News stories describe the bonds that form between soldiers and military dogs in Afghanistan and Iraq, recounting the intensely loving devotion that soldiers express, and the intense mourning on the soldiers' part if these animals die (and also on the animals' part if the soldiers die), and the services these dogs may render for soldiers with PTSD. This seems comparable to the relationship between blind people and guide dogs.

Other service animals include helper monkeys (capuchin monkeys, who often help paralysed people and others with mobility impairments: scratching an itch, picking up dropped objects, turning on a DVD player, turning the pages of a book) and dolphins (who are supposedly therapeutic for depressed and autistic children who swim with them to learn compassion, though Lori Marino and Scott Lilienfeld have done much work to debunk the myth of the supposed benefit to autistic children from swimming with dolphins, and also to expose the trauma that the dolphins themselves experience in this enterprise (2007). Cats are sometimes considered service animals: they can supposedly be trained (though this may seem unlikely) to

alert people to danger by pawing at them, to notice in advance the onset of a seizure, and even to use the phone for help if a person is unable to. More credibly, cats are excellent comfort animals: often used in animal assisted therapy to improve a person's physical, social, emotional and cognitive condition. Monkeys, parrots, lizards, and other animals are also used in this capacity.

As guide dogs are joined by parrots and horses and ducks in the service animal cohort, I wonder what this profuse proliferation means. Are we somehow reverting to the ark-story, where people gather up tokens of every animal in existence and remove them from their natural habitats—enclosing them, capturing them, "saving" them, in a human structure? And then are these animals indebted to us because we have saved them from nature, bringing them into the promised land of human culture?

There is a sense of dominionism, manifest destiny, in our recent additions to the canon of service animals. We are expanding our service corps, expanding the range and realm of "services" they can provide us. As when Europeans began to expand the range of spices, gems, silks, furs that "serviced" their fashion and culinary cultures, to support the expansion of imperialist networks and markets, animals, too, figure as an unexploited resource: here are more services we can harvest from them, augmenting our own potential "wealth."

This profusion perhaps pathologises our socio-ecological isolation as a species: the loneliness, the inadequacy, of the human, the merely human. It is undesirable to be locked inside a bubble, a climate-controlled, pesticide-treated, hermetically sealed capsule designed to efface the outside world. We do need animals. We need comfort; we need to rub up against cats, and worms, and sheep. But balanced against this is the exploitative paradigm by which other animals' existence is appraised in terms of how they may assist us.

Service animals are fetishised: they are so valuable, so "smart," because they help us—because we can use them to remediate clearly-defined human deficiencies. We appreciate them. Does this make us appreciate other animals (those without training certificates) less? Are service animals the exceptions that prove the rule, that most animals do not seem to help us all that much? "The dogs go on with their doggy lives," as W. H. Auden (1989) wrote in Des "Musée de Beaux Arts." Note also that animals do help us in all kinds of ways that may not register in our consciousness: pollinating flowers, fertilising crops, sustaining the ecosystem . . . but in any case, who said it was their job to help us? Where did they sign up for that?. . .

Conclusions

Does the person who depends on a service animal have an admirable relationship to another member of another species, or is he weakened? Is the guide dog smart, useful, valuable, valued? These dogs are, clearly, very intelligent: do we understand that intelligence, do we appreciate it, do we perhaps even take the next step, and extend that insight that *this dog is intelligent* to the larger implication that lots of animals have intelligence that we are not aware of?

Service animals augment our own inadequacies—as do companion animals, military animals, work animals. Guide dogs amply and gloriously fulfil a rubric of value to their human users. But what about annoying animals, scary animals, stupid animals, useless animals? (The question is sarcastic—these are not judgements that are ecologically or ethically proper for people to make, though we make them anyway.)[3] They fare poorly in our rankings. They suffer by comparison to the exemplary animals that work so hard to help us, suggesting the negative repercussions of fetishising of service animals. The "good" animals make the others look lazy, hostile, useless. They set an impossible and ridiculous standard for animals: helping us. What have you done for me lately?! Are service animals the "Uncle Toms" of the animal kingdom? Unthreatening, servile, seemingly happy with their lot; they do not make trouble; they live to serve.

Human expectations of animals' services—our sense of entitlement to these services—exemplifies what Peter Singer (1975: 8–9) calls "speciesism," thus violating Jeremy Bentham's moral principle of equal consideration of interests: "each to count for one, and none for more than one." Just as racism and sexism violate the principles of equality, Singer writes, so too speciesism "allows the interests of [our] own species to override the greater interests of members of other species. The pattern is identical in each case." The discourse of anthrozoology invites the interrogation and deconstruction of even such an intimate human-animal interaction as service animals: one might even say, ". . . *especially* such an intimate human-animal interaction . . ."

As numerous artistic representations suggest, there is at least a subliminal tendency to conflate 'intimacy' and 'equality' when looking at the relationship between a person and a service animal. But this supposition sidesteps a vast tradition of speciesist exploitation in which we are prone to conflate an animal's intrinsic value with his or her usefulness to humans. It is tempting, and flattering, for people to imagine that other animals are eager to help us in our times of greatest need, and that they are gratified by our symbiotic or dependent relation with them.

In closing, there is an alternative perspective, an idealistic ecofantasy, suggesting one way we might problematise, unpack, and co-opt the idea of service animals. On the one hand, envision every animal you see as a service animal—and think about the services they're providing. The bright red cardinal bird is wearing a brilliant new outfit to remind you that it's March, and you should move out of your hibernating winter phase and step into your spring regeneration phase, along with the rest of the natural world. Time for you to put on a bright new outfit, too, and get with the game; be in the season. The elephants you see in a nature documentary service you by spreading seeds in their faeces to replenish the savannahs, by revitalising African grasslands. They dig water holes that assist the survival of other species, thus sustaining biodiversity in their habitats, thus preventing the ecosystemic degradations that lead to global warming, thus keeping our coastal cities from being flooded (for at least a few more years): a pretty vital service rendered.

And on the other hand, besides seeing every animal as a service animal, we may also learn to think of ourselves as service animals: turnabout is fair play. What kinds of services do we provide? What kind of services should we provide? Ecologically, it's symbiotic. Ethically, it's altruistic—but it can also be seen as self-interest (which is often an easier sell than altruism): Do unto others as you would have others do unto you. Think about the ecosocial onus of playing our part as good citizens and rendering services where we can, if only for the selfish reason that this would allow the other animals to continue more easily and more prosperously to render their services back to us.

Earlier I invoked a religious service, the civil service, telephone service: connoting service as a metaphysical calling, a civic mission, a foundation for a more desirable and more functional and durable community. Thinking about how much aid and ability a blind man gets from his guide dog, imagine how amazing it would be if people could render a comparable level of service, a comparable value of service, to some of the other animals who share our world.

Notes

1. Anthrozoology refers to the study of interaction between human beings and other animals.
2. See Nagy K and Johnson P 2013, *Trash Animals: How we live with nature's filthy, feral, invasive, and unwanted species*, University of Minnesota Press, Minneapolis.

References

Auden, W. H. 1989 *Selected Poems,* Vintage, London.

Marino, L. and Lilienfeld S. 2007 'Dolphin-Assisted Therapy: More Flawed Data and More Flawed Conclusions', *Anthrozoos,* vol. 20, no. 3: 239–49.

OED Online, 2004 Oxford University Press <http://dictionary.oed.com/>

The Seeing Eye, Inc. 'Guide Dogs for People Who Are Blind or Visually Impaired,' 20 March 2013 <http://www.seeingeye.org>

Singer, P. 1975, *Animal Liberation,* HarperCollins, New York.

Skloot, R. 2008, 'Creature Comforts,' *New York Times,* 31 December, <http://www.nytimes.com/2009/01/04/magazine/04Creatures-t.html?pagewanted=all >

Tucker, M. 1984, *The Eyes That Lead: The story of guide dogs for the blind,* Robert Hale, London.

RANDY MALAMUD is Regents' Professor and Chair of the English Department at Georgia State University. He has written six books and edited two others, along with 70 essays, book chapters and reviews. He is a Fellow of the Oxford Centre for Animal Ethics, a Patron of the Captive Animals' Protection Society, and an International Faculty affiliate of the New Zealand Centre for Human–Animal Studies at the University of Canterbury.

EXPLORING THE ISSUE

Is It Ethical to Employ Service Animals?

Critical Thinking and Reflection

1. Identify and reflect on the similarities between human beings and animals that you consider to be morally relevant. Why are these similarities morally relevant? How do these similarities affect the moral treatment of animals, especially service animals?
2. Identify and reflect on the differences between human beings and animals that you consider to be morally relevant. Why are these differences morally relevant? How do these differences affect the moral treatment of animals, especially service animals?
3. In addition to concerns about service animals, some philosophers object to the practice of keeping animals as pets (comfort animals). Have you ever had a relationship with a pet (or observed the relationship between another human being and his/her pet)? Do you consider pet ownership to be a moral practice? Why or why not?
4. If humans develop intelligent machines, would it be morally appropriate to use them in place of service/therapy animals? Why or why not?
5. What are the morally relevant similarities and differences between the use of service/therapy animals and the use of low-paid human attendants, such as nursing home attendants? How should these similarities and differences affect the treatment of service/therapy animals? How should they affect the treatment of the human attendants?

Is There Common Ground?

At first glance, the authors appear diametrically opposed. Wenthold and Savage do not question the moral acceptability of the use of animals to assist the disabled, while Malamud finds fundamental moral problems with this practice. If we read carefully, however, we can see subtle points of agreement.

Malamud suggests that humanity needs to rethink its relationship with animals. While he deplores the uncritical placement of animals in a subservient position to humans, he acknowledges the theoretical possibility of a morally acceptable relationship between a disabled person and an animal assistant. In such a relationship, "trans-species harmony, coexistence, mutual support" would predominate. Moreover, Malamud suggests that we can see all animals as service animals by coming to understand what each animal naturally does and recognizing how each animal contributes to the world we share. Meanwhile, Wenthold and Savage describe the ideal relationship between a service

dog and the human whom the dog assists as a bond that can "surpass a species difference" and be "as strong as a family bond." They repeatedly emphasize that those who handle service animals must understand and respect how the animal naturally behaves, learning to work with the animal in the manner that the animal—not necessarily the handler—prefers. All three authors, then, discourage treating animals in a purely instrumental manner and express support for understanding and respecting animals by transcending the boundaries of species.

Additional Resources

Susan Armstrong and Richard Botzler, *The Animal Ethics Reader*, 2nd ed. (Routledge, 2008)

Rebecca Huss, "Why context matters: Defining service animals under federal law," *Pepperdine Law Review* 37:4 (2010)

Robert Garner, *Animal Ethics* (Polity, 2005)

Internet References . . .

Ethics Updates: The Moral Status of
Animals

> **http://ethics.sandiego.edu/Applied/Animals
> /index.asp**

Ethical Considerations in Animal-Assisted
Therapy

> **http://suzanneclothier.com/the-articles/ethical
> -considerations-animal-assisted-therapy**

Animal Welfare: The National Agricultural
Law Center

> **http://nationalaglawcenter.org/research-by
> -topic/animal-welfare/**

Selected, Edited, and with Issue Framing Material by:
Owen M. Smith, *Stephen F. Austin State University*
and
Anne Collins Smith, *Stephen F. Austin State University*

ISSUE

Does Morality Require Us to Switch to Driverless Cars?

YES: **Ronald Bailey**, from "The Moral Case for Self-Driving Cars," *Reason Magazine* (2014)

NO: **Will Knight**, from "Driverless Cars Are Further Away Than You Think," *Technology Review* (2013)

Learning Outcomes

After reading this issue, you will be able to:

- Understand the potential advantages and disadvantages of driverless cars.
- Describe specific ethical considerations that support the use of driverless cars.
- Describe specific ethical objections to the use of driverless cars.
- Formulate your own position on driverless cars and identify evidence supporting your position.
- Identify the main objections to your position and formulate responses to these objections.

ISSUE SUMMARY

YES: Ronald Bailey cites studies that purport to show that the use of driverless cars will drastically reduce the number of accidents, bringing about a great reduction in injuries, deaths, and financial costs that result from accidents. Driverless cars will also revolutionize the transportation system, bringing economic and environmental benefits. For these reasons, we are morally required to change over to driverless cars as soon as they become feasible, or we will waste both money and lives.

NO: Will Knight visits a number of carmakers who caution that driverless cars are not yet ready for the consumer market. In addition to the need for smaller, less-expensive, and more capable sensors, the artificial intelligence required to make driving decisions is not yet capable of the required complexity.

Driving a car requires us to pay constant attention to our surroundings. Indeed, a large part of the stress involved in driving results from the fact that as drivers, we must be vigilant regarding a wide range of factors both inside and outside the car. Am I exceeding the speed limit on this section of road? Is it safe to merge into traffic now? Do I have room to change lanes safely? Is this a good time to pass the car in front of me? Is that car going to pull out in front of me? How fast should my windshield wipers be going? Do I need to turn on my lights? These factors alone would make driving difficult, but the people with whom I must share the road introduce an entirely new set of variables.

I cannot assume that they will always behave in a logical or safe manner, especially if they are inexperienced, impaired by alcohol, or distracted by texting. While most of the decisions made while driving are fairly routine, drivers are occasionally forced to make split-second life-or-death decisions, and these decisions all too often have unhappy outcomes. The National Safety Council reports that in 2013, traffic accidents resulted in 3.8 million injuries requiring medical attention and over 35,000 deaths in the United States alone. Most of these accidents, according to the agency, were the result of human error. Every time we get behind the wheel, we are putting ourselves at risk of serious injury or even death.

Now imagine getting into your car, telling it where to go, and then sitting back as the car itself drives you safely to your destination. As you look out the window, you observe a variety of other motorized vehicles on the road, all controlled by computer and all delivering their passengers and cargo in a safe, efficient manner. You can relax, free from worry about the erratic behavior of pedestrians, bicyclists, and even animals as your car's high-tech scanners easily detect and avoid road hazards. In fact, traffic accidents seldom occur, even in inclement weather, since human error has been eliminated. Such a scenario may sound like science fiction, but it is far closer to reality than many people realize.

A number of car manufacturers are in the process of designing and testing autonomous vehicles and hope to make driverless cars available to consumers within the next ten years. Google, in particular, has made a high-profile foray into the field; not only have they developed cutting-edge technology for driverless cars, they have lobbied for legislation permitting driverless cars in the states where they operate. As of April 2014, their fleet of prototype driverless cars had clocked over 700,000 miles of autonomous driving. They predict that they will have a consumer model available for purchase soon, no later than 2020 and perhaps as early as 2017. Other manufacturers, however, are less optimistic. The scanning technology used in driverless cars is not only bulky, but expensive, and it will be a challenge to incorporate this technology into attractive, affordable vehicles. More importantly, practical problems still await resolution, such as the detection and avoidance of potholes, a task as yet poorly performed by driverless cars.

In the absence of human drivers, computers will be required to make all the decisions required for the operation of the vehicle. The difficulty involved in programming such computers is immense. Indeed, it may be beyond the capabilities of contemporary technology to develop computer programs able to anticipate and respond to the vast number of possible scenarios, many of them unpredictable, that present themselves during the operation of a motor vehicle. So daunting is this task that the initial generation of driverless calls will likely require a human being to monitor the performance of the onboard computer and be able to take control of the vehicle should an emergency arise. Experts are confident, however, that computing technology will eventually advance to the point where computers possess all the abilities required to operate motor vehicles autonomously, ushering in the age of true driverless cars.

However, even after it has become technically, aesthetically, and economically possible to incorporate fully driverless technology into both consumer and commercial vehicles, a significant ethical issue must be addressed before the use of driverless cars becomes widespread: Is it moral to permit computers to make driving decisions that will inevitably cause injury and death to human beings?

The programming of autonomous, vehicle-driving computers must include a protocol for making choices among possible outcomes that all involve harm to human beings. The most likely basis for this protocol is consequentialism, the ethical view that the moral value of an action is determined completely by the consequences of that action. For consequentialists, moral decision-making involves performing a moral calculus that identifies all the possible options available to the moral agent and predicts the benefits and harms that will accrue to everyone who will be affected by the agent's decision. The moral decision would then be to take the course of action that produces the best ratio of benefit to harm. A computer programmed with a consequentialist protocol would perform this type of moral calculus and determine the course of action that would produce the best possible outcome; it would then dispassionately and efficiently implement this course of action.

In the case of driverless cars, the best possible outcome would most often be achieved by avoiding an accident altogether. Indeed, there are good reasons to think that a computer operating a well-designed driverless car would be more successful at avoiding accidents than human drivers. After all, the sophisticated sensors in a driverless car would provide a computer with far more information than human drivers would receive from their senses. Moreover, a computer would have instant access to a database of specific information about vehicle design and performance, whereas most human drivers would be ignorant of this useful information. Finally, and perhaps most significantly, a computer would remain unaffected by emotions such as panic, fear, and anger that afflict human drivers and frequently cause, or at least exacerbate, traffic accidents.

However, a computer making autonomous decisions about driving a car will inevitably encounter a situation in which an accident simply cannot be avoided. Can a computer be trusted to make a decision that is moral? There are inherent problems within consequentialism that cast doubt on the morality of a computer-generated solution to a traffic-related moral calculus.

First, how effectively will computers be able to predict the possible future consequences of their decisions? Predicting the future is, at best, a difficult and imprecise activity; even experts using extensive databases and sophisticated computer models, such as economists, weather forecasters, and sports analysts, frequently make erroneous predictions even about events in the near future. Without a reliable way to identify the consequences of each available option, a computer cannot perform the calculus required to make a moral decision about a traffic incident.

Moreover, in performing a moral calculus, will a computer give equal consideration to every person who would be affected by the moral decision? While consequentialists traditionally consider each person affected by a moral decision to be equally important, a computer may be programmed (or reprogrammed by a sophisticated owner) to assign greater importance to the benefits or harms experienced by particular people. If so, the moral calculus would not produce an impartial decision about the proper resolution of a dangerous traffic situation.

Finally, will a computer even be able to identify the best possible outcome in a situation where people might be injured or killed? After all, no philosophical consensus exists about the meaning of the key consequentialist phrase "the best ratio of benefit to harm." Should the computer choose the action that produces the maximum amount of benefit, even if it produces significant harms? Should the computer try to minimize the total amount of harm, even if significant benefits are eliminated? How, in fact, can benefits even be measured against harms? A human driver would face insurmountable problems in performing a consequentialist moral calculus; a computer would fare no better.

Of course, the computer operating a driverless car would only be implementing the programs installed within it. The computer itself would not be a moral agent; the person who chose the specific programs to install on the computer would be the moral agent. This person would have to make decisions about identifying the consequences of a traffic accident, weighing the importance of the various people affected by a traffic accident, and interpreting the meaning of "the best ratio of benefit to harm." Since a person is selecting the principles used in making moral decisions about traffic accidents, how is this decision-making procedure morally different than the current decision-making procedure, in which the driver of the car makes these determinations? Might the use of computers to operate motor vehicles provide a morally superior decision-making procedure because it permits thoughtful deliberation on moral issues to be introduced into a situation that now is often unreflective, even reflexive?

Ronald Bailey eagerly awaits the imminent availability of driverless cars. In his view, the introduction of driverless cars would not only greatly reduce traffic fatalities, but would also revolutionize the use of motor vehicles in ways that would save fuel, decrease congestion, and reduce environmental damage. While the use of driverless cars will undoubtedly raise certain legal issues, he thinks they can be addressed fairly easily. With regard to the ethical problems associated with driverless cars, he argues that each car should be programmed to protect its occupants first, since that is the choice most drivers would naturally make.

Will Knight is more cautious about trusting the decision-making abilities of driverless cars. As a result, he does not foresee the entrance of driverless cars into the consumer marketplace anytime soon, but rather anticipates a series of intermediate products, such as cars that perform many functions autonomously but still require a human driver for more complex tasks.

YES

Ronald Bailey

The Moral Case for Self-Driving Cars: Welcoming Our New Robot Chauffeurs

Tesla, Nissan, Google, and several carmakers have declared that they will have commercial self-driving cars on the highways before the end of this decade. Experts at the Institute of Electrical and Electronics Engineers predict that 75 percent of cars will be self-driving by 2040. So far California, Nevada, Florida, Michigan, and the District of Columbia have passed laws explicitly legalizing self-driving vehicles, and many other states are looking to do so.

The coming era of autonomous autos raises concerns about legal liability and safety, but there are good reasons to believe that robot cars may exceed human drivers when it comes to practical and even ethical decision making.

More than 90 percent of all traffic accidents are the result of human error. In 2011, there were 5.3 million automobile crashes in the United States, resulting in more than 2.2 million injuries and 32,000 deaths. Americans spend $230 billion annually to cover the costs of accidents, accounting for approximately 2 to 3 percent of GDP.

Proponents of autonomous cars argue that they will be much safer than vehicles driven by distracted and error-prone humans. The longest-running safety tests have been conducted by Google, whose autonomous vehicles have traveled more than 700,000 miles so far with only one accident (when a human driver rear-ended the car). So far, so good.

Stanford University law professor Bryant Walker Smith, however, correctly observes that there are no engineered systems that are perfectly safe. Smith has roughly calculated that "Google's cars would need to drive themselves more than 725,000 representative miles without incident for us to say with 99 percent confidence that they crash less frequently than conventional cars." Given expected improvements in sensor technologies, algorithms, and computation, it seems likely that this safety benchmark will soon be met.

Still, all systems fail eventually. So who will be liable when a robot car—howsoever rarely—crashes into someone?

An April 2014 report from the good-government think tank the Brookings Institution argues that the current liability system can handle the vast majority of claims that might arise from damages caused by self-driving cars. A similar April 2014 report from the free market Competitive Enterprise Institute (CEI) largely agrees, "Products liability is an area that may be able to sufficiently evolve through common law without statutory or administrative intervention."

A January 2014 RAND Corporation study suggests that one way to handle legal responsibility for accidents might be to extend a no-fault liability system, in which victims recover damages from their own auto insurers after a crash. Another RAND idea would be to legally establish an irrebuttable presumption of owner control over the autonomous vehicle. Legislation could require that "a single person be responsible for the control of the vehicle. This person could delegate that responsibility to the car, but would still be presumed to be in control of the vehicle in the case of a crash."

This would essentially leave the current liability system in place. To the extent that liability must be determined in some cases, the fact that self-driving cars will be embedded with all sorts of sensors, including cameras and radar, will provide a pretty comprehensive record of what happened during a crash.

Should we expect robot cars to be more *ethical* than human drivers? In a fascinating March 2014 *Transportation Research Record* study, Virginia Tech researcher Noah Goodall wonders about "Ethical Decision Making During Automated Vehicle Crashes." Goodall observes that engineers will necessarily install software in automated vehicles enabling them to "predict various crash trajectory alternatives and select a path with the lowest damage or likelihood of collision."

To illustrate the challenge, Stanford's Smith considers a case in which you are driving on a narrow mountain road between two big trucks. "Suddenly, the brakes on the truck behind you fail, and it rapidly gains speed," he imagines. "If you stay in your lane, you will be crushed between the trucks. If you veer to the right, you will go off a cliff. If you veer to the left, you will strike a motorcyclist. What do you do? In short, who dies?"

Fortunately such fraught situations are rare. Although it may not be the moral thing to do, most drivers will react in ways that they hope will protect themselves and their passengers. So as a first approximation, autonomous vehicles should be programmed to choose actions that aim to protect their occupants.

Once the superior safety of driverless cars is established, they will dramatically change the shape of cities and the ways in which people live and work.

Roadway engineers estimate that typical highways now accommodate a maximum throughput of 2,200 human-driven vehicles per lane per hour, utilizing only about 5 percent of roadway capacity. Because self-driving cars would be safer and could thus drive closer and faster, switching to mostly self-driving cars would dramatically increase roadway throughput. One estimate by the University of South Florida's Center for Urban Transportation Research in November 2013 predicts that a 50 percent autonomous road fleet would boost highway capacity by 22 percent; an 80 percent robot fleet will goose capacity 50 percent, and a fully automated highway would see its throughput zoom by 80 percent.

Autonomous vehicles would also likely shift the way people think about car ownership. Currently most automobiles are idle most of the day in driveways or parking lots as their owners go about their lives. Truly autonomous vehicles make it possible for vehicles to be on the road much more of the time, essentially providing taxi service to users who summon them to their locations via mobile devices. Once riders are done with the cars, the vehicles can be dismissed to serve other patrons. Self-driving cars will also increase the mobility of the disabled, elderly, and those too young to drive.

Researchers at the University of Texas, devising a realistic simulation of vehicle usage in cities that takes into account issues such as congestion and rush hour patterns, found that if all cars were driverless each shared autonomous vehicle could replace 11 conventional cars. In their simulations, riders waited an average of 18 seconds for a driverless vehicle to show up, and each vehicle served 31 to 41 travelers per day. Less than one half of one percent of travelers waited more than five minutes for a ride.

By one estimate in a 2013 study from Columbia University's Earth Institute, shared autonomous vehicles would cut an individual's average cost of travel by as much as 75 percent compared to now. There are some 600 million parking spaces in American cities, occupying about 10 percent of urban land. In addition, 30 percent of city congestion originates from drivers seeking parking spaces close to their destinations. A fleet of shared driverless cars would free up lots of valuable urban land while at the same time reducing congestion on city streets. During low demand periods, vehicles would go to central locations for refueling and cleaning.

Since driving will be cheaper and more convenient, demand for travel will surely increase. People who can work while they commute might be willing to live even farther out from city centers. But more vehicle miles traveled would not necessarily translate into more fuel burned. For example, safer autonomous vehicles could be built much lighter than conventional vehicles and thus consume less fuel. Smoother acceleration and deceleration would reduce fuel consumption by up to 10 percent. Optimized autonomous vehicles could cut both the fuel used and pollutants emitted per mile. And poor countries could "leapfrog" to autonomous vehicles instead of embracing the personal ownership model of the 20th century West.

If driverless cars are in fact safer, every day of delay imposes a huge cost. People a generation hence will marvel at the carnage we inflicted as we hurtled down highways relying on just our own reflexes to keep us safe.

Ronald Bailey is an award-winning journalist and is currently the science correspondent for *Reason Magazine*. He has written and edited books on economics, ecology, and biotechnology.

Will Knight

 **NO**

Driverless Cars Are Further Away Than You Think

A silver BMW 5 Series is weaving through traffic at roughly 120 kilometers per hour (75 mph) on a freeway that cuts northeast through Bavaria between Munich and Ingolstadt. I'm in the driver's seat, watching cars and trucks pass by, but I haven't touched the steering wheel, the brake, or the gas pedal for at least 10 minutes. The BMW approaches a truck that is moving slowly. To maintain our speed, the car activates its turn signal and begins steering to the left, toward the passing lane. Just as it does, another car swerves into the passing lane from several cars behind. The BMW quickly switches off its signal and pulls back to the center of the lane, waiting for the speeding car to pass before trying again.

Putting your life in the hands of a robot chauffeur offers an unnerving glimpse into how driving is about to be upended. The automobile, which has followed a path of steady but slow technological evolution for the past 130 years, is on course to change dramatically in the next few years, in ways that could have radical economic, environmental, and social impacts.

The first autonomous systems, which are able to control steering, braking, and accelerating, are already starting to appear in cars; these systems require drivers to keep an eye on the road and hands on the wheel. But the next generation, such as BMW's self-driving prototype, could be available in less than a decade and free drivers to work, text, or just relax. Ford, GM, Toyota, Nissan, Volvo, and Audi have all shown off cars that can drive themselves, and they have all declared that within a decade they plan to sell some form of advanced automation—cars able to take over driving on highways or to park themselves in a garage. Google, meanwhile, is investing millions in autonomous driving software, and its driverless cars have become a familiar sight on the highways around Silicon Valley over the last several years.

The allure of automation for car companies is huge. In a fiercely competitive market, in which the makers of luxury cars race to indulge customers with the latest technology, it would be commercial suicide not to invest heavily in an automated future. "It's the most impressive experience we can offer," Werner Huber, the man in charge of BMW's autonomous driving project, told me at the company's headquarters in Munich. He said the company aims to be "one of the first in the world" to introduce highway autonomy.

Thanks to autonomous driving, the road ahead seems likely to have fewer traffic accidents and less congestion and pollution. Data published last year by the Insurance Institute for Highway Safety, a U.S. nonprofit funded by the auto industry, suggests that partly autonomous features are already helping to reduce crashes. Its figures, collected from U.S. auto insurers, show that cars with forward collision warning systems, which either warn the driver about an impending crash or apply the brakes automatically, are involved in far fewer crashes than cars without them.

More comprehensive autonomy could reduce traffic accidents further still. The National Highway Traffic Safety Administration estimates that more than 90 percent of road crashes involve human error, a figure that has led some experts to predict that autonomous driving will reduce the number of accidents on the road by a similar percentage. Assuming the technology becomes ubiquitous and does have such an effect, the benefits to society will be huge. Almost 33,000 people die on the roads in the United States each year, at a cost of $300 billion, according to the American Automobile Association. The World Health Organization estimates that worldwide over 1.2 million people die on roads every year.

Meanwhile, demonstrations conducted at the University of California, Riverside, in 1997 and experiments involving modified road vehicles conducted by Volvo and others in 2011 suggest that having vehicles travel in high-speed automated "platoons," thereby reducing aerodynamic drag, could lower fuel consumption by 20 percent.

And an engineering study published last year concluded that automation could theoretically allow nearly four times as many cars to travel on a given stretch of highway. That could save some of the 5.5 billion hours and 2.9 billion gallons of fuel that the Texas Transportation Institute says are wasted by traffic congestion each year.

But such projections tend to overlook just how challenging it will be to make a driverless car. If autonomous driving is to change transportation dramatically, it needs to be both widespread and flawless. Turning such a complex technology into a commercial product is unlikely to be simple. It could take decades for the technology to come down in cost, and it might take even longer for it to work safely enough that we trust fully automated vehicles to drive us around.

German Engineering

Much of the hype about autonomous driving has, unsurprisingly, focused on Google's self-driving project. The cars *are* impressive, and the company has no doubt insinuated the possibility of driverless vehicles into the imaginations of many. But for all its expertise in developing search technology and software, Google has zero experience building cars. To understand how autonomous driving is more likely to emerge, it is more instructive to see what some of the world's most advanced automakers are working on. And few places in the world can rival the automotive expertise of Germany, where BMW, Audi, Mercedes-Benz, and Volkswagen are all busy trying to change autonomous driving from a research effort into a viable option on their newest models.

Shortly after arriving in Munich, I found myself at a test track north of the city getting safety instruction from Michael Aeberhard, a BMW research engineer. As I drove a prototype BMW 5 Series along an empty stretch of track, Aeberhard told me to take my hands off the wheel and then issued commands that made the car go berserk and steer wildly off course. Each time, I had to grab the wheel as quickly as I could to override the behavior. The system is designed to defer to a human driver, giving up control whenever he or she moves the wheel or presses a pedal. And if all else fails, there is a big red button on the dashboard that cuts power to all the car's computers. I practiced hitting it a few times, and discovered how hard it was to control the car without even the power-assisted steering. The idea of the exercise was to prepare me for potential glitches during the actual test drive. "It's still a prototype," Aeberhard reminded me several times.

After I signed a disclaimer, we drove to the autobahn outside Munich. A screen fixed to the passenger side of the dashboard showed the world as the car perceives it: three lanes, on which a tiny animated version of the car is surrounded by a bunch of floating blue blocks, each corresponding to a nearby vehicle or to an obstacle like one of the barriers on either side of the road. Aeberhard told me to activate the system in heavy traffic as we rode at about 100 kilometers per hour. When I first flicked the switch, I was dubious about even removing my hands from the wheel, but after watching the car perform numerous passing maneuvers, I found myself relaxing—to my astonishment—until I had to actually remind myself to pay attention to the road.

The car looked normal from the outside. There's no place on a sleek luxury sedan for the huge rotating laser scanners seen on the prototypes being tested by Google. So BMW and other carmakers have had to find ways to pack smaller, more limited sensors into the body of a car without compromising weight or styling.

Concealed inside the BMW's front and rear bumpers, two laser scanners and three radar sensors sweep the road before and behind for anything within about 200 meters. Embedded at the top of the windshield and rear window are cameras that track the road markings and detect road signs. Near each side mirror are wide-angle laser scanners, each with almost 180 degrees of vision, that watch the road left and right. Four ultrasonic sensors above the wheels monitor the area close to the car. Finally, a differential Global Positioning System receiver, which combines signals from ground-based stations with those from satellites, knows where the car is, to within a few centimeters of the closest lane marking.

Several computers inside the car's trunk perform split-second measurements and calculations, processing data pouring in from the sensors. Software assigns a value to each lane of the road based on the car's speed and the behavior of nearby vehicles. Using a probabilistic technique that helps cancel out inaccuracies in sensor readings, this software decides whether to switch to another lane, to attempt to pass the car ahead, or to get out of the way of a vehicle approaching from behind. Commands are relayed to a separate computer that controls acceleration, braking, and steering. Yet another computer system monitors the behavior of everything involved with autonomous driving for signs of malfunction.

Impressive though BMW's autonomous highway driving is, it is still years away from market. To see the most advanced autonomy now available, a day later I took the train from Munich to Stuttgart to visit another German automotive giant, Daimler, which owns Mercedes-Benz. At the company's research and development facility southeast of the city, where experimental new models cruise around covered in black material to hide new designs and features from photographers, I got to ride in probably the most autonomous road car on the market today: the 2014 Mercedes S-Class.

A jovial safety engineer drove me around a test track, showing how the car can lock onto a vehicle in front and follow it along the road at a safe distance. To follow at a constant distance, the car's computers take over not only braking and accelerating, as with conventional adaptive cruise control, but steering too.

Using a stereo camera, radar, and an infrared camera, the S-Class can also spot objects on the road ahead and take control of the brakes to prevent an accident. The engineer eagerly demonstrated this by accelerating toward a dummy placed in the center of the track. At about 80 kilometers per hour, he took his hands off the wheel and removed his foot from the accelerator. Just when impact seemed all but inevitable, the car performed a near-perfect emergency stop, wrenching us forward in our seats but bringing itself to rest about a foot in front of the dummy, which bore an appropriately terrified expression.

Uncertain Road

With such technology already on the road and proto-types like BMW's in the works, it's tempting to imagine that total automation can't be far away. In reality, making the leap from the kind of autonomy in the Mercedes-Benz S-Class to the kind in BMW's prototype will take time, and the dream of total automation could prove surprisingly elusive.

For one thing, many of the sensors and computers found in BMW's car, and in other prototypes, are too expensive to be deployed widely. And achieving even more complete automation will probably mean using more advanced, more expensive sensors and computers. The spinning laser instrument, or LIDAR, seen on the roof of Google's cars, for instance, provides the best 3-D image of the surrounding world, accurate down to two centimeters, but sells for around $80,000. Such instruments will also need to be miniaturized and redesigned, adding more cost, since few car designers would slap the existing ones on top of a sleek new model.

Cost will be just one factor, though. While several U.S. states have passed laws permitting autonomous cars to be tested on their roads, the National Highway Traffic Safety Administration has yet to devise regulations for test-ing and certifying the safety and reliability of autonomous features. Two major international treaties, the Vienna Convention on Road Traffic and the Geneva Convention on Road Traffic, may need to be changed for the cars to be used in Europe and the United States, as both documents state that a driver must be in full control of a vehicle at all times.

Most daunting, however, are the remaining computer science and artificial-intelligence challenges. Automated driving will at first be limited to relatively simple situations, mainly highway driving, because the technology still can't respond to uncertainties posed by oncoming traffic, rotaries, and pedestrians. And drivers will also almost certainly be expected to assume some sort of supervisory role, requiring them to be ready to retake control as soon as the system gets outside its comfort zone.

The relationship between human and robot driver could be surprisingly fraught. The problem, as I discovered during my BMW test drive, is that it's all too easy to lose focus, and difficult to get it back. The difficulty of reëngaging distracted drivers is an issue that Bryan Reimer, a research scientist in MIT's Age Lab, has well documented (see "Proceed with Caution toward the Self-Driving Car," May/June 2013). Perhaps the "most inhibiting factors" in the development of driverless cars, he suggests, "will be factors related to the human experience."

In an effort to address this issue, carmakers are thinking about ways to prevent drivers from becoming too distracted, and ways to bring them back to the driving task as smoothly as possible. This may mean monitoring drivers' attention and alerting them if they're becoming too disengaged. "The first generations [of autonomous cars] are going to require a driver to intervene at certain points," Clifford Nass, codirector of Stanford University's Center for Automotive Research, told me. "It turns out that may be the most dangerous moment for autonomous vehicles. We may have this terrible irony that when the car is driving autonomously it is much safer, but because of the inability of humans to get back in the loop it may ultimately be less safe."

An important challenge with a system that drives all by itself, but only some of the time, is that it must be able to predict when it may be about to fail, to give the driver enough time to take over. This ability is limited by the range of a car's sensors and by the inherent difficulty of predicting the outcome of a complex situation. "Maybe the driver is completely distracted," Werner Huber said. "He takes five, six, seven seconds to come back to the driving task—that means the car has to know [in advance] when its limitation is reached. The challenge is very big."

Before traveling to Germany, I visited John Leonard, an MIT professor who works on robot navigation, to find out more about the limits of vehicle automation. Leonard led one of the teams involved in the DARPA Urban Challenge, an event in 2007 that saw autonomous vehicles race across mocked-up city streets, complete with stop-sign intersections and moving traffic. The challenge inspired new research and new interest in autonomous driving, but Leonard is restrained in his enthusiasm for the commercial trajectory that autonomous driving has taken since then. "Some of these fundamental questions, about representing the world and being able to predict what might happen—we might still be decades behind humans with our machine technology," he told me. "There are major, unsolved, difficult issues here. We have to be careful that we don't overhype how well it works."

Leonard suggested that much of the technology that has helped autonomous cars deal with complex urban environments in research projects—some of which is used in Google's cars today—may never be cheap or compact enough to be employed in commercially available vehicles. This includes not just the LIDAR but also an inertial navigation system, which provides precise positioning information by monitoring the vehicle's own movement and combining the resulting data with differential GPS and a highly accurate digital map. What's more, poor weather can significantly degrade the reliability of sensors, Leonard said, and it may not always be feasible to rely heavily on a digital map, as so many prototype systems do. "If the system relies on a very accurate prior map, then it has to be robust to the situation of that map being wrong, and the work of keeping those maps up to date shouldn't be underestimated," he said.

Near the end of my ride in BMW's autonomous prototype, I discovered an example of imperfect autonomy in action. We had made a loop of the airport and were heading back toward the city when a Smart car, which had been darting through traffic a little erratically, suddenly swung in front of me from the right. Confused by its sudden and irregular maneuver, our car kept approaching it rapidly, and with less than a second to spare I lost my nerve and hit the brakes, slowing the car down and taking it out

of self-driving mode. A moment later I asked Aeberhard if our car would have braked in time. "It would've been close," he admitted.

Despite the flashy demos and the bold plans for commercialization, I sometimes detected among carmakers a desire to hit the brakes and temper expectations. Ralf Herttwich, who leads research and engineering of driver assistance systems at Mercedes, explained that interpreting a situation becomes exponentially more difficult as the road becomes more complex. "Once you leave the highway and once you go onto the average road, environment perception needs to get better. Your interpretation of traffic situations, because there are so many more of them—they need to get better," he said. "Just looking at a traffic light and deciding if that traffic light is for you is a very, very complex problem."

MIT's Leonard, for one, does not believe total autonomy is imminent. "I do not expect there to be taxis in Manhattan with no drivers in my lifetime," he said, before quickly adding, "And I don't want to see taxi drivers out of business. They know where they're going, and—at least in Europe—they're courteous and safe, and they get you where you need to be. That's a very valuable societal role."

I pondered Leonard's objections while visiting BMW and Mercedes. I even mentioned some of them to a taxi driver in Munich who was curious about my trip. He seemed far from worried. "We have *siebten Sinn*—a seventh sense," he said, referring to the instinctive road awareness a person builds up. As he nipped through the busy traffic with impressive speed, I suspected that this ability to cope deftly with such a complex and messy world could prove useful for a while longer.

WILL KNIGHT is the online editor of *MIT Technology Review*. His interests include data visualization, the history of technology, machine intelligence, and robotics.

EXPLORING THE ISSUE

Does Morality Require Us to Switch to Driverless Cars?

Critical Thinking and Reflection

1. Suppose that switching to a driverless car would greatly reduce your chances of being killed or injured in a traffic accident. Are there any practical factors that would dissuade you from using a driverless car? Identify these factors (if any) and explain their significance to your decision.
2. Rank the following factors in terms of their importance in the accident-mitigation protocols of a driverless car: the number of persons involved in an accident, the age of the persons involved in an accident, the professions of the persons involved in an accident, the value of the cars involved in an accident, the environmental damage that would be caused by the accident. Explain your rankings. What other factors do you think should be addressed in such a protocol? Why?
3. Should driverless cars use a uniform decision-making protocol to mitigate the severity of a traffic accident? Why or why not?
4. Do you think a practical non-consequentialist decision-making protocol could be developed for computers that operate driverless cars? If so, how might this protocol work?
5. Are there any areas in which moral decision-making should be restricted to human beings? If so, why should computers be excluded from moral decision-making in these areas?

Is There Common Ground?

Ronald Bailey and Will Knight respond quite differently to the development of driverless cars. Bailey awaits the availability of driverless cars with enthusiastic optimism, while Knight advocates a far more cautious and skeptical approach to the adoption of driverless technology.

Despite this difference, both authors agree that the driverless cars would drastically affect the use of motor vehicles in ways that produce substantial benefit. Since the vast majority of automobile accidents involve human error, they agree that driverless cars, once they are fully developed, will significantly reduce the number of fatalities and injuries caused by these accidents. They also envision significant environmental benefits from the use of driverless cars. For his part, Knight envisions coordinated fleets of driverless cars driving very close together, decreasing aerodynamic drag and thereby reducing fuel consumption by as much as twenty percent. Bailey projects that multiple people will share ownership of a driverless car, so that a single vehicle can perform multiple tasks, increasing efficiency and decreasing traffic congestion.

Additional Resources

Michael Anderson and Susan Leigh Anderson, "Robot be good: A call for ethical autonomous machines," *Scientific American* (October 2010)

Noah Goodall, "Ethical decision making during automated vehicle crashes," *Transportation Research Record: Journal of the Transportation Research Board* (2014)

Patrick Lin, "The ethics of autonomous cars," *The Atlantic Monthly* (October 2013)

Gary Marcus, "Moral machines," *The New Yorker* (November 2012)

John Villasenor, "Products liability and driverless cars: Issues and guiding principles for legislation," Brookings Center for Technology Innovation: The Project on Civilian Robotics, April 2014

Internet References . . .

The Center for Ethics in Science and Technology

http://www.ethicscenter.net/

AI Topics: Ethics & Social Issues

http://aitopics.org/topic/ethics-social-issues

The Research Center on Computing and Society

http://ares.southernct.edu/organizations/rccs/category/home/